P9-CDD-932

REDWOOD

LIBRARY
NEWPORT
R.I.

WITHDRAWN

Also by Philip Short

Banda

The Dragon and The Bear

Mao: A Life

Pol Pot

POL POT

Anatomy of a Nightmare

PHILIP

SHORT

A JOHN MACRAE BOOK

Henry Holt and Company | New York

Henry Holt and Company, LLC
Publishers since 1866
115 West 18th Street
New York, New York 10011

Henry Holt® is a registered trademark of Henry Holt and Company, LLC.

Copyright © 2004 by Philip Short
All rights reserved.
Originally published in Great Britain in 2004 by John Murray

Library of Congress Cataloging-in-Publication Data

Short, Philip.
  Pol Pot : anatomy of a nightmare / Philip Short—1st ed.
     p.   cm.
  "A John Macrae book."
  ISBN-13: 978-0-8050-6662-3
  ISBN-10: 0-8050-6662-4
  1. Pol Pot. 2. Genocide—Cambodia. 3. Political atrocities—Cambodia. 4. Cambodia—
Politics and government—1975–1979. 5. Prime ministers—Cambodia—Biography. I. Title.
  DS554.83.P65S53 2005
  959.604'2—dc22   2004054080

Henry Holt books are available for special promotions and premiums.
For details contact: Director, Special Markets.

First American Edition 2005

Printed in the United States of America
1 3 5 7 9 10 8 6 4 2

151935

MAR 16 2005

DS
554.83
.P65
S53
2005

For Mao Mao

Contents

Acknowledgements

History is to a great extent detective work. Contemporary documents, the statements of witnesses, their later recollections, compared and combined with other sources, provide essential clues as to the nature of the 'crime' – that is to say, the historical truth – concealed beneath. The biographer strives to draw from this amorphous mass of detail a credible portrait of the hero, or anti-hero, of his tale.

Many people helped me to assemble the mosaic of fragments of truths, half-truths and lies, related by the perpetrators of the Cambodian nightmare as well as by its victims, on which this book is based. Caroline Gluck gave me the first pointers. Bill Herod and Michael Vickery offered early encouragement. David Ashley, Ben Kiernan, Henri Locard, William Shawcrosss, Sacha Sher and Serge Thion shared documents. Christopher Goscha allowed me to translate the Vietnamese-language copies of dozens of original Khmer Rouge texts which he had been authorised to transcribe by hand at the Military Library in Hanoi. Others assisted with Chinese archival materials. Nil Samom, my Khmer research assistant, spent two years accompanying me across Cambodia, reading and translating, with undented good humour, thousands of pages of opaque Khmer Rouge internal journals, CPK Standing Committee minutes and prison confessions, which form much of the documentation for the later chapters. Stephen Heder and David Chandler generously read the typescript, offering pithy and often pungent comments which gave me much food for thought even if, on certain points, we continue to differ.

Several of the leading protagonists of the Khmer Rouge revolution told me their life stories, often at length over a period of months. They include the former Head of State, Khieu Samphân; Pol Pot's brother-in-law, the Khmer Rouge Foreign Minister, Ieng Sary; Nikân, whose brother, Son Sen, was Defence Minister; Phi Phuon, the Chief of Security at the Khmer Rouge Foreign Ministry; and two other former officials, Suong Sikoeun and In Sopheap, as well as a host of lower-ranking individuals. Their motives were mixed. Some were more truthful, others less so. But like interviewees everywhere, the more they talked the more of themselves they revealed. Without their co-operation, this book would not have been possible.

Some historians argue that anything the former Khmer Rouge leaders say should be disbelieved on principle. I take a different view. If the interviewee has no obvious interest in lying, if his story is plausible and if there is no convincing evidence to the contrary, I tend to believe that he is telling if not *the* truth then at least his version of it. The same applies – although with many more caveats – to confessions obtained under torture at Khmer Rouge interrogation centres. The information they contain cannot be dismissed out of hand simply because the source is nauseous.

Several of the Cambodian students who were with Pol Pot during his years in Paris in the early 1950s, notably Keng Vannsak, afterwards a staunch anti-communist; Thiounn Mumm, who became a Khmer Rouge minister, Ping Sây and the late Mey Mann, also shed light on hitherto unsuspected aspects of his life. Vannsak and Mumm kindly provided previously unpublished photographs from their private collections, as did Bernard Hamel, former Reuters correspondent in Phnom Penh. Youk Chhang and his colleagues at the Documentation Center of Cambodia allowed me access to their holdings of Khmer Rouge documents and pictures. I am grateful to Serge Corrieras, Chris Goscha, Michael Hayes of the *Phnom Penh Post*, Ben Kieman, Roland Neveu and Kathleen O'Keeffe for help in obtaining other illustrations.

My thanks go too, as always, to my editors, Roland Philipps in London and John Macrae in New York; to my agents, Jacqueline Korn and Emma Sweeney; and to Jane Birkett, without whose eagle eye for repetitions, mixed metaphors, lapsed commas and other punctual misdemeanours, this would be a poorer book.

Phnom Penh – La Garde-Freinet,
July 1 2004

List of Illustrations

Section One

Illustration Credits

1, 2, 3, 7 and 11, personal archive of Keng Vannsak; 4 and 5, Vietnamese Revolutionary Museum, Hanoi; 6, courtesy of Ben Kiernan; 8, 12, 13 and 14, personal archive of Bernard Hamel; 9 and 10, personal archive of Thiounn Mumm; 14, AP; 16, UPI; 17, 18, 22, 27, 28, 30, 31, 32, 33, 34 and 37, archives of *Phnom Penh Post*; 19, 20, 21 and 26, Xinhua News Agency; 23, author's collection; 24, private collection; 25, 29 and 36, courtesy of the Documentation Center of Cambodia; 35, Serge Corrieras; 38, Nate Thayer/Tom Keller Associates

Note on Pronunciation

There is no standard system of romanisation for the Khmer language. Thus the village described on maps as Samlaut calls itself Samlot; Kamrieng, on the border with Thailand, is also Kamrean; the port of Kampâng Saom is Kompong Som, and so on. This book employs, wherever possible, either the most commonly used variants or those which approximate best to English pronunciation. None the less, the following basic rules may be helpful:

'a' is intermediate between the English short 'a' and short 'o': thus Saloth is pronounced *Sol*oth, and Samphân, *Som*phân.

'â' lies between the English short 'o' and 'or': Sâr is pronounced *Sor*, Samphân is Sam*phorn*.

'au', as in Pauk, is sounded as in lock; 'ay', as in Chhay and Say, rhymes with sigh.

'eo', as in Keo, rhymes with cow; 'eu' as in Deuch, with book; 'ey', as in Mey, with may; 'ê', as in Chhê, with tie.

'Ch', 'P' and 'T' followed by 'h' are aspirated. Chham is pronounced Cham (whereas *Ch*am, unaspirated, is like *J*am). Phem is *Pem* and Thirith, *Tirit*. Terminal -ch is pronounced -ck, making Pach rhyme with Pack.

Cambodian names, like those in China and Vietnam, are in the reverse order to English. Khieu Samphân's family name is Khieu, his given name, Samphân. However, unlike in China, the polite form of address is Mr Samphân – or simply Samphân – not Mr Khieu. The only exceptions are names which originated as revolutionary aliases. For example, Long Bunruot took the alias Nuon, to which he subsequently added the name Chea. He is therefore Mr Nuon, not Mr Chea. Similarly Pol Pot is addressed as Pol, Vorn Vet as Vorn, and so on. The same distinction applies in Vietnam, where given names are used in formal address because there is such a narrow range of family names that to employ them would be confusing: hence Ho Chi Minh (a revolutionary alias) is President Ho, but Vo Nguyen Giap (a real name) is General Giap.

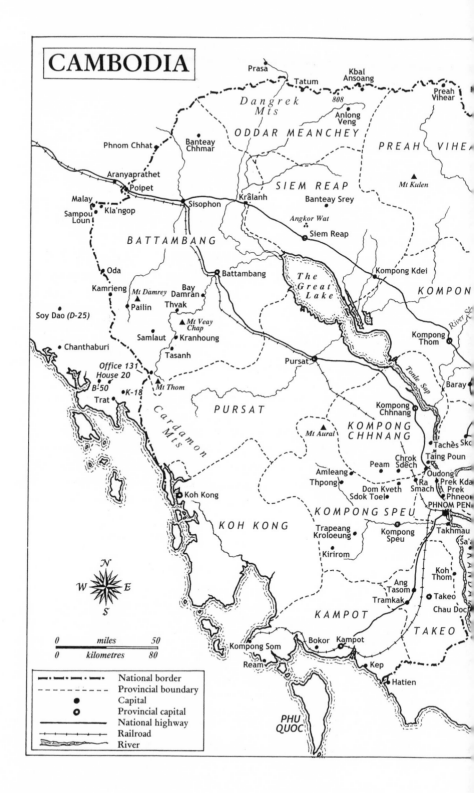

CAMBODIA

Prasa
Tatum
Kbal Ansoang
Preah Vihear

Dangrek Mts
808
Anlong Veng

ODDAR MEANCHEY
PREAH VIHEA

Phnom Chhat
Banteay Chhmar

Aranyaprathet
Poipet

SIEM REAP
▲ Mt Kulen

Malay
Kla'ngop
Sisophon
Krâlanh
Banteay Srey

Sampou Loun

Angkor Wat

BATTAMBANG
Siem Reap

Kompong Kdei

Oda
KOMPON

Kamrieng
▲ Mt Damrey
Bay Damran
Battambang
The Great Lake

Soy Dao (D-25)
▲ Mt Veay Chap
Pailin
Thvak

Chanthaburi
Samlaut
Kranhoung

Kompong Thom

Tasanh

Pursat
River Sk

Office 131
House 20
B-50
K-18
▲ Mt Thom

Trat
PURSAT

Baray

Cardamon Mts

Kompong Chhnang

KOMPONG
CHHNANG

▲ Mt Aural
Tachès Sko

Chrok Sdech
Taing Poun

Peam
Oudong

Amleang
Ra Prek Kda
Dom Kveth
Smach
Prek
Thpong
Sdok Toel
Phneo
PHNOM PEN

Koh Kong
KOMPONG SPEU

KOH KONG
Takhmau
Sa'

Trapeang Kroloeung
Kompong Speu

Kirirom
Koh Thom

Ang Tasom
Takeo
Tramkak
Chau Doc

KAMPOT
TAKEO

Bokor
Kampot

Kompong Som
Kep

Ream
Hatien

PHU QUOC

▬·▬·▬·▬	National border
━ ━ ━ ━	Provincial boundary
●	Capital
○	Provincial capital
━━━	National highway
┽┽┽┽	Railroad
∿∿∿	River

0 miles 50
0 kilometres 80

N W E S

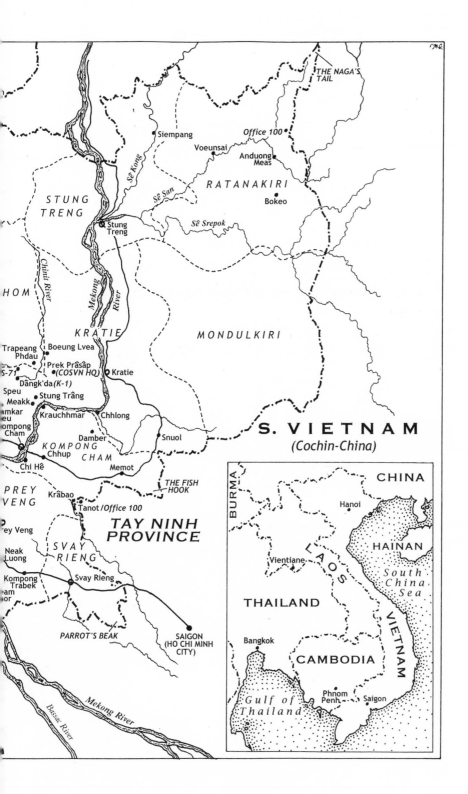

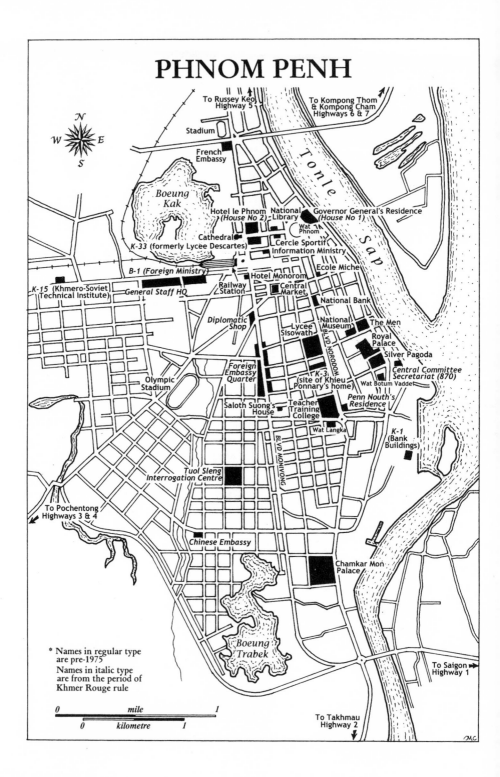

PHNOM PENH

To Russey Keo
Highway 5

To Kompong Thom
& Kompong Cham
Highways 6 & 7

Stadium

French
Embassy

Tonle Sap

*Boeung
Kak*

Hotel le Phnom   National   Governor General's Residence
(House No 2)   Library   *(House No 1)*
                  Wat
                  Phnom
Cathedral   Cercle Sportif
K-33 (formerly Lycee Descartes)   Information Ministry

B-1 (Foreign Ministry)   Ecole Miche
                      Hotel Monorom
K-15 (Khmero-Soviet Railway   Central
Technical Institute) Station   Market
General Staff HQ   National Bank

*Diplomatic   National   The Men
Shop*   Lycee   Museum
               Sisowath   Royal
                                    Palace
                                    Silver Pagoda
*Foreign   *K-3*   *Central Committee
Embassy   *(site of Khieu* *Secretariat (870)*
Quarter*   *Ponnary's home)* Wat Botum Vaddel
*Olympic
Stadium*   *Penn Nouth's
              Saloth Suong's Teacher *Residence*
              House   Training
                              College
                        Wat Langka   *K-1
                                         (Bank
                                         Buildings)*

*Tuol Sleng
Interrogation Centre*

To Pochentong
Highways 3 & 4

Chinese Embassy

                              Chamkar Mon
                              Palace

*Boeung
Trabek*

                                        To Saigon
                                        Highway 1

* Names in regular type
  are pre-1975

  Names in italic type
  are from the period of
  Khmer Rouge rule

0   mile   1
0   kilometre   1

                    To Takhmau
                    Highway 2

Pol Pot

Prologue

THE NEWS REACHED Ieng Sary in Hanoi soon after 10 a.m.
A messenger arrived with a ciphered telegram, transmitted in morse code from Khmer Rouge headquarters north-west of Phnom Penh. When the first few words had been decoded, Sary telephoned the office of the Vietnamese Workers' Party Central Committee and asked to be put through to Le Duc Tho, the Politburo member who the previous year had shared the Nobel Peace Prize with Henry Kissinger for ending the war in Vietnam. Tho had ultimate responsibility for relations with the Cambodian communists.

'We have taken Phnom Penh,' he announced proudly.

A quarter of a century later, Sary still smarted at the memory of the Vietnamese leader's response. 'Be careful not to be misled by false reports!' Tho said acidly. 'Remember what happened when you told us that Takeo had fallen' – a reference to a conversation they had had a week earlier, when Sary had informed him, prematurely, that a town south of the capital had surrendered.

Ieng Sary was then one of the six members of the Standing Committee of the Communist Party of Kampuchea (CPK), the Khmer Rouge supreme leadership. He was fifty years old and balding, with an incipient paunch. A devious, manipulative man, crafty rather than clever, his smooth domed forehead, pale complexion and part-Chinese ancestry gave him a striking resemblance to an ultra-leftist Chinese Politburo member named Yao Wenyuan, one of the so-called 'Gang of Four' headed by Mao Zedong's widow, Jiang Qing. Sary was capable of singular vindictiveness but also of loyalty to useful subordinates, who repaid him with lifelong devotion. He concealed insincerity beneath a calculated ability to make himself agreeable. A British Ambassador who, many years later, attended a lunch with Sary and his wife, Khieu Thirith, likened the experience to having tea with Rosemary West and her husband, two murderous sexual deviants whose names became a byword in Britain for grisly perversion. But that was the distaste of hindsight, at a time when the image of the Khmer Rouge leaders had become inseparable from the abominations their regime had committed. In the early 1970s, the heroic age of Indochinese communism, Sary and his comrades were riding the wave of the future, symbolising for radicals everywhere and for millions of sympathisers in the West hopes of a more just and democratic world.

Sary's chagrin was short-lived. A few hours later, Tho arrived in person, wreathed in smiles, accompanied by aides bearing enormous bouquets of flowers – with a request, slipped in deftly between the Vietnamese leadership's congratulations, that the new Cambodian authorities allow free passage across their territory to Vietnamese troops coming south for the final offensive against the American-backed regime in Saigon.

The request was granted. That day, April 17 1975, the Khmers Rouges could afford to be generous as they savoured a triumph that was all the more gratifying because it had been achieved ahead of their disdainful Vietnamese allies.

They had captured Phnom Penh, as they would never tire of repeating, without outside help. US officials claimed that the final assault on the Cambodian capital was spearheaded by regular Vietnamese units backed by heavy artillery, but, like much else the Americans said at that time, this was false. No Vietnamese main-force unit had fought in Cambodia since 1973. The US had dropped more than 500,000 tons of bombs on Cambodian resistance bases and had spent hundreds of millions of dollars propping up the corrupt and incompetent anti-communist regime of Marshal Lon Nol, who had seized power in 1970 from the country's hereditary ruler, Prince Sihanouk. But it had been to no avail. The Khmers Rouges told themselves proudly that their ill-educated peasant troops had defeated all that the mightiest military power on earth had been able to throw in their direction.

Hubris is the besetting sin of despotisms everywhere. In later years, Khmer Rouge officials, including Ieng Sary himself, contemplating the ruins of the Utopian vision to which they had devoted their lives, would argue that the very speed of their victory in 1975 had held the seeds of their undoing. As a Khmer Rouge village chief put it: 'The train was going too fast. No one could make it turn.'

But even to the extent that it is true, such reasoning is self-serving. There were many causes of the egregious tragedy that befell Cambodia in the last quarter of the twentieth century, and many actors amongst whom responsibility must be shared. The overconfidence of the country's new leaders, above all of its principal leader, the man who would become Pol Pot, was but one element among them and, at the time of the Khmer Rouge victory, it was artfully dissembled.

*   *   *

Another full year would pass before the reclusive figure who had guided the Cambodian communists to victory would emerge from clandestinity and take the name by which his compatriots, and the rest of the world, would remember him.

Even then, he did so reluctantly. For two decades he had operated under multiple aliases: Pouk, Hay, Pol, '87', Grand-Uncle, Elder Brother, First Brother – to be followed in later years by '99' and Phem. 'It is good to change your name,' he once told one of his secretaries. 'The more often you change your name the better. It confuses the enemy.' Then he added, in a phrase which would become a Khmer Rouge mantra: 'If you preserve secrecy, half the battle is already won.' The architect of the Cambodian nightmare was not a man who liked working in the open.

Throughout the five years of civil war that pitted the communists against Lon Nol's right-wing government, most people, inside the country as well as out, were convinced that the movement was led by Khieu Samphân, a left-wing intellectual with a reputation for incorruptibility who had won widespread popular support as a champion of social justice in the time when Sihanouk had been in power. He had joined the maquis in 1967 and, after the Prince's overthrow three years later, became the Khmers Rouges' principal spokesman. As nominal Defence Minister and Commander-in-Chief of the resistance army, Samphân travelled to Beijing to meet Mao. He issued communiqués detailing the war's progress, and in 1973, when Sihanouk, having concluded an improbable alliance with his former communist opponents, visited the 'liberated zones', Samphân acted as host.

But that was a smokescreen. Power lay in the hands of others, whose names were unknown outside the inner circle of the communist leadership itself.

Nuon Chea, for instance, had come to the notice of the colonial government in 1950 as a member of the Issarak movement, fighting for independence from the French, who had established a protectorate over Cambodia almost a century before. But in those days he was called Long Rith. No one ever made the connection between Rith and a portly Khmer businessman, employed by a Sino-Cambodian trading house, who travelled all over the country in the 1950s and '60s, ostensibly selling building materials. Still less did anyone, either in Sihanouk's or in Lon Nol's government, identify 'Nuon' as the Khmer Rouge second-in-command.

And who had heard of Saloth Sâr, who in 1971 was listed merely as one of ninety or so 'patriotic intellectuals' rallying to the revolutionary cause?

A teacher of that name who had frequented 'progressive circles' had attracted the attention of the Phnom Penh police twenty years earlier and subsequently figured on a blacklist of suspected subversives. But there had

never been anything to suggest that he was more than just another disaffected schoolmaster. Even when Sâr's name cropped up again in 1972 as
Chief of the Military Directorate of the Front's guerrilla army, bracketed
with that of Nuon Chea, the Chief of the Political Directorate, they were
assumed to be just two among many, more or less anonymous, second-
echelon figures in the opaque Khmer Rouge hierarchy. During Sihanouk's
visit to the resistance-held areas, photographs show Sâr sitting unobtrusively to one side, leaning forward politely to listen as the stars of the occasion, Khieu Samphân and another former parliamentarian, Hu Nim,
expounded to their entranced royal visitor the prospects for the coming
victory. In other pictures Sâr is barely visible, in a back row at a theatrical
performance or on the fringes of a welcoming party.

Like a Hollywood director making a fleeting, incognito appearance in
one of his own films, Saloth Sâr, the one-time schoolteacher, delighted in
appearing to be what he was not – a nameless face in the crowd, whom
everyone glimpsed but nobody remembered. He had told a follower ten
years earlier:

> The enemy is searching for . . . us everywhere. They are like noodle-sellers
> mincing pork. They mince from the top and the side. The enemy is trying
> to mince us, but they miss us, [they can't do it] . . . That means the enemy
> is weak. The enemy must lose and we must win.

Sihanouk's police in the 1950s, he recalled with his characteristic, gentle
smile, 'knew *who* I was; but they did not know *what* I was'.

As the Khmer Rouge forces rolled to victory in April 1975, that boast
still held good. In the whole country, probably fewer than two hundred
Cambodians – CPK Central Committee members, divisional commanders and their deputies, trusted cadres and personal aides, including his
doctor and his *montagnard* bodyguards – knew *what* Sâr was, and even then,
in most cases, not under that name. One of Lon Nol's secret agents got
close to him in 1974 but did not realise his importance. The CIA knew he
existed but failed to connect him with the mysterious 'Pol', whom the
agency had identified as the head of the Khmer communist movement. It
was hardly surprising when some mid-level officials within the CPK itself
remained ignorant of their leader's identity until almost two years after the
communist victory.

On April 17 1975, Saloth Sâr was at the CPK Central Committee's Forward
Headquarters, in a tract of thick jungle heavily scarred by B-52 bomb
craters, near a wretched hamlet called Sdok Toel, south of Cambodia's
former royal capital, Oudong. Conditions were spartan. The cadres lived

in palmthatched bamboo huts, built on stilts and open to the elements on all four sides. Sâr's hut stood beneath the spreading branches of a banyan tree, whose broad, dark-green leaves provided cover from aerial reconnaissance. He had no furniture and no bed, just a sleeping-mat on the floor. A second hut, thirty yards away, was occupied by Khieu Samphân.

That day, as the radio crackled away bringing news from newly 'liberated' Phnom Penh, they had taken their midday meal together. It was an understated, low-key occasion, 'totally different from the way it would have been in the West', Samphân recalled. 'We avoided showing our feelings. There was no explosion of joy, or anything like that . . . I didn't congratulate him. He said simply that it was a great victory which the Cambodian people had won alone. That was all.' A bodyguard confirmed his account. 'There was nothing special,' he remembered. 'It was just like any other day.'

A few weeks later, diffidence would give way to apocalypse.

April 17 became the day when 'two thousand years of Cambodian history ended' and Cambodians began building a future 'more glorious than Angkor', whose kings, at the peak of their power in the thirteenth century, had ruled an empire stretching from Malaysia to Laos, from Vietnam to Burma. The new regime would reverse the long decline that had lasted ever since. It would build socialism 'without reference to any existing model', Ieng Sary told an interviewer. The CPK would lead Cambodia along roads where 'no country in history has ever gone before'.

It would be impossible, as well as meaningless, to try to pinpoint the moment at which Cambodia's descent into madness began. Like a medieval incubus, it grew from a coalition of differing causes and ideas. But one can fairly ask at what point the nightmare became irreversible. In the autumn of 1974, when the decision was taken to evacuate Phnom Penh? On April 19 1975 – two days after Phnom Penh fell – when Sâr first expounded to the Standing Committee the deceptively simple guideline for the new polity he wished to create: 'Build and Defend!'? Or in January 1976, when the CPK Central Committee formally approved the abolition of money?

The most plausible answer is none of these, but a leadership workconference whose secret was so closely held that for a quarter of a century afterwards no one outside the twenty or so participants knew that it had even taken place.

The Khmer Rouge leaders met in May 1975 at the Silver Pagoda, the holiest of the Buddhist shrines inside the Royal Palace in Phnom Penh, at a time when the regime was still weighing its future course. A new currency had been printed, but should it be circulated or withheld? The capital had been evacuated, but was it to be emptied permanently or just for a time? What role should be assigned to Prince Sihanouk, still in exile in Beijing? What policies should be adopted to meet the perceived threat from Cambodia's larger, more powerful neighbours, Thailand and, above all, Vietnam?

The pagoda, built at the turn of the century for Sihanouk's great-grandfather, King Norodom, is stronger on symbolism than antiquity. Its steeply raked roof, covered in green and gold tiles, with elaborately carved, gilded beams and soaring antler finials, epitomises Khmer tradition. But the so-called Emerald Buddha in its central hall was manufactured by the French glassmaker Lalique, and its stone base is overlaid with Italian marble. The incongruous-looking veranda, ornamented with mock-Grecian columns, was added in the 1960s. There the assembled leaders of the new Cambodia slept, out in the open air, like schoolboys at a summer camp, on iron-framed beds with wooden slats brought from a nearby hospital. The fact that they now held power seemed to have changed nothing. In their minds they were still guerrillas fighting a jungle war.

Only Saloth Sâr chose to sleep elsewhere. His aides set up a bed for him, with a mosquito net, on the raised dais in the centre of the sanctuary normally occupied by statues of the Buddha.

Khmer Buddhist temples rarely inspire awe and exaltation, as great Christian cathedrals do. Bereft of worshippers, the Silver Pagoda is a tawdry place. But it is sacred ground. Sihanouk lived there as a monk during the year of his ordination in 1947, when the divinity of his kingship was ritually affirmed. In the courtyard outside stand four towering, ornately carved white stupas, containing the ashes of dead kings, An artificial hill symbolises Mount Kailash, the Buddhist Paradise. The *enceinte* is surrounded by a covered gallery, 600 yards long, decorated with frescoes depicting the Reamker, the Khmer version of the Ramayana, an epic tragedy of war between the forces of good and evil. One of the cadres, a former professor, explained to Samphân and some of the other leaders the significance of the different scenes, which are crueller and more violent than the Indian original.

Sâr's choice of living quarters revealed more than he knew. Nowhere else in the Cambodian capital do memories of past glory and the mirage of future greatness fuse so easily. No Cambodian leader, however determined to expunge the old, could spend his days in a place so saturated with national identity and still remain insensible to the tenants of history and the legacy of the Khmer race.

In this surreal setting, the arbiters of the world's most radical revolution took the fateful decision, after ten days of discussion, to disband the so-called united front with Sihanouk's supporters and other non-communist groups who had helped them to win power; to jettison the relatively moderate policies that such an alliance implied; and instead to make the leap – the 'extremely marvellous, extremely wonderful, prodigious leap', as the Khmer expression has it – to install, in one fell swoop, full communism, without compromise or concessions. The die had been cast.

While Sâr dreamed his terrible, and terribly beguiling, dreams, the Cambodian people stared into the hallucinative gulf between vision and reality.

The inhabitants of Phnom Penh, as well as many of the urban intellectuals who had joined the Khmer Rouge cause, had expected the war's end to bring a return to normality. Revolution, yes – but peace and a civilised life as well.

Thiounn Thioeunn, the Khmer Rouge Health Minister, and his wife, Mala, were the heirs to Cambodia's two wealthiest aristocratic families. Mala liked to say, only half in jest: 'No one possessed more than we did, except perhaps the King.' They disapproved of Sihanouk, whom they saw as a worthless playboy. Their defection to the Khmers Rouges four years earlier had been the equivalent, in Cambodian terms, of a Kennedy couple joining the ranks of Al-Qaida. Sâr had let it be known that the family enjoyed his personal protection. Thioeunn was a whimsical, otherworldly man, whose life revolved around his work as a surgeon. He had named his eldest daughter, Genevieve, after the car that was the eponymous heroine of a 1950s musical starring Kenneth More and Kay Kendall. The day that Phnom Penh fell, Genevieve was serving as a nurse at a military field hospital not far from the HQ at Sdok Toel. 'We all cheered,' she remembered. 'Everyone started talking about what we'd do when we saw our relatives again, and how, now the war was over, there'd be national reconciliation.' Mala, more down-to-earth, thought of her elderly parents: 'I told myself I'd make them a big cake, with lots of rum in it, and we'd enjoy it together.'

But by the time the Thiounns were allowed back into the city, ten days later, Phnom Penh was already a place of desolation, and rum was the last thing on their minds. Instead of returning to the family home, an immense colonial-style mansion near the palace, they were taken to a barrack-like apartment block at the former Khmer-Soviet Friendship Hospital, where they found that the Khmer Rouge political director had ordered all the mattresses and armchairs removed. 'Luxury poisons the mind,' he told them.

Despite Thioeunn's high rank and his privileged relations with Sâr, Mala was able to meet her parents only once, some months later, for a few hours in a small town in the provinces. Subsequently they starved to death.

All through the late spring and early summer of 1975, columns of evacuees continued to criss-cross the country. Khieu Samphân's colleague, Hou Yuon, whose blunt talking had started to infuriate the higher echelons of the leadership, watched an unending procession of city-dwellers struggling past the bombed-out town of Skoun, fifty miles north-east of Phnom Penh, at the beginning of May. The sight of their fires, burning in the darkness by the roadside, haunted him. 'Those people were truly wretched,' he told Nuon Chea later. 'It's not normal, it's not reasonable, to evacuate everyone like that. What the Standing Committee has done is wrong.'

Two months later, the Cambodian people were still on the move. A Chinese interpreter remembered 'long lines, with sacks of belongings and cooking implements' heading south towards the port of Kompong Som in July. Hunger had already set in; famine would follow. Violence was both random and systemic. Murder had become routine, the administrative tool of first resort. All who had held senior positions in Lon Nol's pro-American regime, officers from the rank of lieutenant upwards, higher civil servants and policemen risked death. So did any others who failed to fit into the Khmer Rouge scheme of things.

Chinese aid experts who had known Phnom Penh in earlier times and now returned to provide 'fraternal assistance' to the new communist government found the city unrecognisable. 'The streets were deserted,' the interpreter reported. 'We saw no one. Some of the doors of the houses were padlocked; others were swinging open. In the factories and at the Ministry, everyone wore black. They had sandals made from car-tyres, and a checkered scarf, a *krama*. We used to try to talk to them . . . But all that came out was propaganda.'

For Cambodian students returning from abroad, it was infinitely more unnerving:

> What I saw was beyond imagining [*wrote one returnee*]. The people [who met us] at the airport were not like human beings. You might have thought they were objects, automatons from another planet. They belonged to a race that was indefinable, neuter, phantoms enveloped in darkness from somewhere very far away. Physically they looked like me, like the rest of us . . . Their appearance was Asian, Cambodian. But it was only their appearance. In every other way, there was nothing in common between us . . . [As we were driven into the city] none of us said a word . . . Was this, then, the new Kampuchea, the new society of equity and justice, without rich or poor? Was this the revolution?

Over the next three years, one and a half million people, out of a population of seven million, would be sacrificed to the working out of Saloth Sâr's ideas. A sizeable minority was executed; the rest died of illness, overwork or starvation.

No other country has ever lost so great a proportion of its nationals in a single, politically inspired hecatomb, brought about by its own leaders.

It is facile, but pointless, to damn Pol Pot and his followers as Nazis or Maoists, visiting a nightmare of imperfectly understood, alien ideas on a supposedly gentle, serene land. It is understandable, but unhelpful, to speak of genocide: the word conveys the magnitude of the horror of what happened in Cambodia but allows Pol Pot's regime to be dismissed, all too conveniently, as a unique aberration. Such terms create a pernicious amalgam, obscuring a reality that was at once more banal and far more sinister.

The sheer scale of death in Democratic Kampuchea, as Khmer Rouge Cambodia was officially known, is part of its gruesome fascination. But beyond the statistics of human callousness lie more troubling issues.

Why did so many Cambodian intellectuals throw in their lot with a movement that turned out to be so ghastly? Why do so many former Khmer Rouge cadres, educated, thoughtful people, including some whose own relatives were murdered under Pol Pot's rule, still maintain that he was a great patriot, whose merits outweigh his faults? Why did the Khmer Rouge revolution go to such implacable, unbearable extremes? Communist regimes everywhere have sought to level income disparities; to make law an instrument of policy; to monopolise the press; to limit movement from the countryside to the cities; and to control postal and telecommunications links with the rest of the world. But Cambodians chose more radical, more insane solutions. Money, law courts, newspapers, the postal system and foreign telecommunications – even the concept of the city – were all simply abolished. Individual rights were not curtailed in favour of the collective, but extinguished altogether. Individual creativity, initiative, originality were condemned *per se*. Individual consciousness was systematically demolished.

There is no straightforward response to such questions, and to the extent that answers exist, they offer scant comfort – to Cambodians and outsiders alike.

Eighteen months after Pol Pot's death in 1998, when the last of his guerrilla armies had laid down their weapons and peace had returned to Cambodia after three decades of war, a sixteen-year-old girl sat down at a stall in one of Phnom Penh's markets and ordered rice soup for herself and her three-year-old niece. A well-dressed woman, accompanied by several bodyguards, came up behind her, grabbed her hair and pushed her to the floor, where the men kicked and beat her until she passed out. Two guards then carefully opened a glass jar containing three litres of nitric acid, which the woman poured over the girl's head and upper body. The pain made her regain consciousness, and she started to scream – splashing acid on the woman and one of the guards, who fled in a waiting car. People in a nearby house doused her with water, but by the time she reached hospital she had third-degree acid burns over 43 per cent of her body.

Tat Marina had been a stunningly beautiful young actress who made her living by appearing in karaoke videos. The previous year she had come to the notice of a Cambodian government minister, Svay Sittha, who had seduced her and installed her in a cheap apartment as his concubine. The attack was carried out by Sittha's wife, Khoun Sophal, whom an American woman-friend would describe later as 'the gentlest soul you could imagine; a truly delightful person'.

The young woman survived, her head and body from the waist up made hideous by scar tissue. Her attackers were never questioned, still less charged with any offence.

Scores of teenage Cambodian girls are disfigured and in many cases blinded in acid attacks by rich men's wives. Older Cambodian women say that Tat Marina and girls like her 'steal other women's husbands' and get what they deserve. Men treat them as disposable, 'like Kleenex, to be used and thrown away'.

The parallel with Khmer Rouge atrocities is striking. One way to try to understand why the Cambodian communists acted as they did is to enter into the mind of a well-educated, intelligent woman, who exacts vengeance by pouring acid over a young girl's head, watching as it eats away her body and every hope of happiness in her life. What can be more odious than to destroy a child's future? The Khmers Rouges, at least, could argue that they were acting for a cause, not out of personal evil. But the result was essentially the same. It was Orwell's vision of the future: 'A boot stamping on a human face, for ever.'

In any violent upheaval, whether war or revolution, innocent people suffer. US officials speak of 'collateral damage'; Maoists talk of breaking eggs in order to make an omelette. In Democratic Kampuchea, 'collateral damage' knew no bounds. Everything outside the 'revolution' became a legitimate and necessary target.

It was not simply that life had no value; that killing became an act of no consequence. An entire country was put in thrall to a dystopian ideal that negated anything and everything that was human. And the question to which all Cambodians ceaselessly demand an answer is: Why? Why did such horrors descend on *us*? Why did it have to happen *here*?

The unstated premise is that the horrors came from without – from the American bombing of Cambodian villages in the early 1970s; from

Maoism; from Stalinism; from the legacy of the French Revolution, transmitted by colonial schoolteachers; from the vicious, warped minds of a small group of evil men.

Cambodians – not just the present government, dominated by former Khmers Rouges who have no interest whatever in raking up the past, but the nation as a whole – are oddly reluctant to look deeper. To do so would require a degree of self-examination for which they are unprepared and which, instinctively, they prefer to avoid. To the extent that people want a reckoning, the goal is to condemn the big fish, the perpetrators – 'them'; not 'us' – the small fry.

No one wants to make 'shrimp soup', as the Cambodian saying has it. The shrimps – the petty thugs and killers – abound in every village. The holocaust that consumed Cambodia required the complicity of so large a proportion of the population that one has to ask how the victims would have behaved if the roles had been reversed.

The question 'Why?' must be rephrased.

The cardinal issue is what it is about Cambodian society that has allowed, and continues to allow, people to turn their backs on all they know of gentleness and compassion, goodness and decency, and to commit appalling cruelties seemingly without conscience of the enormity of their acts and certainly without remorse. It is a question one can ask, in greater or lesser measure, about the Germans (and others) during the time of the Nazis; the Rwandans; the Turks (in Armenia); the Serbs (in Bosnia); the Bosnians (in Serbia); the Israelis in Palestine and the Palestinians in Israel; not to mention all the terrorist organisations occupying the moral high ground inspired by Islamic fundamentalism.

The explanation does not lie in some chromosomal abnormality, some genetic predisposition to violence, a neuropathic 'Bell curve' on the part of the nations concerned. Cambodians, or for that matter Rwandans, are not biologically more prone to cruelty than Americans or West Europeans. The causes are rooted in history – which creates the conditions for nations to seek extreme remedies to perceived ills; in geography – which generates the pressures that seem to justify them (*lebensraum*, said Hitler; 'national survival', said Pol Pot); in culture – which erects or fails to erect moral and intellectual prohibitions against them; and in the political and social system – which affords or denies the individual the right to act according to his own lights.

Context is not all, however. Evil is as evil does.

The individual, whatever the context, has a personal responsibility. Evil, at this level, consists in deliberately ignoring what one knows to be right. The weaker the moral code, the easier evil becomes to commit. Jacques

Vergès, a radical French lawyer who, as a student in the 1950s, befriended many of the future Cambodian communist leaders, maintains that what distinguishes men from animals is *crime*. Nature, knowing no human law, is savage. Man alone is criminal. Or, to put it in Old Testament terms, man alone is evil. When we contemplate what happened in Cambodia, we are looking not at some exotic horror story but into darkness, into the foul places of our own souls.

History, culture, geography, politics and millions of individuals have all played their part in the Cambodian nightmare, albeit in differing measures. The same is true of all such tragedies, which is why the particular agony of a small, distant country has a larger significance, on which those who make policy, and public opinion, would do well to ponder. That is reason enough for recounting the story of the man who became Pol Pot. For if there is one lesson worth retaining from the travails of the Cold War and the miseries it brought in its wake, it is the folly of seeking simple answers to complicated questions. It is a lesson which governments still show no sign of learning.

I

Sâr

THE VILLAGE OF Prek Sbauv extends along the east bank of the River Sên, which flows southward from the town of Kompong Thom to the Great Lake, the Tonle Sap. Wooden stilt-houses stand half-hidden amid orange and purple bougainvillea, morning glory, yellow-flowering *anh kang* trees, cactus hedges and palms. Fishermen row flat-bottomed canoes, with a lazy sweeping motion, standing with a single oar at the stern, to string out nets on stakes in the shallows. The water gleams yellowish-brown. Buffalo with small, erect pink ears peer out suspiciously from the mud. It is a gentle, idyllic place.

Nhep's home is set back about thirty yards from the river, separated from it by a cart-track which leads to the provincial capital, three miles distant. The stilts are a protection against flooding, although severe floods have come only once in Nhep's lifetime, a few years back, the result of uncontrolled logging along the Mekong river, which Cambodians know as the 'Mother of Waters'. As in all traditional Cambodian dwellings, everyone lives in one large room, occupying the whole of the first floor, which is reached by a flight of steep wooden steps leading up from the garden outside. The house where he and Sâr were born stood on the same spot, Nhep says, and was built in exactly the same way. It was destroyed in a bombing raid during the civil war.

The family was well-off, indeed, by local standards, wealthy. Their father, Loth, owned 50 acres of rice-paddy – ten times the average, comparable to the living of a junior mandarin – and their home was one of the biggest among the twenty or so houses in the village. At transplanting and harvest time, Loth hired his poorer neighbours to provide extra labour.

Nhep, the youngest child, was born in the summer of 1927, the Year of the Hare; Sâr, eighteen months older, in March 1925, the Year of the Ox;*

---

*Sâr's officially registered, but false, birth date was May 19 1928. In those days, Cambodian families often neglected to register births until a pressing administrative need – usually connected with school admission – made it necessary to do so. Parents commonly subtracted months or years from a boy's age to comply with school entrance requirements.

and their brother, Chhay, in the Dog Year, 1922. There were three elder
siblings – two boys and a girl – who had also been born within a year or
two of each other, but more than a decade earlier. Three others had died
young. Because they were so close in age, the three youngest were inseparable, particularly Sâr and Nhep. They played and swam in the river
together, and in the evenings, by the light of a rush-lamp, listened to the
old people of the village recounting stories and legends from the days
before the French established the protectorate in the 1860s.

Their grandfather, Phem, was a link with that time. The children never
knew him, but Loth used to tell them of his exploits. Phem had grown up
during what were afterwards called the 'Years of Calamity', when
Vietnamese and Thai invaders vied for suzerainty over what remained of
the old Khmer kingdom, and court poets voiced the nation's fears that soon
'Cambodia would no longer exist'. The Royal Palace at Oudong was razed
and Phnom Penh was destroyed. Among the populace, those who escaped
the corvées imposed by the rival armies 'fled to the forest to live on leaves
and roots'. The Vietnamese were in the habit of gouging out their captives' eyes, salting their wounds and burying them alive. A French missionary who witnessed the devastation left by the Thais reported that they were
little better:

> The Siamese method of warfare is to steal everything they can lay hands on;
> to burn and destroy wherever they pass; to enslave those men that they do
> not kill, and to carry off the women and children. They show no humanity
> towards their captives. If they cannot keep up with the march, they are
> beaten, maltreated or killed. Unmoved by tears and wailing, they slaughter
> small children in front of their mothers. They have no more scruple in kill-
> ing a person than a fly, perhaps less, for their religion forbids them to kill
> animals.

Eventually a compromise was reached between the Thai court and the
Vietnamese Emperor at Hue, peace was restored and Phem prospered. He
became a notable – 'Elder Phem', the villagers called him – and, during
the great rebellion against the French in 1885–6, he organised food supplies for loyalist troops, fighting to preserve the prerogatives of the monarchy against the inroads of colonial rule. But one day, Loth told the children,
Phem and two friends walked into an ambush in a village on the other side
of the river and were killed.

From that time on, the family received the favour of the provincial governor, a staunch royalist named Dekchoa Y, which gave them a place in the
patronage network percolating down from the Throne. Loth's sister,
Cheng, obtained a post in the household of King Norodom, and around

the year of Sâr's birth, her daughter, Meak, was chosen as a royal concubine for the heir apparent, Monivong. The Lady Meak, as she was now
known, bore him a son, Prince Kossarak, and after Monivong became
king, was appointed Head of the Royal Bedchamber with overall responsibility for all the palace women. With her help, in 1930, Loth's eldest son,
Suong, secured a grace-and-favour appointment as a palace officer. Soon
afterwards Meak summoned his sister, Roeung, then sixteen years old, to
join her in Phnom Penh, where she, too, became one of Monivong's
favourites, remaining at the King's side until his death in 1941.

This was not such an unusual story in Cambodia in the early part of the
twentieth century. The mother of Sâr's contemporary Keng Vannsak was
another of Monivong's concubines. The King handed her on to his
brother, but she then fell in love with Vannsak's father and persuaded her
royal master, who had a surfeit of women already, to restore her liberty.
Monivong had more than thirty wives. King Norodom, who died in 1904,
had 360 – as Sihanouk, his grandson and spiritual heir, was forever point-
ing out to justify his own philandering. Even a lesser figure, like the Lord
Governor of Battambang, had more than a hundred consorts and insisted,
to the dismay of the Buddhist clergy who visited him, that all the women
in his household, from the lowest serving girl to his principal wife, should
go about the official mansion nude from the waist up. Polygyny was a sign
of virility, guaranteeing the fruitfulness of the realm.

Cambodian life has an earthy, elemental quality. Nature teems and fruc-
tifies. The sun beats like an iron hammer, the jungle steams, the land pulsates
with the heat and colour of the tropics. In late spring the countryside is blot-
ted out by dense, palpitating clouds of orange butterflies, several miles wide,
which float across plains of lotus blossom and bright green paddy-fields. Girls
flower into women as soon as they enter their teens, and fade when they
reach twenty. Small boys run about naked; girl children stagger under the
weight of their brothers, almost as big as themselves. In the days when Sâr
and Nhep were young, herds of elephant used to pass by Prek Sbauv, heading for the water-meadows beside the Great Lake. At flood time, the villagers organised hunts on buffalo-back, using javelins to spear wild boar. When
Loth's eldest son, Suong, travelled for the first time to Phnom Penh, a hundred miles to the south, the choice was between an eighteen-hour journey
in a Chinese merchant's steam launch or three days in an ox-cart – but only
during the dry season. During the rains, the roads disappeared.

The landscape, and the lifestyle, were, and are still, closer to Africa than
China. Substitute baobabs for bamboo, and papyrus for lotus, and you
could be in Kenya or Tanzania. Dark-skinned Cambodian peasants proudly
call themselves 'black Khmer'. At the country's eastern border, the subtle,

sinicised world of the Vietnamese scholar-official – sustained by a meritoc-
racy based on Confucian notions of propriety and virtue – butts up against
the sensual harshness of Brahminism, against Buddhism and the mind-set
of the Indian states.

Cambodia, even more than the other nations of the region that the
French named Indo-China, lies on the fault-line between Asia's two great
founding civilisations.

Loth's family, like many Cambodians, including the Royal House, was
of Sino-Khmer extraction. Sâr derived his name from his light 'Chinese'
complexion – the word *sâr* means 'white' or 'pale' – a characteristic shared
by his brother Nhep. But race in Cambodia is determined by behaviour
rather than blood line. Loth – or Phem Saloth as he later called himself, to
satisfy the colonial authorities' insistence that everyone must have a family
as well as a given name – did not practise the Chinese rites. He and his wife
did not sweep their ancestors' graves at the Qingming festival, or celebrate
the Chinese New Year. Nor did they speak Chinese. They lived as Khmers
and therefore, racially, they *were* Khmer, in their own minds as well as those
of their neighbours. Their culture was Indianised, like that of the Burmese
and the Indonesians, and all the other serendipitous nations which inhabit
the water margin of Asia, from Sri Lanka to the Timor Sea.

It was, in Nhep's words, a normal, happy family. Loth was a reserved
man, who kept his own counsel. 'He never joked with us, or with anyone
else. If he was angry, he didn't show his feelings or become violent. He
always remained calm. Our mother was the same, and I think that's why
they got on so well.' The younger children closely resembled him, and
Sâr inherited some of his character. He was a disciplinarian, like most
Cambodian fathers, but by the standards of the time the chastisement he
meted out was mild. For those were the days when a village schoolmaster would make a recalcitrant pupil lie down on a red ants' nest to help
him mend his ways. Keng Vannsak endured that once, and never misbe-
haved again:

> I didn't like arithmetic, and I hadn't learnt my multiplication tables. So every
> time we were going to have a lesson, I said that I had a stomach ache and
> wanted to go home. The third time I did that, the teacher said: 'All right,
> you may go. But first recite the seven times table.' Of course, I didn't know
> it. Ai-ya! How he beat me! Kicks and punches . . . he was brutal! Then he
> took me outside, and put me under a grapefruit tree – full of red ants! After
> that, I knew my times tables. I knew them so well that I did all the other
> children's questions, and in return they gave me things from their lunch-
> boxes, because their parents were richer than mine and they had nicer things
> to eat.

Yet punishments like this were so much the norm for Cambodian youngsters that Vannsak remembered that same teacher as 'an adorable, saintly
man' who first instilled in him a love of learning. Certainly he was no worse
than his own father, who used to tie his arms together, throw him on to a
bed and beat him with a cane until he fainted.

Sâr and his brothers were more fortunate. Or, as the people in the village would have put it, it was not their fate to suffer that way: a genie protected them.

Cambodians, at that time even more than today, lived parallel sets of
lives: one in the natural world, among the laws of reason; the other, mired
in superstition, peopled by monsters and ghosts, a prey to witches and the
fear of sorcery. In this sense Cambodia was, and to some extent is still, a
medieval country, where even the King takes no important decision without first consulting the court astrologer. The resemblance to Africa is again
overwhelming. Every village has its witch, or *ap*, and its *k'ruu*, or healer;
each rural community its *neak ta*, the ancestor figure or tutelary genie who
inhabits a stone or an ancient tree and must be propitiated by offerings of
incense and perfumed water. In the countryside, more murders are attrib-
uted to sorcery than to any other single cause. Cambodian officials, university-educated men, still sometimes justify the beating to death of a
suspected witch by a mob by saying: 'The powers of those persons are too
terrible. What else can the peasants do?'

Sâr's earliest memories were coloured by the lore of this nether world.
One story that he would retell as an old man was about a *dhmap'*, or wizard,
whose mouth, as a punishment for his blasphemy, had been shrunk until it
was no bigger than a straw. To feed himself, so the story went, he rolled
dough into fine strips, which was how the Cambodian people came to eat
noodles. He recalled tales about glutton spirits, which, like the ancient
Chinese *taotie*, had only a head and intestines, and fed on foul things that
lived in the mud; and there were gruesome stories of corpse wax, extracted
from the newly dead to make potions, and of foetuses ripped by husbands
from their wives' bellies and mummified as *kun krak*, 'smoke-children',
familiar spirits with magical powers of protection.

Not all Cambodian folk-tales were so grim. The common lore of childhood in Sâr's day revolved around the exploits of Judge Hare and the
human and animal companions he constantly outwitted. Yet here, too, was
an undertow of menace and of the injustice and unpredictability of life.

Unlike children's stories in most lands, in which virtue is rewarded and
evildoing punished, the imagined world from which Sâr and his contemporaries derived their first insights into the ways of Cambodian society had
no such clear-cut rules. In Khmer legend, thieves go unpunished and live

happily to the end of their days. Men are executed for deeds of which they are wholly blameless. Villainy is praised so long as it succeeds. Trickery is admired; honest conduct decried; and goodness regarded as stupidity. There is little place for compassion. Judges are portrayed as fools; true justice can come only from the King, whose rulings brook no appeal.

Through these stories, Sâr and his brothers were introduced to the moral tenets of Theravada Buddhism, which teaches that retribution or merit, in the endless cycle of self-perfection, will be apportioned not in this life but in a future existence, just as man's present fate is the fruit of actions in previous lives.

Prek Sbauv was too small to have a Buddhist temple of its own. But on Buddhist holy days, four times a month, Loth and his wife travelled by oxcart to the great *wat*, or monastery, of Kompong Thom, where their two eldest sons, Suong and Seng, had learnt to read and write. Loth himself had been taught his letters there, and though the boys' mother, Nem, was illiterate, there was enough Chinese ancestry in Loth's make-up for him to understand that education was important. In the early 1930s, rice prices rose. The family prospered and he decided that the time had come to send the younger children to school in Phnom Penh, where Suong, now well-established in his job at the palace, had recently married a young woman from the Royal Ballet corps.

Chhay went first, followed, in 1934, by Sâr. They travelled, not by oxcart, but in one of the new-fangled steam buses the French had just introduced, powered by an engine burning charcoal. Cambodians were being dragged willy-nilly into the modern age. But they went reluctantly, full of backward glances.

Although the reason for sending Sâr to Phnom Penh was to allow him to attend one of the new Western-style primary schools, he did not do so at once. Instead his parents decided he should first spend a year at the Wat Botum Vaddei, a large Buddhist monastery a couple of hundred yards south of the palace.

It was a compromise which reflected, perhaps unconsciously, the anxieties of the time. Tensions were developing between the emancipated, Westernised values transmitted by the French and the immovable, inward-looking conservatism of Cambodian tradition. The anguish this generated was captured in a play by Sâr's future mentor, Keng Vannsak, which took the plight of a gauche young man from a traditional household, torn between the demands of his elderly grandfather and his fashion plate of a lady-love, a thoroughly modern miss infatuated with foreign ways, as a metaphor for that of the Cambodian people, groping their way through a transition they did not understand towards a goal they could not see. A group of intellectuals, led by a young lawyer named Son Ngoc Thanh, began planning the first Khmer-language newspaper, the title of which, *Nagaravatta*, the Pali spelling of Nokor Wat ('Land of the Temple'), evoked the glories of Angkor. Cambodian nationalism was stirring, and the issue of Cambodian identity became its prime concern.

Wat Botum Vaddei, which belongs to the Thommayut order, a small, elitist Buddhist school favoured by the royal court, is a walled village. A warren of narrow lanes and dwellings, sleeping quarters and refectories encircles the temple proper, which stands, hidden in a grove of banyan and palm trees, beside two immense grey-blue stupas. Novices, in indian red robes, squat between the houses, doing washing, preparing rice for the monks' lunch, shouting, fighting, ribbing lay friends who have come to visit. One day, the roles will be reversed: the young acolytes will rejoin the workaday world outside, and their friends will become novices in their place. The *wat* is a revolving door, a place of constant interchange between the hustle and bustle of the city and Cambodians' inner yearning for spiritual release through ritual and meditation.

Each year about a hundred children, between seven and twelve years old, were sent there to be initiated into the mysteries of the Triple Jewel and the Eightfold Path and, scarcely less important, to learn to read and write in Khmer.

The majority, like Sâr, were from the countryside, but there were also boys from aristocratic households, brought by their parents for a few months to fulfil a religious obligation. Many were desperately homesick. Nhep remembered feeling wretched after being packed off to Phnom Penh. But if Sâr missed his mother and father he never spoke of it. On the contrary, in later years he reminisced fondly about the time he had spent at the *wat*, even on various occasions falsifying his biography to make it seem that he had stayed there longer than was actually the case.

It was a crucially important formative period. Monastic discipline was strict. As a novice, Sâr was part of a rigidly ordered community in which, as in all traditional Cambodian institutions, including the court and the Royal Ballet, originality and initiative were discouraged, the least deviation was punished and the greatest merit lay in unquestioning obedience to prevailing orthodoxy. Nhun Nhget, later abbot of Botum Vaddei, was among Sâr's contemporaries:

> In those days, if you came to the *wat* as a novice, you had to study for three months before you were allowed to wear the robe. You were taught the etiquette of a monk: how to put on the robe; how to speak; how to walk; how

to put your palms together to show respect . . . And you were given a thrashing if you didn't do as they said. If you didn't walk correctly, you were beaten. You had to walk quietly and slowly, without making any sound with your feet, and you weren't allowed to swing your arms. You had to move serenely. You had to learn by heart in pali the rules of conduct and the [Buddhist] precepts so that you could recite them without hesitation; if you hesitated, you were beaten.

The boys had dormitories of their own, separate from those of the older monks. They rose at 4 a.m., lit sticks of incense and made obeisance to the Buddha, the Law and the Clergy. Then for two hours they recited sutras, led by a senior monk, before doing their assigned chores – sweeping the temple courtyard, and cooking the rice for breakfast. After two more hours spent memorising the scriptures, they accompanied the monks to beg alms, repeating silently to themselves an impetration in pali to subdue the self. On their return, they prepared the second, and last, meal of the day, consisting of rice and vegetables, which had to be finished by noon – for under monastic rules no food could be consumed between midday and the following sunrise. In the afternoon, they attended classes where, in addition to basic literacy, they were taught from the *cpap*, traditional collections of moral maxims which first appeared in the sixteenth century – the *Treatise on the Morality of Men*; the *Treatise of Ancient Sayings;* the *Treatise on the Glorious Tradition*, and others of the same kind – chanting them aloud until they had them by rote.

The content of these edifying texts was not intrinsically very different from that in China or most other Asian countries, being rooted in respect for parents, for elders and for hierarchy – and, in the case of women, for men. But it was notably more rigid, more intransigent. Where the Confucian primers treat children as individuals, with personalities of their own and talents to be encouraged and drawn out, the *cpap* view them as objects – as 'aggregates of cause and effect', in Buddhist terms – whose behaviour must be moulded to ensure the faithful transmission of immutable values. The *cpap* for boys were stern enough – 'Do not destroy the tradition that your parents pass on to you! Do not oppose their advice!' Those for girls – inevitably, in the feudal scheme of things – were still more stiffnecked and dehumanised:

Never turn your back to your husband when he sleeps and never touch his head without first bowing in his honour . . . Respect and fear [his] wishes and take his advice to heart . . . If [he] gives an order, don't hesitate a moment in responding . . . Avoid posing as an equal to your husband – and never above he who is your master. If he insults you, go to your quarters and reflect, never insult or talk back to him . . .

The *cpap*, at least in the form in which Sâr would have learnt them, had another particularity. They portrayed the Khmers as honest and sincere but 'foolish and ignorant', constantly being duped by their smarter Chinese and Vietnamese neighbours:

Your eyes are open and can see,
But see only the surface of things . . .
Learn arithmetic . . . with all your energy
Lest the Chinese and Vietnamese cheat you . . .
The Khmers are lacking in judgement
They eat without giving thought for what is proper and right,
Each season they borrow from the Chinese,
And the Chinese gain control of the inheritance their parents have
bequeathed.

If the *cpap* were a practical code of conduct to regulate life in the world beyond the monastery walls, the monks also sought to inculcate in their young charges a spirit of detachment. Nhun Nhget remembered that as the hardest thing to accept. 'They taught us to renounce worldly desires, not to covet material things. If you are an ordinary person, you can [behave normally], you can have nice meals, you can marry . . . When you become a monk, you have to forgo all that.'

One wonders whether Sâr, as a child, was also struck by this emphasis on detachment. There is no way of knowing. But subconsciously it must have registered, for in later life the abandonment of personal ties and the suppression of individuality – in both thought and behaviour – would become key elements of his political credo.

In the summer of 1935, at the age of ten, Sâr left Wat Botum Vaddei and went to live with his brother Suong, his wife and their baby son, in a large, rambling wooden house, built on wooden pillars, with a spacious front veranda overlooking a small courtyard planted with trees and tubs of flowers. His older brother Chhay was already staying with them, and soon afterwards Nhep, the youngest, arrived too.

That September, Sâr joined Chhay at the Ecole Miche, named after a nineteenth-century missionary bishop. The lessons were in French, dispensed by Vietnamese and French Catholic fathers, and each day's classes began with an hour spent learning the catechism, followed by a collective recitation of the Lord's Prayer or one of the Psalms. At first sight it might seem an odd choice. Sâr's family had no connection with the Catholic Church. But the school had a good reputation and, catechism apart, the curriculum was the same as at the other main primary school in Phnom

Penh, which was run by the protectorate authorities and catered exclusively for Europeans and a handful of assimilated Khmers from aristocratic families, like Thiounn Thioeunn and his brothers. Even primary schooling was hard to come by in the Cambodia of the 1930s, and the fees at the Ecole Miche, modest though they were, were far beyond the reach of all but a tiny fraction of the population. In the country as a whole, no more than a few thousand children, among half a million of school-going age, had access to even the rudiments of a 'modern' education.

Phnom Penh, at that time, was an unusual capital city. It was strangely un-Khmer.

Visitors found 'tables of chattering Frenchmen . . . Chinese in white suits and helmets, Annamites with bare torsos and full black trousers – and, among them, surprisingly few Cambodians.' Khmers accounted for little more than a third of the population of 100,000. Most of the others were Chinese-speaking merchants, who controlled the country's commercial life, and Vietnamese, who worked as junior civil servants, fishermen or coolies. There was also a scattering of Thais, Malays and Indians from Pondicherry. The few hundred French families formed a tiny, if highly visible, microcosm, who put their stamp on what passed for the cultural and intellectual life of the city, its pavement cafés, tree-lined boulevards and colonial, Mediterranean-style buildings. The result was a cosmopolitan, contradictory place – languid yet bustling – a hodge-podge of conflicting styles:

> The street traffic is a mêlée of rickety native-built gharris [known locally as matchboxes], glittering motorcars, rickshaws, top-heavy omnibuses drawn by tiny ponies . . . and bullock carts exactly like those illustrated on the walls of Angkor . . . all moving against a background of avenues and suburbs full of typically French villas . . . The street-markets of Phnom Penh are peculiarly its own, yet have much in common with those of France . . . The goods are set neatly out on the pavements instead of on raised stalls . . . Flowering plants in home-made basket-pots [stand] in ranks of scarlet and orange, white and mauve, pink and green . . . As the sun moves across the heavens, the goods are [transferred to the other pavement] and laid out patiently and methodically all over again.

Even the King's palace, a gilt-and-gingerbread confection with crenellated yellow-plaster walls, ornately curlicued sentry-boxes and imposing wrought-iron gates – not to mention a *belle époque* summerhouse, used by the Empress Eugénie for the opening of the Suez Canal before being dismantled and shipped to Indochina – seemed to have been created by its French architects with an oriental Monaco in mind.

The foreignness of Phnom Penh, and the leading role played by other

Asians at the expense of Khmers, appear to have had little impact on Sâr. 'It didn't surprise us,' Nhep explained later, 'because . . . there were Chinese everywhere in Cambodia.' Even in a place as small as Prek Sbauv, there was a Chinese shop – the only one in the area – where the merchants from Kompong Thom congregated each year to purchase the rice harvest.

The Vietnamese were viewed differently. Every Khmer child knew the story of the three Cambodian prisoners, whom the Vietnamese buried up to their necks so that their heads formed a tripod on which a kettle could be placed, lighting a fire in the middle and enjoining them not to move lest they 'spill the master's tea' – just as every child knew that sugar palms, or *thnot*, emblematic of Cambodia, stopped growing a few miles before the border 'because they don't want to grow in Vietnam'. That such tales were patently untrue was irrelevant; they summed up a perception of a country which Cambodians viewed as an hereditary enemy. Despite the atrocities committed by the nineteenth-century Siamese, there were no comparable stories about the Thais.

Vietnam was the Cambodian bogeyman. When Khmer children squabbled, one of Sâr's friends recalled, an older child would intervene, reminding them that Cambodians had enemies enough without fighting among themselves. Yet it was above all the *idea* of the Vietnamese that was hated. They seemed to be everything the Khmers were not: a disciplined, vigorous, virile people, whose relentless, centuries-long southward migration had swallowed up Kampuchea Krom, or Lower Cambodia, in the area of what would become South Vietnam, and now threatened a creeping takeover of Cambodia itself, aided and abetted by the French authorities, who encouraged large-scale Vietnamese immigration to staff the lower echelons of the colonial civil service and furnish the skilled manual labour which Cambodians were judged incapable of providing. The result was more than mere racial antipathy. It was a massive national inferiority complex, which took refuge in dreams of ancient grandeur. At a personal level, Khmers and Vietnamese might befriend each other; Khmer pupils often remembered their Annamite teachers with affection. But the cultural fracture between the two peoples – between Confucianism and Theravada Buddhism, between the Chinese world and the Indian – was one of mutual incomprehension and distrust, which periodically exploded into racial massacres and pogroms.

The different quarters of Phnom Penh were strung out along the riverside: the Vietnamese 'Catholic village' in the north; the French district around Wat Phnom, the ancient grave mound from which the city takes its name; the Chinese in the commercial area in the centre; and the Khmers in the 'Cambodian village' in the south.

It was there that Saloth Suong had built his house, on a newly-laid-out street, across fields and marshland, half a mile west of the palace. The city is situated on a flood plain, at the point where the Mekong is joined by two other rivers, the Tonle Sap and the Bassac. In the early 1930s, the French had undertaken a drainage programme and large areas of swamp and lakeland had been reclaimed. Suong's house was in one of these new districts, inhabited mainly by minor officials and palace functionaries. A mile or so to the north, near Wat Phnom, stood the railway station, also built on reclaimed land, where the first train service was inaugurated in 1935. Between the two, on the route which Sâr and Chhay took each morning as they walked to school, a new Central Market was being erected on what previously had been yet another swamp. It was an imaginative, cruciform structure in art deco style with an immense concrete dome (taller than the basilica of St Peter's in Rome, the French architects boasted). In September 1937, Sâr and his brothers watched the grand opening, performed by the French governor, the *Résident Supérieur*, in the presence of the city mandarins and notables.

For the young, Phnom Penh in the 1930s was a place of wonderment. Each November during the Water Festival, the floodwaters that gorge the Great Lake, backed up by the monsoon rains, cause the Tonle Sap to reverse course and flow out towards the sea. The King, escorted by white-robed *baku*, the spiritual descendants of the brahmins of Angkor, their long hair in chignons, bearing trumpets made of conch-shells, boarded the royal barge to watch dragon-boat races, signalling the start of three days of bacchanalian excess when the taboos proscribing flirtation between young men and unmarried girls of good family were temporarily eased. Apart from the Khmer New Year, in April – when Sâr returned to Prek Sbauv to be with his parents – the major ceremonies all revolved around the Throne and the Buddhist faith. Each spring crowds gathered to watch the Royal Oxen plough the Sacred Furrow, from which the King's astrologer would divine whether there would be plenty or famine in the year ahead; and at Tang Toc, the King's birthday, the provincial governors came to pay homage. Royal protocol was draconian. In his palace, if no longer in the colonised state over which he reigned, the King was still an absolute ruler, the 'Master of Life', venerated by the populace as a sacred, quasi-divine figure:

> At royal audiences [*one participant wrote*], the princes, mandarins and other dignitaries crouch on all fours, with their knees and elbows on the floor, and their hands raised together before their heads. The King sits above them, enthroned on a dais, sitting cross-legged like an Indian idol. When he enters or leaves, all present prostrate themselves three times. No one has the right

to speak unless the King addresses him . . . and no one may publicly disagree with anything the King says.

The symbolism was explicit: the heads of the courtiers, in Khmer culture the most sacred part of the body, were beneath the King's feet. A special vocabulary had to be used when addressing him, and all those not of royal blood, even the grandest ministers, were, in the consecrated formula, 'we who carry the King's excrement on our heads'.

Sâr used to visit the palace to see his sister, Roeung, and the Lady Meak, each of whom occupied a small wood-and-brick house in the precinct reserved for secondary wives. There he sometimes encountered Sihanouk's mother, later to become Queen Kossamak. When she passed, he remembered, he and the other children would fall to their knees. Towards the end of his life, he would look back on those visits with nostalgia, speaking of the Queen, in particular, with affection.

There may have been another reason why Sâr's visits to the palace remained engraved on his memory. The harem of a Cambodian king in the 1930s was awash with repressed sexuality. As well as his official wives, King Monivong had innumerable concubines and serving girls, most of them in their teens or early twenties. Monivong was elderly and not in good health. Necessarily, most of these young women were physically unsatisfied.

At fifteen, Sâr was still regarded as a child, young enough to be allowed into the women's quarters. Decades later, two of the palace women, living out their old age on French government stipends in Paris, remembered 'Little Sâr', who used to come to visit them wearing his school uniform, a loose, white shirt with baggy trousers and wooden shoes. The young women would gather round, teasing him, they remembered. Then they would loosen his waistband and fondle his genitals, masturbating him to a climax. He was never allowed to have intercourse with them. But in the frustrated, hothouse world of the royal pleasure house, it apparently afforded the women a vicarious satisfaction.*

Roeung by then enjoyed the King's favour. Monivong himself had supervised the furnishing of her house and had given her jewellery and a motor-car. She, too, recalled Sâr's visits – and she remembered, also, that 'whenever he had something serious to say, he would make a joke of it.'

---

*In large, polygamous households, such behaviour is less unusual than it might seem. In imperial China, palace women, including the Empress Cixi, had liaisons with eunuchs. Pakistani servants in Saudi Arabia and the Gulf States frequently speak of advances from the wives of their employers and also of cases of incest involving adolescent sons.

It would be wrong to read too much into that. In Khmer culture, polite-ness – which, as Nhep noted, was another of Sâr's early characteristics – always implies indirection. None the less, it offers an intriguing glimpse of a child who would spend the rest of his life dissimulating his thoughts behind an impenetrable wreath of smiles and laughter. The sense of fun, moreover, was genuine. Not only Nhep, but all Sâr's friends during his schooldays remembered him as an amusing companion – 'a boy it was nice to be with', as one of them put it – and even Suong, his elder brother, whom the neighbours regarded as rather strait-laced, agreed that young Sâr was an 'adorable child' who 'wouldn't hurt a chicken' and never caused them any worry.

The one black spot was his academic record. Chhay was evidently a gifted student and sailed through his exams. Sâr did not. He should have passed his primary school leaving certificate – the Certificat d'Etudes Primaires Complémentaires – in 1941. But it seems he did not obtain it until two years later, when he was already eighteen, having twice been held back a year, common practice in the French educational system when children have difficulty keeping up. Nhep, who attended an elementary school in the southern part of Phnom Penh, was also an indifferent student and after three years his parents called him home to help on the farm. Chhay went on to study at the highly regarded Lycée Sisowath, the oldest secondary school in Cambodia. Sâr took the admission exam, but failed and was for-tunate to secure a place as a boarder at a newly opened junior middle school, the Collège Preah Sihanouk at Kompong Cham, fifty miles north-east of Phnom Penh on the Mekong river, where he moved in the autumn of 1943.

The first half of the 1940s was a period of jarring change in Cambodia, both for the Khmer population and for its French rulers.

The outbreak of the Second World War in Europe and France's defeat by Germany meant that from July 1940, Cambodia was administered by Marshal Pétain's collaborationist regime in Vichy, under the tutelage of Germany's ally, Japan. The following winter Thailand, sensing French weakness, invaded the border provinces of Battambang, Sisophon and Siem Reap. The imperial Japanese government imposed an armistice on the bel-ligerents and, after negotiations in Tokyo in the spring, awarded most of the disputed area to the Thais. Cambodia was allowed to retain only Siem Reap town and the Angkorian temples. A month later, King Monivong, then sixty-five, humiliated by the loss of territory, died at the hill resort of Bokor, with Sâr's sister, Roeung, at his bedside. Among the hundreds of potential successors, the Pétainist Governor-General, Admiral Jean Decoux, chose eighteen-year-old Norodom Sihanouk, then attending secondary school in Saigon where his favourite subjects were said to be philosophy and music.

It must have seemed a clever manoeuvre – an artsy, teenage monarch who would be putty in French hands. But Sihanouk's accession in April 1941 brought a change of generation and, with time, a change in political style beyond anything the colonial authorities could have imagined.

The French defeat brought other changes, too. In the last years of the Third Republic, political and social life in France had been a gay, decadent cocktail of corruption, incompetence, joie de vivre, prostitution, *pauses-apéritif*, crooked lawyers and dishonest politicians. Vichy's political credo – 'Travail, Famille, Patrie', or TFP, lampooned by its detractors as 'Travaux Forcés en Perpetuité'* – was moralistic and puritanical. At the older-established French schools in Indochina, genuflexions to Vichy's 'National Revolution' were perfunctory at best. But at the new college at Kompong Cham, where the staff had been recruited after the Vichy regime took office, commitment to Pétainist values was a professional requirement.

Instead of reciting the catechism each morning, Sâr and his schoolmates now sang:

> Marshal, here we are!
> Saviour of France, before you,
> Your boys swear to serve you,
> And follow in your path.

There was also a blasphemous prayer – which would not have been lost on Sâr after his time at the Ecole Miche – entreating the aged marshal: 'Our Father, Which Art Our Leader, Glorious Be Thy Name . . . Deliver Us From Evil.' The Pétainist anthem, with its exaltation of order, unity, and labour, stuck in the boys' minds well enough for Khieu Samphân, more than fifty years later, to start singing it when the subject of the war years came up in conversation. There were other aspects of Pétainism, too, which seemed to find unconscious echoes among the Cambodian communists many decades after. Youths were enrolled in mobile labour brigades, *les chantiers de la jeunesse*, or *chalat* in Khmer; officials who womanised or got drunk risked dismissal; the peasantry were romanticised as the incarnation of the nation's vital forces; and city life was decried as inherently depraved.

The weakening of French authority and the growing clout of Japan did not escape the notice of the young men who ran *Nagaravatta*. From 1940, the newspaper acquired a pronounced anti-colonial (and anti-Vietnamese)

---

* 'Labour, Family, Fatherland' or, by a play on its French initials, 'Forced Labour Forever'.

slant, denouncing Annamite domination of the civil service and criticising France's failure to educate Cambodians to the same level. Its founder, Son Ngoc Thanh, and his fellow intellectuals saw Japan as a lever to prise Cambodia from France's grip; Japan saw them as a ginger group, keeping the French off balance.

These conflicting ambitions provided the embryonic nationalist movement with its first martyrs. On July 18 1942, the French authorities arrested two monks suspected of subversive activities. They omitted to obtain the prior approval of the Buddhist hierarchy, as law and custom required. Two days later, Pach Chhoeun, the editor of *Nagaravatta*, led some two thousand demonstrators – including hundreds of saffron-robed monks holding yellow parasols – to protest to the French *Résident Supérieur*. A riot ensued, in which 'the police used their batons, and the monks hit back with their umbrellas.' Pach Chhoeun, Bunchan Mol and the other alleged ringleaders were arrested, sentenced to life imprisonment and transported to the French prison island of Poulo Condor, off the southern coast of Vietnam. Son Ngoc Thanh fled to Thailand and thence to Japan, where he remained until 1945.

The 'Umbrella Revolt', as it became known, was the first major anti-French demonstration for almost thirty years and served as a long-term catalyst for the growth of Khmer nationalism. But it had little immediate impact on youngsters of Sâr's generation. They knew of it – indeed, Sâr himself was almost certainly in Phnom Penh the day it occurred, though it appears he did not witness the event – but even a socially aware student like Keng Vannsak failed to grasp the implications. Among the few who did take note was Ieng Sary, then at school in Prey Veng, near the Vietnamese border. When the news reached the town, he remembered, 'everyone talked about it. It gave me for the first time an understanding of the word, "nation".' Sary was a few months older than the others and had led a much less sheltered life. Born Kim Trang, he was the son of a village notable in a Khmer-speaking district of southern Vietnam. While he was still a small child, the family fell on hard times. His mother managed to send him to elementary school, but at the age of fourteen he was put to work selling ferry tickets at Neak Luong, the main crossing point on the Mekong, forty miles south of Phnom Penh. A year later, with the help of an elder brother, who had secured a job in the provincial governor's office, he moved to Prey Veng, where an elderly *achar*, or lay Buddhist leader, named Ieng, adopted him as his son.

Not even Sary, however, used to read *Nagaravatta*. Among the students at the Lycée Sisowath, only the oldest, like Mey Mann, four years Vannsak's senior, had begun to take a real interest in politics. For the rest, as Sâr's friend and contemporary, Ping Sây, put it: 'We were simply too young. In Europe, when you are twenty, you are an adult. But in Cambodia in those days, people of that age had no idea of what was going on in the world. We matured much later.'

At the college Preah Sihanouk at Kompong Cham, as at the Ecole Miche, Sâr was a mediocre student. Whether this was because he had difficulty keeping up, or because schoolwork did not interest him, is unclear. Either way, he was not academically inclined. He could perhaps be described as a modest all-rounder. Khieu Samphân, who was in the class below him, remembered him playing the violin, enthusiastically but 'not very well', in the school orchestra. Later he took up the *roneat*, a traditional Cambodian stringed instrument similar to a zither. A love of music and romantic French poetry – Verlaine was one of his favourites – remained with him into old age. He liked football and showed a certain flair for the game: one of his friends at the time spoke admiringly, fifty years later, of the 'scissors kick' which Sâr perfected, sending the ball backwards over his head. He was also a member of the school basketball team and a stagehand with the amateur theatrical troupe.

Halfway through his second year at the college, the political situation changed abruptly in a way that even the most inattentive teenager could not fail to notice.

For almost a year, Japan had been losing ground in South-East Asia. By early 1945 it faced the prospect of a massive Allied counter-attack. Tokyo revised its strategy. The priority became to secure the loyalty of the former colonial peoples by playing on their nationalist sentiments. On the evening of March 9, Japanese army units, which, with Vichy's agreement, had been stationed in Indochina since 1941, launched a *coup de force*. French officials in all three territories were placed under arrest and French civilians interned. The operation did not go entirely smoothly: there were numerous instances of Cambodians helping Frenchmen to escape and, in northern Vietnam, communist guerrillas harassed Japanese outposts. But French rule collapsed overnight, and three days later, under Japan's prodding, Sihanouk proclaimed Cambodian independence on the grounds that France was 'no longer in a position to offer its protection'. For Ieng Sary, in his first year at the Lycée Sisowath, as for millions of Cambodians, the unthinkable had happened:

> For the first time I saw a Frenchman tied and bound. I couldn't believe my eyes. Those people were untouchable, they were so high up they were like gods. And this man had his arms tied behind him. It was on the *men* [the

open ground beside the palace], where the Japanese had dug trenches . . .
I watched as he was marched off . . . I was horrified – and fascinated. It made
a very deep impression on me.

Mey Mann, too, remembered discussing the event with his classmates. 'We
saw that a yellow race – the Japanese – had got the better of the white
colonialists, the French. That awakened something in us. It made us start
thinking.'

In April, the leaders of the 'Umbrella Revolt' returned. Sihanouk, on
Japanese advice, appointed Son Ngoc Thanh Foreign Minister and subsequently Premier. Bunchan Mol became a government adviser, aided by his
nephew, Thiounn Mumm, then a nineteen-year-old student at the
University of Hanoi.

Mumm, like Keng Vannsak, was ferociously intelligent. His family's
wealth and connections meant that he was brought up with the children of
the French elite, which made him realise at an early age that he would have
to make a choice between the values of his French playmates and loyalty to
his fellow Khmers. Like his three brothers, Mumm took it for granted that
Cambodians were equal, if not superior, to the French. By the age of fourteen he had concluded that the root of his countrymen's backwardness was
their lack of education, a view he would hold for the rest of his life. He
later became the first Cambodian to attend the Polytechnique, the most
prestigious of the French *Grandes Ecoles*, equivalent to getting a First at
Oxford or *summa cum laude* at Harvard – an achievement designed, he said
afterwards, 'to show Cambodians that it could be done'. But in 1945,
Mumm's concern was how to run the country's secondary schools – of
which there were still only two, the Lycée Sisowath and the Collège Preah
Sihanouk at Kompong Cham – after their French teaching staff had been
interned. Supported by Bunchan Mol and Ea Sichau, another of Thanh's
student aides, he argued that the government should appoint Khmer university students who had returned from Hanoi to fill the vacant posts, rather
than bringing in better qualified Vietnamese professors, as the Education
Ministry wished. After a furious argument at the Cabinet Office, during
which Mumm slapped the Minister's face, the young firebrand had his way.

At Kompong Cham, Sâr and his classmates had other priorities.
Immediately after the coup, the school was closed for an extended New
Year vacation. Khieu Samphân, Sâr and a dozen or so others decided to
take the college theatre troupe on a provincial tour in order to raise money
to visit the temples at Angkor Wat:

We performed comic sketches [*Samphân recalled*], in small towns around
Kompong Cham like Chi Hê and Snuol. I played a girl dancer. Sâr's job was

to raise and lower the curtain. When we had enough money, we rented a charcoal-powered bus and set off. It was 180 miles to Siem Reap, and it took us two weeks to get there and another two weeks to get back. Every couple of miles a tyre would burst, and each time that happened, we would all clap and shout for joy! Because that meant we could get out and explore the villages. The village girls always received us warmly because, for them, college boys like us were really something else! Sometimes we spent the night at a peasant's house, but more often we slept under the bus. We spent three days in Siem Reap. It was tiny then – just a few Chinese shops and nothing else. One night we put on a performance, to earn some money for the trip back. But most of the time we spent going round the temples. Angkor thrilled us. It took our breath away.

For all Cambodians, Angkor was, and remains, the pre-eminent symbol of the country's past greatness. As one of the country's elder statesmen, Penn Nouth, put it: 'Cambodian civilisation attained its high point about the twelfth century . . . But after five centuries of glory, the Khmer Empire succumbed, and ended by crumbling away . . . It is this lesson of history which we do not wish to forget.' Angkor was both a benchmark and a burden – the proof of what Cambodians could achieve and a constant reminder of their failure to attain such heights again. When Samphân was about ten years old, his teacher at primary school told his class about the glories of Angkorian civilisation. 'I can still remember it,' he said, 'and how terribly disappointed I felt when he told us that after the thirteenth century, Angkor had collapsed. One must never underestimate the effect of these centuries of decline on our national subconscious. It is why young Cambodians still ask themselves, almost instinctively, whether Cambodia as a nation can survive.'

The early summer of 1945 was played out to the wailing of air-raid sirens. In February an American Flying Fortress dropped bombs on the Japanese military headquarters in Phnom Penh. They missed their target and fell near the Royal Palace, killing hundreds of Cambodian civilians. Kompong Cham was not attacked, but at each alert the students gathered for roll-call in an arboretum near the school to await the all-clear. In May, the authorities gave up, and everyone was sent home early for the summer holidays. Sâr found a job working for a Sino-Khmer businessman, a comprador who purchased rice from farms along the Mekong on behalf of a French trading house and held the local franchise for the sale of petrol. It was his first and last foray into the world of commerce.

By the time the college reopened that autumn, Thiounn Mumm's efforts to recruit Cambodian teachers had begun to bear fruit. One of the new intake, Khvan Siphan, taught mathematics, physics and philosophy. Not much older than most of his students, Siphan quickly won a reputation for fairness and integrity – 'honest, loving and helpful', as one of them put it. 'He prepared his lessons meticulously,' Khieu Samphân remembered, 'and when he arrived in class he wrote everything up on the blackboard. The students copied it down word for word and learnt it by heart. [He] was strict and he inspired respect . . . No one dared make the slightest sound.' Even at secondary-school level, young Cambodians in the 1940s were still much more comfortable with rote learning, with which they had grown up, memorising the Buddhist precepts and the *cpap*, than with the Western notions of analysis and questioning which their French teachers tried to inculcate. Pierre Lamant, who taught at the Lycée Sisowath, noted:

> In Khmer, the word for 'study' – *riensouth* – is made up of *rien*, which means literally to 'learn by heart', and *south*, 'the sutras'. So 'to study' means 'to learn by heart and recite'. Where is the spirit of criticism? Where is there any analysis, any synthesis? . . . Cambodia's art is extraordinary, its literature is rich and abundant. So the absence of critical faculties does not mean that [Khmers] are incapable or inadequate. But in certain areas, it holds them back.

In Khmer tradition, asking questions was discouraged: young people – and subordinates in general – were expected to listen and obey. Samphân remarked that when foreign teachers tried to force the students to think for themselves, many were unable to follow and lost interest in their studies.

With Siphan's encouragement, Sâr's work improved. The following year he began preparing for the *diplôme*, the examination which, in those days, marked the completion of junior middle school.'*

Meanwhile the defeat of Japan and Germany had opened the way for the return of the French. In October 1945, British troops entered Phnom Penh, ostensibly to disarm the Japanese garrison. A few days later the Prime Minister Son Ngoc Thanh was arrested and packed off to exile in France, where he was sentenced to life imprisonment, later commuted to house arrest. The following January, the Cambodian and French governments signed a *Modus Vivendi*, which provided for the resumption of French rule but also acknowledged Cambodian autonomy, leaving the door ajar for further discussion of the country's political status.

---

* The French education system in the 1930s and '40s comprised three years of elementary school (the first of which would now be regarded as a pre-school year); three years of primary school; four years of junior middle school (or *collège*) – 6ème to 3ème (6th to 9th Grade), and three years of upper middle school (or *lycée*) – Seconde to Terminale (10th to 12th Grade). Children took the *diplôme* or *brevet*, the entrance examination for the lycée, at the end of 3ème (9th Grade). It was the equivalent of British O-levels or CSE.

For the French this was a holding operation, designed to stabilise relations while Paris gradually regained full control. Cambodians saw it very differently. The Japanese occupation had undermined French legitimacy. Independence might have been disallowed, but it was now on the agenda. Not for tomorrow, perhaps, but surely for the day, or the week, or the year after. The principle was not in doubt. All that was uncertain was the timing.

Another factor was at work too. Throughout Cambodian history, politics had been the preserve of the palace. Now, for the first time since the 1860s, a commoner had thrown down the gauntlet to the King. Son Ngoc Thanh's few months in power had given him a claim to leadership which Sihanouk found hard to counter. Even Sâr, whose interest in politics at that time was virtually non-existent, saw Thanh as an heroic figure, for whom arrest and trial by the French had been a consecration. After his arrest, his close followers fled to Vietnam and Thailand where they linked up with clandestine anti-French movements. The most important of these were the Khmer Issarak (literally, Khmer Freedom Fighters, or Khmer Masters), a group founded in Bangkok in 1940 by Bunchan Mol's uncle, Pok Khun. The Issarak were manipulated and partly financed by the Thai government, which encouraged them to harass French outposts as a means of pressing Thai claims to Cambodia's western provinces. During the Vichy period, they were quiescent. But with the war now over and the French demanding the return of Battambang and other Thai-held areas, the Issarak exploded back into life.

In the early morning of April 7 1946, a Sunday, a group of about fifty men, armed with old-fashioned muskets and a couple of machine-guns, attacked the Grand Hotel in Siem Reap, where most of the French officer corps was staying. According to Bunchan Mol, who took part, other, smaller groups tried unsuccessfully to liberate prisoners from the town jail and to attack the houses of government officials. After six hours they were driven off, leaving behind seven French dead and taking with them a quantity of arms. The survivors held out for a week in the ruins of Angkor Wat before retreating to the Dangrek Mountains, a traditional refuge of bandits along the Thai border to the north.

Smaller-scale attacks continued, but they were an irritant rather than a threat to French power. In November of that year, Thailand agreed to return the disputed provinces, and eighteen months later a change of government in Bangkok ended direct Thai support for the rebels. Conditions remained unsettled and many groups turned to brigandage. Agricultural production was disrupted – the economy, in the words of one French observer, was at death's door – and tax revenues fell sharply. But

Cambodian politics would have to evolve further before the Issarak could become a major force again.

In the summer of 1947, Sâr passed the end-of-year examinations and, with a few other children from Kompong Cham, was admitted to the Lycée Sisowath, which was still recovering from the disruption caused by the war and had vacant places in 3ème. For the decidedly average student that he was, it was no small achievement, for the lycée's normal intake was only 120 pupils a year. One of his closest friends at Kompong Cham, Lon Non, whose elder brother, Nol, would become Cambodia's Head of State in the early 1970s, made the move at the same time. With Ping Sây, an extrovert, mischievous youth, a year younger than Sâr, they formed an intimate trio, visiting each other's homes and spending the holidays together. Sâr was once more living with his eldest brother, Suong, who had recently divorced and remarried. His new wife, Chea Samy, had also been a dancer at the palace. She was a cultivated young woman, and Ping Sây was impressed by her. But the house was sparsely furnished, with chairs made of woven bamboo, and Sây remembered thinking that they could not have much money.

Ieng Sary and his best friend, Rath Samoeun, a bright boy from a poor rural family, whom Sâr now encountered for the first time, were in the class above him at Sisowath.

Every Thursday afternoon, they and the other boarders, wearing the school uniform – a white shirt, blue trousers and a blancoed white pith helmet – walked in a crocodile up Boulevard Doudart de Lagrée (named after a nineteenth-century French explorer) as far as the French Quarter, where they were allowed to disperse and spend the afternoon as they wished. The more hard-working among them used to go to the National Library, a yellow-and-white stuccoed building with an imposing Grecian façade and an inscription in French and Khmer, on either side of the main entrance, declaiming prophetically: 'Force binds for a time; ideas enchain forever.' There the politically inclined Mey Mann read the works of Jean-Jacques Rousseau and Victor Hugo's *Les Misérables*. The latter, he acknowledged, was too long for him to finish, but nearly sixty years later, he could still quote from it the words, 'Life is struggle. Those who struggle, live!' Ieng Sary devoured Montesquieu and Voltaire, who advocated constitutional monarchy with an elected parliament, an independent judiciary, equality of the citizenry and fundamental freedoms, all of which were conspicuously absent in Cambodia.

Mey Mann and his friends were not alone in being influenced by the thinkers of eighteenth-century Europe. Sihanouk had also been through the French colonial school system with its – in Cambodian terms – wholly inappropriate emphasis on the French Revolution, and the uncomfortable parallel between the absolutism of the Khmer monarchy and the fate of Louis XVI had not escaped him. In the second half of the 1940s, the young King took the first tentative steps towards liberalising the political system. Under the *Modus Vivendi* Cambodia, no longer a protectorate, was destined to become a member of a still-to-be-established French Union and endowed with a constitution enshrining limited autonomy. To the annoyance of the French – who viewed the new arrangements as no more than a figleaf for the restoration of their pre-war rule – Sihanouk insisted that the text be approved by a consultative assembly elected by universal male suffrage, and that the same system be used in future elections. That made possible for the first time the formation of political parties.

Sihanouk's motives were mixed. As monarch, he had every intention of preserving the reality of undivided power. But he also saw himself as a moderniser and wished to appear to his people as such. Moreover, he had acute political antennae. The continuing popularity of Son Ngoc Thanh (in whose arrest he may secretly have connived) troubled him. So did the nationalists' whispered criticisms over the renewal of his entente with the French following Japan's defeat. By deciding to grant 'his people' the right to involve themselves in the political process, he hoped to refurbish an image that had become tarnished.

Cambodia's first national election, in September 1946, brought to power the Democratic Party, led by Prince Yuthévong, who was named Prime Minister. Yuthévong had a French wife, a doctorate in mathematics and an ambition to install in Cambodia the democratic values and practices that he had come to admire in Paris.

Students flocked to the Democrats' cause. Mey Mann voted for them and helped as a volunteer – preparing the meeting rooms for sessions of the Executive Committee at Yuthévong's headquarters, a villa overlooking the esplanade in front of the city's railway station. In 1947, Rath Samoeun and two other young radicals, Hou Yuon and a boy named Keo Meas, who was studying at the Phnom Penh Teacher Training College, worked in the party campaign office. That April, after only six months in office, Yuthévong died at the age of thirty-four, apparently from lung complications caused by tuberculosis. Thiounn Mumm's brother-in-law, Chean Vâm, who had returned from Europe two years earlier to become, at the age of thirty, the first Cambodian headmaster of the Lycée Sisowath, succeeded him. In 1948, Ping Say joined the party; and in November of the following year – when Sihanouk, exasperated by the Democrats' fractiousness, suspended the National Assembly – Samoeun and Ieng Sary helped to organise a protest demonstration which ended with numerous arrests. Sary was freed a few hours later, but more than a hundred others were held in prison for a week. A student strike was declared, which quickly spread to other cities, and a twelve-man delegation, of which Sary was a member, sought an audience with the King. 'He was quite reasonable,' Sary recalled. 'He heard us out, and then ordered everyone released.'

It was around this time that Sary came across a copy of the *Communist Manifesto* in the library of Yuthévong's brother, Prince Entaravong. Marxism was a taboo subject under the colonial regime. Schoolteachers were forbidden to mention the Russian Revolution in class. But Yuthévong had brought back to Phnom Penh a suitcase-full of 'progressive' works, which Entaravong inherited after his death.

Sary and Rath Samoeun puzzled over the *Manifesto* and argued about what it might mean.

While the Democratic Party was challenging Sihanouk's power, conflict of a different kind was brewing across the border in Vietnam. In the southern provinces of what was then known as Cochin-China, armed clashes had broken out within weeks of Japan's capitulation as local communist and nationalist groups sought to resist the reimposition of French control. The movement, initially piecemeal and poorly organised, was gradually taken in hand by the Nambo Territorial Committee, the southern branch of Ho Chi Minh's Indochinese Communist Party (ICP) which had seized power in Hanoi. It was headed by Le Duan, an intensely nationalistic young southerner who, twenty years later, would succeed Ho as the leader of the communist movement throughout Vietnam. Le Duc Tho, the future Paris Peace Talks negotiator, was his chief assistant. Together they organised guerrilla attacks and sabotage. In Hanoi, Ho strung out the negotiations with France to gain time for the communist forces to consolidate. But by the end of the year his margin for manoeuvre was exhausted. In December 1946, his Viet Minh army, numbering 28,000 men, abandoned the capital to fight the French Expeditionary Corps from the jungle.

The First Vietnam War had begun.

Ever since the foundation of the ICP, in 1930, the Vietnamese communists, encouraged by the Comintern,* had taken the view that they had

---

* The Communist International (Comintern) was established by Lenin in 1919 as an instrument of Soviet control over foreign communist parties. Ho Chi Minh worked for several years at its headquarters in Moscow.

a responsibility to promote revolution not merely in their own country but throughout Indochina. In practice, this had remained a dead letter.

The struggle for independence from France changed that. The Viet Minh, ostensibly an alliance of progressive forces in Vietnam, obtained most of its arms from Bangkok, then the hub of a South-East Asian black market in weaponry left over from the Pacific War. The only way to transport them to southern Vietnam was overland through Cambodia or by sea along the Cambodian coast. The need to secure these arms routes – without which Ho's forces would have been unable to fight the French – gave Cambodia a whole new strategic importance. Defence planners under General Vo Nguyen Giap urged that the country be transformed into a 'logistical support area' for southern Vietnam. That implied the establishment of a Cambodian revolutionary movement, similar to that being created in Laos. The problem was that there was no indigenous Khmer communist structure to build on. Hanoi's only options were to try to co-opt existing non-communist Thai-backed Khmer Issarak groups, or to recruit among the Overseas Vietnamese community, which accounted for almost one in twelve of Cambodia's population, some 300,000 people in all.

In practice, the Vietnamese tried to do both.

First they recruited a former Buddhist lay preacher, calling himself Son Ngoc Minh, to serve as President of a newly-formed Cambodian People's Liberation Committee (CPLC) in Battambang. Minh had been born in a Khmer district of southern Vietnam of mixed Khmer-Vietnamese parentage, which meant he was the nearest the Vietnamese had to an authentic Khmer revolutionary. According to French intelligence, his real name was Pham Van Hua. The *nom de guerre* was intended to capitalise on the popularity of Sihanouk's banished rival, Son Ngoc Thanh, then still languishing in exile in France. Minh spent most of the first two years escorting arms convoys and groups of Overseas Vietnamese recruits through Cambodia to communist-controlled areas in southern Vietnam. But in 1948, the Vietnamese decided that the time had come to try to give the nascent Cambodian movement greater substance. The country was divided into four geographical zones. Minh was placed in charge of the South-West. Dap Chhuon, an army deserter who led an 800-man Issarak band in Battambang province, was assigned to the North-West. Keo Moni, an Issarak chief from Prey Veng province, assisted by another Buddhist preacher, Tou Samouth, had responsibility for the South-East. The North-East, a sparsely populated *montagnard* region where the French presence was tenuous, was for the time being spared Viet Minh attentions.

Attempts were made throughout the areas of Cambodia under guerrilla control to set up an embryonic revolutionary administration – complete with a tax system, land survey, economic and judicial departments, revolutionary tribunals and even a public works service – and on May 15 1948, Son Ngoc Minh sent birthday greetings to Ho Chi Minh on behalf of a purported 'revolutionary provisional government'. But in practice most of the new structures existed only on paper.

The artificial nature of the Vietnamese communist implant in Cambodia, coupled with historical animosities, made it a virtual certainty that relations between the ICP and its Issarak protégés would be uneasy when not openly hostile.

In the 'liberated districts', Khmer leaders, including Son Ngoc Minh himself, could do nothing without the approval of Vietnamese political commissars. A French intelligence officer wrote perceptively: 'The initial Viet Minh plan seems to have been genuinely to transfer control to the [Cambodians] as they acquired the necessary political maturity . . . [However] as their authority steadily grows, [the Cambodian leaders] have more and more difficulty in tolerating Vietnamese [supervision] . . . One can expect that clashes [between them] will increase.' They did. Already in 1945 and 1946, Khmers had slaughtered Vietnamese living in Khmer-speaking districts of Cochin-China. Now incidents began to occur within Cambodia itself. In 1948, Khmer villagers in districts of Takeo province, bordering Vietnam, attacked Viet Minh units, and a massacre of Vietnamese settlers occurred near Phnom Penh. Shortly afterwards a Khmer Issarak commander in south-eastern Cambodia, Puth Chhay, launched an anti-Vietnamese pogrom which so angered the Viet Minh leadership that they despatched a punitive expedition against him. It returned empty-handed.

This resurgence of ancestral hatreds was partly triggered by what Khmers perceived as the condescension of their new revolutionary allies. But it also reflected the mixture of contemporary and historical motives at work on the Vietnamese side: at first internationalist rhetoric was used to justify policies devised for purely national military ends, and then, once the decision had been taken to treat Indochina as a single battlefield, the ICP's long-standing desire to evangelise the Khmers, echoing the 'civilising mission' of the nineteenth-century Vietnamese emperor Minh Mang, had surreptitiously taken over. Almost unconsciously, Hanoi's programme in Cambodia mutated from a strategic initiative into an ideological crusade. Like the Vietnamese Catholic missionaries who had struggled for two hundred years to convert Cambodians to Christianity, ICP emissaries were determined to build a Cambodian revolutionary movement from nothing, regardless of cost or the suitability of the terrain. They would have little more success.

Cambodians, in their immense majority, were simply not interested in the Vietnamese communists' message – in part because they *were* Vietnamese. The history of conflict between the two peoples was merely the visible part of their antagonism. Cambodians assert their identity by means of dichotomies: they *are* in opposition to what they *are not*. Cambodia as a nation exists in opposition to Vietnam (and, to a lesser extent, Thailand). That does not prevent relationships at the level of individuals, but between Cambodians and Vietnamese such personal contacts must take place against the background of an overwhelming, pejorative, nationalist discourse.

The other great problem confronting Vietnam's communist missionaries – like their Catholic predecessors – was that they were trying to cross Asia's deepest cultural divide. Marxism-Leninism, revised and sinified by Mao, flowed effortlessly across China's southern border into Vietnamese minds, informed by the same Confucian culture. It was all but powerless to penetrate the Indianate world of Theravada Buddhism that moulds the mental universe of Cambodia and Laos.

The Vietnamese leaders themselves were aware of these difficulties. '[It is] imperative that nothing be done which might lead our Laotian and Cambodian brothers to think mistakenly that the Vietnamese have come as invaders,' the Defence Ministry cautioned. Hoang Van Hoan, a veteran ICP Central Committee member whom Ho Chi Minh had put in charge of North Vietnam's foreign relations, complained that too many cadres 'apply the revolutionary model used in Vietnam without taking into account the cultural and social differences of western Indochina . . . As a result of such blunders, many Lao and Khmers mistrust them.' He added, in a telling comment, that it was 'necessary to think of the Cambodian and Lao revolutions in terms of benefits for those two peoples, and not just [of advantages] for Vietnam'. Other leaders criticised the 'arrogance' of Vietnamese cadres. To make matters worse, Hanoi's efforts to export its revolution were bedevilled by internal rivalries and conflicting chains of command. It is true that at the time the Vietnamese communists were fighting for their own survival. None the less, their programme for Cambodia was chaotic.

As the 1940s drew to a close, even the little that had been achieved was compromised when Dap Chhuon defected with his forces to Sihanouk, followed by several other Khmer Issarak leaders. French intelligence estimated that, in the entire country, the Viet Minh and their

allies controlled a Khmer population of only 25,000. Out of an estimated 3,000 guerrilla troops in the country, barely 20 per cent were
Khmer – and most of those were Khmer Krom, recruited from Khmer-
speaking districts of southern Vietnam, not from Cambodia itself. The
rest were Vietnamese. The Cambodian revolution was not yet even a
sideshow.

In these circumstances, it was hardly surprising that Sâr and his schoolmates knew little of Issarak and Viet Minh activities. News of the rebels
was censored in the Cambodian press, and such incidents as did occur
were on so small a scale that even politically engaged students like Ieng
Sary and Mey Mann ignored them. Sâr, at that time, was the reverse of
engaged. According to Ping Sây, he never discussed politics while at
Sisowath and, unlike Sây himself and others of their age, he had no contact with the Democratic Party. Apart from his somewhat juvenile admi-
ration for the exiled Son Ngoc Thanh, it seems that the subject simply did
not interest him.

In the summer of 1948, he, Sây and their friend Lon Non sat the
brevet, the exam which determined admission to the upper classes of the
lycée. Sây passed. Sâr and Non failed. Non's parents were wealthy
enough to send him to France to continue his education. Sâr went to
the Technical School at Russey Keo, in the northern suburbs of Phnom
Penh.

It cannot have been a happy move. The place itself was depressing –
two long dormitory huts and a collection of barrack-like workshops that
looked as though they dated from the industrial revolution. For a young
man who had been on track for the *baccalauréat* and the possibility of a
university education, it must have been a dreadful come-down. His
former classmate Khieu Samphân remembered: 'Most students used to
look disdainfully at the boys at the Technical School. No one wanted
to be seen with them.' They had a reputation as toughies. When the
'apprentices', as they were mockingly called, played football against
other schools, the match invariably degenerated into a brawl and they
would bring out the brass knuckles they had made in their metalwork
classes.

But Sâr had no choice. Without a *brevet*, the Technical School was the
only way forward for a Cambodian youth who wished to continue his education. And there did turn out to be a silver lining. The previous year the
government had introduced bursaries allowing the three best students at
Russey Keo to pursue their studies at French engineering schools. This
year there were to be five such scholarships.

In this situation, Sâr's arrival was not entirely welcome. Nghet Chho-pininto, another final-year student, recalled: 'He was regarded as an intruder. If he got better marks than we did, he would get a bursary and we wouldn't. We didn't ostracise him – but he was a rival.' Chhopininto was so keen to go abroad that he made himself a wooden book-stand so that he could revise his lessons in the dormitory under his mosquito net at night. He and Sâr both did carpentry, which was regarded as the easi-est subject. The woodwork teacher, a Vietnamese, was 'a charming man, who always gave everyone good marks'. Whether for that reason, or because Sâr had decided that now he really did need to work, he and Chhopininto both obtained their *brevet* in the summer of 1949 and each was awarded one of the coveted scholarships.* In the end it had been easier than they had thought, for there were only twenty final-year stu-dents at Russey Keo; not all of them passed their exams, and of those who did, not all wished to go abroad. The same was true at Sisowath and at the Public Works School which Mey Mann attended. Under the protec-torate, the French had so neglected higher education in Cambodia that in the late 1940s, fewer than a hundred students a year left secondary school with the requisite qualifications. The problem, whatever Chhopininto may have thought, was not so much a paucity of scholarships as of can-didates. That was especially true in the technical field, where even the humblest posts were filled by Vietnamese because of the lack of trained Cambodians. To the Democratic Party leader, Chhnean Vâm, and his colleagues, remedying this state of affairs was an essential part of the strug-gle for independence.

Even with those caveats, Sâr had become part of a minuscule élite. Although the numbers were rising, fewer than 250 Cambodians had been trained abroad since the beginning of the century, including those sent by their families without government support.

On the eve of their departure, King Sihanouk granted the new bursars an audience amid the opulence and glitter of the palace's Khemarin Hall. At the age of twenty-six, he was only two or three years older than they were, but already had four wives and eight children. Sâr and the others stood in line, self-conscious in their new suits and ties, waiting to be pre-sented by a palace official, who handed the young King an envelope for each of them. It contained 500 piastres (equivalent to about 30 US dollars), an appreciable sum in those days, enough for a student to live on for a

---

*The *brevet d'études techniques* – equivalent to the technical section of a British O-level or CSE – was the highest academic qualification Saloth Sâr ever achieved.

month. Mey Mann, who was there, too, remembered feeling 'very happy and proud. For all of us, it was a unique opportunity. Very few young people in Cambodia had the chance to travel like us.'

Many of those present that evening would later become influential figures on the Cambodian Left. Some were destined to have exemplary governmental careers. Chau Seng, an ethnic Khmer from Ieng Sary's home district of Travinh, across the border in Vietnam, became Sihanouk's Cabinet Director and, later, Minister of Education. Toch Phoeun would head the Public Works Department. Phuong Ton would go on to be Rector of the Royal University.

Others were agreeable but uninspiring youths, for whom even their closest friends could not imagine much of a future. Sâr was one of these. The only thing that distinguished him from the others was that his upbringing had been more eclectic than theirs. Like them, his childhood had been steeped in the legends and superstitions of the countryside and in the moral suasion of the *cpap*. But, unlike most of his peers, he had gone on to a Buddhist novitiate; to catechism at a Roman Catholic primary school; adolescence in Phnom Penh amid the royal harem; a middle school imbued with the values of Vichy France; the Lycée Sisowath, where he had been surrounded by some of the most gifted young minds in the country; and finally, Russey Keo, among student carpenters and boilermakers, tinsmiths and lathe-workers. One might call it a motley training for life or, if one wished to be kind, a variegated education.

However, it gave Sâr one great advantage. He was able to communicate naturally with people of all sorts and conditions, establishing an instinctive rapport that invariably made them want to like him. In this, he was helped immensely by what Mey Mann called 'Sâr's famous smile'. Many years later, Mann still wondered about the smile. 'He never said very much,' he remembered. 'He just had that smile of his. He liked to joke, he had a slightly mischievous way about him. And there was never the least hint of what he would become after.'

Sâr's smile was too open to be enigmatic, too striking to be merely a mannerism. One of Sihanouk's advisers, a Frenchman of left-wing views named Charles Meyer, wrote that the Khmer smile – 'that indefinable half-smile that floats across the stone lips of the Gods at Angkor and which one finds, replicated identically, on the lips of Cambodians today' – served as a mask, 'at the same time ambiguous and likeable, that one erects between oneself and others . . . [like] a screen hiding an emptiness that has been deliberately created as an ultimate defence against any who might wish to penetrate the secret of one's innermost thoughts.' Meyer never met Saloth Sâr. But his words offer an uncanny glimpse into one aspect of his personality.

The morning after the royal audience, Sâr's group, twenty-one young men in all, set out before dawn for Saigon – not in a charcoal-fired bus this time but a modern, petrol-engined vehicle, which completed the 150-mile journey in less than seven hours. They were accommodated at the Lycée Chasseloup-Laubat, where ten years earlier Sihanouk and Thiounn Thioeunn had been classmates. The future South Vietnamese capital was a well-kept, elegant city, bigger than Phnom Penh. 'We felt like bush-monkeys,' Mann recalled. 'We were rustics in from the countryside.' But at the Buddhist *wat* and on the streets, they heard passersby speaking Khmer, 'which gave the older ones among us, including Sâr, a feeling that it was still a Cambodian city'.

Prey Nokor, as they called Saigon, and all the surrounding region, had been Cambodian territory until the mid-eighteenth century. In April 1949, a few months before their arrival, France had incorporated Cochin-China into the new state of Vietnam. Sihanouk had declined to recognise Vietnamese sovereignty.

After a week, their French visas were ready, and on the morning of August 31 they piled their baggage on to bicycle-drawn rickshaws and made their way to the port. Their ship, the SS *Jamaique*, was an elderly passenger liner which had been converted into a troopship for the French soldiers being brought, in ever greater numbers, to fight Ho Chi Minh's communist armies in the north. Sâr and his companions were put with the ordinary ranks, the *marsouins*, travelling fourth-class in the hold, where they slept on narrow bunks, stacked in tiers of three. Many of them were sea-sick throughout the four-week-long voyage, Sâr, Chhopininto and Mey Mann being among the few exceptions. But though that meant there was food in abundance – since the sufferers had no appetite – none of them was yet used to French cooking, and Mann fanned their sense of deprivation by launching into mouth-watering descriptions of Cambodian dishes prepared with tamarind seeds and coconut milk. The ship stopped at Singapore and Colombo – where they bought ebony carvings of elephants – before heading for the Red Sea. By then Sâr had had enough of ship's mutton – 'cooked the French way, we thought it tasted terrible!' Mann remembered – so at the next stopover, in Djibouti, the two of them went to the market and bought lemons, pepper and African spices. After that, he remembered, they were able to eat properly again. Sâr was in charge of the cooking. Mann and another student, who was training to become a vet, assisted.

Sâr's talent as a cook was not the only surprise of the voyage. He struck up friendships with some of the French soldiers, who had a daily ration of red wine and used to give him a *pichet* to share with his friends. As they sailed through the tropics, he and Mann often slept on deck, partly to avoid the smell of vomit wafting up from their stricken colleagues below. 'We talked about our studies,' Mann remembered, 'and we worried about how we would cope with the cold. Politics never came up. Not once. It was just a great adventure.'

2

City of Light

SINCE THE TIME of Beaumarchais and Voltaire, Paris has called itself, with fine indifference to the intellectual claims of other European centres, *La Ville Lumière*, the source of light and of enlightenment for the rest of the civilised world. At times that has been a mixed blessing. It was in Paris, not in Moscow or Beijing, that in the early 1950s Sâr and his companions laid down the ideological foundations on which the Khmer Rouge nightmare would be built.

That this occurred was not – as Sihanouk and his French advisers liked to pretend – because their minds were warped by the Stalinist vision of the world then being propagated by the French communists, the country's largest political party; nor was it due to the influence of Mao Zedong, whose writings the young Cambodians encountered in France for the first time. Stalin and Mao both had their part in the making of Pol Pot's Democratic Kampuchea. So did the Vietnamese and the Americans. But the foreign intellectual legacy which would underpin the Cambodian revolution was first and foremost French.

How, indeed, could it have been otherwise? Language forms the building blocks of thought. The Cambodian students spoke French; they had attended French schools; and they had grown up in a French colony. French was the prism through which they viewed the outside world. And in the Paris of 1950, what an outside world it was! If Saigon had made Sâr and Mey Mann feel like country bumpkins, the French capital seemed to be on a different planet. The young Cambodians climbed the Eiffel Tower and marvelled at the ancient stonework of Notre-Dame and the Ile de la Cité; at the broad, tree-lined boulevards laid out by Baron Haussmann in the 1890s, with their elegant boutiques, classical façades and polished, *belle époque* department stores – 'all the beauty of the structure of the city', as one of them put it – a city, moreover, that had rebounded from wartime austerity and was now experiencing a cultural and social ferment not seen since the 1920s. In the cobbled streets of the Latin Quarter, the heart of the student district, 'bebop' had arrived, scandalising the strait-laced with its 'sensualism and immorality'. Sidney Bechet's New Orleans Jazzband played at the Vieux Colombier, just across from the rue St Sulpice, where Thiounn Mumm's brother, Chum, now a law student, had rooms and the Khmer Student Association (l'Association des Etudiants Khmers or AEK), its headquarters. Mumm himself was at the Ecole Polytechnique, then also in the Latin Quarter not far from the rue de Carmes, where Claude Luter presided over all-night jam sessions at the Lorientais, sponsored by the Hot Club de France.

Existentialism was the rage and St Germain-des-Prés at its apogee. Juliette Greco had become the emblem of an introverted, self-indulgent generation, parodied by the young mime Marcel Marceau. Mey Mann recalled going late one night with a group of friends to a cellar club, where 'everyone was dressed in black'. It was Le Tabou, on the rue Dauphine, where Albert Camus, Alberto Giacometti, Maurice Merleau-Ponty and a certain Jean-Paul Sartre used to gather after the bigger bars closed. The Khmer Student Association's magazine, *Khemara Nisut*, caught the mood of the times – as viewed by Cambodians, at least – in a sketch lampooning the plight of a new arrival from Phnom Penh, who found himself surrounded by 'policemen who gesticulate like opera singers', something called 'autumn' which made the leaves turn red and fall, and 'strange places which deafen you with bawdy, syncopated music, [where] lithe young adonises dislocate themselves, each more frantically than the next, in a kind of collective hysteria . . . and a girl with pouting lips and upturned trousers takes you off to join a group of intense young men, wearing bow-ties and slicked-back hair, who are earnestly discussing whether "essence" precedes "existence" in the case of peas and gherkins, or should it be the other way round?'

Sâr and his companions disembarked into this glittering, chaotic, intimidating new world on the morning of October 1 1949, having travelled up on the overnight train from Marseilles. They were met at the Gare de Lyon by an official of the French Education Ministry, responsible for 'colonials', and, more helpfully, by representatives of the Khmer Student Association.

It was a Saturday and it was raining. The temperature that afternoon was barely 15 degrees centigrade, colder than the worst winter day in Cambodia. None of them had winter outfits. Mey Mann remembered being taken to a second-hand clothes market beneath the iron railway bridge of La Motte-Picquet, on the Left Bank of the River Seine, where he discovered to his delight that they could haggle with the Jewish stallholders just as they did with Khmer traders at home. Then they all went to a student hostel in rue Monsieur-le-Prince, across the road from the Sorbonne, the oldest of the city's universities. But that was only a temporary refuge. Finding permanent accommodation was a student's biggest headache. In principle, the Cambodians were supposed to stay at the

Maison d'Indochine, a well-appointed hall of residence with white walls and fake Vietnamese eaves, supposedly reminiscent of Saigon, at the Cité Universitaire, a park-like campus for non-French students in the south of Paris. But there were never enough rooms to go round. Mey Mann, Nghet Chhopininto and their friends took lodgings in the suburb of Bourg La Reine. Others were happy to find a *chambre de bonne*, a servant's room in a bourgeois apartment, usually a garret, eight floors up, within the city itself.

Sâr was lucky. One of King Monivong's nephews, Prince Sisowath Somonopong, had arrived in Paris a year earlier to study radio technology at the Ecole Française de Radio-Electricité, the same school that Sâr was to attend. Somonopong's mother held a position comparable to that of Sâr's sister, Roeung. It may well have been the young Prince's example that led Sâr to choose the Radio-Electricity School in the first place, for it was not an obvious step for a boy who had been studying carpentry. In any event, Somonopong took Sâr under his wing and found him lodgings with two friends, the sons of the governor of Kratie, not far from the school workshops on the rue Amyot, just behind the Panthéon. Sâr never afterwards referred to this royal connection, saying merely that he had spent the year staying with 'a cousin'.

Despite difficulties with the French language, in which he was never completely at ease, he seems to have had no difficulty settling in.

Encouraged by Somonopong and his two flatmates, Sâr joined the AEK and took part in many of its activities. The following spring, the association organised a memorial meeting for Ieu Koeuss, the leader of the radical wing of the Democratic Party, who had been killed in a grenade attack – allegedly ordered by right-wing opponents – in Phnom Penh in January. There were lavish celebrations in Versailles to mark the Cambodian New Year in April. These included traditional Khmer dances, a midnight ball, and what was termed 'a Pantagruelian feast'. Part of the proceedings were broadcast by French radio. The next month the students held a Cambodian Soirée at the Palais d'Iéna in Paris, with an art exhibition, a play starring a young Khmer actor named Hang Thun Hak (later to become Cambodia's Prime Minister), a poetry recital by Keng Vannsak and dancing until dawn. There was even talk of taking a Khmer play on tour in France and Germany that summer. Sâr's friends regarded him as a 'bon vivant' whose purpose in life was to have a good time.

Shortly before leaving for France, he had acquired a girlfriend, Soeung Son Maly. Her mother was a royal princess, her father a schoolmaster and compulsive gambler who quickly squandered his wife's fortune. Unlike Sâr's adolescent liaisons with the young women of the palace, the relationship with Maly was serious and chaste. She was extremely pretty and was nicknamed 'the Beauty Queen'. It was a standing joke among the students in Paris that, whenever Sâr looked morose, he was pining for his lady-love. Whether or not that was so, there was a solitude about him which others sometimes interpreted as loneliness.

That first year in Paris, he applied himself to his studies and, by his own account, got 'quite good marks'. He narrowly failed the year-end exam but, along with other borderline cases, was allowed to sit it again and passed, which meant he could go on to the second year.

But then, in the summer of 1950, a series of events occurred which would change the direction of Sâr's life. Towards the end of June, the magazine *Khemara Nisut* announced that the Khmer Student Association was offering its members a choice of two trips abroad during the summer holidays. One was a month-long camping tour in Switzerland; the other, participation in an 'international labour brigade' to help with post-war reconstruction in Yugoslavia. The Swiss tour would cost 22,000 francs (about 70 US dollars); the trip to Yugoslavia was free. For Sâr, there was no contest: 'I didn't have money, so I couldn't do as the others and go to Geneva, or to the sea or the mountains, and have a holiday there . . . A group of us poorer students went instead to . . . Zagreb, [where] we worked building a motorway.'

The train journey took forty-eight hours, with lengthy stops and no food to be had – a foretaste of the penury ahead. Nghet Chhopininto, who went with a brigade to Sarajevo a year later, remembered being hungry all the time they were there. The midday meal at the work-site was never enough. Sometimes they went to local restaurants and showed the cooks drawings of the food they wanted. But there was little to be had there either. On the other hand, it was exhilarating to be part of such a massive effort of national reconstruction. 'Everywhere . . . resembles an enormous building site,' one of Sâr's companions wrote later. 'This effort is even more estimable because the force and the faith of the people, united around their leaders . . . allow them to win successive victories, aware that this is a question of national independence.' Foreign volunteers were expected to do manual labour three days a week, from 6 a.m. until noon, and could spend the rest of their time in cultural activities and sports. Chhopininto and a colleague 'got lucky with the local girls', as he put it, which also helped; and he left with happy memories of the camaraderie that came from working together with young people from many different countries.

Not everyone reacted in the same way. Huot Sambath, who had arrived in France a month after Sâr to study international relations and later served as Sihanouk's Foreign Minister, decided that 'the western countries' [post-war] difficulties were being resolved very fast, [whereas] in eastern Europe, the people lacked everything and their lives were not happy at all.' Like other Cambodian intellectuals, he wrote, he was concerned for Cambodia's future: 'There were only two ways to walk: communist or liberal. I had already seen all the facts . . . so I chose the liberal way.'

Sâr was still a year or more away from making that kind of judgement. But Yugoslavia evidently made a favourable impression on him, for he went back there the following summer for a camping holiday.

Back in Paris for the start of the new academic year, he faced other, more pressing concerns. Somonopong had returned home after completing his studies, which left him with nowhere to live. It was then, he recalled, that 'I came into contact with some progressive students . . . I often stayed with them, and little by little they influenced me.' One of these 'progressive students' was Ieng Sary, who arrived at the beginning of November 1950. Sary had obtained the first part of his *baccalauréat* (albeit at the second attempt) in Phnom Penh a year earlier, but had failed the second part, normally a prerequisite for further study abroad. Because the government was in the hands of the Democratic Party, for whom he and his friend Rath Samoeun had campaigned tirelessly, he eventually got his bursary, but not until all the others had left. Samoeun, who had passed his *bac* with flying colours, had reached Paris earlier, and it is possible that Sâr's initial contact was with him. In any event, soon after arriving, Ieng Sary went to pay his respects to Keng Vannsak, who had been four years his senior at the Lycée Sisowath and was now, at the age of twenty-five, among the leading figures of the little Cambodian colony in Paris. He had a friend, he told Vannsak, a young man named Saloth Sâr, who was having great difficulty finding a place to stay. Was he in a position to help?

Vannsak was then living in the rue de Commerce, in the 15th arrondissement, a stone's throw from the market at La Motte-Picquet. He was not long back from London where he had married, at the Hampstead Registry Office, a gifted young Frenchwoman who shared his passion for oriental languages. The couple were, indeed, in a position to help. Just across the road, on the corner of the rue de Commerce and the rue Letellier, was a wine shop which doubled as a café. The vintner let out the rooms above. They were spartan in the extreme – bare, dingy bedsits, in which the bed was the only item of furniture provided – but it was a place to live and Sâr moved in at once. Vannsak lent him a chair and some saucepans, and when the young man went down with flu that winter, his wife, Suzanne, ministered to him with daily injections.

The same month that Sary arrived in France, the AEK elected a new six-man executive committee whose members included Keng Vannsak and Thiounn Mumm. One of its first actions was to set up informal student discussion groups, known as Cercles d'Etudes (Study Circles). There was a Law Circle, headed by Mumm's brother, Chum; an Arts Circle, under the actor Hang Thun Hak; and others concerned with farming, literature and women's issues. The inaugural meeting took place on December 21 1950, when Hak's group – which included Sary, Rath Samoeun and Hou Yuon, then studying for a law degree – debated the relationship between art and society.

A few weeks later Vannsak invited a few friends to a more select, unpublicised gathering in his apartment. This group, which had no name, met two or three times a month to discuss political issues – and specifically the future of Cambodia, now, for the first time, being directly affected by the war in neighbouring Vietnam. Ieng Sary and Rath Samoeun were regular participants. So was Sien An, a former classmate at the Lycée Sisowath, later to become Cambodian Ambassador to Hanoi. Ea Sichau, the president of the Khmer Student Association, and Hang Thun Hak also attended. So did Sâr. The meetings of Vannsak's circle marked the beginning of his political apprenticeship.

In retrospect, October 1 1949, the day when Mao Zedong stood at the Gate of Heavenly Peace in Beijing and proclaimed the founding of the Chinese People's Republic and, coincidentally, the day that Sâr and his companions arrived in Paris, was the beginning of the end of the French presence in Indochina.

All through the 1940s, Ho Chi Minh had been at pains to obscure the reality that the Viet Minh was controlled by the Indochinese Communist Party, even claiming, falsely, that the Party had been dissolved. He presented himself as a nationalist, fighting an anti-colonial war in an area of the world where decolonisation was in full spate. Burma, India, Indonesia, Malaysia and the Philippines were all struggling to free themselves from their respective overlords.

The young Cambodians in Paris saw themselves in the same light. They were first and foremost patriots, engaged, albeit at one remove, in a shared fight for liberty. Mey Mann envisaged Cambodia as 'a little Oriental Switzerland'. Ping Sây's twin ambitions, as a trainee engineer, were to see independence and to build a bridge across the Tonle Sap. Sâr remembered simply being 'patriotic and against French colonialism'. None of them regarded the war in Vietnam as anything other than a colonial struggle. Communism scarcely figured on their horizon. Even Keng Vannsak, more attuned to political realities than most, had unwittingly offended an upper-class French girl a year earlier by suggesting that they spend an afternoon at the 'Fête de l'Humanité', the annual festival organised by the French

Communist Party. 'I had no idea it was communist,' he protested. 'I thought it was just a festival of humanity. She was outraged.'

After the Chinese victory, this age of innocence was left behind. Mao's triumph brought to what had been essentially a little, local conflict, the logic of the Cold War, transforming Indochina from a colonial backwater into a theatre for the Great Powers, whose rivalry would plague the region for the next half-century. The global political shift which had begun three years before, with Winston Churchill's 'Iron Curtain' speech at Fulton, Missouri, had finally reached Asia. In a world divided into two rival camps, Stalin's spokesman, Andrei Zhdanov, proclaimed, Hanoi was associated with 'the camp . . . based on the USSR and the new democracies . . . [It] is backed by the labor and democratic movement and by the fraternal Communist parties in all countries, by the fighters for national liberation in the colonies and dependencies, by all progressive and democratic forces.'

On January 18 1950, China became the first foreign power to recognise Ho Chi Minh's regime in North Vietnam. Moscow and its allies quickly followed suit. Soon afterwards, the US and Britain responded by recognising Cambodia and the other two 'Associated States' of the newly established French Union, Laos and what would become known as South Vietnam. Thailand, put on notice by America to choose between anti-communism and anti-colonialism, did the same, reaping US military aid as its reward. By June, when the Korean War broke out, the logic of containment, with its domino theories and defensive blocs, had become the foundation of American policy.

Vietnamese policy underwent a sea change too.

Communist Chinese occupation of the border areas gave Ho's regime, in the words of the ICP Secretary-General, Truong Chinh, a 'vast and powerful friendly country' as a reliable rear area. The scale of the fighting increased dramatically. Over the following two years, the Chinese formed, equipped and trained six North Vietnamese divisions, capable of waging large-scale mobile warfare, where previously most engagements had been at battalion level or below. The pretence that the Viet Minh was a purely nationalist force was dropped, and the links between the Vietnamese, Laotian and Cambodian revolutionary movements were strongly underlined. General Giap, who in March 1950 was appointed head of an ICP CC Special Committee overseeing Laotian and Cambodian affairs, declared that Indochina was 'a strategic unity'. Truong Chinh insisted that 'the independence of Vietnam will not be assured as long as Cambodia and Laos are not liberated', a statement subsequently repeated *ad nauseam* by every Vietnamese leader from Ho Chi Minh down. The final goal was a 'Democratic Republic of Indochina', incorporating all three countries, to serve as the vanguard of the communist revolution throughout South-East Asia.

In this new geo-political context, the Vietnamese leaders, responding to the French creation of the 'Associated States', decided to establish 'revolutionary counter-states', the Pathet Lao (or Lao Country) and Nokor Khmer (Khmerland), and to endow them with full-fledged political parties which would lay the groundwork for socialist systems modelled on that of North Vietnam.

On March 12 1950, the leaders of the ICP in southern Vietnam, including Le Duan and Le Duc Tho, began a ten-day meeting with the future chiefs of the Cambodian revolution near Hatien, a few miles south of the border. Forty-five Cambodians attended, led by Son Ngoc Minh who the previous autumn had become the first ethnic (or part-ethnic) Khmer to be accepted as a Party member.

The keynote speech was given by Nguyen Thanh Son, whom Giap had placed in charge of Cambodian affairs. He made four main points: firstly, in the absence of a Cambodian proletariat, the Khmer revolution would have to be based on the peasantry; secondly, the overriding priority was to train Cambodian cadres to carry out political work among the Khmer masses and generate popular support for military action – the Vietnamese could help, but Cambodians must take the lead; thirdly, the best way to win Khmer hearts and minds was through the Buddhist monks, for they wielded the greatest influence in the villages; and finally, Vietnamese ideas of communism must be modified to bring them into line with Cambodian reality – it was pointless, for instance, to attack the monarchy because Cambodians would not follow: the correct slogan was 'Liberate the King from the French colonial yoke!'

These were the lessons the Viet Minh had learnt painfully over the previous four years. Now they became official policy. In April 1950, two hundred Khmer delegates, half of them monks, met at Hongdan, just across the border from Cambodia's Peam Chor district, where they approved a new national anthem and flag – a five-towered outline of Angkor Wat in yellow on a red ground – and appointed Son Ngoc Minh head of the provisional revolutionary government. His 'cabinet' included Tou Samouth, who headed the new Khmer National United Front, a broad-based organisation modelled on the Viet Minh, and Sieu Heng, a former aide to Dap Chhuon who had switched sides and was now the principal Issarak leader in the North-West. Samouth and Minh also joined the All-Cambodia Work Committee, a Vietnamese organisation, headed by Nguyen Thanh Son, which had ultimate authority over the Cambodian revolution.

In May, the new leadership issued a Proclamation of Independence, stating: 'We put our confidence in the people's democracies, under the leadership of the USSR . . .' June 19 1950 was designated Independence Day, to be celebrated annually, and thereafter Son Ngoc Minh was venerated as the founding father of revolutionary Khmerland.

The establishment of a Cambodian Party took a further year. In February 1951, the ICP held its last Congress, which approved the formation of a new Vietnamese Workers' Party (VWP), that term being judged more appropriate than 'communist' at a time when it was necessary to rally the whole Vietnamese people against the French. A month later, Truong Chinh informed Stalin that 'people's revolutionary parties' – a name conveying a much lower level of political development – would be established in Cambodia and Laos. During the summer Nguyen Thanh Son's All-Cambodia Work Committee began drafting the statutes and political programme of what was to be known as the People's Revolutionary Party of Khmerland (PRPK). They were promulgated on August 5, and soon afterwards Son Ngoc Minh, Tou Samouth, Sieu Heng, another veteran, Tuk Nhung, and a young man named So Phim were inducted as its founding members. A similarly constituted Laotian Party followed.

Although the issue was fudged, the new Cambodian Party was not, strictly speaking, Marxist-Leninist. The statutes of the PRPK did not even mention the term, nor did they speak of socialism. Rather it was a proto-communist party – not the 'vanguard of the working class' but 'the vanguard of the nation'. Vietnamese officials explained:

> Although Vietnam, Laos and Cambodia have a common enemy – French colonialism – their degrees of evolution differ . . . The mission of the Vietnamese revolution is to liberate the nation, develop people's democracy and establish socialism . . . The mission of the Laotian and Cambodian revolutions is to liberate the nation and establish an anti-imperialist government. For distinct principles and characteristics, distinct parties are needed.

The delays in setting up the PRPK were due partly to the lack of qualified Cambodian cadres. Over the previous three years, various attempts had been made to start cadre training schools in the base areas, but the military situation was unstable and they were difficult to sustain. The courses generally focused on military tactics and on the 'revolutionary situation'. The best students went on to the Truong Chinh Institute, the highest Party school in southern Vietnam, where they spent six months learning Marxist-Leninist theory, Mao Zedong Thought, dialectical materialism, guerrilla strategy and the theory of people's war from lecturers who included Le Duan and Giap. Son Ngoc Minh and other senior Cambodian leaders attended courses there, while lower-ranking Khmer cadres went to a Vietnamese training school at Hon Chong, near the coast a few miles south of Hatien. According to French intelligence, it comprised 'three straw-thatched dormitories, each holding about 60 trainees. Every three months there is a new intake of 150 Vietnamese and 50 Cambodians. At political meetings a red flag with the hammer and sickle is displayed, together with a portrait of Stalin.' Early in 1951, the school was bombed by French aircraft but 'was rebuilt and resumed courses a few days later'.

Gradually a system of local administration was put in place in the communist-controlled districts of Cambodia, starting at village level. It replicated in minute detail the practices developed in Vietnam. Khmerland, too, was to have its equivalent of the Viet Minh 'People's Committees'. In each *khum*, or canton, a guerrilla battalion and a militia unit were organised, and lotteries held to raise funds for the troops. Each Zone had its Women's Front, its Peasants' Front, its Workers' Front, its Youth Front; and each district its Liberation Committee, its Military Committee and its Economic Committee. The Vietnamese even established a Highway Code Committee, to the bemusement of the Cambodians, for whom traffic regulations of any kind have always been a closed book. Khmer cadres were sent specimen forms, translated from Vietnamese, to show them how to file administrative reports. A radio station calling itself the 'Voice of Khmer Issarak' started broadcasting; a Cambodian Information Agency was set up; official telegrams were exchanged between the governments of Khmerland and North Vietnam.

In short, the new polity was carefully endowed with all the trappings of modern statehood. But only the trappings. The 'liberated areas' were still tiny and the Khmerland People's Government's control over them so feeble that for the first two years President Son Ngoc Minh was compelled to live outside 'his' country, across the border at Hatien (just as the Lao revolutionary government was based, for even longer, in northern Vietnam).

In practice, decision-making at every level remained firmly in Vietnamese hands. Truong Chinh noted the VWP's 'right of supervision' over its Cambodian and Lao allies and that the Khmer communists faithfully 'took instructions' from the Party in Vietnam. No Khmer could become a Party member without the prior agreement of Nguyen Thanh Son's All-Cambodia Work Committee, most of whose members were Vietnamese. All appointments, down to the level of village chiefs, required the Committee's approval. Even the commander of the Viet Minh-backed Khmer Issarak forces was Vietnamese until, 'to appease the Khmers', Sieu Heng was given the post, closely supervised by his predecessor, now officially his deputy. No matter how much Hanoi might talk of the need to 'Khmerise' Cambodia's revolution, the reality was that the leaders of Khmerland were little more than a polite fiction masking Vietnamese control.

This was not simply a matter of Vietnam having hegemonic designs upon a weaker neighbour. Rather it reflected the mismatch between two incompatible peoples. To the Vietnamese it seemed that no matter how hard they tried to mobilise Khmer support, the overwhelming majority of Cambodians stubbornly refused to budge. Their frustration at perceived Khmer obtuseness was palpable. At a meeting in the summer of 1950, one of Nguyen Thanh Son's colleagues exploded:

> The Cambodian revolution must be carried out by Cambodians. If the Cambodian people don't wake up, if the Cambodian cadres don't know how to work, then no matter how many millions of cadres we send – how many thousands of tons of arms or how much money we give them – it won't help.

A senior Viet Minh general complained that it was impossible to find Cambodian officer material because they 'lack qualities of command'. In 1951 – despite a recruitment drive and a decision to lower membership criteria for Khmers 'to take account of the insufficiency of their intellectual level' – there were still only 150 Khmer Party members. The Vietnamese, like the French before them, had decided that the Cambodians were apathetic, primitive and incapable of doing anything without the tutelage of a more civilised and vigorous power.

One colonialism was chasing out another. A French intelligence officer wrote: '[This] revolutionary war has an aspect that is truly paradoxical: it is being undertaken by the Vietnamese against the French for the independence of the Cambodian people. It is the deed of one foreign army against another foreign army – the one contesting with the other the right to bring Happiness to the country in question.' The Vietnamese never asked themselves, any more than had the French, whether the Cambodians *wanted* the new system they were introducing. They acted in the unassailable certitude of a superior truth.

The half-dozen or so young men who began meeting in the winter of 1950 in Keng Vannsak's flat in Paris knew little of all this. Although French newspapers were devoting more and more space to the war in Indochina – *la sale guerre*, 'the dirty war', as the French Left called it – it was always in reference to Vietnam. Cambodia hardly got a mention. 'The French press uses "Vietnam" and "Indochina" as though they are interchangeable,' *Khemara Nisut* complained. Mey Mann recalled trying to explain to a group of French students at a holiday camp one summer that Cambodians formed a separate nation, with their own culture and traditions which were nothing to do with Vietnam's. The members of the AEK voted by an overwhelming margin that celebrations to mark the Khmer New Year should never be held in the Maison d'Indochine because the setting was too Vietnamese.

Affirming Khmer identity was a constant struggle, and not only in France: China's Premier Zhou Enlai confessed later that when the Chinese communists began formulating policy in regard to 'Indochina', he and his colleagues initially assumed they were dealing with 'a single country in which the Cambodians were a national minority'.

None the less, by early 1951 it had become clear to the students in Paris that there were three distinct pro-independence movements at work in Cambodia: the original Khmer Issaraks, led by local warlords like Prince Chantarainsey, Puth Chhay, Ouch and Savangs Vong; the so-called 'Khmer Viet Minh', the term used by the French to describe Issarak leaders and others (notably Son Ngoc Minh, Sieu Heng and Tou Samouth) who had thrown in their lot with the Vietnamese; and last, but by no means least, the uneasy partnership between King Sihanouk and the Cambodian parliament, controlled by the Democratic Party, which was seeking to transform 'independence within the French Union' into full statehood through negotiations with Paris. The burning issue for Vannsak's circle was which path to national liberation was most likely to succeed, and how a group like theirs – keenly aware of its responsibilities as Cambodia's future intellectual elite – could best promote that goal. To all of them, independence, not ideology, was the key. The founding of 'New China', the expansion of the war against the French in Vietnam, the independence of India and Indonesia, about which *Khemara Nisut* wrote at length, and the anti-colonialism of the French Left, all combined to put national emancipation at the forefront of their thoughts.

Their discussions were often rather muddled. At one early meeting, Ea Sichau developed a proposal – 'enough to make you fall asleep standing up,' Keng Vannsak grumbled – that Sihanouk should marry an Indian princess so that Nehru would take up the cudgels for Cambodian independence. The anecdote is revealing not just for the lingering influence of the statecraft of the Angkorian kingdom, six centuries before, but for the insight it provides into the mentality of the students in Paris. Even university-educated Cambodians often found the gulf between Western and Asian ways of thinking unbridgeable. As a result, they absorbed European ideas piecemeal rather than as a coherent system of thought. The lack of critical faculties, which Pierre Lamant noted among his pupils at the Lycée Sisowath, was to be an enduring characteristic of many of Sâr's generation: they dreamed dreams, and showed a total disregard for reality.

Another of Sichau's contemporaries, a young man of pronounced right-wing views, wrote a long essay extolling the Soviet collective farm system as a model for Cambodian agriculture without once asking himself what collectivisation would do to Cambodia's social system. A left-wing medical student warned his comrades that 'the sweet, young [French] working girl presents the greatest danger [of venereal disease] because of her inexperience and ignorance of the most elementary rules of hygiene', a comment which, if prophylactically true, was politically indefensible. Even Vannsak, endowed with an alert, questioning mind that far outstripped those of most of his colleagues, embraced an obscure quasi-Buddhist doctrine called ascetology, founded by a paralysed French academic, Dr Gorelle, in the belief that it would help him control his sexual desires at a time when the struggle for independence was paramount.

Vannsak's study circle eschewed political labels. Its members did not claim to be either Left or Right, and the group itself had no name. As he put it, 'It was simply a gathering of friends who liked being with each other, all of whom, in one way or another, regarded themselves as progressive.'

From the outset, however, there were two opposing tendencies. Ea Sichau, Hang Thun Hak and Saloth Sâr believed Cambodia's salvation lay with Son Ngoc Thanh, then still living in exile in Poitiers, and several times in the course of that year travelled there to see the great man and hear his views on the situation at home. Rath Samoeun and Ieng Sary, still under the spell of the *Communist Manifesto* which they had read in Phnom Penh, were more interested in the Viet Minh. Soon after arriving in France they had contacted Jacques Vergès, then a member of the Bureau of the International Students' Union (ISU), a communist front organisation with its headquarters in Prague. He had put them in touch with left-wing Vietnamese student groups.

At this stage, even for Sary, 'independence', not 'communism', remained the overriding goal. But by 1951, the two were becoming intertwined. Since Stalin's recognition of Ho Chi Minh's government a year earlier, the French Communist Party (PCF) had vociferously championed the Viet Minh cause. Many in the Khmer student community began to look on the Party in a new light. Mey Mann remembered thinking that spring that 'the communists were our best friends. They were the ones who supported us. They opposed colonialism . . . Everyone else was against us.' Thiounn Mumm, who spent the first half of the year at a sanatorium at Combloux, near Megève, in the Alps, convalescing from a lung disease, reached the same conclusion. Many of his fellow patients were communists who had been in the French resistance, and from time to time they organised meetings against the Indochina War. 'If you wanted to fight against colonialism,' Mumm decided, 'the communists were the only ones who would help you.'

Within the circle, Vannsak saw himself as a rallying point, bringing the two sides together. But even he recognised that, as the months passed, the gap between the rival tendencies was growing and it was sometimes better that they met separately.

The point of no return came that summer. The World Federation of Democratic Youth, a Budapest-based front organisation from the same stable as the ISU, announced that it was organising a fifteen-day 'World Youth Festival for Peace', to be held in Berlin in August. Sary, alerted by Jacques Vergès, went to see Thiounn Mumm to suggest that the AEK should participate and that Mumm, as one of the most senior and highly qualified of the Khmer community in Paris, should lead the delegation. He agreed. Vannsak, standing in for the Association's president, approved the decision and asked the other two to make sure that everyone had their travel papers. What happened next still made Vannsak fume half a century later:

> They screwed me! They didn't get my papers. The day we were supposed to leave I couldn't go because I had no passport and no visa. Why? Because they wanted to get rid of me, to push me aside. They saw that I wasn't a hardliner, like they were. I thought too much . . . I didn't act pig-headedly, in a fanatical, extremist way. And I had friends among the Thanhists, like Ea Sichau and Hang Thun Hak . . . Ieng Sary himself told me later: 'You're too sensitive. You'll never be a politician. To do politics you have to be tough . . . You can't do it, brother. You're too sentimental.'

Thiounn Mumm, Rath Samoeun, Ieng Sary, Mey Mann and five or six others – all of them sympathetic to Sary's ideas – travelled to Berlin by train through Switzerland. Saloth Sâr was not among them. He was a Thanhist and in any case he had already planned his camping holiday in Yugoslavia.

In theory the Berlin Festival was non-political. In fact it was strongly pro-Soviet, as was made clear by a tract distributed by the CGT, the French communist trade union federation:

> Young working men and women of Paris! Every day you are suffering from the preparations for a new world war [being undertaken] by the [French] government on the orders of its American masters . . . The threat of Gaullist fascism is growing . . . You do not wish to be capitalist cannon fodder [but to] live in peace and win a better life. [In] Berlin, representatives of the young people of the whole world will shake hands and say a resounding 'No!' to all the MacArthurs and Eisenhowers, to the imperialist cannibals thirsting for blood.

The Festival drew 25,000 young people, including 5,000 from France alone. Much of their time was spent watching displays of folk-dancing, and taking part in parades and emotional mass meetings to support the latest Soviet peace campaign. But they also visited the Nazi concentration camp at Ravensbrück and held meetings with delegations from North Vietnam and China. The Chinese, Mey Mann recalled, received the Khmers separately, whereas the Vietnamese insisted on seeing all the Indochinese students together. But it was the officials from Hanoi who made the strongest impression, for they were able to provide the Cambodians with the first reliable news of the Khmer Viet Minh struggle against the French, about which, until then, they had heard only confused rumours. They also gave them a photograph of Son Ngoc Minh, a set of propaganda texts and the flag of Nokor Khmer bearing the five-towered image of Angkor.

From then on, the divergence between the Thanhists and the new *de facto* alliance of Ieng Sary, Rath Samoeun and Thiounn Mumm, became more pronounced. Vannsak swallowed his rage over the Berlin episode and continued to try to mediate between them, joining Mumm in Warsaw in late August for a congress of the International Students' Union. But the fundamental issue in dispute – whether or not to endorse armed struggle against the French – was not one that could be papered over. Mumm said later that he had first realised the importance of a military struggle when his fellow officer cadets at the Ecole Polytechnique (run by the French Defence Ministry) had shown polite interest in Cambodia's campaign for independence and a very different sort of respect for the fight the Vietnamese were waging. 'I understood then that without armed struggle, we could not obtain independence. Ieng Sary felt the same way. And since we didn't want the Vietnamese to have the monopoly of military power, it meant we had to have our own army and fight for our own cause.' After the meeting with the Viet Minh in Berlin, this belief became a certainty. In Vannsak's words, '[they] came back convinced that . . . the Viet Minh were right, that the French had to be forced to yield and armed struggle was the only way.'

Ea Sichau and the Thanhists saw things differently. They argued that to take up arms would be to court Vietnamese domination. Burma and India had both won independence by non-violent means: why could not Cambodia do the same?

Son Ngoc Thanh himself equivocated. Mumm and Sary went to see him at Poitiers, where they noted, disapprovingly, that the *Collected Works* of Marx, prominently displayed in Thanh's library, had never been opened. Thanh's reluctance to commit himself was understandable: he had been trying for years to persuade Sihanouk to grant an amnesty allowing him to return and at long last there were signs that the King might soon do so. Laying himself open to accusations of endorsing armed revolt was the last thing he needed. To Ea Sichau and his supporters, moreover, Thanh's return was the best, last hope of gaining independence without Viet Minh involvement. Sihanouk appeared more than ever a French puppet, a weak, capricious man whom none of the Paris students believed was capable of ending colonial rule. Vannsak, who was deeply mistrustful of Vietnamese motives, also urged Thanh to return and take control of the independence movement so as to forge the disparate Issarak groups into an authentic Khmer force, capable of ousting the French without foreign aid.

In the middle of October, Sihanouk announced that Thanh's exile was to end. Ten days later, accompanied by Ea Sichau, he set out for Phnom Penh, where he was given a hero's welcome by a crowd estimated at 100,000 people, who lined the route from the airport as he drove in an open limousine the five miles into the city, slowing the cortège to walking pace in their efforts to see and touch him. It was the kind of welcome that hitherto had been reserved for Sihanouk alone and it gave the young King much pause for thought. Thanh declined the offer of a government post, and after consultations with Democratic Party leaders, set out on a tour of the provinces, hoping to build his popularity further before making a bid for power. Sihanouk watched uneasily, but could only let events take their course.

The effect of the Berlin Festival and the departure of Son Ngoc Thanh was to move the political centre of gravity of the Khmer student movement in Paris sharply to the left. In October 1951, the AEK chose Hou Yuon as its new president. Nghet Chhopininto remembered him as 'an independent spirit. Once he had traced his path, he followed it.' Of humble origins, Hou was appreciated for the care with which he managed the association's meagre funds and for his frankness and loyalty.

Under Hou Yuon, the AEK established close links with the left-wing French National Students' Union (UNEF) and, through Jacques Vergès, with the ISU and another group he headed, the Liaison Committee of Colonial Students' Associations, which had its headquarters in the rue St Sulpice. From then on, the AEK adopted an openly political stance, approving the 'struggle for national independence in all its forms', a phrase which covered armed struggle as well as negotiation.

But this was merely the outward face of a deeper change. A few weeks earlier, Thiounn Mumm had invited some thirty Khmer students, chosen for their progressive ideas, to a meeting at the home of his French girl-friend's mother in Sceaux, a few miles south of Paris. They heard a report on the Festival in Berlin, followed by a discussion of the best way to promote independence. 'No one used the word, "communism",' Nghet Chhopininto recalled. '[Mumm and Ieng Sary] were very cautious in what they said – and I think if they'd spoken in too ideological a fashion to begin with, people wouldn't have gone along with them. Those who attended were patriots, whose aim was to get rid of the French.' Mey Mann, who was also present that night, agreed. 'The main question was always to get the communists to help us to free ourselves from the colonialists. But the appetite grows with eating. Once you study it, you start to like Marxism because it is so rational and scientific.'

The meeting at Sceaux was designed to test the waters. Soon afterwards, selected participants were approached individually and asked if they would like to participate in a new, secret organisation: the Cercle Marxiste.

The Cercle was built up of individual cells, each comprising between three and six people. It was rigidly compartmentalised: one member of each cell was in contact with a single member of the leadership, and no cell member knew who belonged to the other cells or how many cells existed. Years later Ping Sây and Chhopininto were still unsure who had really been in charge.

In fact the three-man Co-ordinating Committee which ran the Cercle was headed by Ieng Sary, assisted by Thiounn Mumm and Rath Samoeun. Initially there were about a dozen members. One group met at the Hôtel Anglo-Latin on the rue St André-des-Arts, where Ieng Sary and Thiounn Mumm were then living. Keng Vannsak attended the initial meetings but then lost interest, finding the discussions too doctrinaire. Another cell, to which Chhopininto belonged, was based in the suburb of Antony. A third was led by a mathematics student named Ok Sakun and included Ping Sây and Mey Mann. Quite when Saloth Sâr joined is unclear. He may have been at the meeting at Sceaux but, if so, took little part in the discussion, for no one remembers his presence there. Indeed, Thiounn Mumm had no recollection of meeting him at any time in Paris. Nevertheless, some time in the autumn or winter of 1951, Sâr was admitted to a group which met in the rue Lacepède, near the Radio-Electricity Institute. Hou Yuon was in the same cell. So was Sary's friend Sien An, and a boy named Sok Knaol whom Sâr had befriended. Knaol was several years younger than the others and was studying fashion design.

For the next nineteen years, the Cercle operated as a secret core group, manipulating from behind the scenes the AEK and its successor organisations. The French police Special Branch, the Renseignements Généraux, estimated that in 1953, by which time the Cercle had about thirty members, it exerted a direct influence on approximately half the Cambodian students in Paris. That did not mean they were all Marxists. But all had 'progressive' views and saw the communists as allies in the independence struggle.

The cells met once a week, usually for a couple of hours in the evening, to discuss the week's events and to study Marxist texts. They started with Lenin's *ABC of Communism*, followed by the *Communist Manifesto* and Mao Zedong's *On New Democracy*. There were also evenings of 'criticism and self-criticism', when cell members analysed their shortcomings and those of their comrades. Such sessions were relatively benign, one participant recalled, with none of the systematic demolition of personality that would characterise self-criticism in Cambodia when the communists were in power. None the less, there was an undertone of severity, which everyone knew came from Ieng Sary. As Ping Sây put it: 'Sary worked a lot and he was quite broad-minded. But he wasn't amusing like Sâr [or Rath Samoeun] . . . He was tough – and he had a strong character.' Thiounn Mumm charged that some students quit the Cercle altogether because of Sary's excessive demands. Mumm himself and his girlfriend moved to a different hotel after Sary took to banging on their door at six o'clock in the morning to tell him that there was 'political work to be done'. Another Cercle member remembered Sary advising him to masturbate instead of wasting his time with young women. Yet Sary did not always live up to his own exacting standards. A year later, when his fiancée, nineteen-year-old Khieu Thirith, the daughter of a judge, came to join him in Paris, he promptly made her pregnant. Mumm and a couple of friends lent them money to go to Switzerland for an abortion, it being unthinkable for a Cambodian girl of good family – Marxist sympathiser or not – to bear a child out of wedlock. In one sense the incident was banal, proof that Sary was, at heart, no different from other young men of his age. But it reflected a double standard – one set of rules for himself, another for those around him – that would characterise his behaviour all his life.

Thiounn Mumm was a very different character and in later years he and Sary came to loathe each other. Mumm's intellectual brilliance and aristocratic ways gave him a sense of detachment which made him insensitive to the concerns of lesser beings. He was an amoral Utopian, consumed by a voracious curiosity for whatever touched on the realm of ideas but seemingly armour-plated against sentimentality and human weakness.

Of the three leaders of the Co-ordinating Committee, only Rath Samoeun commanded real affection. Khieu Samphân recalled his modesty and kindness; Ping Sây found him 'a gentle man'. To Keng Vannsak he was 'honest and pure'. But Samoeun died before the Khmers Rouges took power. Otherwise he might have been remembered differently.

If Saloth Sâr remained inconspicuously in the background for his first two years in Paris, it was partly his character – as he put it many years later, 'I did not wish to show myself' – and partly because he had yet to find his role. He breathed the 'air of the times', as the French expression has it, and was carried along, with little effort on his own part, by more assured, dynamic colleagues.

Keng Vannsak thought he was 'out of his depth' in France, unable to cope with Parisian ways. To him, Sâr was 'a poor fellow who hardly knew anybody and found it difficult to manage'. That judgement sits ill with the image of the 'bon vivant' that Ping Sây and Mey Mann remembered, and it may say more about Vannsak – whose high opinion of himself was reflected in a certain contempt for those he viewed as less gifted – than it does about Sâr. Yet it held a grain of truth. By the autumn of 1951, Sâr was beginning to worry about what he was going to do with his life. The Radio-Electricity School was leading nowhere: he had lost interest in his studies and that summer failed his second-year exams. His hero Son Ngoc Thanh had returned home. Vannsak's circle he found fascinating, but the discussions were often above his head. The same disdain that the boys at the Lycée Sisowath had shown for the 'apprentices' during Sâr's last year in Phnom Penh had followed him to Paris. 'I only had a middle school certificate,' he recalled. Men like Vannsak and Phuong Ton, preparing doctorates – no matter how sympathetic they might be – did not have a great deal of time for a former carpentry student now training to become a radio technician. Even in the Cercle Marxiste, he admitted ruefully, 'the leaders were appointed on the basis of the diplomas they held – so I was not among them.'

But for Sâr, that winter, something clicked. He found his purpose in life. It was revolution.

He was not alone in that. The discovery of Stalinism – the PCF's official ideology and constant rallying cry – gave the Khmer students in the Cercle something they had all lacked: a sense of belonging and a goal. Suddenly they were part of a world-wide movement endowed with a transcendant mission. Like communists everywhere, they interpreted Marxism through the prism of national culture, in their case an intensely normative form of Buddhism. Unsurprisingly, they saw themselves not as the avatars of a proletarian society which would transform the economic basis of a new, industrialised world, but much more simply – as the incarnation of good that would triumph over the forces of evil.

Most of them, moreover, had only the vaguest notions of Marxist theory. Thiounn Mumm, Khieu Samphân and, a generation later, radical students like Suong Sikoeun and In Sopheap waded through Lenin's *Materialism and Empirio-Criticism* and *State and Revolution*, Stalin's *Economic Problems of Socialism* and other ponderous tomes, but they were the exceptions who proved the rule. Sâr confessed later that when he read 'the big, thick works of Marx . . . I didn't really understand them at all.' Ping Sây, too, thought that 'Marx was too deep for us'. Ieng Sary, as an old man, would still occasionally lapse into Marxist categories when speaking of his Khmer Rouge days, and colleagues recalled how proud he was to have been one of only two Cambodians who had studied at the PCF Cadre School. For the others, Marxism signified an ideal, not a comprehensive system of thought to be mastered and applied.

A few months after the Cercle was established, Sâr joined the French Communist Party. Rath Samoeun, Ieng Sary, Mey Mann and half a dozen others did the same. They attended lectures on communist policy given by PCF leaders in a hall near the Opéra, and meetings of the PCF's Cambodian 'language group', which included both Party members and sympathisers.

In the PCF's scheme of things, Sâr's lack of academic qualifications was not merely of no importance, it was actually an advantage. The French Party in the early 1950s was viscerally anti-intellectual. What mattered most was proletarian origin. Sâr, the former trainee carpenter, was better placed than the others to satisfy class criteria. He may also have been encouraged by Hou Yuon to play a more active role. The members of his cell, he recalled, 'chose me to take charge of research on theoretical and ideological issues . . . My diploma was not as high as the others, and my French was not as good as theirs – none the less, they gave me [this] work to do.' A French militant who met him at that time remembered him as a 'discreet, courteous, polite young man . . . with firm convictions'. He began reading the PCF magazine, *Les Cahiers Internationaux*, and tried to analyse and compare the experience of different countries' revolutionary movements.

Like other members of the Cercle, Sâr also studied Stalin's 1912 essay *Marxism and the National Question* and the *History of the Communist Party (Bolshevik) of the USSR* – both of which, he said later, he found easier to understand than Lenin or Marx. The first sets out a materialist definition of the nation as a 'stable, historically constituted community' with a common culture, language and territory, and explicitly rejects the idea that a nation is a racial blood group – notions that accord closely with traditional Khmer ideas equating both 'race' and 'nation' with cultural behaviour. The second work, written by Stalin in 1938 in the aftermath of the Great Terror, was used as a political primer by communist parties all over the world. The PCF, in its usual, humourless fashion, handed it out free to anyone who bought the first ten volumes of the *Works* of the PCF leader, Maurice Thorez. Mao had it translated into Chinese. Ho Chi Minh issued a Vietnamese version. It cannot therefore, of itself, be blamed for the singular barbarism of future Cambodian communist practice. But it was a crucial formative influence.

The *History of the Communist Party (Bolshevik)* hammered home six basic lessons. Some of them – like the 'need to stay close to the masses', and not to become 'dizzy with success' – were typically honoured in the breach. But Stalin's four other precepts marked indelibly the thinking of the future Cambodian revolutionaries. He stressed the importance of correct leadership – 'without which the cause of the proletarian revolution will be ruined' – and of criticism and self-criticism; he taught that Marxism-Leninism was not a dogma, but a guide to action, constantly enriched by new revolutionary experience; and, above all, he urged eternal vigilance. 'One of the watchwords of the Bolshevik Party', Stalin wrote, is that 'the Party grows ever stronger by cleansing itself of opportunist elements':

> Without waging an intransigent struggle against the opportunists in its own ranks . . . the Party of the working class . . . cannot carry out its role . . . It might seem that the Bolsheviks have spent too much time [on this struggle] and accorded it too much importance . . . That is absolutely false. We can no more tolerate opportunism among us than we tolerate an ulcer in a healthy body . . . There is no way we can allow doubters, opportunists, capitulationists and traitors within the leading headquarters of the working class . . . A fortress is taken most easily from within. To be victorious, we must, before all else, purge the working class Party and its forward citadel, its leading headquarters, of capitulationists, deserters, criminals and traitors.

The *History* offered other lessons, too: on the importance of revolutionaries using both legal and illegal forms of struggle in order to win power; and on the need for a 'monolithic and combative', intrinsically elitist Party, for which candidates must be vigorously screened, rather than a broad-based body to which all and sundry might aspire. But the burden of Stalin's message was that communists must constantly be on guard against 'political crooks', 'tricksters' and 'agents of foreign spy organisations'. Such people, he wrote, would go to any lengths to camouflage their 'vile designs' and worm their way into the Party, using membership as a mask for sabotage and betrayal. The only correct response to these 'dregs of the human species' was 'pitiless repression'.

Stalinism, having been shaped by the legacy of Russian feudalism, resonated with the Khmers, whose culture likewise had little place for the subtle checks and balances that were applied, however imperfectly, in the Confucian world of China and Vietnam. Some members of the Cercle remained unconvinced: Phuong Ton had reservations, and Hou Yuon warned against 'confusing the elimination of the bourgeoisie [as a class] with the elimination of bourgeois [individuals]'. But Sâr, Rath Samoeun and Ieng Sary had no doubts. When the PCF purged two Politburo members, André Marty and Charles Tillon, for breaking Party discipline, Samoeun enthusiastically told a French comrade: 'I've just been waiting for this. I was beginning to think the PCF was too moderate, too legalistic and parliamentary.'

Sary, by this time, had a portrait of Stalin on his wall, as did Thiounn Thioeunn's fellow medical student In Sokhan. That year he confided to Keng Vannsak: 'I will direct the revolutionary organisation . . . I will hold the dossiers; I will supervise the ministers; I will watch that they do not deviate from the line laid down by the Central Committee in the interests of the people.' The words, recalled decades later, may not be exact, but the sentiments ring true. By 1952, Ieng Sary, as head of the Cercle, saw himself as Cambodia's future revolutionary leader.

Saloth Sâr had more modest ambitions. He was slowly beginning to emerge as a 'progressive student' in his own right. He gave talks to the members of his cell. He helped to duplicate the Cercle's clandestine journal, *Reaksmei* ('the Spark', named after Lenin's revolutionary paper), in Ieng Sary's hotel room. There he met for the first time Khieu Ponnary, the elder sister of Sary's fiancée, who was about to return to Phnom Penh to teach at the Lycée Sisowath. Keng Vannsak would say later that Sâr and Sary 'ate and slept revolution'. But Sary was in charge, Sâr followed behind.

He started reading *l'Humanité*, which until then he had avoided, disliking its strident tone. Mey Mann, too, had been repelled by the 'quasi-monarchical' devotion the newspaper showed towards Maurice Thorez, which reminded him of Sihanouk's court. In the early 1950s, *l'Humanité* had no illusions about the kind of stories that would grab the attention of its working-class readership. Alongside articles by Politburo members about the minimum wage and the iniquities of Gaullism were gruesome crime reports with headlines like, 'Amélie Rabilloud shows how she killed and cut up her husband'; 'A baby devoured by the family dog before the eyes of its mother'; and 'Suzanne Feret kept the corpse of her child in a suitcase for 38 days'.

None the less, *l'Humanité* faithfully reflected the PCF's (and Stalin's) priorities: the campaign to ban atomic weapons; the supposed menace of German rearmament; the Korean War; and the battle against French colonialism. Not only Indochina but French North Africa and Madagascar were seething with unrest. Anti-colonial rallies were held at the Salle de la Mutualité in the Latin Quarter, triggering fist-fights with right-wing students on the Boulevard St Michel which often ended with a night in the cells. Khieu Samphân remembered an insurrectional atmosphere in the city, where 'one was almost led to believe that a great revolution was about to break out' – less fanciful than it might seem at a time when communist doctrine proclaimed that the only way to power was through a general uprising.

These were the years when 25 per cent of the French electorate voted for the PCF, more than for any other political party. To be a communist was a badge of honour, the legacy of the glory days when the communists formed the backbone of resistance against Nazi Germany. The PCF leader, Maurice Thorez, travelled in an armoured black limousine to guard against assassination attempts and lesser figures, including Politburo members, were constantly harassed by the police. Left-wing writers and painters like Paul Eluard, Picasso, Louis Aragon and Sartre issued ringing statements of support. The communist journalist André Stil was imprisoned for writing that the US had engaged in bacteriological warfare in Korea. *L'Humanité* urged its readers to draw inspiration from the Paris Commune of 1871, whose eightieth anniversary the PCF marked with grandiose celebrations and whose collapse under the assaults of the bourgeoisie was, in the words of one PCF leader, 'an invitation to redouble our vigilance against the activities of enemy agents'. If that parallel seemed too remote, the East European show trials – of Rajk and Kostov in 1949 and the Czechoslovak leader, Rudolf Slansky, in 1952 – proved to the Party faithful that dangers lurked on every side. The fervour of those who believed was equalled only by the terror unleashed against those who did not.

It was through *l'Humanité* that Sâr learnt for the first time of the heresy of Yugoslavia's President Tito. The Belgrade–Zagreb motorway, on which he and his colleagues had laboured, was now, the newspaper noted smugly, the target of anti-Tito saboteurs. Sâr's views are not recorded but he probably disapproved. According to Nghet Chhopininto, many Cambodian students secretly sympathised with the Yugoslav leader because 'he stood up to Stalin. Apart from Yugoslavia, all the other east European countries were under Soviet tutelage. Tito was the only one who waved the flag of national independence . . . And that pleased us.'

The parallel with Cambodia, likewise struggling to affirm its identity against powerful neighbours, Vietnam and Thailand, did not need to be spelt out.

*   *   *

Another seminal influence, not just for Sâr but for all the members of the Cercle, was Mao's speech *On New Democracy*. Originally delivered to cultural workers in Yan'an in January 1940, it provided a detailed blueprint for revolution in a colonial or semi-colonial state. Ho Chi Minh established the League for Vietnamese Independence (the Viet Minh) on the basis of the principles set out in this speech, and the term 'new democracies' soon became standard communist jargon for countries in transition, on the way to becoming socialist states. The ICP Secretary-General, Truong Chinh, looked forward to the day when 'New Democracy [will] cover a continuous expanse reaching from Central Europe to [Vietnam's] Cape Camau'. The word 'democracy' itself became a synonym for socialism. When Party workers referred to 'democratic publications', they meant the communist press. There were 'people's democracies' in Eastern Europe; a 'Democratic Front' in Asia; and a 'World Democratic Bloc' under the leadership of the Soviet Union. Even Son Ngoc Minh and his Vietnamese mentors adopted the new fashion: Khmerland was referred to as 'Democratic Cambodia' which, with Pathet Lao and North Vietnam, formed the region's three 'democratic nations'.

Mao argued that revolutions in colonies, or semi-colonial semi-feudal states, had to take place in two stages: first, a 'democratic revolution', carried out by an alliance of different classes – the peasants, who provided the main force, the workers and elements of the bourgeoisie; and only afterwards a 'socialist revolution'. The two were fundamentally different and could not be collapsed into one. The first stage would create 'a state under the joint dictatorship of all the revolutionary classes'; the second, a socialist state under 'the dictatorship of the proletariat'. In a world where socialism had become the dominant trend, it was no longer necessary, Mao said, to pass through the phase of bourgeois capitalism, as Marx had assumed. Instead the transition could be accomplished through the establishment of 'a new-democratic republic', which would nationalise banks and major industrial and commercial enterprises while permitting 'such capitalist production as does not dominate the livelihood of the people'. It was true, Mao admitted, that the bourgeoisie were unreliable allies, who would turn tail at the first sign of trouble. None the less, the 'new democracy' phase of revolution was 'necessary and cannot be dispensed with', and since 'we are [realists], not Utopians', it would last for 'quite a long time'.

For students from colonised nations, this was an exhilarating prospect. It meant there was a path to socialism which could elide western-style capitalism. And Mao added, as a further encouragement, that 'the only yardstick of truth is the revolutionary practice of millions of people', which seemed to mean that a revolution could be whatever the masses, or their leaders, wished. 'The universal truth of Marxism,' he explained, 'must be combined with specific national characteristics and acquire a definite national form if it is to be useful, and in no circumstances can it be applied subjectively as a mere formula. Marxists who make a fetish of formulas are simply playing the fool . . .'

Only on one point was Mao, like Stalin, totally inflexible:

> Either you co-operate with the Communist Party or you oppose it . . . The moment you oppose the Communist Party, you become a traitor . . . Whoever wants to oppose the Communist Party must be prepared to be ground into dust. If you are not keen on being ground into dust, you had certainly better drop your opposition.

With Stalin's grim prescriptions for maintaining purity in a revolutionary party and Mao's guide to revolutionary practice, the young Khmer communists-in-the-making seemed to have most of what they needed. None of them, not even Ieng Sary with his much-vaunted 'diploma' from the PCF Cadre School, took much interest in Marxist theory. No one indulged in philosophical speculation about metaphysics or the unity of opposites, as Mao and his companions did at a comparable stage of their careers. Nor, it seems, did they seek out Western accounts of the Chinese and Russian revolutions. Edgar Snow's *Red Star Over China*, Jack Belden's *China Shakes the World* and Agnes Smedley's *China's Red Army Marches* were all available in French translations. But there is no evidence that any Cambodian ever read them. Even a star student like Keng Vannsak was unaware of Maurice Merleau-Ponty's influential work *Humanism and Terror*, an apologium for the Stalinist show trials, despite having the author as his thesis director at the Sorbonne. Still less did any of them study Hegel or Feuerbach or Nietzsche, as their Chinese counterparts had, half a century before.

The Cambodians embraced Marxism not for theoretical insights, but to learn how to get rid of the French and to transform a feudal society which colonialism had left largely intact.

From this standpoint, Stalinism and Maoism both had one great flaw. They dealt with a world in which pride of place belonged to the industrial proletariat. The Bolshevik Revolution had been launched by the workers of Petrograd in a country which was already the world's fourth-ranking industrial power. In 1917, Russia had more than seven million workers. Stalin's vision of socialism reflected conditions in an industrialised state contending for world supremacy with the major capitalist powers. Even Mao, leading what he described as 'essentially a peasant revolution', insisted

71

in the next breath that 'the revolution cannot succeed without the modern industrial working class.'

In Cambodia there was no 'industrial working class', modern or otherwise.

Even the Vietnamese, fired up by their missionary endeavour to create a Khmer revolutionary movement, were compelled to admit that conditions did not exist for 'a socialist revolution, or even a new-democratic revolution, but only [for] a revolution that is national in nature'. For that, a different model was needed – which Sâr discovered one weekend, browsing among the second-hand bookstalls that line the banks of the Seine near the Pont St Michel. Fifty years later, it was the only book from his Paris days whose title he could remember: *The Great Revolution*, by the Russian anarchist Prince Pëtr Kropotkin.

It is a massive volume, running to 749 pages, and Sâr admitted later that he 'did not understand all of it' – unsurprisingly, given that there are long sections on eighteenth-century French feudal land rights, emphyteutic leases, *acapts, arrière-acapts, censives, sur-cens, champarts, lods, quints, requints, soètes, tasques, treizains, venterolles* and other untranslatable fiscal terms – but it held his interest well enough for him to persevere to the end. For the 'national revolution' which corresponded most closely to conditions in Cambodia was not that of China or Russia, but the revolution of 1789, launched by an alliance of bourgeois intellectuals and peasants against the rule of Louis XVI.

Kropotkin set out the aim of his book in the opening paragraph:

> The Revolution was prepared and made by two great movements. One was the current of ideas – the tide of new ideas on the political reorganisation of the State – which came from the bourgeoisie. The other, the current of action, came from the popular masses – the peasants and labourers . . . When these two movements joined together for what at first was a common goal – when for a time they lent each other mutual support – the Revolution occurred . . . The [eighteenth-century] philosophers prepared the way for the downfall of the *ancien régime* . . . But that was not enough by itself to make the Revolution break out. It was necessary to pass from theory to action, from an ideal conceived by the imagination to its practical implementation by deeds. What [we] must study today, above everything else, are the circumstances which permitted the French nation, at a particular moment in history, to make that leap – to begin to make that ideal a reality.

For a young man dreaming of revolution in another feudal kingdom, these were inspirational thoughts.

The story itself was not new to Sâr. All Cambodian children, from primary school on, were taught how the French King was overthrown and the revolutionaries declared a republic of 'Liberty, Fraternity, Equality', whose guiding principles were enshrined in a Declaration of Human Rights. These were recounted as heroic events. 'The King thought he was God's representative on earth . . . The nation . . . was in servitude to royal despotism,' wrote Alphonse Aulard in his *History of France*, one of the most widely read schoolbooks in the 1930s and '40s. Aulard insisted that the monarchy was weak, the republic strong, and the Revolution itself the expression of the noblest, most generous instincts of mankind. Another primary school textbook writer, Ernest Lavisse, declared: 'The soldiers of the Revolution . . . fought not just for France but for the whole of humanity . . . They wanted to deliver people everywhere from their kings so that all men might be free.' The Terror was explained as 'an exceptional measure in exceptional times' which took many innocent lives but saved the French Republic.

That was eighteenth-century France. This was twentieth-century Cambodia. Sihanouk himself was well aware of the precedent, but none of his subjects, nor even the French colonial administrators, seems to have made the connection between his methods of rule and those which brought Louis to the scaffold. With hindsight the parallels cry out. But it was only when the young Cambodians came to France that they allowed themselves to think the unthinkable and the similarities began to register.

Thiounn Mumm found the history of the French Revolution 'exalting'. Ieng Sary held long discussions with other members of the Cercle on the lessons the Revolution might have to offer. Thirty years later, a correspondent of *Le Monde* reported a surrealistic encounter in the jungles of north-western Cambodia with Khieu Samphân, who assured him that 'Prime Minister Pol Pot and I were profoundly influenced by the spirit of French thought – by the Age of Enlightenment, of Rousseau and Montesquieu.' In Sokhan's youngest brother, Sopheap – later Khmer Rouge Ambassador to Egypt – pondered the resemblance between 'the clergy, the nobility and the *tiers état* [commoners]' of royalist France and 'the monks, the mandarinate and the commoners' at home. His contemporary, Suong Sikoeun, afterwards one of Ieng Sary's closest aides, discovered the French Revolution even earlier, sneaking off to the lavatories at his boarding school in Kompong Cham, after 'candles out' at 10 p.m., to read about the Montagnards and their implacable leader:

> Robespierre's personality impressed me. His radicalism influenced me a lot. He was incorruptible and intransigent. [Perhaps] it was the intransigence of youth [that made me feel that way]. If you do something, you must do it right through to the end. You can't make compromises. That was my personal philosophy, my personal ideology. You must always be on the side of the absolute – no middle way, no compromise. You must never do things by halves . . .

73

That was also one of the lessons of Kropotkin's book, though he put it in somewhat different terms. To the Russian prince, Robespierre was an upright man of great moral purity whose revolutionary faith never faltered. But he was also a moderate, an administrator, not a visionary – 'careful not to go beyond the opinions of those who were the dominant force at any given time' – whose power stemmed precisely from occupying the centre ground. The whole problem of the French Revolution, in Kropotkin's view, was that it never went far enough. He warned of the ambivalence of the bourgeoisie, which tried to damp down the revolutionary élan of the masses whenever it sensed that its own interests were threatened. A revolution, he explained, occurred when those in power resisted change until blood ran in the streets. '[It] must never stop half way, for then it will surely fail . . . Rather, once a revolution has broken out, it must develop to its furthest limits. [Inevitably] at its highest point, countervailing forces will combine against it . . . and it will be forced to yield . . . Reaction will set in . . . But the end result will be better than what went before.'

Another of Kropotkin's themes was that the touchstone of revolution was property. Those who owned property were, by definition, against the revolution; those who had nothing were for it. He quoted Robespierre approvingly: 'Only goods in excess may be traded. Necessities belong to all.' The egalitarian principles of the French Revolution, he argued, were in fact the principles of communism. 'Modern [Marxist] socialism has added nothing, absolutely nothing, to the ideas that the French people sought to put into practice in [1793–4] . . . More than that, the people's communism of [those] two years was more clear-sighted, and pushed the logic of its analysis deeper, than today's socialism does . . . The Great Revolution . . . was the source of all the communist, anarchist and socialist concepts of the present age.'

There is much else in *The Great Revolution*. But these three core notions – that revolution requires an alliance between the intellectuals and the peasantry; that it must be carried through to the end, without compromise or hesitation; and that egalitarianism is the basis of communism – would stay with Saloth Sâr for the rest of his life. One may wonder whether he noted another premonitory sentence: 'The powerful currents of thought and action that collided and clashed in the French Revolution . . . are so intimately linked to the very essence of human nature that they will inevitably [do so] again in the future.'

While the members of the Cercle in Paris pondered the tenets of Marxism, at home in Cambodia King Sihanouk was facing more down-to-earth problems. Son Ngoc Thanh, whose old friend Pach Chhoeun was now

Minister of Information in the Democratic Party government, had lost no time gathering together the surviving members of the *Nagaravatta* group and in January 1952, helped by Ea Sichau and monks from the Buddhist Institute, launched a successor paper, *Khmer Krauk* (Khmers Awake!), which poured forth a stream of articles advocating independence along with 'sibylline poems, preaching nothing less than armed revolt'. During a visit to Siem Reap province where, by agreement with France, the Royal Khmer Army had been given responsibility for security, Thanh dropped hints of an accommodation with the Viet Minh. Should they commit 'acts of piracy', he said, they must be opposed; but their 'advance to independence' was a different matter. At some of Thanh's meetings, an American cultural attaché was present, ostensibly to ensure that the public address system, provided with US aid, was functioning properly.

The French were furious, and in February a pro-independence demonstration organised by Thanh's supporters in Phnom Penh was banned. Shortly afterwards he made contact with an Issarak leader named Kao Tak and on March 9, the anniversary of the Japanese *coup de force* which had first brought him to power, he and a few close followers – including Ea Sichau and the young actor Hang Thun Hak – slipped away to a rebel camp in the Dangrek Mountains. From there Thanh broadcast incendiary appeals to government soldiers and police to desert their units and join the rebellion. When these began to bear fruit – in April a Khmer commander sent twelve crates of weaponry to Thanh's Issarak allies – the French army attacked the rebels' bases along the Thai border.

That provoked a series of student demonstrations in Phnom Penh, Battambang and other towns. At Sâr's old college in Kompong Cham, the French headmaster, Monsieur Bourotte, was stoned. Banners in French and Khmer charged French troops with burning down villages suspected of Thanhist sympathies and of 'raping the wives and daughters of our peasants'.

To Sihanouk, it was a replay of 1945. Thanh had seized the initiative and was once more denigrating the monarchy as a passive tool of the French. But now the stakes were higher: if Thanh could forge an alliance with the Democratic Party, the Throne itself might be imperilled. This was not entirely far-fetched. When Thanh had returned in October, the Democratic Party Premier, Huy Kanthoul, had gone to the airport to greet him. The Democrats were widely suspected of having been behind the latest demonstrations. Thanh's radio broadcasts were drawing large audiences and a steady stream of secondary-school students was making its way to join him in the maquis.

Wiser heads might have noted that Thanh's support was limited to the towns and that basing himself in a remote and desperately poor rural area on the Thai border was a serious tactical error. But by this stage neither Sihanouk nor the French were behaving rationally – and rumours that the Americans were eyeing Thanh as a potential republican alternative to Sihanouk's regime were not calculated to improve matters. On June 4, the King broke his silence with a long and vehement speech to the Council of the Throne, in which he warned melodramatically that 'if the current unprecedented crisis is not resolved rapidly and in a radical manner, [it] will precipitate the Kingdom of My ancestors into anarchy and death'. The government, he complained, was equivocating before Son Ngoc Thanh's challenge and the people no longer knew what was right. Most serious of all, the royal family was being discredited:

> There are two injustices which revolt Me! First, that which makes the People believe that those responsible for the [Franco-Khmer] treaty and who continue to have dealings with the French are traitors. Secondly, that which holds that . . . all who do not openly insult and struggle against the French are traitors . . . For Myself, I refuse [this logic] . . . If I am a traitor, let the Crown Council permit Me to abdicate! . . .
>
> I can no longer stand by and watch My country drown and My people die . . . Over these last few months we have no longer dared look each other in the face. In our offices and schools, everywhere people are discussing politics – suspecting each other; hatching plots; promoting this person, bringing down that one, pushing the third aside; doing no constructive work – while, in the country at large, killing, banditry and murder hold sway. Chaos reigns, the established order has ceased to exist . . . The military and the police . . . no longer know where their duty lies. The Issaraks are told that they are dying for Cambodia, and so are our soldiers dying in the battle against them . . . Each day threatens [to engulf us in] a veritable civil war . . .
>
> This is how things now stand, gentlemen. The time has come for the Nation to make clear whether it desires to follow [the way of the rebels], or to continue in the path that I have traced.

It was the first time that the young King, then aged thirty, had deliberately gone beyond his constitutional role and entered the political arena. His performance was not yet vintage Sihanouk – that improbable mixture of rage and self-pity, acid and honey, brutality and sarcasm, passion and wit, which would become his trademark – but the demagogic talents he had discovered as a schoolboy studying rhetoric were already evident. For the next half-century, they would be the weapons of choice in his political armoury.

The speech provoked an open crisis. The Democrats' right-wing adversaries scattered tracts, demanding that the National Assembly be dissolved, the government be dismissed and the King institute direct rule. Dap Chhuon, now commander of the Royal Army in Siem Reap, was rumoured to be marching on Phnom Penh to drive the Democrats from power. Public meetings were banned and on June 8 police searched the houses of four right-wing party leaders, including Lon Nol, who were accused of plotting against the state. On the King's orders, three of them were released after a few hours, but the fourth, Yem Sambaur, a former Prime Minister widely believed to have been behind the assassination of Ieu Koeuss two years earlier, was held overnight. A case of grenades had been found at his home.

The following day, June 9, Sihanouk received the French Commissioner, Jean Risterucci, who called up troop reinforcements from Saigon. They arrived on the 14th. That evening, the King, in the presence of his parents and palace advisers, signed a series of decrees, and Cambodians awoke the following morning, a Sunday, to learn that during the night the government had been dismissed; that Sihanouk had assumed emergency powers and appointed himself Prime Minister; and that he had launched a 'Royal Crusade', pledging to obtain full independence for Cambodia within the next three years. The Democratic Party leaders, the King informed the nation, had confused the interests of the state with their own, grabbing the benefits of high office and excluding others from the spoils.

In this, Sihanouk was not wrong. During the five years they had been in power, the Democrats had shown themselves to be corrupt, feudalistic, incompetent and addicted to Byzantine factional squabbling which paralysed political life. A prominent member of their own party acknowledged: 'They were unworthy. They thought only of themselves . . . All they were interested in was their ministerial career.' Yet it could scarcely have been otherwise. The only indigenous political models were the palace and the mandarinate, which had waxed fat over the centuries by squeezing the population. Parliamentary democracy was a colonial import utterly alien to Cambodian tradition. Sihanouk's reaction, which was to conclude that the institutions of the French Fourth Republic had no place in his oriental kingdom, was short-sighted and did nothing to help Cambodia become a modern democratic state. But the US administration, by instinctively preferring an 'elected government', whatever its defects, to an unelected monarch, was equally simple-minded. It marked the beginning of a process of mutual incomprehension which would not end until America's defeat in the Vietnam War, a quarter of a century later, if indeed it ended then.

For some days after Sihanouk's 'coup', Moroccan infantrymen guarded the parliament building and French armoured cars patrolled the streets. All political meetings were banned. In Siem Reap province the Royal Army launched fresh attacks against the Khmer Serei (or Free Khmers), as Son

Ngoc Thanh's forces now called themselves, and burned down more villages. That triggered fresh protests by secondary-school students and a boycott of year-end exams. The National Assembly was sullenly hostile. But the sharpest criticisms of all came from Paris, where the leaders of the Students' Association rushed out a special issue of *Khemara Nisut*, the centrepiece of which was a vitriolic attack on Sihanouk, penned by Keng Vannsak, bluntly accusing the King of treason and lauding Son Ngoc Thanh and his followers as Cambodia's 'true heroes':

> We, Khmer students of the AEK, consider that Your Majesty has acted illegally . . . and that the policy of the Throne . . . will inevitably lead our Khmer Motherland into an abyss of perpetual slavery. . .
>
> In your message to the nation, [you said that] Cambodia faces ever greater dangers. It seems Your Majesty has only just noticed. The people have known this for a long time, and they know too that their sufferings are the doing of the French imperialists and of the absolute monarchy and its courtiers . . . What should the people think when Your Majesty's Palace has become a lobby for dishonest dealings which place within your hands the riches of the country and the people? . . . Corruption in our country stems from the Throne and spreads down to the humblest officials. The French oppress the whole country, the King trades on his Crown, the Palace and its parasites suck the people's blood . . . These are the main causes of our country's critical situation today. . .
>
> Your Majesty has sought to divide the nation in two: the royalists, and those who struggle for independence. [Your] policy is to set Khmers against Khmers . . . as happened under Sisowath and Norodom, who [also] collaborated with the French . . . Your Majesty is merely following in the footsteps of your ancestors, that is to say, you are selling the blood of your people as the price of your crown. . .
>
> The King considers Cambodia as his chattel . . . His policy . . . is one of destruction – of the people and the life of the Khmer country . . . [But] let Your Majesty be advised that we Khmer students . . . have no intention of judging or condemning you. It will be up to History – the history wrought by Your Majesty and your ancestors – to judge your faults in due time.

Vannsak's attack was all the more wounding because it contained a number of home truths about the personal corruption of Sihanouk's parents. Copies were signed by Hou Yuon, the AEK president; Mey Mann, who had been elected Secretary-General; and by Vannsak and other student luminaries, including Ieng Sary. They were sent to the palace, the National Assembly, the Cabinet Office, the two main Buddhist orders and the newspapers. The King sank into a 'black rage', Vannsak was told later, but was sufficiently lucid to recognise that punishing the culprits would only alienate opinion further. Instead, he sent the most senior of the Counsellors to the Throne, Penn Nouth, to Paris, with instructions first to obtain an apology and then try to smooth things over.

This was easier said than done. Hou Yuon addressed him pointedly as *Monsieur* Penn Nouth, rather than by the royal title, *Monseigneur*, an insult Nouth never forgot. Vannsak refused to see him at all. No apology was forthcoming. Sihanouk was forced to swallow his pride and recall his emissary, leaving behind a warning that the bursaries of those involved were now at risk.

That gave them pause. Vannsak remembered Ieng Sary telling him: 'This is your fault, brother. You've got your degree – you don't need to study any more. We think you should go back to Phnom Penh and try to raise some money, so that we can stay in France.' Whether from guilt – Vannsak loathed Sihanouk and had pressured the others into putting their names to his letter – or from simple lassitude after six years in Europe, he agreed. Ieng Sary and his fiancée, Thirith, took over the apartment in the rue de Commerce, and in October 1952 the Vannsaks set off on the three-day plane journey to Phnom Penh, which included an afternoon stopover in Cairo, to see the Pyramids, and another in Rangoon. Vannsak had warned his wife that they might be arrested on arrival, but in the event the worst that befell him was a dressing-down from an elderly aunt, Princess Peangpas, then Minister of Education. 'Imbecile !' she yelled at him. 'What did you think you were doing, daring to oppose the King?' When he denied responsibility, she demanded to see a specimen of his handwriting. He sat up all night trying to perfect a different script. But next morning the old lady had forgotten about it and instructed her *Chef de Cabinet* to find him a teaching post.

Vannsak had not been alone among the students in Paris in protesting against Sihanouk's actions. Others, with his encouragement, also published articles attacking the King. One, who called himself Khmer Daeum (Old Khmer), entitled his contribution 'Monarchy or Democracy?' Compared with Vannsak's diatribe, it was a rather juvenile effort, but as Saloth Sâr's earliest known piece of writing it provides an insight into his thinking at that time. Plainly influenced by his mentor, Sâr argued that the Khmer monarchy reduced the people 'to the condition of animals which are [treated] like a herd of slaves and forced to work day and night without stopping', whereas democracy was 'priceless as a diamond . . . like a torrent cascading down the mountainside which no person can stop'. Monarchy, Sâr wrote, was 'as foul as a putrefying sore'; 'the King's words are good, but his heart remains evil'. Such imagery, which would become the cachet of Pol Pot's oratorical style, enlivened otherwise pedestrian prose.

Most intriguing was his emphasis on Buddhism. Enlightened monks, he claimed, had 'always understood very well the nature of monarchy' and had written folk-tales like the *Thmenh Chey* (whose hero, one of the best-loved rogues in Khmer literature, famously outwitted the king), in order to show the people that they should not believe in royalty. The Buddha – 'our Great Master' – had abandoned princely life, he went on, in order to become 'a friend of the people'; he had been the first to preach the virtues of democracy and it was the democratic system alone that could defend Buddhism's 'profound values'. As a member of the Cercle Marxiste, Sâr would not have been expected to write in such terms. Ieng Sary or Thiounn Mumm certainly would not have done so. Like his choice of the pseudonym Khmer Daeum, it suggested a conscious desire to identify himself with an authentically Cambodian viewpoint rather than imported, Western ideas.

Sâr's other main historical reference was, unsurprisingly, the French Revolution, which 'dissolved the monarchy and executed the King'. The Russian and Chinese revolutions received passing mention, but for ending monarchical rule, not for their ideological content. There were other allusions which, in the light of later events, assume a significance that was not apparent at the time. Sihanouk, Sâr wrote, had undermined the Buddhist faith by introducing ranks into the monkhood; and he had mortgaged the country's independence. 'History has shown,' he explained, 'that the King who seeks aid from Siam has to pay tribute to Siam; the King who seeks aid from France will have to pay tribute to France.'*

To Sâr and his companions, the King's action was 'a royal coup d'état'. A page had been turned. The French felt it too. 'Democracy had no hope [here],' wrote the French military commander, General Pierre de Langlade. 'The parliamentary experiment has failed . . . The Sovereign remains the only person capable of giving Cambodia political direction . . . [He is] heir to the . . . mystique of the God-Kings, who for thousands of years have guided the destinies of the land . . . Everything in this country has to be done by the King.'

The political instability of the first half of 1952 had allowed the Viet Minh and their Khmer allies to strengthen their grip on the countryside. Son Ngoc Minh's partisans claimed to hold a third of Cambodia with a population of one million. That was an exaggeration. But it was certainly true that large areas in almost every province were now officially declared insecure, and along the Vietnamese border upwards of 200,000 Cambodians were living under communist rule. The French army itself acknowledged

---

* In the 1970s, ranks and foreign aid would be two of the Khmer Rouges' *bêtes noires*.

that – in sharp contrast to the situation three years earlier – the Viet Minh 'have acquired prestige in the eyes of the [Khmer] population'. The one bright spot for the authorities was that Son Ngoc Thanh's efforts to unite the different rebel groups into a single force had fallen flat. In the weeks following his entry into rebellion, individual Issarak leaders, including Chantarainsey and Savangs Vong (an opium-addicted army deserter who led a band of four hundred men in Kompong Speu), had sent him congratulatory messages. But none was willing to give up his autonomy to form a national alliance. Exchanges with the Viet Minh came to nothing when Thanh insisted that any joint force must be under his command.

After Sihanouk's 'coup' in June, the French stepped up what they called their 'pacification efforts' and began to stabilise, then to reduce, the level of Viet Minh penetration. More than 100,000 villagers were gathered into fortified hamlets, protected by watchtowers manned by armed militia. Issaraks who rallied to the government were granted a royal pardon. None the less, it was a delicate game, in which neither side was duped. The French military command knew that if it were to win back the population from Viet Minh and Issarak control, it could only be in Sihanouk's name. The King knew that to win independence, continued insurgency was necessary until the French accepted his 'Royal Crusade' as the only realistic outcome. De Langlade complained that Sihanouk was 'playing into Son Ngoc Thanh's hands' by his 'extreme moderation'.

That summer, there was an unnatural calm. It was plain to everyone that the Democrat-led National Assembly could not cohabit indefinitely with a government, led by the King, which was committed to the Democrats' downfall. Cambodian schools closed for the holidays. Parliament went into recess. The AEK organised a holiday camp at Pornic in Brittany, opposite the island of Noirmoutier, where Thiounn Mumm, Rath Samoeun, Ieng Sary, Sâr and other members of the Cercle swam, went hiking and put on a show of traditional Cambodian dances for a group of French students camping nearby. They also held long discussions about Cambodia's future. No decisions were taken. But when the new academic year began in October, Sary and Thiounn Mumm convened a meeting, attended by about fifteen members of the Cercle, at a farmhouse in the countryside an hour's drive from Paris, owned by a member of the French Communist Party.

There were three questions on the agenda: which rebel organisation they should support, now that Sihanouk had been discredited by his *de facto* alliance with the French; whether anything could still be done to bring the different resistance groups together, following Son Ngoc Thanh's failure to achieve unity; and whether the time had come for members of the Cercle to return to Cambodia to take part in the struggle themselves.

Some of those present argued that Thanh's group, which included former colleagues like Hang Thun Hak and Ea Sichau and had impeccable Khmer nationalist credentials, offered the best hope of wresting power from the French. Others, including Ieng Sary, felt that Son Ngoc Minh's 'Khmer Viet Minh' were more serious, although tainted by their association with the Vietnamese, whose motives the students mistrusted. But as the afternoon wore on, it became clear that they lacked the information on which to base a rational decision. No one in Paris had any idea how strong Son Ngoc Thanh's Khmer Serei really were; of the extent to which the Vietnamese were manipulating Son Ngoc Minh and his followers; or the true stance of independent Issarak leaders like Chantarainsey in Kompong Speu. It was suggested, Sâr recalled, that someone go back 'to carry out a reconnaissance . . . and make an assessment of the different resistance organisations. [Then we would] take a decision over which movement we should support – and which organisation we should join.' The Cercle's Co-ordinating Committee agreed, but added a second task: whoever was sent should also report on the prospects of uniting the main resistance groups. Sâr volunteered to go. Mey Mann, who was present, remembered him being chosen because 'he had a lot of contacts. He knew people at the Palace, and had met Chantarainsey there [as a child] . . . He had known Hang Thun Hak in Paris, and had also met Son Ngoc Thanh.'

Vannsak claimed afterwards that Sâr had jumped at the chance because he was missing his girlfriend, the beautiful Soeung Son Maly. But that was mischievous. It was true that he had failed his exams at the Radio-Electricity School for the second year in a row, which meant his bursary was cut off. However, that had not stopped others staying on. In Sâr's case, he seems to have reached the conclusion that his useful years in France were over and that whatever the future might hold for him, he now belonged at home. He passed on the grim little bedsit in the rue Letellier to a political science student named Son Sen, who came from the same Khmer-speaking district of South Vietnam as Ieng Sary and had arrived in Paris at the same time. In Marseilles, on December 15, Sâr boarded the SS *Jamaique*, the same ship that had brought him to France three years earlier, now making one of its last voyages before being sold for scrap. As before, he bunked in the hold with the soldiers. The atmosphere was no longer as carefree. The war in Indochina was not going well for France. Among each new shipload of conscripts, some would not return.

Even before Sâr left Paris, there had been clear signs that the simmering confrontation between Sihanouk and the Democrats was coming to a head.

In November, students in Phnom Penh and several provincial towns went on strike. When the King appealed to them to return to their classes, more than a hundred took refuge in the National Assembly, which, in a calculated display of defiance, announced that it was setting up a commission to study their grievances. Next came demonstrations by monks, who charged the government with complicity with the French. Then, in December, the Assembly refused to vote the budget on the grounds that it provided too much money for defence and not enough for economic and social purposes. Sihanouk fumed, but his mind was elsewhere: his youngest child, a four-year-old girl whom he adored, had suddenly fallen ill and lay dying.

Sensing weakness, the Viet Minh intensified their attacks, setting ambushes in which a provincial governor and several district chiefs lost their lives. Agitation in the secondary schools, which had momentarily subsided, resumed more strongly than ever. On January 8 1953 a grenade went off in a classroom at the Lycée Sisowath, injuring two students; other devices were defused before they could explode. As usual in Cambodia, the perpetrators were never caught. It was probably a provocation, designed to force Sihanouk to act harshly or to give him justification for doing so. Two days later, the government sought emergency powers, asking the National Assembly to proclaim the nation in danger. It refused.

On January 13, the day that Sâr's ship docked at Saigon, troops surrounded the parliament building in Phnom Penh. In a radio address, Sihanouk announced that he intended to rule by decree. The Assembly was dissolved and civil liberties suspended. 'From now on,' he warned, 'any individual or any political party that opposes My policies will be declared a traitor to the Nation and . . . punished [accordingly].' The King's resolve was said to have been stiffened by a lecture from his mother, the redoubtable Princess Kossamak, who regarded parliamentary democracy as not only inimical to Cambodian tradition but a personal affront. In any event, the French were delighted. 'If Norodom Sihanouk can hold to this new position of firmness,' wrote the Minister for the Associated States, Jean Letourneau, 'we may hope that Cambodia's pacification will make continued progress.'

Over the next few days, nine Democratic Party MPs, including Bunchan Mol and Khieu Ponnary's cousin Im Phon, were imprisoned without trial on suspicion of 'plotting against the state'. In Paris, the AEK, which had been fulminating for months against 'the puppet, Sihanouk' and his 'government of traitors', fired off a telegram of protest.

But the climate had changed. Hou Yuon, Ieng Sary, Son Sen, Mey Mann, Ping Sây, Thiounn Mumm's youngest brother, Prasith, and a dozen others, were informed that their bursaries were terminated. The AEK itself was banned. In Phnom Penh the heads of the two Buddhist orders were treated to a humiliating public admonition against sympathising with the rebels. 'For the first time in my life,' Sihanouk raged, 'I have to grab the monks by the throat. Me! The most religious man in the Kingdom! Because I've had enough – more than enough! My subjects and the elite among my subjects must *obey*!'

An era had ended. The open expression of dissent would never be tolerated again. Cambodia had taken the first, critical step down the road to revolution.

3

Initiation to the Maquis

WHEN SÂR HAD set out for France, three years earlier, one of his companions had remarked that, in contrast to Vietnam, there was 'no fighting in Cambodia'. That was not completely true but it was what most of them believed. When he returned in January 1953, he found a country at war.

The bloodshed was not on remotely the same scale as in neighbouring Vietnam. Nevertheless, that month in Cambodia, according to the French, 115 Issaraks and Viet Minh were killed in clashes with government troops and 220 were taken prisoner. Internal Viet Minh reports spoke of a comparable level of government casualties. Far from being a comic-opera conflict, matching the kingdom's Ruritanian image, it was ugly and brutal. In a typical action in Kompong Cham, a government patrol of fifty men, led by a Khmer sub-lieutenant, was lured into a Viet Minh ambush. The regimental despatch recounted impassively:

> In the first burst of machine-gun fire, Sgt Roeung received a bullet in the head and was killed outright. Cpl Rhek, mortally wounded, crawled back towards our main force. Sub-lieutenant Chhim Yan ran forward to recover Sgt Roeung's rifle and took cover behind an ant-hill . . . when he, too, was hit by a bullet in the head . . . Seeing that the situation was critical . . . our men counter-attacked. Four Viet Minh fell under our fire . . . Our men then formed a square . . . Towards 17.30 hours, the Viets approached . . . from the south-east. They called out to our men: 'Don't shoot. We are friends.' Then they charged. Most of their fighters did not have firearms. They just ran towards us in a compact mass, yelling. We cut them down with machine-gun fire and grenades. Their shouts suddenly stopped as though their throats had been cut . . . The battle ended at nightfall . . . and our men marched back, reaching the HQ at 2 a.m.

In that engagement, the French admitted losing five dead and four injured for thirty-seven Vietnamese put out of action, allegedly including a Viet Minh lieutenant. Both sides habitually inflated casualty figures. None the less, the carnage – especially among the Viet Minh auxiliaries, unarmed villagers from the Khmer districts of Cochin-China who fought with staves and axes – was grim, and French military reports spoke of sorties to 'kill us some Viet' in the same way as Americans would later talk of 'killing gooks'.

To Saloth Sâr, the change was clear the moment he disembarked in Saigon. No longer could one simply go to the bus station and board a coach to Phnom Penh. Now there was a daily convoy, protected by a military escort. Troops patrolled the Cambodian capital. Puth Chhay's men held large areas to the north, west and south of Phnom Penh and the population lived in constant fear of terrorist attacks.

But it was the journey back to Sâr's village at Prek Sbauv that really brought home to him how much Cambodia had altered while he had been away:

> Before I went away to study, my relatives were . . . mostly middle class farmers. When I returned, I took a bus home. [At the terminus], someone – one of the cyclo-pousses – called out to me: 'Oh, you're back!' I looked, and it was one of my uncles. He asked me: 'Do you want a ride home?' I was so shocked! That man used to have land, buffaloes, everything. I wept to see him like that. I rode home with him, and over the next month or so I talked with [other] relatives who had also lost everything . . . The Cambodian countryside was being pauperized. Having lived in Europe, seeing these things hurt my heart.

To Sâr, the cause was colonialism, the remedy, independence, so that Cambodians could run their own affairs under a system that was socially just. The French might retort that the cause was the war and the insecurity it engendered – villagers were unable to harvest their crops; transport was disrupted; the rubber plantations were being sabotaged; and areas producing pepper, the second most important cash crop, had fallen under Viet Minh control. Defence was taking so much of the budget, one official complained, that 'there is nothing left for anything else'. But young nationalists like Sâr were unimpressed. Without colonialism, they argued, there would be no war and therefore no insecurity. The fundamental contradiction was between the continuing French presence and Cambodians' desire for freedom.

The previous winter, Sâr's elder brother Chhay had been appointed Son Ngoc Thanh's representative for much of northern and eastern Cambodia, including their home province of Kompong Thom and neighbouring Kompong Cham. Chhay had little difficulty convincing Sâr that the former Premier was a force to be reckoned with. It was the Thanhists, not the Viet Minh, who controlled Cambodia's secondary schools, and in the urban areas they boasted a sophisticated intelligence network which usually kept them a step ahead of the police.

Apart from the Khmer Serei and the Viet Minh, the only other serious opposition to French rule came from older-generation Khmer Issarak leaders like Prince Chantarainsey and Puth Chhay. But by the spring of 1953, these men were being approached by the palace or its provincial representatives and invited to lay down their arms and join Sihanouk's 'Royal Crusade'. Most succumbed to the royal blandishments. By May only Chantarainsey remained as an independent force. To the French he was useful because he prevented Viet Minh units entering his territory. The French commander, General de Langlade, described him as 'a true feudal lord', but regarded the thousand or so troops that he led as a rabble of bandits and mercenaries. Sâr, who spent two or three months at Chantarainsey's headquarters at Trapeang Kroloeung, in south-west Kompong Speu, in the first half of 1953, reached a similar conclusion. The Prince's camp, of thatched huts, was situated in a poor, arid region of brush and sparse forest. Sâr's report on his stay has been lost, but another student recruit remembered it as 'not well structured or commanded. The men were organised in battalions, and lived with their wives and children . . . When [eventually] they were amnestied, they organised themselves into gangs and went straight back to being highwaymen again, robbing travellers at night.'

Banditry is usually associated with poverty. In many countries, it gives rise to horrific cruelty. Cambodia was no exception. Thiounn Mumm's uncle, Bunchan Mol, one of the founders of the Issarak movement in the 1940s, recounted in his memoirs:

> If we thought a Cambodian was spying for the French, we tortured him and then [killed] him . . . If the executioner clubbed him to death cleanly with a blow on the back of the neck . . . it was not so hard to look at. But sometimes they used other means . . . They had a method called *sra-nge pen*. First they beat up the suspect. Then they made him kneel beside an open grave, with his hands tied behind his back, and formed a circle around him. The executioner took a sharp sword and started dancing round the man and making horrible grimaces. He gradually got closer and very slowly started cutting the man's throat – sucking the blood as it came out and spewing it onto the blade of the sword. It was terrible to see. The victim shook with pain . . . until finally the killer slashed his throat and pushed him into the grave . . . I was against that way of doing things . . . but the other Issarak leaders didn't agree with me. They said the suspect had to be killed like that as a warning to people not to work for the French.

Others had their bellies ripped open while still alive and their livers torn out to be fried and eaten by their accusers, who believed that in this way they would absorb the dead men's strength.

Chhang Song, later a Cambodian senator, remembered how, in his village in Takeo province, the Issaraks would decapitate their victims and stuff their stomachs with grass. 'When as children we went fishing in the ponds,' he recounted, 'we would find severed heads in the water. It didn't bother us; we were used to it. We'd yank them out by the hair, and throw them aside. That was around 1949 . . . I was 10 or 11 years old.'

Many of those killed as spies were framed for reasons of personal vengeance, as Bunchan Mol acknowledged. But while he claimed to be sickened by the violence and said he often thought of quitting the movement, he did not. Nor did he speak out when men he believed to be innocent were being beaten to death in front of him. One reason was that anyone who protested against such punishments automatically fell under suspicion himself. But Mol's silence – the complicity of an educated man confronted with barbarism – also reflected a state of mind in which the mere fact of being accused was regarded as proof of guilt and it was thought better to err on the side of caution, to kill all who *might* be culpable, than to allow an enemy to go free.

Violence walked hand in hand with sorcery and superstition. Issarak leaders like Puth Chhay and Dap Chhuon carried *kun krak* – the 'smoke-children' or mummified foetuses of which Sâr had heard stories as a child – as amulets against enemy bullets. Among the peasants, they were known as *aggi netr*, 'those whose eyes shoot flame', and were rumoured to have occult powers that enabled them to burn a man simply by looking at him. The reality was more prosaic but no less dreadful. 'What it meant,' one veteran recalled, 'was that whenever they saw something they liked – coconuts, chickens, cattle, young women – the people had to offer it to them, otherwise the village would be burned to the ground.' Issarak fighters tattooed their bodies with Buddhist charms; rubbed earth on their heads to symbolise unity with the earth goddess, *mé*; and offered libations at the shrines of the *neak ta*, the tutelary spirits of the forest.

Bunchan Mol remembered a monk once telling them that if they wore his magic *krama*, the bullets would not hit them. One of the men picked up a rifle and shot the monk dead. 'I tried to explain to them,' Mol wrote, 'that we must try to learn combat techniques and not rely on things like that. But they wouldn't listen.'

If the Issarak violated the rules of war, so did everyone else. Colonial troops raped women, burned down villages and destroyed rice stores. A former Cambodian government soldier described how, in Battambang province, he and his comrades 'would move into villages, kill the men and women who had not already fled and then engage in individual tests of strength which consisted of grasping infants by the legs and then pulling them apart'. The Khmer Viet Minh were not much better. Son Ngoc Minh routinely informed his Vietnamese superiors that an enemy agent had been detained 'but despite the tortures we have inflicted on [him], he refuses to talk'. French officials complained that when government troops moved out of a village they had been protecting, the communists immediately moved in and burned it down in reprisal. In disputed areas, Viet Minh assassination squads were sent to murder local dignitaries and political opponents.

Sâr had been the first emissary of the Cercle to return to Cambodia. Others followed. His former classmate, Ping Sây, who arrived two months later, went to the forest of Krâlanh, in Siem Reap province, to meet Ea Sichau. He proposed that the returned students act as a bridge between Thanh's group and the Khmer Viet Minh. 'We talked,' Sây remembered, 'but we couldn't agree . . . Sichau said we were pro-communist which meant we were under the thumb of the Vietnamese, whereas they were pro-American and therefore more independent. If we were to join up with them, we'd have to submit to their rules.' It was exactly the same problem that had prevented Thanh reaching agreement with the other groups a year before: he favoured unity, but only with himself in charge.

When Sây returned to Phnom Penh, he sought out Sâr, now back in the capital after his stay with Chantarainsey, to give him his impressions. The Khmer Serei seemed 'less serious than the communists', he reported, 'and they aren't properly organised.' Moreover, Thanh relied on Issarak forces which had 'been in the forests for years without doing anything spectacular', whereas at least the Khmer Viet Minh had fought against the French. Sây's findings conflicted with the enthusiastic accounts Sâr had heard from his brother, Chhay, and other Thanhists, but they had the ring of truth. One final attempt was made to reach an understanding when, during the summer, Ea Sichau returned incognito to Phnom Penh and had a meeting with Rath Samoeun, who had also now arrived from Paris and was staying with Keng Vannsak at the Lycée Sisowath. But that, too, came to nothing.

In his report to the Cercle, Sâr dismissed Chantarainsey and his band as simple brigands, whom the French were exploiting as a counterweight to the Viet Minh. Son Ngoc Thanh, he wrote, should be taken more seriously, but while 'his forces claim to be resisting the French colonialists, in fact they do nothing; they just stay in an isolated mountain area [in the Dangreks]'. The most promising resistance group, he concluded, was the Khmer Viet Minh or *Moutakeaha* of Son Ngoc Minh, which, through its alliance with the Vietnamese, enjoyed the support of the world communist movement, making it the only rebel organisation to have 'international' connections.

Back in France, Sâr's report was discussed at length in cell meetings. As Mey Mann remembered it, 'We all agreed that Cambodia had to be free of the Vietnamese, but the question was whether we should try to wrest control [from the Viet Minh] by working from within, or externally. If we'd done it from outside [by joining forces with Son Ngoc Thanh] . . . it would have meant fighting them and sacrificing a lot of Cambodian lives. Working within [the Viet Minh movement], we could do it gradually – fewer people would die. So we decided to support the Viet Minh while at the same time trying, little by little, to free the Khmers [in that movement] from Vietnamese tutelage. That was the decision we took in Paris.'

In Cambodia, the Thanhists and the *Moutakeaha*, despite their refusal to join forces, were in regular communication. Saloth Chhay, as Thanh's representative in the North-East, was able to put Sâr in touch with the Khmer Viet Minh Eastern Zone Headquarters in Prey Veng. In August 1953, saying nothing to friends or family, he and Rath Samoeun slipped away from Phnom Penh, bound for the liberated zone.

While Sâr had been staying with Sihanouk's wayward cousin, Chantarainsey, the King himself had flown to France, ostensibly for a rest-cure but in fact to launch his 'Crusade' for Cambodian independence. The French were at first nonplussed, then frankly disbelieving. General de Langlade, their commander in Phnom Penh, on being informed of Sihanouk's demand for complete control of military affairs and an end to extra-territorial privileges for foreigners – who were tried by French, not Cambodian, judges – cabled his superiors that the King's arguments showed 'childish bad faith' and reflected 'a court atmosphere of clans and intrigue worthy of the Middle Ages'. He quoted Prince Monireth, the King's censorious, strait-laced uncle, as having confided to him privately some weeks earlier:

> The terrible thing about my nephew is that when he sleeps, he dreams. He takes these dreams as an inspiration from the Buddha, he gets up in a state of excitement, seizes some paper and starts to write . . . What is even more terrible is that he has a lively pen and a certain literary talent, and, like all *illuminati*, he is imbued with the reality of his dreams . . . And most terrible of all, perhaps, is that when he presents his dreams to you Frenchmen, you are so moved by them . . . that you try to turn them into reality.

That is certainly how the French liked to think of Sihanouk – as a petulant child, to be humoured and then sent off with a hug. When he presented his demands to Vincent Auriol, the elderly French President gave him lunch at the Elysée Palace but made clear that talks on his proposals would be 'inopportune'.

However Sihanouk's sense of theatre, the target of Monireth's jibe, was only one aspect of his volatile personality, as the French would learn to their cost. Once he had determined his course, he was a relentless adversary whose very unpredictability made him all the harder to deal with. Over the next eight months, he played a weak hand with a skill that his great-grandfather, Norodom, would have admired. He, too, in the nineteenth century, had kept his court and his French minders off-balance by mercurial shifts and erratic, arbitrary conduct. It was a character trait that was in Sihanouk's genes and he would use it more and more as his power and confidence increased.

After leaving France in disgust, the King flew home by way of the United States, where his encounters with John Foster Dulles did nothing to improve his mood.

The US Secretary of State had no time for a tinpot monarch who could not seem to understand that the only game in town was the war against communism and that colonialism was a side issue. 'Your difference with France is simply playing into the hands of our common enemy,' Dulles told him. 'Without the French army [to help you], your country would very soon be conquered by the Reds and your independence would be gone.' President Eisenhower apparently felt the same way, for he failed to invite Sihanouk to the customary White House banquet. To add insult to injury, the hapless desk officer in charge of his stay suggested that the King might like to visit a circus – which he took as reflecting the State Department's view of his intellectual level.

Even such gaffes aside, it was a dialogue of the deaf. To Sihanouk, only a genuinely independent Cambodia would be motivated to resist communism. To Dulles, only after communism had been defeated could Cambodia safely become independent. 'Each of us,' Sihanouk wrote later, 'felt the other was trying to put the cart before the horse.'

The visit did have one positive outcome. In an interview with the *New York Times*, Sihanouk warned that if independence were withheld his people might lose patience, overthrow the monarchy and join forces with the Viet Minh, which concentrated minds in Paris sufficiently for the government there to begin talks on speeding up the transfer of powers. But that was the only glimmer of light. Overall the visit was deeply unhelpful to Cambodia's future relationship with the US. Sihanouk's suspicions of American motives, already aroused by maladroit gestures of sympathy for the Democrats and Son Ngoc Thanh, were redoubled. He was appalled by America's brashness and hubris, so different from the old-world duplicity and elegance of his own country and of France. Dulles's Cold War sermonising, which followed him in instalments telegraphically as he travelled back across the Pacific, he found exasperating. The US, he concluded, was a power to be reckoned with, but its values and goals were inimical to Cambodia's desire for freedom on its own terms.

The talks with the French soon bogged down over Sihanouk's insistence on a complete transfer of military powers – including those in the eastern border areas, where Viet Minh penetration was strongest – and the decoupling of Cambodia's economy from that of South Vietnam. For some weeks, there were inconclusive exchanges between the palace and the French High Commission. Then the King's patience ran out.

On June 6, he left Phnom Penh, in order symbolically to distance himself from the colonial authorities, and travelled to Siem Reap, ostensibly to inspect what was known as the 'Khmer Operational Sector', an area where the French had ceded military control to the recently formed Royal Cambodian Armed Forces. Their commander, the Issarak defector Dap Chhuon, who now rejoiced in the grandiloquent name Chhuon Mochulpich ('Diamond-Needle Chhuon'), loathed the colonial authorities and was detested by them in return – De Langlade called him 'a crazed Machiavelli of the forests', 'a dangerously mystic counsellor' – but he had the ear of Sihanouk's mother, Princess Kossamak. In Siem Reap, the King received the surrender of two minor Issarak warlords from the North-West. Then, without informing even his courtiers (and still less the bemused Thais), he crossed the frontier with his personal suite, heading for Bangkok.

The French suspected that Sihanouk had gone for secret talks with the Viet Minh and the Khmer Serei. In fact his aim was merely to sow a little confusion. It was the Norodom syndrome again. 'In this country,' wrote one despairing French official, 'the moment you try to think logically, events will immediately contradict you.' De Langlade thought Sihanouk had been 'overcome by his own rhetoric'. His civilian counterpart in British-ruled Singapore, Malcolm MacDonald, wondered about the monarch's sanity.

How wide of the mark they both were was shown by a secret memorandum which the King drafted in Thailand for the American and British Legations:

> I am asking the U.S.A and Great Britain if, just for once, they will kindly consider the problem of Cambodia from the viewpoint of the Khmers instead of that of the French . . . My people will tell you: 'We don't know what communist slavery means. But the slavery imposed by the French we know well, for we are now living under it. If we fight alongside the French against the Viet Minh and the Issaraks, we are simply strengthening the

chains of that slavery . . .' [The problem is that] in Indochina, you are either a communist or a lackey of the French: there is no middle course. We are not allowed to hope for an independence like that of India or Pakistan within the British Commonwealth . . . The question is: Does French military power on its own have any chance of defeating communism in Indochina? *To fight without having the autochthonous population on one's side makes no sense* . . . What is at stake in this struggle, and what will determine its outcome, is the [native] population. The Viet Minh have understood that from the start. If we [who oppose communism] wish to have the population with us, we must . . . make [our country's] independence . . . real and unquestionable, so that [no one] will listen any more to the Viet Minh propaganda about 'liberation'. . . . This is the whole problem. *It is a political matter.* It has nothing to do with the science of war . . . If France does not boldly face up to [this] . . . then one day, sooner or later, it will be forced to abdicate from Indochina.

At a time when national passions were boiling up uncontrollably, it was a remarkably lucid and sober analysis.

Had the United States been willing to understand the message Sihanouk was trying to convey – had it been able, in his words, 'to consider the problem from the viewpoint of the Khmers' – twenty-five years of war in South-East Asia might have been avoided. But Great Powers are by definition blind to the concerns of lesser peoples. Decades later, after America had been forced to leave mainland Asia, the lesson was still imperfectly learnt and just as quickly forgotten.

The French understood better, not because they were cleverer but because they were a minor power and circumstances left them little choice.

Even before the King's sortie to Bangkok, Risterucci had noticed that the tone of his speeches had changed: he had started haranguing his audiences in terms that, from anyone else, would have been considered seditious. After his return, his appeals to revolt became more explicit. He would not set foot in Phnom Penh or have any further contact with French officials, he said, until France had conceded independence, adding menacingly that 'if we cannot obtain what we want peacefully, the entire Khmer people are resolved to obtain their freedom by other means and are ready to sacrifice their lives'. On June 26, the two main Buddhist orders called for a holy war. Next day, with Sihanouk's encouragement, large-scale desertions began from Khmer units of the French Army. When De Langlade summoned reinforcements from Saigon, the Prime Minister, Penn Nouth, accused France of putting itself 'on a war footing against our country'. Finally, on Sunday June 28, the King called for nationwide mobilisation of all citizens between twenty and thirty-five years old – the *chivapol*, or 'live forces', as he called them — to join the struggle for Cambodian independence.

In Phnom Penh, an 'Assassination Committee' was formed, headed by Puth Chhay's deputy, Seap, to throw grenades into crowded dance-halls and cinemas. Over the next few weeks, twenty-four French soldiers and civilians were killed or seriously injured in such attacks. A French intelligence report noted laconically: 'These incidents have been, if not provoked, at least tolerated by the Khmer authorities, in order to put pressure on us to speed up the re-opening of [independence] negotiations.' But even without terrorism, the situation was moving inexorably in the Cambodians' favour. On July 3, after a new French government had been sworn in, headed by Joseph Laniel, a Social Democrat, De Langlade told Paris bluntly that there was no choice but to accept Sihanouk's demands:

> Let us be logical. If the King calls on the country to rise up, he can count on 7,000 rifles . . . We can rely only on French troops . . . The balance of strength is against us. We cannot carry out a strong-arm policy, because we do not have the means. The King has gone too far to be able to draw back. He will see it through to the end . . . What then can we do? If we pull out, the country will fall into anarchy . . . and the Viet Minh will occupy the whole area East of the Mekong . . . If we fight, we will have to bring in at least 15 more battalions and open up an entire new front, which is something no one wants. If on the other hand, we grant Cambodia complete independence, the government, which knows that our aid is indispensable, will give us all the guarantees we could wish for . . . We need to take into account the pride, the sensitivity and the stubbornness of the Khmer. Confronting him head-on is pointless. But if we yield at the point where his vanity is at stake, we may hope to bind the country to us once more for many years to come.

He stopped short of saying that Sihanouk had been right all along, but his colleague, Risterucci, the civilian commissioner, told a fellow diplomat the same week that 'History is on Cambodia's side'. Similar arguments applied, De Langlade suggested, to Laos and Vietnam.

His advice fell on receptive ears. The Laniel government — like the Nixon administration twenty years later — was bent on finding a way to extract France from an unwinnable and increasingly unpopular war. It announced that it would take steps to 'complete the independence' of the Indochinese states, triggering three months of frantic negotiations as each side manoeuvred to get the best deal it could. All the non-communist Issarak groups, except those of Chantarainsey, Savangs Vong and the Khmer Serei, pledged their support to Sihanouk's cause. More than 150,000 young men and women came forward in response to his mobilisation appeal. The French agonised about the desertion rate from the army

– six hundred officers and men had voted with their feet despite warnings that they risked the firing squad – and about the possibility of Sihanouk striking a deal with the Viet Minh, which would make a negotiated independence agreement impossible. But that did not happen. On October 17, Paris announced the transfer of full military powers to the Cambodian government. Three weeks later, on Monday November 9, Sihanouk took the salute at a march-past of French and Khmer troops in Phnom Penh, joined by 35,000 civilian volunteers. The ceremony ended with his acceptance of the instruments of command, signifying that almost a century of French tutelage was at an end.

It was not quite the 'delirious triumph' that royal propagandists claimed. General de Langlade noted pensively that the crowds acclaiming the King's return were 'smaller and much less enthusiastic' than those which had welcomed Son Ngoc Thanh two years before. Nor was independence yet complete: the disentangling of Cambodia's economy from the institutions of the former French Indochina would drag on for another year. None the less, November 9 1953 was consecrated Independence Day and Sihanouk basked in the glory of it. He had staked his throne on the battle with France and he had won. At thirty-one, he had proved himself a worthy successor to the long line of Khmer kings who, over the centuries, had made the preservation of an independent monarchy, indistinguishable from Cambodia itself, their overriding goal.

When Sâr and Rath Samoeun reached the Viet Minh Eastern Zone Headquarters in August, this fortunate outcome was not yet assured.

There is no record of their journey. Those who set out later were told to go to Prey Chhor district, on the main road from Phnom Penh to Kompong Cham, where they would be met by Viet Minh guides. Mey Mann travelled that way with half a dozen others the following spring, escorted by a Vietnamese who made them march for two weeks through the forest until they reached the outskirts of Stung Trâng, where they were to cross the Mekong. The first attempt, he remembered, ended in disaster. Their sampan capsized and sank, and Mann's prize possession, a new watch he had brought back from Paris, was ruined. At the second try they crossed successfully and then walked for a further ten days through rubber plantations and jungle before reaching the village of Krâbao, at the frontier of Kompong Cham and Prey Veng, about three miles from the South Vietnamese border.

The camp itself was rudimentary. It had been identified by French intelligence two years earlier as the site of the Eastern Zone HQ, and the area was subjected to periodic artillery bombardment and air raids using incendiary bombs. There were no permanent buildings, just canvas shelters in the forest which could be moved at a moment's notice. On arrival each recruit was given a black shirt and trousers, dyed with the juice of *makloeu* berries, a red-and-white checked *krama* and the inevitable car-tyre sandals, with laces cut from inner tubes. 'Everyone wore black,' Mann wrote later, 'even the Vietnamese. That way you melted into the mass of the peasants, and it didn't show the dirt.'

Over the next nine months, a dozen or so members of the Cercle made their way to Krâbao,* along with some secondary-school students from inside the country. The Vietnamese kept them together to make it easier to verify their *bona fides*. Sâr and his colleagues presented themselves as members of the French Communist Party who had come to join the struggle. But if they expected a heroes' welcome, they were sorely disappointed. Sâr remembered:

> As I had just come back from abroad . . . they didn't trust me. [Almost everyone] was Vietnamese – there were just a handful of Cambodians – and everyone spoke Vietnamese. They sent me to stay among this handful of Cambodians. They didn't give me any kind of work to do. All I was allowed to do was cultivate cassava. After a while, they let me work . . . in the canteen. I was the deputy mess officer. The mess officer himself was Vietnamese. [At Krâbao] even the messengers were Vietnamese. The Cambodians were there in name only.

All of them found that hard to stomach. Yun Soeun, who had spent his years in Paris studying eighteenth-century European literature, complained: 'The Vietnamese took all the decisions. We Khmers were just puppets.' Chi Kim An blamed Mey Mann for having persuaded him to come. The Viet Minh, he fumed, were 'just bastards'. Even Mann himself was fed up. 'They left us for months without giving us proper jobs,' he grumbled later. 'We spent our days watering the vegetables, feeding the chickens, things like that. It was because they didn't know who we were . . . they wanted us to prove ourselves.'

The Vietnamese themselves acknowledged as much. 'We were verifying [what they said],' one official explained. 'That's why we let them study . . . but we did not give them any important tasks.' Only after Pham Van Ba, Nguyen Thanh Son's representative at PRPK headquarters, had received confirmation of their claims from the PCF in Paris, via Bangkok and Hanoi, were their communist credentials finally accepted.

* They included Chi Kim An, Hâng Norin, Mey Mann, Mey Phat, Rath Samoeun, Saloth Sâr, Sanh Oeurn, Sien An, Sok Knaol and Yun Soeun. Out of the entire group, twenty-five years later, only Mey Mann and Saloth Sâr were still alive.

At the upper levels of the PRPK, the Vietnamese were equally heavy-handed. Two years earlier, Hanoi had decided – without consulting the Khmer leadership – that the division of Cambodia into four zones should be scrapped and a new system created, in which territory east of the Mekong would be treated as a single Eastern Zone while a new Western Zone would encompass all the rest. This was logical enough: the war in southern Vietnam increasingly depended on arms supplies coming down from the north – by sea from China, via Hainan, and overland through Laos and north-eastern Cambodia, along the network of jungle tracks which would become known as the Ho Chi Minh Trail – so it made sense to tighten control over what was now a vital area. But it caused turmoil in the PRPK. The South-Eastern Zone Secretary, Keo Moni, suddenly found himself subordinate to his former deputy, Tou Samouth, now promoted Eastern Zone Secretary. Son Ngoc Minh, whose power base was in the West, remained Khmerland's 'President' and Party leader, but lost influence as Hanoi's altered priorities gave pride of place to the East. Even Tou Samouth, the beneficiary of these changes, was outraged by Viet Minh high-handedness and the constant use of Cambodians to carry out menial tasks.

Samouth chaired the political training seminars held for the Khmer recruits. But, as one of them noted, 'He *only* presided. It was always the Vietnamese who spoke.' Political study meant learning Vietnamese Party texts, translated into Khmer and explained by Khmer-speaking Vietnamese instructors, led by Pham Van Ba. The study sessions began with a breviary entitled the 'Six Rules of Party Life':

1. Struggle all one's life for communism.
2. Put the interests of the Revolution before everything else.
3. Uphold Party discipline and observe the utmost secrecy about all Party matters.
4. Carry out the Party's decisions with an unshakeable will; never let oneself be downcast no matter how great the obstacle.
5. Be a model for the popular masses.
6. Study!

After the weighty, theoretical volumes they had grappled with in Paris, this seemed simple stuff. Yet between the lines of the 'Six Rules', there were tell-tale clues that Vietnamese-style communism, with its liberal admixture of Confucian ideas, was a very different beast – at least in the form in which it was taught to the Party rank and file – from the system of thought, based on European values, put forward by Marx and Lenin. The Vietnamese 'Rules' stressed the importance of 'struggling for an ideal'; having 'absolute faith'; and maintaining 'a proper conception of life' – none of which had much to do with anything Marx ever wrote. Above all, they emphasised the need for total secrecy:

> The constant growth of . . . the Party's revolutionary potential . . . has led enemy spies, traitors and reactionaries to step up their sabotage activities. This is why the Party must in no way relax its vigilance . . . but, in carrying out its operations, should attach the greatest importance to the preservation of secrecy . . . [To do otherwise] presents a danger of exceptional serious-ness . . . The Party member . . . must observe absolute discretion. . .

At the higher levels of the Vietnamese Party, this distinctive Asian gloss was partly offset by the study of translations from Marx, Lenin and Stalin, which reaffirmed the fundamentals of orthodox communist thinking: materialism, dialectics and historical determinism. In Cambodia, no such translations existed. Members of the PRPK – apart from the handful, like Sâr, who had gone to Paris and tried, with imperfect French, to read the original texts – acquired what little they knew of Marxism via its Vietnamese variant, which they then reinterpreted in cultural terms that were in many ways fundamentally at odds with Marx's materialist view of the world. Even the Vietnamese acknowledged that this often led to 'real difficulty in assimilating the scientific arguments of Marxism-Leninism'.

Despite their subaltern status, none of the young Khmer students – not even the restive Chi Kim An – was seriously shaken from his decision to espouse the communist cause. Sâr himself wrote later: '[Although] I saw that the Cambodian movement was completely controlled by [them] . . . it did not shape my thinking to be anti-Vietnamese . . . I thought we should have a good relationship with Vietnam. I just wanted to make our move-ment independent.'

Moreover, even if the PRPK was not a full-fledged communist party, to Sâr and the other students from Paris much about it was very familiar.

As in the Cercle, the basic unit was the three-man cell, bound by 'iron discipline, freely consented', and 'criticism and self-criticism to maintain unity of belief and action'. Like the French Communist Party, it had a strong anti-intellectual bias. Peasants and workers who had been in the resistance for three months could become Party members after one month's probation; intellectuals were required to spend six months in the resistance followed by three months' probation.

But what set the Cambodian movement totally apart from anything they had experienced before was the context in which it operated. It was one thing to discuss revolution in a comfortable hotel room in the Latin

Quarter, quite another to study the tactics of armed struggle in a clearing in the jungle.

The Vietnamese communists were practical men – the French were constantly surprised by the precision planning of Viet Minh sabotage attacks – and Pham Van Ba and his colleagues regarded it as their first task to teach the young Khmers the nuts and bolts of making revolution among a population of illiterate peasants. Ba remembered instructing Sâr how to 'work with the masses at the base, to build up . . . village committees, one member at a time'. The Vietnamese had a system of 'armed propaganda teams' whose job was to infiltrate Cambodian hamlets and then patiently win over 'progressive elements' until a solid core-group existed, at which point the village would be occupied by force, the old leadership evicted or killed (to serve as a warning to others) and a new revolutionary administration installed in its place.

The mixture of indoctrination and terror was fundamental. 'Making propaganda means mobilising the population to hate the enemy', a Viet Minh broadcast explained. 'Once people have the right feelings in their hearts . . . they will act accordingly.' Winning the support of the masses was the key to everything else. 'Otherwise,' a French officer wrote, 'the Viet Minh could have not existed. They have succeeded because they have been able to channel the confused aspirations of the people, to fire their enthusiasm and to bring them hope.' If the population refused to co-operate, a scorched earth policy was enforced: the village was razed and the inhabitants scattered.

Sâr never forgot those lessons.

He did not see them carried out in practice because the students were not allowed to go out on operations. But after a while the Viet Minh cadres let him visit nearby villages to help out with the farm work, which opened his eyes to the poverty of the border region and enabled him to see for the first time how the peasants adapted to life under a revolutionary regime. Later he made friends with two officers from the Po Kombo Regiment, a nominally Khmer unit of about three hundred men based ten miles to the north-west. The commander, Phay, a former rifleman in the French colonial army, and his political commissar, Chan Samân, were both Khmer, but Sâr noted with disgust that more than 80 per cent of the other ranks were from Vietnam..

It was during this time that he met a young man of his own age who had joined the maquis four years earlier. Keo Meas had hated the French ever since reading *Nagaravatta* as a precocious fifteen-year-old. He dropped out of a teacher training course to join a Khmer Viet Minh group in Svay Rieng province and, in March 1950, was among the twenty-one Khmer members of the ICP who approved the guidelines for the future Cambodian Party during the meeting at Hatien. The following year he was appointed Commissar of the Action Committee for Phnom Penh, and in 1952 travelled to Beijing, where he became the first Khmer to meet Chairman Mao and the Red Army commander, Zhu De, before going on to attend the World Peace Conference in Vienna.

Keo Meas was keenly aware of his high status. He lived with Tou Samouth and the rest of the leadership in a different part of the forest, which was out of bounds to the students. Sâr learnt a lot from him, especially in the later months at the camp, when Meas was put in charge of the new 'Voice of Free Cambodia' radio station and Sâr helped to write the commentaries. How well they liked each other is another matter. Keo Meas already thought of himself as the future leader of the Cambodian Communist Party and Sâr would have been less than human had he not discerned a potential rival. But whatever he may have felt, he showed nothing. Years later, when Meas searched desperately in his memory for clues to the cause of their subsequent estrangement, the idea that it might have stemmed from their months in the maquis together never entered his head.

As proof of his commitment to the cause, Sâr started to learn Vietnamese and eventually, by his own account, could speak and understand it after a fashion. That was more than most of the others could do and it brought him to the notice of Tou Samouth. The Eastern Zone Secretary was a traditionalist – one Vietnamese official likened him to 'an old monk, sweet and good-natured' – and Sâr's Buddhist upbringing and calm, unruffled manner won his confidence. At Samouth's request, Sâr began to act as his assistant, helping him to prepare political seminars. Imperceptibly, he established himself as the older man's secretary and principal aide, a position he would hold for the next five years.

Sihanouk's 'Royal Crusade' had forced the Viet Minh to change tactics. No longer could they claim that the King's heart was with the people but he was a captive of the French. From the summer of 1953, they were caught up in a triangular struggle: the King tried to win over the insurgents; the French tried to deter him from making common cause with the Viet Minh; and the Viet Minh tried to prevent the Khmer rebels from making common cause with the King. For a time, Vietnamese propagandists attempted to fudge the issue, arguing that Sihanouk had been duped. But that was too subtle to be convincing and Hanoi and Beijing soon adopted a harder line. 'This traitorous king has become a lackey of world imperialism,' thundered the Vietnamese Workers' Party daily, *Nhan Dan*. The French were offering 'fake independence' because they wanted to send Cambodians to fight for them in Laos and Vietnam. 'Puppet King Sihanouk is not concerned about the independence of his country or the interests of the Khmer people. He simply wants [American aid] . . .' True independence would be achieved 'only by fighting to the last and . . . eliminating the puppet regime'.

In the villages, it was put in simpler terms, Sieu Heng's deputy, Ruos Nhim, the Khmer Viet Minh military commander in the North-West, told one group of peasants: 'Why doesn't the King ask us to help him [in the struggle for independence]? . . . It is because he is mobilising the Cambodian people to help the French. You will all be sent far from your homes to die. From now on, I forbid you to leave your villages to respond to the King's appeal.'

After the transfer of power from the colonial authorities to Sihanouk in November 1953, the conflict intensified, as the King, backed by the French, on one side, and the Viet Minh and their Khmer allies on the other, manoeuvred for advantage ahead of the Indochina Peace Talks which everyone now realised were only a matter of time.

The Cambodian Army, which had retreated into inactivity throughout Sihanouk's 'Crusade', launched a series of attacks on rebel bases in the southern provinces of Kompong Speu, Svay Rieng and Kampot, followed in December by an operation in Battambang led by the King himself. It was pure public relations: the French ensured that any rebels were kept miles away from the royal person. But it made for lavish photo-spreads in government publications, showing the King marching intrepidly through areas 'infested with booby-traps and mines', braving the Viet Minh's 'craving to kill' in order to free his subjects from 'the whip and lash of communist slavery'. More substantively, in February 1954, the Issarak leaders Chantarainsey and Savangs Vong formally pledged allegiance to the Throne. That left Son Ngoc Thanh as the only non-communist hold-out.

The Viet Minh response was not long in coming.

For the past nine months, Hanoi's master-strategist, Vo Nguyen Giap, had been toying with the idea of a massive assault against eastern Cambodia, comparable to the invasion of Upper Laos in March 1953, when Vietnamese regular divisions had occupied two provinces which became the Pathet Lao 'liberated zone'. That autumn, a mixed force of more than 11,000 Vietnamese, Khmer and Lao troops was assembled (at least, on paper), and by the beginning of 1954 French military intelligence reported that Giap had the material reserves to launch a co-ordinated strike against all of Cambodia east of the Mekong.

In the event, the attack never came. There were logistical problems, and by January, Giap's attention, and that of his Chinese advisers, was directed elsewhere: to the remote mountain base of Dien Bien Phu, two hundred miles west of Hanoi on Vietnam's border with Laos, where the trap was being set which, a few months later, would bring the war with the French to an inconclusive close. Instead of a general offensive, the Vietnamese High Command ordered diversionary actions, first in Lower Laos in January and February and then in north-east Cambodia in March 1954, to distract attention from the Vietnamese battlefield where the end-game was to be played out.

Even that was more than Sihanouk's forces could cope with. For weeks French intelligence had been reporting 'a very serious crisis of morale' in the Cambodian Army. Now it started falling apart. The district centre of Voeunsai was occupied by Viet Minh forces on April 2. Siempang and Bokeo were surrounded a few days later. Sihanouk, showing more courage than his cabinet, which resolved to take no action, set up a temporary headquarters in Kratie to direct the counter-attack. But, as one military observer noted drily, 'the King's army does not seem to follow'. Meanwhile another body-blow was in the making. A Viet Minh column of five hundred men, accompanied by ten elephants carrying heavy equipment and forty ox-carts, had marched across the Cardamom Mountains from the west, terrorising the population into secrecy. At dawn on April 12, the eve of the Khmer New Year, they laid mines along the main railway line to Battambang about fifty miles north-west of Phnom Penh. According to the official report:

> The engine was derailed and 40 carriages overturned. Immediately, [the] Vietminh, armed with sickles, rifles, grenades and automatic weapons poured out of the woods nearby and threw themselves on the defenceless passengers. A regular massacre followed . . . The injured were . . . doused with petrol and burned alive . . . Those who tried to escape were caught and killed slowly with knives . . . In this way, more than a hundred people perished, including 30 monks.

The report claimed, untruthfully, that the train had no military escort. In fact, the forty-five men assigned to guard duty had left their posts and were in the restaurant car or with other passengers, drinking. Another fifty soldiers, with full equipment, were also on board, travelling to Pursat, in the west. They, too, made no attempt to resist. By May the situation had deteriorated further. The government garrison at Pailin, on the Thai border, was under siege, and there were fresh incursions in the South-East as well as in the North. The weekly military intelligence summary warned:

> The regular [Cambodian] forces are disintegrating so fast that any general attack by the V.M. could have the most serious consequences . . . Whole

units have mutinied, refusing to take part in operations. The brief incursion of V.M. Battalion 302 towards Prey Veng triggered scenes of indescribable panic. If this unit launches a concerted action with another V.M. battalion against the main highway to Phnom Penh, it will have every chance of succeeding because [the government] will probably be unable to find any viable force to send there.

The French were puzzled that the Viet Minh did not pursue their advantage. Had they underestimated their own superiority? Were they short of supplies? Or did North Vietnam – or, more likely, its Chinese and Soviet backers – judge that a dramatic extension of the conflict in Cambodia might torpedo the peace talks in Geneva, which had opened on April 28?

Whatever the reason, Hanoi's failure to carve out a communist-administered region to serve as a base for Khmerland on the model of the Pathet Lao dealt the Cambodian communists a fatal blow. Keo Moni and Mey Pho, who travelled to Switzerland to represent the Khmer resistance, could argue as much as they wished that Cambodia was an integral part of the Indochinese battlefield; that stable resistance bases existed in thirty-six out of Cambodia's ninety-eight districts; that Son Ngoc Minh's government had 800,000 people and 40 per cent of the country's territory (more or less) under its control; and that therefore Khmerland should enjoy the same rights as the Pathet Lao and North Vietnam. The fact that they held no clearly defined 'liberated zone' meant that their claims, and their presence, were ignored.

On May 3, the demand of the Khmer 'ghost government', as the Americans called it, to be seated at the head of a separate Khmerland delegation was rejected. Over the next few weeks, Sihanouk's representatives won back at the conference table everything his army's incompetence had lost on the ground. The North Vietnamese Vice-Premier, Pham Van Dong, with support from the Soviet Union, which was far enough away from Indochina to be able to hang tough, but not from Zhou Enlai – who was acutely aware, after China's experience in Korea, of the risk of being dragged into yet another war if the conference should fail – forcefully pressed the Khmer communists' case for two regroupment zones, east and south-west of the Mekong, like those at Sam Neua and Phong Saly in Laos. But Sihanouk refused to budge. In the end, the Khmer resistance was sacrificed to the greater good of communism in Vietnam and Laos. Unlike those two countries, which were divided into communist and non-communist areas, Cambodia emerged from Geneva with its political and territorial integrity intact. Sihanouk's sole concession was to agree that in Cambodia, as in government-controlled areas of Laos and in southern Vietnam, insurgents who did not wish to surrender could accompany the Viet Minh forces being repatriated to North Vietnam.

The ceasefire took effect at dawn on August 7. After technical discussions in New Delhi, the International Control Commission, composed of Canadians, Indians and Poles, began work on the 12th in Svay Rieng. Lon Nol led the government side, Nguyen Thanh Son the joint Viet Minh/Khmer resistance delegation. Almost at once the talks hit procedural problems, which dragged on into September. The deadline for the reintegration of the Khmer rebels came and went. France thought Thanh Son's men were dragging their feet 'to gain time to set up a clandestine propaganda network ahead of the forthcoming elections'.

In fact the explanation was simpler. Time was needed to hide weapons against the day when the struggle would resume. At the Eastern Zone HQ at Krâbao, Mey Mann remembered spending most of August greasing rifles and other weapons with beef fat before putting them in waterproof wrappers for the Vietnamese to bury in the forest.

Time was needed, too, for the Khmer leaders to decide who was to be sent to Vietnam and who would stay behind. In the East, Tou Samouth and one of his district chiefs, Tuk Nhung, made the final selection. Rath Samoeun, Yun Soeun and several other students were among those who left, walking overland to Chau Doc, on the Vietnamese border, where they boarded sampans for the 200-mile river journey across the Mekong delta to Cape Camau. There a Polish cargo ship, the *Jan Kilinski*, was waiting to take them north.

Conditions were grim. On each voyage, 3,000–4,000 troops, most of them Vietnamese, were crammed into the holds with no medical treatment for the wounded, along with arms and munitions and, on one journey, a dozen elephants used by the Viet Minh transport corps.

Altogether 1,900 Khmer men and thirty-six women made that journey. They landed at a fishing port a hundred miles south of Hanoi, and from there were taken in lorries to a camp newly built for them in the high plateaux near the Laotian border, where Son Ngoc Minh, in his speech of welcome, warned them against the rigours of the North Vietnamese winter. They could expect to spend two years in Vietnam, he told them, studying the land reform and undergoing political training.

The last Khmer Viet Minh units left Cambodia on October 18 1954. Sâr, Mey Mann and Chan Samân, the commissar of the now defunct Po Kombo Regiment, were not among them. After leaving the camp at Krâbao, they walked southward by a roundabout route across Svay Rieng as if making for Chau Doc, then crossed into southern Vietnam and headed west for several days before traversing the Cambodian border again and entering Kompong Trabek district in Prey Veng. The journey took a month. Mey Mann remembered that they made frequent stops to disguise their eventual destination. Nguyen Thanh Son's special representative, Pham Van Ba, and his wife travelled with them. After waiting another week in Kompong Trabek, they separated. Sâr took a bus to Phnom Penh, followed, a few days later, by the two Vietnamese. Mann and Samân set out last.

During the political training classes at Krâbao, Pham Van Ba used to tell his Khmer listeners that Cambodia, Laos and Vietnam were 'like lips, teeth and tongue; each needs the other two'. Now, he said, the Cambodians' role had changed. They had to make the transition 'from armed struggle to political struggle'. The three young Khmers discussed this among themselves during the journey. As a proposition, it seemed logical enough. But none of them had any clear idea of what it might involve.

4

Cambodian Realities

A S THE YEAR 1954 drew to a close, Sihanouk found himself confronted with the perils of his own success. The Viet Minh had gone. The French protectorate was finished. Now that he had the plenitude of power, there were no excuses left.

Already, a year earlier, half-jubilant, half apprehensive, he had told the French commander, General de Langlade: 'Getting independence all at once makes it so indigestible I may choke. It was never my intention to go this fast.' His cousin, the Defence Minister, Sirik Matak, predicted gloomily that the withdrawal of the French army would lead 'to the overturning of the Throne and power passing into the hands of Son Ngoc Thanh, which will mean the end of Cambodia.'

In the event, French troops stayed on until after the Geneva talks, which gave the government a breathing space. But under the terms of the peace agreement, elections had to be held in 1955. Most observers, Cambodian and foreign, predicted a Democratic Party landslide. That would open the way for Thanh's return to office and, eventually perhaps, the proclamation of a republic, which the Americans – ever ready to cock a snook at the French – regarded as greatly preferable to the corrupt and decadent Cambodian monarchy and its unreliable King.

Son Ngoc Thanh came down from his mountain lair in the Dangreks, with an escort of two hundred armed men, to pledge allegiance to the government at a ceremony at Siem Reap on September 30. Sihanouk refused to see him. 'Son Ngoc Thanh is not a communist,' Penn Nouth told a French reporter; 'however he is certainly a republican, and that makes him a danger to the regime.' But ostracising the former rebel leader did not make the problem disappear. The Indian Prime Minister, Pandit Nehru, who met Thanh during a visit in October, came away convinced that he would play a key role in Cambodia's future. Washington instructed its Ambassador in Phnom Penh to re-establish contact with him. French intelligence was convinced that Britain was giving Thanh's forces covert aid through its mission in Bangkok. By Sihanouk's own estimate, half the Democratic Party was firmly committed to Thanh's cause, and theirs was

the only party in the country capable of organising a credible election campaign. The King was worried, and showed it; but the only remedy he could
think of was to put off for as long as possible the day when Cambodians
would be called on to vote.

This was the political situation to which Sâr and the others returned.

Viet Minh rules for organisational work in 'enemy-occupied areas',
which the Cambodians tried to apply, laid down: 'Legal, semi-legal and
secret forms of action must be carefully distinguished . . . Groups that work
openly must maintain close links with secret organisations, which should
on no account be dissolved . . . For Party work, secrecy is fundamental . . .'
The overriding priority was to limit to the maximum the consequences of
betrayal or infiltration of Party organisations.

Keo Meas, by virtue of his membership of the old Phnom Penh Action
Committee, was designated acting head of the city's clandestine Party
branch. On Tou Samouth's instructions, Sâr was chosen to handle 'legal'
action, which meant infiltrating the Democratic Party and trying to influence its policies. Meas himself took charge of 'semi-legal' operations and
set up a communist front organisation to serve as the public face of the
Khmer Viet Minh during the coming elections. He wanted to call it Khmer
Toosu (Khmer Resistance). But Sihanouk refused, regarding that name as a
slight on his own 'Royal Crusade'. After an appeal to the International
Control Commission, registration was accorded, but under the more neutral ensign [Krom] Pracheachon (the 'People's Group'). Its statutes contained no reference to communism because under the Cambodian
constitution all political parties had to support the monarchical system.

Keo Meas's group was not alone in viewing the election campaign as an
opportunity to win a place in mainstream Cambodian politics. Sâr's old
mentor, Keng Vannsak, now a teacher at the Lycée Sisowath, had joined the
Democratic Party that autumn. His philippic against Sihanouk two years earlier had been followed by a book of poems, *Virgin Heart*, which used Buddhist
metaphors for coded attacks against the monarchy (portrayed as an enormous
stomach, feeding on its own excrement). To the party elders, Vannsak was a
dangerous if beguiling young firebrand, whose barely concealed republican-
ism and sympathies for Son Ngoc Thanh made him a potential vote-winner.
In September, Thiounn Mumm, the other intellectual force behind the
Cercle Marxiste, had also arrived from Paris. Together he and Vannsak set
about remaking the Democratic Party from within. Four months later, on
January 30 1955, at a rowdy meeting held in one of the city's cinemas, the
old guard was pushed aside. A left-wing prince, Norodom Phurissara, was
elected Secretary-General. Vannsak became his deputy. Ea Sichau and Hang
Thun Hak represented the Thanhists, Thiounn Mumm the Left.

Sâr had gone to see Vannsak shortly after returning from the maquis. 'I asked him what he'd been doing,' Vannsak recalled. 'He laughed a bit shamefacedly and said he'd been stuck with Chantarainsey all the time. He'd never managed to get to the Viet Minh zone!' Sâr's story was sufficiently convincing that, years later, Vannsak continued to insist that reports of his presence among the Viet Minh were mistaken; people were confusing him with someone else. That part of Sâr's life was secret to all except his Party colleagues.

He played his new role skilfully. 'He used to carry my briefcase at meetings,' Vannsak said. 'It wasn't that he was my secretary, he would have been hopeless at that. But he kept me company and he was pleasant to have around.' As the campaign heated up, the two men took breakfast together each morning at Vannsak's house, a two-storey colonial villa in the Lycée grounds, surrounded by palm trees and bougainvillea. Sâr said little, listening while Vannsak held forth on his efforts to weld the three strands of the party – the Thanhists; the Left; and the notables – into a united force.

How much Sâr was able to influence the Democratic Party's policies is a matter of debate. Vannsak has repeatedly claimed that he had no input at all; but it plainly never occurred to him that his protégé might have an ulterior motive. Ping Sây, who was then editing the Democrats' newspaper, *Pracheathippadey*, had a very different impression. 'Sâr had an important role at that time,' he remembered. 'It was he who [helped] lay out the party's political line.' Thiounn Mumm concurred. 'Sâr was manipulating Vannsak,' he recalled. 'When I met him, he told me that since we controlled the Democratic Party, we must take a tough line against the Americans. I didn't agree. I thought it was more important to have a programme which everyone could support. But Vannsak went along with him.'

How to treat the United States was a headache not merely for the Democrats but for Sihanouk as well.

To the King, Cambodia's fate would be sealed if it allowed itself to become just another pawn on Washington's Cold War chessboard. To Washington, in the era of Dulles, foreign governments were either 'with us, or against us'. When the Cambodian Prime Minister, Penn Nouth, declared on Sihanouk's orders towards the end of 1953: 'It is not for us to take sides against communism, so long as the Viet Minh do not try to impose it on our people by force,' President Eisenhower was outraged. On the other hand, at Geneva, which officially enshrined neutralist policies for the whole of Indochina, Washington was agreeably surprised to find that Cambodia, alone of the participating states, adopted an independent stance. But then, on a visit to India, Sihanouk endorsed the *pancasila*, the five principles of peaceful coexistence, which to the Americans put

Cambodia back in the same league as Burma and Red China. Next he delayed approving a US military aid package, saying there were too many strings attached. When that hurdle was passed, he told the American Ambassador, Robert McClintock: 'Nehru thinks he has me in his pocket! He's wrong' – only to launch into a diatribe against American stinginess and interference in Cambodia's internal affairs. 'The US is building engines to go to the moon,' he complained, 'but they won't give us even one airplane. The French are poorer, but far more generous.'

It was a bewildering display of political equivocation. As the King blew hot and cold, he kept America at arm's length while encouraging the belief that one day it would be able to lock Cambodia securely into the Western camp.

The Democrats could find no adequate response to this policy. On the one hand, the left wing of the party would have liked, as Sâr had suggested, to take a stronger anti-American line. But Son Ngoc Thanh and his supporters were pro-American. Moreover, the US administration was sympathetic to the Democrats' republican aims. The result was a flawed compromise: American imperialism was held to be bad, American democracy, good.

Similar confusion reigned in the party's domestic programme. Vannsak and his colleagues could denounce the royal government's corruption and insinuate that the palace was a wellspring of venality. But open opposition to the Throne was impossible because the law forbade it. The best they could do was to plead for a constitutional monarchy and, by means of Buddhist allegories, to trash Sihanouk's image as a providential figure guiding the country's destiny.

Despite their incoherence, the Democrats remained the favourites to sweep the board at the elections. In February 1955, Sihanouk called a referendum on the pretext of seeking approval of his 'Royal Crusade'. It was intended to provide a springboard to kick off his campaign, and it was shamelessly cooked. Voters were told: 'If you love the King, [choose a] white ballot. If you don't love the King, a black ballot.' Of those voting, 99.8 per cent chose white ballots. But the turnout was disappointingly low. At the end of that month, when the Democrats held a weekend rally in a Buddhist *wat* in southern Phnom Penh, Sihanouk went secretly to a nearby villa to listen to the proceedings, which were carried over loudspeakers. On hearing the enthusiastic reception accorded to the speakers, he wept with rage.

Three days later, on Wednesday, March 2 1955, Radio Phnom Penh broadcast a statement which the King had recorded on a dictaphone that morning. Not even his parents had been told what he was to say. It was the announcement of his abdication:

My enemies work against Me ceaselessly . . . Certain of our students, who love injustice . . . are determined to serve the Democrats and Son Ngoc Thanh . . . The educated, the highly-placed and the rich . . . spend their time throwing up obstacles [to My work] for the sake of their own interests and ambitions. All this has completely discouraged Me and prevents Me continuing to reign . . . If I remain on the Throne, I will be unable to work in your interests, My poor and humble subjects . . . Freed from My golden cage in the Royal Palace, I offer My life and My strength to My people . . . For though I leave the Throne, I shall not shirk My duty to serve.

In the words of an official chronicler, 'tears flowed from people's eyes . . . and their hearts refused to believe'. But Sihanouk was unmoved. Two days later his father, Suramarit, was enthroned in his place. Freed from the constraints of kingship, Sihanouk could throw himself into the political arena and fight for power like anyone else – except that, unlike his opponents, he retained what one observer called 'a quasi-mystical eminence that transcends politics', which made it, in this respect at least, a rather one-sided contest.

It was, as Keng Vannsak acknowledged, a stroke of genius.

The elections, due in April, were postponed until the autumn to give Sihanouk time to organise a new political formation, the Sangkum Reastr Niyum, which meant literally the 'People's Community', though by homonymy it also implied 'Socialist', a deliberate play on words to undercut his left-wing rivals. Conservative politicians from Lon Nol to Dap Chhuon dissolved their own political parties and flocked to the Prince's standard. So did some of the older Democrats, like the Economics Minister, Son Sann, and Sim Var, who had worked on *Nagaravatta* in the 1930s. But the mainstream of the Democratic Party held firm, as did its base of support – the civil servants, Buddhist monks, teachers and secondary-school students. The Sangkum had no policies other than supporting Sihanouk and projected no clear image. To its opponents it was a dog's breakfast of a party, made up of 'ideological bric-à-brac'. For all the Prince's efforts, the Sangkum, in the judgement of the French Ambassador, Pierre Gorce, was 'by no means assured of success'.

Sihanouk himself evidently reached the same conclusion. Around the end of July, he asked the Indian chargé d'affaires, Sir Dhirendra Mitra, to sound out Keng Vannsak on the possibility of the Democrats and the Sangkum joining together to form a government of national union. Vannsak convened his Executive Committee, which saw the offer as a sign of weakness and rejected it, confident in its own strength.

That decision marked a turning point.

Since the spring, the police had been putting pressure on the anti-Sangkum parties, harassing their candidates and threatening their supporters. Already in June, the *Pracheachon* newspaper had been banned and its editor, Chi Kim An, jailed for three months for *lèse-majesté*. An arrest warrant was issued for Sâr's brother, Saloth Chhay, who was editing another left-wing journal, *Sammaki*. He took refuge with their sibling, Suong, whose status as a palace official meant that the police were unable to intervene. But after a week-long stand-off King Suramarit ruled that Chhay must give himself up.

Five weeks before the vote, massive intimidation began. Keng Vannsak recalled:

> The evil genius behind the repression was Sam Sary – a bestial man. As an investigating magistrate in the 1940s, he had beaten suspects to death with his own hands. Then he went to study in France. In 1955, he joined the Sangkum and became Sihanouk's closest aide . . . After Sihanouk decided to use strong-arm tactics, Sary handed out money and arms to hired ruffians to come and break up our meetings . . . Kou Roun, who was then police chief, sent men with gongs and drums, mounted on bicycle carts, to drown out the speeches . . . We could do nothing. It was a provocation. If we'd reacted, the police would have had an excuse to intervene and we'd have fallen into the trap.

The Pracheachon suffered even more severely. In the provinces, several of its candidates were shot dead by unknown assailants, and more than twenty others were arrested. When polling day finally arrived, it was able to field candidates in only thirty-five of the ninety-one constituencies.

The Democrats maintained their full list, which included Mey Mann and Ping Sây, both of whom had been party activists in the 1940s, and two other former members of the Cercle Marxiste, Toch Phoeun and Mey Phat. But at the height of the campaign Thiounn Mumm disappeared. It later transpired that his mother, warned privately by the Queen to get her son out of harm's way, had bundled him on to a plane to Paris. On the eve of polling day, Sunday September 10, Keng Vannsak was arrested after a bystander was shot dead at one of his rallies. The gunman accused the Democratic Party leader of having hired him to assassinate a right-wing opponent. In court, the man retracted. Vannsak remained in prison. A month later he sent a grovelling letter to Sihanouk, promising never again to engage in politics, which secured his immediate release and the dropping of all charges.

When the results of the voting were announced, the Sangkum had swept the field. Not one Democrat or Pracheachon candidate had been elected.

The outcome was not due solely to electoral fraud. Sihanouk was revered in the countryside. But intimidation was the key. 'The Cambodians are not brave when faced by firmness on the part of the authorities,' the British chargé d'affaires noted. Vannsak was blunter: 'The Khmers have been slaves for centuries. In the face of authority, they bow down. Those who use violence know that – they know how the people react.'

Most left-wing voters stayed at home. If they did pluck up the courage to go to the polling stations, the conditions they found there were such as to discourage the boldest among them. First they had to run a gauntlet of police and soldiers. Then they were handed coloured voting slips, representing the different parties, one of which had to be placed in an urn under the watchful gaze of local officials. If that were not enough, the count was falsified. 'The heads of the voting stations were all the Prince's people,' Sâr recalled. 'So they put all the votes indiscriminately as being for the Sangkum.' In some constituencies, when it was found that Sihanouk's candidate had finished second, the voting slips were destroyed and the winner murdered. Officials in an electoral district of eastern Cambodia, known for years as a Viet Minh stronghold, solemnly reported that the Pracheachon candidate did not receive a single vote. Even with such flagrant gerrymandering, three Pracheachon candidates were reported to have won more than a third of the vote in their respective constituencies, and in the four southern provinces of Kampot, Takeo, Prey Veng and Svay Rieng, the group averaged 16 per cent. In an incautious moment two years later, Sihanouk acknowledged that in fact thirty-six electoral districts had voted 'red or pink', in other words, Pracheachon or Democrat, in 1955. Officially, at the time, none was admitted to have done so. The Democrats were said to have obtained 12 par cent of the vote nationally, the Pracheachon, 4 per cent.

In a fair fight, the two left-wing parties might well have gained enough seats to form a government. At the very least, the Sangkum would have faced substantial parliamentary opposition. Instead Cambodia became, in every material respect, a single-party state, led by a narcissistic, whimsical, charming and utterly ruthless autocrat who was beholden to no one but himself. When a French correspondent suggested that there might be 'reservations about certain aspects of the voting', the International Control Commission promptly ruled that it had been 'correct' and foreign embassies in Phnom Penh, led by the French and the Americans, conscientiously closing their eyes to the irregularities, vied with each other in heaping praise on the ex-King for his electoral triumph.

The blatant manipulation of the polls, following Sihanouk's *coup de force* against the Democrats three years earlier, extinguished any hope that the

Left might take power by parliamentary means. 'Taking part in elections is just for propaganda,' Sâr concluded. 'An election is a power struggle. The one who has power in his hands is the one who controls the outcome.'

Over the next few months, many Democratic Party leaders either abandoned politics altogether – like Keng Vannsak and Thiounn Mumm – or joined the Sangkum. The Cambodian communists hesitated. Logically, in such circumstances, the next step for a revolutionary party would have been to renew the armed struggle. But in Cambodia, the movement was too weak and its Vietnamese allies too preoccupied with their own domestic concerns for that to be an option. As long as the Pracheachon and the Democrats had a chance of forming a government, the Vietnamese had supported them. But once Sihanouk emerged victorious and it became clear that he was the man they would have to deal with, the pragmatists in Hanoi changed tack.

Even before the elections, the Viet Minh had treated Cambodia with kid gloves. Since the Geneva accords, far fewer communist-provoked incidents had been reported there than in Laos or South Vietnam. The French concluded that there was more to this than met the eye. An informer had told the SDECE, the French counterpart of the CIA and MI6, that the godfather of Cambodian communism, Nguyen Thanh Son, had reached a secret agreement with Sihanouk at the time of the Viet Minh withdrawal, under which limited numbers of Viet Minh cadres would be allowed to operate clandestinely in certain parts of Cambodia, notably the border regions, to promote the struggle in South Vietnam, in return for assurances that the Vietnamese communists would not interfere in Cambodia's internal affairs.

The agreement, detailed in an intelligence report dated September 16 1954, has never been officially confirmed. But for the next sixteen years, the trade-off it described was followed to the letter.

By the time of the elections, moreover, Sihanouk's regime looked much more attractive to the communist powers of Asia than had been the case a year before. In contrast to US client states like Thailand and the Philippines, Cambodia had refused to join Washington's military arm in the region, the South-East Asian Treaty Organization, SEATO. That spring, at a summit in Bandung, Sihanouk had become one of the five founder members of the Non-Aligned Movement, along with Zhou Enlai, Marshal Tito of Yugoslavia, Indonesia's President Sukarno and Egypt's Gamal Abdel Nasser. The Vietnamese soon concluded that they had everything to lose and nothing to gain by undermining his regime. On that basis, towards the end of 1955, they issued new instructions to the Khmer Party:

> The goal is to . . . cooperate with and to support Sihanouk's government, which is following a policy of peace and neutrality, and to struggle to push it still farther down that road in order to strengthen and develop national independence. At the same time the [Cambodian Party] should fight against the meddling of American imperialism and its invasion [of the region]; and it must struggle to eliminate or correct the negative aspects of the [Sihanouk] government which run counter to the people's interests.

The directive reiterated that armed struggle was over. In its place the Cambodians should carry out 'political struggle, accompanied by other forms of legal, semi-legal, illegal, overt, semi-overt and secret struggle'.

It was hardly the kind of programme to mobilise enthusiasm for revolutionary change. Apart from opposition to the US, it offered no clear policy direction. It was ambiguous and difficult to grasp; and it unashamedly sacrificed the Cambodian Party's interests to those of Vietnam. None the less, this was the policy the Khmer communists were stuck with for the next ten years. Neither their leaders nor, still less, Sâr and the returned students, had any say in the matter.

Sihanouk's use of police methods to crush the opposition led the communists to impose a more rigorous separation of 'legal', 'semi-legal' and 'secret' work than had been the case before. Legal activities virtually ceased as the Democratic Party was reduced to a shell. Ping Sây started a new journal, *Ekhepheap* ('Unity'), which defended neutralist (and hence, anti-American) theses, not very different from those of Sihanouk himself. But the mere fact that it was not under the government's control made that unacceptable. When temporary closure orders failed to make Sây see the light, the police arrested him on his wedding day and put him in prison for seven months.

The Pracheachon – the Party's 'semi-legal' arm – survived despite constant government harassment. Keo Meas remained its leader but gave up his position as Secretary of the clandestine Phnom Penh Party Committee. The other members of the group – Non Suon, a young peasant from Kampot province who had risen to become South-Western Zone Secretary during the war against the French; Ney Sarann, a member of the Khmerland provisional government set up in April 1950, who was close to the Eastern Zone military commander, So Phim; Chou Chet, a young PRPK cadre from Kompong Cham; two returned students, Chi Kim An and Ieng Sary's former classmate Sien An; and two journalists, Nop Bophann and Penn Yuth – had all worked with Meas as members of Nguyen Thanh Son's Viet Minh delegation at the ceasefire talks in Svay Rieng.

To the Cambodian government, and to foreign embassies in Phnom

Penh, the Pracheachon were 'the communists' – or as Sihanouk began calling them around this time, the 'Rouges', to distinguish them from the 'Khmers Roses', the pink liberals in the Democratic Party. That there might be an inner, secret Party organisation, for which the Pracheachon was merely a façade, seems never to have crossed anyone's mind. Initially the group tried to act as a loyal opposition, applauding the Prince's journey to China in February 1956, Zhou Enlai's return visit that autumn and the establishment of diplomatic relations with the Soviet Union and other Eastern Bloc countries – moves viewed with grave misgivings, not only by the United States but also by Britain and France, which wondered anxiously whether the Prince would be able to cope with the forces that his 'slide to the Left' unleashed. But Sihanouk was more adept than his critics gave him credit for. The tilt towards communism abroad was matched by increased repression of communism at home. The Pracheachon became the Prince's whipping boy, denounced at public meetings as a treacherous fifth column serving foreign masters.

With time, the group acquired, in the public mind and in the minds of its own members, a distinct identity. It still took orders from the secret Party leadership. But in practice it became a separate faction, or at least a separate sensibility, rather than the semi-public face of one and the same revolutionary organisation. It was the price the movement paid for splitting its activities into discrete branches which, for security reasons, kept contact with each other to a minimum.

The secret Party leadership itself, appointed by the Vietnamese in the winter of 1954, consisted of a five-man provisional Central Committee. Sieu Heng was Secretary, in place of Son Ngoc Minh, with Tou Samouth as his deputy. Minh himself, who had been given responsibility for the two thousand Khmer Viet Minh regroupees in Vietnam, ranked third. So Phim, representing the Eastern Zone military, and Tuk Nhung, the rural base areas, filled the remaining places.

Sieu Heng was a surprising choice. During the Royal Crusade, when Sihanouk had offered an amnesty to Khmer Viet Minh leaders who rallied to his cause, he had wavered and by some accounts came close to surrendering. Nguyen Thanh Son, however, regarded him as the brightest of the Cambodian communists. The North-West Zone military commander, Ruos Nhim, who worked with Heng, put it somewhat differently. 'He knew how to please the Vietnamese,' he said, 'and as a result, he was promoted.' Seconded by the veteran Tuk Nhung, Heng had responsibility for the 140 Party cells in the countryside. Tou Samouth was in charge of urban Party organisations. But the new arrangements broke down almost at once. Son Ngoc Minh was in Hanoi; Sieu Heng stayed in South Vietnam until

1956; Tuk Nhung abandoned the struggle altogether; and So Phim fled into the jungle. The rural Party organisation was left leaderless and slowly withered away. Of the five nominal leaders, only Tou Samouth was active inside the country. Since his primary responsibility was for the urban areas, the centre of gravity of the Cambodian movement shifted from the countryside to the towns.

Throughout this period, Sâr was living a double life.

After his return from the maquis, he had rented a house in a marshy area of southern Phom Penh known as Boeng Keng Kâng. 'It was ideal for someone who wished to be anonymous,' Ping Sây remembered. 'The whole place was a maze of crooked little wooden houses, built on stilts, joined by flimsy, bamboo walkways, just above the level of the swamp, with dozens of ways in and out.'

Sâr's house was simplicity itself. The only furnishings were a sleeping-mat on the wooden floor and a pile of books he had brought back from Paris. There was no street lighting and at night, when the district was in darkness, he could meet colleagues who were working openly, like Sây and Thiounn Mumm, as well as secret emissaries from Tou Samouth, without anyone being the wiser. Keo Meas and Ney Sarann, from the Pracheachon, came to the house to co-ordinate the group's campaign activities with those of the Democratic Party; and Sâr, in turn, visited the Pracheachon offices – but, just as he had managed his association with Vannsak without attracting the attention of the police, so too his meetings with Meas passed unnoticed. Even Non Suon, Meas's deputy, who saw him come to call several times, always wearing a white short-sleeved shirt, did not learn the visitor's identity until much later. This gift for subterfuge, coupled with an ability to combine 'open' and 'secret' work, put Sâr in a strong position. All contacts between the Pracheachon and the Democrats passed through him, as did most, though not all, communications with the underground Party apparatus.

But there was also a second Sâr, who seemed to have little in common with the first. This Sâr drove a black Citroën sedan of a type which, not many years earlier, had been reserved for the exclusive use of the French *Résident Supérieur*. Admittedly, it was not new – it had apparently belonged to his sister Roeung, the ex-royal concubine – but it enabled him to cut a figure before his society belle, Soeung Son Maly, whom he was once again courting assiduously. Keng Vannsak let them meet at his house at the Lycée Sisowath while he and his wife were out teaching. He was sure, he said later, that 'nothing untoward happened . . . They probably sat some way apart, talking about their feelings for each other . . . Maly wouldn't have let it go further because she was waiting for him to get a proper position. Her idea was that when the Democratic Party triumphed, Sâr would become an important official and then they would be able to marry.'

It is not easy to reconcile the dedicated young activist, plotting revolution from his empty house in the slums, and the elegant young man-about-town arranging trysts with his lady-love. But it would be wrong to assume that the second was simply a cover for the first.

Sâr was no ascetic. His youthful escapades with the young women of the palace, his reputation in his first year in Paris and earlier as a young man 'who likes to have a good time', his love of music and of dancing – 'he dances very well, in the Western style with a girl in his arms,' one of his colleagues noted a few years later – all suggest that if he was playing a part, it came naturally to him. One may wonder how the story would have ended if the Democrats had won in 1955 and Sâr obtained the post that Maly hoped for. But the Democrats lost and she dumped him, becoming a few months later the junior wife of Sam Sary, the nemesis of the Left and the second most powerful politician in the land after Sihanouk himself.

Keng Vannsak claimed later that this dual setback touched off a cycle of sexual and political frustration which embittered Sâr for the rest of his life. That is excessive. But at a political level, the events of 1955 undoubtedly steeled Sâr's determination to hold to his revolutionary course, and over the next five years, while the Party gradually imploded and a less engaged man would have given up – as many did – his commitment did not waver. At a personal level it led him to marry – 'on the rebound', as Vannsak put it – a fellow revolutionary whose convictions were equal to his own.

Sâr and Khieu Ponnary, the elder sister of Ieng Sary's wife, Thirith, whom he had first encountered in Paris, had met up again after his return from the maquis. Vannsak remembered her as one of a group of Democratic Party women who always sat in the front row at rallies. She was also, which Vannsak did not know, the main point of contact between Phnom Penh and the Viet Minh prior to the Geneva accords. A messenger would come at night from Prey Chhor to a meeting place near the house on rue Dr Hahn which Ponnary shared with her mother, just behind the palace. Then she would take him to a rendezvous, always in a different place, to meet students waiting to be escorted to the camp at Krâbao. She was a person who could be relied on, and after the turmoil of the election defeat and Maly's betrayal, reliability was something Sâr desperately needed. Towards the end of 1955, he left the bare, wooden house at Boeung Keng Kâng, and took lodgings with Ponnary and her mother. Six months later they married.

A Vietnamese Party historian, alluding to their revolutionary credentials, described it, only partly tongue-in-cheek, as a 'marriage made in heaven'. In fact, it was a very odd union. Sâr was thirty-one; his bride, thirty-six – an age difference still more unusual in Cambodia, where men normally take much younger wives, than in the West. Moreover, Sâr had charm and good looks. Ponnary was prim and proper, and behind her back was nicknamed 'the old maid'. Even her best friend could not have claimed she was beautiful; she had had smallpox as a child and her face bore the scars. Yet marry they did, at a three-day-long ceremony, conducted by Buddhist monks, chanting and swinging censers of incense in accordance with Khmer custom, which culminated in a huge banquet on Saturday, July 14 1956, attended by Mey Mann, Ping Sây, other friends from Sâr's Paris days, and scores of guests from the village of Prek Sbauv and from Ponnary's family.

The choice of the wedding day, Bastille Day, was not fortuitous. But revolutionary symbolism took second place to Khmer tradition. As the high point of the ceremony, Sâr insisted that his new wife prostrate herself before his father, then in his seventies. Ponnary, a well-educated, self-aware woman, who had been one of the first two Cambodian girls to pass the *baccalauréat*, reluctantly complied. Ieng Sary, when told about the incident later, was shocked. 'No one could understand why he did that,' he said. But Ponnary, too, was deeply conservative, and at one level this deference to ancient customs may not have displeased her. When the old man died, two years later, she accompanied Sâr to Prek Sbauv for the funeral. One of her students remembered her as

> a very traditional Khmer woman – no lipstick or anything like that. Her sister, Thirith, was more modern, more liberal if you like. Thirith would say what she thought, like a European. She was more direct, more open. Ponnary didn't do that . . . She was very *Khmer*. [Sâr] had that quality, too. Her way of behaving, her way of approaching people, were very authentic, reflecting Khmer culture and custom . . . The way she dressed wasn't excessively prudish; it was traditional, that's all. She was modest. She had a sense of humour but did not always show it – I wouldn't say she was full of laughs. But she was thoughtful and she was interesting to be with. We all respected her immensely.

When Thirith and Ieng Sary returned to Phnom Penh from Paris in January 1957, they spent six weeks with the Sârs at the house at rue Dr Hahn. 'They lived in a very old-fashioned way,' Sary remembered. 'In theory, [Sâr] believed women should be equal. But with his own wife, for some reason he didn't see it the same way. She was an intellectual. But when she talked to other people [instead of remaining silent, deferring to her husband in the traditional manner], he didn't appreciate that. . .'

In the months before her marriage, Ponnary had become more outgoing. Another student remembered that she started to wear a little make-up
and even jewellery. 'She seemed so happy,' he recalled, 'and we were happy
on her behalf.' But it proved short-lived. The following year, she found she
had uterine cancer. The operation was successful but it meant that she
could not have children. Sâr's eldest brother, Suong, and his wife had
hoped that having a family might make Sâr settle down. It was not to be.

In the winter of 1955, the underground Party apparatus was reorganised.
Tou Samouth, who had spent most of the election campaign outside
Phnom Penh, moved into a small house which Sâr had had built for him
on land owned by Ponnary's family near Tuol Svay Prey, the 'Hill of the
Wild Mango', on the south-western outskirts of the city.* It was surrounded by a tall hedge of water tamarinds. A group of cyclo drivers hung
around outside during the day and slept there at night, acting as bodyguards.
    Samouth chaired the Party's Urban Committee, which initially consisted
of himself, Nuon Chea – who had replaced Keo Meas as Secretary of the
Phnom Penh City Committee – and the trio who had returned together
from the maquis a year before, Sâr, Mey Mann and Chan Samân. Mann
dropped out some months later, ostensibly to devote his energies to reviv-
ing the now moribund Democratic Party. In fact he was excluded because
he made clear that he was not prepared to sacrifice his family life to the cause,
which earned him recriminations for 'sentimentality and lack of courage'.
    Nuon Chea had come to the communist movement by a different path
from the others. Two years older than Sâr, he had grown up in Battambang.
During the Thai occupation of the province in the 1940s, he attended secondary school in Bangkok and worked for a time as a clerk at the Thai
Foreign Ministry before enrolling at Thammasat University, where he studied law. While there, he became a member of the Thai Communist Party,
but left in the late 1940s to join his cousin, Sieu Heng, at the North-
Western Zone headquarters in the mountains of Samlaut district, not far
from Pailin. His Party membership was transferred to the ICP and, in
September 1951, he was appointed to the newly created PRPK Central
Committee. Subsequently he spent a year studying at the Vietnamese
Higher Party School. The most secretive of all the Khmer revolutionaries,
he returned unobtrusively to Cambodia in the summer of 1955 and found

---

* Tuol Svay Prey would later acquire a sinister reputation as the site of the Khmer Rouge
torture centre, S-21, set up after 1975 at the Tuol Sleng secondary school. In 1955, a primary school stood on the site, but most of the surrounding area was still undeveloped.
Samouth's home and another house used by the Party lay just north of the school, between
Tuol Sleng and what was then the horse-racing track, now the Olympic Stadium.

employment with a Sino-Khmer trading company, where he would remain, under deep cover, long after his colleagues had fled back to the maquis.

Sâr, meanwhile, had taken a job teaching history and French literature at a private school not far from his old home in Boeung Keng Kâng. Chamraon Vichea (Progressive Knowledge) was one of three such establishments in the city where young radicals who lacked the qualifications to teach at state schools were able to find work. Here, a third Sâr emerged, complementing the revolutionary and the smartly dressed young man of the world. Having been a mediocre student, he proved an unusually gifted teacher. Soth Polin, later a well-known Khmer novelist, studied French literature with him:

> I still remember [Saloth Sâr's] style of delivery in French: gentle and musical. He was clearly drawn to French literature in general and poetry in particular: Rimbaud, Verlaine, de Vigny . . . He spoke in bursts without notes, searching [for his words] a little but never at a loss, his eyes half-closed, carried away by the lyrical flow of his thoughts . . . The students were enthralled by this teacher who was so approachable, always dressed in a short-sleeved white shirt and dark blue trousers.

On this point, all testimonies concur. He was 'a self-composed, smooth-featured teacher who was fond of his students, eloquent, unpretentious, honest, humane'. One young man, struck by Sâr's evident good nature and attractive personality, declared after their first meeting: 'I [felt] I could easily become his lifelong friend.'

The new leadership met at Tou Samouth's home, once every two or three weeks, to discuss the political situation and how best to promote the communist cause. It was an uphill struggle. The agreement, tacit or otherwise, whereby Sihanouk turned a blind eye to the Vietnamese communists' activities on Cambodian territory provided they kept out of its internal affairs, had freed his hands to carry out a harsh but highly effective campaign of repression against former Khmer Viet Minh activists. By 1957, the number of Party members had been halved, from 1,670 at the end of the war to 850. Most of the former rural leaders were inactive. Ruos Nhim, in the North-West, was living on a farm in Battambang. Ke Pauk, who would later head the Northern Zone, had gone back to his home village to work as a peasant. So Phim, the fourth ranking member of the provisional Central Committee, had made his way to Phnom Penh, where Mey Mann and Toch Phoeun, then a senior official in the Public Works Department, found him and a group of thirty followers employment as carpenters on government building sites.

When Ieng Sary returned from Paris that January, leaving the Cercle Marxiste in the hands of Khieu Samphân, who was studying for an economics doctorate, he came to the conclusion that the movement was moribund.

Part of the reason was that the Vietnamese, the begetters of the Cambodian communist movement, were overwhelmed by their own problems. A shadowy 'Work Committee', headed by a southern Vietnamese who used the alias Hay So, had been set up in Phnom Penh by the VWP's Southern Bureau, the future Central Office for South Vietnam (COSVN), to handle liaison with the Khmers.* But its main concern in the late 1950s was the safety of its own leadership. In 1957 the Southern Bureau itself was forced to take refuge in the Cambodian capital to escape the wave of repression unleashed by the South Vietnamese President Ngo Dinh Diem. Le Duan, soon to be designated Ho Chi Minh's heir apparent, was based there for part of that year. The Southern Bureau continued to operate clandestinely from safe houses in Phnom Penh until 1959, when guerrilla fighting resumed in the south and it re-based inside Vietnam. In practice, so long as the Cambodian Communists did nothing which might jeopardise Hanoi's relationship with Sihanouk, they were left to go their own way. The links with the Vietnamese 'elder brother' slowly weakened. Speaking many years later, Sâr argued that this had been a good thing because 'it gave us the chance to be independent and to develop our movement ourselves'. But to the beleaguered little group of Khmer communists, trying desperately to survive on their own, it cannot have seemed like that at the time.

More fundamental, however, was the Cambodian Party's crisis of identity. The PRPK, to which all Khmer communists theoretically belonged, was not even a proper communist party. How could one be a communist as a member of a party which was not?

Those like Sâr, Sok Knaol and Mey Mann, who had belonged to the French and Indochinese Parties, insisted in later life, not always truthfully, that they had never been officially inducted into the PRPK but had been members of 'the Cambodian section of the ICP'. In Mann's words: 'It was all very vague. There wasn't a proper structure . . . We had a leadership core . . . and [we] worked together. We felt we were members of the Communist Party, but what communist party I couldn't say.' Sâr spoke in similar terms. From the mid-1950s, they began referring to their movement among themselves not as 'the Party' but as *angkar padevat*, the 'revolutionary organisation', or more often just as Angkar.

In 1957, Tou Samouth, Sâr and Nuon Chea began drafting a new political programme and statutes for a re-launched Cambodian Party to replace

---

*Ieng Sary claimed not to know Hay So's real name. He has been identified as Nguyen Van Linh, who became Vietnamese Communist Party leader after Le Duan's death in 1986.

the PRPK, which they regarded more and more as an alien implant. The revived party would be allied with, but not subordinate to, the Vietnamese. A recruitment drive was launched, based on the Viet Minh principle of 'quality rather than quantity'. In practice, this meant building up core groups, 'one member at a time', as Pham Van Ba had taught them in the maquis, and then gradually, after a lengthy apprenticeship, inducting into the movement those who had proved themselves. Suong Sikoeun, then nineteen years old and in his final year at the Lycée Sisowath, was among the new intake:

> We used to meet once a week at a worker's house in the southern part of the city. Every time I left home, I wondered whether I would get back that night. Because it was clandestine. I used to imagine that someone might shoot at me. We always told the cyclo driver to drop us some way beyond, and then walked back making sure that no one was following. . .
>
> The meetings used to last about two hours, from 8 p.m. to 10 p.m. . . . Mainly we talked about the political situation – there was very little discussion of ideology . . . The [political] line was essentially the same as what we read in the left-wing press: neutrality, a parliamentary system, multi-party democracy and constitutional monarchy. The difference was that now we were members of an organisation, with its own internal discipline and rules . . . [One of the rules was that] we each had to contact three or four potential sympathisers and then observe them over a long period to see how they behaved. Eventually, the most progressive element among them might be asked to join the cell . . . They were cells, not discussion groups. But they were the cells of a party that was still in the process of being formed.

To Sikoeun, the conspiratorial side of the movement was part of the attraction. That was true for Sâr, too. He did not take part in cell meetings – nor did Tou Samouth or Nuon Chea – to avoid the risk of exposure. But he organised informal gatherings with groups of students at his home, a brick-built Chinese-style house, not far from Tou Samouth's dwelling, to which he and Ponnary had moved soon after Ieng Sary's return. The house was spotlessly clean, one participant remembered, but almost bare except for a few books and some Chinese prints on the walls. Sâr led the discussions and encouraged the others to speak out, but apart from criticising corruption never revealed his own political stance. Ieng Sary and Son Sen who, after returning from France, had become Director of Studies at the Phnom Penh Teacher Training College, chaired similar discussion groups and participated in cell meetings like those which Suong Sikoeun attended. At a still more restricted level, Samouth, Sâr and Nuon Chea held political training seminars in safe houses for the most reliable elements, essentially those who had joined the PCF or the ICP in the pre-Geneva period and a handful of younger people who had proved their loyalty.

The movement was hardly flourishing, but by the summer, at least in Phnom Penh, it was no longer in decline. Chamraon Vichea and the two other 'progressive' schools in the capital, Kampuj'bot and Sotoân Prychea In, were staffed largely by communists, and growing numbers of students were being attracted to the cause. Core groups existed at the Lycée Sisowath, where Ponnary and her sister Thirith taught; at the Teacher Training College; and at the Sisowath Alumni Association, headed by Sâr's protégé Sok Knaol. Similar networks were being built up in provincial cities, including Battambang and Kompong Cham.

Sihanouk, whose intuition in such matters was finely honed, sensed the danger.

In August 1957, he summoned the leaders of the Democratic Party, whose continued existence afforded a kind of vicarious protection for all with left-wing views, to a debate at the Royal Palace before an audience packed with his own supporters, which was broadcast over loudspeakers to a crowd of several thousand outside. As they left, after five hours of public humiliation, they were dragged from their cars and beaten with rifle-butts by palace guards. For the next two nights, soldiers from the Phnom Penh garrison, encouraged by the right-wing Chief of Staff, Lon Nol, rampaged through the streets, shouting 'Death to the Democrats' and molesting indiscriminately any Cambodian, Chinese or Vietnamese unfortunate enough to cross their path. To demonstrate Sihanouk's magnanimity, the party was not banned outright but allowed to limp on until the parliamentary elections next spring, when it decided not to field any candidates.

The following month, September, the Prince announced the foundation of a government movement, the Royal Socialist Khmer Youth, whose primary mission was to prevent young people being seduced by communist propaganda.

Next came the turn of the Pracheachon, which decided, 'not without courage . . . given the physical risks involved', as one Western Ambassador noted, to put up candidates in the capital and four rural constituencies. Sihanouk seized the occasion to launch a violent anti-communist crusade, travelling in person to all five electoral districts to denounce his opponents' 'anti-national' policies. His movement, the Sangkum, put up gory posters of communist terror attacks against Khmer civilians, dating from the war, and Radio Phnom Penh accused the Prince's opponents of being puppets of the hated Vietnamese. The Pracheachon ran a skilful campaign, presenting its candidates as local men, who 'travel on foot and by ox-cart and understand local problems', unlike their rivals from the Sangkum, who came in fleets of American cars. But it made no difference. Systematic intimidation forced four of the five to drop out. The only one who stayed the course, Keo Meas, in Phnom Penh, was credited with a mere 396 votes from an electorate of more than 30,000.

As if that were not enough, later the same year it was discovered that the Party leader Sieu Heng, and a Pracheachon member, Penn Yuth, had been working as government informers. Exactly when their betrayal began was never clearly established. Nor was it known how much Sieu Heng had told the police. He had been under suspicion within the Party for some time and Tou Samouth had taken steps to limit his access to information. But it is also likely that he held back much of what he knew, for his niece was married to Nuon Chea, and neither Nuon nor any of the other central leaders appears to have been compromised by his betrayal. The most serious effect of his action was to sever all communication between Phnom Penh and the rural networks. Already sorely tried by lassitude and government repression, these now imploded altogether. Of the 850 Party members in 1957, by the end of the decade only 250 remained.

Treason was in fashion in Cambodia in the late 1950s.

Sihanouk had a keen nose for those who showed signs of acquiring more power than was good for him. In the summer of 1957, he began to smell trouble in the shape of his Minister of State, Sam Sary, whom he packed off to London a few months later to serve as Ambassador to the Court of St James's. Unfortunately, Sary was still the same 'sulfurous and vindictive personality' who, as a young magistrate, had gained a reputation for beating prisoners. This time he beat up a young woman, described at first as his children's governess. Soeung Son Maly, Saloth Sâr's old flame, now Sary's junior wife – for apparently it was she – went to the British police. The Embassy then issued a statement claiming that such behaviour was normal in Cambodia. The resulting scandal, amplified when the newspapers discovered that the 'governess' was in fact Sary's concubine and had recently borne him a child, led to his immediate recall.

Sâr's reaction is not recorded. But Sihanouk was furious. Not, as he explained later, because of what Sam Sary had done, but because of the discredit his behaviour had brought on Cambodia. Over the next few months, the ex-Minister moved gradually into open opposition, launching a newspaper to propagate his views and attempting, unsuccessfully, to form his own political party as a rival to the Sangkum. The Americans and their regional allies, the Thais and the South Vietnamese – ever anxious to find a counterweight to Sihanouk, if not an outright replacement – egged him on from behind the scenes.

Then, at the beginning of 1959, the Chinese and French governments got wind of a plot by Cambodia's two neighbours to overthrow the monarchy, proclaim a republic and install Son Ngoc Thanh, who had been in exile in Thailand since the 1955 elections, as Head of State. The French took the affair seriously enough for their Foreign Minister, Louis Joxe, to warn the US Ambassador that in France's view, such a move would be 'a huge mistake' and against Western interests. When Sihanouk was told, he immediately assumed that Sary was implicated. Fearing for his life, on January 20 the ex-Minister fled to Thailand where he joined Son Ngoc Thanh, thereby confirming the Prince in his conviction that Thanh, Sary, the Thais, the South Vietnamese and, at least tacitly, the Americans, were all party to a vast conspiracy which he baptised the 'Bangkok Plot'. Whether Sary was really involved or fell victim to a machination that was not of his making is another matter. For the next three years he was described as one of the leaders of Thanh's Khmer Serei movement until, during a visit to Laos, he disappeared. It emerged later that he had been murdered, either by Sihanouk's agents or by his own associates.

If Sary's role remains obscure, no such doubt exists about the 'Bangkok Plot' itself.

Shortly before Sary's departure for London, another pillar of the regime, Dap Chhuon, was also removed from the government, in which, as Security Minister, he had been one of Sihanouk's favoured instruments for terrorising opponents.

Chhuon returned to his old fiefdom of Siem Reap with the title of Royal Legate, which in practice gave him vast powers over most of northern Cambodia. But Sihanouk must have wondered whether such an energetic and unscrupulous man, having experienced national office, would be satisfied indefinitely with a provincial post, no matter how important, and when Chhuon asked to be made Legate of Battambang, which since the days of the Thai occupation had been the most rebellious province in the country, he prudently refused. Over the next twelve months, Chhuon's disaffection grew. In private, he denounced what he called Sihanouk's 'pro-communist policies' and ostentatiously refused to participate in 'voluntary' manual labour, which the Prince, inspired by the example of China's Great Leap Forward, had made compulsory for all government officials. He toyed with the idea of splitting Siem Reap from the rest of the country and setting up an independent northern Cambodian regime with the support of the Thais (which was exactly what Sihanouk had feared he might do, had he become Legate at Battambang). But before he could make up his mind to act, South Vietnam's President Ngo Dinh Diem, infuriated by Cambodia's tolerance of Viet Minh activities on its territory, approved a proposal by the South Vietnamese Ambassador to Phnom Penh, Ngo Trong Hieu, to 'organise a coup d'état to get rid of Sihanouk'. In December 1958, they approached Chhuon to carry it out.

This was the plot which the Chinese and French intelligence services had uncovered.

In February, a month after Sam Sary's defection, the conspirators went into action. Several planeloads of arms arrived in Siem Reap from Thailand, and Ngo Trong Hieu himself flew in from Saigon with 100 kilograms of gold bars to finance the rebellion. A few days later, another Vietnamese plane arrived bringing two powerful transmitters, to be used for propaganda broadcasts by the new regime.

It is possible that by then Chhuon had got cold feet and decided to change sides. In this version of events, he himself tipped off Phnom Penh that the South Vietnamese were trying to suborn him and assured Sihanouk of his loyalty. If so, the Prince was sceptical. He ordered his Chief of Staff, Lon Nol, to nip the rebellion in the bud, recover the gold ingots and kill Chhuon and his closest associates. When Nol's troops invested Siem Reap on February 22, they encountered no resistance. Chhuon and several of his officers were captured and afterwards killed. Three other Cambodians, including Chhuon's brother, and two Vietnamese, were sentenced to death by a military tribunal and executed in public by firing squad.

But the story did not end there.

Six months later, in an attempt to put relations back on a more normal footing, Sihanouk visited Saigon at Ngo Dinh Diem's invitation. Four weeks after his return, on August 30 1959, two gift boxes were delivered to the palace, one for the royal chamberlain – which, on being opened, was found to contain an elegant set of smoking implements – the other for Queen Kossamak. The chamberlain had no opportunity to give the second box to the Queen until the following evening. On her instructions he began to unpack it, at which point the King, who was also present, remembered that a group of officials was waiting for them in the audience chamber. Moments after they left the room, the box exploded with such force that it blew a hole in the reinforced concrete floor, killing the chamberlain and another official instantly. A third man died later from injuries and two others were seriously hurt. Once again, the finger of suspicion pointed at South Vietnam.*

These bizarre events had far-reaching repercussions.

Political murder, which until then had been limited to peripheral excesses by low-level officials, mainly during election campaigns, moved

*The suspicion was justified. Ten years later, Diem's Director of Intelligence, Tran Kim Tuyen, described how the gift boxes had been prepared in Saigon on the orders of the President's brother, Ngo Dinh Nhu. It had been assumed that, after unpacking his own present, the chamberlain would give the other to the Queen, who was known to enjoy opening gifts herself.

on to the national stage. A taboo had been broken. Cambodian politics had never been for the faint-hearted, but now the risk of violent death became a recognised part of the political game.

Relations with both Cambodia's neighbours took a nosedive from which they never recovered. Diplomatic ties with Thailand, suspended in October 1958 over a territorial dispute, were finally broken off in 1961 and with South Vietnam in 1963.

But most serious of all, Cambodia's relationship with the United States was damaged beyond repair. Behind Bangkok and Saigon, behind Sam Sary and Dap Chhuon, behind Ngo Dinh Nhu's parcel bomb and Son Ngoc Thanh's Khmer Serei, Sihanouk saw the malign hand of Washington. At the time, his claims seemed far-fetched and, to most Americans, downright absurd. But the evidence that emerged later was damning. The low blows to which Cambodia was subjected from the mid-1950s on, in total disregard of the accepted principles of international relations, were almost without exception the result of secret US government directives.

In 1956, when Cambodia became the first non-communist country to be granted Chinese aid, Thailand and South Vietnam, at America's prompting, imposed an economic blockade. Under pressure from US allies, it was lifted. But the CIA continued to cultivate Son Ngoc Thanh – still viewed in Washington as a possible alternative to Sihanouk – and the US Embassy in Phnom Penh had standing orders to seek out other personalities and political forces to counter the Prince's 'left-wing policies'. Sam Sary, acclaimed by the State Department as 'the staunchest friend of the United States in Cambodia', had been sent on a three-month study visit to America, as had Dap Chhuon's brother. Chhuon himself was viewed favourably by the administration as 'an anti-communist warlord'. Surreptitious support for Sihanouk's pro-Western opponents 'to reverse the drift towards pro-Communist neutrality' was reaffirmed in a National Security Council directive in April 1958. By then, there was serious tension on the border with South Vietnam. But when Sihanouk threatened retaliation, he was told by the US Ambassador that if American-supplied equipment was used against 'a friendly power', military aid would be suspended. The contrast with US behaviour towards countries it considered to be allies was flagrant. When Thai troops occupied an ancient Cambodian temple complex on their common border, the Americans remained silent.

To Washington's extreme displeasure, the Prince then upgraded relations with China, which had previously been at the level of trade missions, by approving an exchange of resident ambassadors. The US began actively seeking ways to bring him down.

After Sam Sary's efforts came to naught – efforts, the French Foreign

Ministry noted in a secret memorandum, 'which the United States probably . . . did not initiate, but certainly knew of and did nothing to discourage' – the Americans switched their attention to Dap Chhuon. Here the US
role was more direct. President Eisenhower was informed in January 1959
that preparations for a coup were under way. A CIA agent at the American
Embassy in Phnom Penh, Victor Matsui, was detailed to liaise with the
rebels and gave Chhuon a transceiver 'to keep the Embassy informed'.

The third attempt to destroy Sihanouk, by parcel bomb, may have been
mounted without American knowledge. But it certainly would not have
occurred had South Vietnam believed the US would disapprove, any more
than Thailand would have provided hospitality to Sihanouk's enemies, Sam
Sary and Son Ngoc Thanh, without US acquiescence.

American policy in the 1950s was founded on a Manichean vision in
which – decades before President Reagan coined the phrase – the US led
the forces of good in an apocalyptic struggle against the empire of evil. In
this polarised mental universe, there was no place for a middle road. 'All
those who are not with us are against us' became the intellectual underpinning that led America to its calvary in Vietnam. In fairness to policy-makers
in Washington, it must be added that, in the 1950s and '60s, not to speak of
half a century later, such attitudes were consistent with the beliefs of the
majority of Americans. Korea had barely dented America's confidence in
its self-ordained role as leader of the Free World. It would take the Vietnam
War to make Americans question established certitudes, and then not for
very long. In the meantime, Washington insisted on viewing the world
through a deforming prism that blinded it to the realities of the countries
with which it had to deal. In Cambodia's case, as in many others, this produced results exactly opposite to those America desired. Sihanouk sought
closer ties with China, and eventually with North Vietnam. The US dream
of an anti-communist alliance stretching 'from the 17th parallel to the
border of Burma' was definitively shattered, largely by its own maladress.

The same instinctive wariness that had caused Sihanouk in 1957 to distance
himself from right-wing leaders like Sam Sary and Dap Chhuon – the
'Bleus', as he took to calling them, in contradistinction to the 'Rouges' –
led him to restructure his own political power base. In one sense he had no
choice. The Sangkum members of the National Assembly elected in 1955
had shown themselves to be corrupt, fractious, undisciplined and, worst of
all, incompetent. Having gone through ten different governments in less
than two and a half years, destroyed the Democrats and intimidated the
Pracheachon, the Prince decided that the time had come to broaden his
political base. That meant bringing the Left, or what remained of it, back

into Cambodian politics, not as opponents but as part of the national union the Sangkum was supposed to represent.

Already, two years earlier, he had made tentative moves in this direction. Keng Vannsak was given a senior post in the Education Ministry. Ea Sichau returned to work at the Treasury. Thiounn Thioeunn, Mumm's eldest brother, was invited to join the government but declined.

In the 1958 elections, the opening to the Left became a priority. While Keo Meas and his Pracheachon colleagues were being flayed by Sihanouk's propaganda machine, the victorious Sangkum candidates, selected by the Prince in person and allowed to stand unopposed, included two former members of the Cercle Marxiste, Hou Yuon and Uch Ven, and three other young leftists, all but one in their late twenties and all far better educated than the outgoing members they replaced. Hou Yuon was the most controversial of the new intake. Before joining the Sangkum, he, too, had been a Pracheachon member. Shortly after his election, it was discovered, to the government's embarrassment, that there was a court case pending against him for fomenting an illegal strike. The charges were hurriedly dropped. Uch Ven, who had travelled to France with Sâr aboard the SS *Jamaique*, was a teacher, as was the third of the new recruits, So Nem. The last two – Hu Nim, a brilliant student from a poor peasant background, who had become, at the age of twenty-six, Director of the Treasury; and Chau Seng, the most ambitious of the group, who had married the daughter of a PCF mayor in the South of France – were not Party members but espoused radical ideas. On his return to Cambodia, Chau Seng had become Sihanouk's private secretary. After the elections, he and Hou Yuon were appointed junior ministers. The other three would hold ministerial posts intermittently over the next few years in accordance with the Prince's pleasure and the political vagaries of the moment.

Sihanouk's motives were mixed. The leftists were never more than a token force in the Sangkum. But they were young, dynamic and intelligent – qualities Cambodian politics sorely lacked – and their presence served as a safety valve for frustrations which might otherwise have sought more dangerous outlets. He also hoped that the temptations of power would erode the young men's idealism. Above all they provided a counterweight to the Right, which enabled him to assume the political role he liked best – that of supreme arbiter, playing off one side against the other.

The 1958 elections set a pattern that lasted for the next eight years. Within the Sangkum, the radicals were afforded certain freedoms provided they accepted the rules that Sihanouk laid down. Beyond that limit they were ruthlessly repressed.

The new climate of political violence that followed the parcel-bomb attack at the palace in August 1959 quickly made itself felt. On the evening of October 9, the editor of the Pracheachon's weekly paper, Nop Bophann, was shot as he left his office. He died two days later. Unsurprisingly his killers were never caught: they were members of the security police. His death was probably intended as a gesture of reassurance to the Right that, notwithstanding Cambodia's difficulties with America, the communists would be held in check. But, deep down, Sihanouk's feelings were much more ambivalent. In an article suffused with despair, published the same week, he wrote for the first time of communism's 'irresistible global advance' and the West's seeming inability to counter it:

> The constant progression of communism throughout the world is undeniable, and I cannot see what will stop it and make it retreat . . . The Western conception of Democracy seems to me the only one that is worthwhile from the viewpoint of the human condition, of human rights and freedoms. Its superiority resides in the fact that it places Man at the summit, while Communism reduces him to the state of a slave to an all-powerful State . . . But the great weakness of Western Democracy is its failure to deliver social justice . . . In most of the countries where they build up military forces as a rampart against totalitarian, freedom-hating communism, our American friends close their eyes to the violations of Democracy perpetrated by the governments concerned – violations which lead to a system no less totalitarian than the one they are fighting against, and without the latter's advantages . . . The West must try to understand that . . . its aid will never cure the Red fever if it is used to prop up regimes which lack the support of their own people.

Within this unpromising global context, Cambodia's fate, Sihanouk concluded, depended largely on factors over which it had no control. The realisation marked the beginning of a long and perilous tightrope walk, balancing between East and West – leaning first one way, then the other – that Sihanouk would execute in bravura fashion throughout the next decade, keeping Cambodia insulated from the firestorm in neighbouring Vietnam until, finally, the forces that the war had unleashed overwhelmed him, dragging him and his country into the inferno.

At home, repression spread in all directions. 'Arrests and searches are taking place everywhere,' wrote one diplomat, shortly after Nop Bophann's murder. 'People in Phnom Penh are frightened, and this is exacerbated by rumours of the brutal treatment the security police are said to be inflicting on those they interrogate.' By the spring of 1960, some two thousand people, Vietnamese, Chinese and Khmer, were being detained in a holding camp on the outskirts of the city.

The Vietnamese, prime targets of suspicion, were the object of a full-scale witch-hunt. While Sihanouk maintained publicly that his 'constant aim' was 'sincere reconciliation with [Vietnam]', he sent a secret memorandum to his cabinet stating that security measures must be based on the explicit premise that 'all Vietnamese, no matter what group or political party they belong to, constitute an *eternal* and *mortal* danger for the Khmer nation'. The government acted accordingly. Vietnamese communist cells – reimplanted in eastern Cambodia to prepare for the resumption that summer of communist insurgency in South Vietnam – were smashed and their members arrested. Khmer Krom saboteurs sent in by Son Ngoc Thanh's Khmer Serei movement from CIA training camps across the border in South Vietnam were hunted down and killed. In one celebrated incident, probably imagined by the Prince himself, the two targets were combined: the security services detained and 'turned' a naïve young member of a Viet Minh cell in Svay Rieng, who was then sent to the US Embassy to ask for help with a plan to assassinate Sihanouk. The Americans, as might have been expected, handed him over to the police. But the result was an embarrassing scandal in which all the Prince's adversaries – the US, the communists and the Vietnamese – were dragged through the mud. The unfortunate youth at the centre of the affair, who had apparently been told he would be released as the price of his co-operation, was sentenced to death.

A Military Tribunal, whose judgements were not subject to appeal, dealt with state security offences. In its first two months of operation it handed out twenty-two death sentences to associates of Sam Sary and Dap Chhuon, generating what one observer termed 'a psychosis of fear'. Another nine death sentences followed that spring. The verdicts, the French Embassy noted, were decided by Sihanouk in person, 'without the least concern to maintain even the appearance of judicial independence' and in flagrant disregard of the evidence, or rather the lack of it, against the individual accused:

> Over the last eighty years . . . Cambodia has grown unused to such outbursts of [royal] hatred which do not spare even women and children. Many Cambodians are talking privately among themselves of the odious nature of the sentences. Unfortunately, in this country . . . few dare speak out openly . . . [for] it is true that opposition is neither possible nor feasible in the presence of a Prince who will not tolerate even the slightest infringement of his authority.

After the death of his father, King Suramarit, in April 1960, Sihanouk's 'façade of liberal democracy, concealing the reality of personal dictatorship', became a little more threadbare. The Prince's mother, Queen Kossamak, a strong-willed, highly political woman, whom Zhou Enlai once compared to a scheming Chinese empress, made clear that she wanted the throne for herself. After weeks of Byzantine palace intrigue, Sihanouk forced her to accept a powerless, ceremonial position as Guardian of the Throne, while a constitutional amendment was pushed through making him Head of State for life. It was a coup d'état in disguise.

Meanwhile the left-wing press became a special target for attack.

The most dramatic incident involved a French-language newspaper called *l'Observateur*. It had been founded the previous autumn by Khieu Samphân, Ieng Sary's successor at the head of the Cercle Marxiste, who had returned to Cambodia from Paris after completing his doctorate (and, along the way, becoming a committed member of the French Communist Party). With Sary's encouragement, he had followed Hou Yuon's example and joined the Sangkum. But then, to the dismay of his elderly mother, who expected him to begin a lucrative career as a high official, he invested his savings in a stock of lead type and began producing a twice-weekly broadsheet. His assignment from the underground Phnom Penh City Committee was to rally intellectual support and reach out to potential communist sympathisers in mainstream political life. It was a role to which Samphân was well-suited. He was an idealist, in whom personal morality and social conscience were indissolubly linked. To help make ends meet, he taught maths at a private school at weekends. One of his students remembered:

> He was always punctual and there were no jokes in his lessons, but he was a good teacher who won our respect. He would insist on our homework being done on time and we obeyed him even though he never punished us . . . He used to say, 'I can't understand why the trees are planted in the countryside but they fruit in the capital,' by which he meant that the hard work of the farmers turned into wealth for the city people . . . His clothes were simple and he drove a rusty old sky-blue Mobylette. We used to laugh about the noise it made, like a tubercular cough . . . He dressed like a peasant, with sandals instead of shoes. His house was simple and small. In all these things he was setting an example. Above all, he disliked the corruption of the capital.

Samphân had a nimble, even mischievous mind, a ready pen and a dry sense of humour; but there was also something blinkered about him, an austere side to his character which treated life as though it should be lived along geometrical lines of discipline and self-denial. His younger brother, Khieu Sengkim, remembered how one day Samphân had invited him out to dinner:

> He told me to order anything I liked. I ordered duck. When I had finished, he asked me: 'Was it good?' I said, 'Yes, very good.' His face darkened and

he levelled a finger at me. 'You ought to be ashamed of sitting here eating such good food when most people who work ten times harder than you have nothing at all!'

In Paris, friends recalled how he had fallen in love with a French girl but had broken off the affair after deciding that his personal happiness should take second place to the quest for social justice at home.

L'Observateur infuriated Sihanouk because, while plainly subversive, it was so carefully written that it was hard to establish seditious intent. It was anti-American and anti-colonial; it campaigned against the use of French in the lower classes at primary school on the ground that children from poor backgrounds were disadvantaged by not being taught in Khmer; and it carried a regular column, of which Samphân was particularly proud, which chronicled the wretchedness of the city's poor – the water-carriers; the coolies who worked in the market, 'so used to being beaten by police truncheons that they don't even cry out, their skins hardened to the blows'; bicycle repairers; slum-dwellers; rickshaw men. Official spokesmen charged that it 'never [contains] any constructive suggestion – and [there is] always complete silence about the social measures the government has taken.' In short, the newspaper unctuously flattered the Prince's person while perfidiously deploring the social ills that resulted from his policies.

That spring Khieu Samphân was summoned by the Security Minister, Kou Roun, 'a thuggish individual', as one diplomat described him, and crudely put on notice that the government would not answer for the consequences if he did not fall into line. In the next issue of *l'Observateur*, Samphân printed a record of the conversation, 'omitting neither threats nor blows ... something which,' the French Ambassador noted, 'very few Khmers would have dared to do'.

At lunchtime on Wednesday, July 13, Kou Roun put his threat into effect. As Khieu Samphân was leaving his office on his motor-scooter, a dozen or so cyclo drivers suddenly blocked his path. When he enquired what they wanted, they pinned his arms behind his back, beat him up and stripped off all his clothes. One of his assailants took a photograph of him standing naked in the street, after which they made off. A passer-by gave him a *krama* to cover himself. He then walked to the Central Police Station, a few hundred yards from where the attack occurred, lodged a complaint, and next day wrote a detailed account of what had happened, in which he accused the security police of responsibility for the outrage.

When parliament summoned the Minister to explain himself, Kou Roun baldly declared that it was not the job of the police to protect opponents of the regime. The National Assembly, he added menacingly, itself contained people of that ilk, and he proceeded to name Hou Yuon, Hu Nim, So Nem, Uch Ven and Chau Seng (who happened at the time to be a fellow member of the cabinet). Uch Ven, on behalf of his colleagues, then tabled a censure motion. But before it could be debated, Sihanouk issued a statement sharply reprimanding the deputies for their 'hostile attitude' towards his security chief and denouncing the Left in general and Khieu Samphân in particular as irredeemable troublemakers. Shortly afterwards, Hu Nim, the political director of the Prince's newspaper, *Réalités Cambodgiennes*, who had used its pages to express his indignation against what he termed this 'cowardly [and] brutal intimidation', was sacked. Two days later, fifty more leftists were taken in for questioning and *l'Observateur* and three other pro-communist papers were closed. Fifteen of those detained, including Khieu Samphân and a group of Pracheachon leaders, headed by Non Suon, were placed in preventive detention in police cells. The Prince told a cabinet meeting that they were guilty of treason and 'sowing hatred of the monarchy', and that the Pracheachon's 'moral and political swindle' could not be allowed to continue. But no charges were brought and a month later they were all freed.

In one sense the targeting of the Left was almost a compliment. The contrast between 'this small group of resolute men . . . [who] put their beliefs before their own safety' and the 'spinelessness' of the mass of the Sangkum, in Ambassador Gorce's words, cried out for all to see. Sihanouk himself had written earlier that year that though there were 'probably only a few dozen true communists in Cambodia, they are militants of real worth, deeply convinced in their beliefs, doctrinally rigid but flexible in their tactics, capable of any sacrifice – even of their own self-respect – in order to attain their goals.' But at another level the systematic resort to illegality, justified, when not instigated, by Sihanouk himself, augured ill for the future.

To most Westerners, the early 1960s were a golden age for Cambodia. One American resident recalled: '[There was] complete peace and internal security, something which the country has not known within living memory . . . By 1960 . . . one could travel anywhere without danger from outlaws or hindrance from the authorities.' The same week that Khieu Samphân was imprisoned, Sihanouk presented the prizes for 'the most glamorous motor-car and owner' at a *Concours d'Elégance* at Kep, won by Miss Kenthao de Monteiro and her Ford Thunderbird, with a Dutch businessman's wife the runner-up. To the affluent, Cambodia was an oriental paradise ruled by an entrancing playboy prince. The other side of the coin was better not thought about. 'He is so thirsty for power that he can admit no opposition,' Gorce had written that spring. 'The system [he has created] accepts no contradiction. [To maintain it] the police impose a sort of reign of terror.'

In wonderland, the worm was in the fruit.

While Sihanouk tilted quixotically at the communists' public emanations, the movement's secret leadership went ahead with preparations for a Party Congress to transform the PRPK into an authentic Marxist-Leninist party. The original intention had been to meet in 1958, but the Vietnamese, whose approval had been sought, hurried slowly, rightly suspicious that the Khmers wanted to strike out on their own. Finally, however, Hanoi was persuaded that the existing structure, with separate rural and urban organisations, must be changed, and it was agreed that a Congress should take place in the second half of 1959. Then came Sieu Heng's defection. Everything else was pushed into the background; the priority became damage control.

Tou Samouth, Nuon Chea, Saloth Sâr and a fourth man, probably So Phim, formed a 'General Affairs Committee' to head the movement nationally, pending the election of a new leadership. In Phnom Penh, Nuon Chea remained Secretary of the City Committee, but delegated the running of it to Sâr, who brought in Ieng Sary and a younger man named Vorn Vet, whom he had known at Krâbao, to help him. In the countryside, repression intensified. The Vietnamese spoke of a campaign of terror; a Cambodian communist document charged that Sihanouk's police were 'slaughtering everyone'. The physical destruction of the rural bases was aggravated by a breakdown in communications. In some cases, contacts between the Party leaders in Phnom Penh and surviving rural networks remained severed for four years. In the summer of 1960, Sâr himself set out for Kompong Cham, to follow up, apparently successfully, a chance report that a group of former guerrillas were eking out a living as charcoal burners in a remote, forest area of Krauchhmar. Others, like Ke Pauk's district committee in nearby Chamkar Loeu, would remain out of touch until 1963.

The draft statutes and political programme which the leadership had prepared were circulated to Party cells in the spring of 1960, together with a set of 'rules for Party members'. Sâr claimed later that he had done most of the drafting himself, but officially the documents were presented as a collective effort. The programme of the new Party, which was to be called the Kampuchean Labour Party, one step up from a 'People's Revolutionary Party' but not quite on a par with the 'Workers' Party' in Vietnam, was in most respects orthodox enough. It was defined as 'a Party of the working class . . . [taking] Marxism-Leninism as its foundation, closely linked to the masses, organised on the basis of democratic centralism and [using] criticism

and self-criticism as its guiding principle'. The issue of exactly who constituted this 'working class' was fudged, but that could hardly be otherwise in
a backward, agricultural country with virtually no industrial proletariat. As
Sâr knew from his reading in Paris, China had taken similar doctrinal liberties – as indeed had Vietnam. That apart, the programme's analysis of the
classes in Cambodian society was conventional (albeit rather woolly), and
the Party's declared aims – 'to nationalise the main means of production . . .
to realise the people's democratic dictatorship . . . [and then] go on to construct a fully worked out socialist system on the basis of the slogan "From
each according to his abilities, to each according to his work", under the
dictatorship of the proletariat, in order to advance towards communism' –
were textbook Leninism.

Buried among the platitudes were two neuralgic issues: the relationship
between the new Party and the Vietnamese communists; and policy
towards Sihanouk's regime.

In practice, the two were inseparable. In a letter to the Cambodian leaders at the end of 1959, the Vietnamese Party had reiterated the policy of
qualified support for Sihanouk's government that they had first laid down
four years earlier.

The validity of this approach, at least in Vietnamese eyes, had been
underscored by Khrushchev's concept of a 'parliamentary road to socialism', proclaimed at the Soviet 20th Party Congress in February 1956 and
subsequently enshrined as the doctrine of 'peaceful transition' at the World
Communist Conference held in Moscow a year later. The idea was that,
in the era of peaceful coexistence between the two world blocs, communist parties could achieve power through elections, rather than by class
struggle and revolutionary violence. To Sâr, after the Cambodian Party's
experiences in 1955 and 1958, this rang very hollow. But for Hanoi it was
a useful weapon to keep the Khmers in line (since they were in no position to argue that the entire world communist movement was wrong), and
from 1956 onwards, Sieu Heng, with Vietnamese encouragement, had
urged that parliamentary rather than class struggle be given priority.

He was not alone. Keo Meas and the *Pracheachon* group also favoured
'peaceful transition'. So did So Phim and Mey Mann. Ieng Sary, who had
watched the PCF grappling with Moscow's new line shortly before he left
Paris, likewise spoke in favour of it during discussions at cell meetings. On
the other hand, it was plain that it was not a concept the Vietnamese
accepted for themselves. In January 1959, the VWP Central Committee
authorised the resumption of armed struggle in South Vietnam on the
grounds that Ngo Dinh Diem's government was 'a US tool for aggression
and enslavement'. By 1960, widespread insurgency had broken out and, in

mid-September, the VWP's Third Congress approved the launching of a full-scale guerrilla war. At about the same time, armed struggle resumed in Laos. It was hard for the Khmers to understand why they alone should be bound by a doctrine which their communist allies breached.

Two weeks after the VWP Congress ended, twenty-one delegates gathered at the home of Ok Sakun, a member of Vorn Vet's North Phnom Penh Party branch (and a veteran of the Cercle Marxiste) who held a senior post at Cambodian Railways and occupied a government villa not far from the Phnom Penh station. To avoid attracting attention they arrived singly or in small groups, and Sakun posted watchers to give the alarm if strangers approached. They met for three days, from September 30 to October 2. 'During that time, none of us was allowed to leave,' Ieng Sary recalled. 'We slept on the floor, piled together like logs. It was hot and we couldn't wash properly – and the whole place started to smell.' No record of the discussion has survived and it is probable that none was kept. But the programme approved by the meeting marked a crucial first step towards an independent political line.

The 'feudal ruling class led by S[ihanouk]', they declared – far from playing a positive role, as the Vietnamese argued – was 'the most important enemy of the Kampuchean Revolution' and 'a tool of the American imperialists'. The plight of the Cambodian people was 'two or three times worse' than before 1955 (when Hanoi had imposed the policy of co-operating with Sihanouk). Cambodians would therefore have to struggle to 'annihilate the feudal regime' – peacefully or otherwise:

> The Kampuchean Revolution must have [the option of] two forms of struggle: peaceful means; and means that are not peaceful. We will do our utmost to grasp firmly peaceful struggle, for that form of struggle does not cause heavy losses to the people. However, [we] must be ready at all times to adopt non-peaceful means of struggle if the imperialists and feudalists . . . stubbornly insist on forcing us to take that road . . . [If and] when the enemies of the revolution force us to arm ourselves, the countryside will provide us with favourable . . . conditions . . . For that reason, the revolution [should make use of] its potential to build, consolidate and develop its strength in the rural areas . . . The countryside is an important base for the revolution because in Kampuchea, like all undeveloped countries, the national revolution is a peasant revolution. The cities are . . . the nerve-centre of the ruling class and the imperialists, the places where the enemies of the revolution can concentrate great power to suppress [us].

The arguments, and the conclusion, even down to the phrase 'non-peaceful means of struggle', echoed, word for word, those employed by the Vietnamese themselves eighteen months earlier to justify to the

Russians the resumption of their own armed struggle. The only argument Hanoi could raise against it – that Sihanouk's policy of neutrality made him fundamentally different from Ngo Dinh Diem, in South Vietnam, or Phoumi Nosavan, the right-wing leader of Laos – the Cambodians implicitly rejected. The underlying message was that, regardless of Vietnam's preferences, the possibility of armed struggle was once again firmly on the Cambodian Party's agenda. But since the Khmers' position was couched in such careful terms, there was little the Vietnamese could do except reply in the same veiled fashion. Three weeks after the Congress, Ho Chi Minh sent birthday greetings to Sihanouk, wishing him 'good health and happiness in order that you may lead the Kingdom. . . to everlasting progress and stability'. Subsequent Vietnamese messages to the Cambodian Party leadership urged patience and promised that after South Vietnam and Laos had won their freedom, 'the Cambodian revolution will also triumph.'

There were other signs of a growing divergence of views. The Cambodian programme did not mention neutralism or the ICP or the PRPK, and it contained only one brief reference to Vietnam and Laos. Instead of Indochinese solidarity, the new Party's stated goal was to 'secure total independence . . . construct a national economy [and] build one Cambodian nation, independent, sovereign and prosperous'. Vietnam's hopes of an Indochinese Federation were fast receding.

The Congress elected a new leadership. Tou Samouth became Secretary with Nuon Chea as his deputy and Saloth Sâr in the third-ranking position. All three were full members of the CC Standing Committee. Ieng Sary, whose only real qualification was to have headed the Cercle Marxiste in Paris, was promoted over the heads of the former resistance leaders to become fourth in the hierarchy – a striking demonstration of the growing power of the returned students. He and So Phim, who ranked fifth, were alternate Standing Committee members with the right to participate in the Committee's deliberations but not to vote. Then came two other veterans of the Indochina War – Mang, the Zone Secretary of Son Ngoc Minh's former base area in the South-West, and Prasith, an ethnic Thai from Koh Kong province. Minh himself, who did not attend, was in tenth position, while Keo Meas was placed eleventh and last in the rank order.* According

---

*Vietnamese documents name the eighth- and ninth-ranking members of the CC as 'Keo Can ma li' and 'Ray Thon'. According to Ieng Sary, the first of these was probably Thang Si (a veteran ethnic Lao leader from Stung Treng); the second may have been Non Suon (who was also called Chey Suon). Those known to have been present at the Congress were Tou Samouth, Nuon Chea, Saloth Sâr, Ieng Sary, So Phim, Mang, Prasith, Keo Meas, Ping Sây, Non Suon, Vorn Vet, Thang Si, Vy (a former student, subsequently a journalist with

to Ping Sây, the question of appointing Rath Samoeun and other Hanoi regroupees to the Central Committee was not raised because 'they were regarded as having excluded themselves'.

The 1960 Congress was the first at which the Khmer communists had chosen their own leaders and defined their own political strategy free of Vietnamese tutelage. Previously such decisions had been taken for them by Nguyen Thanh Son's All-Cambodia Work Committee. This time, not only was no Vietnamese Party delegate present, but the Party programme – while clearly drafted with Hanoi's reactions in mind – was not submitted to the Vietnamese in advance. As Keo Meas put it, 'From now on we were responsible for our own fate. We dealt with them as equals.'

To underline the fresh start, all members of the movement were required to reapply for Party membership.

At the same time, a major effort began to rebuild the rural bases, which would be the key to the Party's future if, as the Standing Committee plainly expected, 'peaceful struggle' led nowhere. Mang and Prasith returned immediately to the South-West; Ruos Nhim left his farm in southern Battambang to restore the old Issarak networks in the hill districts around Samlaut; So Phim went back to the Eastern Zone. Even the citified Ieng Sary was reported to have travelled through the provinces trying to revive dormant cells. As things turned out, it was a wise precaution.

Throughout 1961, Sihanouk was obsessed by the deteriorating relationship with Thailand and South Vietnam and the threat from Son Ngoc Thanh's Khmer Serei movement. For the communists, the pressure was off. The government announced that it was dropping legal proceedings against the *Pracheachon*, *l'Observateur* and two other left-wing newspapers suspended the previous autumn, and that their printing presses and equipment would be returned 'because gagging or imprisoning convinced militants has never served any purpose . . . except to turn them into martyrs'.

But the communist challenge was not forgotten. During a tour of the provinces that summer, the Prince delivered a series of harsh – and prophetic – warnings about the Khmer communists' ultimate aims. A communist regime in Cambodia, he said, might achieve more than the Sangkum had done, but at the price of 'depriving the individual of all that

---

the Pracheachon group, who went on to become deputy Zone Secretary in the North-East) and 'another, unnamed cadre from the North-East'. It is almost certain that Chan Samân, Ney Sarann, Ruos Nhim and Son Sen were also there. Others who may have attended include Mok, who worked with Mang in the South-West, and Kong Sophal, shortly afterwards to become head of the new Party Youth League. Ok Sakun was present but took no part in the debates.

is dear to him – basic freedoms and the joys of family life – and turning him into a producing machine which over time has all human values sucked out of it'. Such a system 'reduced men to the level of brute beasts'. Cambodians would gain nothing and had everything to lose by adopting it. His statements reflected the bitterness and frustration of a man who saw disaster approaching but felt he could do nothing to avert it. 'Sooner or later the communists will win,' he warned glumly. 'Laos is lost already. So is South Vietnam. Cambodia's turn will follow.' American policy was so inept and so out of touch with Asian realities, he concluded, that the precarious power balance that enabled Cambodia to live at peace would inevitably collapse – and not to the West's advantage.

The months of tergiversation that these bleak forebodings engendered came to an abrupt end on January 10 1962.

That day twelve members of the Pracheachon were arrested in the province of Kompong Cham for allegedly collecting military intelligence on behalf of the Vietnamese communists, trying to suborn the monkhood and to infiltrate the Sangkum. The so-called 'plot' was a government fabrication timed, like the 1958 campaign against the *Pracheachon*, to unite the country behind Sihanouk ahead of the parliamentary elections which were due in June. But this time the stakes were higher. 'I will not pardon these traitors, I'll have them shot . . . because that's what they were planning for me,' Sihanouk raged. On January 12, Non Suon was detained, followed by the *Pracheachon*'s editor, Chou Chet. Keo Meas went into hiding: But the newspaper refused to be silenced. 'Our country is [supposed to] have a constitution . . . and to have proclaimed its attachment to the Declaration of Human Rights,' it protested. 'Yet our staff are under day-and-night surveillance by armed police with binoculars and cameras.' Shortly afterwards it accused the government of 'harsh oppression, contrary to democratic principles', and appealed to Britain and Russia, the co-Presidents of the 1954 Geneva Conference, for the release of Non Suon and Chou Chet. More arrests followed and on February 10 the newspaper's offices were sealed. A month later, the only other surviving 'progressive' mouthpiece, a weekly called *Pancasila*, was also closed. The pretext was that it had reprinted an eighteenth-century Khmer poem which urged court functionaries not to mistreat people.

So ended the communists' first and last attempt to operate legally in Sihanouk's Cambodia. On the Prince's instructions, the Military Tribunal condemned Non Suon and his companions to death. No Pracheachon candidate stood in the 1962 elections and to all intents and purposes the group ceased to exist. But there was still a left-wing presence in parliament. Bluff, outspoken Hou Yuon and Hu Nim, the former Treasury Director, both won re-election and Khieu Samphân became an MP for the first time and soon afterwards a cabinet minister.

In July 1962 the Left suffered another body-blow when the Communist Party Secretary, Tou Samouth, was arrested and killed. He had been living, disguised as a labourer, in the southern part of Phnom Penh. One day he left home to buy medicine at the market for his sick child. The security police were waiting. They allegedly took him to a house belonging to the Defence Minister, Lon Nol, where he was tortured but refused to talk; then he was killed and buried on a piece of wasteland in the Stung Meancheay district of the city.

It was never convincingly established who betrayed Samouth. But it was a setback to the Party's urban networks scarcely less damaging than Sieu Heng's defection had been to its rural organisations.

It also opened the way for Saloth Sâr to become Party leader.

Here, too, fate played its part. Normally Nuon Chea, as Tou Samouth's deputy, should have become acting Secretary. But a year earlier Nuon had fallen under a cloud. The Vietnamese communists' Work Committee in Phnom Penh, headed by Hay So, had given him a substantial sum of money – 10,000 Vietnamese dong – to purchase a house. The transaction, which was supposed to be secret, had been approved by Hay So's deputy. But word leaked out and rumours started circulating that Nuon had obtained the money improperly. There was muttering about his loyalty, and the fact that he was related by marriage to the defector Sieu Heng. According to the Vietnamese, who worked with him closely at this time, he became depressed and for much of the next year, withdrew from Party work. Sâr, as the third-ranking member of the leadership, became Samouth's *de facto* deputy. As a result, when Samouth disappeared, Sâr, rather than Nuon, became acting leader in his place.

Samouth's murder raised the question of whether the leadership should leave the capital for the safety of the countryside. Sâr argued against it. An election would have to be held to elect a new Party leader, and he was well aware that his chances of success in Phnom Penh were far better than in an unfamiliar rural area, where the influence of resistance veterans like So Phim was preponderant.

Over the next six months, the situation appeared to stabilise, and in February 1963, while Sihanouk was on a visit to China, it was announced that the sentences on Non Suon and his companions had been commuted to life imprisonment. At the end of that month, the Party convened its Second Congress.

The meeting was held in the apartment of a Sino-Khmer sympathiser, in the centre of Phnom Penh just west of the Central Market, and lasted a single day.* According to Ieng Sary, only seventeen or eighteen people attended, fewer than in 1960. Sâr was elected Secretary of a new four-man Standing Committee; Nuon Chea remained Deputy Secretary; and Sary and So Phim became full members. Four new Central Committee members were also appointed: Mok, a former monk from Takeo, who had become Mang's deputy in the South-West; Ruos Nhim from the North-West; Vorn Vet from Phnom Penh; and Son Sen. Keo Meas and the mysterious 'Ray Thorn' (almost certainly Non Suon) were dropped. The Party's name was changed – it now became the Kampuchean Workers' Party, which put it on the same level as the Workers' Party in Vietnam – and its programme was modified to pay lip-service (in Cambodian conditions it could hardly have been more than that) to the November 1960 Moscow Declaration, which reaffirmed the validity of the parliamentary road to socialism.

The Congress was held not a moment too soon.

Throughout the winter of 1962, student agitation had been growing. In February, a banal protest over the right of schoolchildren to cycle along footpaths in Siem Reap degenerated into rioting after it was learnt that one young demonstrator had died in police custody. Two officers were beaten to death in revenge. Faced with the fury of the mob, the police and provincial militia fled and took refuge in the forest. For three days, from February 24 to 26, Siem Reap was in the hands of the students. Police headquarters were ransacked, filing cabinets emptied and their contents burned. Next day the Minister of Education arrived to negotiate with student leaders. He and his officials were taken hostage and paraded through the streets before a jeering crowd.

When Sihanouk returned from Beijing on March 1, he was beside himself with rage. Over the next forty-eight hours he publicly berated the Prime Minister, Prince Kantol, for incompetence, dismissed the government, announced the dissolution of the Sangkum and of parliament and ordered new elections. He then asked Keng Vannsak, at the time Dean of the Literature Faculty of Phnom Penh University – who had visited Siem Reap shortly before the rioting occurred and whom he suspected of fomenting the unrest there – to become Prime Minister. Vannsak politely declined. In a show of force, troops were sent to occupy the radio station and other key installations.

Two days later, on March 4, with political tensions at their peak, Sihanouk published a list of thirty-four known and suspected leftists drawn

---

*Ieng Sary told a French Maoist delegation in September 1978 that the Second Congress took place on March 2 1963. Earlier Khmer Rouge documents, issued in 1971 and 1973, said it was held on February 21–22 1963. Vietnamese Party histories do not give a precise date.

up by the security police,* and after treating them as 'cowards, hypocrites, saboteurs, subversive agents and traitors', demanded that they form a new government (reserving for himself, however, the right to name the Police, Interior and Defence ministers), 'in order to show the country what they are capable of'. On March 7, he summoned the entire group to a meeting at the Prime Minister's Office, where each of those present was asked to put in writing whether or not he agreed to form a government. To no one's surprise, they all wrote that Sihanouk himself was the only man capable of guiding the country forward.

Two of the thirty-four failed to appear. Chou Chet, who had been released from prison three weeks earlier, had already left for the maquis. Saloth Sâr went into hiding as soon as the list was published.

By mid-March, the storm had passed and Sihanouk's imprecations against parliament, the government and the Sangkum were quietly forgotten. It was, one Western Ambassador grumbled, 'a crisis Cambodia could have done without'. Yet there was method in the Prince's madness. After spending three weeks in China, singing the praises of a foreign communist state, he had given Cambodians a trenchant reminder that communism had no place in his own kingdom. From now on, each new opening to communism abroad would be matched by increased repression at home. The thirty-four named leftists found police guards posted outside their houses. The schools where many of them taught, Chamraon Vichea, Kampuj'bot and Sotoân Prychea In, were placed under surveillance, and several left-wing newspaper editors imprisoned for 'causing trouble and disorder'.

The clamp-down on the communists that spring was the signal for the withdrawal to the countryside that had been in the air since 1960. To Sâr, with the leadership election over, there was no longer any reason to delay. For the first time in his political career, the veil of anonymity that cloaked his activities had been rent, leaving him suddenly exposed. It was not an experience he enjoyed.

Ieng Sary took a different view. He claimed later to have argued that the possibilities for legal and semi-legal activities were not yet exhausted and that to abandon Phnom Penh was premature, but Nuon Chea – whose name had not appeared among the thirty-four, and whose cover was appar-

---

*The thirty-four comprised Keng Vannsak and Son Phuoc Tho (both left-wing Democrats); Hou Yuon, Chau Seng and Khieu Samphân (then members of the cabinet); Uch Ven, Son Sen, Toch Phoeun, Thiounn Prasith, Sim Son, Saloth Sâr, Ieng Sary, Sien An, Tiv Ol, Siet Chhê, Sok Lay, Chou Chet, Keat Chhon, Hu Nim, Ping Sây, Chi Kim An and Ok Sakun (who would all eventually be revealed as communists) and twelve others.

ently intact – had insisted that those in the Party leadership whose identities had become known should not continue clandestine work lest they
inadvertently expose others. Moreover, he told Sary, a spell in the maquis
would help to get rid of his 'petty bourgeois Parisian attitudes' and develop
a 'proletarian spirit'. Reluctantly, Sary acquiesced.

Sâr set out first, on March 31, with a guide provided by Hay So's successor, a South Vietnamese communist named Sau Kouy. Two weeks later,
on April 13, Sary followed. He left Phnom Penh at ten o'clock at night,
he recalled, hidden under sacks of charcoal in the back of an ancient lorry.
'Every time we stopped at a checkpoint, the driver got out and gave the
soldiers money to let us through without a search. For once I was glad
Cambodia was corrupt.' Next day they arrived at the commune of Snuol,
on the border of Kratie and Kompong Cham. From there, he walked for
a day through the jungle to an encampment of the South Vietnamese communists, the Viet Cong, concealed in thick forest just across the
Cambodian border. Son Sen followed the same route a day later.

The communist leaders were rational men. The decision to re-base in
the countryside marked the same kind of tactical retreat that the Chinese
Politburo had made in abandoning Shanghai in 1933 and the Vietnamese
when they left Hanoi in 1946.

But Sâr and his companions were not Chinese or Vietnamese, they were
Khmer. Just as Sihanouk always consulted an oracle before taking any grave
decision, and Cambodia's agricultural plan was determined, with all the
seriousness in the world, on the basis of such astrological portents as the
royal oxen's choice of grains after the ploughing of the sacred furrow, so
too the Cambodian communists inhabited a mental realm in which the
irrational had an accepted place. Outwardly the Cambodian revolution was
returning to its roots, to the maquis where the Issarak had fought.
Psychologically the transition was more complex. In Khmer thought, the
fundamental dichotomy is not between good and evil, as it is in Judaeo-
Christian societies, but between *srok* and *brai*, village and forest.
Subconsciously the centre of gravity of the revolution had shifted from the
civilised regions, the towns and settlements, where man dominated nature,
to the jungles, the wild places, where dark, unknown forces roamed and,
throughout the centuries, sages – the Khmer Daeum of Cambodian antiquity – had repaired to seek spiritual power.

5

Germinal

L IFE AT THE Vietnamese base was dire. Ieng Sary said later that Sâr had
sent him a message a few days after arriving to tell him not to come,
but the letter never reached him. The camp itself was spartan: a few peasant huts scattered in the forest, backed up by a system of tunnels and bunkers. It was close to the headquarters of the South Vietnamese National
Liberation Front (NLF) in the village of Ta Not, though Sâr and his colleagues were probably at first unaware of the NLF base's presence. Sunlight
could not penetrate the jungle canopy, and Sary remembered that their
faces took on a waxy pallor, 'a jaundiced, sickly look'. Truong Nhu Tang,
afterwards Justice Minister in the South Vietnamese Provisional Revolutionary Government, spent several years working in the area:

> We lived like hunted animals . . . [Each of us had] two pairs of black trousers
> and shirts, a couple of pairs of underpants, a mosquito net and a few square
> yards of light nylon (handy as a raincoat or roof) . . . The rice ration for both
> leaders and fighters was 20 kilos a month . . . a nutritional intake which left
> us all in a state of semi-starvation . . . Food was a continual pre-occupation;
> the lack of protein especially drove us to frenzied efforts at farming or hunt-
> ing whenever it was feasible . . . I will always remember one chicken feast,
> where we shared out a single bird among almost 30 of us . . . I think I have
> never eaten anything quite so delicious . . . Elephants, tigers, wild dogs, mon-
> keys – none of these were strangers to our cookpots . . . Another dietary sup-
> plement which I eventually learned to eat was . . . jungle moth . . . With the
> wings off and barbecued quickly over a flame it wasn't exactly a tasty morsel,
> but it wasn't that bad either . . . But [nothing] alleviated the chronic malnu-
> trition or the tropical diseases that battened on the weakened men.

For the Khmers, these discomforts, which Sâr had already experienced,
albeit in milder form, at the old Khmer Viet Minh base at Krâbao, just
across the border three or four miles away, were compounded by physical
and mental isolation.

For the first few weeks there were only three of them – Sâr, Ieng Sary
and Son Sen. As at Krâbao, nine years earlier, they were advised not to leave
the camp or to have any contact with nearby Khmer villages. The South

Vietnamese air force was already carrying out bombing raids along the border, and if the base's location had become known, not only the Khmer encampment but the much more important NLF headquarters would have risked attack. None the less, it was galling. Sâr and his colleagues were no longer naïve young students but the leaders of a national communist party which, in theory, at least, was the equal of Vietnam's. At Ta Not, they felt treated as outcasts. They could listen to the radio and once a week they had a meeting with their Viet Cong 'hosts', who briefed them on current events. That was it.

As the government crackdown in Phnom Penh intensified, the size of the Khmer contingent gradually increased. Keo Meas and his family, who had been in hiding in the Eastern Zone, arrived during the summer. A courier office was established in a Cambodian village about four hours' walk from the base, enabling Sâr to send out messengers independent of the Vietnamese. But by the end of the year, there were still only six or seven of them. It was a strange, artificial existence, like being inside a pressure cooker. There were explosions over trivial incidents. Keo Meas, in particular, felt excluded by the others, who had been together in Paris. In reality all of them were in limbo.

Early in 1964, Sâr persuaded the Viet Cong to allow the Khmers to set up their own camp 'to avoid political complications and build the revolution step by step by ourselves'. The new base, known as Office 100, was also on the Vietnamese side of the border and, like its predecessor, under tight Viet Cong control. Ney Sarann, who arrived from Phnom Penh in August to become the base administrator, found that they had to 'rely on the Vietnamese for everything, food, materials, security, the lot . . . To go from one bureau to another, we had to have a Vietnamese guard to escort us . . . They were the hosts and we had to obey.' But Sarann also noted that, in terms of policy and ideology, 'little by little . . . we were developing an independent stance.'

The first concrete sign of that came in the autumn, when an enlarged plenum of the Central Committee – the first such meeting the Cambodians had ever held* – took place in a forest on the Cambodian side of the border. It lasted several weeks and ended by producing a draft resolution which endorsed 'all forms of struggle', including 'armed violence' against Sihanouk's government, and emphasised 'self-reliance', the Khmers' codeword for freedom from Vietnamese control.

---

*The meeting was apparently attended by all twelve members of the Central Committee – except Son Ngoc Minh and possibly Thang Si – and by Chan Samân, Chou Chet, Keo Meas, Kong Sophal, Koy Thuon, Ney Sarann and Sien An. No CC Plenum had taken place between 1960 and 1963, and before 1960 there had been only a provisional leadership. The holding of regular CC meetings was a further step towards the respect of Party norms.

Copies were run off using a glass bottle as a roller, stencils of waxed paper on which a text was scratched by hand with a stylus, and ink made by burning rubber, and despatched throughout the country. Son Sen's younger brother, Nikân, remembered that the messengers hid them in cakes or bottles of *prahoc*, the pungent fish relish which is the Khmers' national dish, or rolled them inside tubes of bamboo, to avoid discovery by Sihanouk's police.

In January 1965, the Central Committee met again to put the resolution into its final form. The version approved by this Second Plenum attacked 'modern revisionism' — meaning Khrushchev's ideas about the 'peaceful transition' to socialism — and affirmed the role of 'revolutionary violence' in the struggle against 'imperialism and its lackeys'. To the Khmers, Sihanouk was just such a 'lackey' — 'a chieftain of the feudalists and imperialists [wreaking] terror on the Cambodian people', as one of their pamphlets put it — and therefore a legitimate target. To the Vietnamese, he was a patriot. But this and other issues which risked creating discord — such as the Central Committee's decision not to accept Vietnamese advisers — were either finessed or omitted from the written text altogether.

Alongside these incremental, snail's-pace steps towards an independent Khmer communist identity, Sâr began to reflect on the kind of system he wanted to create in Cambodia.

'After 1963,' he explained, 'when I withdrew to the countryside, my opinions and my thinking and views changed a lot, because I was in a very isolated, remote, rural area, far from the city . . . I lived among the masses [and] I realised I could trust them.' Towards the end of his life, he spoke again of this period on the border. In Paris, he said, he had understood little, because he had been surrounded by intellectual high-fliers; in Cambodia, he was in contact with 'the lower levels, the monks, the ordinary people, so I understood the problems.' In the villages his modest educational level was not only no hindrance but in many ways a help, for he was closer to peasant realities than his university-trained colleagues. Nevertheless, it was a journey in the dark. 'We applied ourselves to [define a direction] and then to put it into practice without knowing whether it was right or wrong.' There was no model, no blueprint, but rather 'a mixture [of influences], a little of this, a little of that . . . I copied no one. It was what I saw in the country that made an impression on me . . .'

Those remembered fragments are revealing. Not for Sâr and his colleagues the certainties of 'scientific socialism', in which the writings of Marx and Lenin, of Mao and Stalin, would provide ready-made answers for every problem that might arise. The Cambodians sought their path to communism intuitively. 'Marxism–Leninism,' Sâr said later, 'resides within the movements forged by the people, and the people's movement in each country puts together [its own] Marxism–Leninism. Cambodia is also [able to] contribute to the building of Marxism–Leninism.' The inference was that there was no need for Party members to study the Marxist classics and therefore no need to translate them into Khmer. Sâr acknowledged that foreign experience could provide useful lessons. But the goal was an authentically Khmer doctrine, rooted in Cambodian identity.

Such an unschooled, almost mystical approach to communism had no precedent either in Chinese or in European Marxism.

There were superficial parallels in Mao's writings. Sâr believed, like him, that revolutionary truth came 'from the masses, to the masses'. Both romanticised the peasantry. To Mao, in his more megalomaniac moments, the peasants were pure and unsullied, 'poor and blank . . . Poor people want change, want revolution. A clean sheet of paper has no blotches, and so the purest and most beautiful words can be written on it.' To Sâr, like Jean-Jacques Rousseau, they epitomised the noblest, most profound yearnings of their race. But Mao's revolutionary romanticism was tempered, in theory at least, by an awareness of reality. As he had explained in *On New Democracy*, which Sâr had read in Paris: 'We are not Utopians and cannot divorce ourselves from the actual conditions confronting us.' It was necessary to 'seek truth from facts' and 'test the correctness of ideas in action'.

To Sâr and his colleagues, such considerations simply did not apply. What mattered was the vision, the inspiration. Whereas Mao was the product of an intensely rational, literate society, with highly developed traditions of philosophical debate, Sâr's cultural heritage was irrational, oral, guided by Theravada transcendentalism and by *k'ruu*, spirit-masters, whose truths sprang not from analysis but from illumination. As the Cambodian communist leaders groped towards a model for their future revolution, they never once, either at Office 100 or later, carried out any form of investigation of the social conditions in which that revolution was to occur. The contrast with Maoist China could hardly be greater.

What the two countries did have in common, as did Vietnam, was that the bulk of the population were peasants. Accordingly, the Cambodian Party identified lower-middle peasants as the 'semi-proletariat' of the countryside and poor and landless peasants as a 'core element of the working class . . . the lifeblood of the revolution' – a heresy in Marxist terms, which it tried to gloss over by insisting on the leading role of the country's minuscule industrial workforce, at the time only 10,000 strong. But efforts to create clandestine pro-communist workers' associations were unsuccessful, partly because no senior Khmer communist had a working-class background. Whereas Mao had started his communist career as a trades union organiser and Ho Chi Minh had been a deckhand and a washer-up in a London restaurant, neither Sâr nor Nuon Chea nor Ieng Sary nor So Phim nor any other Cambodian leader had experience of working-class life. They were peasants, students of peasant origin, or both: to all of them, industry was a closed book.

The Cambodian Party's inability to penetrate the country's nascent proletariat was to have far-reaching consequences. Sâr and his colleagues did not ask themselves what they were doing wrong. Instead, in a pattern of behaviour that would be repeated whenever they were faced with failure, by 1965 they decided that the factories had been 'infiltrated' and 'the workers transformed into enemy agents'. From then on, factory workers were systematically refused admission to the Party.

For a communist party, whose *raison d'être* is to represent the working class, this was an astounding decision. Khieu Samphân would argue later that the Party had no choice:

> [It is true that] the Cambodian communist party was based on the poor peasantry rather than the working class . . . But you can't use that as an argument for saying it wasn't a Marxist party, or that there was no economic basis for a communist party in Cambodia. In fact, we applied the criterion of 'material conditions' quite correctly, because the poor peasants were the most impoverished, the most oppressed class in Cambodian society, and it was this class that was the foundation of the Cambodian Party.

The problem with this approach was that it stood Marxism on its head. To Marx, the industrial proletariat represented progress; the peasantry represented backwardness and petit-bourgeois extremism. For the peasantry to develop proletarian characteristics, its role in society would have to change in ways that, to an orthodox Marxist, could come only from the transformation of its economic role.

To Sâr, the way out of this difficulty was provided by Buddhism.

The Khmer word *viññān*, which is derived from the Sanskrit *vijñāna*, 'to distinguish or comprehend', represents, in Theravada metaphysics, the last of the five sensorial aggregates which condition life. It is usually translated as 'consciousness' and is the animating force of all human endeavour. To 'proletarianise' the peasantry, all that was needed, in this Buddhist-inspired scheme of things, was 'proletarian consciousness'. Class, which to Marxists everywhere else, including the Chinese, was determined by a person's economic activity, was for Cambodian communists a mental attribute.

That this was totally heretical did not matter. To Khmers, it seemed an attractive and logical idea.

Theravada Buddhism is intensely introspective. The goal is not to improve society or redeem one's fellow men; it is self-cultivation, in the nihilistic sense of the demolition of the individual.

In the 1960s even more than today, religious belief provided the primary value-system of ordinary people throughout South-East Asia. Sâr himself had been a Buddhist novice. The first communists, like Tou Samouth and Son Ngoc Minh, had studied at the Higher Pali Institute. So had younger leaders like Siet Chhê and Mok. Both within the Party leadership and among the rank and file, the grammar of Theravada Buddhism permeated Khmer communist thought, just as Confucian notions helped to fashion Maoism. In neither country was this a conscious undertaking. Sihanouk had called his policy 'Buddhist Socialism', and his doctrine of neutrality, the Buddhist 'middle path'. The Cambodian communists eschewed such labels. But just as Mao had sinified Marxism, Sâr gave it a Buddhist tincture. The result, in both cases, was that it ceased to be a foreign transplant and flourished in autochthonous minds.

The idea that 'proletarian consciousness' could be forged, independent of a person's class origins or economic status, became the central pillar of Khmer communism.

The distinction between peasants and workers was gradually elided. They were described as 'worker-farmers', led by a Party composed of 'proletarianised peasants' and intellectuals who had 'reformed their thought and overcome their origins . . . to build [their] class position'. Beneath the thinnest of Marxist veneers, this was the same alliance of 'peasants and intellectuals' that Kropotkin had seen as the motive force of the French Revolution in 1789, and with the same primary goal: to overthrow the King – in other words, the feudal system personified by Sihanouk – and install an egalitarian communist polity based on a refurbished version of the old revolutionary trinity, '[collective] liberty, [mass] equality and [militant] fraternity', all endowed with a distinctive Khmer flavour.

Nineteen sixty-three was a fateful year. It was when the seeds were sown from which, a decade later, Cambodians would reap the whirlwind.

A month after Saloth Sâr fled to the maquis, China's President Liu Shaoqi came to Phnom Penh to pay a goodwill visit. It was emblematic in several respects. Shortly before Liu's arrival, the Cambodian security services, alerted by Chinese intelligence, uncovered a Taiwanese plot to plant explosives in a tunnel under the highway from the airport and blow up the royal limousine as he and Sihanouk drove by. Given Taiwan's alliance with the US and recent precedents involving South Vietnam, the Prince concluded that the CIA was still bent on replacing him with someone more to Washington's liking, a conviction that would be amply confirmed in the course of the next few years. The visit itself, meanwhile, signalled Cambodia's increasing tilt towards Beijing, the bale-fire of Asian communism – complemented, but in no way diminished, by stepped-up repression of communists at home.

This pattern of growing amity with left-wing regimes abroad matched by increased reliance on right-wing forces domestically would continue and amplify throughout the decade.

Sâr remembered it as 'a black time', when 'the enemy furiously arrested and killed our Party members and [we] suffered great losses'. That was certainly true in Phnom Penh, where Khieu Samphân and Hou Yuon were both forced to resign their ministerial portfolios (albeit retaining their parliamentary seats), and Vorn Vet's city committee was under intense pressure. It was standard practice for a Party or a Youth League member in the capital to know only two others – his immediate superior, who gave him instructions, and the next man below him in the chain. Nuon Chea, the *éminence grise* of the clandestine Party in Phnom Penh, explained:

> Operating secretly, our organisation has the following rules. Three members are required to form a cell . . . If there are [more than three] people, we form two separate cells, having no contact with each other . . . If the enemy discovers one cell, the other can continue its work. There are no direct contacts among cells.
>
> In each factory [or school, or university], there is one leading cadre. Only he knows this . . . Contacts between [him] and the leadership . . . are arranged through a third person. If the enemy captures the leading cadre, he will not be able to identify the leadership, only the go-between . . . [Such designated leading cadres] should not live with their families. When they do, things get complicated. [If they have to leave in a hurry], it takes them longer to escape. We have had some bitter experience with these things . . .
>
> Contacts between publicly well-known leaders, such as those who work in parliament, and secret leaders are arranged through two or three other persons. We employ various . . . signals, such as a scarf in front of a house. If the scarf is in place, it is safe to enter; if not, it means the enemy is there* . . . [Our] couriers are not allowed to know our real places of residence. Otherwise captured couriers could be forced to reveal them . . . We have learned to abandon a safe house at once if a messenger is two or three hours late.

---

* Like many other Khmer Rouge techniques, this was inherited from the Issarak. Thiounn Mumm's uncle, Bunchan Mol, described in his memoirs how, at a bar where Khmer nationalists used to meet in the 1940s, a picture of a dog would be displayed whenever a French informer was present.

By the early 1960s, Phnom Penh had one policeman for every sixty inhabitants, one of the highest urban ratios in the world. A significant number came from a special security unit reporting directly to the Prime Minister's Office. Communist Party organisers, if caught, were shot without trial. Charles Meyer, who was one of Sihanouk's close advisers throughout the 1960s, wrote that 'several hundred' disappeared in this way. The figure seems exaggerated, but the practice was not. Even sympathisers put their lives on the line. One youth from a suburban lycée was detained at pistol-point by plain-clothes police, stripped naked and thrown into a small cell, just big enough to stand up in, before undergoing a week-long interrogation, accompanied by beatings during which his head was immersed in water until he passed out. No charges were brought. He spent the next two years in prison.

In the provinces, on the other hand, the communists fared better. The rural networks that had been destroyed under Sieu Heng were gradually rebuilt, and by 1965 the Party's strength was back up to 2,000 members, the same level as at the time of the Geneva Conference, ten years earlier.

Still more encouraging for the long term was that, after a decade in which it had seemed that none of the conditions was present for a communist movement to exist in Cambodia, Sihanouk's policies were at last beginning to create a social and political climate more favourable to communist goals.

The student population had decupled. By the time Sâr left Phnom Penh, 600,000 young people were in full-time schooling. But the only posts they wanted were in the administration where there were limitless possibilities for 'squeeze' and, in consequence, more than a hundred candidates for every available position. The result, as the Prince himself noted, was to throw into unemployment ever-increasing numbers of disaffected, semi-educated young men, too proud to work in the rice-paddies as their parents had done but unable to find anything better. At a humbler level, peasants, ruined by bad harvests and usurious interest rates, flooded into the towns to form a lumpen-proletariat of coolies and *cyclo-pousse* drivers living at the margins of society, often in wretched conditions. Everywhere, living standards stagnated when they did not actually fall – except among the elite, where, in the words of one observer, there prevailed 'a total absence of civic sense and insatiable appetites for gain'.

Foreigners liked to say that Sihanouk himself was honest but those around him were not. That was too kind. As Head of State, he had no need to be corrupt. Years later, when opponents accused him of selling Cambodia to the Vietnamese, an old lady in the suburbs of Phnom Penh demurred. 'It's his country, isn't it?' she said. 'He can sell it if he likes.'

Sihanouk's rule was a continuation of the tradition that makes the verb 'to reign' translate into Khmer as 'to eat the kingdom'. His mother, Queen Kossamak, his consort, Monique, and her relatives, did just that. So did hundreds of lesser figures: ministers, civil servants, courtiers and cronies whom Sihanouk could never bring himself to discipline, let alone dismiss. He was well aware of the consequences. 'This ball and chain of corruption will finish by bringing me down,' he wrote in 1962. But the one serious attempt to do something about it, by his high-minded uncle, Prince Monireth, was countermanded before it began lest it incriminate his entourage.

Sihanouk's political sleight of hand, which in the early days had dazzled and bemused supporters and opponents alike, now began to pall. To many, even within his own circle, it seemed that Cambodia was being ruled by whim and royal bullying. The new French Ambassador, Jean de Beausse, likened him to a satrap, subjecting all around him to public ridicule:

> The Prime Minister, members of the Cabinet, MPs, civil servants, no one is spared! All have to stop their official business and submit to the Prince's fantasies. Last year it was manual labour. [Everyone had to spend one day a month working on dams and irrigation canals.] This year it's sport. A small thing, you may say . . . but infuriating for middle-aged men who have to display themselves in volley-ball and basket-ball matches, which naturally the Head of State's team . . . always wins. [They] make a sorry spectacle in athletics shorts . . . and are roundly jeered by the good people of Phnom Penh, whom the Prince invites to watch . . . There was a time when, to succeed in life, one had to be seen at the Court of Versailles. Here it is at the sports field of the princely residence at Chamkar Mon that anyone who is anyone in Phnom Penh has to be seen . . . The country, or rather the Prince, is in a frenzy. Everything is sacrificed to sport. A fifth of the annual budget is being spent on preparing the South-East Asian Games which are to be held in Phnom Penh in December . . . At a time of acute financial crisis . . . [in a country] where hospitals are cruelly lacking, such expenditure is scandalous.

For more and more young Cambodians, Sihanouk was not the solution but the cause of their country's problems – the 'incarnation', to use his own word, of an outdated, venal, feudal system which had brought the appearance of modernisation but not the reality.

Teachers like Ping Sây and Dam Pheng in Phnom Penh, Koy Thuon in Kompong Cham, Tiv Ol in Prey Veng and Nikân at Kompong Kdei led 'strings' of colleagues who sought out promising students to join 'core groups'. The most committed among them would be invited to become members of Kong Sophal's Revolutionary Youth League, which made them feel 'that we were part of the leadership of Angkar, because the Youth

League was associated with the Communist Party – so we were above the ordinary people.' Phal, a twenty-year-old at the lycée at Takhmau in 1965, later a Khmer Rouge military commander, was one of this new generation of communist recruits:

> The teachers . . . were closely watched by Lon Nol's police. They couldn't do anything – even if they went out to a restaurant together it would attract the attention of the police. But we students could meet as we liked, and no one could claim there was anything wrong in it. So it was the senior students who recruited the younger ones. That was happening at lycées all over Cambodia.
>
> At that time, everything was by word of mouth. We had no documents. I never read any books in French about Marxism or Mao's ideas. Nor were there any books in Khmer for us to read. What we knew about communism came from the senior student who led our 'string' . . . One senior student might be in charge of several 'strings' of younger students, each with three or four members [who would] meet and hold discussions. [To us], communism meant the hope of a better and more just society. I joined the movement because I was against injustice . . . That was something that we heard about from the old people; they would tell us stories of how they had been oppressed. I wanted to overthrow the government, and that was the goal that Angkar – the revolutionary organisation – was striving for. Maybe I didn't have any clear idea of what kind of system we were going to put in the place of the old one, once it had been overthrown. But I knew I wanted to overthrow the existing government.

By the mid-1960s Cambodia's schools had become a breeding ground for anti-royalist youth in the same way that, fifteen years earlier, teachers committed to the Democratic Party had fostered student networks supporting Son Ngoc Thanh. Clandestine pro-communist 'strings' were bolstered by legal organisations – the General Association of Khmer Students (AGEK), set up in 1964 by a law graduate named Phouk Chhay; and a Teachers' Association, founded by Uch Ven and based at Kampuj'bot. Both were secretly controlled by Vorn Vet's Phnom Penh city committee. In Paris, the AEK's successor, the Union of Khmer Students (UEK), manipulated by the Cercle Marxiste, which Thiounn Mumm now headed, ensured that Angkar would not lack intellectual supporters when the revolution finally came. A similar organisation was set up among Khmer students in Moscow. There were even attempts – partly successful, judging by the portraits of Mao Zedong that the authorities sometimes found in the dormitories of the younger monks – to recruit inside the Buddhist *wats*, which in earlier times had been a source of support for both the Thanhists and the Issaraks.

Sihanouk's domestic policies and, even more, his style of rule, gave the communists all the scope they needed to build the peasant–intellectual alliance which Sâr viewed as the driving force of the future revolution. Certain aspects of his foreign policy also helped their cause.

Every time the Prince proclaimed, as he did with increasing frequency from 1962 onwards, that within ten years South Vietnam would turn communist and Cambodia would inevitably follow, the effect was to boost the Party's appeal. His aim was to shock the West into adopting wiser policies in Asia. But at home his message was taken literally: it meant that the monarchy was doomed and communism was the country's future. The same was true of the tilt towards China. The more the Prince praised the Chinese, the more China's experience appeared to be a model for Khmers to emulate.

Ultimately even more dangerous for Cambodia's stability was the slow derailment of the Prince's neutrality policy.

This was not entirely Sihanouk's fault: it is hard to maintain a balance between East and West when the intelligence service of one side keeps trying to assassinate you for fear you might get too close to the other. But the effects were profoundly destructive. In November 1963, South Vietnam's President Ngo Dinh Diem and his brother were murdered after an American-inspired coup. Three days later, incandescent with fear and rage, the Prince announced the rejection of all future US military and economic aid. 'Look what happens when you put your trust in the Free World,' he spat. 'The Americans have so many ways to eliminate those they no longer need.' The killings confirmed his belief that the US would not rest until Cambodia became part of an anti-communist front and was sucked into a war which America was doomed to lose. When Diem's murder was followed by the assassination of President Kennedy and the death of another American ally, the Thai Premier, Field-Marshal Sarit, Sihanouk gloated that 'our enemies have departed one after the other . . . Now they are all going to meet in hell, where they will build military bases for SEATO . . . The gods punish all the enemies of peaceful and neutral Cambodia.'

Two other major decisions were taken that November.

Sihanouk announced the nationalisation of the banks, insurance companies and import-export businesses – a move intended to compensate for the ending of US aid by giving the Cambodian economy a dose of austerity: instead, it alienated businessmen and created huge, new opportunities for corruption among the political elite. Then, a few days later, the Prince took public and very feudal vengeance on a hapless young Khmer Serei who had fallen into the government's hands. The man, Preap In, had entered Cambodia from South Vietnam on a safe-conduct from the governor of Takeo which had been authorised by Sihanouk himself. He was arrested and brought in an iron cage to a hastily arranged Sangkum Congress. When he refused to recant, a mob of the Prince's supporters screamed abuse and pelted him with refuse for two hours until he was hauled away to face a military tribunal. It was, a Western diplomat commented, 'an odious proceeding . . . a spectacle from another age – a mixture of buffoonery and barbarism as a man was pilloried in total disregard of assurances given for his safety.' Preap In was sentenced to death and, a few weeks later, taken before a firing squad. His execution was filmed and, for the next month, a fifteen-minute newsreel, showing his last moments in unsparing detail, was screened before every séance in every cinema in the country. Decades later, people still squirmed at the memory. It was a reminder of Khmer savagery that Cambodians, in the 1960s, would have preferred to forget.

For the next eighteen months, relations with the US continued to deteriorate until, in May 1965, Cambodia severed diplomatic ties. South Vietnamese raids on frontier villages, occasionally with the participation of American advisers, had become an almost weekly occurrence, leaving dozens of villagers dead or injured. Then, as the first US marines waded ashore at Danang, hawks in Washington began urging the right of 'immediate pursuit' into Viet Cong sanctuaries. In response, Sihanouk sought closer ties with North Vietnam and the South Vietnamese NLF. The result was a structural distortion, a skewness, in Cambodian policy. No longer could he be the tightrope walker, balancing leftists against rightists in Cambodia and Americans against Chinese abroad. Instead, the communists who supported him in Beijing and the anti-communists who supported him at home were tugging in opposite directions. It would take another five years before the tightrope snapped. But as Sihanouk himself later admitted, the fatal error had been made in the *annus horribilis*, 1963. 'There is perhaps one thing I regret,' he conceded tetchily twenty years later. 'This was to have rejected . . . the humiliating aid accorded by the United States to my army and my administration.'

In January 1965, the same Central Committee plenum that approved the use of 'revolutionary violence' had decided that Saloth Sâr should lead a Cambodian Party delegation to Hanoi. Up till then the Khmer communists had been in contact only with the VWP's Southern Bureau. Now the aim was to establish full Party-to-Party relations and to agree guidelines for the Cambodian Party's future strategy in light of the spreading war between the communists and the American-backed government in southern Vietnam.

By the time Hanoi's agreement had been obtained, it was the beginning of April. Sâr set out on foot for north-eastern Cambodia, accompanied by Keo Meas. They then took the Ho Chi Minh Trail, at that time no more than a network of footpaths used by porters, across the mountains of southern Laos to the Annamite cordillera. The journey took two and a half months.

On arrival, Sâr met Ho Chi Minh – whom he would see twice more during his stay – and Le Duan, the VWP General Secretary, who had had dealings with the Cambodian communists as head of the Southern Bureau in the 1940s and '50s. Le Duan was twenty years Sâr's senior, a dour, rather uninspiring man who owed his rise to his bureaucratic skills and unquenchable patriotism. Over the next five months they met more than a dozen times. But if Sâr had hoped for Vietnamese support for the launching of armed struggle against Sihanouk, he was sorely disappointed. Hanoi would have been reluctant in any circumstances to see insurgency spread to Cambodia. But since the beginning of the year, a number of events had occurred which made it unthinkable. The entry into the war of American ground troops had focused all Vietnam's attention on the south; the last thing it wanted was a risky distraction elsewhere. Cambodia's decision to break diplomatic relations with the US meant that objectively Sihanouk had become an ally. Still more important, during the spring, probably in March or April, the Prince had agreed to allow the South Vietnamese NLF to establish permanent sanctuaries on the Cambodian side of the border, rather than simply turning a blind eye to Viet Cong incursions, as had been the case before. Negotiations were also under way for an agreement to allow arms shipments from China to the NLF to pass through the Cambodian port of Kompong Som, to supplement the supplies being laboriously manhandled down the Ho Chi Minh Trail.

Le Duan tried his best to persuade the Cambodians that political struggle was a noble end in itself and an 'organisational and military preparation for armed struggle', and he assured them that 'if the Americans widen the war, we will make the transition to armed struggle accordingly'. But the bottom line, bereft of high-sounding phrases, was that, for the moment at least, Sihanouk must be left in peace. To Sâr, Vietnamese policy was still stuck in the same groove it had been in since 1955.

A more subtle negotiator, a Zhou Enlai or a Ho Chi Minh, might have been able to sweeten the pill. That was not Le Duan's style. He showed an almost visceral insensitivity to Cambodian concerns. All the old Vietnamese hobby-horses were trotted out anew: the Khmer struggle was inseparable from those in Vietnam and Laos; Vietnam had had to wait for the success of the Chinese revolution before it could defeat the French, similarly Cambodians would have to wait for a Vietnamese victory before their revolution could triumph; after Vietnam won its freedom, Cambodia's would automatically follow. The Cambodian Party's stress on 'self-reliance' was excessive, Le Duan argued. The principal contradiction in the world was between socialism and capitalism, not between the oppressed peoples and imperialism as the Cambodians wished to believe, and in these circumstances what mattered was international solidarity. To bolster his case, Le Duan proposed that the Cambodian leader review the history of the two Parties' relations from texts in the Vietnamese archives – certain that the accounts of Vietnam's heroism and selflessness in aiding the Khmers' struggle over the years would win him round. Sâr spent days poring over Party documents and drew his own conclusions:

> I found that from 1930 . . . to 1965, all the Vietnamese Communist Party documents depicted the Cambodian . . . and Lao People's Revolutionary Parties as branches of the Vietnamese Party . . . Both [Parties] implemented the rules, the political line and the strategy of the Vietnamese Party. Until I read these documents myself, I trusted and believed the Vietnamese. But after reading them I didn't trust them any more. I realised that they had set up Party organisations in our countries solely to achieve their aim of the Indochinese Federation. They were making one integrated party to represent a single, integrated territory.

The Vietnamese leader apparently assumed that his arguments had carried the day and that, even if the Cambodians had reservations, in practice they would do as they were told. Sâr remembered the talks as 'uncongenial'. The Vietnamese paid lip-service to the Khmer Party's independence, he said later, but 'in their bones they did not recognise us [as equals] . . . We had many differences. We were unable to reach a common view.' Characteristically he hid his feelings behind a wreath of smiles. His hosts failed to register the malaise developing between them.

Accompanied by Son Ngoc Minh, now Secretary of the Hanoi-based branch of the Party, Sâr also addressed a meeting of former Khmer Viet Minh 'regroupees', many of whom had taken Vietnamese wives and found jobs as public servants in the Vietnamese administration.

He appears to have said little about the proposed shift to 'non-peaceful struggle' or about 'self-reliance' – partly, no doubt, to avoid irritating Le Duan, but also out of wariness towards this group of Khmer communists, four or five hundred strong, representing almost a fifth of the Party's total strength, who had lived outside Cambodia for ten years, whose thinking was deeply influenced by Vietnam and whose allegiance must have seemed uncertain. The Vietnamese, too, despite their ostensible embrace of the new Cambodian Party leader, showed proof of a certain caution. After Sâr had left, they distributed to the Khmer colony in Vietnam copies of Lenin's text *Left-wing Communism: An Infantile Disorder*, as a warning against Cambodian 'adventurism'; and a secret military unit, codenamed P-36, was set up under Le Duc Tho to train Khmer officers, so that if and when armed struggle did break out in Cambodia, Vietnam would have its own force of tried and tested Khmer cadres, loyal to Hanoi, ready and waiting to assume the leadership of native Khmer communist units.

The 1965 visit was a watershed. Until then, the Cambodians had chafed at what they saw as heavy-handed Vietnamese paternalism, but had never seriously questioned that they shared a common objective. After the talks in Hanoi, Sâr concluded that Vietnam's interests were incompatible with, if not inimical to, those of Khmer communism. On ground made fertile by old hatreds, the seeds of enmity were re-sown. But that was not apparent at the time, and both sides continued to act as though they were brothers-in-arms.

The Vietnamese put Sâr in contact with the Lao Party leadership and then arranged for him to fly on alone to Beijing, while Keo Meas, who had a gall-bladder condition, remained in Hanoi for medical treatment.

Sâr arrived in the Chinese capital towards the end of December and spent about a month there. He stayed at the *Ya fei la peixun zhongxin*, the Chinese communist training centre for African, Asian and Latin American revolutionaries situated near the Summer Palace, a few miles north-west of Beijing. Officially his host was Deng Xiaoping, then CCP General Secretary. However, most of his meetings were with Peng Zhen, Deng's deputy and Mayor of Beijing. He also saw the Head of State, Liu Shaoqi, who had just played host to Sihanouk on a goodwill visit to China, but not Mao or Zhou Enlai. Four months later, Peng would become the first top-level victim of the Cultural Revolution, and Liu and Deng would quickly follow. But in the winter of 1965, that great upheaval was still only a sardonic twinkle in Mao's eye. None of the Chinese Politburo as yet had any inkling of the cataclysm about to be unloosed – still less a young Cambodian communist who did not speak Chinese.

Nevertheless, there was already an impassioned, radical edge to the political climate in Beijing which Sâr found exhilarating after his tribulations in Hanoi. Where Vietnamese minds were focused on the practicalities of war with America, China was caught up in a vast ideological campaign – the 'Socialist Education Movement' – to transform the thinking of hundreds of millions of Chinese peasants. While the Vietnamese worried about sanctuaries and logistics, the latest weaponry from Moscow and munitions flows from Beijing, the Chinese published a seminal article, under the signature of the Defence Minister, Lin Biao, entitled 'Long Live the Victory of People's War!' Its message – that the peoples of Asia, Africa and Latin America were now the standard-bearers of the world revolution, who would storm the citadels of capitalism in the United States and Europe – galvanised communists throughout the developing world. To Sâr, here was the justification for all his arguments that had fallen on deaf ears in Vietnam:

> The liberation of the masses is accomplished by the masses themselves – this is a basic principle of Marxism-Leninism [*the Chinese leaders wrote*]. Revolution or people's war in any country is the business of the masses in that country and should be carried out primarily by their own efforts: there is no other way . . . It is imperative to adhere to the policy of self-reliance, rely on the strength of the masses in one's own country and prepare to carry on the fight independently even when all material aid from outside has been cut off . . . In the last analysis, whether one dares to wage . . . a people's war . . . is the most effective touchstone for distinguishing genuine from fake revolutionaries . . . The peasants constitute the main force of the national democratic revolution against the imperialists and their lackeys . . . The countryside, and the countryside alone, can provide the . . . bases from which the revolutionaries can go forward to final victory.

The principal contradictions, the article said, were 'between imperialism and the oppressed peoples . . . [and] between feudalism and the masses' – which was the Cambodian Party's position – not between 'the imperialists and the socialist camp', as the Vietnamese maintained. It added, for good measure, that the outcome of revolutionary struggle was decided not by weapons but by 'the proletarian revolutionary consciousness and courage of the commanders and fighters . . . The experience of innumerable revolutionary wars has borne out the truth that a people who rise up with only their bare hands at the outset finally succeed in defeating the ruling classes who are armed to the teeth.'

Rhetoric aside, the Chinese were, at heart, no more anxious than Vietnam to see armed struggle develop in Cambodia – and for exactly the same reasons: Sihanouk's co-operation was vital to the pursuance of the war in the South.

But Peng Zhen and his colleagues found cleverer ways to say so. They approved of the Cambodian Party programme; endorsed its anti-revisionist stance; praised its 'authentic Marxism-Leninism' and its reliance on the peasantry; and encouraged Sâr to 'struggle actively . . . to confront American imperialism'. Two younger men – a radical theorist named Chen Boda, who had been for many years one of Mao's secretaries; and Zhang Chunqiao, an up-and-coming Shanghai leader – were particularly supportive. Together they discussed 'the concept that political power comes from the barrel of a gun, class struggle and proletarian dictatorship'. The Chinese Party even offered material support, which Sâr politely declined on the grounds that the time was not yet ripe. Of course, it was easier for China to appear sympathetic to the Khmer communists' cause. Unlike Hanoi, Beijing was not directly at war with an American expeditionary force which, by early 1966, numbered 300,000 men. The Chinese were always looking for new allies in their dispute with the Soviet Union – indeed, had there been no Sino–Soviet dispute Sâr's task would have been far harder – and despite the fraternal relationship between Vietnam and China (which, throughout the 1950s and '60s was far and away Hanoi's biggest provider of military aid), the emergence of an independent Khmer Party to offset Vietnamese dominance in Indochina was certainly not against Chinese interests.

The month Sâr spent in Beijing marked the start of a *de facto* alliance. 'If we want to keep our distance from Vietnam,' he told Keo Meas on his return, 'we will have to rely on China.' He was much encouraged, he said, by the warm welcome he had been given, and 'reassured to have friends in China . . . who give us spiritual, political and strategic support . . . [Now] we need have no more doubts about the correctness of what we are doing.'

In February 1966, after a final meeting with Le Duan in Hanoi, Sâr and his companions set out for home along the Ho Chi Minh Trail. The journey took more than four months, almost twice as long as the outbound trip, because of massive American bombing to disrupt North Vietnamese supply columns. Office 100 also suffered from the intensification of the war. Towards the end of 1965, the US government had authorised B-52 raids along the length of the South Vietnamese/Cambodian border. They were audible as far away as Phnom Penh, reverberating like distant thunder. After being forced to move several times to avoid enemy 'search-and-destroy' operations, Ieng Sary, Son Sen, Ney Sarann and most of the rest of the communist leadership were taken by the Viet Cong in January 1966 to a more secure camp at Loc Ninh, fifty miles further east in a thickly forested, mountainous region adjoining Cambodia's Memot district. Three young Khmers, together with twenty Viet Cong guards, stayed behind to assure communications with the interior.

At Loc Ninh, the top military leader of the COSVN, General Nguyen Chi Thanh, took aside Ieng Sary and Nuon Chea, who was then passing through on one of his periodic visits from Phnom Penh, and urged them to continue supporting Sihanouk's neutrality policy, the same argument that Le Duan had advanced the previous autumn. Thanh's action angered Sâr, saw as an attempt to go behind his back. In this mood he summoned members of the Central Committee and senior Zone officials to an enlarged Third Plenum in September to discuss an entirely new Party programme, inspired by the Maoist credo that the world as a whole, and Asia in particular, were in the throes of a revolutionary upsurge in which imperialism was doomed to extinction in the flames of 'people's war.'

The meeting lasted six weeks. By the time it ended, on October 25 1966, the Cambodian leaders had taken three crucial decisions.

They changed the name of the Party: instead of being a 'Workers' Party', like that of Vietnam, it would henceforth be known as the Communist Party of Kampuchea (CPK). The decision was kept secret, however. The Party rank and file were not informed. Nor were the Vietnamese.

They decided to move the Party headquarters from Office 100, which had resumed operations during the summer, to Ratanakiri, in the far north-east. The excuse given to the Vietnamese was that the expanding war in the south made it necessary to find a safer location. But the real reason was to escape COSVN surveillance. At Office 100, Ieng Sary complained, 'even telegrams from Nuon Chea in Phnom Penh had to go through the Vietnamese first'. In Ratanakiri, the Cambodians would have a base of their own, free from Vietnamese snooping and, unlike Office 100, it would be on Cambodian territory.

They also agreed that each Zone Committee should begin making preparations for the launching of armed struggle in the rural areas. The wording was still cautious. The Cambodians were not yet ready openly to defy their Vietnamese 'elder brothers'. But they approved the expansion of underground networks in the towns; a more active political struggle; and the development of 'political violence' and eventually 'armed violence' when circumstances warranted. There was nothing in this that Hanoi could seize on as unacceptable, but between the lines, one participant noted, it prefigured 'the start of the internal war', signifying an implicit rejection of Le Duan's plea that the Khmers wait patiently for the Vietnamese to decide when they should begin to act.

The Party leaders' decision to adopt a more aggressive stance towards Sihanouk's regime was vindicated by events in Phnom Penh.

That summer, the Prince had called parliamentary elections. For the first time since the 1950s, he did not choose the candidates himself. It was an odd move on his part, though not exactly a surprise: he had been threatening something of the sort for the previous three years. It may be that, after ten years of hand-picked parliaments which constantly failed his expectations, he wanted a change – and, in the absence of any better method, determined to 'let the dice fall where they may'. If so, the results were not what he had hoped for. The new Assembly, elected on September 11, was more conservative than its predecessors, being composed almost entirely of bureaucrats and businessmen. A month later, the Prince sprang a second surprise. Instead of designating the Prime Minister and the cabinet himself, as was his custom, he invited the Assembly to make the choice. Again, the result was not to his liking. On October 18, the deputies selected Lon Nol, who a week later inaugurated a government made up entirely of right-wing sympathisers. 'The only thing the new members of the cabinet have in common,' the

French Ambassador cabled Paris, 'is that none of them is a Sihanouk loyalist and, in all likelihood, none would have been chosen by him.'

It is not easy to understand, even with hindsight, what led the Prince to administer this self-inflicted wound. He had been leading Cambodia for twenty-five years, first as King, then as President of the Sangkum, finally as Head of State. The corrosion of power, the weariness that comes from a satiety of one-man rule in a country where absolutism masquerades as democracy and judgement is sapped by the fawning of courtiers, is certainly part of the answer. By the mid-1960s, Sihanouk's photograph was on every page of every Cambodian newspaper, accompanied by articles of nauseating servility. If a Western journalist incautiously described Cambodia as 'minuscule', newspaper editors around the world would be inundated for weeks afterwards with letters, signed by the Prince himself, listing all the thirty-nine United Nations member states with smaller territories and the fifty-four with smaller populations. His susceptibility became so outlandish that illiterate villagers at provincial rallies were treated to long, ranting accounts of articles in *Le Monde* or the *New York Times* supposedly denigrating their ruler.

It was not that he was unhinged. But the nature of the system he had inherited and built was such that none of his closest advisers dared reason with him. 'There is a malaise developing,' one diplomat wrote before the election. 'The Prince's behaviour is plunging even his most faithful supporters into perplexity and dismay.' Earlier that year Indonesia's President Sukarno had been eased out of power in an army coup. Lon Nol – an imperturbable, heavily-built man, who professed a mystic loyalty to the monarchy – might have no thought of emulating the Indonesian military. But it was better not to tempt fate. For the next six months, Sihanouk worked assiduously, and not without difficulty, to circumscribe the new Premier's powers. Assailed by self-doubt, he took refuge in amateur film-making. In the 1950s one canny observer had compared Cambodia to a stage-show in which the Prince had the starring role. Now theatre and reality were one. He wrote, directed and starred in a series of maudlin romances with his wife, Monique, as the leading lady, and sundry members of the government, including the Chief of Staff, Nhek Tioulong, in supporting roles. Sihanouk monopolised the screen as he did his country. Neither his films nor, from then on, his policies, would have any lasting success.

To Sihanouk, Lon Nol's emergence as Prime Minister at the head of a right-wing government more independent than any that had gone before was a challenge that needed to be blunted. To the Cambodian communists, it was a godsend. As Defence Minister for more than a decade, Nol had been in charge of anti-communist repression. As Prime Minister, he was the ideal target against which to mobilise opposition to Sihanouk's regime. A week after his appointment, the CPK Central Committee denounced his government as 'lackeys of the United States' and attacked Sihanouk by name 'not just as a King who reigns but worse, a reactionary . . . who should be overthrown'. Lon Nol's nomination justified 'the use of political violence at a high level', it declared. The revolutionary movement had arrived at the stage of the 'direct seizure of power . . . and if [Lon Nol] oppresses and terrorises [the population] strongly, we will have to resort to armed struggle'.

The fate of the Indonesian Communist Party, which had supported Sukarno, gave legitimacy to this new strategy. After his overthrow, some 300,000 Indonesian Party members had been slain in anti-communist massacres. The lesson for Sâr was that the bourgeoisie could not be relied on. The Vietnamese strategy was wrong. It was not possible for the communists to 'live together with Sihanouk' because the contradictions between them were too deep. Policy towards non-Party sympathisers was therefore modified. In theory, the guideline remained 'to unite with all those who can be united with', but in practice the movement behaved more and more as though 'all those who are not with us are against us'. Khieu Samphân, Hou Yuon and Hu Nim, who had kept their seats in the September elections, began to distance themselves from the Prince. It marked the start of the politics of exclusion that would become one of the hallmarks of the Cambodian Party's style. From now on, the CPK required its supporters 'to draw a clear line of demarcation between the enemy and ourselves'.

The new line on armed struggle was first applied in the North-West, where Ruos Nhim had strong support in the villages south of Battambang.

Nhim's career as an Issarak commander stretched back to the 1940s. When the idea of relaunching guerrilla activity was broached at the Central Committee meetings of late 1964 and early 1965, he had immediately started preparing his followers. One of their first actions had been to mine a railway bridge over the Dam river, between Battambang and Poipet, damaging a passenger train. After that, Lon Nol and Nhek Tioulong began installing guard posts in the villages and new roads were driven through the jungle to make troop movements easier. The soldiers' presence, in turn, brought petty exactions and harassment, fanning local discontents. In December 1966, after the CPK's Third Plenum had endorsed the principle of 'armed violence', Nhim stepped up his campaign. 'We decided to arm the people . . . [to] attack Lon Nol's secret police and soldiers,' one of his aides wrote later. 'The government then sent in reinforcements.' The spiral of violence and counter-violence was beginning to bear fruit.

The following month, Sihanouk, still preoccupied with what he saw as the political challenge from the Right, departed for his annual dietary cure in France. His absence, he thought, would be salutary, making it possible for him to install after his return a cabinet more responsive to his wishes.

In the event that was what happened, though not for the reasons Sihanouk anticipated.

Lon Nol spent much of January and February in Battambang supervising state purchases of the rice harvest. The previous year 60 per cent of the crop had been sold to Chinese middlemen acting for the Viet Cong and smuggled out to liberated zones in South Vietnam and Laos, creating a huge shortfall in state revenues. The problem, as a US National Security Council study noted, was that the Vietnamese communists paid far higher prices than the Cambodian government. To make the peasants sell to the state, compulsion was necessary. In southern Battambang, where centrifugal tendencies were strong because of the province's links with Thailand, where Phnom Penh had always had difficulty in making its writ run and where Ruos Nhim's communist agitators had been hard at work for two years, this was a recipe for disaster.

It is impossible to tell which of the various factors involved was most responsible for the events that followed. Kong Sophal, who had become North-West Zone Deputy Secretary, remembered 'pushing the peasants more and more strongly until early 1967, at which point the conflict became ripe for the internal war to explode'. The villagers were angry over the forced rice sales and the corruption of local officials. There was resentment at the authorities' demands for free labour and 'voluntary financial contributions' to carry out government projects, and over the seizure of peasant land-holdings, which were given to army officers for development as large, private estates or redesignated as youth settlements to provide work for the urban unemployed. There was friction, too, caused by the resettlement in the area of Khmer Krom refugees who had fled from South Vietnam, a group notably recalcitrant to authority and – understandably, after two hundred years of persecution by the Vietnamese – obsessed with its own survival.

Whatever the precise mix, the pot soon boiled over. In mid-February clashes occurred between soldiers and local people in the gem-mining town of Pailin on the border with Thailand. Anti-government demonstrations broke out in Battambang, where three city officials were hacked to death. In the thickly wooded hill-country around Samlaut – which had been an Issarak stronghold twenty years before – village armouries were raided and the population fled into the jungle. On March 11, protesters demanded that the Pailin garrison be withdrawn, a call which Sihanouk, just back from France, angrily rejected.

Thereafter the situation degenerated rapidly. On the morning of April 2, villagers in Samlaut attacked a group of soldiers overseeing rice purchases, killing two of them and stealing several rifles. Two hundred peasants then marched to the nearby village of Kranhoung, the site of a large youth settlement, a fitting symbol for all the aggravations the authorities had made them endure, which they proceeded to burn to the ground. By nightfall, army posts in two other villages had been attacked and a commune chief killed. Over the next four days more attacks followed, two road bridges were destroyed and another local official was executed. Then the first units of paratroops arrived to begin what Sihanouk euphemistically called 'repression and pacification'.

By late April, two hundred rebels had been captured and nineteen killed, against four dead on the government side. The Prince himself visited Samlaut, offering an amnesty and making liberal distributions of food and clothing. However, attacks on army posts continued, and the inhabitants of three more villages fled their homes to join the rebels. Communist cadres, accompanying a force of five hundred peasants, some of them armed, retreated to Mount Veay Chap, a highland area covered by dense jungle some twenty-five miles north-east of Samlaut. But the army poisoned wells and seized and burned their rice stocks, and by mid-May their position was critical. At that point Nuon Chea conveyed to Nhim and Kong Sophal a directive from the CPK Standing Committee 'to stop the war and negotiate with the enemy'. Shortly afterwards talks began with the newly appointed Battambang governor, In Tam, through the intermediary of the Abbot of Wat Thvak, a large Buddhist monastery near the mountain. The government undertook not to carry out reprisals – a promise which it did not keep – and a month later, on June 20, Sihanouk was able to announce that the rebellion was over.

The 'Samlaut events', as they became known, posed problems both for the Communist Party and for Sihanouk.

For the former, the welling up of peasant anger had been too good an opportunity to miss. But it had happened too quickly for the Party to be able to exploit it to the full. 'Non-peaceful means of struggle' had been on the agenda as a principle ever since 1960. But the Central Committee's Third Plenum, in October 1966, had fixed no date for it to begin and still less a co-ordinated programme for a nationwide uprising. That was to await the establishment of Sâr's new headquarters in Ratanakiri and the organisation of a courier service capable of assuring communications with the rest of the country. In the meantime all that had been decided was to start 'active preparations' for rebellion. On the other hand, having ordered a vigorous campaign against the compulsory rice purchases, Sâr could hardly ask Nhim and Sophal to douse the anger they themselves had fanned. Yet the fact was that the Samlaut peasants were out on a limb. Only in one small area, covering about 300 square miles, where communist influence was strongest, did the countryside catch fire. By May it was obvious that unless a peaceful outcome could be found, the movement would be ruthlessly crushed.

Sihanouk, too, was in a quandary.

The idea that Cambodian peasants, his children, as he liked to call them, should rise up against him – *Samdech Euv*, 'Monseigneur Papa', the father of the nation – was politically intolerable, and he flew into a rage when *Le Monde* and other French newspapers interpreted the unrest in those terms.

His explanation was that it was the work of Khmer Viet Minh cells which had been left behind in the former Issarak base areas in 1954 and lain dormant ever since, awaiting their opportunity. Their 'backstage bosses', he claimed, were none other than the three left-wing Sangkum MPs, Khieu Samphân, Hou Yuon and Hu Nim, who were deliberately stirring up trouble to destabilise Lon Nol's right-wing government. How much of this the Prince actually believed is another matter, but it was his story and he stuck to it. He therefore followed a two-handed policy, showing royal indulgence to the majority of the four to five thousand rebel villagers who eventually returned to their homes, but giving the army a free hand to take vengeance on the rest as soon as the insurgency was over.

The punitive raids which followed took hundreds of lives and left much of the population of Samlaut and the surrounding area irremediably hostile to the regime. The communists' jungle bases were bombed, villages strafed and burned to the ground. 'The pacification of the disturbed region,' wrote Donald Lancaster, a Briton who was then working in Sihanouk's office, 'was undertaken with the rude vigour peculiar to soldiery who have been promised a monetary reward for each [rebel] head they might forward to military headquarters.' Another foreigner, returning to Cambodia after a year's absence, found Phnom Penh alive with 'ghoulish details . . . of trucks filled with severed heads that were sent from Battambang . . . so that Lon Nol should be assured that his programme was being followed.'

Whether or not this was actually true, it was what everyone, both senior Cambodian officials and foreign ambassadors, believed, creating an expectation of brutality that would increasingly affect the behaviour both of the regime itself and of its left- and right-wing opponents.

A striking example of this concerned Khieu Samphân, Hou Yuon and Hu Nim. On April 22, Sihanouk announced on the radio that the three MPs might be brought before the Military Tribunal for a confrontation with their accusers, after which, if appropriate, the government would bring charges. This was not a threat to be taken lightly. Two days later, Samphân failed to return home. 'My mother served dinner as usual at 7.30 p.m.,' his younger brother, Khieu Sengkim, remembered. 'The two of us sat at the dining table and waited for [him] to arrive . . . We stayed there till 11 without eating, listening for every footstep and every sound. Then my mother broke down and began to cry. She cried all night.'

When it was learnt that Hou Yuon had also vanished, most people assumed that Lon Nol and, in the background, the Prince himself, were responsible. Grisly rumours began to circulate about the way their bodies had been disposed of, later confirmed by one of the Prince's long-time French advisers. He told guests at a private dinner party hosted by a cabinet minister that he knew precisely how the two MPs had been killed. 'He said one was burnt alive with sulphuric acid,' one of them recalled. 'The other was crushed by a bulldozer.' There was a thoughtful silence, he remembered, as the Cambodians present looked at their plates. 'Everyone knew that was exactly the way Sihanouk would have behaved.'

In fact the rumours were false. On April 23, the day after Sihanouk's threat, Khieu Samphân spoke to a contact in the Party's clandestine network in Phnom Penh. Next day, police spies reported, he and Hou Yuon met twice. As instructed, Samphân said nothing to his family. Yuon, a less disciplined, more sentimental man, probably warned his wife. That evening at dusk, they were collected by a driver, who took them to an isolated spot in Ang Tasom district, 50 miles south of Phnom Penh on the road to Kampot. There they linked up with cadres from Mang's South-Western Zone Party Committee, who guided them to a hamlet in the woods about a mile from the main road. The half-dozen families who lived there were all related, which, as Samphân said later, meant 'there was no risk of betrayal because they were bound by the fidelity of blood'. None the less, the cadres, all veterans who had fought with the Viet Minh, took no chances. After three months in a village house, the two men were moved to a makeshift wooden cabin deeper in the forest. Samphân, a fastidious man, insisted on a daily bath, and each night after dark was accompanied by two village girls to a stream a couple of miles away to perform his ablutions. 'I was on my guard,' he said primly. 'Having left Phnom Penh for reasons of principle, I wasn't going to sully myself with a village woman.' Apart from a radio set and occasional contacts with the villagers, they were completely cut off from the outside world. Hou Yuon railed at their enforced inactivity. Samphân, being of a very different temperament and never having lived in the countryside, followed the cadres' instructions to the letter, dreamily contemplating, like his hero, Jean-Jacques Rousseau, the mysteries of peasant life.

The disappearance of Khieu Samphân and Hou Yuon embarrassed Sihanouk and helped trigger the resignation of Lon Nol, who was replaced as Prime Minister at the end of April. The new government, headed by the Prince himself, included several moderate left-wing ministers as well as elder statesmen like Son Sann and the former Democratic Party leader, Prince Norodom Phurissara, who became Foreign Minister. On the strength of these changes, Vorn Vet, the top Party leader in Phnom Penh, told Hu Nim, who had also been planning to flee, that he should stay on to see how the situation developed. A few days later, Nim issued an effusive statement of loyalty, declaring that he would 'remain a loyal member of the Sangkum until the end of [my] life'. But Lon Nol's departure changed little: the repression did not let up. In October, Nim, too, slipped away. His home was under round-the-clock police surveillance, but on the night of his disappearance there was a torrential downpour. An official inquiry found later that the surveillance team had taken refuge with a neighbour to get out of the rain. Soon afterwards Phouk Chhay, the head of the left-wing General Association of Khmer Students (AGEK), was arrested and sentenced to death, subsequently commuted to life imprisonment, and the Association banned. The same week, Nim's brother-in-law died in unexplained circumstances while in police custody and a left-wing entrepreneur, Van Tip Sovann, who owned the *Pracheachon*'s printing press and other front businesses, was tortured to death at the Central Commissariat. A visiting Australian historian wrote that people spoke 'with a mixture of repugnance, fear and gallows humour' about the expeditive methods of Sihanouk's security services. The trickle of intellectuals who had been making their way to the maquis since 1965 became a stream. They went, he noted, not just because they were afraid for their lives but out of a growing conviction that radical left-wing change was inevitable.

The twelve months that had passed since the CPK's Third Plenum had not been easy for Sâr either. The rebellion in the North-West and the subsequent flight of Khieu Samphân and the others had proved his strategy correct: legal, parliamentary struggle was impossible; the use of armed force against Sihanouk was now the only recourse. Nevertheless, Sâr had to acknowledge that he had failed to move quickly enough to take advantage of the peasant resentment that had built up in Battambang and as a result the rebellion had had to be called off because communist networks in the rest of the country were not yet ready to follow.

Some time in the late spring of 1967, probably at the beginning of June, the four Standing Committee members, Sâr, Nuon Chea, So Phim and Ieng Sary, met at Office 100 and agreed that a fresh attempt should be made to launch a general uprising, this time on a nation-wide basis, the follow-ing winter. Sary was appointed North-Eastern Zone Secretary and despatched to Ratanakiri to organise the new Central Committee HQ. That autumn, after four years on the Vietnamese border, Office 100 was finally dissolved. Some of its staff were transferred to other zones, others to the new base in the north. Soon afterwards Sâr wrote to the Chinese Party Central Committee:

> We have reached an important turning point. We have mastered how to undertake the revolution in our country . . . Our past experiences, notably . . . in using political violence and, in part, armed violence, from the end of 1966 to the middle of 1967 have convinced us that organisationally and ideo-logically our people are ready . . . to launch a true people's war. We are now exerting leadership [to that end] in the country as a whole.

The letter went on to lavish fulsome praise on the Cultural Revolution, which, as Sâr put it, 'we have studied, are studying and are determined to go on studying continuously and without let-up', and on Mao, its archi-tect, 'the great, guiding star who brings unceasing victories'.

Like all communications between the Cambodian Party and Beijing at this time, the message was transmitted through the Vietnamese, who opened and read it before delivering it to the Chinese Embassy in Hanoi. Not surprisingly, it set off alarm bells. That the Cambodians should eulo-gise China's leader in so slavish a fashion must have stuck in Vietnamese gullets, but they knew that in 1967 such phrases were an unavoidable part of Mao's cult. That the peasants of the North-West should rebel against local oppression was also understandable. But that the Cambodians should tell the Chinese they were about to launch a 'people's war' was a totally different matter.

Hanoi despatched two of its top political and military leaders in the south – Nguyen Van Linh who, as Hay-So, had headed the Vietnamese communists' Work Commitee in Phnom Penh; and General Tran Nam Trung – to try to dissuade Sâr from his project for a general uprising. After ten days, they departed without reaching agreement.

It is hard to see how it could have been otherwise. If the choice is to wage or not to wage war, there is no middle way.

All the Vietnamese could do was to refuse to help. They did. Cambodian requests for weapons were systematically rejected, and when Sâr asked the VWP Central Committee to allow the Khmer 'regroupees' in Vietnam to return to Cambodia to join the struggle, the message went unanswered. But there was a point beyond which the Vietnamese felt unable to oppose their Cambodian allies. By 1968, each side needed the other and both knew it. Sâr might speak privately, in terms strikingly similar to those employed by Sihanouk, of using China as a counterweight to Vietnamese domination. Le Duan might bridle at what he and the rest of the Hanoi leadership saw as Khmer bloody-mindedness. But the Cambodians knew they were condemned by geography to look to the Vietnamese for support; and the Vietnamese relied on Cambodian co-operation to keep open their supply lines at the southern end of the Ho Chi Minh Trail and to provide cover for the Viet Cong hospitals, sanctuaries and command posts – including the COSVN headquarters itself, concealed in a rubber plantation at Memot – along the entire length of the Cambodian side of the border. In the late 1960s, Khmers and Vietnamese were uneasy bedfellows, but bedfellows all the same.

Ratanakiri was a prime example of this forced cohabitation.

With the two neighbouring provinces of Mondulkiri and Stung Treng, it occupied almost a quarter of Cambodia's total land area but contained less than 2 per cent of the population, fewer than 100,000 people. Almost all were from tribal minorities – Brao, Jarai, Kachâk, Krâvet, Krüng, Lamban, Lao, Rhade, Stieng, Tampuon – whose natural affinities were not with lowland Cambodians but with their fellow *montagnards* in Laos and Vietnam.

These *Khmer loeu* (Highland Khmer), as they were called, wore loincloths, practised slash-and-burn agriculture, worshipped their own gods and spoke their own tribal languages. They had nothing in common with the Buddhist, rice-eating Khmers and saw little benefit from their presence. In the entire region, until the late 1950s, the Cambodian government had built three primary schools and the same number of medical clinics to serve an area the size of Denmark. Only when signs of tribal unrest and strategic concerns about security on the frontier with Vietnam began to concentrate minds in Phnom Penh were the first timid efforts made to bring development to the area.

By then the Vietnamese communists had been active in Ratanakiri for more than a decade, building support networks to shield their bases along the border. But no Khmer revolutionary had yet penetrated the region. A handful of minority cadres, like the Lao veteran, Thang Si – who attended the 1960 Party Congress – were in contact with the leadership in Phnom Penh. It was not until the end of 1964, when Sâr despatched a young man named Vy, a former *Pracheachon* journalist, to create a CPK network in the North-East, that the first Khmer communists entered the province. In January 1965, local Viet Cong officials introduced Vy and his companion, Man, to *montagnard* representatives from Ratanakiri's three districts, telling them, as one participant remembered: 'These men are Khmers . . . From now on you have your own leadership. You should follow them.'

By the time Ieng Sary arrived, two and a half years later, district Party committees had been set up and a Zone Headquarters, Office 102, established near the hamlet of Kang Lêng in dense forest about seven miles south of the district centre of Anduong Meas. A second encampment was built later about half a mile away, on the bank of the Toek Chrâp stream, for use as the Central Committee HQ. Like its precursor in Tay Ninh, it was referred to as 'Office 100'. Between the two lay a third cluster of thatched huts which served as a reception centre for couriers and visiting cadres from other parts of the country. Sary, as Zone Secretary, took direct responsibility for Ratanakiri; Son Sen, who became Deputy Secretary, was put in charge of Stung Treng, and Ney Sarann of Mondulkiri.

Sâr himself stayed on in the south until early November 1967, delayed first by the preparations for the uprising and then by the talks with Nguyen Van Linh. The journey from Tay Ninh took more than a month. In the final stages he had to be carried, prostrate from malaria, in a hammock, slung from a bamboo shoulder-pole between two bearers.

With him came Pâng, the youth who had run the printing press at Office 100 and now headed the Messenger Unit; two other Khmer assistants; and a group of *montagnard* bodyguards. After crossing the San river – one of the principal affluents of the Mekong which bisects north-eastern Cambodia, flowing in a long westerly arc from its source in the central highlands of Vietnam – they had made for a Viet Cong medical facility, 'Hospital No. 5', on the border close to Mount Ngork, where quinine was available.

Malaria was, and still is, endemic in the jungles of Indochina. Khieu Samphân recalled marching in Indian file through the forest with a guerrilla escort and watching the man in front of him 'jerking about uncontrollably as he walked as though he had the palsy'. Hu Nim lost most of his hair after a malarial attack. In 1968, Mang, the South-Western Zone leader, died from it. A senior Viet Cong official remembered malaria being a worse problem than the Americans: 'For each of my years in the jungle, I spent approximately two months in the hospital, battling the high fevers and general debility of the disease . . . We lost more people to malaria than we did to the enemy.'

Sâr recovered and a few weeks later was carried on a litter to Office 102, where he remained until his own headquarters, Office 100, was ready. But for the rest of his life he would suffer relapses. The following summer, Khieu Ponnary arrived to join him, accompanied by her sister, Thirith, and Son Sen's wife, Yun Yat.

In the North-East, for the first time since they had left for the maquis, the CPK leaders were truly their own masters. The new Office 100 was a wholly Cambodian outfit, with a Khmer cook and a 'doctor', Dam, who had been a medical student before dropping out to join the revolution. Like other bases in the area, it was equipped with primitive but lethal defences:

> It was surrounded by dozens of pit-falls, containing sharpened bamboos and spears. Along the paths we suspended traps from the trees. We had no mines in those days. But the guards patrolled in five-man groups with bows and poisoned arrows. We had guns, old-fashioned Enfields from the First World War; a few Kalashnikovs, but very few; and muzzle-loaders that the local tribesmen used for hunting.

Sâr travelled little during this period. He had time to plan and think, free from outside influence, in an area of Cambodia where the government's writ did not run. The population at large – a prey to the exactions of rapacious officials, sent from faraway Phnom Penh, and to what one diplomat called the 'overweening superiority complex' of lowland Cambodians – had no love of Sihanouk's regime. To Sâr, the *montagnards*, even more than the Khmer peasantry, were Rousseau's 'noble savages' – simple, pure, fanatically loyal, unsullied by the decadence of Cambodian life. Ieng Sary, too, remembered them as 'men who would give their lives for you without a thought . . . With a Khmer soldier you never knew how he'd react. But a Jarai would make sure I was safe no matter what it cost.'

By December 1967, plans for the uprising were complete. As before, it was to start in the North-West, in the area around Samlaut. But this time, instead of remaining confined to southern Battambang, it would spread in stages to the rest of the country. That month Nuon Chea met Vorn Vet, the South-West Zone Secretary, Mang, and Kong Sophal at a safe house in Phnom Penh, and gave them their final instructions.

'I rushed back,' Sophal recounted, 'and told everyone that we would start the rebellion in all the villages on the same day and they must start preparing their weapons.' Word spread quickly. Khieu Samphân, in his forest hideout, noticed an unusual excitement among the young peasants guarding him and puzzled over what it might mean:

> Then one day one of the cadres came to see me and said: 'Now it's decided: we are going to take up arms. You are to come with us' . . . So, just like that, we set off through the forest . . . Some of them belonged to the [government's] provincial guard, which had Enfields. They had 'borrowed' these guns on the pretext of going hunting . . . and they now used them to attack government arms depots.
> At night, we slept in the jungle with a piece of plastic cloth suspended

between the trees above our hammock as protection against rain. Even that was only for the cadres. The peasants made themselves a covering of straw or a lattice of leaves. Each group consisted of between 10 and 20 men, and there were several groups in our part of the forest. [At first] we ate rice. Each night, the men would go back to their villages and bring back food which their families had left for them at the edge of the forest . . . They also had a dog, which caught turtles and big lizards. I saw them tickle fish with their bare hands in the streams . . . But after a certain time, the villages were sealed off [by government soldiers] and we couldn't get supplies any more. Then we ate roots and tubers that the men found in the forest.

The uprising was launched on January 18 1968 with a dawn raid on an army post at Bay Damran, twelve miles south of Battambang. This feat would later be celebrated as marking the start of the revolutionary war. In fact the operation had been betrayed by an informer and the rebels, led by Sophal himself, were driven off with two men killed. But they were able to seize a number of weapons and, in other villages, three policemen were caught in ambushes and killed. A week later another group of rebels attacked a guard post at Thvak, shooting dead several defenders and seizing fifty rifles. The same month, the first incident occurred in Ratanakiri, when a group of Jarai tribesmen with two muskets and a rifle ambushed a military transport on a jungle track in Bokeo. On February 25, Mang's followers launched co-ordinated attacks in five provinces in the South-West. By nightfall they had seized several dozen rifles, two machine-guns and cases of ammunition, destroyed bridges and burned official buildings. Over the next few weeks they acquired another two hundred guns. In early March, the North – where Son Sen's former student, Koy Thuon, had become Zone Secretary, with Ke Pauk as his deputy – and the Eastern Zone, under So Phim, followed suit. In the country as a whole, more than 10,000 villagers left their homes to join the rebels.

Like most revolutions it started on a very small scale, with a handful of determined men patiently building support, rifle by rifle and one villager at a time. But Sihanouk was not deceived by the insurgency's modest beginnings. He found it more and more difficult to maintain the fiction that the troubles were remote-controlled by Cambodia's enemies abroad and began for the first time to speak of the risk of all-out civil war.

The rebels did not have things all their own way, however.

The leadership had been able to co-ordinate the launching of the uprising. But it took a month for a message, hand-carried by courier on foot or elephant-back, to get from one Zone HQ to another and still longer to Ratanakiri. Once the rebellion was under way, a centralised chain of command became impossible. Each Zone fended for itself.

At the end of January, Sihanouk brought back Lon Nol, who had been in semi-disgrace since his resignation as Premier eight months earlier. That signalled the resumption of the scorched-earth tactics that had been used the previous spring. The air force was called in to bomb and strafe rebel-held areas; efforts were made to interdict food supplies; and people living in isolated hamlets were resettled in fortified villages. Diplomats reported that the army acted 'without restraint and at times with great brutality'. At the beginning of April, after artillery and aerial bombardment, government soldiers overran the North-Western Zone HQ on Mount Veay Chap. Part of the guerrilla force, accompanied by more than 4,000 civilians, fled south towards the Cardamom Mountains. The rest scattered. By the autumn, some two hundred guerrillas had regrouped at Mount Damrey, near Pailin, but soon found themselves 'in a critical situation, with only wild roots and papaya to eat'.

In the South-West, where Mok – the 'skinny, bony ex-monk from Takeo', as one fellow townsman remembered him – took over as acting Zone Secretary after Mang's death, the insurgency settled into a pattern of hit-and-run attacks. In the North and East, where the rebellion had begun later, the government pre-empted weapons seizures by withdrawing police posts that were judged vulnerable and disarming village militias. As a result, it was not until July that So Phim's Eastern Zone detachments – which in theory should have been among the strongest in the country – were able to obtain a stock of rifles. The situation in Siem Reap and Sâr's native province of Kompong Thom was scarcely more encouraging. 'In the East . . . our bases were destroyed and our people killed or driven away,' Sâr wrote later. 'In the North . . . we experienced considerable difficulties.'

Only in the vast, uninhabited expanse of the North-East were the insurgents able to hold substantial swathes of territory.

In Ratanakiri, thousands of *montagnard* villagers were moved from their homes along the San river to the security of the high mountains, where they built new 'strategic hamlets' out of reach of government troops. By the autumn, according to Ieng Sary, the Zone Secretary, the rebels occupied thirty-one of the province's thirty-five communes, and Sihanouk himself admitted that in areas of the province bordering Vietnam 'we are no longer in control'. The insurgents' cause was aided by the callousness of the provincial military governor and the barbarity of the Second Parachute Regiment which was sent to quell the unrest. As at Samlaut, a year earlier, bounties were offered for each rebel head brought in, 'but officers soon learnt to demand a rifle as well as a head, because the soldiers started killing ordinary tribesmen to get heads for a reward', Sihanouk himself set the tone by telling a mass rally in Bokeo in February that 'traitors' would be treated with 'extreme harshness'. Three months later he announced at Stung Treng that he had personally ordered 'several dozen *montagnards*' taken before a firing squad and shot, bringing to 'around 200 the number who have been exterminated'. 'I do not care if I am sent to hell,' he cried defiantly, 'I will submit the relevant documents to the Devil himself.' The result, the French Ambassador noted, was 'a vicious cycle of reprisals and counter-reprisals', more likely to 'harden the Khmers Rouges' attitude than to make them submit'. The severed heads of captured rebels were displayed in district centres and photographs published in the Khmer-language press. An Eastern Zone Khmer Rouge cadre was disembowelled by government soldiers. In Kompong Cham, townspeople spoke of mass executions of leftists; and in a particularly ghastly incident near Phnom Penh, troops took two children, alleged to be communist messengers, and sawed off their heads with jagged fronds from a palm tree.

As the bloodshed continued, the Buddhist hierarchy showed growing misgivings. So did other establishment figures who could hardly be accused of communist sympathies. When two right-wing deputies, Sim Var and Douc Rasy, protested at the army's conduct, Sihanouk warned that he would 'send them into the next world without even troubling to lift their parliamentary immunity'.

By the summer of 1968, the government's 'search-and-destroy' operations in Ratanakiri were coming dangerously close both to Office 100 and to a military camp further south, known as K-1, where Son Sen had started training revolutionary guard units to form the nucleus of the future Khmer Rouge army. It was decided that the entire leadership should move thirty miles to the north, into the mountainous area known as the Naga's Tail, where the frontiers of Cambodia, Laos and Vietnam meet. The new base, near the village of Nây, inhabited by Kachâk tribesmen, was given the codename K-5. It was three days' march from K-12, a Viet Cong transit base on the Laotian border at the southern end of the Ho Chi Minh Trail, and about six miles from the border with Vietnam.

At K-5, Sâr began to emerge more and more not just as first among equals in a collective leadership, but as *the* Cambodian Party chief. The living arrangements told the story. At Office 100 in Tay Ninh, everyone had shared and shared alike. At Office 100 in Kang Lêng, Sâr and Ponnary had their quarters in the same camp as Vy's deputy, Man, and other local cadres. At K-5, Sâr had an entirely separate encampment, with his own personal staff and guards, to which no outsider was allowed access unless an escort was sent out to fetch him. As at Kang Lêng, Sâr rarely moved outside, even to go to nearby villages. But he held lengthy debriefings with the cadres and intellectuals who were now arriving in Ratanakiri in ever-increasing numbers from other parts of the country, and Ponnary travelled extensively on his behalf, reporting back on conditions in the different areas she visited.

It would be wrong to read too much into this hermetic existence. At a time when the US and South Vietnam were stepping up cross-border bombing and raids by special forces, there were both security and policy reasons for Sâr to remain under deep cover. Nevertheless, it reflected a pattern which would continue for the next thirty years. As he concentrated power in his own hands, reality was kept at one remove, not grasped directly but through the eyes of others – as though to maintain a screen, filtering out inconvenient facts, between the leader and the nation that he sought to transform. It was a style of leadership that sat perfectly with Sâr's reclusiveness, his indirection, his penchant for concealing his intentions. It already contained the seeds of the high tragedy that would follow.

As 1968 drew to a close, rebel activity was reported from at least twelve of Cambodia's nineteen provinces. In Ratanakiri, Sâr took over Ieng Sary's responsibilities as North-Eastern Zone Secretary so that Sary could spend more time in the two districts where the insurgency was strongest, Anduong Meas and Bokeo. The government's intelligence services estimated that, in the country as a whole, there were about 1,500 rebels, supported by several times that number of unarmed villagers. The core of the insurgent force was composed of armed peasants from former Khmer Viet Minh strongholds led by old-style Issaraks like Ruos Nhim, Mok, Ke Pauk and So Phim, who had acquired their military skills in the war against the French. Only in the North-East were 'intellectuals' like Sâr, Ieng Sary and their followers directly in charge.

This duality reflected the Party's origins. The mismatch between the indigenous, largely uneducated, rural movement, fostered by the Vietnamese, and the citified elite that had been superimposed upon it, made up of schoolteachers, students and civil servants, had been papered over in the 1950s when urban cadres assured the organisation's survival and the rural networks were shattered or went into hibernation. Tou Samouth had been a leader whom both the Issaraks and the 'returned students' could accept. But when Sâr took over two years later, the consensus frayed. In Hanoi in 1965, he told Le Duan that 'the problem of unity within the Party is the most difficult thing we have to deal with'. With hindsight he was franker: 'From 1961 to 1967,' he said, 'there were separatist tendencies . . . The Party was split.'

Other Khmer Rouge accounts bear that out. Ruos Nhim, Ney Sarann and Ke Pauk had little time for the returned students. So Phim was quoted as saying disparagingly: 'Those intellectuals only have [posh] city homes and theory'.

Phim was a quintessential warlord. At the Second Congress in 1963, he shocked even Mok, hardly the gentlest of men, whom he had been asked to propose for election to the Central Committee. 'He was blind drunk,' Mok remembered. 'I saw it and I thought – with a leader like that, it's not proper. [Phim] could really drink! [Afterwards], we went to study [Party documents] together. He didn't know his arse from his tit!' Phim's wild ways continued. In 1968, Doeun, a young student from Kompong Cham, later to become head of the Central Committee's General Office, encountered him for the first time 'drinking wine . . . and in a black mood'. The rebellion in the Eastern Zone was going badly and Phim was depressed. 'He was outrageous. When he spoke . . . everyone was afraid. No one dared go near him . . . I tried to cheer him up, hoping that it would make him behave better . . . because he was one of the Party's top leaders and I didn't want people to look down on him.' That year, Phim had a row with his deputy, Phuong, which ended with both men drawing their pistols. He was a womaniser and an autocrat: when others offended him, he threatened to have them shot.

Mok, surprisingly, given his subsequent reputation for brutality, appears to have been the most understanding of the group. 'He was a peasant,' Khieu Samphân said later. 'He never spoke about theory and ideology, things like that. But he was broad-minded: he realised we [intellectuals] weren't used to the life in the countryside and he tried to make things easier for us.'

That became increasingly necessary as police surveillance in the towns intensified and the numbers of left-wing teachers fleeing to the countryside grew. It was enough for a teacher to be seen attending a picnic with his pupils, to fail to put in an appearance at a ceremony where Sihanouk was present, or to criticise the misdeeds of a long-dead monarch in a classical literature class, to be listed as a subversive. In the three months from November 1967 to February 1968, more than thirty teachers quit their posts. Most of them made their way to Mok's HQ near Mount Aural, though a few reached the Central Committee base in Ratanakiri. They were as unprepared for what lay in store as were their rural 'hosts' to receive them:

> I had been told that Mok's base was very well-organised, just like the Chinese revolutionary bases during the civil war [*one aspiring young radical remembered*]. There was even supposed to be electric lighting, decent lodging for cadres, offices with typewriters . . . I couldn't wait to get there . . . What did I find? Khieu Samphân, Hou Yuon and Hu Nim were almost unrecognisable: Nim had lost most of his hair . . . Hou Yuon, who used to be so well-built, was as thin as a nail . . . Another comrade lay beside them,

shivering and groaning with fever, and talking deliriously to himself in French . . . The bodyguards were asleep on a bed nearby, under which were stocked provisions of dried elephant meat. They all had skin diseases and kept scratching themselves as they lay on top of our one, very tasteless, source of protein. When I saw all that, 'I became as light as cotton and my liver flew out of my body'.

As the rebellion continued, the two groups were forced to come to terms with each other. In Sâr's vision of the future, it was imperative that they should. But to weld two such disparate forces into a single political grouping required exceptional pressures. In 1968 and 1969, the waging of a 'people's war' against a more powerful adversary, the repression that rained down impartially on the Party's urban and rural networks alike, the belief that communism was the wave of the future and that an egalitarian victory would soon be shared by all, created the necessary conditions. For the first time, a truly national revolutionary movement was coming into being. Yet the graft remained imperfect – an unavoidable but unnatural alliance which Sâr and his companions would devote extraordinary ingenuity to justifying and maintaining.

The onset of armed struggle, prefigured by the Samlaut rebellion, coincided with a sharp deterioration in Cambodia's relations with China, which until then Sihanouk had viewed as his country's most loyal friend. Not that the Prince had any illusions about the nature of Beijing's interest in the region. But, much like Kim Il Sung in North Korea, with whom he had developed an improbable but enduring friendship, he had seen China as a trump card, to be used to counter US ambitions and extract aid from the Soviet Union and its allies. The relationship helped to keep domestic radicals in check and provided a barrier against the Vietnamese, communist or otherwise.

In the spring of 1967, with the Cultural Revolution at its height and the discourse of Chinese foreign policy rising to a shriek, this carefully-thought-out strategy began to fall apart. Chinese aid experts waved Mao's 'Little Red Book' and proselytised their Khmer co-workers, while their Embassy in Phnom Penh sent strident letters to Khmer newspapers berating them for failing to understand 'the Great Proletarian Cultural Revolution'.

There were limits to the agitation: the powers-that-be in Beijing had decreed that Mao's works should not be translated into Khmer. But French-language versions were freely available; young Cambodians began sporting Mao badges; and the police reported that groups of students, emulating the Red Guards, had put up wall posters critical of the regime.

More disturbing, there were signs that the Sino-Khmer community, some 400,000 strong, which until then had remained largely apolitical, devoting itself to mercantile concerns, was beginning to respond to the propaganda barrage from Beijing calling for 'revolutionary patriotism' and 'loyalty to the [Chinese] motherland'.

In public, Sihanouk sought at first to minimise the problem, arguing that 'errors' and 'excesses' committed by individual Chinese in no way reflected the views of the Chinese government. The wearing of Mao badges was banned, and schools operated by the Chinese community, which had been teaching 'Mao Zedong Thought', were threatened with closure unless they reverted to the government-approved curriculum. But as the year wore on, the Prince's mistrust of Beijing's intentions deepened. The French Ambassador reported in June that, after having long denied any connection with the internal unrest, the government was now beginning to suspect that the Chinese were 'colluding with the Khmers Rouges and . . . trying to capitalise on the movement they have launched'.

Matters came to a head on September 1, when Sihanouk ordered the dissolution of the Khmer-Chinese Friendship Association, which he accused of acting as a Khmer Rouge fifth column to undermine his regime. Three days later, ultra-leftist officials in Beijing fired off a telegram which, in barely veiled terms, denounced the Cambodian government as 'reactionary'. At that, the Prince's patience snapped. Cambodia, he said, was facing an 'ideological invasion, and would take legitimate measures of self-defence'. Chau Seng, who had made public the telegram, was sacked from his post as Economics Minister. All non-government newspapers were banned. The New China News Agency bureau in Phnom Penh was closed, and it was announced that the Cambodian Ambassador in Beijing and all his staff would be brought home.

This last move succeeded in getting the Chinese leadership's attention.

On September 14, Zhou Enlai made a personal appeal to the Prince to reconsider. After a short interval, he agreed, and to outward appearances, relations slowly returned to normal. But the honeymoon was over. For more than a decade the entente with China had been, in Sihanouk's words, 'the cornerstone of Cambodian foreign policy'. Now China had shown itself as fallible a friend as any other.

The crisis provoked a further shift to the right. After September 1967, no left-wing minister would again serve in Sihanouk's government, nor any left-wing MP sit in parliament. In foreign relations it helped tip the scales in favour of a reconciliation with the Prince's *bête noire*, the United States. Sihanouk remained convinced that the Americans were doomed to lose the Vietnam War and that his strategy of accumulating political credit with the communists, the future winners, was therefore correct. However, pressure from the Pentagon for tougher measures to foreclose the Cambodian sanctuaries and the Prince's own concern at the Viet Cong's increasingly open use of the border areas demanded a more balanced policy, less obviously favourable to Vietnamese communist interests. In November he invited Jacqueline Kennedy to pay a private visit to Phnom Penh and Angkor as his personal guest. Her stay was a success – Sihanouk's gloating at her husband's assassination four years earlier was conveniently forgotten – and in January 1968 another US emissary arrived, a more political figure this time, in the shape of Chester Bowles, special envoy of President Johnson. According to the State Department, they reached an informal agreement to permit US forces to enter the sparsely inhabited border areas of Ratanakiri and Mondulkiri – though not the more densely populated regions further south – in pursuit of Viet Cong guerrillas.

Over the next few months, other factors strengthened this trend towards rapprochement. Sihanouk declared the Khmer Rouge insurgency to be part of a 'global strategy by Asian communism' to win control of all of South-East Asia, a view consonant with that held in the US. Even so, he could not resist a jibe at Washington's simplicity:

> America says it is fighting against communism. Which communism? Chinese communism? If so, Washington [should realise that] the communism it is in the process of destroying – Vietnamese communism – is in no sense inspired by China, but is hostile to Chinese expansionism. It is actually a nationalist barrier between China and the rest of South-East Asia. The truth is that America, by waging war against Vietnam, is playing China's game. And indirectly, by preventing Vietnam from becoming strong, it is also helping Cambodia.

Paradoxically the opening of peace talks in Paris between the US and the Vietnamese communists strengthened the Prince's belief in the importance of the American presence. As soon as peace was restored, he argued, a reunified Vietnam would once again turn its energies to subjugating its smaller neighbours. Laos, in his view, was already doomed to become a Vietnamese satellite. The only power that could help Cambodia resist a similar fate was America. Until 1968, Sihanouk had doubted Washington's ability to play such a role, even if it wished to. But the massive build-up of American forces in South Vietnam persuaded him that the US might after all continue to be a force in the region for longer than he had previously thought.

Reversing course was a delicate exercise. The US, under pressure from its allies, Thailand and South Vietnam, had refused to recognise Cambodia's existing borders, which to Sihanouk was the *sine qua non* for normalising relations; and botched B-52 raids along the frontier wiped out Khmer hamlets with such regularity that the Cambodian army concluded they must be deliberate. Equally problematic was the need to conduct the rapprochement in a way which would not anger China, still a major aid donor, or the Viet Cong, which, with Sihanouk's complicity, continued to receive munitions through the port of Kompong Som and to buy – through corrupt intermediaries, including Lon Nol and the entourage of the Prince's wife, Monique – most of the surplus Cambodian rice harvest. The amounts of money involved were colossal. The North Vietnamese Premier, Pham Van Dong, told Mao in 1968 that payments for rice and transport fees, financed by the Chinese government, 'exceed 20 million dollars a year, [and allow the Cambodians] to gain both a good reputation and profits'.

It is never simple to support both sides in a war. Yet that was the logic of the Prince's position. It was a policy which required constant ambiguity. Inevitably his margin for manoeuvre became more and more restricted.

In March 1969, President Nixon ordered the US air force to begin secretly bombing the Cambodian sanctuaries. Over the next twelve months, B-52s would fly more than 3,000 sorties over the eastern part of the country in an operation codenamed 'Menu'. Sihanouk chose not to protest, not because he agreed with the bombings but because, at a time when his priority was to mend relations with America, all the alternatives were worse. In April, with beguiling cynicism, the United States finally accorded its long-delayed recognition of Cambodia's borders. Diplomatic ties were restored soon after, offset, in Sihanouk's mind, by simultaneous Cambodian recognition of the Viet Cong Provisional Revolutionary Government of South Vietnam. But the Prince reaped little direct benefit. Instead the Americans' return boosted the morale of the Right, which started to behave more and more like a full-fledged opposition. All those in the army and in middle-class circles in Phnom Penh who had opposed the rupture in the first place took it as an admission of error. Under more normal circumstances, Sihanouk could have roused the left wing of the Sangkum to counter such criticisms. But the Khmer Rouge rebellion had made that impossible. The parliamentary Left had ceased to exist. Its chief spokesmen, Khieu Samphân, Hou Yuon and Hu Nim, had fled, and moderates like Chau Seng were in disgrace.

Sihanouk had backed himself into a corner. The rebellion was not dying down, the communist underground was growing ever bolder, and Lon Nol's security forces were the only weapon he could use against them.

In Phnom Penh in the summer of 1968, the Prince had been outraged

to learn that communist agents had distributed Khmer Rouge tracts to delegates at his own Sangkum congress. Lon Nol, now back as Defence
Minister, organised a series of police raids which produced alarming evidence of the scope of the communist network in the capital. During the
drag-net, a young man named Kac Sim was killed in a shoot-out with
Special Branch agents. Forty suspects – most of them student drop-outs
who had taken jobs as labourers or cyclo-pousse drivers, but also 'officials
at the Public Works Department, the Posts and Telegraphs, the National
Bank, the Railways and even the Justice Department' – were arrested and
subsequently executed.* They included, the government newspaper,
Réalités Cambodgiennes, reported breathlessly, 'a woman courier who was
carrying secret messages in her bra and panties', a revelation judged sufficiently titillating to be placed in italics. More importantly, the police found
complete sets of field surgery instruments, waiting to be sent to the maquis;
arms and ammunition; duplicating machines and rebel tracts; and several
powerful radio transmitters, including one that operated on the same fre-
quencies as the security service at Sihanouk's official residence.

The raids gave the authorities their first insight into the systems for
'secret work' that Nuon Chea had devised. 'The organisation is highly
compartmentalised,' a police report stated. 'The members know only those
in their own cell and communicate with other echelons by secret messages,
transmitted via several successive intermediaries. Thus, if "No. 25" wishes
to write to "No. 1", he gives the letter to "T" who gives it to "No. 26"
who has a meeting with yet another person that was fixed some time before
. . . It is a real Chinese puzzle.'

But while the Special Branch men were able to seize a Jeep and an Opel
saloon, used by the head of the clandestine network, the mysterious
'No. 1', and even to learn that he was named Pen Thuok, the man himself
slipped through their hands. In fact, they had got much closer to him than
they realised. Pen Thuok was Vorn Vet, and he had been at Kac Sim's house
the night it was raided. The shoot-out had been a diversion to allow him
to escape.

Another important figure had also been in Phnom Penh that day: Sâr's
wife, Khieu Ponnary, was staying in another safe house in the city, on her

---

* It was later reported that 'on Sihanouk's own orders, 40 schoolteachers suspected of treason were thrown to their deaths from the mountainous heights of Bokor above the provincial capital of Kampot', a story which may well have originated with these arrests. It was
probably no more true than the grisly claims of Khieu Samphân's death in an acid bath or
Hou Yuon's under a bulldozer. But like those tales, it was universally believed. Cambodians
expected the Prince to treat his opponents with atavistic cruelty and it suited his purposes
that they should think so.

way from Ratanakiri to Mok's headquarters at Mount Aural, when the raids occurred. She, too, evaded capture.

The crackdown that autumn did not wipe out the city network. Vorn Vet patiently rebuilt his smashed 'strings'. Nuon Chea, the opaque master of the underground, undetected by the authorities, continued to devote himself to what was now his main task – using his cover as a commercial traveller to send rifles, grenades and ammunition to the rebels in the bush.

None the less, it showed how far the rebellion had extended its tentacles into the capital itself and offered fresh proof, if proof were needed, of how indispensable Lon Nol had become. In December 1968 he was named acting Prime Minister, standing in for the ailing Penn Nouth. Seven months later he was still serving in that post while concurrently Defence Minister and Chief of the General Staff. It was the first time the Prince had allowed anyone to combine the top military and civil offices. He had no choice.

Sihanouk was also forced to retreat over economic policy. That same December he announced that the programme of nationalisations and state control of foreign trade, launched five years earlier, would be modified to give more scope to private enterprise and that the government would accept foreign aid 'no matter where it comes from'. The rationale was the same as had led him to restore diplomatic relations with the US. To arm itself against a potentially unified, communist-ruled Vietnam, Cambodia needed to strengthen its ties with the West. That meant reorientating its economy along capitalist lines and joining the International Monetary Fund and other Western-run aid institutions.

To Cambodian right-wingers, here was yet another case of the Prince reversing himself after belatedly discovering that his earlier policies had been wrong.

Once more, Sihanouk was disarmed.

With no left wing to fall back on, he had to confront his critics himself. The following spring, for the first time, parliament defied his authority by refusing to bury a corruption inquiry involving one of his cronies. The resulting row lasted three months and ended only after the Prince had been forced into an unprecedented public climb-down, an episode which left him smarting. By then another crisis was brewing. To try to balance the budget, Sihanouk had granted, for an annual fee of 80 million francs – a huge sum at that time, equivalent to a third of all Cambodia's foreign aid – licences for two casinos. Financially they were an immense success. Socially they were a disaster. Phnom Penh was soon alive with stories of people committing suicide after losing their life-savings. Business activity slumped as factory owners, government officials, shopkeepers and labourers spent their days and nights courting ruin at the betting tables. To right-wing MPs like Sim Var and Douc Rasy, it was the perfect symbol of the bankruptcy of Sihanouk's regime.

In July 1969, the Prince decided that Lon Nol's confirmation as Premier could no longer be delayed. The US chargé d'affaires, Mike Rives, was due to arrive the following month. If Cambodia wanted the Americans to take it seriously, it could not continue indefinitely under a caretaker government. Lon Nol, Sihanouk believed, was personally loyal to him – which men like Sim Var were not – and he commanded the support of the Right. In any case, there was no alternative. The Khmer Rouge threat showed no sign of receding, and the Vietnamese were finally beginning to give their Khmer allies small quantities of arms. Moreover, their own forces in Cambodia had undergone a massive expansion, growing from 6,000 in mid-1968 to an estimated 30,000 a year later.* Nor were they now confined to the sanctuaries. The secret 'Menu' bombings had not only failed in their primary mission – neither COSVN headquarters nor the Viet Cong bases had been destroyed – but had driven the Vietnamese communists further and further into the Cambodian interior.

One may legitimately wonder whether, behind the rhetoric, Nixon's objective all along was not to spread the war to Cambodia in order to divert attention from the withdrawal of US troops from Vietnam. Certainly it worked out that way. One senior American general said later that the US aim in Cambodia was to mount 'a holding action. You know . . . the troika's going down the road and the wolves are closing in, and so you throw them something off and let them chew it.' By mid-1969 Cambodia was being sucked into a conflict it had done everything to avoid, and which, until Nixon's election, Sihanouk's see-saw diplomacy had managed to keep at arm's length.

Nowhere were these developments watched more closely than in Beijing and at Sâr's headquarters at K-5.

That spring Zhou Enlai told the North Vietnamese Premier, Pham Van Dong, that China was 'not [too] optimistic' about the situation in Cambodia. The parallel with Sukarno had not escaped the Chinese leaders,

---

* In 1968, Viet Cong and North Vietnamese penetration of the border areas began to grow exponentially. That September, French military analysts concluded that there were nine Vietnamese bases in Cambodia – three in Ratanakiri and Mondulkiri, including a transit facility at the end of the Ho Chi Minh Trail (probably in the same area as the Khmer Rouge camp, K-12); and six further south, among them two logistics bases in southern Memot district, near COSVN, and at the eastern tip of the Parrot's Beak in Svay Rieng, a sanctuary in Snuol district and another in Kompong Thmey. The French estimated that there were up to 6,000 Vietnamese soldiers on Cambodian soil at any one time. In September 1969, Lon Nol estimated their strength at 32–35,000. Three months later the figure had reached 40,000.

any more than it had Sihanouk himself. They did not rule out the possibility of an American-backed military coup.

By the middle of 1969, the latent conflict between Sihanouk and the Sangkum right wing was also exercising Sâr. But where the Chinese leaders saw a threat to the flow of arms to the Viet Cong, Sâr saw an opportunity the Khmer communists could exploit. In July, Nuon Chea travelled secretly to Ratanakiri for an enlarged meeting of the CPK Standing Committee, which approved a major change of political line. For the previous three years, the CPK had targeted Sihanouk as the chief symbol of the 'reactionary, monarchical system' it wanted to overthrow. Henceforth, the Standing Committee resolved, the Party's main line of attack should be directed against Lon Nol and the pro-American right. This did not necessarily mean, as Sâr and other communist leaders later claimed, that they had 'foreseen' that a coup was imminent. But certainly they understood sooner than most that a new and fundamental fault-line had developed in Khmer politics. The Party's prime task, Sâr now argued, was to isolate the rightists and mobilise 'all forces capable of being mobilised' into a united front against them. Consequently, anti-Sihanouk propaganda was to cease.

To underline the importance of the change, the Standing Committee censured Khieu Samphân, Hou Yuon and Hu Nim, who had recently written a tract denouncing the Prince, for acting 'counter to the Party's line on the National United Front'. Theoretically this was justified because the 1960 Party Programme mentioned the need for front work 'to win over intermediate forces'. But until then the stress had been on 'quality not quantity', on revolutionary purity rather than gaining dubious allies. After mid-1969, the Party itself remained as secretive and puritan as ever, but its tactics changed.

The resolution called for renewed stress on political struggle in areas such as the North-East, the Cardamoms and Mount Aural, where the movement enjoyed the protection of a substantial Vietnamese presence and had the possibility of establishing 'revolutionary bases'. The prime task of the guerrilla forces in those regions, it said, was to protect the bases and the civilian population which lived there. They were to serve as a springboard for resistance in the event of a coup, and as prototypal liberated zones, a pole of attraction for urban sympathisers repelled by the rise of the Right.

Efforts were also made to win over the former Khmer Viet Minh who had settled in North Vietnam after the Geneva accords. In August, Sâr despatched Keo Meas, who had spent the spring in Beijing undergoing medical treatment, to act as the CPK's unofficial representative in Hanoi. His brief was to work with Son Ngoc Minh, and 'to try, step by step, to take over the political education of the regroupees . . . [but] to do so secretly, not openly'. It was an all but impossible task. Minh was out of touch with events at home and deeply suspicious of the younger men who had supplanted him. With Vietnamese support, he used his rank as a Central Committee member and Secretary of the Hanoi branch of the Party to ensure that Meas's contacts with the exiles were kept to a minimum.

That same month, as Nuon Chea was making his way back from K-5 to inform the Zone committees of the new strategy, Lon Nol was sworn in as Prime Minister of a 'Government of Rescue and National Salvation', more openly pro-American and more right-wing than any administration Cambodia had known before. Sihanouk announced that the new Prime Minister had *carte blanche* to take whatever measures he thought necessary to revive the flagging economy and end the Khmer Rouge rebellion, the only proviso being that the policies of neutralism and non-alignment must remain intact. In fact, their relations were marked from the start by a climate of mistrust, which Lon Nol did nothing to diminish by appointing the Prince's arch-enemy, Sirik Matak, as his deputy.

Nol might be loyal to the Throne, but he had been burned by Sihanouk's duplicity during his previous stint as Prime Minister in 1966. Sirik Matak, a man of sterner stuff than his Prime Minister, was determined to prevent a repetition. This time the government insisted on governing. Within weeks, diplomats were reporting open conflict between the two sides. The Prince was increasingly restricted to his constitutional role. He found it intolerable.

'Formerly everything came down from Sihanouk,' commented the French chargé d'affaires, Robert Mazeyrac. 'Today, Cambodia's domestic policy is almost entirely out of his hands.' In October the Prince branded the National Assembly 'a gang of evildoers, traitors and criminals', refused to attend the state opening of parliament and issued a decree banning MPs from attending all official ceremonies he presided over 'from now until the end of my life'. The bluster had no effect. Nor did his jibes, a few days later, at 'the headless government' of Lon Nol (who had left for medical treatment in Switzerland), which was not 'a government of rescue' but 'a government of drowning'. By the end of the year, there was a perfect stalemate. Government and parliament stood together. Sihanouk's relations with both were execrable. No one, neither Lon Nol, nor Sirik Matak, nor even the Prince himself, could see how it would end.

For Sâr, too, the last months of 1969 had been frustrating, if less dramatic. The rebellion was slowly gathering strength and the new 'united front' strategy was beginning to bear fruit. CPK 'armed propaganda teams', closely modelled on those the Viet Minh had brought to

Cambodia in the early 1950s, were gradually building support in the villages. But the insurgents were still extremely short of weapons, and without external support, it looked as though the current stand-off – in which neither side had the strength to inflict decisive damage on the other – would continue indefinitely.

In November, Sâr, accompanied by Khieu Ponnary, his assistant, Pâng, and two bodyguards, set out once again on foot up the Ho Chi Minh Trail to Hanoi, to try to persuade Le Duan and Pham Van Dong that the time had finally come for the Vietnamese communists to aid the rebellion directly.

The moment was ill-chosen. Sihanouk himself had travelled to Hanoi two months before to attend the funeral of Ho Chi Minh and had made clear to the Vietnamese leaders that if they wanted to keep Cambodia 'neutral' and open to the transit of supplies to the Viet Cong, they would have to show support for him. Sâr's importunities got nowhere. Le Duan urged him to call off the rebellion altogether and revert to political struggle. 'The talks took place in a very tense atmosphere,' Sâr wrote later. 'The contradiction between [us] was unbridgeable.' There were differences on other issues, too. When the Vietnamese suggested that he travel on to Moscow, he said he did not wish to become involved in the Sino–Soviet dispute. When, in turn, he proposed visiting Pyongyang, the Vietnamese replied, mendaciously, as he learnt later, that the Korean Party leaders were 'not ready to receive him'. His request to visit the Pathet Lao was likewise deflected. By the time he flew to Beijing in January, nothing had been resolved and no progress made on any of the issues he had discussed.

Sihanouk was equally unsuccessful in extricating himself from his dispute with Lon Nol. At one point, according to his cousin, Prince Sisowath Entaravong, he considered having himself crowned King again, but was dissuaded by his mother, Queen Kossamak, who told him he would look ridiculous after his repeated promises never again to wear the crown. Then, at the end of December, he ordered four government ministers, all long-time Sihanouk loyalists, to submit their resignations in the hope of triggering a cabinet crisis. The four complied. But no crisis ensued. A few days later, in a black depression, Sihanouk retired to the French hospital in Phnom Penh, suffering from nervous exhaustion. On January 6 1970, with only a few hours' warning to his wife and family and none at all to the government or the diplomatic corps, the Head of State flew out to France for a much-delayed rest-cure at a clinic in the Mediterranean town of Grasse.

It was three years, almost to the day, since he had left, in similar circumstances, during Lon Nol's first premiership. On that occasion, his absence had helped to unblock another difficult situation. This time, with Sirik

Matak in charge and Lon Nol convalescing in Europe, the Prince felt that by 'standing back at a distance', he would give his troublesome cousin enough rope to hang himself. As the new decade began, for Sihanouk, as for Sâr, everything was still to play for.

6

The Sudden Death of Reason

UNTIL THE SPRING of 1970, nothing that Saloth Sâr had done or permitted to be done by the Party he led gave any intimation of the abominations that would follow.

To all appearances, he was still the same soft-spoken, smiling, amiable man who, as a student in Paris, was remembered for his sense of fun and good companionship; who later, as a teacher in Phnom Penh, had been adored by his pupils; and who finally, as a communist, was valued for his ability to bring together different tendencies and groups. His revolutionary alias in the 1960s reflected his reputation. He called himself Pouk, meaning 'mattress', because his role was to soften conflicts.

True, under his leadership the Cambodian Communist Party had started a guerrilla war against Sihanouk. But that was a decision which, to a great extent, had been forced on him. As the portly young banker Pok Deuskomar had explained two years earlier, shortly before setting out for the maquis: 'there are no legal avenues of struggle left to us, so we have to take up arms.' By the late 1960s, Sihanouk's inability to tolerate criticism or even argument, his conviction that no one knew better than he on any conceivable subject, had killed political debate in Cambodia. Those who might have formed a constructive opposition had been silenced or forced to flee. In a deeply corrupt state, ruled by an autocrat and racked by social and economic injustice, armed rebellion had become not just the natural but the inevitable choice of any idealistic young man or woman committed to the country's good. Moreover, the rebellion was not, in the early stages, markedly different from similar conflicts elsewhere. Village headmen and others who collaborated with the government were brought before mass meetings and publicly executed. But the same thing was happening in neighbouring Vietnam and on a far larger scale. There were acts of petty banditry which the government assimilated to terrorism – an attack on a bus in Koh Kong in which five people died; and random shootings near Phnom Penh during the New Year holiday – but nothing remotely comparable with terrorist incidents in South Vietnam or even with the train massacre perpetrated by the Khmer Viet Minh in 1954. Most rebel attacks were carefully targeted to serve political or military goals and the groups involved were so small that 'excesses' were rare. The atrocities, in these first years of the war, were the work of government troops.

That is not to say that the forces which would give the Khmer Rouge revolution its peculiarly malignant form were not already at work. In retrospect it is clear that the ground had been prepared, the seeds of the future polity were already sown. But at the time no one foresaw – not the Vietnamese, not the intellectuals who flocked to the CPK cause, not even Sâr himself – the poisoned harvest that would follow. Questioned about the way the communist guerrillas treated their opponents, one of Sâr's bodyguards, who had fought in Ratanakiri, responded thirty years later:

> You're asking me if we took prisoners? No . . . and on our own side we had orders not to allow ourselves to be taken alive. If we captured a villager, and it was someone from the area, we sent him back home. But if we caught a government soldier, we killed him. There wasn't any explicit guideline to that effect, but everyone understood it was what we should do. It was a struggle without pity. We had to draw a clear line of demarcation between the enemy and ourselves. That was the guiding principle.

That was also how the government troops acted. They, too, took few prisoners. But the justification of the communists – 'drawing a clear line of demarcation' – raised different issues. Government forces killed their prisoners because Sihanouk had ordered exemplary repression. The Khmers Rouges did so because 'enemies' were defined as irredeemably hostile. This was not yet an article of faith: there were cases in the early 1970s of Khmers Rouges releasing their prisoners in the hope that they would mend their ways. But the Maoist approach, instrumental in achieving victory in the Chinese civil war, that enemy prisoners could and should be won over to fight for the communist cause, did not come naturally to Cambodians. In the Confucian cultures of China and Vietnam, men are, in theory, always capable of being reformed. In Khmer culture they are not. The 'line of demarcation' is absolute. Just as Cambodians are what they are because they are not Vietnamese or Thais, just as the village exists in opposition to the forest and what is civilised in opposition to what is wild – so those beyond the 'line' are irretrievably divided from those within. Their existence has no value.

This attitude informs much Khmer thought and behaviour, but its application depends on circumstances. Eventually, it would come to dominate every aspect of CPK policy and practice. But not in the spring of 1970. The tragedy that was about to unfold did not have to happen.

The same was true of other facets of the emergent Khmer Rouge movement.

Sâr's insistence that the revolution be led by an alliance of peasants and intellectuals was, in orthodox Marxist terms, a recipe for extremism. Both classes, according to Marx – and to Mao – had the characteristics of the petty bourgeoisie: individualism, volatility, indiscipline and a tendency to metaphysics and anarchism. They would behave as revolutionaries only if led by the proletariat. But extremism was a risk, not a certainty. It was not set in concrete that a revolution led by intellectuals and peasants had to be a blood bath.

The same applied to the CPK's obsession with secrecy. In the conditions of Sihanouk's Cambodia, a revolutionary party had no choice but to be secretive. The CPK's Vietnamese mentors themselves insisted on it. It was from Hay So, Teur Kam and the other pseudonymous Southern Bureau comrades in Phnom Penh in the 1950s that Sâr and Nuon Chea had learnt to use aliases and code numbers rather than place-names – 'Office 100'; 'Office 102'; K-1; K-5, K-12; and all the bewildering array of messenger offices (designated by the letter 'Y'), bureaux ('S'), logistics and medical units ('V' and 'P') that followed. The Chinese communists never used such codes: they were a purely Vietnamese invention. So was the system of naming leaders. Ho Chi Minh chose aliases for his Politburo colleagues on the model of the Vietnamese family, in which the siblings are numbered in order of seniority. When Sâr visited Hanoi in 1965, the Vietnamese addressed him, likewise, as *Anh Hai*, '[First] Brother', the eldest member of the Cambodian revolutionary 'family', and thereafter he used the soubriquet *Hay* whenever he dealt with Vietnam. The Khmers subsequently adopted these appellations as their own. Sâr was known among the Party elite as *Bâng ti moi*, 'First Brother', and Nuon Chea as 'Second Brother'.* The Orwellian overtones conveyed in western languages by the usual translation, 'Brother Number One', are absent in Khmer. 'First Brother' was chosen precisely because it was reassuring and ordinary, a familiar name for an eldest brother in every family everywhere in East Asia. But whatever meanings are read into these names, the conspiratorial system of which they formed part was not uniquely Khmer.

Other characteristics of the Cambodian movement were also less singular than hindsight made them appear. Despite or perhaps because of the

---

*The system is in fact slightly more complicated. In Vietnam, the first child is called the second, for superstitious reasons similar to those which lead some Western hotels to omit the thirteenth floor: evil spirits will be tricked into thinking they have already carried off the missing 'first' child and leave the 'second' alone. Ho Chi Minh, the notional 'Second Brother', accordingly named his deputy, Le Duan, 'Third Brother'; Pham Van Dong, 'Fourth Brother'; Truong Chinh, 'Fifth Brother', and so on down to Pham Hung ('Youngest Brother'). Sâr's title in Vietnamese, *Anh Hai*, literally meant 'Second Brother', but with the sense, in Vietnamese usage, of 'First Brother'. In Cambodia (and China, where different tricks are used to confuse the spirits), this refinement is ignored. *Bâng ti moi* in Khmer is both literally and figuratively 'First Brother'.

fact that the Party was led by intellectuals, it was contemptuous of book-learning: from the mid-1960s on, students were encouraged to show their revolutionary commitment by dropping out and joining the maquis, rather than completing their studies. But the PCF and other European parties had the same anti-intellectual bias.

Even the absence of any serious effort to translate Marxist texts into Khmer could be explained by the orality of Khmer culture.

The one thing that really did set Khmer communism apart at the end of the 1960s was its monastic stress on discipline. Son Sen's younger brother, Nikân, spent three months holed up in a peasant's hut in rural Kompong Cham while he was on the run in 1968. He was not allowed to go outside to wash or even to use a latrine, ostensibly for security reasons but in fact to temper him, enabling him to prove that his loyalty to the Party had no limit. Khieu Samphân endured similar isolation when he first arrived in the maquis. Others spent years immured in secret hideouts in Phnom Penh. It was behaviour more appropriate to a religious sect than a political movement. In retrospect, it contained the germs of the systematic destruction of the individual that would later become a hallmark of Khmer communist ideology.

But no one saw that at the time. It seemed then to be merely a reaction against the careless, laissez-faire ways of a gentle, laid-back people whose would-be leaders had to be constantly on their guard in order to escape the attentions of Sihanouk's security police.

In short, at the beginning of 1970, none of the elements that would fuse into the murderous specificity of the Khmer Rouge regime in power was unambiguously present. The ideological potential was there. But it was not preordained to take the form it did.

Similar considerations applied to Sihanouk's position. He, too, had reached an invisible crossroads. Rumours that Lon Nol was plotting to overthrow him surfaced at the beginning of January. But by then there had been so many false alarms that the French Ambassador reported dismissively to Paris that it was mischief-making by Soviet-bloc diplomats with nothing better to do. Western chancelleries had been preparing contingency papers about the possibility of a military coup for the best part of a decade, but it was not a prospect they took seriously – any more than did the Prince himself.* To the outside world, Sihanouk personified Cambodia. Even the

---

*The Viet Cong also heard the coup rumours and did take them seriously. A new headquarters for the COSVN was prepared in Kratie province, 60 miles north of the existing base at Memot, and escape routes mapped out through Prey Veng and Kompong Cham, in case a pro-American regime took power in Phnom Penh and the fighting in the border areas intensified. They also made contingency plans for a further retreat, should it become necessary, either west of the Mekong or northwards into Laos.

Americans, who had unsuccessfully sought his replacement by a more congenial figure in the 1950s and early '60s, were wary of becoming involved in any fresh attempt to unseat him. In January 1970, there seemed no reason to suppose that he would not be able to turn the tables on his adversaries by some dazzling pirouette, as he had done so many times in the past.

Over the next few weeks, all these comforting certitudes would prove hollow. For Sâr, for Sihanouk, for the Khmer people, the world would be turned on its head with brutal thoroughness. The ideology of the Khmers Rouges, hitherto confined to the thoughts and private discussions of Sâr, Ieng Sary, Nuon Chea and a handful of others, found its *lebensraum*. For them, as for the Prince, the moment of truth had arrived.

On March 8, a Sunday, demonstrations against the presence of Viet Cong guerrillas took place in the provincial capital of Svay Rieng and several district centres. By then the Parrot's Beak, as the area was called, was reluctant host to some 20,000 Vietnamese communists. To Sihanouk, the build-up was one more factor sucking Cambodia into the Vietnam War. His efforts the previous autumn, when he had attended Ho Chi Minh's funeral, to persuade Hanoi to exercise restraint had been to no avail. Now the time had come to get nasty. He planned to travel home from France via Moscow and Beijing to ask the Soviet and Chinese leaders to put pressure on their protégés to be more discreet. To dramatise his plea, he had proposed to Lon Nol that 'spontaneous protests' be organised against the Vietnamese a few days beforehand.

The following morning, students in Phnom Penh demonstrated outside the National Assembly, where they presented a motion demanding that the Viet Cong withdraw from Cambodian territory. Two days later, on the 11th, tens of thousands of people, many of them civil servants who had been given time off for the purpose, marched on the Embassy of the South Vietnamese Provisional Revolutionary Government. While the police stood by, the crowd, egged on by government agents, overturned and set fire to diplomats' cars, and a squad of soldiers in plain clothes stormed the Embassy buildings, throwing filing cabinets, books and papers out of upper-storey windows and setting fire to whatever was left within. After spending an hour or so looting, the mob moved on to the Embassy of North Vietnam. That, too, was systematically wrecked. By contrast, the Chinese Embassy was guarded by a cordon of Cambodian troops with strict orders to shoot any demonstrator who tried to cross the line. Rioting continued sporadically, and in the course of the next two days two Vietnamese Roman Catholic churches and a number of shops and private homes in the city came under attack.

Whether or not Sihanouk had intended the protests to go as far as the sacking of the embassies is moot. Whether Lon Nol and Sirik Matak saw the rioting simply as a complement to the Prince's diplomacy; whether they viewed it as a way for the government to take control of a key foreign policy issue, confining Sihanouk to his constitutional role; or whether they hoped that the climate of violence, fuelled by popular anger against the 'hereditary enemy', would create the political conditions for more drastic action against him, is also uncertain.

What is clear is that the Prince's reaction set off alarm bells.

For months, Sirik Matak and Lon Nol had been turning over ideas to restrict Sihanouk's powers and – at least in Sirik Matak' s mind – if all else failed, to remove him from office. But they had reached no conclusion. On the evening of the 11th, however, the Prince issued a statement in Paris deploring the incidents and denouncing unnamed 'personalities who are aiming at destroying beyond repair Cambodia's friendship with the social-ist camp'. When he returned home, he added menacingly, he would ask Cambodians to choose between himself and these recreants.

In all probability, Sihanouk was merely positioning himself for the coming talks in Moscow and Beijing. If he could demonstrate that he was trying to hold the line, not only against an inflamed public opinion but against his right-wing ministers, his appeal for restraint by the Viet Cong would stand a better chance of being heard.

But Sirik Matak read it differently. To him, the burden of the message was that he and Lon Nol would become scapegoats for actions the Prince himself had approved, a conviction reinforced when his brother, Sisowath Essaro, informed him from Paris that Sihanouk had been talking darkly of having the leaders of the government shot. It was typical hyperbole, as Matak well knew, but the timing was unfortunate.

The sequence of events then accelerated. Next day, Thursday March 12, the CIA Station Chief in Saigon told Washington that Matak had opted for a showdown and the army was ready for a coup 'if Sihanouk refused to support the current government or exerted pressure upon [it]'. A few hours later, Lon Nol issued a statement apologising for the damage to the two embassies but demanding, with a straight face and total lack of realism, that all Vietnamese communist forces must leave Cambodian territory by dawn on March 15. Neither he nor Matak had a direct channel to the Americans, but both were convinced that a change of regime would have Washington's blessing. Lon Nol had been talking to Son Ngoc Thanh, the leader of the Khmer Serei, since the previous autumn. Another US client in the region was also in touch with the plotters. At midnight on March 12, the Vice-President of South Vietnam, Nguyen Cao Ky, landed at Phnom Penh's

Pochentong Airport, in total darkness and with the runway lights extinguished, aboard a DC-4 from Saigon, for the first of two secret, late-night visits. There is no record of what he discussed, or with whom, but he certainly opened the door to the idea of an alliance between Cambodia and South Vietnam.

On Friday March 13, Sihanouk, after much hesitation, left Paris as planned for Moscow. It was an uncharacteristic misjudgement, of the kind that politicians make after too many years in power. Had he returned directly to Phnom Penh, as at one point he intended, the plot would have fizzled out. But Sihanouk had told the Cambodians for so long that the country could not do without him that he had come to believe it himself. In the end, he was the victim not of the CIA, as he claimed, but of his own hubris.

The last days were a blur. Both the Russians and the Chinese wanted the Prince to return home without delay. He would not listen. In Phnom Penh, Sirik Matak had the Police Minister, Oum Mannorine, Sihanouk's brother-in-law, placed under house arrest. Violent demonstrations against the Vietnamese continued in the provinces. The capital was alive with rumours of strange portents, spread by those with a vested interest in such tales. A white crocodile was said to have been sighted; for three days, the moon was encircled with a halo the colour of blood; a peasant soothsayer had arrived at the palace with a message from a long dead king that Sihanouk was about to fall.

Finally, in the early hours of March 18, Sirik Matak and two army officers confronted Prime Minister Lon Nol. Matak was a haughty, sophisticated man, born to palace intrigue, who greeted callers wearing a silk dressing gown and lived in a princely mansion full of sumptuous furniture and marble statuary. Lon Nol was a commoner and rejoiced in the common touch. In true Khmer style, his home, a rambling estate on the road to the airport, was always full of relatives and hangers-on. He encouraged his troops to call him 'Black Papa', to underline that he was a dark-skinned Khmer, without foreign blood. Sihanouk's French advisers remembered him as 'a rock-like figure . . . silent as a carp'. He did not impress by his intellect. Charles Meyer, who dealt with Lon Nol frequently, wrote later that by using him as 'a fascist scarecrow to frighten the left-wing opposition', Sihanouk had convinced him that he was a strongman with a national destiny. 'In fact he was none of that. He was withdrawn and full of confused ideas, expressing himself in obscure parables whose significance only he could see . . . [and] capable of following his pet projects with all the subtlety of a bulldozer in the jungle.' Nol and Sirik Matak were an improbable pair. Yet they had been friends since their schooldays and had worked together in the right-wing Renovation Party during the struggle against the French in the late 1940s.

Lon Nol prevaricated. Everything he had achieved in his life had been due to Sihanouk's patronage. He knew the Prince trusted him. But he was ambitious and profoundly influenced by esoteric Buddhism. The mystics and seers he frequented had persuaded him that his fate was to restore the glories of the ancient Khmer-Mon empire by waging war against the *thmil*, the hated 'unbelievers' from communist Vietnam. Now was the moment, if ever, to assume that destiny.

Matak presented him with a draft decree approving the Prince's overthrow. According to one of those present, when he continued to tergiversate, Matak cried: 'Nol, my friend, if you don't sign this paper, we'll shoot you!' Weeping, the Prime Minister signed. A few hours later, armoured cars surrounded the radio station, three tanks took up position in front of the parliament building, international telephone and telegraph lines were cut and the country's airports closed.

At 9 a.m., the National Assembly and the Council of the Kingdom, a consultative upper chamber, met in joint session. For two hours, MPs poured out, with rare unanimity, their accumulated bile at all the humiliations Sihanouk had made them endure over the previous three years. Not one voice was raised to defend him. For the first time in his life, the Prince was subjected, *in absentia*, to the same lynch-mob instincts that he himself had used so often to crush his opponents at Sangkum congresses. When the vote was called, one MP walked out. The other ninety-one approved a motion 'to withdraw confidence in Prince Norodom Sihanouk [who], as from one o'clock on March 18 1970 . . . shall relinquish his office as Chief of State'. In accordance with the constitution, the President of the National Assembly, Cheng Heng, was to act in his place pending new elections.

Sâr heard the news in China. Sihanouk was told in Moscow by Premier Alexei Kosygin as they were driving to the airport for his departure to Beijing.

It was not the first time the Russians had played host to a third-world potentate who suddenly found himself dispossessed of his country and Kosygin politely made clear that there was not a lot the Soviet Union could do.

The Chinese reacted very differently. Since 1965, China had viewed its relationship with Vietnam through the prism of the Sino–Soviet dispute. Beijing was still Hanoi's biggest source of military aid. But Mao had reacted sharply against Le Duan's decision, apparently taken without Ho Chi Minh's knowledge, to open peace talks in Paris, seeing it as a step towards a US–Soviet global condominium. Vietnam already dominated Laos. In Zhou Enlai's judgement, a pro-American regime in Phnom Penh –

especially one led by Lon Nol, whom he had met and instinctively distrusted – would sooner or later collapse, opening the way for Vietnamese,
and in a worst case, Soviet, hegemony over the whole of Indochina.

The following morning, when Sihanouk's plane landed in Beijing, he
found the entire diplomatic corps, ambassadors and heads of mission representing forty-one states, including Britain and France, lined up on the
tarmac to greet him. Zhou Enlai himself was there. As they drove into
Beijing, the Chinese Premier enquired about his intentions. 'I am going to
return home and fight,' Sihanouk replied. Zhou was not taken in. He
warned that a war would be 'long, hard, dangerous and sometimes dis-
couraging', and suggested that Sihanouk give himself a day to reflect. That
evening, the Chinese Politburo met and agreed to allow the Prince to
remain in Beijing if he so wished and to make statements to the press.

In fact Sihanouk was anything but certain of what he wanted to do. In
the plane he had talked with his wife, Monique, of retiring to their villa at
Mougins on the Côte d'Azur. One of his first actions after arriving was to
sound out the French Ambassador to China, Etienne Manac'h, on the possibility of France granting him asylum. There was a precedent for such a
step: the Vietnamese Emperor, Bao Dai, had ended his days on the Riviera;
so had Egypt's King Farouk. But these were not men Sihanouk admired.
To accept exile would be an act of cowardice. His resolve was bolstered by
the vilification to which he was subjected by the new regime. François
Ponchaud was then a young Roman Catholic missionary in Phnom Penh:

> I think Sihanouk would have accepted being overthrown. But the Khmers . . .
> don't understand the difference between criticism and calumny. I used to read
> the Khmer newspapers. There were pictures of a naked man with Sihanouk's
> head and a naked woman with the face of Monique. When I saw that, I said
> to myself: 'Sihanouk can never accept that.' That was my immediate reaction.

Next day, the Prince told Zhou his mind was made up. In a message to the
Cambodian people, broadcast by Radio Beijing, he denounced the coup-
makers and promised to fight for 'justice', by which he meant revenge.

On March 21, the North Vietnamese Premier, Pham Van Dong, flew
to Beijing. He asked Sihanouk whether he was willing to co-operate with
the Khmers Rouges, adding that if the answer were yes, there would have
to be contacts both at leadership level and among the rank and file. 'He
said nothing beyond giving general consent', Dong told Zhou Enlai afterwards. 'He did not say what he wanted us to do.' Even with those caveats,
the fact that Sihanouk consented at all was an extraordinary step. He had
said often enough that if communism triumphed in Cambodia, its people
would be enslaved. Since the mid-1960s he had ordered, or at least

approved, policies of pitiless repression. But he had also given warning, ten years earlier, of what would happen if the United States forced Cambodia to abandon its neutralist course: 'There will be a monarchical-communist revolution . . . [and it will be] a catastrophe for the Free World.' The prophecy had come to pass and, from a mixture of motives – betrayal; a desire for vengeance; and an ancestral obligation to try to preserve the monarchy – Sihanouk decided that it was his fate to put it into execution.

The North Vietnamese leader also met Sâr, who found him in a very different mood from their last encounter two months earlier. Now it was all 'friendship and solidarity [and] friendly words and embraces . . . It was a change of 180 degrees.' To Hanoi, if Cambodia entered the war, the whole of Indochina would once again, as in the 1950s, become 'a single battlefield'. An alliance between Sihanouk and the Khmer communists would then be in all their interests.

The problem was that neither Sâr nor Pham Van Dong nor Zhou was yet sure that Sihanouk could be relied on. 'We should support [him] for the time being and see how he will act,' the Chinese Premier said. 'We will see whether he really wants to establish a united front against the US . . . Because of the circumstances he may change his position.' All three, therefore, kept their options open. China and Vietnam maintained contact with the new authorities in Phnom Penh in the faint hope of preserving the Viet Cong supply line through Kompong Som. And Pham Van Dong gave the Prince a formal assurance, 'on oath', as he put it, in Zhou Enlai's presence, that Vietnam would respect the 'independence, sovereignty and territorial integrity' of Cambodia 'within its present borders'.

Two days later, on March 23, Sihanouk announced that he was forming a political movement to be called the National United Front of Kampuchea, known by its French acronym, FUNK, and appealed to his compatriots to launch a campaign of guerrilla attacks and civil disobedience against the Lon Nol government. Those with 'the necessary courage and patriotic spirit' would receive arms and military training – the former (although he did not say so) to be provided by China, the latter by North Vietnam – and as soon as practicable a National Liberation Army would be formed, which would fight under the orders of a Cambodian Royal Government of National Union (GRUNC).* The political complexion of the new movement was not explicitly spelt out, but the statement stressed the role of 'the progressive, industrious and pure working people'; promised 'social

---

*North Vietnam's Defence Minister, General Vo Nguyen Giap, assigned hundreds of Vietnamese instructors to train a 'Sihanoukist' army in the 'liberated zones' of Cambodia, which eventually numbered some 15,000 men.

justice, equality and fraternity among Khmers'; underlined the solidarity of 'our three peoples, the Khmers, Vietnamese and Laotians', and claimed the 'complete support' of 'anti-imperialist countries and peoples, near and far'.

As the language indicated, the 'Appeal of March 23', which Sihanouk liked to compare with De Gaulle's appeal to the French in 1940 to resist Nazi Germany, was not all his own work. A draft had been given to Zhou Enlai, who in turn had shown it to Sâr. He had proposed certain changes, the main one being to excise all references to socialism. During the meeting the Chinese Premier told him: 'The Cambodian communists should think about the overall situation of the country, and not dwell on past quarrels. Prince Sihanouk is a patriot and his international reputation is high . . . [You] should co-operate to form a joint government against the common enemy.' Sâr needed no persuading. But instead of agreeing to meet the Prince, as Zhou had expected, he drafted a message of support for the Front over the signatures of the men the Americans called the 'three Ghosts', Khieu Samphân, Hou Yuon and Hu Nim, who most Cambodians believed had been killed on Sihanouk's orders three years earlier. It was delivered on March 26 and purported to have been sent from a resistance base inside Cambodia. Sihanouk was never told of Sâr's presence in Beijing, and when it was publicly confirmed eight years later he refused to believe it.

The supposed 'message from the maquis' was an astute move. By presenting Khieu Samphân and his colleagues as the principal Khmer Rouge figures (as Sihanouk himself had always believed) the secrecy surrounding the CPK leadership and the Party's existence was preserved. All three men were widely respected for their probity and courage. In terms of image, Sâr could hardly have done better.

The resistance was Cambodian, patriotic and led by a Khmer king. Lon Nol's claims that it was 'communist' and 'controlled by the Vietnamese' faced an uphill task.

Sihanouk's appeal amounted to a declaration of war. Every Khmer was now forced to choose sides. In China, the Prince was joined by the few Cambodian ambassadors who had remained loyal to him, including Sarin Chhak from Cairo, Huot Sambath from the United Nations and Chan Yourann from Dakar; by Chau Seng, his former minister and gifted bad boy of Phnom Penh's 'drawing-room Left'; and by Thiounn Mumm and a group of colleagues from the Parisian Cercle Marxiste. For the next year, they and another former cabinet member, Keat Chhon, formed the administrative backbone of Sihanouk's government-in-exile.

Political matters remained under the watchful eye of the Chinese. They alone, in that first year, were in contact with the CPK leaders inside

Cambodia. It was they who, on April 24 and 25, organised an Indochinese summit between Cambodia, Laos and Vietnam – officially held in the jungle 'on the border of China and Vietnam' but actually at a luxurious hot springs resort in the suburbs of Canton – to demonstrate the new-found solidarity of the Indochinese peoples.* It was the Chinese, too, who told Sihanouk at the beginning of May that it was time to form a government; and Vice-Foreign Minister Han Nianlong who summoned Thiounn Mumm to draft its political programme. This was a moderate, nationalist document which, even more than Sihanouk's appeal in March, eschewed communist goals, and was deliberately designed to win the widest possible support both inside and outside Cambodia. This time there was no input from 'the interior'. Mumm remembered receiving only a single message, passed on by the Chinese, requesting that half the posts in the new government be given, notionally at least, to cadres inside Cambodia.†

---

*The summit nearly came to grief because of a row between Sihanouk and Penn Nouth, who had been with him at the time of the coup and accompanied him into exile. Sihanouk wanted to appoint Huot Sambath, whom Penn Nouth detested, to a cabinet position. Nouth threatened to retire to France; Sihanouk dug in his heels. Eventually a solution was found, but not until the early hours of the morning of the day the conference was to open. Thiounn Mumm had a surrealistic 3 a.m. meeting with Vice-Minister Han Nianlong, in his bedroom wearing undershorts, at which it was agreed that it would have to be post-poned. Zhou Enlai had wanted the summit to start on April 23, to coincide with the launch-ing of China's first satellite. Instead it began a day later. Disputes over personalities were a characteristic of Cambodian politics under Sihanouk and have remained so ever since.

†The composition of the GRUNC, taking into account later reshuffles, was as follows (with the names of ministers living in the maquis in italics):
Prime Minister: Penn Nouth
  Vice-Minister in the Prime Minister's Office: Keat Chhon
Deputy Prime Minister and Minister of Defence: Khieu Samphân
Foreign Minister: Sarin Chhak
  Vice-Minister: Pok Deuskomar
Information Minister: Hu Nim
  Vice-Minister: Tiv Ol
Interior Minister. Minister of Co-operatives: Hou Yuon
  Vice-Minister of the Interior and National Security: Vorn Vet
Minister of Economy and Finance: Thiounn Mumm
  Vice-Minister: Koy Thuon
Minister for Special Missions: Chau Seng
Minister of Co-ordination: Thiounn Prasith
Minister of Education and Youth: Chan Yourann
  Vice-Minister Khieu Thirith
Minister for Armament: General Duong Sam Ol
Minister of Justice: Chea San
  (later Prince Norodom Phurissara)
Minister of Rites and Religious Affairs: Chey Chum
Minister of Public Works: Huot Sambath

The GRUNC was formally proclaimed on May 5 and immediately recognised by China, North Korea and Vietnam, as well as by Cuba and a
handful of other third-world states. It was housed in the *Youyi binguan*
(Friendship Hostel), a residential and office complex in north-western
Beijing originally built for Soviet aid personnel in the 1950s. Sihanouk
lived in the former French Legation, a turn-of-the-century mansion set in
formal gardens, surrounded by high walls, in the heart of the city's government quarter. The Chinese paid all costs. Sihanouk and his suite were not
used to penny-pinching. Zhou Enlai had asked Thiounn Mumm to work
out a suitable budget. The figure he came up with was five million dollars
a year. 'Zhou said "No",' Mumm remembered. 'He doubled it. We were
to use half ourselves. The other half was to be sent to the interior.'

There were practical reasons for this division of funds. The Khmers
Rouges acquired part of their weaponry from corrupt officers in Lon Nol's
army who would sell to anyone prepared to pay them in hard currency.
Each year, for that purpose, five million dollars in notes was wrapped in
layers of waterproof paper, packed in rucksacks, and carried down the Ho
Chi Minh Trail by Khmer porters, usually students or returnees, who were
told they were transporting 'secret documents'. But the equality of treatment between Sihanouk and the Khmers Rouges was also a reminder to
both sides that China considered them to be playing equally valuable, but
quite separate, roles. With hindsight, it was the separation that was most
striking. Non-ruling communist parties always keep their distance from the
public front organisations they manipulate behind the scenes. The relationship between the communist COSVN and the non-Party NLF was a typical example of the genre. But in the Cambodian case, there was not even
manipulation. Once Sihanouk had accepted the principle of co-operating
with the Khmers Rouges, he was free to lead the diplomatic battle for
international recognition as he thought fit. Sâr had the same liberty to conduct policy at home. Each had a distinct agenda. Sihanouk wanted vengeance. The Khmers Rouges needed his name. It was not even a marriage
of convenience. They shared different beds with different dreams.

At the beginning of April 1970, Sâr flew back to Hanoi, where he and
Khieu Ponnary were fêted by Le Duan, Pham Van Dong, Vo Nguyen Giap
and other VWP Politburo members. Before they left on the long trek back

---

Minister of Public Health: Ngo Hou
   Vice-Minister: Chou Chet
Phurissara resigned as Lon Nol's Foreign Minister a few days after the coup. He fled with
his wife to the maquis in January 1972.

down the Ho Chi Minh Trail, Le Duan proposed a meeting to discuss military co-operation.

In Sâr's absence, Nuon Chea – who, on the day the coup occurred, had been with So Phim at Krâbao attending a meeting of Eastern Zone CPK officials – had given instructions that, wherever possible, the Khmer Rouge 'armed propaganda groups' working in the countryside should seize control of village, commune and district administrations. A week later, after Sihanouk's appeal, Vietnamese officials approached him with a proposal for joint military action. Nuon initially demurred, but when the Vietnamese made clear that, in their own interests, they intended to secure their sanctuaries in Cambodia regardless of Khmer views, he agreed in principle that the two forces should co-operate. However, Nuon did not commit himself on details. Instead he sent a message to Hanoi, explaining what was being proposed, to await Sâr's arrival. Now Le Duan wanted to know what were the CPK's intentions.

It was, by Sâr's account, a rather awkward discussion. The Vietnamese began by offering 5,000 rifles to equip Khmer Rouge units, which the Cambodians accepted. But then Le Duan proposed setting up mixed commands. To Sâr, that brought back memories of the 1950s when Khmer 'commanders' had been assisted by Vietnamese 'deputies' who had taken all the decisions. The Cambodians would once again be under Vietnamese tutelage. Sâr took refuge in a syllogism, saying he had no mandate from the CPK Central Committee to discuss the issue. But his 'personal view', he added, was that it would be counter-productive: the 'experience of past struggles' had shown that mixed commands were a source of conflict; and politically it would give the impression that the Cambodian resistance was dependent on Vietnam, which neither Sihanouk nor the Khmer people would find acceptable. Le Duan took the point.

Other, more fundamental, problems were less easily resolved.

Even before Sihanouk's appeal, the Vietnamese had drawn up plans for an offensive against Lon Nol's forces if, as they expected, negotiations with the new government failed. On March 19, the day after the coup, without waiting to see what happened in Phnom Penh, COSVN moved to a pre-prepared base in the Prek Prâsâp district of Kratie. Soon after this, the Vietnamese leaders concluded that Lon Nol and Sirik Matak had accepted a Faustian pact to enter the war on the American side in return for US aid and that continued contacts would achieve nothing. On March 27, the last Vietnamese diplomats in Cambodia were flown out to Hanoi.

Two days later the 40,000 Viet Cong and North Vietnamese troops in Cambodia, hastily reinforced by additional units from the communist 5th, 7th and 9th divisions, launched co-ordinated attacks against government positions. On April 20, Viet Cong units came within fifteen miles of Phnom Penh before being beaten back. By the end of the month, they had occupied most of Ratanakiri and Mondulkiri, parts of Stung Treng and Kratie and a swathe of territory stretching through six other provinces, from Kompong Cham to Kampot.

At that point President Nixon announced that the US and South Vietnam would launch what was officially termed 'a limited incursion'. For the next two months, 30,000 Americans and more than 40,000 South Vietnamese swept through Svay Rieng and Kompong Cham ostensibly seeking the elusive, and long since departed, COSVN headquarters, but actually trying to keep Lon Nol's flailing government afloat.

There were short-term benefits. The US forces and their allies seized mountains of communist weaponry and equipment and killed large numbers of Viet Cong. But the long-term effects were disastrous. The invasion ratcheted up still further domestic US opposition to the Vietnam War and triggered the first of a long series of congressional amendments, restricting the US government's freedom of military action. For Lon Nol, whom the White House had omitted to consult or even inform, it destroyed the government's case against Sihanouk: there was no point telling Cambodians that the Prince was a lackey of the hated Vietnamese if Lon Nol's own regime was being propped up by Saigon. But worst of all, the offensive was militarily counter-productive. To silence criticism at home, Nixon had had to promise that all US units would be pulled out by the end of June and that the invasion force would not penetrate more than twenty-one miles into Cambodian territory. The effect was to complete what the 'Menu' bombings had started: the Vietnamese communists were spread all over Cambodia.

For Sâr and his colleagues, this posed a real dilemma. On the one hand, the more territory the Vietnamese seized, the more recruits there would be for the resistance army and the bigger the 'liberated zones' for the Khmers Rouges to administer. On the other hand, the CPK leaders were acutely aware of the danger of going too fast. 'They told us, in effect,' a Vietnamese historian wrote later: 'If you, our brothers, help us to do everything too quickly, we won't be able to keep up with you, and then, the moment you leave, we will have nothing.'

When Sâr had met Le Duan in Hanoi, he had made clear that the Cambodians needed weapons, not troops: they had to build up their own armed forces, not rely on Vietnam's. The implication, which he did not spell out, was that the Khmers Rouges sought a protracted war, not a speedy victory.

Khieu Samphân argued later that the coup and its aftermath vindicated

Sâr's decision in the mid-1960s to initiate an armed struggle, because it meant that in 1970 a rudimentary Khmer Rouge guerrilla force was already in existence. But it was only two to three thousand strong, outnumbered twenty to one by its Vietnamese brothers-in-arms. The result was that, except in the North-East, where a local Khmer Rouge administration was already in place, the Vietnamese brought with them administrative offices, hospitals, military and political training schools, and all the paraphernalia of an occupying force. In Takeo province, a local cadre remembered:

> Some Vietnamese came up from Vietnam to organise the village adminis-
> tration . . . They [called it] a mixed Khmer–Viet Cong administration, but
> it was actually run by the Viet Cong. For instance, they appointed a Khmer
> commune chief. But in practice he answered to a Viet Cong official at the
> same level. It was like a colonial system. They appointed Khmer officials,
> but they were under Vietnamese supervision.

This was not an isolated case, it was official COSVN policy. Sâr complained afterwards that the Viet Cong had set up a 'parallel state power' in the 'liberated zones' and established their own guerrilla detachments, independent of the Khmer Rouge command structure, 'without the CPK Central Committee's knowledge'. In fact, the Cambodian leaders knew very well what the Vietnamese were doing. They did not like it, but there was no choice. In most of Cambodia, the Khmers Rouges had neither cadres to administer the newly gained territories nor soldiers to defend them.

Nevertheless it stuck in their gullets to see Angkor Wat, the very symbol of Khmer sovereignty, which fell to the resistance in May, occupied not by their own troops but by the Viet Cong.

The Vietnamese communists understood that. Khmer susceptibility was not new. In terms almost identical to those Nguyen Thanh Son had used in the early 1950s, COSVN urged its cadres to 'treat Cambodians as equals' and 'be patient in providing help for their movement . . . Eliminate the thought that we are "big country" and that [they] are poor and weak.' But alongside the protestations of good faith, the same old condescension was in evidence: 'Although the Cambodian revolutionaries are enthusiastic, they are incapable', another document stated. 'The Cambodian revolution is weak and its organisation loose. We have to strengthen it.' It was all too true. But to Sâr, these were the honeyed words of Vietnamese duplicity.

The Cambodians were torn between the fear that their Vietnamese allies would withdraw as soon as the war ended, leaving them high and dry, as had happened in 1954, and the even greater fear that they would stay. The ancestral dread of Vietnamese domination, shared by Sihanouk and Lon Nol, emerged in 1970 as one of the driving forces of CPK policy. But for the communists the threat came not from enemies but from friends, not from adversaries but from allies – which was far more insidious.

From the outset, the civil war in Cambodia was marked by savagery. A week after the coup, peasant demonstrations broke out in Kompong Cham and a number of local officials were beaten to death. Troops opened fire to disperse rioting crowds. Next day, March 26, a mob sacked the governor's mansion and the courthouse. Radio Phnom Penh described it as 'a provocation by people with a Viet Cong mentality', which raised the tension another notch. At dusk, two local MPs arrived from Phnom Penh to try to mediate. They were set upon and killed. Their livers were then cut out and borne in triumph to a local restaurateur who was ordered to cook them. Afterwards pieces were handed out to the crowd. The same evening Lon Nol's half-brother, Nil, was slain in similar circumstances at a nearby rubber plantation. His liver, too, was cooked and eaten.

That night about a thousand people from Kompong Cham set out in lorries and buses for Phnom Penh, bearing portraits of Sihanouk. At the city outskirts they were joined by another column from Siem Reap. Again troops opened fire to drive them back. Some 10,000 peasants, following on foot, then sacked the government offices at Skoun. This time the army used heavy weaponry, killing and wounding about sixty people. At the weekend, another two hundred died when troops with tanks and armoured cars broke up protest marches in Takeo and Prey Veng.

In the provinces, the repression had predictable results. 'I ran away with my teachers and fellow-students,' one young demonstrator recalled. 'Fifty or sixty of us met up [in the jungle] . . . We hated the troops for what they had done and we wanted to fight back.' Sihanouk's appeal of March 23 prompted a wave of desertions from the army, most notably in Kratie, where the local commander sent all his men home and handed control of the region to the resistance. Viet Cong propagandists played recordings of the Prince's broadcast in the villages. To the peasants, the coup was sacrilege.

In Phnom Penh the reaction was quite different.

The middle classes heaved a sigh of relief that at last they were rid of the playboy Prince with 'his damn film shows', as one young man put it, 'and endless radio speeches in that singsong voice'.

For them, too, the point of reference was the French Revolution, with Sihanouk in the role of Louis XVI. But their model was the revolution of Mirabeau in 1789, when the bourgeoisie seized power, not that of Robespierre and Saint-Just. At heart, in 1970, Cambodia remained a feudal country, and the coup was seen in feudal terms. In the first months, moreover, it was middle-class youths who provided the core of the regime's support. After a couple of days' military training at the city's golf course, they were bussed down towards the border to face the Viet Cong. 'Every day they could be seen setting out,' one observer wrote, 'hanging on the sides of Coca-Cola trucks or brightly painted buses, wearing shower clogs or sandals, shorts or blue jeans, parts of very old French uniforms or over-sized American fatigues.' They carried sticks and cardboard suitcases, and occasionally a rifle.

When cannon fodder was found to be no defence against the hereditary enemy, Lon Nol's government vented its fury on Vietnamese civilians. A curfew was declared – for Vietnamese only – and, 'for their own safety', families were herded into makeshift camps. Unlike the pre-coup demon-strations, in which Vietnamese had lost property but no one had been hurt or killed, this time there were full-scale pogroms. In the space of a single morning, four hundred bodies, with gunshot wounds and hands bound behind their backs, were counted floating down the Mekong river at the ferry point of Neak Luong, just below Phnom Penh. That same day, April 10, at Prasaut, in the Parrot's Beak, camp inmates were told of an immi-nent Viet Cong attack and ordered to flee. As they ran, Cambodian guards opened fire with machine-guns. At least 3,000 people, all males over the age of fifteen, were rounded up in Vietnamese villages in the suburbs north of Phnom Penh, taken downriver and shot. The women left behind were raped. A few days later, Vietnamese 'refugees' being housed at a primary school in Takeo province met a similar fate. Mark Frankland of the London *Observer* witnessed the aftermath:

> It looked and smelt like a slaughterhouse . . . The cement floor was covered with pools of coagulated blood. Three corpses covered with bloody cloth-ing were in one corner. About 40 Vietnamese men and boys lay or squat-ted on the far side of the classroom, as far as possible from the several hundred Cambodian soldiers milling around in the open . . . It was difficult to see exactly how many were wounded since everyone had been splattered with blood. One man . . . had stuffed clothes into an open stomach wound . . . The inside of the classroom's single wall was peppered with bullet holes, but not the outside.

The government denied point-blank that any massacres had taken place. Those who died, officials said, were the victims of cross-fire during attacks by the Viet Cong. It was an archetypal Khmer reaction. In a culture where people go to immense lengths to avoid causing others loss of face – where a man's instinctive reaction in the face of the slightest conflict is to pull back, be it at the cost of sacrificing his own interests – embarrassing questions are simply not asked. If uncouth Westerners insist on doing so, they should not be

surprised when they are told lies. In Khmer terms, they have put their inter-
locutor in a situation from which a lie provides the only possible way out.*

The corollary of this visceral desire to avoid confrontation at all costs is
that debate and argument do not function as a means of resolving differences. Between the extremes of acquiescence and violence there is no
middle ground. The French archaeologist Bernard-Philippe Groslier, who
spent his life studying Angkor, wrote of Cambodia that 'beneath a carefree
surface there slumber savage forces and disconcerting cruelties which may
blaze up in outbreaks of passionate brutality'. Sihanouk himself acknowledged that 'the Khmers can be violent, their gentleness and good fellow-
ship can hide terrible explosions'. The one is the inescapable complement
of the other. When the strains and pressures of existence reach a point
where there is no longer the possibility of graceful withdrawal, when the
smiling façade cracks, violence – 'running amok', as Sihanouk put it –
becomes the only alternative. It is not an aberration. It is an intrinsic part
of Khmer behaviour – the same reflex that leads a kindly middle-aged
woman to pour nitric acid over the body of a teenage girl who has become
a rival for her husband's affections or a villager to tear out another man's
liver. In normal times, the line of fracture remains hidden. Once crossed, it
is the signal for appalling acts of inhumanity undertaken without remorse.

In 1970, all of Cambodia, city and countryside, prince and peasant,
crossed that line.

Eight weeks after the coup, Lon Nol made a radio broadcast announcing the start of a chiliastic religious war against the Vietnamese communists. They were 'the enemies of Buddha', he declared. All Vietnamese,
communist or not, must leave the country and return 'home'. The
pogroms, which Lon Nol had halted after horrified protests abroad, not
least from his South Vietnamese allies, were now followed by mass depor-
tations. Over the next year, 250,000 Vietnamese residents of Cambodia
were forced to abandon their homes and belongings – 'to be taken care of

* In interviews with former Khmers Rouges, I was frequently made aware by a change of
tone or expression that I had overstepped the bounds of what was deemed to be acceptable
questioning, and that the answer given would then be a transparent fiction. This was even
more true of Western-educated leaders like Khieu Samphân than of unlettered peasants.
There was no embarrassment about the lie: it was the answer such a question merited.
Cambodian officials under Sihanouk, Lon Nol, Pol Pot and Hun Sen – not to mention the
leaders themselves – have all, in their different ways, been insouciant of truth, viewing it as
a practical, not a moral commodity. In communist Vietnam and China, the approach is
different. Lying is equally common (as indeed it is in Europe and America) but efforts are
made to cloak the deception in verisimilitude, and political statements, even when riddled
with distortions and omissions, usually have some basis in fact. In Cambodia, they are often
pure invention.

by their neighbours', as the government cynically put it – and placed in concentration camps pending their expulsion. And still the violence did not stop. In May, a Khmer general took about a hundred camp inmates, including women and children, to Khieu Samphân's old constituency of Saang. There he forced them to march, holding white flags, towards Viet Cong positions, using megaphones to urge the communists to surrender while acting as a human shield for the Cambodian soldiers behind. The Viet Cong were unimpressed. They opened up with machine-guns and the 'new tactic of . . . psychological warfare', as the general had explained it, collapsed in a bloody heap. Christian churches, frequented mainly by Vietnamese converts, were bombed by the Cambodian air force on the grounds that they might provide refuge for communist guerrillas.

There was a price to be paid for this policy of hate. The South Vietnamese troops who had flooded across the border in April were ill-disciplined even in their own country. In Cambodia they had a massacre of their compatriots to avenge. American forces pulled back as planned by late June. The South Vietnamese stayed on to terrorise the countryside – raping Khmer women, stealing cattle, pillaging homes. The result was a recruiting opportunity made in heaven for the Khmers Rouges. The Viet Cong had been exemplary guests, leaving payment for anything they took and going to enormous lengths to avoid offending against Khmer customs. Lon Nol's South Vietnamese allies were bandits. Before long, tens of thousands of villagers voted with their feet, swelling the population under communist control and sending their sons to join the resistance army.

The pogroms were not the regime's only self-inflicted wound.

In April, Lon Nol had announced that the monarchy would be abolished. 'An oracle has predicted,' he said, 'that everybody will enjoy equal rights . . . The bad king will flee, a comet will appear . . . and Cambodia will become a republic.' To many peasants that meant nothing less than the end of the world as they knew it. 'How shall we tend our rice-paddies, now that the King is not here to make it rain?' Father Ponchaud, the Catholic missionary, was asked. Sihanouk, despite his abdication, was the 'Master of Life', the Brahmanic overlord whose symbolic power held the Khmer nation together. To a medieval people, his overthrow was a cosmic event. Had a new king been crowned, as Prince Sirik Matak wished, the outcome might have been different. But Lon Nol, encouraged by his younger brother, Sâr's old schoolmate Lon Non, and by a group of intellectuals led by the anti-monarchist Keng Vannsak, decided that the regeneration of Buddhism required a complete break with the past. In this he was not wrong: many of the country's ills stemmed from the feudal system which the monarchy perpetuated. But in practice Cambodia was no more ready for republican democracy than England under Henry the Eighth. The proclamation of the Khmer Republic was a monumental strategic error, definitively alienating the rural population.

The slide over the edge of reason, into the abyss, was not confined to the regime in Phnom Penh. If, to Lon Nol's government, all Vietnamese were communists, to the Khmers Rouges all foreigners were enemies. By the end of April, twenty-six Western journalists had 'gone missing' in Cambodia. Those fortunate enough to end up in the hands of the Viet Cong were usually freed, as was the practice in Vietnam, at a moment of maximum political advantage to their captors. With three exceptions, all those captured during the war by the Khmers Rouges – priests and aid personnel, as well as journalists – were killed. Once again it was a matter of 'drawing a clear line of demarcation between the enemy and ourselves'.

As the fateful year, 1970, lengthened, attitudes on both sides hardened. This was not inevitable. It was not just a response to the widening war. Each side was deliberately cutting loose from its traditional points of reference: the monarchy, in Lon Nol's case; the legacy of Indochinese communism in the case of the Khmers Rouges. The normal restraints on thought and behaviour were eroding, Cambodia was moving into unknown territory.

Sâr bade farewell to his Vietnamese escort at K-12, at the southern end of the Ho Chi Minh Trail, in June. He and Khieu Ponnary, accompanied by Pâng and their two Khmer bodyguards, had made the entire journey once again on foot, travelling across the Annamite cordillera and then through Attopeu in southern Laos.

Ponnary had started behaving oddly while they were still in Beijing. A Chinese official who met her then remembered her being 'so anti-Vietnamese it wasn't possible even to mention the word "Vietnam" in her presence'. He wondered at the time what had happened to make her so unbalanced. By the time they set out from Hanoi she was seriously ill and for the last weeks of the journey she had to be carried on a stretcher. Only much later was her illness diagnosed as chronic paranoid schizophrenia. By then it was too late to attempt treatment. Sâr's cook, Moeun, recalled an aide putting out a glass of water for him one day. 'She screamed at him not to drink it because the Vietnamese had put poison in it,' Moeun said. 'Then she took the glass away, and brought him another one. I remember the look of pity on his face.' After the initial acute spasm, Ponnary appeared to recover, but periodically afterwards suffered bouts of agitation and restlessness when 'she would shout that Vietnamese troops were coming and they were going to kill us'. Eventually Sâr, who at the best of times suffered from insomnia, sent her to stay with Moeun whenever she had an attack to prevent her keeping him awake all night as she ranted in fear at imaginary enemies. For some years, she enjoyed long periods of normalcy, when she appeared completely lucid. But over time she developed the classic symptoms of the illness, withdrawing into herself, refusing to wash or to respond to those around her, and growing obsessed by nightmarish visions of Vietnamese atrocities.

The root causes of paranoid schizophrenia are poorly understood. It is known, however, that stress often acts as a catalyst, rendering the condition acute. In Ponnary's case, an early and basic cause of stress was undoubtedly her sterility. Friends remembered that in later life she loved to surround herself with children and that their presence seemed to make her behave more normally. She must have known that Sâr, too, had wanted children, but had buried his longing deep within himself.

However, the trigger for the episode that began on the Ho Chi Minh Trail was obviously more recent. 'Something must have happened to her in Vietnam or China,' Moeun speculated later. Sâr himself provided a clue to what it may have been. During the talks in Hanoi in December 1969, he wrote, 'The Vietnamese delegation . . . could neither bridle its violent hostility . . . nor control its fury . . . The [Cambodian] delegates [felt] they could easily resort to assassination . . . The atmosphere . . . was so tense that some members of the delegation, who were not used to such tests, were greatly shaken.' The description is overblown, but it may have reflected what Ponnary, who was present, had felt. Her schizophrenia was in a sense merely a clinical manifestation of a wider, national paranoia, whose focus was Vietnam but which would progressively invade every aspect of Cambodian life. Her madness had nothing to do with Sâr and still less with Khmer Rouge policies which had not even been formulated, let alone applied, at the time her mind began to crumble. Rather it was a metaphor – a tragic, personal metaphor – for the fate which was awaiting the country as a whole.

Sâr spent the next two months at his old headquarters at K-5, three days' march south of the border. He had brought with him radio transceivers powered by hand-cranked generators, which meant that, for the first time since the Ratanakiri base had been established, he could communicate by morse with Hanoi and with the Chinese Party's International Liaison Department in Beijing. Three Khmer 'regroupees', who had been trained as radio technicians during their exile in Vietnam, served as operators. They were among the first of some 1,500 exiles who made the journey home that year. Kit Mân, one of the few women in the group, who had been trained as a doctor in Vietnam, left Hanoi in early April, a few days after Sâr's own departure:

Before leaving we were given two weeks' training. They made us carry a heavy rucksack and climb a hill, then come back down, then climb it once more, over and over again. Then we set out, 60 or 100 of us, escorted by Vietnamese guides . . . The journey took three months. But there were resting places in the jungle along the trail, maintained by the Vietnamese, where they had hammocks for us to sleep in . . . In the regions the Americans were bombing, we marched at night with little pocket lights.

Sâr's aide, Pâng, set up a reception post at a village on the Lao border, from which the returnees were directed to destinations further south. Mân was sent to Kratie, which had been occupied by the Viet Cong in May. The Northern Zone Secretary, Koy Thuon, had established his headquarters in the forest of Speu on the banks of a tributary of the Chinit river, which rises in the hill-country of Preah Vihear and describes a long south-westerly arc before emptying itself into one of the affluents of the Great Lake. There, with two other Vietnamese-trained doctors and a group of nurses, Mân set up a primitive hospital for the use of the Party leadership.

Other groups followed over the next twelve months. Most were assigned to the Eastern Zone, where they occupied middle-level posts in the emerging Khmer Rouge regional and district administrations.

At the end of July, Sâr himself set out for the south, accompanied by Ponnary, Tiv Ol, the dandified young secondary-school teacher from Prey Veng who had joined them in Ratanakiri two years earlier, and by seventy *montagnard* bodyguards.

On the eve of their departure, Sâr called the leaders of the group together. 'Now we are going down to the plains,' he told them. 'Today, we will all change our names. I will no longer be Pouk. From now on I will call myself Pol.' He then gave the others their new aliases, which he had chosen himself. His Jarai assistant, Phi Phuon, who was with him that day, received the name Cheam. It was a rite of passage, opening the way from one existence to another. Khmer men took new 'names-in-religion' when they became monks; Khmers Rouges did so when they took on new responsibilities. Son Sen had changed his name in 1969, when he was appointed Chief of Staff, responsible for the revolutionary guard units. Formerly he had been Khamm, 'the Biter'; now he was Khieu ('Blue').

Pol – or Pol Pot, as he would later call himself, following the custom of adding an euphonic monosyllable, in the same way that Vorn made his name Vorn Vet and the eldest of the Thiounn brothers was called Thiounn Thioeunn – never explained why he had chosen his new name. However, the Pols were royal slaves, the remnants of an aboriginal people, 'noble savages' in Rousseau's terms, and it is tempting to see in the soubriquet a sardonic reference to Sâr's alliance with Sihanouk which made him, metaphorically, the 'slave of the King'. It may also have harked back to his use of Khmer Daeum (Old Khmer) as a pseudonym while a student in Paris, for the Pols were Khmers Daeum; one of his fellow students at that time had used an even more explicit pen-name, Khmer Neak Ngear (Khmer hereditary slave) to sign an attack on the monarchy. Whatever the reason, for the next decade Sâr would be known as Pol.

The journey south was slow and, apart from sporadic American bombing, uneventful. The transmogrified Pol Pot and his escort reached their initial destination, a temporary camp on the border of Kratie and Kompong Thom about thirty miles north-east of Koy Thuon's headquarters, towards the end of September. There he convened an enlarged meeting of the CPK Standing Committee. No record of who took part has survived. Khieu Samphân had reached the area a few days earlier and was told that he was being given responsibility for liaison with Sihanouk, but he did not attend the leadership discussions. Although Pol himself claimed later that it was 'a full meeting of the Central Committee', evidently to underline its importance, it appears that the only senior Party figures present were himself, Nuon Chea and So Phim.

The resolution they issued set out for the first time the principle of 'independence-mastery', which was to be the Party's watchword for the next nine years. Like many Khmer Rouge terms, the word was a neologism derived from Pali, the language of the Buddhist monks. It proclaimed the Cambodian communists' right to determine their own strategy, free from outside interference – a message hammered home by reference to the 'betrayal' of the Khmer revolution by the Vietnamese at the Geneva Conference of 1954:

> The Cambodian Party has traced its own revolutionary path . . . We must not permit other powerful states to decide the destiny of our nation, our people and our revolution. At present [these states] still nurture this ancient longing . . . [In the past] we held our destiny firmly in our own hands, and then we allowed others to resolve it in our place. We must never allow this historical error to be repeated . . . Aid from abroad, even if healthy and unconditional . . . can never play a decisive role, either in the short term or the long term . . . We must always hold firmly to the stance of independence-mastery, rely on our own forces and endure difficulties and suffering. On that basis, whether we accept or do not accept aid will depend on whether or not we think it is necessary, on whether we find it useful or harmful, and also on the manner in which that aid is to be used.

This was the theoretical text on which the independence of the Cambodian Communist Party was to be based. The time had not yet come to give it practical effect. For all their fine words, the Cambodians knew they still needed Vietnamese support. But Hanoi was not wrong in seeing it as a fundamental shift in the CPK's position.

The meeting also approved the sending of Ieng Sary to Hanoi and Beijing as 'Special Representative of the Interior' charged with foreign policy matters, a formulation which, to non-initiates like Sihanouk, continued to disguise the reality of communist power.

While Pol was laying down the principles of future Khmer Rouge policy in the jungles of Kompong Thom, Lon Nol ploughed relentlessly on with his plans for a republic of the Cambodian middle classes. That summer Sihanouk and eighteen of his closest supporters were sentenced to death in absentia. Two months later, on October 9, a grand ceremony was held in front of the Royal Palace, at which Lon Nol, Sirik Matak and In Tam, the President of the National Assembly, resplendent in white dress uniform, worn with a silk *sampot*, the traditional divided skirt used on great occasions, presided over the abolition of the thousand-year-old monarchy. To mark the advent of the Khmer Republic, as Cambodia was now to be called, a 101-gun salute was fired. On the fifteenth salvo, the cannon exploded, killing one of the gun crew. The news was around the city like wildfire. The *tevoda*, the nation's guardian deities, were warning of fell times ahead.

7

Fires of Purgation

IN THE FIRST half of the 1970s, the Khmers Rouges fought not one war but four.

The first was waged by the United States, using heavy bombers which flew in from Guam. Their targets were Viet Cong and Khmer Rouge troop concentrations, but the bombs fell massively and above all on the civilian population. Bill Harben, a disaffected political officer at the US Embassy in Phnom Penh, made a simple experiment. He took a cardboard cutout delineating the 'box', half a mile wide by two miles long, that represented the area of devastation from a B-52 bomb-load, and placed it on a large-scale map. In much of central and eastern Cambodia, he discovered, there was nowhere the box could be placed which did not include hamlets or villages.

The second war, not always well co-ordinated with the first, was waged by Lon Nol's forces on the ground. There was a third war, sometimes latent sometimes overt, between the Cambodian and the Vietnamese communists. And finally there was a struggle for influence, which never quite spilled over into open warfare but teetered on the brink, between Sihanouk in Beijing and the resistance leaders inside Cambodia.

The air war was by far the most dramatic.

B-52 raids resumed on July 27 1970 after the Pentagon realised that the 'limited incursion' during the spring had resolved nothing. They were directed at targets throughout the Eastern Zone and later in much of the rest of Cambodia as well – necessarily so, since the incursion had spread the Viet Cong over a much larger area. Truong Nhu Tang, the Viet Cong Justice Minister, wrote later:

> Nothing the guerrillas had to endure compared with the stark terrorisation of the B-52 bombardments . . . It was as if an enormous scythe had swept through the jungle, felling the giant teak and *go* trees like grass in its way, shredding them into billions of shattered splinters . . . It was not just that things were destroyed; in some awesome way, they had ceased to exist . . . There would simply be nothing there, in an unrecognisable landscape gouged by immense craters. . .

The first few times I experienced a B-52 attack it seemed, as I strained to press myself into the bunker floor, that I had been caught in the Apocalypse . . . The concussive *whump-whump-whump* came closer and closer . . . Then, as the cataclysm walked in on us, everyone hugged the earth, some screaming quietly, others struggling to suppress attacks of violent involuntary trembling. Around us the ground began to heave spasmodically, and we were engulfed in a monstrous roar . . . The terror was complete. One lost control of bodily functions as the mind screamed incomprehensible orders to get out.

On one occasion a Soviet delegation was visiting our ministry when a particularly short-notice warning came through. When it was over, no one had been hurt, but the entire delegation had sustained considerable damage to its dignity – uncontrollable trembling and wet pants the all-too-obvious signs of inner convulsions. The visitors could have spared themselves their feelings of embarrassment; each of their hosts was a veteran of the same symptoms . . .

Sooner or later, though, the shock of the bombardments wore off, giving way to a sense of abject fatalism. The veterans would no longer scrabble at the bunker floors, convulsed with fear. Instead people just resigned themselves . . . The B-52s somehow put life in order . . . It was a lesson that remained with me, as it did with many others.

The United States dropped three times more bombs on Indochina during the Vietnam War than were used by all the participants in the whole of the Second World War; on Cambodia the total was three times the total tonnage dropped on Japan, atom bombs included. Party cadres, committed to the cause, might rationalise the dread inspired by the B-52s. The peasants lapsed into blind terror. 'Their minds just froze up and [they] would wander around mute and not talk for three or four days,' one young villager remembered. 'Their brains were completely disoriented . . . They couldn't even hold down a meal.'

The effect was twofold. Hundreds of thousands of villagers fled to the cities, where they eked out a precarious existence on the edge of starvation. The population of Phnom Penh, which had been 650,000 at the time of the coup, exceeded a million at the end of the year and would reach 2.5 million by 1975. Provincial towns still in government hands, like Battambang, Kompong Thom and Siem Reap, swelled to bursting point.

Hundreds of thousands of others fled in the opposite direction, into the forests, the eternal refuge of Khmer peasants in times of war and desolation. By the end of 1970, US intelligence estimated that more than a million people were in areas controlled by the Viet Cong, the North Vietnamese and the Khmers Rouges, whose grip now extended to more than half the country's territory.

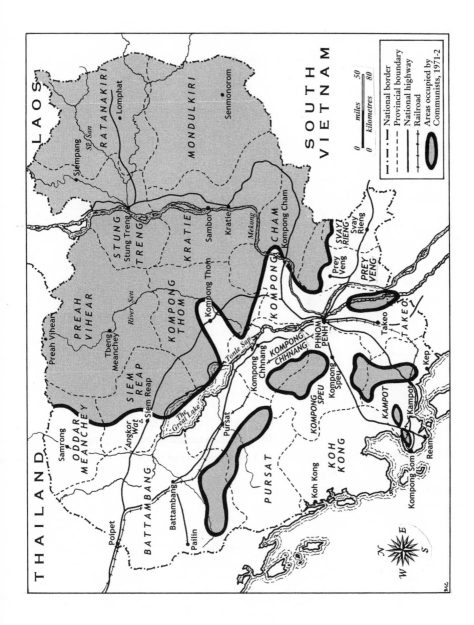

It would be wrong to suggest that the intensity of the bombing brutalized Cambodians and thereby contributed to the nature of the regime which Pol and his colleagues installed. A far greater quantity of high explosive fell on Vietnam, yet the Vietnamese did not establish a system like that of the Khmers Rouges. The bombing may have helped create a climate conducive to extremism. But the ground war would have done that anyway. The Khmers Rouges were not 'bombed back into the Stone Age'. Even had there been no B-52 strikes at all, it is unlikely that Democratic Kampuchea would have been a significantly different place.*

Instead, the B-52s placed a millstone round the government's neck by inundating the cities with a demoralised detritus of human misery that the authorities could not relieve, and gave the Khmers Rouges a propaganda windfall which they exploited to the hilt – taking peasants for political education lessons among the bomb craters and shrapnel, explaining to them that Lon Nol had sold Cambodia to the Americans in order to stay in power and that the US, like Vietnam and Thailand, was bent on the country's annihilation so that, when the war was over, Cambodia would cease to exist. 'What they said was credible because there were just so many huge bombs,' one man remembered. 'That was what made it so easy for the Khmer Rouge to win the people over.' In warfare, destruction breeds hatred; hatred is assuaged by more destruction. Villagers who had lost family members or seen their homes destroyed in bombing raids were filled with hatred. The ranks of the Khmers Rouges grew – to an estimated 12,000 regular soldiers at the end of 1970 and four times that number two years later – while on the government side, as corruption escalated to levels unheard of even in Sihanouk's day, the moral high ground was definitively lost.

In the everyday chronicle of the fighting, especially in the early days, both sides showed unsuspected strengths and weaknesses. Government troops, poorly trained, badly officered and often unpaid, sometimes fought with astonishing bravery. The French archaeologist François Bizot witnessed one such clash in which a sergeant whose unit was on guard duty at a

---

* William Shawcross, in *Sideshow: Kissinger, Nixon and the Destruction of Cambodia*, has argued the contrary case, writing eloquently of 'peasant boys and girls, clad in black, moving slowly through the mud, half-crazed with terror as fighter bombers tore down at them by day, and night after night whole seas of 750-pound bombs smashed all around'. He noted that Khmer Rouge casualties were often well above levels where, in orthodox military doctrine, units suffer 'irreversible psychological damage', and quoted Zhou Enlai as saying that the longer the war continued, 'the more extreme and harsh will be the final victory'. All that is certainly true. However, policy was made not by the peasants but by Pol and the other members of the CPK Standing Committee, men who did not experience the bombing at first hand. The pitiless absolutism of Khmer Rouge rule after 1975 had other causes.

bridge on the outskirts of Siem Reap got the better of a mixed Khmer Rouge–Viet Cong detachment:

[He] had the black skin of the true Khmer, very dark with a coppery sheen. Hard eyes, a square chin, and short teeth, like blocks worn down from the top . . . His half-open shirt revealed ritual tattoos, and he wore a tangle of necklaces, bearing images of the Buddha, tigers' teeth and amulets, which knocked against each other, giving off a protective clinking which we would hear all night . . . The sergeant busied himself, giving orders, checking the foxholes where the young men under his command [were dug in]. . .

Suddenly, a voice resonated through a loud-hailer . . . 'Comrades! We are brothers! We are fighting for Sihanouk and to liberate our beloved home-land!'. . .

The man spoke with a Phnom Penh accent: 'Comrades!' he said again. 'You are here in a miserable hole while Lon Nol sleeps with his wife in bed . . .' It was a technique that had proved itself elsewhere and the attackers did not expect much resistance. But they hadn't reckoned with the obstinacy of the sergeant, who bounded from one hole to the next, putting spine into the men who were paralysed by fear . . . In the darkness, the encirclement tightened . . . and the voice reverberated again, this time more boldly. 'Comrades, look at me! I am your brother! Let's talk! I will show myself to you unarmed! Don't fire, but watch!' . . . Fifty yards away, a man stood up, holding out his right arm and shining a pocket-lamp onto his own face . . . Mesmerised by his courage, no one dared move.

Seconds later a violent explosion shook the air. The sergeant had thrown a grenade . . . setting off a fusillade in all directions which continued [until] the sunrise put the attackers to flight.

More typical were two big land offensives, both baptised 'Chenla' after an ancient Khmer kingdom of that name, which Lon Nol launched to try to relieve the provincial capital of Kompong Thom, besieged by communist forces. They were commanded by an eccentric figure named Um Savuth, 'an astonishing personality, a thin, twisted man who walked with a long white cane, [who] drove his jeep at terrifying speeds and was nearly always drunk'. As a young officer he had ordered a subordinate to place a cat on his head, retire to a distance and then shoot it off, a moment of high spir-its which blew away part of his brain and left him paralysed down one side of his body. One US adviser maintained that 'Savuth drunk was better than most Cambodian officers sober', but that was as much a reflection on the calibre of the Cambodian officer corps as on Savuth's own qualities.

His first attempt to reach Kompong Thom foundered when his combat battalions, with their families straggling along behind, set out northwards along a narrow, raised causeway between flooded rice-paddies. The extended line made a perfect target for communist artillery, and Viet Cong sappers blew up the bridges behind them faster than they could be repaired. Thousands of men, women and children were slaughtered. After two months, Lon Nol declared victory and, with some difficulty, the survivors were brought home. The second attempt was initially more successful. Savuth's forces reached Kompong Thom and duly 'liberated' it. In the process, however, the American commander in Saigon, General Creighton Abrams, noted grimly, 'they opened a front forty miles long and two feet wide' which the Vietnamese promptly cut in half. As Savuth's men fled across the rice-fields, abandoning their equipment, including tanks, armoured personnel carriers, lorries, scout cars, 105-mm howitzers which they neglected to spike and countless lighter weapons, hundreds died. Savuth told friends afterwards that he had found the Vietnamese troops 'impressive', and had been amazed by the amount of American weaponry they were carrying.

The Khmer Rouge forces were a mixed bunch too. Alongside veterans of the civil war of the late 1960s were raw recruits from the villages no better than the cannon fodder of Lon Nol's army. But where Lon Nol, from the summer of 1970, had introduced conscription, the Khmer Rouge recruits in the early days were all volunteers. Some, like Pol's future secretary, Mey Mak, joined because they liked the idea of becoming soldiers. Others became guerrillas 'because the girls teased us if we stayed behind – they said boys should be at the front'. Yet others went to fight for Sihanouk, or because their friends did so, or simply to get out of their villages. Their first memories of the resistance were usually much the same:

> I remember that they came to the village – it was a mixed group of Khmers and Vietnamese – and they just asked people to join. So I joined. They were all in uniform – the Khmers wore black clothes; the Vietnamese had green uniforms. It was in 1971 some time . . . maybe in May or June . . . They didn't give us any training. They just picked me to be a group leader, gave me a gun and then put me in a truck and sent me off to the battlefield . . . I fought in three battles – in Angkor Borei; in Prey Pk'oam, and Takoep. I was terrified. After those three battles, I hung my rifle on a tree and fled back home. There were so many people who were killed in those battles. It was infantry fighting. I killed some enemy soldiers myself – I shot them. But I was afraid that I would die too if I stayed in the resistance army. It was the sight of all the bodies that made me run away . . . I was a group leader for about three months before I deserted. When I got home, nothing happened to me. The village chief didn't say anything. After a while, people came to look for me to ask me to rejoin my unit. But I didn't go.

There were nuances. Some remembered the Viet Cong wearing black like everyone else. Most new recruits were terrorised by their first battles, but not all deserted. Enough did so, however, for deserters to be treated leniently. The iron discipline which already existed within the Party did not yet extend to poor peasant soldiers. There were differences in training, too. The majority received none. But for those judged capable of becoming commanders, there were intensive six-month courses, nominally under a Khmer Rouge cadre but with instruction given by Khmer-speaking Vietnamese. Mey Mak attended one such course at a forest encampment in Tramkak, the home district of the South-Western Zone leader, Mok. Six hundred men took part, he remembered. Mok's son-in-law, Muth, was in charge, and the Vietnamese taught 'combat technique . . . how to use weapons, how to crawl undetected, strategy and tactics for attack'. There were also political education meetings, at which the instructors – again Vietnamese – explained that the Khmers must fight to liberate their country from the Americans and to free the people from the oppressing classes.

The Khmers Rouges' weaknesses in those first years were more than compensated for by the strengths of their allies. It did not matter if most of their recruits were untrained, if there were not enough weapons to go round and if some of them deserted. Throughout 1970 and 1971, the brunt of the fighting in Cambodia was borne by the Vietnamese. The Khmers Rouges were a leavening, to make Vietnamese units appear more acceptable to the population at large, or, if they fought separately, an auxiliary force, to occupy the terrain once the Vietnamese had passed. It was not a Khmer Rouge unit that stormed the airport on the outskirts of Phnom Penh, but Vietnamese commandos from the elite Dac Cong brigade who, in a four-hour assault which left at least forty dead, blew up the whole of Lon Nol's air force – ten MiG-17s, five T-28 trainers, ten transport aircraft and eight helicopters – and two ammunition dumps. The same group later destroyed 60 per cent of Cambodia's oil refinery storage in a raid on Kompong Som.

All that stood between Lon Nol and defeat, one American military historian commented bleakly, 'was US aid, Allied airpower and [the] 11,000 South Vietnamese troops [still] in south-eastern Cambodia', the latter being in any case a mixed blessing, given their propensity for slaughtering Cambodian civilians.

Unlike the communists, Lon Nol did not have the backing of ground troops provided by his principal ally. Even for Nixon, that was politically impossible. When Kissinger's military assistant, General Alexander Haig, informed Lon Nol early on in the conflict of the limits of US involvement, the Prime Minister began to weep. 'He walked across to the window and stood there, his shoulders shaking, his face turned away.' It was the fatal error of the coup that Nol and Sirik Matak had set in motion. They had staked all on the support of a government whose overriding preoccupation was not to be drawn further into the Indochinese quagmire but to get out.

In these circumstances, the American panacea was to bomb, until Congress ended that option too. But bombing without ground support was no more effective in Cambodia than it had been in Vietnam, or would be in any of the conflicts American presidents would subsequently launch, claiming they could win victories without body-bags flying home.

In the end, even if the US had sent in troops, it would probably have done no more than drag out the inevitable. But victory in Cambodia was never the Americans' goal. If it had been, the US would have replaced Lon Nol, who suffered a debilitating stroke in the spring of 1971, leaving him, as the US Ambassador, Emory Swank, reported in cablese, 'not in emotional or physical state to bear burdens of his office'. The Nixon White House did no such thing. Instead it made sure that the ailing marshal would stagger on for four more surrealistic years, submitting his generals to long harangues about ancient Khmer history, setting up a special bureau to teach his troops 'traditional Khmer-Mon occult practices of warfare', and eventually, when all else failed, having a line of coloured sand drawn around Phnom Penh to give the city magical protection.

To the Nixon administration, Cambodia was a means of gaining time to extract US troops from Vietnam. Time was vital for the Khmers Rouges too. Nixon's endgame was exactly what they needed.

At the beginning of November 1970, Pol, Khieu Ponnary, their entourage and bodyguards, about a hundred people in all, accompanied by Koy Thuon and other Northern Zone cadres, arrived at their new base, code-named K-1, at Dângkda, north-east of Speu commune. It was spartan. There were three stilt-houses, thatched with palm leaves: one for Pol; one for Nuon Chea; the third for 'invited guests'. The guards and lower-ranking cadres were billeted in the surrounding forest.

For the next twelve months, everything Pol did was geared to one overriding priority: the creation of a Khmer communist army and administration capable of assuming the conduct of the war when the peace talks in Paris between the US and North Vietnam produced a settlement in the south and Hanoi's forces withdrew. The implications of this strategy were threefold.

Militarily it meant hurrying slowly, consolidating advantages on the ground before attempting further advance. As a result, throughout 1971, the battlefield situation remained unchanged: communist forces continued to hold more than half Cambodia's territory; Lon Nol's rare offensives were repulsed or, where they succeeded, the terrain was reoccupied after government units withdrew; but there were no major gains.

The second imperative was to clarify the Khmers Rouges' relationship with the Viet Cong and the North Vietnamese. In late November 1970, Pol and Nuon Chea had a week-long meeting with the two top leaders of the COSVN, Nguyen Van Linh (still known to them as Hay So) and General Tran Nam Trung, at a camp midway between K-1 and the COSVN headquarters in Kratie, forty miles to the east. Three decisions were taken. The Vietnamese agreed to withdraw their civilian cadres from the administration of the 'liberated areas' as soon as they could be replaced by Khmers; they undertook to step up their military training programme, so that Khmer Rouge units could bear a larger share of the fighting; and they promised that in areas where mixed Khmer Rouge–Viet Cong battalions had been formed, notably in the East and the South-West, they would gradually be dismantled and replaced by all-Khmer units. After this meeting, friction between the two sides, which had led to armed clashes in the autumn of 1970, markedly declined.

The third aspect was political. At a time when overall strategic considerations required an improvement in relations with the Vietnamese as well as the rapid growth of Khmer Rouge military strength, an intensive political education campaign was needed to ensure that the resistance remained loyal to Cambodian, not Vietnamese, goals, and that the CPK itself was welded into a still more tightly disciplined force, capable of enforcing 'independence-mastery' throughout the communist-held areas. Accordingly, from December 1970 onwards, recruits for the army and for FUNK were accepted regardless of their background with no questions asked; but entry qualifications to the Party were made even stricter. Students and 'middle peasants', defined as those with enough to eat all year round, who in the 1960s had been readily admitted as candidates for Party membership, were now turned down flat or, at best, allowed to join the Youth League. Only 'poor peasants' were deemed to have the right class origin for admission to the Party ranks.

At the end of 1970, Pol and Nuon Chea moved to a new base about five miles away on the northern side of the Chinit river. It was bigger than the old one, with twenty or thirty straw-thatched houses, guardrooms, a messenger office and a printing shop. K-1 became a support facility. The whole Central Committee area now bore the code name S-71. At the same time, the Northern Zone HQ was transferred to Dângkda and by the spring of 1971 accommodated some two hundred people, including a troupe of sixty musicians and dancers, who toured the Zone giving 'revolutionary performances' to inspire the masses.

Indoctrination, by whatever means, was crucial because communications difficulties made referral to a centralised hierarchy impossible – and the Party's enforcement mechanism, the Santebal or political police, did not operate nationally until 1975. Unity had to be achieved, not through a vertical command system but through the inculcation of shared beliefs, both within the Party and among the population at large. One of Pol's first moves after reaching Kompong Thom had been to set up an information section, headed first by Tiv Ol, the former teacher who had accompanied him from Ratanakiri, and later by Hu Nim, to provide articles for the FUNK radio in Hanoi. The office, known as S-31, housed many of the 'progressive figures' who had flocked to the CPK standard – Sihanouk's cousin, Prince Norodom Phurissara, the GRUNC Justice Minister; Hou Yuon, the Interior Minister, who had accompanied Hu Nim from the South-West; Toch Phoeun from the Cercle Marxiste, now Public Works Minister; and Pok Deuskomar, the ribald Vice-Foreign Minister who, in a pre-Khmer Rouge incarnation, had once remarked to a friend that his girth was 'very good for the fucking, keeps the stomach against the woman!' Khieu Samphân also spent time at S-31 but, because of his role in liaising with Sihanouk, was soon moved to a compound nearer Pol's headquarters.

Another, more secret office, known as L-7, headed by Son Sen's wife, Yun Yat, produced the Party's internal monthly journal, *Tung Padevat* (Revolutionary Flags), which appeared in two versions – one with five flags on the cover, destined for senior cadres; the other with a single flag, for the Party rank and file.

Ping Sây worked at both S-31 and S-71, where he served as Pol's confidential secretary. His most abiding memory was of the draconian security restrictions under which everyone lived. Pol himself set the tone. In Ratanakiri, he had suffered from chronic gastric ailments which became associated in his mind with the risk of poisoning. Whenever he was given medicine, he would demand proof that it was what it claimed before agreeing to take it. At S-71, even Zone Secretaries had to leave their bodyguards outside the perimeter before being escorted in, alone and unarmed:

> The base was in a part of the jungle that was reserved exclusively for the leaders. No one was permitted to go there. It was a forbidden zone . . . You had to be accompanied at all times by a messenger, normally a montagnard . . . Once you were inside, you did not have the right to leave the sector to which you had been assigned . . . Even within the Information Section, you couldn't move about freely. If you had tried, someone would have seen you and you would have been told: 'Stop it! Why are you going from place to place?'
>
> The huts where we lived had thatched roofs and walls, a hard bed of woven bamboo and a desk and chair, also bamboo, all very simple and rustic . . . They were 20 or 30 yards apart – sometimes as much as 50 yards – and separated by thick hedges, so you couldn't see from one to another. They were built in the same way as at the Issarak camp I'd visited in 1951, but

under Pol Pot they were better made and the camp was better organised . . . The Issaraks threw their rubbish everywhere, the place was a mess. [Here] there were strict rules of hygiene . . . We ate rice [and] sometimes meat or fish, but usually just rice with *prahoc* [fish sauce] and wild vegetables we found in the forest.

At that time, I didn't even know where [Pol's] Office was. Everything was kept rigorously separate . . . The offices were only a mile or two apart, but each in its own area. In Pol's Office, the living conditions were much the same as everywhere else . . . But let me tell you a story. When I arrived, I said to the others, without thinking – 'I see you always build your camp by a water-course' – because Pol's Office, like S-31, was on the bank of a stream. That was reported back, and two or three days later Yun Yat summoned me. She said I must not speak like that, I must show 'revolutionary vigilance' . . . In one way, she was right; if it had come to the notice of the enemy, it would have been a clue about where the HQ was located. But when she said that, it made me realise that these people had a sense of 'revolutionary vigilance' that was really quite disturbing. They were very, very secretive. Even inside their own headquarters.

It was a shared neurosis. Pol's deputy, Nuon Chea, was equally wary. The primary cause was the leadership's conviction that, in Khieu Samphân's words, 'Khmers cannot keep secrets', and therefore exceptional means had to be used to compel them to do so. Almost all the later excesses of the Khmer Rouge regime can be traced back, at least in part, to this perception that the innate failings of the Cambodian people could be overcome only by a totalitarian absolutism so severe and all-embracing that no evasion was possible and everyone would be forced to engage, for the good of all, in selfless and unremitting collective endeavour.

In mid-January 1971, the Central Committee met for the first time since October 1966. The three-day meeting took place at S-71 and was attended by twenty-seven delegates.* Hu Nim, Hou Yuon and Khieu Samphân –

---

* Those present were: Pol, Nuon Chea, So Phim, Vorn Vet, Mok, Prasith, Ruos Nhim (all members of the previous CC); Chou Chet and Sê, from the South-West; Kong Sophal and Tol, the chief of the Mount Veay Chap base in the North-West; So Phim's deputy, Phuong, and two other Eastern Zone leaders – Sok Knaol and Siet Chhê; Vorn Vet's deputy in the Special Zone, Cheng On; Koy Thuon, Ke Pauk and Doeun from the Northern Zone; Hang, who had succeeded Vorn as underground Party chief in Phnom Penh; Va and Hâng, from Preah Vihear; Yem [Sin Son], later Khmer Rouge Ambassador to Pyongyang, and three others from Kratie; Khieu Ponnary, in her capacity as President of the Women's League of Democratic Kampuchea; and Pâng, to assure the secretariat. Of the five other CC members elected in 1963, Mang had died; Ieng Sary and Son Ngoc Minh were in Hanoi; and Thang Si and Son Sen, together with the other North-Eastern Zone leaders, were instructed to stay at their bases, presumably because it was felt they had already been sufficiently briefed before Pol's departure from Ratanakiri.

then being presented to the outside world as the chiefs of the Cambodian resistance – did not take part. All three were Party members, having been inducted by Mok in 1969, but even Khieu Samphân, the most trusted of them, was not yet judged sufficiently sure to be admitted to the CPK's inner councils.

Pol's message to the assembled leaders was pragmatic. The CPK must maintain good relations with the Vietnamese 'because we are fighting a common enemy'. The Party line was, as Ieng Sary put it later, 'United we win; divided we lose':

> Our Party holds that there are three battlefields [in Indochina] which cannot be separated from each other . . . If we break up into two or three strategic lines in terms of dealing with the enemy, it will be difficult for us. At the same time, however, within the three battlefields there are three different peoples. Thus an important point for our Party is that every country must be self-reliant and must struggle.

In this scheme of things, the Cambodians' role was to launch guerrilla activities – 'a people's war which must be the affair of the whole people' – cutting communications links and harassing isolated government units in support of the Vietnamese main force. The Khmer resistance, Pol told the delegates, was still at the stage of a 'national-democratic revolution'. Talk of socialism could come later. The immediate priorities were to seize weapons from the enemy and to build the broadest possible united front, in order to create a self-sufficient force which would permit the implementation of 'independence-mastery'.

Much of the meeting was taken up with 'housekeeping'. New boundaries were agreed for the Zones, together with a new set of code numbers: the North-East became 108; the East, 203; the North, 304; the South-West, 405; and the North-West, 506. Subsequently a new zone was created around Phnom Penh, designated, as in Issarak times, 'the Special Zone', under the control of Vorn Vet. The Zones were in turn divided into regions, each also with its code number.

Shortly afterwards the former Pracheachon spokesman Non Suon, who had been released from prison as part of a post-coup amnesty, was appointed head of Region 25 in the Special Zone. But none of the Hanoi returnees was given responsibilities at this level. Pol held that they had been away too long and were out of touch with the CPK's thinking.

The meeting also approved the setting-up of three distinct sets of military forces on the Viet Minh model: the *chhlorp*, or village patrols, which combined security and militia functions; regional troops, operating at district level as a territorial defence; and main-force units, organised in the Zones, which were destined to take over the conduct of the war from the Viet Cong and the North Vietnamese when the latter eventually went home.

The task was immense. At the end of 1970, the biggest Khmer Rouge units were of battalion strength, usually comprising three or four hundred men. The first regiments would not be established until 1973. The Vietnamese had been fighting under divisional commands since the 1950s. None the less, the decisions taken in January 1971 gave the CPK for the first time a blueprint for a civil and military organisation covering the whole of Cambodia. Most of the next eighteen months would be spent on the wearisome nuts and bolts of turning it into reality. CPK directives spoke of the need to 'exercise mastery over the revolutionary movement in every way . . . [to] get a tight grasp [and] filter into every corner', a message which was repeated, mantra-like, at political education seminars all over the country. Pâng remembered conducting five training sessions for local officials in Preah Vihear, each lasting ten days and attended by eighty people, over a period of two months. In July and August, Pol himself presided over a month-long 'nationwide training' for some two hundred district, region and zone cadres at Koy Thuon's Northern Zone HQ. Afterwards selected participants were escorted by *montagnard* guides to a specially prepared camp in another part of the jungle, about fifteen miles away, to attend the CPK's Third Congress. It turned out to be a wise precaution, for, whether by accident or design, shortly after they moved, the whole of the Northern Zone HQ area was heavily bombed.

Some sixty delegates attended the Congress, including all the Regional and Zone Secretaries, military commanders such as Ke Pauk and Kong Sophal, representatives of the 'intellectuals' like Hou Yuon, Hu Nim and Khieu Samphân, and a token group of Hanoi returnees. By the time it ended in mid-September, they had approved new Party statutes, ratifying the name, 'Communist Party of Kampuchea', adopted five years earlier; confirmed Pol as Secretary of the Central Committee and Chairman of its Military Commission (rather than merely Standing Committee Secretary, which he had been until then); and elected a new CC of thirty members, including Chou Chet from the South-West, Koy Thuon and Pauk from the North, Vy from the North-East, and Khieu Samphân and Khieu Ponnary as alternates. Hou Yuon and Hu Nim were not included. Neither was Non Suon or any of the Hanoi group.

By the beginning of 1972, Pol felt sufficiently confident to make his first extended journey through the 'liberated zones' to see how the new political and military structures were taking shape. Apart from his travels to and from Ratanakiri and to Vietnam and China, he had remained confined to his own headquarters for almost nine years. Escorted, as always, by *montagnard* bodyguards, he went first to Vorn Vet's HQ in Peam commune, fifteen miles west of the old royal capital of Oudong, and then to Mok's base in the hill-country near Amleang, where Ponnary had spent much of the previous spring. From there he travelled on elephant-back across the Cardamom Mountains to Koh Kong, on the Thai border in the far south-west. Every-where he went his message was the same: 'independence-mastery'; self-sufficiency; and 'the need to take our own forces as the main factor, even though we co-operate with others'.

The three months Pol was away were a time of rapid change. Phi Phuon, his Jarai aide-de-camp, remembered how, week by week, the local cadres in the areas they traversed seemed more self-assured. On the outward jour-ney, Pol's guards took him across Kompong Thom province, avoiding the more densely populated areas further south. When they reached the Great Lake, they lost their way for three days in the water-marshes which form when the floods recede at the end of the rainy season. The whole journey was made on foot and took six weeks. For the return trip they travelled the forty miles from Amleang to Tachès by Land-Rover and crossed the River Sap in motorised canoes at a point only thirty miles north of Phnom Penh. Another jeep took them to the Northern Zone HQ at Dângkda.

There, in May 1972, Pol summoned another meeting of the Central Committee, at which he spoke of his impressions during his journey and the conclusions he had drawn. The burden of his message was that the rev-olution was going too slowly. The decision adopted at the Third Congress, nine months before, to 'start sweeping away the socio-cultural traits of the old regime . . . the traits of feudalism, reaction and imperialism', had remained a dead letter, he said. At his urging, the Committee issued an 'urgent directive' calling on the Party to strengthen its 'proletarian stance' and to intensify the struggle against 'the various oppressive classes . . . [who] want to conserve their rights under our new regime'. The participants also approved plans for the collectivisation of agriculture and the suppression of private trade as soon as the situation permitted.

It was a turning point.

The Khmer Rouge army by then numbered 35,000 men, backed by an estimated 100,000 guerrillas, more than enough to hold their own against Lon Nol's increasingly demoralised troops even if the Vietnamese did one day withdraw. They had sufficient weaponry. The five million dollars in cash which China provided each year for buying arms from government forces was supplemented by income from sales of rubber produced at the former French-owned plantations in the Eastern Zone, now under communist control – which was exported with the connivance of corrupt officials in Phnom Penh. At the same time, Chinese weaponry flowed down the Ho Chi Minh Trail, enlarged a year earlier by Chinese engineering teams and equipped with a flexible petroleum pipeline which reached as far south as the Laotian border. Throughout the 'liberated zones', a stable administration was in place. A third of the population, more than two million people, was living under communist control.

The time had come to move on to the next stage. The social revolution was about to begin.

For the first two years after Sihanouk's overthrow, Khmer Rouge policy in the countryside had been remarkable mainly for its moderation. Within weeks of the coup, district-level CPK cadres, presenting themselves not as communists but as representatives of the FUNK, and often, in the Eastern Zone, accompanied by Vietnamese, began organising commune and village-level elections throughout the 'liberated areas'. All the candidates were local peasants, most supported the FUNK because they wanted Sihanouk to return, and, with rare exceptions, none had any connection with the Communist Party.

In one sense this was making a virtue out of necessity. The CPK barely had enough cadres to head the district administrations, let alone appoint them to commune- and village-level posts. Accordingly, the *wats* continued to function normally; religious festivals and holy days were observed as before; families continued to farm individually and to buy and sell at local markets. In some areas, the peasants were encouraged to form small-scale credit co-operatives and mutual aid teams at harvest time. One or two evenings a month, a village assembly was held, with much singing of revolutionary songs and exhortations to support the resistance.

But if expediency played a part – the Khmers Rouges went easy on the villagers because the only way to win support was to improve their lives – there was also a powerful streak of idealism, a desire to 'be together with the people and serve the people', comparable to the early days of the Chinese and Vietnamese revolutions. 'The [Khmers Rouges] would sometimes pick fruit,' a government official in Siem Reap recalled, 'then they would leave payment at the foot of the tree. The local [people] would think they were very fair.' Ith Sarin, a Khmer Rouge defector with every reason to show his former comrades in an unflattering light, reported that in the Special Zone:

> If a peasant is sick, the Khmer Rouge will often go to the house to give an injection or leave medicine, even at night or during a storm. In ploughing, transplanting, harvesting or threshing seasons, each office will send out its cadres to help . . . These kinds of psychological activities were really successful and deeply affected the people . . . The farming people of the base areas who knew nothing of socialist revolution quickly began to support Angkar because of its sentiments of openness and friendliness.

Certainly the new system was more puritanical than Cambodians were used to. Extramarital affairs were frowned on, gambling was banned and alcohol discouraged. But, at the same time, theft was stamped out and corruption, the besetting sin of government in the past, even at village level, was virtually eliminated.

For those who were prepared to co-operate, the regime was comparatively benign. Probably the most galling restriction was on individual movements: a peasant who wished to travel outside his commune had to obtain an official pass. But that was presented as a matter of wartime security.

For those perceived to be hostile it was a different story. Opposing the revolution, whether in word or deed, usually meant death. In most cases, the offender was summoned to the district headquarters and never returned. Less commonly, exemplary punishment was meted out. In the autumn of 1970, a village whose inhabitants had rebelled and killed three district cadres was encircled by Viet Cong and Khmer Rouge soldiers, and the families of the three alleged ringleaders, twenty-four people in all, including children and infants, were publicly beaten to death. A year later, mass graves containing more than 180 bodies were found near Kompong Thom. But these were the exceptions. Until the end of 1971, Khmer Rouge jails held few prisoners, and in the villages arrests of suspected spies and 'enemies' were still a rarity. Even the US Defense Intelligence Agency acknowledged that 'on the whole [Khmer communist cadres] have attempted to avoid acts which might alienate the population, and the behaviour of Vietnamese communist soldiers has generally been exemplary . . .'

After the Central Committee meeting in May 1972, all that began to change.

That spring, Cham Muslims in Vorn Vet's Special Zone were ordered to stop wearing Islamic dress – colourful clothing for women and white tunics with baggy cotton trousers for men – and to adopt the same black peasant garb as the poorest Khmer villagers. Upswept hairstyles and the wearing of jewellery, characteristic of Cham women, were also forbidden. The Chams were singled out because they are culturally distinct: they live together in their own villages; they have their own mosques; they marry among themselves and they keep to their own ways. But the primary motivation was not racist. Soon afterwards similar prohibitions were extended to the population as a whole. The Chams were merely the earliest victims of a general policy aimed at the cultural, social and economic levelling of all Cambodians, regardless of race or creed.

By the summer the same principle was applied to land ownership and certain private possessions. Richer peasants were divested of part of their land-holdings, which were given to poorer families, so that, by the end of the year, each family had exactly the same acreage. In some provinces, like Kampot, the quota was set at five hectares; in others, where population pressure was greater, it might be as little as one hectare. Unlike the land reform in China, which was based on the number of mouths to feed, in Cambodia the benchmark was uniformity. In any given village, each family was treated identically. At the same time the revolutionary administration requisitioned or taxed out of existence all private motor transport.

The result, and the intention, was that no one had anything different from anyone else.

The poorest and lower-middle peasants, whom the CPK regarded as the strongest supporters of the regime, did well out of these arrangements. They had no motor-cycles to lose and they were given extra land. But even for richer families, the reform was relatively mild. Everyone continued to farm individually, or at most in mutual-aid groups of four or five families; they grew enough to feed themselves; they retained ownership of livestock and poultry, and while restrictions were imposed on the slaughter of cattle, other animals could be killed and sold at market. Co-operative stores were set up to sell household necessities, including cloth, kerosene and medicines, imported from Vietnam, thereby eliminating the Sino-Khmer merchants who had kept a stranglehold on village commerce. In some areas, pressure was put on wealthy families to sell their household furniture, another mark of difference, for poor peasants possessed no furniture and slept on a mat on the floor. Ostentatious weddings, traditionally an occasion for finery, expensive gifts and extravagance even in the poorest communities, were at first discouraged and then stopped altogether, on the grounds that all energies should be devoted to the war and young people who wished to marry should wait until it ended. The sale of bottled beer and cigarettes, previously smuggled into the countryside from Phnom Penh, was likewise halted because only the richer peasants could afford them. After 1972 only locally made palm wine and roll-your-own tobacco were available.

None the less, a schoolteacher who left the Special Zone in January 1973 and defected to the government – therefore in principle not a sympathetic witness – felt able to write that 'the local people [see] they have a fairly easy life and no one is oppressing them . . . They are grateful, they are happy, they are enjoying themselves.' That may have been a partial view, based on experience in a single area. However, it is clear that in much of the countryside, the new regime won acceptance with little difficulty, for the good and simple reason that, for the poorer peasants, who made up half the rural population, the first years of Khmer Rouge rule were better than what had gone before and for most of the other half not markedly worse.

What would have been, and later was, a hell on earth for town-dwellers was not a huge change for those who had always lived that way. In the 1970s, large parts of the Cambodian countryside remained mired in autarchic poverty beyond the imagining of the educated elite. The American historian Michael Vickery recalled visiting an area in the north-west near the Angkorian site of Banteay Chhmar, where, along the roadside, 'wild-looking boys [were] carrying [home for supper] dead lizards strung on sticks like freshly caught fish . . . The people seemed strangely hostile [and] . . . we heard mutterings that they did not like city people, because their arrival usually meant trouble.' The villagers ate forest tubers; there was no rice because of a three-year drought. They made their own silk, but refused to sell or exchange it because 'there was nothing they wanted to buy.' That was in 1962. Forty years later, long after the Khmer Rouge regime had come and gone, another American visited a village in the hinterland of Kompong Thom. 'They live completely apart,' he reported. 'No one has a radio or a motorbike. Everything they need they make for themselves; nothing comes in from outside.' Some time afterwards, two of the villagers came to Phnom Penh to visit him. 'To try to put them at ease,' he said, 'I took them to eat at a stall in the market, the simplest place I could think of. They had no idea how to behave. They weren't comfortable. They didn't know how to sit on a chair. Everything in Phnom Penh was strange and they hated it.'

The overriding, if unstated, objective of Khmer Rouge policy from 1972 on was to refashion the whole of Cambodian society in the image of this authentic, autochthonous peasantry, unsullied by the outside world.

But there was another purpose, too, both Khmer and communist, underlying the Party's emphasis on social and economic levelling to force everyone into the same poor-peasant mould: the eternal Buddhist goal of demolishing the individual, but this time in new garb – not as a path to *nirvana* ('nothingness'), but to remove what was seen as the biggest obstacle to the establishment of a collectivised state: the innate and essential egoism which characterises Khmer behaviour. Whatever shortcomings attach to such cultural generalisations, that was the way Cambodians saw themselves. Sihanouk called individualism 'a national failing'. Ith Sarin came back from nine months in the Special Zone convinced that it was 'the fundament of the Khmer personality' and therefore communist policies could not succeed. Years later, a prominent Khmer businessman argued that the reason there are few Cambodian restaurants in Paris but innumerable Khmer taxi-drivers and pharmacists is that the latter occupations are suitable for a single man or a couple; to start a restaurant, several Khmer families have to pool their resources and the venture inevitably founders amid recriminations and jealousy.

The organisation of life in Khmer villages reinforces that perception. Where Vietnamese and Chinese villagers live cheek by jowl, animating a communal existence by means of countless associations and benevolent institutions, each Khmer family is an island, living on its own land, united only by membership of the *wat* and a shared belief in Buddhism. If Khmer Rouge attempts to set up village associations failed, it was precisely because of the absence of a co-operative tradition in Cambodia.

Pol and Nuon Chea preferred to close their eyes to all that, emphasising instead the rare occasions when Khmer villagers did work together – at harvest time, for instance, or to help a neighbour build a new house. But they were also aware that Angkor, the timeless symbol of Cambodia's glory and the inspiration of their own future regime, had been built not by free Khmers but by slaves. A Western diplomat, reflecting on Sihanouk's political difficulties, had written in the 1960s: 'Khmers, born individualists, predisposed to egocentrism, require a unifying bond to bring them together and the use of effective force to maintain their unity.' In his mind, the Throne was the bond and the 'effective force', the Sangkum. Ten years later, Pol and his colleagues reached the same conclusion. But now the bond was revolutionary consciousness and the 'effective force', Party coercion, which, as time went on, emulating Vietnam's experience, relied increasingly on terror.

If, among the population at large, levelling was imposed from above, among the Khmers Rouges themselves* the methods of choice were 'criticism and self-criticism', manual labour, and the study – *riensouth*, 'learning by heart and reciting' – of Communist Party texts.

Criticism and self-criticism took place at so-called 'lifestyle meetings', held in small groups, usually twice a week but in some units every evening. Members of each section met together – kitchen staff, for instance; or guards; or cadres who worked together in the same bureau – under the leadership of an older member, and each in turn would publicly confess his errors in thought and deed since the previous session. Khieu Samphân called them 'a daily accounting of revolutionary activities'. At the jungle prison where he was held in 1971, the French archaeologist François Bizot watched his warders go through the nightly ritual:

*In the 1970s, the Khmer Rouge movement consisted of four different categories of people: non-Party elements; 'core elements' (those awaiting admission to the Youth League or, more rarely, directly to the Party); Youth League members; and Party members. The last two groups were subdivided into candidate and full rights members.

'Comrades', began the older man who was leading the séance, 'let us all give account of the day that has passed, to correct our faults [and] purge ourselves of the sins that are holding back our beloved Revolution.'

Then the first one spoke: 'For myself', he said, 'I was supposed today to replace the rod where we hang the washing to dry, behind the northern hut, but I didn't. I was lazy . . .' The older man said nothing, and pointed to the next one. 'I fell asleep after the meal', this man said, 'and I forgot to check whether the prisoners' urine pots had been emptied properly . . .'

When they had all spoken, they went on to the next stage . . . One of the youngest ones raised his hand . . . 'This afternoon,' he began, 'I happened to go into the dormitory, and I saw Comrade Miet hiding something in his bedding . . .' With a gesture of his head, the older man sent someone to search the hammock. He ran back, holding a notebook. Young Miet burst into tears.

Bizot never did learn what the notebook contained. It was probably nothing culpable. But that was not the point. The aim of these 'introspection meetings', as they were also called, was to make the participants look into their own souls and strip away everything that was personal and private until their individuality was leached out, their innermost thoughts exposed before their peers and existence outside the group made meaningless. Mutual surveillance and denunciation were a key part of the process, which required a climate of perpetual vigilance and suspicion. Like monks at confession, opening their hearts to God, the young Khmers Rouges 'gave themselves to the Party', becoming one with a revolution which, in theory at least, replaced all other relationships.

Bizot, who was in Cambodia to study Khmer Buddhism, was struck by the paradox. 'The Party theoreticians,' he wrote later, 'had substituted *Angkar* ("the Organisation") for the *Dhamma*, the primordial Being who [in Buddhism] personifies the notion of "Instruction".' In place of the monk's ten vows of abstinence (*sila*), the Khmers Rouges had 'Twelve commandments' (also called *sila*). Like the 'Three Main Rules of Discipline and Eight Points for Attention', which Mao issued to the Chinese Red Army after 1927, and the 'Twelve Points' used by the Vietnamese communists, these enjoined the cadres 'not to touch even a single pepper or can of rice belonging to the people', to 'act properly towards women', and 'to be modest and simple'. But there were also significant differences. Mao's injunction to his troops 'not to ill-treat captives' was absent from the Cambodian list. Instead the Khmers Rouges were urged to 'have burning rage towards the enemy', 'not to depend on foreigners', 'not to be individualistic' and to 'follow the traditions of the people'. Angkar was absolute and impersonal, as Buddhism was, Bizot wrote, and it demanded the same unconditional determination, refusing 'to take into account the human aspect of things, as though it were dealing solely with matters of the spirit'.

These were not parallels that the CPK leaders willingly acknowledged, but unconsciously they resonated in the minds of their followers. To youthful Khmer Rouge devotees, echoes of the novitiate placed the new communist teaching in a familiar setting.

Criticism, self-criticism and 'introspection' were not only for the young and malleable. All Khmer Rouge cadres, at whatever level, were required to take part. At Pol's headquarters on the Chinit river, Central Committee meetings always started with a week-long session of 'criticism and self-criticism', led by Pol himself or Nuon Chea. Only afterwards would they get down to the real business at hand. 'We all had to go through it,' Khieu Samphân remembered. 'You had to examine your own thinking, and analyse your failings and your strongpoints.' Only members of the Standing Committee – which in practice meant Pol and Nuon – were exempt.

'Introspection' and 'study' were two sides of the same coin, and much of Pol's time during the first years at the Chinit river base was taken up with writing training documents on such topics as 'Class Struggle', 'How to Fight Individualism [and] Liberalism' and 'Building Proletarian Principles'.

To 'build', in Khmer Rouge parlance, meant to refashion a person's consciousness. Mental training was one means to that end. The other was manual labour. As with many Khmer Rouge practices, this had been copied from China and Vietnam. Manual labour had been made compulsory for Chinese Communist Party cadres at Yan'an in the 1930s. The goal then was essentially practical: self-sufficiency in food in a drought-ridden border region. Even Mao had his vegetable plot. In the early 1950s, the Viet Minh used it to temper new arrivals – as Pol and the others had cause to remember from their days at Krâbao – much as army sergeants in the West put raw recruits to cleaning out latrines. Later Mao made it part of a campaign to bridge the gap between manual and mental labour and, through the Great Leap Forward, to harness the nation's energies for development. It was in that form that Sihanouk introduced it to Cambodia in the mid-1960s.

All these elements – self-reliance; showing humility; being close to the masses; combining mental and manual labour; mobilising the nation for development – were incorporated into the Khmer Rouge approach.

But to Pol, manual labour had another, more important purpose. It was a means of forging 'proletarian consciousness', that immaterial, indefinable quality that, contrary to all Marxist principles, Pol had viewed since the late 1960s as the touchstone of revolutionary virtue. This 'theory of proletarianisation', as it was called, held that through manual labour, anyone, whatever his class origin, could acquire 'the materialist discipline of the factory worker . . . the idea of respecting the rhythm of discipline, the tempo of work, the rhythm of life' that characterised the working class. Those considered most apt for this transformation were the poor peasants, the backbone and model of CPK support. Others, including intellectuals, could in theory reforge themselves, but it was inherently more difficult.

Manual labour under the Khmer Rouge had another purpose, too, more far-reaching than in China or Vietnam.

The cadres' goal was not to become merely 'close to the people' but indistinguishable from them – not merely to work but 'to speak, sleep, walk, stand, sit, eat, smoke, play, laugh . . . like the people'. Eating in a revolutionary manner meant eating meagrely, out of respect for the peasants' poverty, even if plenty of food were available. Dressing in a revolutionary manner meant that everyone without exception, including Pol himself, should wear black peasant clothes, with a red-and-white checkered *krama* around the neck and sandals cut from car tyres. Men wore Chinese-style peaked caps, and women had their hair severely bobbed. Thiounn Thioeunn's wife, Mala, remembered that when she and her husband left for the Special Zone in January 1971, the first thing she did, after depositing the family jewellery with her sister in Phnom Penh, was to equip herself with the regulation black trousers and jacket. 'They told us it was safer like that, because you couldn't be seen from the air. If you lay on the ground, the spotter planes thought you were a burnt log,' she recalled. 'So we all became crow-people.'

By the beginning of 1972, relations with the Vietnamese were going downhill again. Hou Yuon dated the change to the end of the previous year.

The key factor was the increase in the military strength of the Khmers Rouges. With 35,000 men under arms, clashes with Vietnamese units were inevitably more frequent than when there were only a tenth of that number. As the CPK forces grew more confident of their ability to handle the war on their own, pressure increased for the disbandment of the remaining Khmer-Vietnamese mixed units and for the Khmers Rumdoh (Liberated Khmers) – the 'Sihanoukist' troops trained by the Vietnamese in the early months of the war – to be brought under Khmer Rouge command. Officially, relations were still close, but with an undertone of mistrust. In the summer of 1971, the Vietnamese had proposed a second Indochinese summit as a follow-up to the Canton meeting a year earlier. Pol had refused, seeing it as another attempt by Hanoi to dominate the Lao and Khmer 'junior partners'. 'There was no [open] conflict with Vietnam', an Eastern Zone official recalled, 'but [we] were watching each other very closely.' Non Suon quoted Vorn Vet as saying in the autumn of 1971 that when problems arose with Vietnamese units, 'avoid using arms if possible . . . Try to use political methods.'

In 1972, liaison offices were set up at district and regional level, answering to a special bureau at Pol's headquarters, codenamed D-3, to provide a mechanism to resolve disputes and reduce friction. Then, after a series of allegedly 'spontaneous' anti-Vietnamese demonstrations, new regulations were introduced requiring Viet Cong and North Vietnamese units to be billeted well away from Khmer population centres, to give advance notice of troop movements, and to produce passes, signed by both the Vietnamese and the Khmer Rouge commands, whenever they travelled through Khmer Rouge territory. An internal Eastern Zone directive justified the new restrictions but acknowledged that the fault was not all on one side:

> Some Vietnamese [soldiers] have no papers, and don't want to submit to our checkpoints for fear they will be arrested or have their guns confiscated. So they threaten our sentries . . . They behave aggressively because they are frightened [and] they think our sentries are interfering with their freedom of movement . . . [But] the real problem is that there is too much coming and going [which] gives . . . the enemy an opportunity to infiltrate the liberated zones. . .
>
> If two or more Vietnamese soldiers wish to pass [a checkpoint], so long as one has a Khmer *laissez-passer* all should be allowed to go through. They should not be obstructed or arrested . . . The Khmer pass must be printed in bold characters; handwritten or typewritten passes are not valid . . . Glued to the back of the Cambodian paper, there should be a pass from the Vietnamese Command which must specify the exact number of weapons the unit is carrying.
>
> NB: It must be noted that one reason for the continuous, successive, and more and more numerous incidents which are chipping away at Khmer–Vietnamese solidarity in a number of localities is that our side keeps making mischief by stealing the Vietnamese troops' rifles and ammunition.

By the beginning of 1972, Vietnamese main-force divisions had started pulling out of Cambodia. It was later claimed that they had been forced to withdraw and that their expulsion had been decided by the CPK at the highest level. This was untrue. They left of their own accord – indeed, according to Vietnamese documents, over the Cambodian leadership's objections – because they were needed for the offensive against Saigon and because, in Hanoi's judgement, the Khmers Rouges could now cope on their own.

Their departure should have eased the strains. It did not.

Over the next two years, the CPK imposed ever tighter controls on Vietnamese troops who sought sanctuary in Cambodian territory; on the amount of food the 'Vietnamese friends' could purchase from Khmer villages; and, eventually, on Vietnamese civilian refugees living in the border areas who, 'to protect the Cambodian revolution' – in other words, to deprive the Viet Cong of a support base among sympathetic compatriots living on Cambodian soil – were ordered to return to their homes in South Vietnam. The directives were worded with care. 'We must not resolve these problems by violence, but by lawful means', one typical CPK document declared. 'We must be calm, just and patient.' Vietnamese settlers were to be allowed to harvest the rice they had planted (but not to use this as an excuse for delaying their departure unreasonably) and attempts to confiscate their belongings or to force them to sell their livestock were forbidden. None the less the sense was clear: the Khmers Rouges, now the dominant military force in the 'liberated zones', were reasserting sovereignty over their own territory.

In the same vein, the Khmer Viet Minh 'regroupees' who had returned via the Ho Chi Minh Trail in 1970 and 1971 were increasingly viewed as a potential Vietnamese fifth column. '[They] have lost their national character,' Pol wrote. 'They've been spoiled, and some have political problems.' Khmer Rouge cadres were scandalised by the returnees' enthusiasm for taking new Cambodian wives when they already had families in Vietnam and began speaking of them disparagingly as 'Khmers in conical hats', an allusion to the headgear worn by Vietnamese peasants. From early 1972 some of the Hanoi Khmers were discreetly removed from sensitive positions, especially in the Special Zone and the South-West, to be given lower-ranking posts or sent to 'reforge themselves' through manual labour. Although there was no general purge – transfers were made on a case-by-case basis – it prompted a number of defections by former Khmer Viet Minh, who either crossed the lines to join the government side or made their way back to Hanoi, thereby reinforcing the CPK leaders' doubts about the group's reliability.

This growing mistrust of Vietnamese intentions, felt by Pol and the rest of the Standing Committee no less than by lower-level cadres, was not simply the product of atavistic fears.

Even the Soviet Ambassador in Hanoi, Ivan Shcherbakov, a pro-Vietnamese source if ever there were one, told Moscow that the Vietnamese leaders still spoke of their old dream of a 'socialist Indochinese Federation'. Hanoi's 'narrowly nationalistic approach' and its attempts 'to subordinate the problems of Cambodia and Laos to the interests of

Vietnam', he warned, risked alienating the communist movements in both those countries – exactly the same problem that had soured relations with the Khmers in the early 1950s. To Pol, the experience of the alliance with the Vietnamese during the resistance war in 1971 and '72 showed, even more clearly than Vietnam's refusal to help him against Sihanouk in the late 1960s, that only *force majeure* would ever bring Hanoi to accept the reality of an independent Cambodian revolution and that, for the CPK to be in a position to resist Vietnamese control, it would have to build up its forces militarily and politically until they had sufficient strength to make attempts at interference unprofitable.

At this juncture, another factor intervened. The peace talks with the Americans, which had been under way in Paris for the previous four years, suddenly picked up speed. In mid-1972, for the first time, a real possibility emerged of a negotiated settlement.

For Pol this presented both problems and opportunities. Until then, the Vietnamese and Cambodian communists, whatever their political differences, had been bound together by the war against the United States. If Hanoi now signed a separate peace, the biggest factor uniting them would disappear. If, on the other hand, Vietnam's forces left Cambodia after a negotiated accord, the Khmers Rouges would at last have *carte blanche* to follow whatever policies they wished without having constantly to look over their shoulders to gauge Vietnamese reactions. However they would also come under pressure to negotiate with the US themselves, a course which Pol regarded as diametrically opposed to the CPK's long-term interests, even without the precedent of Geneva in 1954.

It was this last prospect that he found most worrying. That spring President Nixon had met Mao to lay the foundations of a strategic partnership with China against the Russians. Would the Americans try to use this new relationship to reach a separate deal with Prince Sihanouk, who for the past two and a half years had been acting as the public face of the resistance from his gilded exile in Beijing? If they did, how would the Chinese react? And the mercurial Prince himself – which side would he come down on?

For the first year Sihanouk spent in Beijing, he had been both physically and politically in an orbit entirely his own. In the city beyond, the harsh values of the Cultural Revolution prevailed. But behind the walls of his princely mansion, the Cambodian leader lived like the King he still was, with a phalanx of chefs to turn out gourmet dishes of Chinese, Khmer and French cuisine, a private swimming pool, a tennis court, a cinema and the best wine cellar in Red China. He entertained diplomats and sympathetic journalists like the French writer Jean Lacouture, at a table groaning with foie gras and guinea-fowl – 'from my good friend, [the North Korean leader] Kim Il Sung' – and made broadcasts to the Cambodian people over the FUNK radio in Hanoi, extolling the feats of arms of the resistance and denouncing the treachery of Lon Nol and his 'pro-American clique'.

But he had no direct contact with the Khmer Rouge leadership.

It was as though the GRUNC, in Beijing, under Prime Minister Penn Nouth, with its attendant apparatus of ministries and ambassadors, existed in total isolation from the reality of the war being fought on the ground. The rare messages from 'the interior faction', as the CPK was euphemistically called, were sent in the name of Khieu Samphân, now officially presented as 'Commander-in-Chief of the People's Armed Forces for the National Liberation of Kampuchea', and transmitted via the Chinese Foreign Ministry.

The propaganda display in Beijing was useful. The Chinese understood that the resistance stood a far better chance of international recognition with Sihanouk at its head than if it were led by a group of anonymous revolutionaries in the jungles of Kompong Thom. Sihanouk was no dupe either: he said privately from the outset that the FUNK would exist only for as long as the Khmers Rouges needed him, and later told the *New York Times*: 'They will spit me out like a cherry pit the moment they have won.' But it was in the Prince's interest, too, to portray himself as resistance chief. He maintained close contact with the Vietnamese, who delighted him when he visited Hanoi by letting him stay in the apartments formerly occupied by Ho Chi Minh. Nominally he headed the Khmers Rumdoh, who were distinguished from Cambodian communist units by a badge bearing the Prince's effigy which they wore on their uniforms. In reality, however, these troops were a Vietnamese creation. As Sihanouk noted bitterly, there was no chain of command stretching back to the GRUNC in Beijing. The 'Sihanoukist army' took its orders from Hanoi.

It was a role Sihanouk understood well: as King, under the French, he had also served as a national symbol, with no overt executive role. But in those days he had been able to transmute the aura of kingship into political power.

Now, confined to faraway Beijing, that became much harder – and from mid-1971 onward, when Ieng Sary came to China as 'Special Representative of the Interior', his margin of manoeuvre was restricted still more. Sary had reached Hanoi from Ratanakiri in December 1970. He spent the next three months reorganising the 'Voice of FUNK' Radio (which he placed under the control of his wife, Khieu Thirith) and trying to impose the new Party line, emanating from the maquis, on Son Ngoc Minh and the rest of the fractious Khmer community in North Vietnam. In April 1971, he travelled secretly to Beijing, where he spent the summer incognito in talks with the Chinese Communist Party's International Liaison Department, his presence unknown even to his fellow Khmers. Finally, in August, the Chinese announced his arrival with much fanfare and he was officially installed in a villa in central Beijing about half a mile from Sihanouk's residence. There a teletype circuit was installed, giving him a direct link to Pol's headquarters at S-71, and he began to build the core of the future Khmer Rouge Foreign Ministry. Thiounn Mumm, his brother Prasith, and the asthmatic Keat Chhon were inducted into the CPK, followed shortly afterwards by several other young radicals from the Cercle Marxiste.

Sary had a triple mission. He was to liaise with the Chinese and Vietnamese leadership on behalf of the CPK; to keep an eye on the GRUNC's foreign policy, which until then had been the exclusive preserve of Sihanouk and Penn Nouth; and to ensure that the Prince hewed to the Party line at a time when CPK and Vietnamese policies were diverging.

This last task was not made easier by the fact that Sihanouk took an instant dislike to him. Sary was a slippery, duplicitous introvert, contemptuous of the Prince in private and intimidated in his presence, 'falling over himself, not knowing where to put his hands when he tries to make a reverence', as one observer put it. Sihanouk in turn tormented him, telephoning him in the small hours of the morning to check that he was not meeting Zhou Enlai (who, like Mao, kept impossible hours) and inviting him to watch risqué films borrowed from the French Embassy, an experience Sary loathed. For a time, the Prince managed to maintain the outward appearance of concord. But occasionally the mask would drop. 'That abominable Ieng Sary is always spying on me,' he told the Swedish Ambassador, Jean-Christophe Oberg, who visited him at the state guesthouse in Hanoi. 'Mr Ambassador, if you look at the bottom of the curtain as you go out of the room you will see his feet. He is always standing there listening in.' Eventually, during a visit to Algiers, the Prince could contain himself no longer, telling journalists that his Khmer Rouge minder was 'my worst enemy . . . What is more, I find him antipathetic. But what does that matter? . . . What sort of patriot would I be if I made everything revolve around . . . my personal likes and dislikes?'

The looming peace accord on Vietnam exacerbated the differences between Sihanouk and his communist allies.

To the Prince, it opened the prospect of a negotiated settlement for Cambodia whereby, with American and Chinese backing, he could return to Phnom Penh as head of a 'third force' government, made up of moderates from the Lon Nol regime and men like Khieu Samphân, Hou Yuon and Hu Nim (whom he mistakenly believed were key figures in the communist resistance). The Vietnamese favoured this solution and Zhou Enlai gave him to understand that China was not opposed either. The Khmers Rouges were adamantly against it. In July, Pol called a ten-day meeting of Zone and military leaders at which he insisted that there would be 'absolutely no negotiation'. Whatever the Vietnamese might do, the Cambodians would go on fighting. Three months later, he repeated this to the new COSVN head, Pham Hung, during an acrimonious four-day meeting near his headquarters on the Chinit river. Soon afterwards, the chief Vietnamese negotiator at the Paris Peace Talks, Le Duc Tho, warned Kissinger that while Vietnam could ensure that the Pathet Lao would acquiesce in a peace accord, it could not deliver the Khmers Rouges. Kissinger refused to believe him. Only when it became clear that the Vietnamese would not budge did the Americans reluctantly agree that, in Cambodia's case, the accords should contain a non-binding commitment, which Kissinger later explained at a press conference as an American 'expectation that a de facto ceasefire will come into being' there as well as in Laos.

Pol's view was that while 'up to now, Sihanouk's position is one of unity with us, some elements of his approach are unstable . . . We must therefore continue to draw him over to our side.' Accordingly, he decided that the Prince and his wife, Monique, should be invited for the first time to tour the 'liberated zones'.

This was something that Sihanouk had been requesting ever since 1970 but the Khmer Rouge leadership had always refused, claiming that it was too dangerous. In fact they were afraid that, in the words of one Khmer Rouge cadre, 'if Sihanouk comes back, all the people will unite behind him and we will be left bare-arsed'. Khmer Rouge wariness over the Prince's popularity meant that their troops wore no Sihanouk badges; the CPK did not display his portrait; and he was rarely mentioned at meetings. Within the Party, behind closed doors, he was condemned as a feudalist, but a Central Committee directive laid down that such views 'must absolutely not be made known to the masses . . . [and] can be disseminated only within our own ranks'.

By late 1972, such concerns seemed less pressing. The communists were solidly in power in the areas they controlled. To Pol, the key consideration became to stiffen Sihanouk's resolve and to equip him to serve as the voice of an independent Cambodian nationalism, not simply as a spokesman for the Khmer resistance in an Indochina-wide war.

It proved a very necessary precaution.

Three days before the signing of the Paris accords on January 27 1973, Pham Hung returned to the Chinit river to present Pol with the text of the peace agreement. That same week Ieng Sary began extended talks in Hanoi with Le Duan and other members of the Vietnamese Politburo. Extracts from the minutes circulated internally in Hanoi show the Vietnamese leaders walking on eggshells. Le Duan suggested to Sary that the CPK 'consolidate the victories already achieved, and then move forward'. The Premier, Pham Van Dong, urged him to 'take the initiative. Maybe they will meet your demands, maybe not . . . Why does your country still hesitate?' But when, at the end of the month, Sihanouk offered publicly to meet Kissinger, promising 'a rapid reconciliation with Washington' if the US would agree to recognise an independent and non-aligned Kampuchea, Hanoi was compelled to row back. On February 7, a joint statement issued by the GRUNC and North Vietnam said the war in Cambodia would continue. Four days later, Le Duc Tho proposed to Sary that Pol should visit Hanoi to discuss 'the diplomatic struggle'. He went on: 'Among Cambodia, Vietnam and China, we should be of the same mind about how both to fight and to negotiate . . . in order to bring America down . . . Otherwise [Cambodia] will meet difficulties like Thailand, Malaysia and Burma [with] endless guerrilla warfare, no assistance [from outside] and the situation will not progress.' Sary was non-committal but promised to transmit Vietnam's views.

Soon afterwards he accompanied Sihanouk and Monique down the Ho Chi Minh Trail. It was a very different journey from the one he had made two years earlier, when he had walked the entire way. This time they travelled in a cavalcade of Russian-made jeeps and lorries with an escort of more than a hundred Vietnamese guards, drivers, cooks, servants and a full medical team. Thanks to the peace accord there was no bombing. Each night they stayed in a wooden guest cottage, specially built for the purpose and equipped with running water and plumbing, where they were served French meals with freshly-baked baguettes. It was a fitting start for an altogether surreal homecoming.

The couple were welcomed at K-12, the transit station on the Laotian border, by Hu Nim, Khieu Samphân, Son Sen and Ney Sarann, the North-Eastern Zone Secretary. After donning black Khmer Rouge peasant garb and checkered red *kramas*, they spent the next six days being driven some three hundred miles along bumpy dirt roads through the northern provinces of Stung Treng and Preah Vihear, to Mount Kulen, north-east of Siem Reap. To avoid spotter planes, much of the journey was made at night. No Vietnamese was permitted to accompany them, but a Chinese film unit recorded their progress.

Like a latter-day Marie-Antoinette vaunting the rustic joys of the Petit Trianon at Versailles, Monique went into raptures over the traditional

Khmer stilt-house that the Northern Zone Secretary, Koy Thuon, had prepared for them at their destination. 'It's our White House in the liberated
zone!' she wrote excitedly in her diary. 'There's a study, a little salon and a
curtain separating these from the "bedroom" – there's even a carpet on the
floor and curtains in the windows.' Almost every Khmer Rouge luminary
of note was there to honour them, although some, like Pol, concealed their
identities. The Prince was fêted with theatrical performances, a meeting to
mark the third anniversary of his 'Appeal of March 23' which had launched
the FUNK, and visits to the temples of Bantei Srey and Angkor Wat, where
he and Monique were photographed beneath thirteenth-century friezes of
Angkorian overseers and slaves under the watchful gaze of their modern
cohorts.

For all its aura of guerrilla chic, the trip was not without danger. The
US had stopped bombing Vietnam and Laos but not Cambodia, and the
day after the Prince's party started back, the road they had taken was oblit-
erated by B-52s. In propaganda terms, it was a coup, and when the first
photographs appeared in April, flabbergasted American diplomats insisted
they must be fakes. Two months later, to press home his advantage,
Sihanouk set out on an extended tour of sympathetic states in Africa, Asia
and Europe, his second since his overthrow, and afterwards announced that
the resistance government was being transferred from Beijing to the 'liberated zones'. The goal was to convince a majority of United Nations
member states that the GRUNC, rather than Lon Nol's regime, should
hold Cambodia's UN seat. The effort failed by a handful of votes, mainly
because of US pressure but also in part because of the ambiguities of
Sihanouk's own position. Despite his enthusiasm over his homecoming, he
had been lucid enough to realise that his hosts had systematically prevented
him from having any contact with the population, and in a series of interviews that summer he reflected bleakly on his future under a Khmer
Rouge administration. His relationship with Ieng Sary deteriorated further
and at one point he informed his entourage that he intended to resign.
Zhou Enlai dissuaded him, as he had during an earlier tantrum in 1971.

Meanwhile pressure for a negotiated settlement continued. Pol declined
Le Duan's invitation to talks in Hanoi, pleading ill-health. But over the
next two years he had to combat peace initiatives not only from Vietnam
but also from other 'friendly powers', including Algeria, Romania,
Yugoslavia and, more subtly, from China itself, which wanted an early end
to the war so as to be able to concentrate Asian minds not on US imperialism, now, in its view, in decline, but on Soviet 'social-imperialism', which
it saw as the main threat to the region.

In fact, the idea of a 'third force' solution was doomed before it began.

Lon Nol showed little interest in a negotiated peace in Cambodia – which, whatever else it might do, would certainly remove him from power – and Nixon and Kissinger none at all. Nevertheless, the impression grew abroad that the Khmer Rouge leadership was fanatical, obdurate, intransigent if not actually irrational, while at home the campaign against 'third force' elements and the tendencies to pacifism and compromise which they were held to represent made all forms of moderation suspect.

This was not an isolated trend. In 1973 every indicator of policy pointed to the same conclusion: the Cambodian revolution was entering a phase of comprehensive radicalisation.

On February 9, two days after Sihanouk and the Vietnamese leaders had proclaimed that the Cambodian resistance would fight on, the United States resumed bombing. Over the next six months, until Congress imposed a halt, B-52s and other aircraft dropped 257,000 tons of high explosive on Khmer villages, nearly half the total in five years of war. In part this was because Cambodia, in the words of the CIA Director, William Colby, was now 'the only game in town'. As a result of the Paris accords, the US was hamstrung in Laos and Vietnam. Cambodia was the one place in Indochina where it could flex its military muscle and show that, even in retreat, it was still capable of something. Bombing became a virility symbol. 'The President wanted to send a hundred more B-52s,' the Air Force Secretary, Robert Seamans, recalled. 'This was appalling. You couldn't even figure out where you were going to put them all.' In the event, B-52 sortie rates peaked at eighty-one a day, a third higher than in Vietnam, and air traffic congestion became so acute that bomb-loads sometimes fell dozens of miles off target.

The deluge of fire from the sky saved the Lon Nol government, which most observers, including Americans, had expected to fall that year. It also sent tens of thousands of new recruits to join the ranks of the resistance or to become refugees in Phnom Penh and other government-held towns, as peasants fled devastated villages in far greater numbers than ever before. More importantly, it provided the conditions for a mutation of Khmer Rouge policy, which would have come about anyway over time but now occurred much more quickly.* The outcome was a harsher,

---

*There is a close precedent in China, where the outbreak of the Korean War in 1950 created a climate of patriotic exaltation which permitted a marked acceleration in the dispossession of the landlords, the creation of agricultural co-operatives, the elimination of 'counter-revolutionaries' and the nationalisation of commerce and industry. As a result, social and economic changes which had been expected to take twenty years were completed in five.

more repressive regime under which the suffering of individuals became unimportant because there was so much of it.

Ostensibly to avoid the bombing, whole villages were uprooted and moved to new locations. Smaller-scale population movements had already occurred in 1972 – and even, in Ratanakiri, as early as 1968 – but then it had been a matter of removing people from government control by transferring them deeper inside the 'liberated zones', where they lived in conditions not too different from those they had known before. Now they were sent to remote mountain and jungle areas. Their original homes, if not already destroyed, were burned down to stop them returning. Instead of working individually or in small mutual aid teams, they were dragooned into co-operatives of thirty or forty families who farmed the land in common. Here, too, there were precedents: in the South-West and the Special Zone, attempts had been made to introduce co-operatives after the May 1972 Central Committee meeting. But they had been unpopular and the authorities had not insisted. Now collectivisation was imposed by force throughout the 'liberated zones'. Even in the Eastern Zone, where the cadres were reputed to be more easy-going than in other parts of the country, in half a year some 30,000 people were moved away from areas adjoining Vietnam. Kenneth Quinn, then a US consular officer just across the border at Can Tho, pieced together what had been happening from interviews with refugees:

> Families were forced to abandon [everything] except for basic necessities. Others reportedly committed suicide rather than face the loss of all their worldly possessions. Stories carried back by those who had survived earlier relocations told of people dying en route and forced labour after arrival . . . Village officials fled rather than carry out the directives from higher head-quarters. Anyone protesting these policies was arrested, taken away and never seen again. Despite this, people . . . still fled . . . By November [1973] . . . a depopulated buffer zone had been established . . . [Intelligence] officers who flew along the border were able to observe deserted villages, empty roads, abandoned rice-fields and abandoned towns. . .
>
> Conditions in the new locations are reportedly not good. [Those] who have escaped say they are crowded, dirty places where people suffer from lack of food and [there is] a great deal of sickness . . . All land is organised and worked in common . . . and even though production has increased through the use of fertilisers and other scientific methods, people are [said to be] unhappy because they are forced to work constantly and do not have land of their own.

Internal Khmer Rouge reports bore out his account. A senior Eastern Zone leader acknowledged that many villagers killed their livestock for meat, rather than see the animals become collective property. 'When everything was communally owned,' he said, 'the cattle and poultry became sick and died. Farm implements were damaged because no one maintained them any more, and no one took care of the fields.'

The new policy was officially launched on May 20 1973. Pol justified it partly on practical grounds. Co-operatives were necessary to prevent the peasants selling their produce to the Vietnamese or to traders from government-held areas, who offered higher prices than the Khmer Rouge administration. They were a means of ensuring sufficient food supplies for the constantly expanding army and, in areas where most of the able-bodied men had left to fight in the war, of guaranteeing subsistence rations for the women, children and old people who had remained behind. But there was also an ideological rationale. The CPK's goal was to 'build a clean, honest society'. Private trade, like private ownership, implied the pursuit of gain and attachment to individual possessions. It was by definition dishonest.

In the first six months after the collectivisation programme began, some 60,000 people fled the 'liberated zones' to cross into government-held areas or take refuge in South Vietnam.

The 25 per cent of the rural population that had never owned anything, and therefore had nothing to lose, went along with the new system. The problem was the other three-quarters. They, too, were poor. Rural Cambodia, in the early 1970s, was less developed than many parts of sub-Saharan Africa. But most of the peasants who supported the Khmers Rouges in their fight against the Americans, sending their sons to join the resistance and rice to feed the army, were not seeking a fundamental change in their way of life. Pol would later twist the figures to claim that 75 per cent of the population was virtually destitute. It was a claim he must have known was absurd, an ideological figleaf to cover a political decision taken for other reasons. But once proclaimed, it became holy writ.* For the Khmers Rouges, from 1973 onwards, co-operative policy was framed on the premise that most Cambodians had lived in semi-starvation under the old society and therefore the co-operatives had to be an improvement. Since the majority were 'content with and faithful to the new collective system', as Pol put it, dissent was ipso facto the mark of a class enemy. Like many of the policies he imposed, it was a case of 'cutting the feet to fit the shoes'.

The new regime was applied with particular vigour in the Northern Zone, as Ping Sây discovered when he travelled to Pol's HQ on the Chinit river in the summer of 1973:

---

*Suong Sikoeun has said that when he worked at the Democratic Kampuchea Foreign Ministry after 1975, he found repeated errors in Pol's speeches and other documents. But when he proposed a correction, 'What do you think I was told? That I was casting doubt on the abilities of the leadership!' After that he kept quiet.

I met some relatives on the way [who] told me that in all that region there were no markets any more . . . Life was very harsh, very difficult. The revolution was not at all what they had expected. So when I arrived I met Khieu Samphân and Hu Nim, and I said to them: 'We ought to set up a trade office to sell things to the people. They don't even have any salt or relish for their rice.' They didn't answer. But they must have reported back what I had said, because afterwards Hu Nim told me: 'Your views are unacceptable' . . . I often wondered what happened to make them so hard and pitiless.

The following year, Pol himself gave Sây part of the answer. ' "If you could see how the revolutionary army fights to defeat the enemy," he said, "I think perhaps you wouldn't like it." He said that to my face. And maybe he was right: because the destruction in those battles was incredible. For him I wasn't tough enough.' It was the same accusation that Ieng Sary had thrown at Keng Vannsak twenty years earlier, when they were students in Paris, and which others would make against Mey Mann. They were 'excessively sentimental'.

Sentiment has little place in any revolution. Robespierre's France and Stalin's Russia, the two revolutionary braziers which the young men of the Cercle Marxiste knew best, were prime examples. But in Cambodia in the mid-1970s, the glorification of violence went further. In Pol's mind, bloodshed was cause for exultation. Humane feelings were a sign of weakness and should be ruthlessly suppressed. Nor was this one man's aberration: the other Khmer Rouge leaders felt the same. CPK directives ritually enjoined Party members to embrace 'suffering and hardship' in exactly the same way as the early Christians were urged to embrace martyrdom. The Democratic Kampuchea National Anthem, which Pol sanctioned if not actually wrote, resembles nothing so much as the sanguinary paeans of nineteenth-century Catholicism:

> Bright red Blood covers the towns and plains
> of Kampuchea, our Motherland,
> Sublime Blood of the workers and peasants,
> Sublime Blood of the revolutionary men and women fighters!
> The Blood changes into unrelenting hatred
> And resolute struggle,
> [Which] . . . frees us from slavery.

There is nothing comparable in Chinese or Vietnamese communist literature. Mao, who presided over slaughter on a far greater scale than Pol Pot, did not glory in the destruction caused by the Chinese revolution. To him it was a necessary evil, not an index of revolutionary virtue.

The same deliberate extremism was translated into the conduct of the war at all levels. Until late 1972, atrocities were most often associated with government troops. Communist prisoners were routinely killed, to the despair of the Americans who found themselves deprived of potentially valuable intelligence because the men they hoped to question were dead by the time they arrived. Lon Nol's soldiers massacred Vietnamese civilians and called in bombing strikes against Khmer villages, indifferent to civilian casualties, on the off chance that communist guerrillas might be hiding there. That is not to say the CPK forces were any better. They, too, killed and disembowelled prisoners and executed suspected collaborators. On the communist side, however, it was only after 1973 that such exactions became systematic.

The Khmer Rouge soldiers in the field felt the change too. No longer were deserters treated with indulgence. Now they were killed. Discipline was ferocious for all ranks. That summer, the resistance launched its first major onslaught on Phnom Penh, in which 20–25,000 men, representing half of all Khmer Rouge main-force units, were mobilised to take part. By the time the offensive was beaten back in late July, thanks largely to US bombing, at least 30 per cent were dead. To meet the growing need for cannon fodder, conscription was introduced. The casualty rate on the government side was equally horrific: 1,000 men a week dead, injured or missing, according to the Commander-in-Chief, Sosthène Fernandez. But while government units sometimes turned and ran, there was no report of any Khmer Rouge unit breaking ranks or surrendering.

US military intelligence claimed later that the forward commanders had 'direct orders to take the city before August 1973', when, at the behest of Congress, the American bombing runs were to end, 'so they could prove to the world that they could humble the US.'

Pol's insistence on an all-out assault at the height of the rainy season, when the entire area surrounding the capital was flooded and conditions for the attackers were at their worst, was certainly, in military terms, futile, and showed total disregard for the lives of his own men. Had the Khmer Rouge commanders husbanded their forces and waited until the start of the dry season in December, the result might have been very different. As it was, the South-Western Zone troops who bore the brunt of the fighting had still not recovered from their ordeal a year later.

But the Americans were wrong in concluding that Pol was bent on their humiliation. The real objective of the summer offensive was to force the hand of the Vietnamese.

Since the Paris accords, the leadership in Hanoi had been in a quandary. Pol's refusal to negotiate a ceasefire raised the spectre that they might lose control of their prickly Cambodian allies. Their first reaction was to make good the warning that Le Duc Tho had given Ieng Sary in February, when he had spoken of the danger of the Cambodians having to fight on with 'no assistance from outside'. That spring the flow of arms down the Ho Chi Minh Trail from China was mysteriously interrupted. In April the Vietnamese Prime Minister, Pham Van Dong, told a Soviet diplomat that Vietnamese aid to the Cambodian communists was 'decreasing, and its scale is now insignificant'. But squeezing the Khmer Rouge supply line did not produce the desired results. The Cambodians responded by raising the stakes. Pol gave orders that the Hanoi returnees, apart from a small minority who had proved their loyalty, should be rounded up and taken to a detention centre in Chhlong district, on the west bank of the Mekong, as suspected Vietnamese agents. At political training seminars, cadres began for the first time to speak of 'those with Khmer bodies and Vietnamese minds'. Most of the returnees would eventually be executed.* Clashes between Khmer Rouge and remnant Vietnamese units escalated sharply: in July alone, there were two hundred Vietnamese casualties from incidents involving 'friendly forces'. By late summer, only 2–3,000 Vietnamese combat troops and about 2,000 civilian cadres, plus the special units in the North-East guarding the Ho Chi Minh Trail, remained on Cambodian soil. All Vietnamese civilians, not merely refugees but also long-term residents, came under pressure to 'return home' on the grounds that the war in South Vietnam was now over. When the alternative was being herded into co-operatives, they needed little persuasion.

At the same time the Khmers Rouges stepped up the military pressure. The river convoys supplying Phnom Penh came under sustained attack. Two cargo ships and several barges were sunk and eight other vessels damaged. The seaside town of Kep was captured. Takeo was surrounded.

* According to Pol's aide-de-camp, Phi Phuon: 'After the Paris peace accords, all the former Khmer Viet Minh had problems . . . Some of them disappeared altogether; others were dismissed from their posts; still others had their responsibilities reduced.' It appears that the killing of the returnees began in earnest in the autumn of 1974, but it was not systematic: some of those at Chhlong survived until at least mid-1976 and possibly as late as mid-1978. Among those who were left at liberty, but with diminished responsibilities, were Yun Soeun, who had been with Pol at Krâbao in 1954; Mey Pho, one of the group of Young Turks who had taken Sihanouk prisoner in the abortive coup of August 1945; and a young man who became Ieng Sary's private secretary and managed to hold the post throughout the time the Khmers Rouges were in power. One of the unresolved mysteries of the period is what happened to Rath Samoeun, Sary's close friend and co-founder of the Cercle Marxiste. He was last seen in Hanoi in mid-1970 by Thiounn Mumm's younger brother, Prasith. Sary has claimed that he was killed 'immediately after returning to Cambodia'. However, in 1976 he was still referred to as a Party 'comrade', which would not have been the case had he been liquidated. It seems most probable that, like Uch Ven and Pok Deuskomar, he died from illness while in the 'liberated zone'.

Rockets fell for the first time on Battambang. Finally, on August 12, government forces abandoned the strategic road junction at Skoun, 25 miles north of Phnom Penh. All the main land routes in and out of Phnom Penh were now insecure or cut and the capital relied increasingly on a US airlift for food, fuel and munitions.

By the time the US bombing raids ended, refugees fleeing the countryside had swollen the population of the capital to nearly two million, three times the pre-war level. Around the city and along the banks of the Mekong as far as the Vietnamese border, the land was so pitted with craters that it looked, in the words of one diplomat, 'like the valleys of the moon'. The Khmer Rouge attacks of that summer, undertaken in total disregard of the human and material cost, had created a momentum that was unstoppable. Kissinger later acknowledged that, after mid-1973, he had known Cambodia was lost.

In Hanoi the Vietnamese Politburo was compelled to make a painful reassessment. The Khmers Rouges now controlled more than two-thirds of Cambodia's territory and almost half its population. With US bombers grounded, it was clear that they would win whatever Vietnam did. Hanoi's original strategy – to establish a unified communist Vietnam, which would then 'liberate' its younger siblings, Laos and Cambodia, earning their undying gratitude – was dead in the water. By continuing to push Pol to start peace talks which he did not want or need, the Vietnamese communists risked losing what little goodwill from the Khmers Rouges remained.

The arms flow along the Ho Chi Minh Trail was quietly restored.

Other gestures followed. Vietnamese heavy artillery was despatched to help in the siege of Kompong Cham. A South Vietnamese NLF delegation toured the Eastern Zone and was given a red-carpet welcome from Pol himself, Nuon Chea, Khieu Samphân, Hou Yuon and other CPK luminaries. But the damage had been done. In July 1973, the CPK Central Committee held its annual plenum at K-30, Pol's new headquarters a few miles north of S-71, which had been abandoned the previous winter. The delegates agreed that in future Vietnam should be treated 'as a friend, but a friend with a conflict'.

That autumn, Pol travelled again to the Special Zone, where a new forward base had been established near the village of Chrok Sdêch, 'The Gate of the King', in the eastern foothills of the Cardamom Mountains, on the old royal road from Oudong to Pursat. The area was thickly forested, crisscrossed by tracks no wider than an ox-cart, which were hidden from the air by a dense canopy of foliage of immense tropical hardwoods. As the crow flies, it lies about thirty miles north-west of Phnom Penh.

Pol and his entourage lived in thatched huts, built beside a stream amid a cluster of century-old mango trees. Mok's South-Western Zone troops had set up their main camp, equipped with bunkers and trenches for protection against bombing, in rough, broken country, studded with rocky outcrops, a few miles further into the hills. Thiounn Thioeunn ran a military hospital, with six long barrack-like wards, in the nearby village of Boeng Var. Down the cart-track leading southward towards Phnom Penh was Vorn Vet's Special Zone headquarters, concealed in a grove of sugar palms that towered over the surrounding plain.

In theory, operational control of the Khmer Rouge army lay with Son Sen, whom Pol had summoned from the North-East to resume his role as Chief of Staff. His command post was ten miles to the south-east, near the railway halt of Ra Smach on the now abandoned main line from Phnom Penh to Battambang. It was in an area dotted with giant anthills up to twenty feet high, with trees and clumps of bamboo growing out of their sides. Sen's brother, Nikân, recounted:

> We built the command offices half-underground, with trenches and bolt-holes inside the anthills, and a system of tunnels to communicate from one anthill to the next. When there were bombing raids, we hid inside – as though we were ants ourselves. Then, when the danger was past, we would emerge and resume our work. Usually when we built trenches, we lined them with wood and a layer of rice-husks to absorb the shockwaves from the bombs. But earth that has been worked by ants resists the blast even better. And the bamboos provided camouflage.

Messages were carried to the front by courier. Pol distrusted radio traffic for fear of enemy monitoring. Although the resistance had captured US-made transceivers from Lon Nol's forces, they were used mainly to listen in to enemy communications and occasionally to mislead enemy commanders, as on one notable occasion when a quick-witted Khmer Rouge operator tricked the navigator of an air-force transport plane into parachuting a precious cargo of 105-mm artillery shells, destined for government forces, into a resistance-held area, by providing false map co-ordinates. At battalion level and below, Khmer Rouge forces had no radio equipment. Where the Chinese communists, at a similar stage in their civil war, had used bugles to communicate, the Cambodians employed wooden flutes, whose banshee-like wails, echoing through the night air, instilled terror into their opponents.

Pol took two major decisions during his stay at Chrok Sdêch.

The first was systematically to tighten the noose around the capital by cutting, as far as possible, road and river communications with the rest of the country, in preparation for an all-out offensive either the following spring or, if that proved impossible, during the dry season a year later. The second was to tighten security in the Special Zone to prevent infiltration by government spies. This had become a real problem. Serge Thion, a French sympathiser who had visited the Special Zone a year earlier, had been astonished by the ease with which people could cross between government and communist-controlled areas. As a result, Lon Nol's intelligence service was remarkably well informed.*

Now all that changed. Kong Duong, then a sixteen-year-old student at the Lycée Yukanthor in Phnom Penh, recalled what happened when he tried to visit relatives near Oudong the following spring:

> I had a guide from the liberated zone, a peasant who had come to take me across. But we were both arrested by the *chhlorp*, the village militia. They said we were spies . . . My arms were bound behind me and they used a length of rope to pull me along. They sat me down under a tree . . . Then they announced that they'd caught a spy – and all the villagers came to look. When my sister and brother-in-law saw it was me, they came up and vouched for me. That was my good luck – because I was arrested at 4 p.m. If there'd been no one around who could recognise me and say who I was, I'd have been killed. They asked me questions. 'Where are you from? What do you do? How long have you been a spy? You are here to find out where are the places to bomb!' It was the militia chief of the commune who decided I should be spared. But if later I had turned out to be a spy after all, my brother-in-law and his whole family would have been executed. The guide who had brought me over wasn't so lucky. When we were arrested we were separated. He was taken to another village. No one knew him there and he was killed.

Purges also began among the local population. Duong, who afterwards spent fifteen years as a Khmer Rouge cadre, remembered how in his village 'they killed anyone who had an education'. It was not that they had been ordered to do so. But that was how the peasants interpreted the call

---

* This was amply demonstrated by the accuracy of a contemporary Interior Ministry report on Thion's visit: 'Agent 044 reported that in early January 1972, a Frenchman, name unknown, thin and tall with a pointed nose, red hair and sandals, left Phnom Penh on National Road 5 for Thpong district of Kompong Speu in enemy-controlled territory in the South-West. When he reached [their area], he presented the enemy with a pistol. On January 13 1972, the Frenchman was seen taking part in a celebratory meeting at Wat Krang Phngea, Sangkat Veal Pun, in Oudong district of Kompong Speu. He carried a notebook and a bag full of documents. The source stressed that those Khmers [Rouges] strictly banned the Frenchman from seeing any Vietnamese.' In December 2001, the village chief of Ra Smach, who had escorted Thion thirty years earlier, confirmed that they had indeed been under instructions to prevent their visitor seeing any sign of the Vietnamese presence.

for heightened vigilance. 'To them, rich people and educated people were the same: they both looked down on the poor.'

New prisons were built – one near Vorn Vet's headquarters; two others further up in the mountains, beyond Chrok Sdêch – where alleged infiltrators, if they survived the militia, were sent for interrogation. Long afterwards local people still shivered at the names of these places – Sdok Srat, Phnom Prateat and K'mab – 'to which men were taken, but none came back'. Monks arriving from the capital were also viewed as potential spies and confined to a holding centre in the village of Dom Kveth. Ethnic Chinese and Sino-Khmers, who had at first been among the strongest supporters of the resistance, were now denounced as 'capitalists who suck the Cambodian people's blood'. There was growing concern, too, about the attitude of the Chams, who were numerous in the Special Zone. In November 1973, a Cham revolt had broken out in the East, in protest against the communists' attempts to force them to abandon their customs and live in co-operatives like everyone else. At the end of the year, most of the leaders of the movement were still in hiding in the jungle. The Zone Secretary, So Phim, acting on Pol's instructions, gave orders that those captured be treated with exemplary severity:

> The leaders must be tortured fiercely in order that we may obtain a complete understanding of their organisation. Then we should wait for a time before deciding what to do with them. Lower-level leaders should also be tortured harshly, but they need not be killed . . . Their followers should be re-educated . . . Then they can be released to act as political bait and kept under surveillance . . . All methods, and all political and military measures, must be employed . . . to prevent them hiding and regrouping their forces.

This idea that all who diverged from the revolution were human vermin and should be treated accordingly, analogous to the medieval Christian notion that sinners merit the torments of Hell, also coloured the Party's attitude to the inhabitants of Phnom Penh, including the peasant refugees who had streamed into the city. They had chosen their side, sitting out the US bombing in safety while the revolutionaries were blown to smithereens. They therefore merited whatever punishment rained down on them. From late December 1973, Chinese-made 107- and 122-mm rockets were fired into the city, often falling on the poorest quarters and causing hundreds of casualties. The following spring, these were supplemented by captured 105-mm artillery, firing at maximum range from positions south of the capital. Already in 1971 and 1972, the Viet Cong had launched occasional rocket attacks as a means of psychological warfare, to demonstrate that the Lon Nol government was incapable of protecting the population. Now it became a daily blitz of indiscriminate terror.

During the winter Pol travelled back to the Chinit river base to confer with Nuon Chea and Ieng Sary, who had arrived from Beijing. While he was there, twenty-five Khmer Rouge battalions stealthily took up position around Oudong, the former capital, north-west of Phnom Penh. The assault force included two all-women battalions, the only ones in the communist army. They had an unhappy record, for, as one cadre explained, 'the moment it was known they were there, they attracted the enemy like magnets.' By the time the war ended, they had each lost 60 per cent dead.

Oudong was attacked at 3 a.m. on Sunday, March 3 1974. By morning, most of the defenders had been driven back to a narrow perimeter centred on a temple south-east of the town. After a three-week siege, the redoubt fell and several thousand government soldiers and civilian refugees were massacred. It was said afterwards that many 'turned their [guns] on their own families' – the eternal camp-followers of Cambodian military campaigns – 'before killing themselves to avoid capture and torture'. The population of the town, some 20,000 people, was rounded up and marched to the forest of Palhel, an uninhabited area to the east of Chrok Sdêch, where Mok had a military base, before being resettled in co-operatives in the Special Zone and the South-West. Officials and uniformed soldiers were separated from the rest, led away and killed.

The resistance did not have everything its own way. South-Western Zone troops laid siege to Kampot but were beaten back. Government forces eventually recaptured what was left of Oudong, now an empty wasteland of razed buildings and burnt earth. Some 40,000 villagers in the Northern Zone, driven to desperation by the harshness of the regime imposed by Ke Pauk and Koy Thuon, took advantage of a thrust by government troops to flee the 'liberated areas' en masse and take refuge in the town of Kompong Thom. Their accounts of the brutality of Khmer Rouge cadres, of forced labour, hunger and executions, foreshadowed the regime that would descend on the whole country little more than a year later. For a few weeks, republican forces fought with renewed vigour. But then the grim images of life on the other side were rationalised away as refugees' exaggerations and quietly forgotten.

At the end of March, Pol left Chrok Sdêch to visit the battlefield at Kampot before travelling on to Kep, which had been captured six months before. It is an area of pristine, white-sand beaches and limpid turquoise water, formerly the summer playground of the Cambodian elite. Now it was totally deserted. To mark the victory at Oudong, Pol knotted a *krama* around his waist and, like Mao signalling the start of the Cultural Revolution by swimming across the Yangtse, plunged into the sea. His *montagnard* bodyguards had never seen the ocean before and waded in uneasily after him, holding their AK-47s above their heads. It was the month of his forty-ninth birthday. The vice around Phnom Penh was slowly tightening.

The war remained Pol's chief concern in 1974, but it was not the only one. Although theoretically Cambodia was still in the midst of what Marxists termed a 'national democratic revolution' – which required the broadest possible united front to overthrow the right-wing government and install a progressive regime – Pol's mind was beginning to turn to the next stage, the 'socialist revolution', whose purpose was to transform root and branch the nature of Cambodian society. Collectivisation and the elimination of private commerce were already under way. Now, he decided, the time had come to start speaking openly of socialism as Angkar's political goal, to launch a secret campaign to oppose the influence of Sihanouk and to sharpen the 'consciousness and revolutionary stand' of every Party member in preparation for the day when the new policies could be put into effect nationwide.

In September, Pol summoned the Central Committee to the village of Meakk, in Prek Kok commune, eight miles south of the old Northern Zone base at Dângkda, for its annual plenum. There, at his urging, the assembled CPK leaders took three crucial decisions, which together helped to define the nature of the Khmer Rouge system over the next four years.

The first concerned the population of the towns.

As early as 1971, Pol and others had been struck by the speed with which the urban centres in the 'liberated zones', given half a chance, reverted to their bad old, capitalist ways. In March that year, Pol's former companion at Krâbao, Yun Soeun, had been dismayed to discover during a visit to Kratie:

> The town market was even more crowded than before liberation . . . It was full of people at every hour of the day and night . . . There were Khmers, Chinese and Vietnamese merchants, buying and selling. People came on bicycles, on motorbikes and up the river by motor-boat. At the port, boats were coming and going all the time. There were drinking shops, brothels and gambling dens, and many cases of robbery . . .

Two years later, Pol wrote subsequently, nothing had changed. The merchants 'did not want to work with us . . . At first, it wasn't our intention to ban them. But . . . they cheated us all the time . . . In Kratie . . . we could not control the population because the traders . . . controlled the distribution of goods . . . They were arrogant, and did not want to subordinate themselves to us.' The only answer, he concluded, was 'to send them to work in the fields'. Otherwise, 'if the result of so many sacrifices was

that the capitalists remain in control, what was the point of the revolution?'
Kratie was evacuated in the second half of 1973. At about the same time,
Khmer Rouge forces attacking Kompong Cham drove 15,000 town-
dwellers from their homes and forced them to accompany them back into
the 'liberated zones'. Some died of hunger and from bombings along the
way, but most were resettled in villages where, as one peasant put it, 'they
lived a normal life'. Finally, in March 1974, came the evacuation of
Oudong. According to Pol's aide, Phi Phuon:

> It worked well in the sense that there weren't any big problems [for us] in
> resettling the evacuees from Oudong in the countryside and, on their side,
> the town-dwellers didn't cause any special difficulties either. It was a radical
> solution designed to foil any attempt by the enemy to destabilise our forces
> – and at the same time it was an internal measure, because for our cadres, if
> they were living close together with the urban population, there was a risk
> that they would be politically and ideologically corrupted. They might be
> influenced by the new urban environment . . . If the town-dwellers were
> evacuated, that risk was avoided. You must understand that the final goal was
> the liberation of Phnom Penh, and to that end we had to sharpen our polit-
> ical and ideological stance. Was it so our cadres would avoid 'the sugar-
> coated bullets of the bourgeoisie?' Yes!

There were other, less clearly defined reasons, too. All through history,
peasant revolutions have been characterised by resentment of the cities.
Not just in Asia but in early-twentieth-century Europe, men like the
Bulgarian Agrarian Party leader, Aleksandr Stamboliski, 'hated the town
and both its categories of inhabitant, bourgeois and industrial workers
alike'. Populists in Serbia, in Poland and Russia held similar views. The
CPK did not put it in quite those terms. But the wellsprings of its action
– the peasant resentments which, in a primitive agricultural society like that
of Cambodia, provided the only possible motor for revolution – were
exactly the same. The town-dwellers were to return to the land to reforge
themselves, to reconnect with their Khmer roots. It was a trial, a rite of
passage, from which they were expected to emerge strengthened, purified
of the filth that came from city life.

Whatever the precise mix of arguments, the outcome was a unanimous
decision that Phnom Penh and all other Cambodian towns should be evacuated as soon as they were 'liberated' and the population sent off to start a
new life in the villages.

The second issue before the Committee concerned money.

A year earlier, shortly after Sihanouk's visit to the maquis, it had been
agreed that a new currency should be printed for use in the 'liberated
zones'. The previous December, Ieng Sary had brought sample notes from

Beijing for Pol's approval. Thereafter, the use of government currency had been gradually phased out in the communist-controlled areas and replaced temporarily by a barter system with a view to introducing the new, revolutionary money by the end of 1974. The Central Committee did not call into question the principle of these decisions, but decided that the new currency should be put into circulation only after the whole country had been brought under communist control.

The third and, in many ways, the most difficult problem had to do with Party unity.

Since 1968, when the infant Cambodian communist movement had officially launched its armed struggle, the different groups and patronage networks that made up the CPK had made a real effort to come together. But it did not last. Five years later, cracks were appearing in the façade of Party brotherhood. In the Northern Zone, the military commander, Ke Pauk, a former Issarak, was constantly at odds with the Zone Secretary, Koy Thuon, who came from an intellectual background. There were similar, though more muted strains between Ruos Nhim in the North-West and his military commander, Kong Sophal. But Pauk and Sophal enjoyed Pol's favour; their civilian counterparts did not.

In the Eastern Zone, where Vietnamese influence had traditionally been strongest, the problems were of a different order. Men like Chan Chakrey, a flamboyant ex-monk who became commander of the Khmer Rouge 170th Division, made no secret of their preference for a less extreme communist system, one more tolerant of human failings. That was true, too, of the former Pracheachon leader Non Suon, who watched with dismay as members of his group were relegated to minor posts in the new CPK hierarchy. The conflict, dormant since the mid-1960s, between the 'thatched huts' and 'brick houses' – the former Issaraks with their roots in the 'nine years' war' from 1945 to 1954, and the urban-educated radicals like Pol and Ieng Sary – came to the fore again. Adding to the tension, Hou Yuon, who never minced words, had begun openly to criticise certain CC decisions, often giving voice to what others felt but dared not say. In 1974, Yuon accused the Standing Committee of cheating the peasantry by refusing to honour IOUs issued for requisitioned rice. He told Pol and Nuon Chea that the co-operative system, of which he was nominally in charge, was being imposed too fast and allegedly warned: 'If you go on like this, I give your regime three years. Then it will collapse.'* Yuon was a jovial, open

---

*The quotation may be apocryphal. Certainly, in the light of later events, it reads a little too pat. However it is frequently cited in Khmer Rouge circles, and the fact that, from 1974 onwards, Hou Yuon had disputes with Pol over policy is widely attested.

man, 'a good leader . . . popular among his comrades and the population at large'. His loyalty to the cause, and his friendship with Pol, dating from their Paris days, saved him from real trouble. None the less, he was sent to do penance planting vegetables at an isolated base called K-6 in the Chinit river headquarters area and thereafter remained under a political cloud.

Matters came to a head in the South-Western Zone where there had been a long-standing feud between Mok, the Zone Secretary, and the Koh Kong leader, Prasith.

Ostensibly it was over 'revolutionary morality': Prasith and another senior Zone official, Chou Chet, were both notorious skirt-chasers. Mok was a puritan. Chou Chet made his peace with the Zone Secretary. Prasith did not. But there were also deeper issues. Prasith, who had joined the Central Committee in 1960, had been passed over eight years later when Mok had been appointed Zone chief. Since that time Prasith, who had a strong following among the peasantry in the Thai border area, had manoeuvred against Mok to maintain his independence. To what was essentially a struggle for power were then added political differences. Prasith was a moderate in Khmer Rouge terms – 'a gentle, simple, methodical man, a good organiser . . . who mixed easily with the people', as Phi Phuon described him. He ran Koh Kong on more liberal lines than other South-Western Zone regions: private trade was permitted until the beginning of 1974 and villagers were allowed to travel back and forth across the border with Thailand. Mok, by contrast, like Ke Pauk in the North, enforced Standing Committee directives on collectivisation and the suppression of private property with the utmost vigour.

Early in 1974, Mok went to Pol, claiming that Prasith had been in contact with In Tam, whom Lon Nol had put in charge of a programme to encourage Khmer Rouge cadres and their troops to defect. The allegation was almost certainly untrue, as were Mok's other claims – that Prasith, an ethnic Thai, was working for the Bangkok government and the CIA.

The latter charge was less outlandish than it might seem. From the late 1950s on, Sihanouk had claimed constantly in speeches and radio broadcasts, sometimes with good reason, that the CIA was working for his downfall, to the point where, to many Khmers, the Agency's name had become just a synonym for 'enemy'. Mok, in particular, saw CIA agents everywhere.* In 1971, he had been convinced that the French archaeologist François Bizot was working for the CIA and had tried to convince Pol and Vorn Vet of his guilt. When Pol had ordered Bizot's release, Mok flew into

---

*So did Ke Pauk. His Northern Zone troops regularly executed villagers after US bombing raids, claiming they must be CIA spies who had called in enemy air strikes.

a fury: 'This fucking Frenchman is CIA,' he yelled at Vorn and Bizot's jailer, Deuch. 'The upper brothers want him freed. But we, who work at the grass-roots, see things better. It's out of the question to let him go.' At Vorn's insistence, Bizot was liberated. Prasith was not. Nor apparently was he given any opportunity to state his case. Instead, with Pol's agreement, Mok's troops took him into the forest and killed him. His death was followed in April by a purge of ethnic Thai cadres in Koh Kong who were suspected, by virtue of their nationality, of being in sympathy with him.

Prasith was not the first CPK cadre to be liquidated. Mok had already eliminated a number of lower-ranking officials. Others in the East and the North-West had been killed in local power struggles. Some of the Hanoi returnees had also been executed, though most were still in detention camps, ostensibly undergoing 're-education'.

This was the first time, however, that intra-Party conflict had reached into the ranks of the Central Committee. It was the first time, too, that the Party leadership had authorised the execution of one of its own number. Prasith's case was discussed at length during the plenum at Meakk. 'Pol explained', his aide-de-camp Phi Phuon remembered, 'that the class struggle had become extremely acute, and we had to take a resolute, decisive stance against our enemies. He said that anti-communists and counter-revolutionaries had to be dealt with categorically.' But Phuon was not entirely convinced. 'Prasith,' he told himself, 'was from a national minority, as I am. Is that how they think they can treat people like us?'

By the time the meeting ended, Pol's explanation of the purge had been accepted. But all present knew that a line had been crossed.

The recapture of Oudong by Lon Nol's forces in the late spring of 1974 was the last throe of a dying regime. Thereafter its position steadily deteriorated. For much of the previous two years, the dwindling energies of the half-paralysed, self-proclaimed 'Marshal' had been more occupied with political intrigues to shore up his personal position than with trying to save his government. Those he saw as potential rivals – Sirik Matak, Son Ngoc Thanh and In Tam – were successively sidelined. Nol himself was elected President in a fraudulent referendum where, but for massive vote-rigging by his younger brother, Non – Pol's one-time classmate – he would have been soundly defeated.

The US Embassy's political counsellor, William Harben, before his acerbic despatches led to his transfer from Phnom Penh, noted in his diary that Washington was 'supporting a regime which is almost a caricature of the ideal opponent for Marxist-Leninists'. His Ambassador, Emory Swank, told the State Department that Nol was mentally, as well as physically, ill.

The government's inability to protect even its own ministers was dramatically exposed by an incident in June 1974, when two members of Lon Nol's cabinet, taken hostage by demonstrating students, were shot dead by a CPK hit man who vanished into the crowd. The same month, the new Prime Minister, Long Boret, had a narrow escape from a communist rocket attack.

On the battlefield, communist forces continued to have the upper hand. Lon Nol's troops, a US military historian wrote later, were hampered by 'chronic deficiencies of poor leadership, corruption, inadequate training and poor morale'. Their main achievement that year was to prevent Khmer Rouge gunners from establishing secure positions closer than eight or nine miles from the capital, just beyond rocket and howitzer range of the central part of the city, which meant that incoming ordnance fell mainly on the suburban slums, teeming with malnourished refugees. But Phnom Penh was already rotting from within. It was not just a matter of the venality of officials at all levels, the opium parlours, the catamites, the brothels offering *fillettes*, the depravity of a regime where everything and everyone was for sale; more telling than any of that was the fact that most of those with a spark of integrity now supported the other side. The former Democratic Party Prime Minister, Chean Vâm, and Thiounn Thioeunn's younger brother, Chum, worked secretly with urban radicals like Mey Mann to send to the resistance medicines and military maps, often bought from Lon Nol's own officers. To circumvent government checkpoints, they were couriered out by a network of blind and maimed beggars. The banker Sâr Kim Lomouth served as the movement's occult treasurer.

In the diplomatic field, too, the resistance was gaining ground. By 1974, sixty-three countries had recognised the GRUNC. That year, Lon Nol's government retained its seat at the United Nations by a mere two votes. Khieu Samphân went to China to meet Mao, the first Cambodian communist to do so since Keo Meas in 1952, and then set out with Sihanouk on a two-month-long tour of GRUNC allies in Africa, Asia and eastern Europe. The aim was not merely to build support for the future Khmer Rouge regime, but, more importantly, to ensure that the Prince's commitment did not waver. Though he strongly denied it, he had not completely abandoned the idea of a negotiated settlement that would enable him to return at the head of a coalition of moderate republicans, Khmers Rouges and monarchists.

But Kissinger's mind, in the autumn of 1974, was still on extricating America from Vietnam. The Khmers Rouges, who held the guns and therefore called the shots, adamantly opposed all talks. By the time Nixon's successor, President Gerald Ford, authorised serious overtures to the Prince, it was already far too late.

Pol made final dispositions for the dry-season offensive against Phnom Penh at a meeting in early December at B-5, a new forward base near Taing Poun village in Kompong Tralach, about five miles north of Oudong. Son Sen was named front commander, with the Northern Zone Secretary, Koy Thuon, as his deputy. The assault began at one o'clock in the morning of January 1975, with a massive artillery bombardment by captured 105-mm howitzers and Chinese-made rocket launchers, as 30,000 infantrymen advanced on the capital from the south, west and north.

The first week went badly. The skies were clear and on New Year's Eve there was a full moon. This time it was the Northern Zone troops who suffered most, as wave after wave of Khmer Rouge foot-soldiers, advancing across the brightly lit floodplain, were mown down in counter-attacks by government forces which had dug in on every patch of rising ground.

The second stage of the plan was more successful. Vorn Vet and So Phim had been given the task of stopping the river convoys on the Mekong, if possible by the end of January. They achieved it with five days to spare: the last convoy reached Phnom Penh on January 26. By then, Chinese-made floating mines had been brought down the Ho Chi Minh Trail by a CPK delegation led by Ieng Sary.* Ney Sarann met the group at the Laotian border and the mines were taken by lorry to the front. Ten days later, on February 5, the river was blocked by sunken vessels south of the ferry crossing at Neak Luong. Until then, river convoys had provided 90 per cent of the government's supplies. Now, American naval experts concluded, the waterway was definitively closed.

Son Sen was charged with blocking the US airlift, which was the only other way of supplying Phnom Penh. In the first twelve days of January, more than a hundred 107-mm rockets hit the airport and nearby city suburbs. As the siege of the capital intensified and the howitzers were able to move closer, the frequency of shelling increased until the runways were being pounded more than a hundred times a day. In mid-March, after a 105-mm shell went through the cockpit of an aircraft coming in to land and several passengers were killed by shrapnel, the airlift was halted. But it

---

*It is frequently claimed that the Khmers Rouges purchased the floating mines from China with the promise of rubber exports from the formerly French-owned estates in eastern Cambodia whose nationalisation Sihanouk had announced the previous autumn. This is untrue. All Chinese military assistance to Cambodia, both before and after 1975, was made in the form of grants, as was China's far greater military aid to Vietnam during a quarter of a century of Indochinese wars.

resumed two days later as American officials realised they had no alternative. At its height, 600 tons of ammunition were being flown in each day from Thailand and more than 400 tons of rice.

On February 25, Ke Pauk's Northern Zone troops captured Oudong for the second time and began moving down Highway 5, closing in on Phnom Penh from the north-west. South-Western Zone troops under Mok advanced along Highway 4, from the direction of Kompong Som, while a Special Zone division moved up the salient between Highways 2 and 3, from Kampot and Takeo.

At the beginning of March, Pol moved his headquarters to the hamlet of Sdok Toel, barely twenty miles from the city, and an observation post was set up on Mount Chitrous, the site of the Royal Tombs at Oudong, offering a panoramic view of the Khmer Rouge army, swarming like a black mirage across the gridiron-flat plains.

By then, France and Japan had ordered the departure of all non-essential personnel from Cambodia and the Americans were dusting off evacuation plans, codenamed Operation Eagle Pull, drawn up two years earlier, when it had first seemed that the regime might collapse. Sihanouk announced in Beijing that when Phnom Penh fell, the 'seven arch-traitors' – Lon Nol, Sirik Matak, In Tam, Cheng Heng, the army commander, General Sosthène Fernandez, Lon Non and Long Boret – would be executed, but others would be spared. Over the next few weeks the list would be expanded to include a total of twenty-three names. But the implicit promise of an amnesty for everyone else was maintained. On April 1, Lon Nol allowed himself to be persuaded 'temporarily' to step down and, consoled by a draft for a million dollars from the Cambodian National Bank, flew off to exile in Hawaii. The same day, the ferry crossing at Neak Luong, which had held out since January, was overrun by Eastern Zone troops, who then advanced to a line just south of Takhmau.

At this point, the Vietnamese, who had expected to wage a lengthy campaign to take Saigon, realised that strategic blunders by President Nguyen Van Thieu had opened the prospect of a quick victory. Their old plan to conquer the south before the Khmers Rouges took Phnom Penh suddenly seemed feasible after all. An undeclared race got under way. In practice it should not have mattered, but psychologically it was key. The last thing Hanoi wanted was for the Cambodians to win first. Far from helping, as the Americans claimed, they dragged their feet. Khmer Rouge officials complained about Hanoi's miserliness in sharing munitions. Much later the Vietnamese themselves confirmed this: an internal military history, published in Hanoi, described how, in late March, Vietnamese officers refused to hand over a convoy of Chinese army trucks until the

Khmers signed a document thanking Vietnam, not China, for providing them. In desperation the Cambodians complied.

By early April, life in Phnom Penh had become totally unreal.

Those with money and connections scrambled for seats on the last planes out. The two and a half million others existed in suspended animation. Despite the airlift, the city was getting only half the rice it needed. There was no medicine, few hospital beds and, in a country drowning in blood, none left over for transfusions. Once one of the loveliest capitals of South-East Asia, Phnom Penh had become a bloated caricature of the plight of poor countries everywhere, in which the misery of the many is matched only by the shameless consumption of the few. While rice prices rose astronomically and, in the shanty towns, thousands of children and old people starved to death, restaurants like the Sirène and the Café de Paris still offered foie gras, venison and fine French wines. At the venerable Hotel Phnom, the oldest and most respected establishment in Cambodia, a French girl made love one evening in the swimming pool – once at the shallow end, once at the deep end, with two different men – to cheers from other guests sipping poolside drinks. It was as if the city were determined to prove itself the cesspit of decay and turpitude that the Khmers Rouges claimed it was – the ideal target, ready and waiting, like a diseased whore, for the purifying fires of an incandescent revolution.

By April 10, some 800 US Embassy personnel and assorted 'experts' had been flown out to Thailand. Kissinger, having realised, months too late, that a deal with Sihanouk was the only possible way of avoiding total defeat, tried to keep Ambassador John Gunther Dean and a skeleton staff in Phnom Penh while feelers were put out to the Prince in Beijing. The effort was doomed before it began. Two days later, the Secretary of State had to bow to the inevitable. On Saturday, April 12, the Ambassador and his colleagues were helicoptered out to US naval ships standing by off the Cambodian coast. Cambodia's acting President, a veteran army general named Saukham Khoy, went with them. After spending nine billion dollars, equivalent to nearly ten years of Cambodia's national income, most of it on aerial bombardments, and leaving half a million inhabitants dead, America's adventure in Cambodia had finally reached its term.

Next day, New Year's Day by the Khmer calendar, a Supreme National Council was formed. It was headed by the new army commander, Sak Sutsakhan, who had studied in France at the same time as Pol and, by one of those family ironies with which Cambodian politics abound, was cousin to the CPK Deputy Secretary, Nuon Chea. That did not help him. Sutsakhan's name was promptly added to the list of traitors.

The Year of the Tiger gave place to the Year of the Hare, an auspicious year in Cambodian legend. For a few hours, the daily rocket attacks tailed off. Ignoring the round-the-clock curfew, families met to celebrate and look ahead to happier times. At Pol's forward base at Sdok Toel, the Khmer Rouge leaders celebrated too. Over lunch that day, the South-Western Zone leader Mok pooh-poohed the military talents of Son Sen and Vorn Vet. 'Without me, you wouldn't be anywhere near taking Phnom Penh,' he crowed. 'You're a bunch of layabouts.' Phi Phuon, who was present, remembered that a 'heated discussion' followed. Pol, he noticed, 'tended to pay more attention to Mok's views than those of the other two'. It was the harbinger of an improbable complicity between the two men, one the unruffled theorist of the Khmer Rouge revolution, the other a crude, peasant warlord, noted for his cruelty and for the devotion of his followers.

The pause in the fighting was short-lived. On Monday morning the shelling resumed as fiercely as ever, triggering fires in various parts of the city which raged out of control for days. Hundreds of slum-dwellers perished in the flames. Takhmau, six miles south of the capital, was occupied by Mok's troops. The airport was surrounded by Special Zone forces. Two days later, on April 16, the Supreme Council decided to leave the city and set up a temporary seat of government in the north-west, near the border with Thailand. But that night the helicopters which were to fly them out failed to appear. Years later, people had differing memories of the next few hours. Some spoke of an eerie calm. Others wrote of continuing bombardment which made the buildings shudder, and of gun and rocket fire drowning out conversation. All effective resistance ceased. By dawn, individual Khmer Rouge commanders were discussing with their republican counterparts arrangements for surrender.

The war was over. The peace was about to begin.

8

Men in Black

THE YOUNG MEN who appeared from nowhere in the centre of Phnom Penh soon after first light did all the things that victorious rebels are supposed to do. They drove about in jeeps flying a strange flag, a white cross on a blue-and-red field, acknowledging the cheers of the crowds as they passed. They seized control of key installations including the Information Ministry and the radio station, and fraternised with government troops, who threw away their weapons and waved white flags in surrender. 'People began kissing and hugging each other,' the French missionary François Ponchaud remembered. 'We foreign onlookers were utterly amazed . . . Were these men, looking so well-fed and so few in number, the dreaded revolutionary troops?' Others had doubts, too. An American photographer decided they 'weren't for real'. The British correspondent Jon Swain thought their leader swaggered about like 'a playboy [in] a black uniform [that] looked as if it had been tailored by Yves St Laurent'.

None the less, a mood of euphoria took hold. People tied white hand-kerchiefs to the aerials of their cars and the handlebars of bikes. The armoured personnel carriers outside the Hotel Phnom were festooned with bunches of yellow *anh kang* flowers. One young woman remembered neigh-bours singing and dancing in the streets. 'An almost physical sense of relief led to general rejoicing,' Ponchaud wrote. 'No more rockets to fear. No more compulsory military service. No more of this rotten, loathed regime.'

At midday the Khmer Rouge local radio, which had been broadcasting since the spring from a small mobile transmitter near the Great Lake under the name, the 'Voice of the FUNK of Phnom Penh City', announced that the capital had fallen. But virtually no one in the city heard it, and it was not until half an hour later that the mysterious insurgents were able to find two technicians capable of operating the radio studios. Their leader, Hem Keth Dara, then broadcast a pre-recorded statement on behalf of the organisation he claimed to head, the Monatio or National Movement, confirming Phnom Penh's capitulation and proposing a round-table meet-ing 'to discuss a settlement'. Under his aegis, the Supreme Patriarchs of the two Buddhist sects and a senior Republican general, Mey Sichân, made appeals for calm and for government troops to lay down their weapons. But suddenly, as Sichân was saying reassuringly that he would 'make arrangements with representatives of the other side' to ensure a peaceful transfer of power, another, harsher voice broke in. 'We are not coming here to negotiate,' it said. 'We are entering the capital through force of arms.' After that the radio went dead.

The charade was over. The Khmers Rouges, the real ones this time, had taken charge.

Hem Keth Dara and his friends were students manipulated by Lon Nol's younger brother, Non, to make a last-ditch attempt to win a place in the new order by pretending to be revolutionary sympathisers. That such a hare-brained scheme could have been contemplated, let alone carried out, showed how utterly detached from reality the republican leaders had become. But the gamble also reflected an almost universal belief that, whatever the political colour of the new regime, after a period of transition the *mores* of the old society would reassert themselves and life would go on much as before.

In retrospect, it is hard to understand why the Cambodian elite refused so stubbornly to see the writing on the wall.

Sihanouk's presence at the head of the resistance was one factor. The reassurance of the FUNK's political programme, with its artful guarantees of religious and personal freedoms, leniency toward opponents, national reconciliation and the 'inviolability of the person, property and wealth', drafted by Thiounn Mumm, was certainly another. So was the prominence given to Khieu Samphân, who was widely viewed as a good and honest man. Moreover, many of the Phnom Penh bourgeoisie had friends or relatives who had quietly slipped away to join the other side. But beyond all this lay a deep weariness, a belief that the new regime, whatever it was like, could not possibly be worse than what had gone before. Pin Yathay, an engineer with a senior post in the Lon Nol government, remembered arguing with his parents: 'Some of those people are my friends . . . They're patriots first and communists second. They will abide by the will of the people.' Others told themselves that if things went really wrong, they could always go abroad, as the FUNK programme had promised.

Lon Non, who through his role in government intelligence was one of the best-informed men in the country, was not alone in judging that it was worth the risk of staying on. Prime Minister Long Boret, although listed as one of the arch-traitors the Khmers Rouges would execute, also declined to leave. So did Boret's predecessor, Hang Thun Hak, who had known Saloth Sâr as a student. None of them seemed to have any inkling of what was about to be unleashed. Or, if they did, they refused to think about it.

While Hem Keth Dara and his followers were being disarmed, men and women in black of a very different stamp moved soundlessly through the city, methodically taking control of each intersection, collecting weapons, searching vehicles and ordering government troops to remove their uniforms. Son Sen's younger brother, Nikân, was with the vanguard, entering the city with a Special Zone division:

> We moved in from all sides. Altogether there were fourteen different jumping-off points for the final push. The main concentration was in the West . . . That was where the bulk of our forces were based. Son Sen divided his time between his HQ at Ra Smach and a forward post on Mt Chitrous, from which he was able to watch the advance. We had expected the town to fall between 10.30 a.m. and noon, but in fact it was an hour earlier. For us, it was such joy and happiness! All our strategic objectives had been met. I remember thinking how everything would change, how the peasants would finally have a better life. . .

Mok's South-Western Zone troops advanced from the south, up Highways 2 and 3. Special Zone forces came in from the west, past Pochentong Airport, where resistance from a government paratroop regiment delayed them for several hours. Northern Zone troops took the area around the French Embassy and the Hotel Phnom, as far south as the railway station. Chan Chakrey's Eastern Zone division – which was originally supposed to stay on the far bank of the Mekong – occupied the riverfront area up to Boulevard Norodom, including the Royal Palace.

To Nikân, 'it was a perfect victory. Justice was on our side.'

To the population at large, the carnival atmosphere – the 'village fete' that Sihanouk had predicted when peace finally returned – soon yielded to alarm and a sinking sense of dread. 'I had a physical sensation,' François Ponchaud wrote later, 'that a slab of lead had suddenly fallen on to the city.'

The newcomers were 'covered in jungle grime, wearing ill-fitting black pajama uniforms with colourful headbands or peaked Mao caps', one woman remembered. 'They seemed ill at ease . . . [with] a wary, exhausted look.' To the Khmer journalist Dith Pran, they were from 'a different world . . . They never smiled at all. They didn't even look like Cambodians.' Ponchaud, too, remembered their faces, 'worn and expressionless, speaking not a single word and surrounded by a deathly silence', as they marched in Indian file along the boulevards as though the city were a forest.

They were indeed from a different world – the world which Michael Vickery had glimpsed a dozen years earlier in the dirt-poor villages of Banteay Chhmar, where illiterate, near-destitute peasants lived as their ancestors had, without running water or electricity, without schools, without mechanical devices of any kind, without even a proper road, wholly untouched by the surface modernity that the Sihanouk years had brought to the towns and villages along the main highways. These were boys from the Cardamoms, from Koh Kong and Pursat, from the hills north of Siem Reap, Preah Vihear and Stung Treng, where, in the words of a rich peasant, 'they had never seen money, they didn't know what a car was.' In those benighted regions of the Cambodian hinterland the Khmers Rouges had built their strongholds and recruited their first followers. They were places which town-dwellers never visited and whose very existence they found hard to imagine. Yet peasants from such areas were no less Khmer than their city cousins, and to Pol and his colleagues in the CPK leadership, they were purer and more authentic, the primal gene-pool from which the revolution would be forged. These poorest of the poor became the model for all the rest. Those from better-off regions, who joined the revolution later and in time made up the vast majority of the Khmer Rouge soldiery, were pressed into the same mould.

Two Cambodias, which until then had been kept rigorously apart, collided that April day in 1975.

The urban elite discovered with horror how primitive the conquering forces were. Soldiers drank water from toilet bowls, thinking they were what city people used instead of wells. 'They were scared of anything in a bottle or a tin,' a young factory worker remembered. 'Something in a tin had made one of them sick, so they mistook a can of sardines, with a picture of a fish on it, for fish poison.' Some of them tried to drink cans of motor oil; others ate toothpaste. The archaeologist François Bizot, returning to his house after a Khmer Rouge unit had carried out a search, found broken chairs, smashed glass and, in the bathroom, a bidet overflowing with excrement. Decades afterwards, Thiounn Mumm, who had been a Khmer Rouge minister, still shook his head over the way the children of high-ranking peasant cadres wiped their bottoms with tree-branches after relieving themselves and left the soiled sticks lying around the house.

The soldiers were equally repelled by what they saw as urban vice.

Many of them were teenagers, some only twelve or thirteen years old, not much taller than the AK47s they carried manfully on their shoulders. In their eyes, city girls wearing lipstick and youths with long hair were prostitutes and perverts, the proof of all they had heard about the bourgeoisie's loathsome ways. Had not Hou Yuon warned, in a broadcast three months before the city fell: 'If you, brothers and friends, continue to live in the extremely anti-national and arch-corrupt militarist, dictatorial and fascist republic, you can be sure of dying uselessly . . . Your only way out is to follow the path of resolute struggle'? By ignoring such appeals and remaining in enemy territory, Phnom Penh's inhabitants had shown where their true loyalties lay. Now they were 'prisoners of war' and everything they possessed was legitimate war booty. Shortly before the final assault, division commanders from the South-West, the East, the Special Zone and the North had ordered their troops not to loot or to kill unless they met with resistance. In the event, for many of them, the temptation was too great. It was not money or jewels they coveted: a bemused city-dweller watched one man open a packet containing 10,000 US dollars and throw it disgustedly into the river, unwilling to touch such imperialist filth. They wanted cars and motor-bikes, whose unfortunate owners were asked politely but firmly to 'lend them to the revolution', whereupon, having no knowledge of gears or steering wheels, they drove them straight into trees or walls, walking away bruised and laughing to try all over again. Crashed and abandoned vehicles were stripped of their tyres, which were cut up to make rubber sandals. Ballpoint pens with click-in tips were especially coveted, and Ponchaud saw young guerrillas 'with four or five wristwatches on one arm'. The troops broke into Chinese merchants' stores and slashed open bales of cloth, not out of vandalism, as some city people thought, but to make bags to hold their newly acquired gadgets. Television sets, fridges and expensive furnishings – emblems of the bourgeoisie – were ignored or thrown aside.

Hate played its part in the events that followed, and some of those involved later admitted as much. But it was not the dominant emotion that day. More common, especially among the younger troops, was a slow, sullen anger, directed against the city and all its works. 'The city is bad because there is money in the city,' a Khmer Rouge cadre told Ponchaud. 'People can be reformed, but not cities. By sweating to clear the land, sowing and harvesting crops, men will learn the real value of things.'

The anger of the young men who had emerged from the jungle was directed at those who had continued living in comfort, oblivious to their misery, while they had fought against all odds to defeat the 'imperialists and reactionaries'. It was directed against those who were better-educated or better-off. Above all it was directed at anyone and anything linked to the American bombing of their villages. In Battambang, communist troops tore apart two T-28 bombers with their bare hands. 'They would have eaten them if they could,' one resident wrote later. At Pochentong Airport, where Mey Mak's unit was based, the troops systematically smashed every runway light before anyone could stop them.

'There was something excessive about their anger,' a Phnom Penh doctor reflected. 'Something had happened to these people in their years in the forests. They had been transformed.'

Right: The only known picture of Saloth Sâr as a young man, taken at Kep, probably in 1954, when he was twenty-nine.

Below left: Ieng Sary (*left*) and Keng Vannsak, at the latter's apartment in Paris, c.1951.

Below right: Sary's close friend, Rath Samoeun, co-founder of the Cercle Marxiste.

A portrait of Son Ngoc Minh, the first Cambodian communist leader, is carried in procession by Party militants, *c.*1952.

His successor, Tou Samouth, who became Party Secretary in 1960.

Keo Meas, leader of the Pracheachon group.

Khieu Ponnary (*right*), with her sister, Thirith, and Keng Vannsak's mother-in-law, Madame Collineau, in Paris, *c.*1950.

King Sihanouk is borne in state beneath a palanquin to preside over the ceremony of the sacred furrow.

Above: Khieu Samphân in the role of Sitha, the heroine of the *Reamker*, at celebrations in Paris marking the 2500th anniversary of the birth of Buddha (1957).

Below: (From right) Keat Chhon, Thiounn Mumm, Prince Sihanouk and (*upper left*) Chhorn Hay, at the same occasion.

Right: Son Sen as Director of Studies at the Phnom Penh Teacher Training College, 1958.

Left: Sihanouk and Queen Kossamak with Jacqueline Kennedy, who visited Cambodia in 1968.

Below: Government-sponsored mob sacks the North Vietnamese Embassy in Phnom Penh in March 1970.

On Sihanouk's orders, the army commander, Lon Nol (*above left*), organised public executions of captured Khmer Serei in the 1960s. In the civil war which followed, government troops took the heads of communist soldiers as trophies.

Saloth Sâr, shortly before he took the name Pol in Ratanakiri in 1969, and (*below, front row, centre*) at the CPK's Third Congress held in the jungle near the Chinit river in 1971, in a hall decorated with portraits of Marx, Engels, Lenin and Stalin.

Prince Sihanouk and his wife, Monique, in Khmer Rouge uniform, outside what she described as 'our White House in the liberated zone', at Mount Kulen in 1973.

Sihanouk with (*from right, front row*) Hu Nim, Khieu Samphân and Monique at Stung Treng, at the start of their visit to the 'liberated zone', and (*below*), inspecting a Khmer Rouge field kitchen.

Khmer Rouge women's battalion on the march, *c.*1974. The scene is reproduced on one of the Khmer Rouge banknotes printed in China the following winter. The notes, which were never issued, show Angkor Wat and other historic monuments as well as idealised scenes of the society Pol Pot wished to create.

Above: Ieng Sary and Ambassador Sun Hao (*second and fourth from right*) with Chinese diplomats at their jungle 'embassy' near Tasanh, April 1979.

Left: Chinese government passport issued to Ieng Sary, under the assumed name of Su Hao, following the Vietnamese invasion.

Below: Deng Xiaoping greets Sihanouk at Beijing Airport on January 6 1979.

Pol Pot celebrated his sixtieth birthday by remarrying and starting a family. One of the cruellest of the Khmer Rouge leaders, Nuon Chea (*above*), living up to his alias, 'Grand-Uncle', holds Pol's daughter, Sitha, at the age of six months, in October 1986. Pol poses with the children of his aides (*below left*), and goes sightseeing in Thailand with his wife, Meas (*far left*), probably the same year.

But few of his colleagues lived to see his new-found domesticity.
(*From left to right, top*) Vorn Vet, Siet Chhê and Ney Sarann, and (*bottom right*)
Koy Thuon, were all killed on his orders at the Tuol Sleng interrogation centre in
1977 and 1978. So Phim (*bottom left*, with Pol) committed suicide rather than
face arrest.

Left: Heng Samrin, installed by Vietnam as Cambodian Head of State in 1979.

Right: Khieu Samphân, beaten by a mob sent by Hun Sen's government, after his return to Phnom Penh in November 1991 to implement the Paris peace accords.

Below: Pol Pot, being carried in mountain chair during a visit to Mao's old guerrilla base at Jinggangshan, in southern China in 1988, and (*facing*), his two principal military supporters, Ke Pauk (*left*) and Mok.

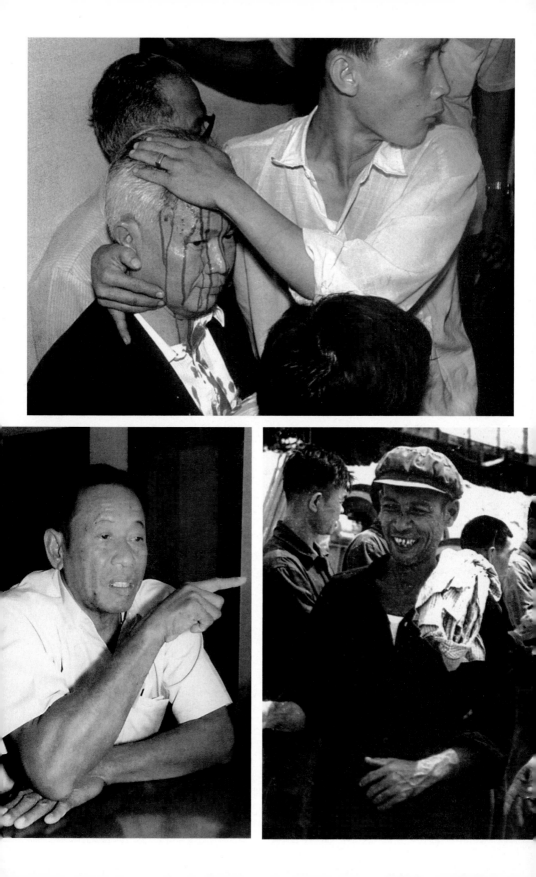

In July 1997 Pol Pot was brought before a mass meeting near Anlong Veng and sentenced to 'life imprisonment'. He died peacefully in his sleep nine months later.

Yet it could have been far, far worse; After a five-year civil war in which half a million people had died and both sides were guilty of widespread atrocities, the fall of Phnom Penh was not marked by rivers of blood. At the Hotel Monorom, a few blocks south of the railway station, where the deputy front commander, Koy Thuon, established his headquarters, a 'Committee for Wiping Out Enemies' was set up. Its first action was to approve the execution of Prime Minister Long Boret, Lon Non, and other senior republicans, who were taken out and killed in the grounds of the Cercle Sportif, not far from the Information Ministry where they had been detained. Altogether, in the following days, seven or eight hundred politicians, high-ranking officials, police and army officers were killed and thrown into common graves on the road to the airport. So much for Sihanouk's assurance that only the named 'arch-traitors' would be punished. But at least, in these early stages, there was no large-scale violence against the population as a whole. It would have been superfluous: people were so relieved that the war was over, they would have done anything the new authorities demanded. Most government troops simply abandoned their weapons and uniforms and fled. There were some exemplary killings, of long-haired youths, civilian looters who were caught pillaging shops or the occasional man or woman rash enough to defy a direct order, but usually a soldier had only to loose off a few rounds into the air to secure instant compliance. Of the eight hundred or so foreigners who gathered in the French Embassy, some had been put in great fear for their lives; yet none was wounded, let alone killed.

Early in the afternoon, the next phase began. Soldiers went from house to house, telling the inhabitants that they must leave 'just for two or three days', on the pretext that the Americans planned to bomb the city. Officers with loud hailers repeated the order.

The idea was not, in itself, far-fetched. Provincial towns overrun by the Khmers Rouges had often been bombed afterwards by government aircraft. The Viet Cong had used a similar subterfuge, likewise asking people to 'leave for three days', when they evacuated Hue during the Tet offensive in 1968. In both cases, the assurance that they would soon return disarmed potential resistance and, in theory at least, reduced the quantities of personal possessions the evacuees carried with them – which to Pol was important, since one unstated aim of the exodus was to strip bourgeois families of their worldly goods as a step towards reforging them in the mould of the poor peasantry amongst whom they were now to live.

But there the parallels end. The Viet Cong operation – like the Khmer Rouge evacuations of Oudong and Kompong Cham – was small-scale, tightly controlled and meticulously planned.

The evacuation of Phnom Penh was a shambles.

It could hardly have been otherwise. To move more than two and a half million people out of a crowded metropolis at a few hours' notice, with nowhere for them to stay, no medical care, no government transport and little or nothing to eat, was to invite human suffering on a colossal scale. Although the great majority – the two million displaced peasants who had fled their villages to escape the war – were only too pleased to leave the slums and shanty towns and return to their rural homes, they would have preferred to go at their own pace and in their own way, not amid a river of human detritus, expelled volens nolens by an avenging power. For the others, the 600,000 or so authentic city-dwellers, who had lived in Phnom Penh since before 1970, evacuation meant leaving behind everything they held dear and entering an unknown world for which they were totally unprepared.

To confound the confusion, troops from the four different Zones responsible for occupying the city issued contradictory orders.

In the North, Koy Thuon's forces had been informed of the evacuation order weeks in advance and began turning people out of their houses soon after midday, giving them only a few minutes to pack some food and a few pots and pans. Buildings were systematically searched; arms and valuables confiscated; and there was widespread looting. Nowhere was exempt. The locked doors of the Soviet Embassy were blown open with a B-40 rocket and the diplomats pushed out at gunpoint. Within minutes, all streets leading northward were blocked by a seething mass of townspeople, urged on by soldiers firing into the air. One of them wrote later:

> It was a stupefying sight, a human flood pouring out of the city, some people pushing their cars, others with overladen motorcycles or bicycles overflowing with bundles, and others behind little home-made carts. Most were on foot . . . The worst part of the whole march was the stopping and starting: there was such a crowd that we could never go forward more than a few yards at a time before we had to stop again. . .

April is the hottest month in Cambodia. The land swelters under a leaden sun as men and animals await the coming of the rains. In five days, the main body of the cortège had covered only eight miles:

> Sick people were left by their families at the roadside. Others were killed [by the soldiers] because they could walk no further. Children who had lost their parents cried out in tears, looking for them. The dead were abandoned, covered in flies, sometimes with a piece of cloth thrown over them. Women gave birth wherever they could: in the road or under the trees. We didn't have the energy even to think about eating. At night we fell down with

weariness and slept with everyone else at the edge of the highway. When
we awoke at dawn, we realised we had been sleeping next to the bodies of
some soldiers who had been killed the previous day.

The hospitals were emptied. From the episcopal palace, opposite the Hotel
Phnom, François Ponchaud witnessed 'an hallucinatory spectacle':

> Thousands of the sick and wounded were abandoning the city. The strong-
> est dragged themselves pitifully along, others were carried by friends, some
> lying on beds pushed by their families with their plasma and IV drips bump-
> ing alongside. I shall never forget one cripple who had neither hands nor
> feet, writhing along the ground like a severed worm. Or a weeping father
> carrying his 10-year-old daughter wrapped in a sheet tied round his neck
> like a sling, or the man with his foot dangling at the end of a leg to which
> it was attached by nothing but the skin.

When Phnom Penh fell, there were an estimated 15–20,000 people in the
city's hospitals. Many doctors had already fled abroad and conditions in the
wards were like those of the Crimean War, giving the sick and injured little
hope of survival. But the evacuation decision, and the ruthlessness with
which the Northerners carried it out, left them no chance at all.

Another French priest wrote of an unnerving calm, 'no indignation, no
revolt, the most complete resignation'. When the column reached the
Northern Zone checkpoint at the village of Prek Phneou, army and police
officers from second lieutenant up and government functionaries were
asked to come forward and identify themselves. They were informed that
they would be taken back to Phnom Penh to help Angkar reorganise the
city. That was indeed the destination of the most senior among them,
including the former Premier, Hang Thun Hak, and another ex-Minister,
Pan Sothi. Both men were taken to Koy Thuon's HQ at the Hotel
Monorom and then killed. The rest were simply led across the rice-paddies
into nearby scrubland and bludgeoned to death. The remainder of the
column, purged of these remnants of republican power, went on to Prek
Kdam, where it divided into two – one part heading along the western bank
of the Great Lake, towards Pursat and Battambang in the North-Western
Zone, the other towards Skoun, to be resettled in co-operatives in the
Northern Zone provinces of Kompong Thom and Kompong Cham.

Troops from the other Zone commands had been less well briefed.

South-Western and Special Zone units received the evacuation order
only on April 16 or, in some cases, the early morning of April 17, and at
first there was a mix-up about how long it was to last. Some soldiers assured
residents that they would be allowed to return after three hours, with the
result that many simply closed their doors and stayed put. Hospitals in the

southern districts of the capital continued functioning, and when eventually it was made clear that everyone would have to leave, the troops gave people time to pack and let them take as much as they could carry. Looting was rare and when, years later, former residents of these areas returned, they found their homes much as they had left them: one man reported that the only item missing was a file of photographs and newspaper cuttings about his student days in Paris, which had been removed from a locked cabinet.

Initially the southward evacuation was even slower than that by the northern route. Many people were still only a few hundred yards from their homes seventy-two hours after setting out. This was in part deliberate. As the tide of humanity unfurled along Highway 1, towards Svay Rieng, and Highway 2, to Takeo and the lower reaches of the Bassac river, many dragged their feet in the hope that after three days they would be allowed to return. The Khmers Rouges responded with random killings, and recalcitrants were executed in public as a warning to the rest. But on the whole the South-Westerners, who answered to Mok and Chou Chet, used the velvet glove more than an iron fist. One deportee remembered them 'shepherding [us] quietly along, without too much brutality'. Pin Yathay found them 'as polite as they were implacable'.

Mok's troops allowed them to make for their home villages, even if it meant leaving the main column. Yathay was able to drive his car as far as Koh Thom, forty-five miles south of Phnom Penh, and when eventually it was confiscated he was given a receipt. In the North, such niceties were unknown. The South-Westerners were also more selective in their treatment of republican soldiers. Some, but not all, senior officers were killed, and junior officers and NCOs were spared. The Special Zone troops on Highways 3 and 4, leading to Kampot and Kompong Som, who answered to Vorn Vet, adopted a similar approach.

Eastern Zone units were even less well-informed about the modalities of the evacuation than the other groups, no doubt because originally they were not intended to enter the city at all.

On the afternoon of April 17, a senior Eastern Zone officer assured an emissary from the Buddhist Patriarch, Huot That: 'I can give you my word of honour that I have never heard of this [evacuation] order. It is an imperialist manoeuvre . . . to sow seeds of panic among the population.' But when, later, Mey Mann went to the headquarters of Chan Chakrey's 170th division and asked point-blank whether he and other 'progressive figures' in the communists' urban support network could stay in the city, Chakrey said he would have to consult higher authorities. Two days later, the answer came. 'The *Khmers Rouges* say no,' Chakrey told him, rapping out the words as if to distance himself from a message with which he disagreed.

'You must leave with the others.' Deportees who travelled eastwards down Highway 1 gave glowing accounts of their treatment by the green-uniformed Easterners who, in contrast to the callousness of the men in black, 'helped everyone who was overloaded . . . carrying babies for the mothers [like] good commie soldiers!' But it was a difference of style, not of policy. Once the evacuation order had been passed down, Eastern Zone units, like everyone else, ensured that the areas under their control were emptied of inhabitants.

Mann went with his family to his home village in Prey Veng. Thiounn Mumm's brother Chum, and his brother-in-law, the former Prime Minister Chean Vâm, were sent to a co-operative in the Special Zone. Pol's brother, Loth Suong, the palace official with whom he had lived as a child in Phnom Penh, joined the crowds walking north and eventually reached a co-operative in a remote area of Kompong Thom. There he was reunited with his youngest sibling, Nhep, and their sister Roeung, King Monivong's concubine.

Pol's favourite brother, Chhay, had spent the previous few years editing a republican newspaper. On the way north he collapsed and died, becoming just one more meaningless statistic on the balance sheet of those for whom the deportation became a death march. Altogether it is estimated that some 20,000 people lost their lives during the evacuation of Phnom Penh. The figure itself, while appalling, is not exceptional in the aftermath of a civil war. In France in 1945, in the first months after the German retreat, 100,000 people died in revenge killings, murders and the settling of scores between those who had collaborated and those who had not. The population of France being seven times that of Cambodia, the proportion of deaths was not that different. But in France, the killings, the forced suicides, the shaming of women who had shared their beds with the enemy, were the work of individuals, acting alone or in mobs. In Cambodia it was the result of a deliberate policy decision taken by the country's highest authorities: Pol and the CPK Standing Committee.

Day One of the new regime was marked by sporadic clashes between the different Khmer Rouge units in Phnom Penh along the boundaries of the areas each controlled.

Some were straightforward turf fights. Others stemmed from uncertainties over individual soldiers' identities in an army without uniforms or badges of rank, a problem graphically illustrated by the Hem Keth Dara incident. In theory all Khmers Rouges carried identification papers, but that was little help when most of the guards manning the checkpoints were illiterate. A recurrent image in city-dwellers' accounts of this period is of a black-clad male or female combatant, glaring suspiciously at a passport or some other official document, held upside down.

Scattered pockets of resistance came from remnants of Lon Nol's forces. There were also incidents involving looters. Parallel to the urban exodus, peasants from co-operatives in the Special Zone and the South-West streamed into the city to loot 'useful goods' – axes, hoes, spades, fencing wire and sacks of rice. The departing townspeople looted, too. And there were 'authorised' looters. Pol's aide, Phi Phuon, drove in with a group of bodyguards from Sdok Toel and returned with an American jeep and a Land-Rover to expand the Party Secretary's motor pool. Other units raided the city's pharmacies, taking truckloads of drugs to Thiounn Thioeunn's field hospital near the village of Bek Chan and to the Zone command posts.

On Day Two – Friday, April 18 – Son Sen and his staff drove in from Ra Smach and established their headquarters at the Phnom Penh railway station.

One of his first acts was to summon the division commanders from all four Zones to delineate clear limits for each sector. Tensions continued, and during the weekend, in one of the strangest incidents of that week, the National Bank was blown up with dynamite. François Bizot, at the French Consulate a mile further north, remembered 'a fearful explosion shaking the air' followed by a huge column of smoke climbing into the sky. It was never completely clear who was responsible, but the bank was at the limit of Eastern and South-West Zone control. The likeliest explanation is that it was pillaged by men from Chakrey's Eastern Zone headquarters. The perpetrators allegedly made off with 200 kg of gold and then blew up the building to make the theft appear to be the work of gangsters profiting from the confusion.* After this incident, co-ordination improved and open clashes between troops from different units ceased.

New guidelines were also issued to harmonise the evacuation procedures in different parts of the city. No longer could people choose for themselves which road to take. Those in the north went north, up Highway 5, even if their home villages lay in a quite different direction; those in the west were marched along Highways 3 or 4, towards Kampot or Kompong Speu; those in the south towards Takeo or Svay Rieng. The entreaties of husbands and wives or parents and children who happened to

---

*The one certainty is that the bank was *not* deliberately blown up by the new regime itself. Not only were other, more visible symbols of capitalism, like the Central Market, left untouched, but in April 1975, the Khmer Rouge leadership had every intention of issuing currency and establishing a banking system of its own. A month later, when the preparatory team started work, it was based in an undamaged area of the bank premises.

find themselves in different parts of the city were ignored: they went the same way as everyone else in their sector. Searches were stepped up for those trying to stay behind. The old and bedridden were simply killed.

Similar scenes, with local variations, occurred all over Cambodia.

The only major Zone command not to have sent troops to the battle for Phnom Penh was the North-West. On April 18, its soldiers occupied Battambang, where they acted more circumspectly, but even more brutally, than the Northerners in the capital. Soon after arriving, they ordered the prices of foodstuffs in the market to be cut fifty to a hundredfold, to the delight of the population and the despair of the Chinese stallholders. The acting provincial governor, a republican colonel, then appealed over the radio to all soldiers to report with their arms to the Prefectural Office. There they were divided into three groups: officers, NCOs and enlisted men. Most of the latter were marched westwards, towards Samlaut, and set to clearing the forest for new settlements and paddy-fields. But some of the NCOs were taken away in trucks, one group leaving for Siem Reap, another for Phnom Penh, supposedly for retraining. About twenty miles out of the city, they were ordered to get off and assemble in nearby fields, where their arms were bound and they were killed.

The officers were initially told to stay at home and await further instructions. Five days after the city's fall, on April 23, they were ordered to report, wearing dress uniform, for departure to Phnom Penh to greet Prince Sihanouk, who was about to return from Beijing. Several prominent local businessmen were asked to join them. As they headed down Highway 5 towards the capital, the convoy stopped near Mount Thippadey. There, according to one of the few survivors, they were machine-gunned by Khmer Rouge executioners hiding in ditches by the roadside.

Similar massacres occurred throughout the North-West. At Pailin, the gem-mining town on the Thai border, the Khmers Rouges arrived on April 20, 'People [streamed] in from neighbouring villages', one resident remembered. 'They were all singing and dancing for joy, beating drums to make noise and shouting, "Long live peace!" . . . [They] sang and danced all night long as though it was the New Year.' As in Battambang, prices in the markets were slashed. The officers from the republican garrison, about forty in all, were taken off in trucks 'to help train our soldiers to drive tanks, operate radios and use artillery'. At the Samlaut crossroads, fifteen miles to the east, they were all killed. So were eighty city officials. On April 26, the townspeople were driven out. Most were rehoused in primitive settlements in the jungle on either side of the Pailin–Battambang highway. Those who went further encountered a flood of people coming from the opposite direction – the inhabitants of Battambang, which had been evacuated two days earlier. They, too, were marched deep into the forest, often miles from the nearest road, where they built themselves bamboo huts and began preparing for the planting season to grow food for the coming year.

In the course of these first weeks, the deportees were progressively stripped of their possessions. In some cases, individual Khmer Rouge soldiers 'requested' them: woe betide the rash owner who refused, for such 'requests', in the stilted, saccharine jargon which the revolutionary movement affected, were always made in the name of Angkar, a term which the deportees were now hearing for the first time and did not understand beyond associating it with fear. Pin Yathay recalled how his sister was forced to give up her motorcycle:

> 'Angkar needs that motorbike,' the soldier repeated . . . Then, as polite as ever . . . he said: 'Angkar *proposes* to borrow it from you. Do you accept, yes or no?' [She replied:] 'I'm sorry . . . I need it. How else can I carry my baggage?' The soldier's eyes widened. He unslung his rifle [and] said: 'You dare say "no" to Angkar?' . . . Then suddenly he fired into the air right in front of her face . . . She burst into tears [and] ran to my mother, who took her in her arms. The soldier glared round at us all, as if daring us to move. I was frozen with fear . . . [Then he] settled the rifle back on his shoulder, slowly untied [my sister's] baggage, handed it carefully to my father, mounted, kicked the engine into life and rode off.

For the better-off, who owned cars or trucks, there was a second stage in this creeping pauperisation. Many had left Phnom Penh and other towns with vehicles 'overflowing with bundles of clothing, curtains, and incongruous but treasured items – cookers, sofas, cupboards . . . symbols of former wealth [like] televisions and tape-decks.' Haing Ngor, later to achieve fame in the film *The Killing Fields*, contemplated the efflux of consumer durables and thought how strange were the things people valued and that they should fail to realise that electric fans and televisions would be of no use in villages without electricity. In the event, these cherished icons of the consumer society never got that far. When the order came for private cars and trucks to be abandoned, their contents were left scattered by the roadside: refrigerators, suitcases, sewing machines, armchairs – even a grand piano, which was sighted three years later, the lacquer peeling from its frame, marooned in the middle of a rice-field. For some it was all too much. Several deportees remembered seeing 'a shiny new Peugeot, driving down the riverbank':

> It was one of those events that happened faster than its meaning can be absorbed . . . The car drove into the water with a splash and floated forward,

until the river current spun it round and took it slowly downstream. There were people inside. A man in the driver's seat, a woman beside him and children looking out the back with their hands pressed against the windows. All the doors and windows stayed closed. Nobody got out . . . We just stared as the car settled lower and the waters closed over the roof. A rich family committing suicide.

As well as cars and consumer goods, money itself lost its value. For some days, traders continued to set up stalls, offering cakes, cigarettes, barbecued chicken and eggs, fruit and vegetables, laid out on tarpaulins by the roadside, for ever-increasing quantities of the old Lon Nol riels. The Khmer Rouge might warn that the old currency had been abolished, but market instincts died hard. Only when it became clear that riels were useless, and the roads passing through the suburbs were, in the words of one deportee, 'covered in a thick carpet of banknotes' whose usefulness was now limited to lighting fires, did the traders finally resort to barter.

By this stage, rich and poor alike were reduced to taking only what they could carry on their backs. And the levelling-down continued. On every road leading out of Phnom Penh or Battambang or smaller provincial towns, checkpoints were set up where each deportee's baggage was searched. Cameras, radios, tape recorders, wristwatches, books in any language, documents, foreign currency – in short, all those things which, in former times, set the elite apart from the peasantry as defined by the condition of the very poorest among them – were confiscated. There were no body searches, partly because it was assumed (often correctly) that, at the mere mention of Angkar, people would obey to the letter, and partly, it seems, because to have soldiers body-searching deportees, especially women, would have violated the communists' moral code. As a result, many families managed to hide jewellery, gold and medicines, and even in some cases dollars, which would later serve as a medium of exchange for favours from village cadres and for extra food, until that resource, too, was exhausted.

For those who survived the march and the spot checks to which former army officers and civil servants were subjected, there remained one further test. When they reached their home villages, or in some cases even before, adult deportees were required to write a short autobiography. This was a technique devised by the Chinese Communist Party in the 1930s to test applicants for Party membership and as a vehicle for self-criticism during rectification campaigns. In the 1940s and '50s the Viet Minh went a step further, making the repeated writing of life-stories the central plank of a sophisticated process of indoctrination aimed at non-communist intellectuals. The Cambodian communists took the process to its logical extreme, eventually requiring virtually everyone in the country to write out a personal history describing their family background, their activities since childhood, and above all how they had spent the years when Lon Nol was in power. Educated people were judged by the style and language they employed as well as the content of what they wrote. Scribes assisted the illiterate. As ever, Khmer Rouge cadres promised clemency, assuring all who had held posts in the republican administration that, if they were honest about their past, the new regime would make use of their talents.

Many fell into the trap. But what happened to them next varied enormously, depending on who they were and, above all, to which part of the country the exodus had brought them.

Technicians and skilled workers were sent away in lorries after being promised that their families would be allowed to join them later. When nothing further was heard from them, many deportees concluded that they had been killed. In fact, most were taken to Phnom Penh to help restore production in the factories where they had worked previously. In provincial towns, where the evacuation was on a smaller scale and consequently better managed, factory employees were told at the outset to remain at their places of work.

Former military men, civil servants, architects, doctors, engineers, lawyers, schoolteachers and university students were sent for 're-education'. For the first two categories, this was often a euphemism for death. But not always. At Sramar Leav, in Takeo province, in the heart of Mok's South-Western Zone, reputedly a tough area, those who had served in the army and the civil service under the Lon Nol regime were assigned separate living quarters but otherwise treated identically to other deportees. In a commune in the supposedly liberal East, sixty former civil servants and professional people underwent a three-month 're-education course' consisting of intense physical labour, a starvation diet and repeated interrogations. All but three died. In the North-West and the North, where the evacuation itself had been conducted with especial harshness, all those with university training underwent re-education involving extremely hard physical labour for between three months and a year. Yet in both Zones large numbers of intellectuals survived.

The evacuation of Cambodia's towns and its immediate consequences – the relocation of the entire population to the countryside; the killing of former opponents; the reform or elimination of all regarded as potentially hostile – were an almost perfect paradigm for the three years, eight months and twenty days of Khmer Rouge rule that followed.

That most city-dwellers were taken completely by surprise merely showed how little attention they, and the outside world, had paid to the

Khmers Rouges and their methods during their long years in the wilderness. What happened in mid-April 1975 was the fruit of policies that had been in gestation since the 1960s and had their origins in a still earlier time. It was not fortuitous that six of the principal Zone leaders – Ruos Nhim and Kong Sophal in the North-West; Pauk in the North; Ney Sarann in the North-East; So Phim in the East; and Mok in the South-West – had started their revolutionary careers as Issaraks during the war against the French.

They showed the same extreme single-mindedness, the same excessive simplification, the same ruthlessness and contempt for human life, as the rebels of thirty years earlier. They also showed the same fractiousness and diversity. Unlike orthodox communist states, where decision-making is highly centralised and implementation is in theory monolithic, Khmer Rouge Cambodia was unruly. That combination of attributes would prove one of the most enduring features of Pol's regime and eventually a prime cause of its downfall. Directives from the CPK Standing Committee were obeyed, but each Zone interpreted them in its own fashion. Hence the welter of conflicting signals during the evacuation of Phnom Penh. What was true of the Zones was also true at lower levels. A battalion commander from the South-West maintained that 'whether different units were soft or strict depended on the individual commanders – not on the Zone they came from'. Deportees might be treated harshly in the supposedly moderate East, or with moderation in the supposedly harsh North.

The prevailing image of the Khmers Rouges as uniformly mindless automatons, bent on destruction, was fundamentally wrong. What the deportees themselves experienced was a mosaic of idealism and butchery, exaltation and horror, compassion and brutality, that defies easy generalisation. That, too, would continue throughout the Khmer Rouge years.

Even those who acted most harshly oscillated between thuggery and nerveless calm. The young soldier who furiously loosed off a volley in the face of Pin Yathay's sister as he stole her motor-bike, afterwards 'slowly untied [her] baggage and handed it carefully to [her] father'. At one level it was the eternal Khmer dichotomy between serenity and uncontrollable violence, with no middle ground between. 'We try to stay polite,' Haing Ngor explained, 'because it is easier that way. To be in conflict forces us to treat each other as enemies, and then we lose control.' In a revolutionary context, where violence was the norm, the politeness of the Khmers Rouges was all the more telling. Often it had a sinister coloration: a woman overheard a soldier telling a group of prisoners who had just been savagely beaten: ' "So you don't feel too well? Just wait, you'll feel better in a little while . . ." Those sugary words, that irony, I recognised all that, it was the way the soldiers talked.' Yet there were also cadres who were genuinely 'not

oppressive or threatening [but] quiet and polite'. The two were not necessarily in conflict. Pin Yathay noted that the soldiers went about their work,
'preparing death with unfailing courtesy'.

Alongside terror and cruelty, virtually every deportee had a story to tell
of at least one 'decent' Khmer Rouge, who offered help when it was least
expected. A young woman recalled a black-garbed cadre who noticed her
sick niece and 'in an inexplicable humane gesture, used his influence to
secure the streptomycin that saved [her]'. Another deportee remembered
a soldier helping a small boy and his elderly grandmother at a Phnom Penh
hospital. 'He left them alone for five minutes, then came back with a hospital cart loaded with ten big loaves of bread, some grilled fish and some
pork.' Haing Ngor recognised a regional Secretary in the North-West as
one of his former teachers, a man who had lived 'a simple, spartan life . . .
He was very pure and intellectual . . . typical of the idealists who joined
the communists in the 1960s and then vanished into the forests.'

There were many reasons for the disparities in Khmer Rouge behaviour.

One was the entrenched individualism of Khmer society. Despite constant indoctrination and ferocious discipline, the communist troops
remained Khmers, heirs to a culture which holds – in contrast to that of
China and Vietnam – that each family, each individual, is an island, and its
primary task is to defend its own. To such a people uniformity does not
come easily, especially not to those among them who hold a particle of
power. It produced, in the case of the Khmers Rouges, a system which was
not so much 'communist' as inherently unpredictable. The replacement of
a cadre, the vagary of fate that led a deportee to settle in one village rather
than another, could mean literally the difference between life and death.
Capriciousness and uncertainty were as characteristic of the Khmer Rouge
regime as violence and barbarism.

Differences were exacerbated by the high level of illiteracy and the paucity of qualified cadres. No matter how detailed the guidelines prepared by
the CPK Standing Committee, the fact that they had to be transmitted
orally to low-level officials meant that only the most simplistic, broad-
brush principles were retained. All the rest was improvisation. The way in
which policies were carried out depended on the whim of the individual
and the attitude of the higher-ups in his *k'sae*, a word which means literally 'string' but has the sense of a vertical patronage network through which
a mandarin distributes largesse and receives support from subordinates.
Under the pre-colonial monarchy and under Sihanouk, such networks
were the principal channels for the exercise of power in Cambodia.
Revolutions, even as they destroy, build on the model of what has
gone before. Power relations among the Khmers Rouges continued to be

channelled through *k'sae*, with the Zone Secretaries, latter-day mandarins, in the role of provincial warlords, loyal to the CPK Centre yet with considerable latitude of their own.

The other defining features of the evacuation – the systematic stripping away of the possessions of the rich and not-so-rich; the writing and rewriting of autobiographies to identify potential opponents; the summary executions; the near-total absence of resistance by millions of people, uprooted from their homes and going like sheep to the slaughter – were equally a foretaste of the regime to come.

The united front that had linked the Khmers Rouges with Sihanouk and other 'bourgeois progressives' had expired in fact, if not in name, the day Phnom Penh fell. Far from trying to broaden the communists' support base, the CPK had reverted to its pre-1969 strategy of 'quality rather than quantity', promoting a narrow, puritanical regime, fit for carrying out an ultra-radical revolution and guided by the principle that it is always better to go too far than not far enough.

That doctrine lay at the root of many of the abuses both of the evacuation itself and of the years that followed.

Every rank-and-file soldier and village chief knew that insufficient vigilance against enemies would bring certain punishment, but excessive zeal in pursuing suspects would not. Thus, there was no central directive from the Party leadership ordering army clean-up squads in Phnom Penh and other towns to kill elderly and sick people who had stayed or been left behind during the evacuation – but the troops did so because they had been told to ensure that the area was emptied and that was the simplest way of doing it. There was no central directive, either, to loot libraries, scientific laboratories and research institutes, and to burn Buddhist and Western books. None the less, it happened. François Bizot saw the holdings of the Ecole Française de l'Extrême Orient, 'precious works, laboriously collected by scholars, which we had deliberately kept in Phnom Penh to show our commitment to future generations of Khmers', being thrown from the first-floor windows to be consumed in a 'pathetic *auto da fé*'. Another foreigner watched piles of books from the library of the Roman Catholic cathedral being burned on the lawn in front of the bishopric. Months later, Thiounn Mumm, then a senior adviser to the Khmer Rouge Industry Ministry, stumbled across a laboratory formerly used for agronomical research. 'The soldiers had smashed everything . . . They didn't do it for any clear reason – but if you leave a house full of ten-year-olds for three or four days without the presence of adults, you know what the result will be.' The explanation is self-serving but not without truth. The destruction of Western things was not ordered from on high, nor was it universal.* It was the visceral reaction of men who had been force-fed with the idea that imperialism and all its works were absolute evil.

Soldiers everywhere are trained to secure their objectives without paying too much attention to the damage they cause along the way. In the case of the Khmer Rouge, this was compounded by ignorance and extreme youth. None the less, the political context which allowed them to act as they did had been defined over the previous decade by Pol and the CPK Standing Committee.

It need not have been so.

In April 1975, popular disgust with Lon Nol's republic was at its zenith and the majority of the urban population was ready and willing to support virtually any policy the new regime chose to introduce. Different leaders, with a different ideology, might have chosen a policy of national reconciliation. Pol decided otherwise. To him, the city-dwellers and the peasants who had fled to join them in the dying months of the war were *ipso facto* collaborators and had to be dealt with as such. Only when they had been subjected to the regenerative power of manual labour and the rude battering of peasant life would the survivors emerge from purgatory, just as the Khmers Rouges themselves had emerged, toughened and purified, from their own years in the maquis.

Suffering and death were an essential part of this process. Mey Mak's commanding officer told him: 'If we worry about that sort of stuff, we are no longer revolutionaries.' Soldiers were urged to 'cut off their hearts' towards potential enemies, a category which included all urban deportees. It might be argued that such behaviour comes more naturally to Cambodians than to other nations because their culture regards forgiveness as a form of weakness. Buddhist detachment, in the shape of indifference, is so widespread that a Khmer proverb asks: 'The marrow has pips: why has man no heart?' But the argument does not hold up. War and revolution are by definition heartless, no matter where they are made. The only distinction that can be drawn is quantitative. As Cambodians were discovering, some revolutions are crueller and more unforgiving than others.

The urban deportees, the jetsam of the Cambodian revolution, tried in different ways to make sense of the sudden implosion of their lives. Many saw the evacuation, and the brutality with which it was carried out, as reflecting the Khmers Rouges' numerical weakness, where 'two or three

---

* The National Library, for instance, was protected throughout the period the Khmers Rouges were in power. The pulping of its collections did not occur until 1979, when the government of Heng Samrin ordered it as a stopgap measure at a time of an acute shortage of paper.

brainwashed teenagers with rifles' had charge of thousands of displaced town-dwellers.

Others regarded it as an act of collective revenge by a neglected underclass against anyone who by birth, education, official position or wealth, had been privileged under the old regime. Revenge is the timid man's weapon and, in Cambodia, where people flee open confrontation, it is a weapon of choice. *Kum*, that 'particularly Cambodian mentality of revenge', one deportee wrote, 'is the infection that grows on our national soul . . . If I hit you with my fist and you wait five years and then shoot me in the back one dark night, that is *kum* . . . Cambodians know all about *kum*.' To yet others it was a practical measure, designed to disorientate the town-dwellers and place them in a position of dependency vis-à-vis the country's new rulers.

But the great majority, especially among the poor, interpreted what happened in April 1975 in terms that were not rational but reached back to the wellspring of Cambodians' cultural identity. The *Puth Tumniay*, a book of Buddhist prophecies, written in the nineteenth century but imitating much earlier works, had warned of a dark age, a black time, when hooligans would rule, the cities would be emptied, 'people will be so hungry that they will run after a dog to fight for a grain of rice that has stuck to its tail', the monkhood would be destroyed and a demon king would come, who would 'make people think that wrong is right, black is white, good is bad'.

The predictions of the *Puth Tumniay*, like those of Nostradamus and the oracles of old, were framed so elastically as to fit a wide range of situations. None the less, to Khmers trying to understand an incomprehensible revolution, they offered a familiar and traditional means of coming to terms with the events they were living through by placing them within the cyclical flow of Buddhist history. In Theravada lore all over South-East Asia, there are tales of flesh-eating ogres and evil spirits who gather to attack the Buddhist religion. The Khmers Rouges were equated with the '500 Thieves', a legendary group of millennial bandits who 'rob us of all the things we possess – our families, our children, our property and even our lives'. Another version described how 'black crows will scatter *lvea* fruits throughout the land'. The *lvea* fruit is round and green, with a beautiful shiny surface. But when it is opened it is full of lice. The 'black crows' were the Khmers Rouges; the '*lvea* fruit' the alluring ideas of Utopian communism; and the 'lice' the reality of killings, famine and privation. The one consolation was that all the prophecies agreed the black time would be of brief duration.

9

Future Perfect

I T WAS NOT the triumphal entry that most insurgents dream of.
Three days after the fall of Phnom Penh, on the morning of April 20,
Pol returned to the city he had last seen twelve years before. Then he had
been a fugitive, hidden in the back of a lorry, fleeing to Vietnam. Now he
was escorted from the forward headquarters at Sdok Toel in a captured
armoured car, surrounded by a phalanx of jeeps carrying the leaders of the
three Zones which had co-ordinated the offensive – Mok from the South-
West; Koy Thuon and Ke Pauk from the North; Vorn Vet and Cheng On
from the Special Zone – Pol's deputy, Nuon Chea; Khieu Samphân; the
Chief of Staff, Son Sen, and the four chief division commanders, San,
Saroeun, Soeun and Thin.

But old reflexes die hard. Instead of proceeding directly down Highway
5, which would have taken them past dense crowds of urban deportees, the
convoy took a devious back route, along narrow dirt roads through
bombed-out hamlets and paddy-fields, to emerge near Pochentong Airport
and enter the city from the west. At the railway station, where communist
Cambodia's new leaders would spend the next few weeks, there was no
honour guard. 'Pol's arrival was secret,' his aide, Phi Phuon explained.
'There was no announcement, no ceremony, nothing to show he was
there.'

The railway station had been chosen because it stood well apart from
other buildings and was easy to defend. It had been built in the 1930s to a
French-Cambodian colonial design, with an art deco, Mediterranean-style
façade of concrete latticework, decorated in ochre and white, for light and
ventilation, and inside, above a cavernous passenger hall, a single floor of
offices. It was there, in a large, open work area with three small enclosed
bureaux on either side, that Pol and his colleagues spent their days discussing the outline of their new state, sleeping at night on rattan mats spread
out on the concrete floor.

Nuon Chea and Khieu Samphân were sent to inspect the Northern
Zone checkpoint at Prek Kdam, on Highway 5, while Mok shuttled back
and forth to the South-Western Zone HQ near Takeo. All three reported

that the evacuation was proceeding smoothly. And, to them, it was. For the CPK leadership, 20,000 dead was a small price to pay for demolishing, at a stroke, Cambodian capitalism, and erasing the social frontier between the city and the countryside.

Yet, crucial though the evacuation was for the future Khmer Rouge polity, the leadership did not find it easy to justify.

Pol himself offered two contradictory sets of reasons. To Westerners he maintained that 'this action was not pre-planned . . . It was the realisation that a food shortage was imminent . . . and that there was a plan by US lackeys to attack us that prompted [it].' None of that was true. Not only were food supplies adequate, but it was far more difficult logistically for the Khmers Rouges to provide grain to moving columns of deportees than it would have been if they had stayed put. The 'plan by US lackeys' was a figment of Pol's imagination. Moreover, the evacuation had indeed been pre-planned, and not, as he asserted on another occasion, equally untruthfully, in February 1975, but the previous October. He was more honest at a meeting with Chinese journalists, when he admitted: 'Until we had smashed all kinds of enemy spy organisations, we did not have enough strength to defend the revolutionary regime.' That much at least had a basis in fact. CIA officials, including the Chief Strategy Analyst in Saigon, Frank Snepp, later confirmed that the evacuation of the towns, where the agency had established secret radio terminals and clandestine spy cells, 'left American espionage networks throughout the country broken and useless'.

However, the real reasons for the evacuation were more complex. According to Ieng Sary, Pol cited the example of the Paris Commune, whose eightieth anniversary they had celebrated together as students in France. The Commune had been overthrown, Pol said, because the proletariat had failed to exercise dictatorship over the bourgeoisie. He would not make the same mistake.

An internal Central Committee study document stated that, besides ensuring security, the evacuation was designed 'to preserve the political position of cadres and combatants; to avoid a solution of peaceful evolution which could corrode [the revolution] from within; to fight corruption, degradation and debauchery; to get the urban population to take part in [agricultural] production; [and] to remove Sihanouk's support base.' The students and intellectuals among the deportees had been 'extricated from the filth of imperialist and colonialist culture', and 'the system of private property and material goods [was being] swept away'. Most of the deportees had reached the countryside empty-handed, Khieu Samphân explained, adding with evident satisfaction, 'The few belongings [they] were able to carry with them will be worn out or used up within two or three years.' Indeed, it had been to limit the amount they could carry with them that people had been ordered to leave at such short notice in the first place. But in all public pronouncements, these strategic aims were passed over in silence.

Thus the new regime began with a lie, and lying would remain one of its defining characteristics. After April 1975, nothing the Cambodian leaders said could ever be taken at face value. They lied to hide unpleasant truths; they lied because they could not be bothered to remember what had really happened; they lied by mistake, by accident, out of laziness, or for no discernible reason at all. The lie became an instrument of rule, enveloping policy in a miasma of uncertainty, secrecy and dissimulation.

But in the case of the evacuation, behind the lies stood a truth. It was not, as many deportees alleged afterwards, the first step in a process deliberately designed to exterminate an entire class, whether town-dwellers in general or intellectuals in particular. Some Khmer Rouge soldiers and grass-roots cadres interpreted it that way in their dealings with individual deportees, and in a society where power and powerlessness are traditionally viewed as reflecting merit or the lack of it in a previous life, and therefore ineluctable, they had the latitude to do so. But it was never CPK policy. Pol's aim was to plunge the country into an inferno of revolutionary change where, certainly, old ideas and those who refused to abandon them would perish in the flames, but from which Cambodia itself would emerge, strengthened and purified, as a paragon of communist virtue.

The goal was not to destroy but to transmute. The evacuation, Pol wrote later, was 'an extraordinary measure . . . that one does not find in the revolution of any other country'. It was the nub of the Party's political and economic strategy, which was then being elaborated at a series of Standing Committee meetings held first in the railway station and, subsequently, at the former republican Finance Ministry, a sprawling complex of office buildings a couple of hundred yards to the south, where Pol moved his headquarters in early May.

When the full leadership met at the Silver Pagoda soon afterwards to discuss the new guidelines, they decided to give absolute priority to raising farm production. 'Agriculture is the key both to nation-building and to national defence,' Pol declared. 'We must take the measure of this problem. Understanding it properly will show us the road to follow and enable us to make quick progress.' It was agreed that the overall goal should be to attain 70 to 80 per cent farm mechanisation in five to ten years; and to build on that foundation a modern industrial base in fifteen to twenty years.

To achieve this the new Cambodia would rely essentially on its own resources.

Foreign assistance was not completely ruled out, but it was seen as intrinsically pernicious. Already as a student in Paris, Pol had written that '[he] who seeks aid from France will have to pay tribute to France'. Sihanouk's experience with the Americans had confirmed that belief. 'If we go out and beg for help we would certainly obtain some,' he told the Standing Committee, 'but this would affect our political line.' He was equally wary of foreign imports, which, he argued, risked blunting the country's drive for autonomous development: 'Imported iron would not provide mastery. Buying from others would conflict with our own strategic plans . . . If we . . . [take that route], there's no way of knowing when we shall have our own industry.'

There was also the matter of face. After the communist victory, Western aid organisations in Thailand waited in vain for authorisation to fly in relief supplies following the end of the US airlift of rice. 'We had to . . . preserve our independence and our dignity without asking for help from any other country,' Ieng Sary explained. In fact, substantial food aid did come in from China, but it was never publicly acknowledged. The meagre rations provided to the deportees during the exodus from the towns and their first months in the rural areas came mainly from strategic stockpiles which the Khmers Rouges themselves had established in the 'liberated areas' in 1974 and from what remained of the US supplies provided to Lon Nol.

The case for autarky had been made by Khieu Samphân in his doctoral thesis presented at the Sorbonne in 1959. 'International integration,' he had written, 'is the root cause of the under-development of the Khmer economy.' Foreign aid made the country dependent on world markets, over which Cambodia had no control because they were dominated by foreign interests. Foreign trade drove local entrepreneurs out of business by flooding the market with cheap imports. Autarky, or 'self-conscious autonomous development', as Samphân preferred to call it, was therefore an objective necessity. To bring that about, it was necessary to restrict free trade and to redefine the relationship between the individual and the state:

Individuals are grouped in nations with whose prosperity they are closely associated [and they] cannot separate their fate from that of the nation to which they belong . . . *The fundamental fact which economists ought to take into consideration is therefore not the individual but the nation* [emphasis in the original].

The greater the reduction in the number of individuals engaged in general social organisation, the larger will be the number of people who can contribute to production and the faster the nation will acquire wealth . . .

> A rational ordering of society must therefore strive to restrict unproductive activity so as to employ the maximum number of people in production.

Among the 'unproductive activities' Samphân identified were commerce and the government bureaucracy.

Hou Yuon, as a doctoral student in France, had put forward similar ideas. But it would be wrong to see in those early writings a blueprint for the economic system that the Khmers Rouges introduced in Cambodia in 1975. Both men stressed the role of technology, which was marginal to Pol's vision, and Samphân even argued that Cambodia needed a form of 'autonomous national capitalism'. Yuon insisted on gradualism in developing collective practices. None the less, their theses provided the stuff of debate among Cambodian radicals in the 1950s and 1960s, and many of the key concepts of the Khmer Rouge experiment – economic primacy for the nation rather than the individual; a conscious decision to turn inward and sever foreign relations; and a radical restructuring of society to maximise agricultural production – can be traced back to the discussions that took place at that time. Such a programme would entail 'a step backwards', Samphân acknowledged, but it was the only way to build the nation's productive forces for the future.

In the mid-1970s this hermetic approach to development did not seem nearly as outlandish as it would in the internet-linked, globalised world of thirty years later.

A group of Western social scientists, asked in 1976 to draw up a 'blueprint for the future of Thailand', proposed a programme with more than a passing resemblance to the radical measures then under way next door: relocation of the surplus urban population to the countryside; confiscation of unproductive wealth from the rich; and increased investment in agriculture. David Chandler, the doyen of Western historians of Cambodia, wrote the same year that 'autarky makes sense'. Joel Charny, an American aid expert who headed Oxfam's operations in South-East Asia, declared that Pol's rural development plans – digging irrigation canals, clearing new land for rice and mixing biofertilisers, with minimal use of fossil fuels and virtually no imports – 'were they found in a consultant's report, would win the approval of a wide cross-section of the [Western] development community'.

None of these authors was remotely left-wing. All were acutely aware that the conventional development strategies of the 1950s and '60s had failed Cambodia – Sihanouk's emphasis on prestige projects and turnkey industrial plants had been, in the words of his French adviser, Charles Meyer, practically an object lesson in how not to go about it – and they were willing to look with a new eye at radically different approaches.

The strategy mapped out by the CPK Standing Committee in May 1975, however, posed an insuperable problem for even the most sympathetic foreign observer. It was not so much a matter of its content, even though this was far more extreme and unrelenting than anything Khieu Samphân and Hou Yuon had envisaged. The problem lay in the way it was to be implemented – 'not irrational or utopian', as a French specialist put it, just 'cruel and inhuman'.

What Pol and his colleagues approved that spring was a slave state, the first in modern times.

The term is emotive and requires definition. Stalin, Hitler and a plethora of Third World despots enslaved their peoples metaphorically by depriving them of basic rights and freedoms. Pol enslaved the Cambodian people literally, by incarcerating them within a social and political structure, a 'prison without walls', as refugees would later call it, where they were required to execute without payment whatever work was assigned to them for as long as the cadres ordered it, failing which they risked punishment ranging from the withholding of rations to death. Food and clothing were, in theory, provided by the state. But there were no wages. In the Soviet Union during the period of 'War Communism' in the early 1920s, in the Yan'an period in China a decade later, or even in contemporary North Korea, workers were paid at least a pittance. No matter how paltry the sum, it meant they had some measure of choice, even if it amounted to no more than whether to buy a packet of cigarettes or a tablet of soap once a month. There was a minuscule space for the exercise of free will. In Khmer Rouge Cambodia, there was none – which marks a qualitative difference that only those who have experienced it can comprehend. Not only were there no wages, there were no markets. With time, as the system grew more rigid, even barter was discouraged. Like true slaves, the inhabitants of Pol's Cambodia were deprived of all control over their own destinies – unable to decide what to eat, when to sleep, where to live or even whom to marry.

The Khmer Rouge leaders, Pol first and foremost, would have objected to that description. And it is true that, in some of his speeches, he called on local cadres 'boldly to encourage democracy'. But by that he meant merely that 'the masses' should be urged to give the regime active support, rather than 'simply performing their tasks like machines'. It is also true that the way the new system was interpreted varied hugely from zone to zone, region to region and even village to village. In some areas, cadres were lenient; in others, harsh. But in both cases the people – the slaves – had no say in the matter. They merely endured whatever degree of leniency or harshness the 'upper levels' decided to mete out.

Why did the Cambodian communists institute such a system?

The motive was not revenge against a particular class or group, for even though the vindictiveness of individual cadres affected the way the policy was applied, the stratification of society under the Khmer Rouge was theoretically fluid.

From 1975 onwards, all those living in rural co-operatives, in other words, virtually the entire population, were reclassified into three groups: full-rights members, candidates and depositees. The first, usually poor and lower-middle peasants, were entitled to full rations; to hold political posts in the co-operative; to join the army and to apply for Party membership. Candidates were next in line for rations and could hold low-level administrative positions. Depositees were 'last on the distribution lists, first on the execution lists, and had no political rights'. Initially the first two categories consisted exclusively of 'base people', who had lived in the 'liberated areas' before the communist victory, while urban deportees, or 'new people', all became depositees. Previous status also played a part, and in many cases former rich peasants were lumped together with the 'new people' in the lowest category. But the latter could in theory become candidates, and they in turn could become full-rights members, if they showed appropriate zeal for the revolutionary cause.

In practice, the new tripartite division was introduced unevenly – in some areas it was already in force in 1975, elsewhere not until 1977 or later – and the basic dichotomy remained between 'base' and 'new' people. The difference in status between these two groups was immense, especially in the first year of Khmer Rouge rule. The 'base people' could grow their own food to supplement communal rations and, if they offended against revolutionary discipline, were often let off lightly or given the benefit of the doubt. 'New people', by contrast, were always suspected of the worst. Pol himself urged local cadres to tread a careful line between, on the one hand, 'treating everyone indiscriminately, without reference to the positions, principles and viewpoint of the Party', and on the other, 'treating all new people as enemies'. But that was asking too much of the poorly educated peasants who made up the village administrations. In many areas 'new people' continued to be viewed, as they had been during the exodus, as 'prisoners of war'. Unsurprisingly, most concluded that the system was deliberately designed to exterminate them, leaving the 'base people' as the country's sole class. In fact that was never the intention. What occurred was rather a dysfunction of the Khmer Rouge polity, one of many that prevented Pol's vision of the future ever being carried out and which were intrinsic to it, for they stemmed from a fundamental incompatibility between the vision and Cambodian reality.

If the institution of a system of slavery was not motivated by class revenge, it cannot be explained either by what one writer has called a 'narcissistic turning back' to the grandeur of the Angkorean kingdom.

Certainly Angkor was the benchmark, the point of reference, for the Khmers Rouges, no less than for every previous regime. 'If our people can make Angkor,' Pol said in 1977, 'they can make anything.' It is also true that there were numerous parallels between the Angkorean kingdom and the system Pol sought to install. Both aspired to total independence. Both sought an unattainable perfection – one in temples of stone glorifying the Hindu deities, the other as a model of communism. Both executed enemy officers and sent their followers to do forced labour; both stressed irrigation and rice-growing as the mainstay of the economy; and both employed slaves. Moreover in the 1970s the Cambodian peasantry, who formed the basis of the Khmer Rouge revolution, did not live much differently from their forebears six centuries earlier, using less farm equipment than French peasants in the Middle Ages.

But none of this meant that Pol wished to recreate the past. The goal was not to imitate Angkor but to surpass it.

The first step, the destruction of the feudal elite which for centuries, in the revolutionaries' view, had exploited the country for its own ends, had been accomplished by the communist victory and the evacuation of the towns. The second and third steps – 'to build and defend', in Pol's phrase – meant mobilising the entire nation to develop at breakneck speed, in order to prevent Cambodia's sempiternal enemies, Thailand and Vietnam, from taking advantage of its enfeebled state. This last consideration was crucial.

For centuries, Cambodia had been mauled by its two powerful neighbours. Colonisation by the French, followed by the US war in Vietnam, had brought a hundred-year-long respite. But now that the Great Powers had departed, Cambodia, Thailand and Vietnam were left to their own devices. To Pol, in 1975, this did not mean that a new regional conflict was imminent. But the constant sparring for influence between the Cambodian and Vietnamese communists during the civil war, the frequent clashes between supposedly allied Khmer and Vietnamese troops and the troubled history of border skirmishes during the Sihanouk years, convinced him that Cambodia needed to gird itself against future challenges from Hanoi. As he told the Standing Committee, 'If we run really fast, Vietnam won't be able to catch us.'

Even without that spur, Pol would undoubtedly have driven the country to the limits of endurance and beyond. 'If we wish to defend the fruits of the revolution, there must be no let-up,' he told his colleagues. 'We must strike while the iron is hot.' The economy was just another battlefield to be conquered by brute force:

> How must we organise [our] action? It is the same as in war. There we raised the principle of attacking . . . wherever the enemy was weak. The same goes for the economy. We attack wherever the opportunities are greatest . . . We must prepare offensives for the whole country . . . We learned from the war. If the command was strong, we would win. If the command was not strong, we would not win. The same goes for building up the economy.

It was the same approach that had thrown tens of thousands of men into repeated offensives against Phnom Penh, undeterred by casualty figures that would have stopped any other army dead in its tracks. In 'building socialism', as in waging war, Pol declared,

> the Party leadership must exercise its leading role by the use of cutting-edge violence . . . This is the most important factor, the decisive factor, which is the power that drives things forward.

Ieng Sary commented years afterwards – somewhat belatedly, it might be thought – that his brother-in-law had 'a very simplistic vision of things'.

In terms of development policy, this brought a militarisation of thought and language. People 'struggled' to catch fish or to collect fertiliser; they 'waged continuous offensives' to grow 'strategic crops'; they attacked 'on the front lines' (at dam and canal sites) and 'at the rear' (in the village rice-fields); they formed sections, companies, battalions, mobile brigades and regiments; they showed 'fighting solidarity' to win 'victory over nature'.

It was the doctrine of the bludgeon. By 1975, it was written into the Party's genes. No other way was imaginable. Yet it was also true that Pol and the rest of the CPK leadership faced a genuine and all but insurmountable problem, which had defeated the French, defeated Sihanouk, and has defeated every Cambodian government since.

The problem was: how to make Khmers work.

Putting it in those terms will raise hackles. But the issue is too important to be brushed aside with comforting platitudes. The witticism of an anonymous civil servant in colonial Indochina – 'The Vietnamese grow the rice; the Khmers watch it grow; the Laotians listen to it grow' – has a sufficient core of truth to put out of countenance the most convinced Cambodian nationalist. The perception of indolence has become part of the country's self-image, an explanation for its failure to keep up with its neighbours economically.

Khieu Samphân and Hou Yuon, in their doctoral theses, argued that the low output of the peasants was not the result of laziness, but of an 'economic and social structure which prohibited [them] from developing their full potential'. Many French experts in the early part of the century shared those views. Why should Khmer peasants exert themselves, they asked, when all but subsistence earnings were seized for taxes or went to line the pockets of Chinese moneylenders? Instead the farmer 'makes himself as poor as possible as a defence against the rapacity of the mandarin . . . Why do more when, whatever happens, he will be left with less? . . . [His] inertia, his passivity, is in the final analysis nothing more than a form of resistance against a system that is weighted against him.'

But that was only part of the truth. Even Khieu Samphân estimated that on average Khmer peasants worked only six months of the year, and sometimes much less. Theravada Buddhism has never placed much value on the acquisition and consumption of wealth. Sihanouk has recounted the experience of an American aid expert in the 1950s who convinced a group of villagers to use chemical fertiliser, promising that it would enable them to double rice production: 'Sure enough, at harvest time, the yield was doubled. Everyone was delighted . . . [But] when the official came back [the following year] he was horrified to find that each peasant had cultivated only half his land. "Why," said the peasants, "cultivate the entire area when you can get just as much by cultivating half?"' Fifty years later, a Khmer businessman, seeking a regular supply of palm sugar for sweetmeat manufacture, encountered exactly the same problem. Once the peasant farmers he employed had earned enough for the year, they stopped work, and neither blandishments nor the promise of more money could make them start again. 'From their point of view it was logical,' he acknowledged. 'Once they had paid their family's expenses – seed for the next planting; fertiliser; clothes; offerings to the monks; school fees for the children – what would they spend it on? There was nothing more they wanted.'

To some, that may be indolence; to others, it is wisdom. But in either case it flies in the face of the way the modern world runs. To Pol, it was a roadblock obstructing his ambition to make Cambodia prosperous and strong, and it had to be demolished. He explained his views to a sympathetic fellow communist, the Thai Party Chairman, Khamtan: 'The characteristics of peasants,' he said, 'are often negligence, lack of zeal and lack of self-confidence. They know only how to work by following orders.' Already, before the communist victory, a perceptive American journalist, Donald Kirk, had noted that the Khmers Rouges had deliberately adopted policies of extremism to move 'the inert peasant mass'. After 1975, that approach was applied throughout the country.

Its implementation became the prime task of the faceless, clandestine, collective leadership still known to the population only as Angkar. It was a word with multiple uses. Angkar was the regime at all levels, from Pol and the Standing Committee to the lowest village militiaman. It was omnipotent and baleful, impersonal and remote, the incarnation of revolutionary purity, demanding and receiving quasi-religious reverence from all with whom it dealt. Pol's old mentor, Keng Vannsak, called it

> an immense apparatus of repression and terror as an amalgam of Party, Government and State, not in the usual sense of these institutions but with particular stress on its mysterious, terrible and pitiless character. It was, in a way, political-metaphysical power, anonymous, omnipresent, omniscient, occult, sowing death and terror in its name.

Pol, of course, did not see it that way, any more than he thought of the population as slaves. On the contrary, he assured his colleagues, 'with time the masses will draw closer and closer to the Party.' Nor should that be dismissed as propaganda: Pol did believe that he was acting for the common good and that sooner or later everyone would recognise that. The fascination exerted by power – of wielding absolute control over every detail of the lives of a whole people in the service of a grand design to which he alone held the key – certainly played its part. But the aim was not to 'compel'; rather it was to make them 'see the necessity for work'. It was a nuance that escaped his fellow citizens.

In late April 1975, even before the fall of Saigon, Pol decided that the entire Standing Committee should travel to Hanoi in a spectacular gesture of goodwill. The calculation was simple. If, as Pol believed, Vietnam was the main, potential long-term enemy, prudence required the maintenance of good relations at least until Cambodia was strong enough to meet an eventual Vietnamese challenge.

The need for a conciliatory approach towards the 'hereditary enemy' soon received striking confirmation. On May 4, Cambodian and Vietnamese naval units fired on each other near the island of Phu Quoc, which lies about ten miles off the Cambodian coast near Kampot. It had been administered as part of South Vietnam ever since the colonial period, but the issue of sovereignty had never been resolved. Other incidents quickly followed and on May 10 another small Vietnamese-held island was occupied by Cambodian troops based on Wai Island, eighty miles southwest of Kompong Som. Two days later, into the midst of this offshore skirmishing blundered an elderly American container ship, the SS *Mayaguez*, which was promptly intercepted and boarded by Cambodian coastguards. What followed was pure farce, or would have been but for the loss of life it entailed. President Ford, smarting from the US withdrawal from Saigon less than two weeks before, decided to hang tough and ordered an aerial bombardment to interdict access to the ship. In Phnom Penh, Pol summoned the Standing Committee, who agreed that the crew should be released and the vessel sent on its way, as had happened a week earlier in the case of a Panamanian ship. Instructions to that effect were radioed to the local commander and an announcement prepared for the following day. But by then the President had already decided to send in the marines for a heliborne rescue attempt. Over the next few hours, fifteen marines and twenty-three American airmen were killed, US bombers destroyed the oil refinery at Kompong Som and the nearby airfield at Ream, and an undetermined number of Cambodians died. In the meantime, unknown to the rescuers, the crew of the *Mayaguez* had all been released unharmed. Mr Ford said later the raid gave 'a whole new sense of confidence' to the American people and helped put the Vietnam War behind them.

For Vietnam and Cambodia, the *Mayaguez* affair was peripheral to the main business at hand: the fight for possession of the offshore islands. None the less it was a salutary reminder of Cambodian weakness. At this juncture, Pol was laid low by a severe attack of malaria, a legacy of his years in the maquis. Fearing that the US might next launch air attacks against Phnom Penh, he moved his headquarters to the Silver Pagoda, inside the Royal Palace, while Ieng Sary asked the Chairman of the Non-Aligned Movement, President Boumedienne of Algeria, to reassure Vietnam of Cambodia's peaceful intentions. Two weeks later, on June 2, the new COSVN Chairman, Nguyen Van Linh, drove up from Saigon to see Pol on behalf of the Vietnamese Politburo and was assured by the Khmer Rouge leader that what he called these 'painful, bloody clashes' were not the result of central policy, but rather of local troops' 'ignorance of geography'.

That was not quite the end of the matter. A year earlier, Vietnam had lost the Paracel Islands, which had been occupied by China. Hanoi wanted to make crystal clear that it was not about to yield sovereignty over islands in the Gulf of Thailand, least of all to a nominal ally which had come to power through a war in which 25,000 Vietnamese soldiers had died fighting on Cambodian soil. Once they had recovered the territory the Cambodians had initially seized, Vietnamese units attacked Wai Island, which they occupied on June 10.

In these circumstances it was plainly unwise for the entire leadership to be out of the country at the same time, so the three Zone secretaries, Ruos Nhim. So Phim and Vorn Vet, stayed behind, while Pol, Nuon Chea and Ieng Sary left as planned for Hanoi, where they proposed that the two countries conclude a Friendship Treaty.

It was an astute move. Pol's old adversary, Le Duan, who led the talks on the Vietnamese side, could not openly rebuff such an overture. Yet it underlined that in the Cambodian view, future ties between Phnom Penh and Hanoi should be bilateral, between equal, sovereign nations, rather than part of a larger grouping of all three Indochinese states as the Vietnamese would have preferred. The visit, like all Pol's activities in 1975, was secret. There was no announcement, no communiqué, no way for anyone outside the two Party leaderships to know what had transpired. But the talks were evidently successful in reducing political tensions. Pol offered ritual thanks for Vietnamese aid, 'without [which] we could not have achieved victory', and though he could not bring himself to utter the term 'special relationship', he did say, masking his feelings behind his eternal smile, that 'the great friendly solidarity among the parties and peoples of Cambodia, Vietnam, and Laos . . . is the determining factor in all [our] victories to date as well as a decisive factor in [our] victories to come.'

At the beginning of August Le Duan paid a return visit to Phnom Penh, which the Vietnamese Party newspaper, *Nhan Dan*, characterised as 'cordial', and a few days later Nguyen Van Linh informed Nuon Chea that Vietnamese units had evacuated Wai Island and were preparing to release six hundred Cambodian soldiers they had taken prisoner. Subsequent exchanges of messages included ringing declarations of 'militant solidarity' and 'indestructible friendship'. Liaison offices were established in the border provinces and armed clashes all but ceased.

True, the repatriation of Vietnamese families from Cambodia continued: from April to December 1975, an estimated 150,000 Vietnamese returned to Vietnam, while thousands of Cambodian refugees, who had fled the Khmer Rouge advance, were sent back the other way. None the less, as the year ended, the Vietnamese Politburo concluded that relations were 'slowly improving' and that, despite strains, the alliance was intact.

This was a fatal error. As the Vietnamese Foreign Minister, Nguyen Co Thach, subsequently acknowledged, 'In 1975 Vietnam evaluated the situation in Cambodia incorrectly'. Khieu Samphân said later that Pol was simply playing for time.

A week after the talks in Hanoi, Pol flew to Beijing. Again the visit was secret. This time he was accompanied by Ieng Sary, Ney Sarann and Siet Chhê. Symbolically the highpoint of his stay was a meeting with Mao, which took place beside the Chairman's private swimming pool, at his home near the Forbidden City, on the afternoon of June 21. The Chinese leader was old and ill; he had to be helped to his feet, and on bad days even his secretary-companion, Jiang Yufeng, who had learnt to lip-read, had difficulty understanding what he said. But Mao's mind was as nimble as ever. The Cambodian communists intrigued him. This, therefore, was a good day, or would have been had he not insisted on trying to convey some of his thoughts in English, a language he had been trying and failing to learn for the previous forty years. Whether Pol felt intimidated in Mao's presence, or whether his interpreter was overwhelmed by the challenge of rendering into Khmer Mao's elliptical reasoning, the Chinese transcript shows that he said nothing of substance. Mao, on the other hand, had a lot to say. He began by declaring his approval of the Cambodian revolution:

> You have a lot of experience. It's better than ours. We don't have the right to criticise you . . . Basically you are right. Have you made mistakes or not? I don't know. Certainly you have. So rectify yourselves; do *rectification*! . . . The road is tortuous . . . Now our situation [in China] is exactly as Lenin predicted – a capitalist country with no capitalists . . . Salaries are not equal. We have a slogan of equality – but we don't carry it out. How many years will it take to change that? Until we become communist? Even under communism, there will still be a struggle between what is advanced and what is backward. So this matter is not clear. [Emphasis in original]

On close reading, it was strangely ambivalent. Mao's repeated references to criticism and mistakes, at a meeting with a friendly delegation, were unusual. Moreover, the last sentence seemed to throw doubt on whether the perfect egalitarianism Pol advocated, however desirable, could ever in practice be realised: 'this matter is not clear'.

The Chairman's mind was harking back to the infancy of his own revolution when the Chinese communists in Jiangxi in the 1930s – just like the Khmers Rouges, forty years later – had burned down villages, displaced populations, terrorised rich peasants and executed Party dissidents under the slogan, 'Better to kill a hundred innocent people than let one truly guilty person go free'. That period had ended with the Long March, when Mao developed the doctrine of rectification to provide a subtler means of dealing with intra-Party disputes. Now he was urging the Cambodians likewise to 'do rectification!', implying that the time had come for them, too, to abandon their early extremism. This message was woven between the lines of everything Mao said that day. By using snatches of English, by referring to Pol's Cambodia as 'a socialist *wat*', by citing Huxley, Kant, and the fourth-century Buddhist missionary Kumârajîva,* and finally by offering to

---

*Mao quoted Kumârajîva, as saying: 'If you copy everything I do, it will be a fatal mistake'. He did not explain the story behind it, which recounts that the Buddhist master had numerous mistresses. When his disciples started to follow his example, Kumârajîva filled his alms bowl with sharp iron needles and, showing it to them, said: 'He who wants to do as I do must first eat this; then he will be able to keep women.' He took a spoonful of needles and ate them as easily as rice. The disciples were mortified and mended their ways.

give Pol '30 books written by Marx, Engels, Lenin and Stalin' to study, Mao sought to convey the idea that the Cambodian leaders should open their minds and place their revolution in the context of the wider world.

How much of this any of them understood – indeed, how much survived the translation – is another matter. The one idea that clearly did resonate, because afterwards Pol frequently repeated it, was Mao's injunction to his visitors not to copy indiscriminately the experience of China or any other country, but 'to create your own experience yourselves'.

Notwithstanding Mao's reservations about the system Pol wished to build – reservations shared by Zhou Enlai and Deng Xiaoping – China had already decided to give his regime all-out support. For China, as for Cambodia, the key factor was Vietnam. There was a near-perfect symmetry to the three countries' relations. China was to Vietnam as Vietnam was to Cambodia – a vast and powerful neighbour, which threatened hegemony. Both had made huge sacrifices, in men and money, to help their allies' revolutions, only to have them bridle against their suzerainty. Relations between Hanoi and Beijing had begun to cool in the late 1960s. By 1975, the Chinese leaders saw Vietnam as a Soviet bridgehead in Asia, which Moscow would try to use to spread its influence throughout the region. The Laotian communists were too weak, and historically too close to Hanoi, to act independently. That left Cambodia as the one country on Vietnam's western flank which might be expected to resist the expansion of Vietnamese, and hence of Soviet, power.

In the end it was *realpolitik*, far more than ideological affinity, which brought China and Cambodia together.

That is not to downplay the importance of the beliefs they shared: the primacy of men over machines; the exaltation of the human will (in China) and 'revolutionary consciousness' (in Cambodia); the pre-eminence of ideology over learning (being 'red' rather than 'expert'); the strategy of using the countryside to surround the city and the need to eliminate the differences between them; the concern to bridge the gulf between mental and manual labour; and the view that revisionism, in the shape of bourgeois thought, grew spontaneously within the communist movement itself.

Mao was entranced by Pol's boldness in emptying the cities. That autumn he asked Le Duan whether Vietnam could do the same. When the Vietnamese leader shook his head, Mao paused for a moment and then agreed: 'No. We couldn't do it either.'

At the end of his long life, the Chairman was lucid enough to realise that the new world the Cambodians dreamed of would prove to be a mirage. China had tried that route already. It too had considered doing without money, but rejected the idea as impractical. The temporary closing of schools and universities during the Cultural Revolution had brought as many problems as it had solved. Even Mao himself now accepted that the Great Leap Forward in the late 1950s – a Utopian mass movement which was intended to allow China to overtake Britain and America in economic output and proceed directly to communism, but instead resulted in 20 million deaths from starvation – had been a disaster. Yet when later a frail Zhou Enlai, in hospital suffering from cancer, tried to caution Khieu Samphân that the road to socialism was long and Cambodia should not repeat China's errors, he drew only a non-committal smile.

From then on, the two Parties rarely discussed ideological matters, and when they did they failed to agree.

The relationship was pragmatic. China offered Cambodia large-scale economic aid, technical training, military supplies and a market for its meagre exports; Cambodia provided a secure forward base for China's strategy to contain Vietnam. The *quid pro quo* had been established within days of Phnom Penh's fall when, on April 19, Ieng Sary had flown from Hanoi to Beijing to ask that military supplies henceforth be channelled through the port of Kompong Som, rather than through Vietnam. Four days later, on April 23, the Deputy Director of the Chinese Communist Party's International Liaison Department, Shen Chien, at the head of a small fact-finding team, had accompanied Sary to Phnom Penh on the first flight to Cambodia since the end of the civil war. To underline the importance of the mission, Pol himself had gone to the airport to greet them. In June, following his encounter with Mao, Pol had a series of meetings with Deng Xiaoping in Beijing and Shanghai to discuss Cambodia's aid requirements. Deng told him that military assistance would be provided free, and that – in the words of the final accord, signed the following February – 'it will be up to the Cambodian government to decide how the [Chinese] military equipment and supplies are allocated and used. China will not interfere, nor impose any condition, nor demand any privilege.' The list was long, and included:

Complete equipment for three artillery regiments, including a total of 108 pieces of 85-mm, 122-mm and 130-mm ordnance and 13,000 shells.
Complete equipment for two anti-aircraft regiments and an anti-aircraft battalion, including 150 pieces of 100-mm, 57-mm and double-barrelled 37-mm cannon.
Complete equipment for a signals regiment.
Complete equipment for a pontoon battalion.
Equipment for a tank regiment, including 72 light tanks and 32 amphibious tanks.
Equipment for a radar battalion, including 20 sets of search-and-guide radar.

30 fighter aircraft and six trainers.

15 bombers and three trainers.

12 high-speed torpedo boats, 10 escort ships, 4 anti-submarine vessels, with corresponding armament; 4 landing craft, one 80-ton minesweeper and one 300-ton tanker.

It was to be delivered by sea over a three-year period ending in 1978. In addition, China undertook to repair and refurbish US equipment seized from Lon Nol's army, including sixty more aircraft; to furnish 50,000 complete sets of infantrymen's equipment; to build a new military airport at Kompong Chhnang, fifty miles north of Phnom Penh, a naval base at Ream, near Kompong Som, a munitions depot and a communications workshop; and to enlarge an existing weapons repair works. All this was on top of 10,000 tons of military equipment, including 100 120-mm artillery pieces and 1,300 military vehicles, the delivery of which had been held over from 1975 following Ieng Sary's request that transport via Vietnam be discontinued.

The quantities of economic assistance pledged were equally impressive. Pol asked that priority be given to restoring road and rail links, especially from Phnom Penh to Battambang and to Kompong Som, and that China provide barges for river transport. Next came the reconstruction of war-damaged factories processing export commodities: rubber, tropical hardwoods and fish products. By the end of the year agreement had also been reached on building, or more often, rebuilding, twenty-nine industrial enterprises, including the oil refinery destroyed by US bombers during the *Mayaguez* affair; textile mills; glass and tyre factories; a paper mill; fertiliser and pharmaceutical plants; a phosphate mine and a cement works.

In addition, more than three hundred Chinese army officers and technicians and a larger number of civilians were sent to Cambodia to conduct training programmes, while nearly six hundred Khmer trainees went to China.

The true financial cost of these measures is difficult to establish. In September, diplomatic sources in Beijing reported that the Chinese commitment exceeded a billion US dollars (equivalent to 3.4 billion dollars in today's money). If anything, that is probably on the low side. The Chinese government later revealed that economic assistance alone to Cambodia in 1975 totalled more than 300 million dollars, and that, like the military aid, it was provided in the form of grants. The one-billion-dollar figure had begun circulating a few days before Le Duan arrived in Beijing to seek Chinese help for the post-war reconstruction of Vietnam. It was almost certainly leaked to underscore China's refusal to give further aid to Hanoi.

Explaining that decision, Mao baldly told the Vietnamese leader: 'Today you are not the poorest under heaven. We are. We have a population of 800 million.' Deng Xiaoping then berated Le Duan for anti-Chinese statements in the Vietnamese media and treated him to a lengthy disquisition on Mao's 'Three Worlds' theory, which held that the Soviet Union and the United States were both hegemonist powers, each as bad as the other.

Barely five months after the fall of Saigon, it marked the parting of the ways.

Le Duan returned home in a cold fury, having refused to issue a joint communiqué and, in what one Chinese official called 'an extraordinary gesture for a fraternal Party leader', cancelled the customary return banquet for his hosts. In October he travelled to Moscow, where the Russians promised three billion dollars for Vietnam's five-year plan. Beijing and Hanoi were slowly moving towards a collision course in which Pol's Cambodia would play the starring role.

It did not seem like that at the time. To Pol and his colleagues, their first year in power had begun rather well. The alliance with China was solidly in place. After his stay in Beijing, Pol had paid a secret five-day visit to North Korea, where President Kim Il Sung had promised to send aid experts to help with agricultural and hydroelectric projects. Through China's good offices, relations with Thailand had stabilised. Talks between provincial officials on the border during the summer were followed by a visit by Ieng Sary to Bangkok, which led to the setting up of a permanent liaison office near Poipet. Such incidents as did occur were the result of fishing disputes or the work of the Khmer Serei and other exile groups, and after the Cambodians had mined the land border, even that irritant diminished. Overtures were made to Laos, which sent its Foreign Minister, Phoune Sipraseuth, to Phnom Penh to discuss the possibility of using the Cambodian port of Kompong Som. Even with Vietnam, relations were correct. There were minor incidents in the North-East, where Vietnamese units which had been guarding the Ho Chi Minh Trail delayed their departure longer than the Cambodians would have wished. But by the following spring Pol felt able to report that the situation on all the country's borders had 'very greatly eased'.

Pol stayed on in China to have a medical check-up after the rest of the delegation had left. As well as malaria, he was plagued by gastric ailments. So it was not until mid-July that he flew back to Phnom Penh to begin work on the nuts and bolts of putting the new administration together.

The first task was to restructure the army.

On July 22, Pol addressed a unification rally, attended by 3,000 soldiers, followed by a military parade at a stadium near the former French Embassy. Flanked by the seven Zone secretaries – Koy Thuon, Mok, Ney Sarann, Ruos Nhim, So Phim, Vorn Vet and Chou Chet (in charge of a new Western Zone) – he announced the formal incorporation of their forces into a national Revolutionary Army, headed by Son Sen, Chief of the General Staff. They had dared to wage 'a struggle completely different from that of revolutions elsewhere in the world', he declared. Now that they had won, their main task was to ensure security in the capital and to guard against espionage and internal saboteurs.

It was all just a little bit too late. If the CPK Military Committee, which Pol headed, had been able to impose its authority on the forces of the Zone commanders a year or two earlier, many of the problems which followed might have been avoided. But Pol, unlike Mao, had never led his men into battle. He was a political, not a military strategist. Even Mao had taken ten years to unite the People's Liberation Army, which then fought for twelve more years before achieving victory. In Cambodia, victory had come far faster. As a result, the CPK, in appearance, at least, seemed to be united, but the army, from which its power derived, was not. In Phnom Penh, the different sectors of the city were guarded by units which, while nominally under unified command, continued to answer to divisional commanders from different Zones. Pol never succeeded in creating a military force which was loyal to him personally and, in the end, that would prove his undoing.

The matter of forming a new government was also troublesome.

In theory the GRUNC, headed by Penn Nouth, continued to govern Cambodia. But Nouth himself and his Foreign Minister, Sarin Chhak, were still in Beijing. Two other ministers – Hou Yuon (Interior) and Norodom Phurissara (Justice) – had been rusticated just before the fall of Phnom Penh. Phurissara had been sent to reform himself through manual labour in a remote village in Preah Vihear, near the border with Thailand. Hou Yuon, who was now seen as excessively liberal, sat out the first weeks of 'liberation' in a deserted camp near Oudong. After being allowed to spend a day visiting Phnom Penh at the end of May, he was put aboard a river steamer for Stung Trang, on the Mekong. There he was held with two other Party miscreants – Ping Sây and another former Cercle Marxiste member, Chhorn Hay – under a loose form of house arrest.* Of the eight

---

*It is commonly asserted that Hou Yuon was executed as an opponent of the regime in August 1975. This appears to be untrue. According to Yuon's former bodyguard, Pol sent a Jarai messenger to escort him back to Phnom Penh. Either the Jarai mistook Yuon's gesture and thought he was reaching for his pistol, or, fearing that he was about to be arrested, Yuon attempted to commit suicide, but in any case the man shot him dead. While the details

remaining cabinet posts, half existed only on paper. Khieu Samphân was no more responsible for Defence than the Western Zone Secretary, Chou Chet, was for Religious Affairs. They were ghost portfolios, announced in January 1975, four months before victory, to make it appear that the Khmers Rouges had a viable government-in-waiting.

The first step towards installing a new order was taken in August, when three additional vice-premiers were appointed: Vorn Vet (Transport and Industry); Ieng Sary (Foreign Affairs) and Son Sen (Defence). But then the process stalled. There was too much uncertainty over the future role of Prince Sihanouk, whiling away his days at the palatial home Kim Il Sung had built for him in Pyongyang, awaiting the call to return; over the choice of Prime Minister; and over domestic policy, which had been left in abeyance during the summer while the Standing Committee concentrated on relations with China and Vietnam.

Pol spent August travelling in the South-West and the Eastern Zone to see for himself how the rural areas were coping with the flood of urban deportees. Then, in mid-September, he convened a Central Committee plenum in Phnom Penh, at which he laid out in detail his vision of Cambodia's future:

> We must fix quotas for [agricultural] production and for the distribution of the resultant capital at all levels – the villages, the districts, the regions and the zones . . . Part should go . . . to the people for their food and to exchange with the State for medicines and other articles of prime necessity. Part should go to the State, to be used to improve the people's living standards, for defence and for national construction . . . Later, [when] cooperatives have been established everywhere . . . they will take on the task of building schools, dispensaries and workshops . . . The districts can keep a little capital, but not much, just enough to coordinate the labour force. The regions can have a bit more, to build hospitals of some size, to buy medicines, and to undertake agricultural research and maintain a corps of technicians. . .
>
> [To] develop public health [we should] both use traditional medicine [and] buy modern medicines abroad in exchange for [exports of] rice and rubber . . . [We must] eradicate malaria . . . There are other illnesses, too, to fight, like leprosy, tuberculosis and goitre. For each illness, we must work out a strategy.
>
> We must set up creches and kindergartens to free the energies of our women . . . We must think of the development of education and culture.

---

remain obscure, it seems certain that his death was accidental. It may also have taken place a year later than is generally believed: Ping Sây says he was told that Yuon was still at Stung Trang in August 1976. Thereafter, Khmer Rouge cadres often referred to him as a traitor. But by late 1978 that charge was no longer heard; it was officially claimed that he had died 'while on a mission for the Party'; and Pol himself, in conversations with aides, described him as a 'comrade', indicating that he was not suspected of treachery.

The State must provide schools, exercise books and pencils. Don't forget that later on we will need more advanced technology. But scientific and technical education must obey the general principle that technicians and scientists must temper themselves first in the movement of the masses.

The basic production quota, Pol announced, to be applied throughout the country, was three tons of paddy, or unmilled rice, per hectare.* On paper this was not totally unreasonable, at least as a long-term goal. Sihanouk himself had proposed a target of two tons per hectare, and experimental farms had had no difficulty in reaching 3 or 4 tons. But in a country where historically yields had averaged just over one ton of paddy per hectare, among the lowest in Asia, it was still a tall order. Moreover, to achieve it would require massive use of chemical fertiliser, which was exactly what Cambodia did not have: instead, Pol proposed using 'animal manure, alluvial soils, earth from anthills, bat guano and so on', which while ecologically sound was incapable of producing the yields he demanded. In that contradiction lay one of the major causes of the vicious circle of repression, famine and more repression that would eventually bring the regime down.

Another equally fateful decision was taken by the delegates that month: not to use money.

A year earlier, at Meakk, the Central Committee had agreed that the new currency, printed in China, should be issued as soon as possible after the fall of Phnom Penh. In January 1975, Ping Sây had travelled with a delegation bringing wooden crates full of the new banknotes down the Ho Chi Minh Trail. Shortly afterwards he and Hou Yuon attended a meeting of the National Bank Preparatory Committee, chaired by Khieu Samphân, at B-20, a camp near Pol's old headquarters on the Chinit river. In May, the work conference at the Silver Pagoda which approved the new strategic line of advancing directly to communism, decided that the riel should be put progressively into circulation, with appropriate measures to guarantee its value, in order, as Pol put it, 'to demonstrate to the people the reality of our state power'. Non Suon, the former Pracheachon leader, was appointed National Bank Chairman with a brief to get the new system up and running. That summer, posters showing the new bills were sent to the provinces along with supplies of notes pending final approval from Phnom Penh. In August, Suon was succeeded by a young regional commander from the Northern Zone, Pich Chheang, who had married Pol's former cook, Moeun. Chheang started a training programme for sixty peasant youths, who were to run the bank's branches in the regions and, as a trial

---

*Three tons of paddy is equivalent to just under two tons of milled rice. In this book, all references are to unmilled rice, unless specifically stated otherwise.

run, at the beginning of September, allowed the new currency to circulate in his home area, Region 41 of the Northern Zone, north-west of Kompong Cham.

By then, however, a number of influential CPK leaders were questioning the wisdom of these moves. Pol's aide, Phi Phuon, remembered informal meetings of the Standing Committee at the Silver Pagoda in late August where Mok, in particular, spoke out against the use of money:

> Mok favoured a barter system. He said some regions were rich in rice, others had different products: the answer was a system of exchange. He also said if there were no money, it would remove the problem of corruption and curtail the activities of enemy agents. 'When a wound is not yet healed,' he said, 'you shouldn't push a stick into it. You must leave it alone, otherwise it will get worse.' So Phim and Koy Thuon supported him. They agreed with his views.

Pol, too, found Mok's arguments convincing. Beyond practical considerations – the regime's 'lack of experience', as he put it, a reference to the difficulty of turning semi-literate young men with politically correct, poor peasant origins into capable bank tellers – there were more important ideological reasons. The question of whether or not to use money, he told the Central Committee, concerned the essence of the Khmer Rouge state:

> The State is an organism whose purpose is to maintain the power of one class by exercising dictatorship over others in all domains . . . But the State is also an instrument that creates a privileged social stratum which, as it develops, becomes cut off from the proletariat and from labour. This has happened, for example, in the Soviet Union . . . and [to some extent] in [North] Korea and in China. In conformity with Marxist-Leninist principles, it is necessary to . . . reduce progressively this defect which is the State until it is extinguished completely, giving place to [a system of] self-management of factories by the proletariat and of agriculture by the peasants. The privileged upper stratum will then disappear altogether.
>
> Up to now, the fact we do not use money has greatly reduced private property and thus has promoted the overall trend towards the collective. If we start using money again, it will bring back sentiments of private property and drive the individual away from the collective. Money is an instrument which creates privilege and power. Those who possess it can use it to bribe cadres . . . [and] to undermine our system. If we allow sentiments of private property to develop, little by little people's thoughts will turn only to ways of amassing private property . . . If we take that route, then in one year, or 10 or 20 years, what will become of our Cambodian society which up to now is so clean?
>
> Money constitutes a danger, both now and in the future. We must not be in a hurry to use it . . . We need to think more deeply about this matter.

On September 19, the conference resolved not to issue the new currency, a decision confirmed at the CPK's Fourth Congress four months later. The supplies of currency which had already been distributed were gathered up and put in storage in Phnom Penh.

The other major theme of the September plenum was the need to improve rural living standards. Manufacturing industry was to concentrate on turning out light industrial goods for daily use – bicycles, clothing, mosquito nets, fishing lines, cigarettes and lighter flints – and simple agricultural machinery. Commerce, in the absence of money, would be limited to barter between co-operatives and the state. Koy Thuon, who had championed this system, was given responsibility for making it work and he and Khieu Samphân drew up a notional price-scale to be used in barter transactions. How well it functioned is another matter. Thiounn Mumm, who had just arrived in Phnom Penh from Beijing, was horrified:

> I found myself in the Ministry of Industry, working under Vorn Vet. What did I see? First of all, there was no administration. The cadres sat outside under a tree. When someone arrived, they'd ask him: 'What d'you need? You need oil? Go and get it from such-and-such a factory.' And they'd give him a voucher. They didn't even keep a copy. Sometimes the man would get to the factory only to be told there wasn't any oil. No one knew. No accounts were kept!

This was a problem of Pol's own making. If there were few qualified cadres, it was because he refused to employ those with non-revolutionary backgrounds. But it also reflected his ignorance of economics. He once told the Central Committee that 'if we have a million riels, we use it all for national construction and defence . . . [Other socialist countries] spend half of it on wages and only half on building and defending their country. That puts them half a million riels behind us.' Those like Mumm and Khieu Samphân, who did have an economic training, kept their mouths well shut.

Pol's approach to the welfare of the population was equally simplistic. His visit to the South-West in August had finally made him understand what the rural cadres had known for months – that 'shortages of food and medicine are affecting the labour force . . . Those who are suffering most are the urban deportees from Phnom Penh.' It was not the suffering that bothered Pol; it was the fact that lack of food might reduce their ability to work. Rather than bringing in rice from other areas, the best solution, he decided, was 'to redistribute the labour force in a balanced manner in accordance with the production needs of the different regions'. That became the signal for another wholesale movement of the population. In April the priority had been to empty the towns as quickly as possible. No one had paid much attention to where the deportees ended up. As a result, most settled in the East, the South-West and the North. Now, just as the crops were ripening and they were looking forward to the fruits of their labour, they were uprooted to go to other areas where their muscle-power was needed more.

As always, the regime cloaked its intentions in a lie.

This time the story was not that the Americans were about to launch bombing raids, but that Angkar was calling for volunteers to return to their home villages, or to Phnom Penh or Battambang. In the event, most of the 'volunteers' went to the North-West, traditionally the rice-bowl of Cambodia. By year's end, more than a million people had left their adopted villages to be resettled in sparsely populated areas where manpower was lacking. In the context of a despotic state, it was not an illogical policy. But the timing was terrible. There was no way the North-West could cope with hundreds of thousands of extra mouths which arrived too late for their owners to grow new crops but in time to require feeding from the wholly inadequate harvest planted for a much smaller population several months before. Moreover, it underlined the principal lesson of the April evacuation. To Pol and his colleagues, the Cambodian people were no longer individual human beings, each with hopes and fears, desires and aspirations. They had become soulless instruments in the working out of a grand national design.

During a period of singular megalomania, in the late 1950s, Mao had likened the peasantry to a blank sheet of paper on which 'the newest and most beautiful words can be written, the newest and most beautiful pictures can be painted'. The Khmers Rouges, more prosaically, adopted the ox as their model. 'You see the ox, comrades. Admire him! He eats where we [tell] him to eat . . . When we tell him to pull the plough, he pulls it. He never thinks of his wife or his children.' A young deportee confided to her journal the oxen's response: 'Slaves we are,' she wrote, 'and as slaves are we treated.'

In October 1975, a month after these decisions had been taken, the first large group of Cambodians abroad was authorised to return to Phnom Penh. Among them was Suong Sikoeun's wife, Laurence Picq, and the couple's two small daughters. Like the others, she had been working for the FUNK in Beijing. Unlike them, she was French.

Laurence Picq would become one of only two non-Asians to spend the Khmer Rouge years in Cambodia. This was due to the intervention of Ieng Sary. In Beijing, Sikoeun, emulating other Khmer Rouge cadres married to foreigners, had asked to be allowed to divorce her to prove that his devotion to the revolution outweighed family ties. Normally this was CPK policy: a foreign spouse was a security risk. But in Sikoeun's case, Ieng Sary refused. Their Chinese comrades, he explained, liked and respected Picq, a lively, bright woman of strong left-wing convictions, then in her late twenties. It 'might not be understood' if they were to split up. She herself suspected, probably correctly, that she was an alibi, there to prove that the new Cambodia, or at least its Foreign Minister, was not only not xenophobic but broad-minded enough to accept non-Khmer sympathisers.

Unlike the 'new people', the urban deportees who had been swept up by the revolution and forced to live terrifying new lives wholly against their will, Laurence Picq and the thirty or so Cambodians who flew back with her were ardent supporters of the Khmer communist cause. All were intellectuals. All had voluntarily given up comfortable lives in the West or, in some cases, in Cambodia itself, to join the resistance in Beijing. Now they were brought face to face with the reality of the regime they had championed through five years of civil war:

> Along the roadside, cars lay abandoned and stripped, dozens and dozens of them, with their doors and windows open . . . The houses, too, had gaping black openings, like haunted buildings. In the courtyards and on the pavements, crockery, cooking stoves, fridges, lay scattered . . . What were they doing there? . . . On both sides of the road, an apocalyptic landscape rolled past us, as though a powerful shock-wave had wiped out any human presence . . . An unspeakable weariness overcame us. No one spoke. People averted their eyes . . .

To those, like Sikoeun, who had spent time in the rural bases before coming to Phnom Penh, the desolation could be rationalised away as an inevitable consequence of war. To those returning directly from abroad, it was traumatic. The image that sprang to Laurence Picq's mind was of Guernica: 'That silence. A terrible silence . . . It resonated with the pain of a people that had been torn apart, their cries of despair, their distress, a suffering beyond measure.'

Yet by the time the Beijing group arrived, Phnom Penh was actually in better shape than it had been when the communists had taken over six months earlier.

The indiscriminate looting which had been a feature of the city's 'liberation' had stopped almost at once. 'War booty,' the Party had decreed, 'is what is seized during wartime. Now the war is over so booty belongs to the State.' The 'State', initially, meant the Zones. For weeks, the deportees saw convoys of trucks and requisitioned cars, loaded with bicycles, furniture, electrical appliances, motor-bikes, pharmaceutical goods and radio sets, heading towards the Eastern Zone, the South-West and the North. The Zone Secretaries, true warlords that they were, feuded among themselves over how the plunder should be divided. By summer, removal teams were going from house to house in Phnom Penh with instructions to leave the 'revolutionary minimum' – defined as a bed without a mattress, a chair without a cushion, and a table; to remove whatever they thought might be useful for storage in state warehouses; and to burn the rest. In the central districts of the capital, which in April, when Lon Nol's regime fell, had been piled high with filth, uncollected rubbish and the debris of buildings destroyed in Khmer Rouge rocket attacks, soldiers swept the pavements each morning. The shanty towns on the outskirts, where millions of peasant refugees had lived out the last year of the war in misery and squalor, were razed.

The Foreign Ministry, codenamed B-1, headed by Ieng Sary, took over a complex of buildings, occupying an entire city block, which in Lon Nol's day had housed the Prime Minister's Office. Situated just south of the railway station on the main road to the airport, it adjoined the General Staff Headquarters, which Son Sen had established in the former republican Defence Ministry next door. Each was a self-contained community, a *munthi*, as it is called in Khmer, where the cadres and their wives lived – often in separate dormitories – worked, tended collective vegetable plots in what had once been the Ministry gardens, participated in political study and sent their children to the Ministry crèche. In three years, Laurence Picq was allowed outside the B-1 compound fewer than half a dozen times, usually to see theatrical performances, and never on her own.

That first year, when Cambodia was still almost totally cut off from the outside world – with no international telephone, telegraph or postal links, all land and sea borders closed, and no scheduled flights to anywhere – there was little work for diplomats.

In Sopheap remembered making by hand the first passports for the new regime: 'We typed the pages, put them between two sheets of cardboard and stapled them together . . . Later we had passports printed in China, but that was how we began.' Sikoeun found some teletype machines to monitor foreign news agencies and compiled a daily digest which was circulated to the Standing Committee. But most of the Ministry personnel were sent to the countryside to reforge themselves through manual labour.

The few who remained spent their days sweeping offices, cleaning graffiti off the walls and scrubbing lavatories. 'It was a chance to show their revolutionary mettle,' Picq recalled. 'Normally Khmers are extremely squeamish about faecal matter . . . But now it was too good an occasion to miss. Some used rags, some buckets of water, but the boldest used their hands, scraping off the dried excrement with their finger-nails.' Another

Ministry team set about cleaning the former Governor-General's Residence and the Hotel Phnom, nearby, which were rechristened 'House No. 1' and 'House No. 2' and were to be used for government receptions and to accommodate distinguished guests. 'Pol himself came to inspect our work,' a member of the team remembered. 'At one point someone opened a cupboard door and a little dog jumped out. We all froze, we were terrified. It could have been taken as a serious breach of security. Fortunately he smiled.'

By then Pol had moved from the Silver Pagoda to a new permanent headquarters in what were known as the Bank Buildings. A seven-storeyed L-shaped apartment complex – at the time the tallest in Phnom Penh – built in the 1960s to a design by a Cambodian architect, it had formerly housed senior civil servants and officials from the National Bank. Ieng Sary chose it as the Party leaders' residence because it stood on its own in a park at the 'Four Arms', the point where the River Bassac, the two streams of the Mekong and the Tonle Sap meet, which meant that it was easy to protect and had access to the three main highways leading north, south and west. Pâng, who had been appointed Pol's Chief of Staff, had bamboo palisades erected around it, with troops manning machine-guns on all four sides and multiple checkpoints along the single approach road. K-1, as it was called, was home not only to Pol, but to the other three Phnom Penh-based members of the Standing Committee – Nuon Chea, Sary himself and Vorn Vet – as well as Khieu Samphân, whose relationship with the Party Secretary, despite his junior status, was becoming increasingly close. Like the Foreign Ministry cadres, they lived apart from their wives, whom they saw once a week – 'as though you were going to visit your mistress', Vorn Vet used to complain – and at Pol's insistence, in order to 'proletarianise themselves', they had to clean their own rooms and help with other domestic chores. To Pol, that was no hardship: as Party leader, he was exempt and he lived as a bachelor anyway. Khieu Ponnary's schizophrenia had worsened and she had been assigned a house in Boeung Keng Kâng, in the southern part of the city, where relatives of other leading figures, including Khieu Samphân's elderly mother, also lived.

Later in the year, Pol began using Ponnary's old family home on rue Docteur Hahn as an additional residence. The whole block, which was known as K-3, was barricaded with corrugated-iron sheeting and barbed wire, and patrolled by guards. The other buildings were used for meetings and to accommodate Central Committee members when they came to the capital for the annual plenum. Subsequently Pol acquired a third home, a villa near Sihanouk's former palace at Chamkar Mon, also in the southern part of Phnom Penh.

The Central Committee Secretariat, codenamed 870, was housed in a shabby, two-storey office building behind the National Assembly. Doeun, a protégé of Koy Thuon and a member of the Northern Zone CPK Committee, was appointed Political Director, with Khieu Samphân as special assistant responsible for united front matters, the economy, commerce, industry and tariffs. Samphân was also entrusted with missions which Pol judged too sensitive for others to handle.

But if the basic framework of the future Khmer Rouge administration was being put in place, and the worst eyesores of the war removed, normalcy, in Phnom Penh, remained a very relative term.

The Roman Catholic Cathedral was demolished, not so much as an anti-Christian or even anti-foreign gesture, but because its French missionary founders, with typical nineteenth-century arrogance, had built it directly opposite Wat Phnom, which in Khmer tradition is sacred ground.* The National Bank was left in ruins. The rest of the city's building stock, unoccupied and unmaintained, slowly rotted in the tropical heat and damp. The city's parks and gardens were given over to 'useful' trees and plants: frangipane, for traditional medicine; guavas; bananas; and, along the pavements, coconut palms. Pigs and cattle, belonging to the various ministries, roamed the streets – until Son Sen's office issued a circular, warning that unless livestock were controlled, it would adversely affect the country's image in the eyes of visiting delegations. But the principle that each *munthi* should be self-sufficient was not called into doubt. If Phnom Penh itself could not be physically uprooted and transferred to the countryside, as its population had been, nature would be allowed, wherever possible, to reassert its rights, eliding the difference between worker and peasant, mental and manual labour, and exerting a pristine, regenerative influence on the new revolutionary elite.

The physical changes in Phnom Penh, disconcerting enough in themselves, were as nothing compared to the psychological shock of re-entering a familiar community to find that its members now inhabited a different mental plane.

---

*Despite their reputation for iconoclasm, the Khmers Rouges preserved the most important Cambodian historical monuments. The Buddha's Tooth Stupa in front of the Phnom Penh railway station survived Khmer Rouge rule unscathed, as did the Royal Palace and the National Museum. So did all the major Buddhist monasteries in Phnom Penh and in most provincial towns. So, too, did Angkor Wat and the other Angkorian sites. The French-trained Khmer conservationists were kept together and given special protection at a co-operative in Bakong, in Siem Reap province, evidently with the intention that their skills would be used again when economic conditions improved.

Laurence Picq found that old friends from her days in Paris and Beijing were now unrecognisable. 'Their behaviour was studied, measured . . . When they spoke it was in the same official formulae that we had heard from countless other cadres . . . Every action, every word, was placed in a defined political and ideological context.' Yet she was seduced by the monastic simplicity of the way of life she was offered in this new society which preached poverty, moral integrity and the renunciation of personal belongings. It was a society, she wrote, whose goal was to achieve harmony by surmounting the contradictions inherent in life or, in Buddhistic terms, where the reason for living was 'not to have but to be', a society 'without desire, without vain competition, without fear for the future'.

For Picq and her companions, the 'renunciation of personal belongings' was relatively civilised: shortly after they arrived, each was asked to unpack their bags and keep only the indispensable minimum, giving the rest to Angkar. For those who came later, from Europe and the United States, where, it was presumed, they had sat out the war in comfort, the regime was harsher. As had happened to the urban deportees, their bags were searched by soldiers, who threw out anything they considered superfluous, publicly stripping them of their dignity and their identity as individuals. Ong Thong Hoeung, who had given up a doctorate in French literature to return, remembered 'blouses, trousers, skirts, underpants, bras, beauty products, medicine, books . . . all scattered on the ground . . . We felt humiliated . . . But no one dared say a word.'

For everyone, regardless of when they returned, there came next a period of testing, which might last anything from six months to several years. All, virtually without exception,* had to undergo it – just as Pol, Rath Samoeun, Mey Mann and their comrades had had to prove themselves to the Viet Minh at Krâbao a quarter of a century before. In 1972 and 1973, the first groups of student volunteers who had returned from Beijing had been sent initially to a boot camp called B-15, in a clearing in the jungle a day's ride by ox-cart from Pol's headquarters on the Chinit river. One of them, Long Nârin, described how they built themselves wooden huts and spent a year growing their own food and living the lives of peasants:

---

* Apart from Sihanouk and his immediate entourage, Thiounn Mumm appears to have been the one man who escaped this rule entirely. He never went to the maquis; nor did he do manual labour or live in a co-operative. In Sopheap and Suong Sikoeun were allowed to go directly to K-33 (the Information Ministry) and B-1 respectively, but both had spent a year working at the FUNK radio station in Hanoi before returning to Phnom Penh in May 1975, and both were regarded as essential personnel to get the new administration running. For the same reason Ok Sakun, Thiounn Prasith, and possibly one or two others, spent only a few weeks at co-operatives before Ieng Sary recalled them to Phnom Penh.

B-15 was new. When we arrived there was nothing. We had to do every-thing for ourselves in accordance with the principle of relying solely on our own strength. To start with, we were six or seven intellectuals. We had a group of teenagers to look after, mostly the children of leaders, aged between twelve and fifteen – the children of Hu Nim, Hou Yuon and Tiv Ol were there – it was tough for them because they were young and on their own. Altogether, including local peasants, there were about seventy of us. There was never enough to eat. For the whole group, we had 500 grams of rice a day: we mixed it with bananas, sweet potatoes and manioc, which we grew ourselves, just to give the impression that there was rice. It was enough to survive, but everyone was hungry all the time.

At one level they were being tempered, in the same way as the urban deportees would be tempered, and for essentially the same reason: to prove their revolutionary devotion. Every evening there was a 'lifestyle meeting', like those which François Bizot had witnessed at his prison in the Special Zone, three years earlier, where each participant gave an account of his acts during the day and criticised himself and his colleagues. To Laurence Picq, at B-1, such meetings were 'a ritual . . . which none of us could have done without . . . goading the group to new efforts, stronger, more united, more steeled . . . with ever greater intensity to do more and better'. There were also twice-weekly study meetings where, in Long Nârin's words, 'we had to wash away our intellectual mode of thinking'.

Even these basic forms of thought control were undertaken with a sever-ity 'as tough', as Picq put it, 'as anything to be found in the harshest re-education camps in China'. If, after six months, or a year, the postulant was assigned a responsible post, it meant he or she had passed the test. But not everyone did so. In her group, some were never able to convince Angkar that they should be allowed to return to Phnom Penh. Long Visalo, who had a doctorate in cartography from Budapest and returned six months after Laurence Picq, compared the experience to crossing a river: 'There will always be people who don't make it, who can't get over and fall in the water. You can't leave those people behind, so eventually you kill them.'

Along with other returnees from Europe and America, Visalo stayed at the former Khmero-Soviet Technical Institute, which had been renamed K-15 and transformed into a holding camp for intellectuals. The work regime was tougher and the food more meagre than at B-1 or B-15. Ong Thong Hoeung found that friends who had left Paris only three months before were now 'as thin as nails, skeletal, not just thin but dirty, covered in rashes and sores, with blackened and missing teeth . . . They looked as though they had come from a Buddhist hell or out of a concentration camp.' He was struck even more by their expression, 'a strange, enigmatic, disconcerting smile, expressing sadness but also something else, which I couldn't fathom. I couldn't bear to look at them. How had they got into this state?' The answer, he discovered, lay not only in the physical conditions, but in the mental indoctrination to which they were subjected. The way Long Visalo remembered it:

> They told us to plant rice on a basketball court. On reinforced concrete! They didn't want us to break the concrete, but to cover it with a layer of earth . . . I thought: 'These people are mad' . . . But then you start to realise, a basketball court is a place where the bourgeoisie play during their leisure. The peasants have to work to live . . . Take a city street. It's where the bourgeoisie drive their cars. The peasants don't have cars. So destroy the street! In [southern Phnom Penh] I planted tomatoes in the street. I dug holes a metre deep through the tarmac and filled them with straw and shit with my hands. You have to like that! You have to like shit, because it gives life! The street doesn't give life. You can't eat the street. But once you've grown tomatoes you can eat them . . . It's not important how much you produce: you can grow tons of vegetables, but in itself that means nothing. What matters is to change your mentality.

Exactly what was involved in 'changing your mentality' was made clear to the new arrivals at a month-long seminar conducted by Khieu Samphân:

> How do we make a communist revolution? [he asked us]. The first thing you have to do is to destroy private property. But private property exists on both the material and the mental plane . . . To destroy material private property, the appropriate method was the evacuation of the towns . . . But spiritual private property is more dangerous, it comprises everything that you think is 'yours', everything that you think exists in relation to yourself – your parents, your family, your wife. Everything of which you say, 'It's mine . . .' is spiritual private property. Thinking in terms of 'me' and 'my' is forbidden. If you say, 'my wife', that's wrong. You should say, 'our family'. The Cambodian nation is our big family . . . That's why you have been separated: the men with the men, the women with women, the children with children. All of you are under the protection of Angkar. Each of us, man, woman and child, is an element of the nation . . . We are the child of Angkar, the man of Angkar, the woman of Angkar.
>
> The knowledge you have in your head, your ideas, are mental private property, too. To become a true revolutionary, you must . . . wash your mind clean. That knowledge comes from the teaching of the colonialists and imperialists . . . and it has to be destroyed. You intellectuals who have come back from abroad bring with you the influence of Europe, what we may call the 'sequels of colonialism'. So the first thing you must do to make yourselves fit to participate in the communist revolution, [to put yourself on a par with] the ordinary people of Cambodia, the peasants, is to wash your mind . . .

If we can destroy all material and mental private property . . . people will be equal. The moment you allow private property, one person will have a little more, another a little less, and then they are no longer equal. But if you have nothing – zero for him and zero for you – that is true equality . . . If you permit even the smallest part of private property, you are no longer as one, and it isn't communism.

Samphân cautioned them that they should keep these ideas to themselves, because 'if the masses knew what we had been discussing, they might become discouraged'. Yet more than twenty years later, Visalo, by that time a government minister, still felt that 'in principle, all that he said was just. Whether it could be put into effect is another matter. It was idealistic . . . But when I listened to him, I felt it was right. His arguments were reasonable.'

They resonated for several reasons. Cambodians are naturally attracted to extremes (which is no doubt why Kropotkin's dictum, that the French Revolution should not have stopped halfway, influenced Pol so strongly in his student days in Paris). Even Mao had faltered, by Khmer Rouge standards, by allowing the need for wages, for knowledge and family life. The Cambodian communists would go where none had gone before. 'Zero for him, zero for you – that is communism,' Khieu Samphân had said. The idea that property is baneful is rooted in the Buddhist creation myth, which depicts a golden age, when rice grew in abundance and men ate as they wished, before greed for private possessions perverted the primeval commonwealth. When the French had introduced land rights, a century earlier, Prince Yukanthor commented: 'You have established property, and you have created the poor.' Men like Visalo, and the thousand or so Khmer expatriates who returned before and after him, came from a Europe fired up by the ferment of May 1968 and an America tearing itself apart over the war in Vietnam – a world where the old ways had been found lacking and a shining, new future beckoned to those with the courage to believe. The returnees did believe. In choosing to come home, they had consciously rejected what they called 'the orchestrated calumnies, the campaigns of intoxication . . . the claims of massacres and forced labour', spread by the US media, and proclaimed their faith in the 'prodigious achievements [and] sublime ardour' of the Cambodian people under their new leaders. Despite the appalling conditions they encountered after they arrived, many continued to believe until the regime fell.

At B-1, where the Foreign Ministry staff, having already completed their period of testing, were held to be ideologically more advanced than the returnees, the séances of introspection, criticism and self-criticism were fiercer.

The ultimate aim was to demolish the personality, 'that hard, tenacious, aggressive shell which in its very essence is counter-revolutionary', as one Khmer Rouge cadre put it; the preferred method, a 'surgical strike' to destroy 'the individual', who, in contradistinction to 'the people', defined as the embodiment of good, was seen as the root of every imaginable evil. Personality was a 'property of the bourgeoisie, whereby they crush the masses . . . It is what enables them to throw out their chests and hold their heads high . . . It is the stuff of which imperialists and colonialists are made.' The ultimate goal for a Khmer Rouge was 'to have no personality at all'. To eradicate it, the 'strike' was directed at the individual's most vulnerable point – his family relations, perhaps, or educational background or ties with a foreign country – in order to decondition him, liberating his behaviour from the acquired reflexes of his former life, before building a new persona on the basis of revolutionary values. The process was repeated with increasing refinement, through self-examination and public confession, until a new man emerged who embodied loyalty to Angkar, alacrity and non-reflection.

Laurence Picq, reflecting on her life at B-1, compared it to membership of the Moonies. In all sects, indoctrination is accomplished by extreme mental and physical pressure. In Khmer Rouge Cambodia, that meant hunger, lack of sleep and long hours of labour. 'All our thoughts were constantly on food,' Picq wrote. 'When political education drips into minds emptied by hunger and weariness and cut off from the outside world, the effects are prodigious.' The same was true in reverse. During the twice-yearly seminars held by Ieng Sary at B-1, the diet of thin soup and mouldy bread suddenly improved: there was fruit and fresh-water crayfish, vegetables and rice. The combination of indoctrination and good treatment had 'a psychological impact that was frightening . . . It acted on collective attitudes and behaviour with such power that the participants emerged feeling they were capable of anything.' As the ideological fetters tightened, people no longer saw themselves as individuals, but as cogs in an occult machine whose workings, by definition, they could not fully understand.

No other communist party – whether in China, Vietnam or North Korea – has gone so far in its attempts directly to remould the minds of its members. Under Pol's leadership, the CPK was unique in its determination to create a 'new communist man' by pushing the logic of egalitarianism, co-operative self-management and the withering away of the state to its uttermost limits. The ideals of the French Revolution, the practices of Maoist China, the methods of Stalinism, all played their part. But the specificity of Pol's revolution lay in its Khmer roots.

The destruction of 'material and spiritual private property' was Buddhist detachment in revolutionary clothes; the demolition of the personality was the achievement of non-being. 'The only true freedom,' a study document proclaimed, 'lies in following what Angkar says, what it writes and what it does.' Like the Buddha, Angkar was always right; questioning its wisdom was always a mistake.

To the former town-dwellers, adjusting to life in the countryside was even more traumatic than Phnom Penh was for the intellectuals. For both, it was a double blow. Physically they were deprived of the creature comforts they had taken for granted throughout their lives. Psychologically they were enslaved, confined within a political and ideological strait-jacket that grew steadily tighter. The deportees were at one end of the Party's scale of concerns, the intellectuals at the other. But its approach to both was the same.

The physical change was so overwhelming for the 'new people' that at first it drowned out every other consideration. Many were terrified. 'We had the impression,' one wrote, 'of having been abandoned in the middle of a hostile land.' They arrived in villages 'that seemed frozen in time', where people still suffered from yaws, dropsy and other diseases which were supposed to have been eradicated from Cambodia decades before. Like the intellectuals, the deportees had to learn everything from the bottom up – to build primitive wooden huts; to plough; to plant vegetables and rice – usually in conditions far harsher than the returned students endured. Like the peasants, they used potash extracted from the cinders of wood fires as a substitute for soap. In the flooded rice-paddies, they wrapped cloths between their legs as protection against minuscule leeches which could enter the penis, the anus or the vagina, causing excruciating pain until, days later, they detached themselves and were flushed out.

That first year, in most areas – except for parts of the North-West and western Kompong Chhnang, where the distribution system collapsed under the weight of the population increase – food supplies, while meagre, were enough to ward off starvation. Women stopped menstruating, as they did even in Phnom Penh where food was more plentiful; some suffered prolapsed uteruses, and nursing mothers had no milk. Malaria was rife. By the following spring, local cadres were reporting 40 per cent of the population incapacitated by fever. None the less, the deportees foraged for snails and lizards, crabs and spiders, and wild vegetables in the jungle, and bartered for food with the 'base people' what remained of the gold and jewellery they had managed to bring with them from the towns. Like the French, who survived the Second World War as well as they did in part because they were close to the soil, urban Khmers were at heart less removed from peasant life than they sometimes tried to pretend, and it stood them in good stead.

In retrospect, one of the most astonishing aspects of the Khmer Rouge period is that so many academics and professional people were able to 'use the hoe as a long pen and the rice-field as their paper', as the cadres liked to say, keeping themselves and their families precariously alive. The exceptions were the 'Chinese', the Sino-Cambodian businessmen who had no rural roots. They died in larger numbers.

Within this overall context, local variations were extreme. Even in the North-West, where conditions were generally worst, there were villages where the 'new people' had as much rice as they could eat – 'too much', one man remembered. At the same moment, in Pursat, thirty miles to the south, others were so desperate for food that cannibalism was rife and a third of the deportees died before the year was out. Local leaders looked after their own: what happened in the next district, the next village, was not their concern. It made a mockery of central directives, as Pol was well aware. 'It's impossible to solve problems when walking on a narrow path,' he complained to the Central Committee. But feudalistic, patron–client relationships were too deeply rooted in Cambodian culture for even the Khmers Rouges to change. 'There was no established rule for the whole country,' the former government engineer Pin Yathay concluded. 'Discipline varied at the whim of each village chief.' There were 'good' villages in the worst regions, and 'bad' villages in the best.

Hunger was a weapon in the countryside no less than in the re-education camps. Lenin's dictum, 'He who does not work, does not eat', was applied in the Cambodian co-operatives with a literalness the Russians had never dreamed of. In a bad area, a day's work earned one bowl of watery rice soup; those too ill to work got nothing. Illness itself was often equated with opposition to the regime, or at least a lack of 'revolutionary consciousness' which was considered almost as bad, and the rural clinics, where untrained nurses doled out traditional medicines, were no more than charnel-houses.

But hunger, compounded by non-existent health care, was a double-edged sword.

For the local cadres, food was an essential means of control, calibrated by the differing treatment of 'new' and 'base' people. For the 'base' people, life was bearable. The plight of the 'new people' was a constant reminder to them of their own relative good fortune, which in turn was designed to incite the former to work harder to reforge themselves, in order to progress from being depositees to candidate or full-rights status with a corresponding improvement in rations. That, at least, was the theory. In practice, it rarely worked that way. The Khmer Rouge system was essentially coercive. Yet at the same time there was a genuine shortage. Even with relief rice from China, grain stockpiles after the war were dangerously low. When 'new people' starved to death that winter, it was not a matter of policy but because the system had failed.

Pol wanted more, not fewer people. He called for a doubling or tripling of the population, to '15 or 20 million people within 10 years', to implement his plans to make Cambodia prosperous and strong. But how was that to be achieved if women were unable to menstruate because of malnutrition? How could the existing population work effectively if it were half-starved? The leadership recognised the problem. Standing Committee resolutions at that time, and Pol's speeches at closed Party meetings, are full of references to the need to ensure an adequate diet, defined as an average of 500 grams of paddy per person per day. 'The [most] important medicine is food,' he told a conference in the Western Zone. 'Resolving the food problem is the key.' Two months later he made the same point again: 'We must solve the problem of the people's livelihood and we must solve it rapidly . . . [Otherwise] contradictions [will] spring up among us.'

But the contradictions were already embedded in the policy. In a period of generalised penury, cadres were expected to ensure a healthy minimum diet for all, while maintaining a hierarchy of rations between 'new' and 'base' people. This meant guaranteeing that those in responsible positions, who lived apart from the masses – co-operative and district leaders, soldiers, militia and certain other privileged groups, such as railway workers, whose loyalty was crucial to the regime – were fed not merely adequately but well, with meat or fish in addition to rice; yet at the same time retaining the use of hunger as a means of discipline, since there was no obvious alternative.

It added up to so many conflicting imperatives that in practice most cadres opted for the simplest solution: they and the 'base' people ate well; the 'new' people ate badly; hunger remained a punitive weapon; the death toll from malnutrition and related diseases stayed high; and the health and strength of the 'new' people continued to decline.

There was a similar dilemma over how hard people should work, and how much 'cutting-edge violence' should be used to make them do so.

The Standing Committee had decreed one free day in each ten-day week – a system copied from the French Revolution – and up to fifteen days' holiday a year. 'There's not enough food for people to work all the time,' Pol explained. 'If a person doesn't rest, he gets ill. It is a strategic objective to increase the strength of the people. Therefore, leisure should be considered fundamental.' But in practice the weekly day off, when granted, was devoted to political meetings, and the proposed annual holiday was never implemented.

That left the question of daily work quotas.

If they were set too high, those who failed to meet them were punished, either by being given extra tasks, or less food, or both, frequently leading to illness and death. But if they were lowered, the targets set by the region and the Zone would not be fulfilled. Grass-roots leaders met this challenge in different ways. Some tried to strike a balance – especially in the Eastern and South-Western Zones; in Kratie; and in the more fertile districts of the North-West. Others resorted to terror. The indiscriminate killing of former republican army officers and senior civil servants which had marked the first months of the regime had stopped during the summer. But in the co-operatives, executions of supposed 'bad elements' and others who allegedly violated collective discipline continued. A young village militiaman explained:

> Those we surprised at night in the act of saying bad things, we educated, which means that they worked harder than the others. If they repeated the offence, they were killed with a cudgel or a pickaxe. Then they were buried and that was that . . . Children were also killed if they made a lot of mistakes . . . I agreed with the executions . . . Those who made mistakes had to take responsibility for their errors.

Carried out at night and in secret, they inspired a morbid jingle: 'Angkar kills but does not explain'. But this method too had a drawback: every person who died was one person less to work.

By the winter of 1975, if not sooner, the mass of the Cambodian population had become, in the eyes of the leadership, digits on a national balance sheet. It was implicit in the menacing couplet which the cadres used when a person was about to be killed: 'To keep you is no profit, to destroy you is no loss'. A villager remembered it as a time when 'a person's worth was measured in how many cubic yards of earth he could move'. Like the oxen they were supposed to emulate, people were a commodity to be fed, watered, housed and worked. When they were executed, their clothes were removed by the soldiers and handed on to others to wear; their corpses were often buried beside fields, in the belief that the rotting flesh would fertilise the soil. Those who died in village clinics were cremated and the bone ash used for phosphate. As in death, so also in birth: when women still menstruated, cadres noted the dates of their periods so that their husbands might be brought to sleep with them at the time they were most likely to be fecund, to swell the population.

While life for those in the co-operatives was physically extremely harsh, the indoctrination to which they were subjected was correspondingly mild.

In part this was a conscious decision. At the end of 1975, the CPK's existence was still secret. Another year would pass before it would be hinted publicly that the mysterious Angkar might in fact be a communist organisation. Only a third of the co-operatives then had Party branches – total Party membership for the whole country was probably less than 10,000 – and, as Khieu Samphân had noted, the time was not yet ripe for communist ideas to be disseminated openly among the masses.

There were also practical reasons. In the rural areas the aim was not to demolish personality – that treatment was reserved for intellectuals – but to make the deportees shed their bourgeois outlook and think and act as peasants. The nightly lifestyle meetings concentrated on planting schedules, increasing fertiliser production, the digging of irrigation channels and disciplinary violations. 'The bourgeoisie . . . have been subordinated to worker-peasant power. They have been forced to carry out manual labour,' the Party journal, *Tung Padevat*, explained, 'but their views and their aspirations remain.' Once they had reforged themselves, the differences between 'new' and 'base' people would disappear and the next stage could begin, which would be to instil in them the 'proletarian consciousness' that alone would permit the modernisation of agriculture and industry which was the regime's ultimate goal. In Samphân's words:

> The workers are the most revolutionary class, because they do not possess property and they work in an organised manner at regular hours. The peasant possesses land on which to grow his crops; he is disorganised and negligent; he works when he feels like it. The worker owns nothing; he earns his living with the strength of his arms. That is how we, too, should be . . . So in this first stage we have a peasant revolution; but later, to advance to communism, we must make a proletarian revolution.

That should not be seen as an affirmation of Marxist orthodoxy: the real flesh-and-blood workers in the factories of Phnom Penh and Battambang were distrusted as much as ever. 'Proletarian consciousness' was an ideal, to be achieved through 'illumination',* not, as Marx had held, the reflection in the social superstructure of a particular pattern of economic organisation – and in any case it was for the future.

For now, the nightly message was 'to work hard, produce more and love Angkar', to 'build and defend the nation' and to reject the selfish, individualistic values of Western-style capitalism.

It was government by incantation. The village leaders knew their lines so well, one man noticed, that 'every time they spoke they put the punctuation marks exactly where they had been the day before.' The repetition

---

*The term 'illumination' was used not only by the Cambodians but also by Vietnamese communists, whose vocabulary was likewise Buddhist-influenced. But whereas in Vietnam it was simply a metaphor, denoting understanding of Marxist-Leninist ideas, the Cambodians used it literally in its original Buddhist sense. It is not found in Chinese or Korean communist texts.

was deliberate, the cadres emphasised. It was designed, like a Buddhist sermon, to 'impregnate' people's minds so deeply with a single idea that there would be no room for any other.

Radio Phnom Penh did the same, repeating stereotyped phrases with mantra-like regularity. Pol told the Information Minister, Hu Nim, that the announcers should have clear, strong voices 'like the monks who lead the prayers at a *wat*'. In more prosperous communes, the daily homily was broadcast over loudspeakers. Invariably it was accompanied by a song illustrating the chosen topic – the need for greater efforts in pig-breeding or the digging of irrigation canals – set to a lilting traditional air. Despite the dreariness of the subject matter, the music, one deportee remembered, made it a 'most effective tool – you started to believe in it'. Like the *cpap* of Pol's childhood, it was an aid to memorisation and an ideological guide, depicting the world as it should be, a place of joy and exaltation, where everyone struggled constantly to build a better life, seethed with class hatred against the exploiters of old and showed absolute faith in Angkar, the 'correct and clear-sighted revolutionary organisation'. 'The implication,' one woman wrote, 'was that if we did not share the general joy, the fault lay with us. We must work harder . . . to weed out selfishness, laziness and desire.'

From the winter of 1975, the radio started urging people to 'fight non-revolutionary moral and material concepts, including those of private property, personality [and] vanity, and . . . [to] adopt the stand of collective ownership and austerity'. It called for 'renunciation' – another Buddhist notion – which the cadres explained meant devoting oneself body and soul to the collective without being swayed by personal interests:

'Renunciation of feelings of ownership' meant that one must concentrate completely on the task at hand without thinking of oneself, as in Buddhist meditation. 'Renunciation of material goods' implied detachment from one's wife, one's children and one's home, just as Buddha once renounced those things. 'Renunciation of control over one's own life' meant digging out from oneself the roots of pride, contempt for others and complicated thoughts, as the monks used to preach before. The 'renunciation of the self' is particularly necessary as it concerns the emotional ties within the family – between husband and wife, parents and children, and children and parents. [They used to tell us:] 'You should purify yourselves, free yourself from emotional bonds'; 'You still have feelings of friendship and goodwill. You must eliminate from your mind all [such] individualistic notions.'

However, indoctrination was carried out principally through the practice of daily life.

Language was stripped bare of incorrect allusions. Instead of 'I', people had to say 'we'. A child called its parents 'uncle and aunt' and other grown-ups, 'mother' or 'father'. Every relationship became collective; words distinguishing the individual were suppressed or given new meanings. Terms denoting hierarchy, like the dozen or so verbs meaning 'to eat', whose use depended on the rank and social relationship of those involved, were replaced by a single verb previously used only by peasants. Nuon Chea, who masterminded these changes, devised neologisms, often based on scholarly Pali terms, to convey political concepts for which no equivalent existed in Khmer. Other new coinages were taken from peasant slang: *bokk rukk*, 'to launch an offensive', meant literally 'to ram a stake into a hole', with the sense of violent buggery. The sexual connotation was odd in such a puritanical regime, but it conveyed well enough the idea of an elemental, brutish struggle to overcome material obstacles and bend nature to man's will. Nuon, as the final authority, other than Pol himself, in all matters concerning propaganda, also supervised Radio Phnom Penh. At his insistence, words conveying lyrical or 'bourgeois' sentiments, like 'beauty', 'colourful' and 'comfort' were banned from the airwaves. The goal was that described in Orwell's *1984*, a book which neither Pol nor Nuon had read but whose principles they grasped intuitively:

> The whole aim of Newspeak is to narrow the range of thought . . . In the end we will make thoughtcrime literally impossible, because there will be no words in which to express it. Every concept that will ever be needed will be expressed by exactly *one* word, with its meaning rigidly defined and all its subsidiary meanings rubbed out and forgotten . . . Every year fewer and fewer words, and the range of consciousness always a little smaller . . . In fact there will be no thought as we understand it now. Orthodoxy means not thinking . . . Orthodoxy is unconsciousness.

Reality mirrored the notions this new language conveyed. The family continued to exist but, as Orwell had imagined, its primary purpose became 'to beget children for the service of the Party'. Ties between individual family members were diluted within the larger community. 'Mothers should not get too entangled with their offspring,' Pol told the Central Committee. Similarly, if a man felt a sentimental attachment developing with a woman, he should 'take a collectivist stand, and resolve it . . . To do otherwise is to have a strong private stance.' Marriage – not merely between Party members, as Orwell had envisaged, but between any two people – was a Party, not an individual affair. Khieu Samphân married in December 1972 because Pol told him he should and personally served as his go-between. Traditionally, in Khmer society, marriages had been arranged between families. Now Angkar played that role. 'Free choice of spouses' was explicitly condemned. To underline the social aspect, weddings were celebrated collectively for a minimum of ten couples. After a marriage had been consummated the couple often lived apart.

Illicit love affairs were punished by death. Women wore their hair short in a regimented Maoist bob with shirts buttoned to the neck. At work the sexes were segregated, regardless of age. Sport was banned as 'bourgeois'. So were children's toys. There was no free time. The only reading materials were two Party journals, which were exclusively for cadres, and a fortnightly newspaper, *Padevat* (Revolution), which circulated within the ministries in Phnom Penh. The Buddhist *wats*, formerly the centre of village life, were closed. Some were demolished, as the Catholic cathedral had been, to recover the iron struts that reinforced their concrete frames. Others were turned into prisons or warehouses, much as Cromwell's New Model Army in seventeenth-century Britain had turned the churches into stables. Because they lived on charity, the monks were regarded as parasites: in Khmer Rouge terminology, they 'breathed through other people's noses'. Along with expatriate intellectuals and officials of the republican regime, they were designated a 'special class' – a singularly un-Marxist category – and within a year had been defrocked and put to work in co-operatives or on irrigation sites.

In short, everything that had given colour and meaning to Cambodian life was comprehensively suppressed.

Certain groups had special difficulty in accommodating to the new regime. As in Lon Nol's time, Christians were suspected of being Vietnamese. Sino-Khmers were forbidden to speak Chinese, on the grounds that Khmer, or Kampuchean as it was now termed, was the single national language. The Chams, already under suspicion during the civil war, had the worst of all worlds, since their history, religion and culture made them a people apart. The Khmers looked down on them because their kingdom, Champa, had been overrun by the Vietnamese in the fifteenth century, an event constantly cited as a warning of Cambodia's fate if its resolve weakened. Moreover, the fact that they lived and intermarried in self-contained communities, often having little contact with other Cambodians, was a security concern. In 1974, the CPK had begun speaking of the need to 'break up this group to some extent; do not allow too many of them to concentrate in one area.' A year later, the dispersal of the 150,000 Chams in the Eastern Zone to villages in the North and North-West became established policy.

This was not racism in the normal sense of the term. The aim was uniformity – a country where, as Mey Mann put it, 'everyone was exactly 1m. 60 tall' – not the suppression of a particular group.

In practice, local cadres sometimes simplified their own lives by singling out such people for punishment, not because of anything they had done but because they were seen as more likely than others to deviate from Khmer Rouge norms, in the same way as anyone wearing spectacles was regarded as bourgeois or an intellectual or both and hence untrustworthy. The Issarak, twenty-five years earlier, had acted in much the same way. They, too, had killed people who wore glasses. It was the right to difference that was at stake. The Chinese suffered disproportionately because they found it harder than others to adjust to peasant life. The Chams, having lost their own country, were more reluctant than other groups to abandon the cultural and religious specificity that constituted the only identity they had left. The result was a vicious circle: the more the Chams were perceived as anti-revolutionary and anti-national, the more they were repressed. But there is no convincing evidence that Chams died in vastly greater numbers during the Khmer Rouge period than did other racial groups. The criterion was not ethnicity; it was whether people behaved like Khmers or, as they were now called, Kampucheans, a term that had been adopted for the nation as well as the language precisely in order to avoid the impression of racial exclusiveness. That may have been disingenuous, but it was in line with the traditional thinking which had always defined the 'Cambodian race' as those who lived like Khmers. Until recent times, the Khmer language employed the same word for race and religion: to be Khmer was to be Buddhist. Cambodia has never seen itself as a multicultural state. 'This is not America!' Khieu Samphân exclaimed when asked why the Vietnamese had been repatriated in 1975.

Even for the Chams, moreover, the first year of Khmer Rouge rule was not unbearably harsh. That may seem a paradoxical statement when, all over the country, families were being torn apart and tens of thousands of people died. But revolution, like war, is an abomination *per se* – fine for theoreticians, but dreadful for most of those who have to live through it. What happened in Cambodia in 1975 was not qualitatively different from what had occurred in China or Russia, or the killings that accompanied the communist power-seizures in Albania, North Korea or Mongolia.

The vast majority of the population adapted and survived, in many cases far better than anyone could have expected.

Alongside the horror stories, many deportees described work in the cooperatives that first year as having been 'not hard' – in some cases easier than in the factories of Australia or the US where they went later as refugees. In Thmar Puok, in the North-West, it had been 'a happy time' and people 'really liked the cadres, who were lenient and kind'. In the East, living conditions were often 'good' or 'tolerable' and 'controls were very loose'. Even usually critical sources, such as Pin Yathay, in the South-West, acknowledged that daily existence was 'not brutal; just steady, undifferentiated purgatory,' or, in the phrase of a deportee in Prey Veng, 'not too onerous, but dirty and monotonous'. Haing Ngor, the future star of *The Killing Fields*, thought that if the regime had relied less on fear and allowed a little more freedom, 'I would have accepted my fate and become a rice farmer with all my heart and soul'. A Chinese businessman said drily that it was 'pretty much life as usual except that you couldn't spend money'. Such fortitude from men and women who a few months earlier had constituted a privileged elite offered a sobering lesson in the resilience of the human spirit. The 'base people' were not tested in the same way. The freedoms the town-dwellers missed were freedoms they had never had.

Drear and joyless it was, certainly. But that was what its leaders intended. Theravada Buddhism taught that *nirvana*, the realm of selflessness, could be attained only when the 'thirst for existence', made up of worldly and emotional attachments, had been totally extinguished. Under Pol's rule, love, sorrow, anger, passion and all the other feelings that make up everyday life were seen as emanations of individualism to be banished for the collective good. In some parts of the country, it was forbidden even to laugh or sing. In pursuit of illumination, the people had to suffer.

10

Model for the World

WHILE POL AND his colleagues were laying the foundations of the Khmer Rouge state, Prince Sihanouk spent the summer of 1975 kicking his heels in Beijing and Pyongyang. Neither of his 'good friends', Mao and Kim Il Sung, thought it necessary to mention to him that during that time, Pol had come secretly to their capitals to discuss the outline of their future relations, and Sihanouk did not learn of his presence until many years later. Power had slipped away from him while he had been in exile. Now that the Khmers Rouges had won, he was barely even a figurehead. But his prediction that, after victory, 'they will spit me out like a cherry pit', proved wrong. To Pol, the prospect of leaving Sihanouk abroad to serve as a rallying point for opposition was much more disturbing than the inconvenience of having to accommodate him at home. His presence in the new regime would reassure expatriate Cambodians and sympathetic foreigners, of whom there were many in this immediate post-war period, of its bona fides. His stature in the non-aligned movement was an asset not to be squandered. Moreover, it was clear that both China and North Korea, Cambodia's two main allies, wanted Sihanouk to remain in office.

Mao had asked Khieu Samphân a year earlier, half in jest: 'Do you intend to overthrow these two princes, Sihanouk and Penn Nouth?' On being assured that he did not, the Chairman had urged 'small arguments, big unity'. In August 1975, Zhou Enlai met Ieng Sary to discuss 'the way Sihanouk will be treated after his return' and was told that he would have the post of Head of State for life. Only then, it seems, did the Chinese advise the Prince that the time was right for him to go back to Phnom Penh. 'Don't be frightened of having to work with a hoe in the fields,' Mao told him a few days later. 'None of you will have to do that, but you might use a broom and sweep a bit'. He counselled Khieu Samphân not to make Monique and their two children do manual labour either. Then he held up his hand and bent down one of his fingers: 'Between the Khmers Rouges and Sihanouk,' he said, 'there are four points of accord and only one of disagreement.'

On September 9, the Prince returned to Phnom Penh, to be greeted by saffron-robed monks – among the last not to have been defrocked – chanting victory psalms; black-clad Khmer Rouge girls scattering flowers at his feet; a carefully selected crowd of revolutionary soldiers and workers, and representatives of Angkar, led by Khieu Samphân. It was a moment to savour and Pol himself came to watch, hidden behind the pack of welcoming officials. Sihanouk did not see him and was never told that he had been there.

For the next three weeks, he was treated royally. On Ieng Sary's instructions, Long Nârin, now a Foreign Ministry official, had spent the whole of August with a group of workmen cleaning up the Royal Palace for the Prince and his suite, a bizarre assembly of relatives and hangers-on, which included his mother-in-law, the notoriously corrupt Madame Pomme; his aunt, Princess Mom; one of his daughters, Sorya Roeungsy, and her family; his aide-de-camp and chief of protocol; and three ladies-in-waiting for Princess Monique. Essential supplies, like foie gras and truffles, had been sent ahead of him from Beijing, and fine wines were obtained from the Central Committee commissariat, which had been set up behind Wat Langka as a repository for foodstuffs, porcelain, jewellery and other valuables recovered from the houses of the wealthy after the evacuation. Chhorn Hay, the former Cercle Marxiste member who had been doing penance at Stung Trang with Ping Sây and Hou Yuon, was summoned back to serve as Sihanouk's Khmer Rouge major-domo; and a Chinese doctor and nurse, sent from Beijing, were permanently on hand should he or any of his entourage fall ill. The Prince was entranced that several of his Khmer Rouge minders used the special court vocabulary to address him. He was less pleased to discover that the soldiers had appropriated gold ceremonial chains from the Throne Room to use as leashes for their dogs. But he still felt able to say that they were 'very polite and obliging'. He was allowed to carry out funeral ceremonies in the Silver Pagoda for his mother, Queen Kossamak, who had died in China in April. Khieu Samphân took him to visit a textile factory and on a boat trip along the Tonle Sap, and afterwards, with other leaders (though never Pol or Nuon Chea), joined him for banquets at the palace, where they assured him that he and Princess Monique would be able to travel back and forth to Beijing and Pyongyang as often as they wished and that their two sons could continue their education abroad. The Khmers Rouges, Sihanouk conceded, were 'behaving like gentlemen'. Life might be tolerable after all.

This 'strange idyll', as he later called it, was of short duration.

In October the Prince addressed the United Nations General Assembly. Third-world delegates gave him a standing ovation for his anti-American rhetoric and defence of the Khmer Rouge regime. The following month he started a six-week-long tour of Africa, the Middle East and Europe, from which he returned via Paris in December. While there, he had a meeting with Cambodian students. By this time the atmosphere was already beginning to sour. Shortly after his UN speech, a former aide had given Western newspapers a lurid description of life in revolutionary Phnom Penh, said to be based on the confidences of members of his suite. Khieu Samphân had responded by sending Sihanouk what the Prince later called a letter 'of rare insolence', warning that 'by choosing a wrong road, you have nothing to gain and everything to lose'. Yet in his address to the students, he took care to say nothing which might show reservations about Khmer Rouge rule. This duplicity would have terrible consequences for the young men and women who drank in his words.

The Prince was more truthful with the members of his entourage, whom he warned to choose carefully between remaining in exile and accompanying him back to Phnom Penh. In the end, more than half preferred to stay abroad. In another ominous development, the communist leaders began omitting the adjective 'Royal' from the GRUNC, referring merely to the 'Government of National Unity of Cambodia'. They neglected to inform Sihanouk that a new constitution had been drafted, changing the country's name, abolishing the monarchy, omitting most basic rights and freedoms and setting out procedures for a simulacrum of parliamentary elections, or that all the country's ambassadors were being recalled, ostensibly for ten days' 'training' but actually to be replaced.

By the end of the year, every political indicator pointed the same way: Cambodia's institutions were being turned upside down to bring them into line with the realities of Khmer Rouge rule, and Sihanouk, the prime symbol of the society that the revolution had overthrown, would have no influence at all in the new system that was emerging. Yet on December 31, after a farewell meeting with Deng Xiaoping, he boarded a Chinese Boeing 707 and flew back to Phnom Penh, accompanied, this time, by a much-reduced suite. The atmosphere at the airport confirmed all his misgivings: no monks, no red carpet, no girls strewing petals at his feet, but instead a sombre crowd, chanting slogans glorifying Angkar and the revolutionary army. 'It was Kafkaesque', Sihanouk reflected afterwards. 'The smile frozen on my face must have looked ridiculous.'

Why, then, did he go back?

At one level, he owed it to the Chinese and to Kim Il Sung, who had supported him in the dark days and were entitled to be repaid in kind. Had he chosen exile, he could have lived in France – but at the risk of the same ignoble comparisons with Bao Dai that had haunted him at the time of the coup, five years before. That was not how Sihanouk wished history to remember him. He claimed later that he felt a visceral need to be among his people in their hour of trial. But he also understood intuitively that he had to remain in Cambodia if he were to have any hope of ever regaining power. It was a gamble, and a courageous one, and in the end it would pay off. But not until he had endured a multitude of tribulations.

For the moment, the Prince went through the motions expected of him by his new masters. On January 5 1976 he chaired a cabinet meeting which promulgated the new constitution of the country that would henceforth be known as Democratic Kampuchea, a name which carefully avoided the words 'Khmer' and 'Republic', associated with Lon Nol. Kampuchea, the indigenous pronunciation, was preferred to the Westernised Cambodia, and the adjective 'democratic' harked back to the 'new democracy' in vogue during Pol's political apprenticeship in the early 1950s. Democracy was a word Pol liked. He spoke of a 'democratic', not a 'socialist' revolution, arguing that 'it wasn't socialism that mattered, but rather the social results'.

The Khmer Rouge constitution was a radical manifesto, not a legal document, and as such very different from the constitutions of other Asian communist states. After proclaiming baldly that 'every Cambodian has full rights to the material, spiritual and cultural aspects of life' (except 'reactionary religions', which were banned), it asserted state ownership of the means of production, the equality of men and women, the mastery of the workers and peasants over their factories and fields, and the right and obligation of every Cambodian to work. 'Worklessness,' it warned, 'is absolutely non-existent in Democratic Kampuchea.' State power was to be embodied in a three-man Presidium which, it was expected, Sihanouk would head.

His other main function was to host receptions for Phnom Penh's minuscule diplomatic corps, made up of the Chinese Ambassador, Sun Hao, as doyen, followed, in order of arrival, by the envoys of North Vietnam, North Korea, South Vietnam, Albania, Yugoslavia, Cuba, Laos and, later, Egypt, Romania and Burma.

This was a delicate task, for Phnom Penh soon acquired a deserved reputation in foreign chancelleries as the world's one real hardship post. Apart from the Chinese, who were allowed to retain their old Embassy in the southern part of Phnom Penh, the other countries were assigned living and working quarters on Boulevard Monivong, not far from the railway station. The side roads were barricaded off, and the diplomats were not permitted to walk more than 300 yards up and down the street without an escort and official permission. Initially, food was delivered three times a week from a state farm where, unbeknown to them, their former colleagues, Cambodian diplomats who had returned from abroad, laboured to reforge themselves. Conditions eased a little in the spring of 1976, when a diplomatic store, the first and only shop in Democratic Kampuchea, was opened near by, stocking wines, spirits and some consumer goods as well as basic foodstuffs. But embassies were not allowed to employ Cambodian staff, which meant the diplomats had to cook, wash and clean for themselves. They were not allowed cars. They were not allowed to visit the Foreign Ministry – their rare meetings with Cambodian leaders took place at guest-houses in the city – and the one-way telephone system which operated meant that the Ministry could call them but they were not allowed to call out.

In part these measures reflected the suspicion in which the Cambodian government held even friendly foreign states. Pol told the cabinet that spring:

> Diplomatic missions are there to check on us . . . to analyse our [situation] so that they can act in their own interests . . . [Although] these governments are our friends, some of their diplomats may be bad people serving as CIA agents . . . [Therefore] we must be very careful in our contacts with foreigners. We should be cordial, sincere and polite, but secret – because secrecy is the basis of being careful . . . We should let them talk more than we do. We just listen . . . If we talk a lot we can make mistakes . . . Our principle is that we don't want them to know about us, because . . . [then] they cannot attack us . . . If they know about us in advance . . . during negotiations they will put pressure on us in order to dominate us.

These were essentially the same principles that applied within Cambodia itself. What seemed in diplomatic circles an unconscionable restriction of liberty was less severe than the regimentation within the Cambodian administration. For an official from one Ministry to visit another required special authorisation. To travel from one part of the capital to another required a special pass. Members of the Standing Committee, including Pol himself, were stopped at military checkpoints. After late 1975, when large-scale population transfers finally came to an end, similar restrictions on movement were imposed in the rural areas.

Sihanouk was brought face to face with the awfulness of life in Democratic Kampuchea for the first time during two provincial tours he made that winter in the company of Khieu Samphân, one to the Eastern and Northern Zones, the other to the North-West. '[It] bowled me over,' he wrote later. 'My people . . . had been transformed into cattle . . . My eyes were opened to a madness which neither I nor anyone else had imagined.' His account of those journeys is self-centred and self-pitying. He often seemed more outraged by Khmer Rouge table manners, or the decrepitude of buildings where he had once entertained state guests 'like Prince Raimondo Orsini of Italy or the great German actor Curt Jurgens' than by the wretchedness of his compatriots, labouring in the fields. Yet there is no doubt that he was deeply shocked. The question was posed: Could he continue to lend his name to a regime which inflicted such egregious suffering?

In his memoirs, Sihanouk wrote that he had made up his mind to resign even before he got back to Phnom Penh. In fact, he hesitated. To step down, barely two months after returning home, was to invite a head-on confrontation with the Khmer Rouge leadership, with unpredictable consequences. Nor could he be sure how China would react. His old ally, Zhou Enlai, had died in January and the ultra-leftists, headed by Mao's wife, Jiang Qing, were in the ascendant. Penn Nouth advised him to stay his hand. So did his wife, Monique. But then, in the first week of March, Sihanouk learnt that, in violation of all the rules of protocol, Ieng Sary had despatched new Democratic Kampuchean ambassadors to Beijing, Hanoi, Pyongyang and Vientiane without asking him, as Head of State, to sign their letters of credence. It seems to have been the straw that broke the camel's back. Pol acknowledged later: 'Although an incident of no importance, it made him feel that we no longer needed him. It raised the question of [his] status.'

On March 10, Sihanouk gave the palace factotum, Chhorn Hay, his letter of resignation, in which he pleaded health problems. He wished to step down, he said, before March 20, when parliamentary elections were to be held, and to go to China for medical treatment.

Next day Pol called a meeting of the Standing Committee to discuss the Prince's request. In one sense the timing was fortunate. The imminent appointment of a new State Presidium offered a perfect occasion to replace him if he insisted on going. But Pol still hoped that might be avoided. 'Our position,' he told the meeting, 'is always to recognise his noble contribution, his deeds and efforts for the country, particularly in the international arena. The nation owes him its gratitude.' Khieu Samphân and Son Sen were instructed to try to change the Prince's mind. Two days later, Samphân reported that they had failed: Sihanouk was adamant, his decision irrevocable. The Committee then decided that the Prince should be denied further contact with foreigners and refused permission to travel abroad – not because he himself would behave badly, but because his wife, 'who has no patriotic spirit', and her mother were untrustworthy. For the same reason, the couple's sons, the Princes Narindrapong and Sihamoni, were to be brought back from Moscow and Pyongyang in order to 'solve this problem once and for all'.

None the less, Pol did not give up hope entirely that Sihanouk would reconsider. The Prince might look fierce, he said, but he was now 'an old, meek tiger, all skin and bones with no claws or fangs', incapable of doing harm. If he withdrew, it would be the revolution's loss. Moreover, he warned, China and North Korea, both of which viewed Sihanouk as 'a long-standing and very dear friend', might think the Khmers Rouges had 'chased him away' and react negatively.

Shortly after the elections, a second delegation went to see the Prince, this time led by Penn Nouth and including all three vice-premiers. Again, he refused their entreaties. On the morning of April 2, after being informed that his resignation had been accepted, he recorded a farewell statement in French and Khmer, which was broadcast later the same day. His voice, bleached of emotion, testified to his distress. Yet, however difficult it was for him at that moment, and whatever the true reasons for his action – which were certainly less altruistic than he claimed – the move was inspired. Like his abdication in 1955, it left him uniquely placed to play a pivotal role in the future.

If there was a price to pay, it was paid mainly by those around him. Relatives who until then had been spared were sent to the countryside, where none survived. His aide-de-camp 'disappeared'. But Sihanouk himself and his immediate family – his two sons, Princess Monique, her mother and a young cousin – were too important politically and diplomatically to suffer the same fate.

Even by his own account, the 'golden cage' to which he had returned – he had used the same term for the kingship, twenty years earlier – was none too arduous. For the next year, he retained the services of his Khmer Rouge 'retinue'. Khieu Samphân continued to invite him on visits to the provinces, which he apparently refused.

Although forbidden any contact with the world beyond the palace walls, other than listening to radio broadcasts, Sihanouk's material needs were amply provided for – to the point where, in his memoirs, he grumbled about running out of rum to make *bananes flambées* for dessert. At a time when hundreds of thousands of his compatriots were dying of starvation, the complaint rang a little hollow. He was allowed to have air-conditioning because he was averse to the heat. Although the Chinese doctor attached to the palace was withdrawn, he had access to hospital treatment from the same medical and dental teams that cared for Pol and his colleagues. To reassure China and North Korea, the government declared him to be a 'great patriot', announced that a monument would be built in his honour and that he would receive a state pension of 8,000 dollars a year, promises observed in the breach but indicative none the less.

Sihanouk's decision to separate himself from the Khmers Rouges in April 1976 had unintended repercussions.

It ended the last pretence that Democratic Kampuchea had a united front government, in which key posts were held by men outside the revolution-ary ranks. Instead of Sihanouk, Khieu Samphân – the 'dauphin', as Thiounn Thioeunn and his wife started calling him – now became Head of State, a ceremonial post, admittedly, but beyond his wildest expectations only a few weeks before. To Sihanouk, Samphân was 'a figurehead, a dummy'. But Pol placed growing trust in him. He appreciated his patience and perseverance, and the fact that when he was given a task, he would carry it out to the letter, doing neither more nor less than he was asked. Samphân was one of only two Khmer Rouge leaders Pol ever singled out for public praise (the other being Nuon Chea). He was passive, but loyal; incorruptible, but small-minded.

Initially it had been intended to have Penn Nouth, the outgoing Premier, take the post of Vice-President. But in the end that idea was dropped too. The new government was purely Khmer Rouge.

To Pol, notwithstanding the disadvantages, Sihanouk's departure had a silver lining. The monarchy and the legacy of feudalism, he declared, had been definitively dismantled and foreign policy would be more clear-cut. 'Our government is not mixed, as before,' he told the new cabinet at its first meeting. 'We alone now have total responsibility for what goes right and what goes wrong, what is good and what is bad, what we lose and what we gain . . . No one rules the country except us.'

Nuon Chea was appointed President of the Standing Committee of the National Assembly, a post which, like many others in Democratic Kampuchea, existed only on paper. Pol became Prime Minister, assuming at this point the name by which the world would remember him: Pol Pot. It was a decision he took with some reluctance. In February, the Standing Committee had designated Son Sen as Premier. But after Sihanouk's resig-nation, Pol had second thoughts. 'The new government must have prestige at home and abroad,' he said, 'and it needs sufficient authority.' Son Sen, he argued, had his hands full at Defence. Penn Nouth, though competent and trustworthy, was not Khmer Rouge material. That left only himself.*

---

*The new government comprised:

Pol Pot	Prime Minister
Ieng Sary	Vice-Premier, Foreign Affairs.
Vorn Vet	Vice-Premier, Economy
Son Sen	Vice-Premier, Defence
Keat Chhon	Minister in the Prime Minister's Office
Hu Nim	Minister of Information
Khieu Thirith	Minister of Social Affairs
Yun Yat	Minister of Education and Culture
Thiounn Thioeunn	Minister of Health
Kang Chap	Minister of Justice
Toch Phoeun	Minister of Public Works

In hindsight this was perhaps the most important effect of Sihanouk's departure. After a lifetime spent in the shadows, hiding from the limelight, Pol was forced to take centre stage.

It was not a role which came to him easily. At first, Cambodian officials were told to say the new Premier was 'a rubber plantation worker' from the Eastern Zone, and a fictitious biography was circulated, claiming that he had fought with the Issarak during the Japanese occupation. In Paris there was speculation that 'Pol Pot' might be an alias for Rath Samoeun. When the first photographs of him appeared, old friends from his student days, like Nghet Chhopininto, to say nothing of his own brothers, working as peasants in Kompong Thom, were amazed to discover that their new leader was the self-effacing Saloth Sâr. It was the old instinct, born of years of clandestinity, that information must be jealously guarded and the less that got out, the better. As Nuon Chea explained:

> Even now, after 'liberation'. . . secret work is fundamental in all that we do. For example, elections of comrades to leading work are secret. The places where our leaders live are secret. We keep meeting times and places secret . . . On the one hand this is a matter of general principle, and on the other it is a means to defend ourselves from enemy infiltration. As long as there is class struggle or imperialism, secret work will remain fundamental. Only through secrecy can we be masters of the situation . . . We base everything on secrecy.

Other considerations, stemming from a much older tradition also came into play. A popular Buddhist text explained that the happiness of the people was in proportion to the wisdom of the King. In a revolutionary context, it depended on the Party leadership, which must therefore be defended at all costs. In Nuon Chea's words:

> If we lose members but retain the leadership, we can continue to win victories . . . As long as the leadership is there, the Party will not die. There can be no comparison between losing two to three leading cadres and two

---

Non Suon	Minister of Agriculture
Cheng On	Minister of Industry
Doeun	Minister of Commerce
Mey Prang	Minister of Transport
Phuong	Minister for the Rubber Plantations

The last six cabinet members, while holding ministerial status, were officially described as Committee Chairmen and reported to Vice-Premier Vorn Vet. None of the four Sihanoukist ministers in the previous united front government – Penn Nouth, Norodom Phurissara, Sarin Chhak and Chey Chum – was reappointed. Nor were Hou Yuon (Interior Minister) or two Khmer Rouge vice-ministers, Tiv Ol and Chou Chet. Koy Thuon, who had been designated Commerce Minister, never took up the post. From May 1976, Doeun and Non Suon shared responsibility for his portfolio. Doeun became titular Minister later the same year.

to three hundred members. Rather the latter than the former. Otherwise the Party has no head and cannot lead the struggle.

This was the Angkorian model of statecraft, dressed in communist clothes. There were no intermediate layers of power, no pyramid of responsibilities, as in a modern state. The feudal system which Cambodia had inherited had comprised Sihanouk and a handful of mandarins who held office at his pleasure – and his subjects. The King was now replaced by Angkar, personified by Pol Pot – and Sihanouk's 'subjects' by 'the masses'.

Throughout the years of revolutionary struggle, the demands of secrecy had meant that this mysterious and omnipotent leadership had remained anonymous. Now, for the first time, the 'Comrade Secretary', like the god-kings of old, had to reveal himself with a human face.

It was a face that was very hard to fathom.

'Pol Pot,' Ieng Sary recalled, 'even when he was very angry, you could never tell. His face . . . his face was always smooth. He never used bad language. You could not tell from his face what he was feeling. Many people misunderstood that – he would smile his unruffled smile, and then they would be taken away and executed.' Sihanouk admired Pol's eloquence and charisma. 'He seduced you,' he wrote, 'speaking softly [and] always with courtesy.' Kong Duong, who worked with him in the 1980s, remembered his warmth and his obliquity:

> He was very likeable, a really nice person. He was friendly, and everything he said seemed very sensible. He would never blame you or scold you to your face. He would imply things, so that we would have to think about them ourselves . . . [Because of this indirectness], it was sometimes very difficult to figure out what he was getting at. So we were very cautious, because we used to worry about misinterpreting his meaning.

Mey Mak, later one of his secretaries, recalled one such allusive parable:

> He once called me over to sit near him and told me a story. It was about a king and an official. The official was very clever and the King valued him. The King called him to come and play chess. But he laid down one condition. 'If I lose the game,' the King said, 'I will let you rule the kingdom in my place. But if I win, I will send you to work in the countryside as a peasant.' While they were playing, the official saw an opening to win. But he didn't follow up. Instead he found a way to allow the King to break through his defence. So finally, he lost. The King was very happy. And because he was very happy, instead of sending him to the countryside to become a peasant, he promoted him to a still higher post. Pol Pot told that story because he wanted us to think about it. He said: 'You must interpret it as you think.'

The anecdote is intriguing for the layers of subterfuge and ambiguity it reveals. Ieng Sary might condemn Pol's ideas as simplistic, but he also acknowledged that his character was complicated. The Khmer sociologist Vandy Kaonn, who survived the Khmer Rouge years by pretending to be mad, saw no contradiction in that. '[Pol] demanded a radical, intransigent application of the principles adopted,' he wrote, 'but at the same time he required maximum creativity and tact.'

More ominous were Pol's silences. When he 'sat quietly and did not reply', it was the prelude to political disgrace. Those Pol trusted might be granted uncommon latitude. But once a grain of suspicion had taken root in his mind, there was no way to stop it growing.

The verbal precautions with which he cloaked brutally simple policies lent his pronouncements an enigmatic quality. Thus, agricultural mechanisation was the aim, but to get there it was necessary to use as little machinery as possible. Cambodians must reject private ownership, but that did not mean they could not have 'numerous possessions' – this was 'a false contradiction . . . The material livelihood of the people must be encouraged'. 'New people' were unreliable and in many cases unreformable; yet it was wrong to treat them all as enemies. None of these statements was incoherent *per se*: even the puzzling reference to private property merely meant that poverty was not the goal; the more possessions people had, the better, provided they were collectively owned. Like the *k'ruu*, the sages of Khmer antiquity, who spoke in riddles, imparting wisdom in return for obedience and respect, Pol preferred not to be explicit. He believed the revolution would prosper only if the cadres developed a 'revolutionary consciousness' which enabled them to act on their own with a minimum of guidance.

The result was that he was constantly disappointed by his subordinates' capabilities. That fuelled the purge of elements judged to be disloyal. It also made him spend time on trivia that would have been better left to others. Like Sihanouk, who personally inspected the place-settings before official banquets, Pol approved the menus for state receptions, sent laundry lists* of instructions to provincial officials receiving government guests, chose the announcers for Radio Phnom Penh and supervised the programme

---

* In the case of the visit to Sisophon by the Thai Foreign Minister, Chatichai Choonhavan, in November 1975, this was literally true. Pol personally inspected the bedroom slippers, soap and bath-towels sent from Phnom Penh for the occasion. Hun Sen, who eventually succeeded him as Cambodian Prime Minister, showed the same tendency to concentrate all power in his own hands. In the 1990s, speeches by Chea Sim – then the second most powerful man in the kingdom – were vetted and where necessary corrected in Hun Sen's own hand before they were delivered.

schedules. In a society where the word of the King had always been law, initiative was still-born. To Suong Sikoeun, 'micro-managing the smallest details was part of Pol's conception of leadership. A firm hand, with no sharing of power. He wanted to monopolise everything.'

Over time, this tendency became more pronounced.

In theory, meetings of the Standing Committee were conducted on the principle of democratic centralism or, as it was rendered in Khmer, 'the collectivity decides; the individual is responsible for implementation'. In practice, Khieu Samphân said, from 1976 on, Pol decided alone:

> He would listen impassively and with immense patience to detailed reports from lower-level officials. . . . He liked to hear the views of many different people . . . The more information the better. He would retain whatever was relevant to the problem at hand, and work out an initial hypothesis, which he would keep to himself. When he had refined it and reached a conclusion which satisfied him, he would make his decision, which then became irrevocable. Afterwards he would call a meeting [of members of the Standing Committee], explaining the problem before them in such a way that, without anyone realising it, the discussion was orientated towards the result he desired . . . After everyone had spoken, he would make the summing up – selecting points from their speeches which buttressed his position. He would relate these to a number of fundamental principles, including the Party's political line and the dialectical rule that all things are linked and exist in relation one to another. Then he would announce the decision, making it appear that everyone had contributed to its formulation. There was no vote. It was stated: 'The collectivity has decided.'

Imperceptibly, Pol slipped into the role that his position as Premier required. He gave his first interviews to communist journalists. He chaired cabinet meetings. When Mao died in September, Pol delivered the memorial speech. In Sopheap, who heard him speak at Party meetings, was struck both by his personality and by the cultural roots on which he drew:

> Pol Pot liked to talk about his ideas. Whether he was a 'great communicator', I don't know . . . But in any case, he spoke well. He was very Khmer . . . He could find the words that went to your heart, that touched every fibre of your being. To Europeans, his way of reasoning may have seemed outlandish. But for Cambodians, it worked . . . When he spoke he hardly moved . . . He never raised his voice. It's a very Cambodian way of behaving . . . He was serene, like a monk. For a monk, there are different levels. At the first level, you feel joy. And it's good. Then there's a second level. You no longer feel anything for yourself, but you feel the joy of others. And finally, there's a third level. You are completely neutral. Nothing moves you. This is the highest level. Pol Pot situated himself in that tradition of serenity.

Elizabeth Becker of the *Washington Post*, who saw him two years later, also found him 'not what I expected . . . His gestures and manner were polished . . . Not once, during a violent [diatribe], did he raise his voice or slam his fist on the arm of the chair. At most he nodded his head slightly, or flicked his dainty wrist for emphasis.' When he spoke to Khmer audiences, he usually carried a fan, emblematic of the monkhood.

The formation of the new government marked the end of one phase of the Cambodian revolution – the 'national revolution', when the Khmers Rouges had been allied with more moderate groups – and the beginning of another, the 'socialist revolution'. The goal now was to make a leap – 'an extremely marvellous, extremely wonderful, prodigious leap' – into full communism.

This was not what Zhou Enlai had advised. It was not what Mao's successors, Hua Guofeng and Deng Xiaoping, thought best for Democratic Kampuchea. But realism has never been the strongpoint of Khmer politics. Sihanouk spent his life insisting that his country was not 'minuscule'. Lon Nol dreamed impossible dreams of restoring a Mon-Khmer Empire.

Belief in Angkor as the eternal reference point of Cambodia's glory and the imperative need to deny that it was a small, poor country that had to accommodate powerful neighbours were not Pol Pot's inventions: they were rooted in the Cambodian psyche. Self-absorption and self-aggrandisement mutated into self-deception. In Pol's case, the almost supernatural ease with which the Americans had been forced to flee Cambodia exacerbated the problem. The fact that the US had been bent on getting out of Indochina whatever the cost, and that Sihanouk and Lon Nol, during their years in power, had so crushed all domestic opposition that by the time the Khmers Rouges arrived no moderate alternative remained, was ignored. 'In the entire world,' Pol proclaimed in July 1975, 'no country, no people and no army has been able to drive the imperialists out to the last man and score total victory over them. Nobody!' Not only was this wholly untrue – the Vietnamese, whose help Pol categorically denied receiving, had achieved a victory a hundred times more impressive – but it bespoke a degree of hubris that was riding for a fall.

To Pol, Democratic Kampuchea was an island of purity 'amid the confusion of the present-day world', 'a precious model for humanity' whose revolutionary virtue exceeded that of all previous revolutionary states, including China:

The standard of the [Bolshevik] revolution of November 7, 1917, was raised very high, but Khrushchev pulled it down. The standard of Mao's [Chinese] revolution of 1949 stands high until now, but it has faded and is wavering:

it is no longer firm. The standard of the [Cambodian] revolution of April 17 1975, raised by Comrade Pol Pot, is brilliant red, full of determination, wonderfully firm and wonderfully clear-sighted. The whole world admires us, sings our praises and learns from us.

Another Central Committee study document asserted: 'Not using money, prohibiting markets, using a supply system to meet people's needs . . . the world never thought of such policies before. This new line has successfully resolved the . . . contradiction between town and country, an intractable problem that mankind has been wrestling with for centuries.' A Khmer Rouge song portrayed Democratic Kampuchea as 'a place of pilgrimage'. If Cambodians could defeat imperialism, Radio Phnom Penh declared, 'all people, including the American people, will certainly achieve victory'.

Underpinning this vision of a new global revolution was the idea that the other Marxist-Leninist parties in the region were poised to follow Cambodia's lead. This was not, at the time, far-fetched. In the mid-1970s, the West was being battered by the effects of the oil shock and world communism was at its apogee. Thirty-two nations, more than ever before or since, were ruled by Marxist or pro-Marxist regimes. Singapore's tough-minded Prime Minister, Lee Kwan Yew, remembered: 'The communists were on the ascendant, and the tide looked like flowing over the rest of South-East Asia'.

Over the next two years, Pol and Ieng Sary courted communist leaders from Burma, Indonesia, Malaysia and Thailand, and officials of the East Timor Liberation Front. Several parties, including the Indonesians, sent groups for military training in Democratic Kampuchea. The Thais, in whom Pol placed particular hope, were permitted to build bases along the two countries' common border. When, in October 1976, the Thai army seized power in a bloody, right-wing coup, sending hundreds of Thai students fleeing to join the communist insurgency, the Cambodians were not alone in thinking that another domino was about to fall. A leading American specialist wrote that the Thai revolutionaries had 'growing capability . . . To a great extent the future of Thailand now rests in their hands.' With hindsight, such a judgement seems absurd. But to many Thai intellectuals, as well as Western scholars, that was how it looked at the time.

The idea that Democratic Kampuchea was a model for revolutionaries elsewhere had as its corollary the view that the Cambodian revolution was genetically original. Like the chiliastic movements of medieval Europe, each of which was seen as 'an event of unique importance, different in kind from all other struggles known to history, a cataclysm from which the world [would] emerge totally transformed and redeemed', Cambodia was undertaking 'a revolution without precedent'. In Pol's words:

> We do not have any preconceived model or pattern of any kind for [our] new society . . .
>
> The situation is completely different from other countries. We are not con-fused, as they are . . . Ours is a new experience and people are observing it. We do not follow any book.

Ieng Sary went further, telling an interviewer in 1977: 'We want to achieve something that has never occurred before in history.' To do so, he said, the Khmers Rouges eschewed theories but 'relied on [revolutionary] con-sciousness and carried out the struggle in a practical way'.

That raised the question of whether Cambodian 'communism', in the fully developed form it assumed after mid-1976, could be considered Marxist-Leninist at all. 'Certain [foreign] comrades,' Pol acknowledged, 'take the view that our Party . . . cannot operate well because it does not under-stand Marxism-Leninism and the comrades of our Central Committee have never learnt Marxist principles.' His answer was that the CPK did 'nurture a Marxist-Leninist viewpoint', but in its own fashion. To some extent this was true. Party members studied texts on dialectical materialism, the dictatorship of the proletariat and other Marxist concepts. But the Cambodian Party had never been an integral part of the world communist movement – until 1975, its only foreign contacts were with China, Vietnam and Laos – and it took from Marxism only those things which were consonant with its own world-view. Socialism, to Pol, was a means to an end, a way of making Cambodia strong, 'of defending the country and preserving the Kampuchean race forever'. His ideological soul mates were not Stalin or Mao, but the sixteenth-century Englishman Thomas More, the Hébertistes of the French Revolution and the utopian socialists of nineteenth-century Russia, whom Lenin had castigated as 'the carriers of a reactionary petty bourgeois ideol-ogy [promoting] stagnation and Asiatic backwardness'. The difference was that Pol had power and could put his ideas into effect.

In the summer of 1976, the Khmers Rouges were at last in a position to strike out on their own.

There was a change of style. Democratic Kampuchea had a new name, a new leader, a new government, a new self-image. The desire to win acceptance from the rest of the world yielded to a sentiment that others would have to accept the regime on its own terms.

The previous spring Pol had insisted that the parliamentary elections be 'carefully prepared . . . so that our enemies cannot criticise us'. He had instructed Hu Nim to organise radio broadcasts of campaign meetings with peasants, workers and soldiers, and interviews with candidates, to prevent the foreign press claiming the procedures were undemocratic. It was a charade. As Pol himself acknowledged, 'This isn't a capitalist election; we apply proletarian class dictatorship.' The only area in the country to have multiple candidates was Phnom Penh, where Sihanouk and Khieu Samphân cast well-publicised votes. Everywhere else there was only one name on the list, and in many, though not all, areas, 'new people', having no political rights, were not allowed to take part. When the new parliament convened some weeks later, the fiction continued. Radio Phnom Penh announced that the deputies had met for three days to discuss the composition of the government before solemnly voting it into office. In fact, they met for three hours; there was no discussion and no vote. But the public façade was there to show the outside world the trappings of a proper state. The same was true of most of the public meetings which the Khmers Rouges claimed to have held over the previous two years. The Second FUNK Congress in February 1975; the Special Congress in April, which supposedly created a commission of 1,200 members to elaborate the new constitution; the Third Congress in December which approved that constitution – all existed only on paper. They never met, at least not in the form that was claimed. They were simply press releases, dreamed up to give a semblance of normalcy to a minimalist regime.

From mid-1976 onwards, that changed. For all practical purposes the legislature, the executive and the judiciary, to the extent that they had ever existed, fell into disuse. Parliament, which was supposed to hold two sessions a year, never met again. Cabinet meetings ceased. Ministerial portfolios were left vacant. Two years later, only half of the sixteen government posts were still filled. The pretence was over. Power resided where it had always been: in the hands of the CPK Standing Committee and its Secretary, Pol Pot.

There was also a change of substance.

The first stage of the socialist revolution, which had begun in April 1975, had seen the establishment of village-level co-operatives throughout the country. In October the Standing Committee agreed to take the process a step further. Several villages were now to be linked in a single co-operative of 500 or 1,000 families, with the eventual goal of forming commune-sized units with twice that many people. At the same time, communal kitchens were organised. In practice, this 'unity of feeding', as the Khmers Rouges called it, meant that each family had to surrender its cooking pots and dishes, keeping only a kettle to boil water and a spoon for each family member. In parts of the Northern Zone and the

North-West, the new system took effect from December 1975. Elsewhere, notably in parts of the Eastern Zone, family meals continued until mid-1977. Sometimes neighbouring districts applied the new rules months apart. Villagers forced to eat communally on one side of a highway enviously watched their neighbours on the other side of the road cooking supper outside their huts. Like much in Khmer Rouge Cambodia, it all seemed to depend on the whim of the local cadres.

Communal eating quickly became one of the most detested aspects of life under the Khmers Rouges.

In theory it made things easier for all concerned. 'They have no need to cook,' Ieng Sary's wife, Thirith, enthused. 'They just do the work and then they come back and eat.' And some did see it that way. Laurence Picq, at B-1, felt that however disagreeable it might be at a personal level, communal cooking had great practical advantages. Some Sino-Khmer families, at a loss to fend for themselves in the countryside, found it less trouble. But everyone else hated it. The food supply sharply diminished, as the cooks pilfered provisions for their own use or for the village chiefs. The cohesion of the family, already under pressure, was weakened further. Women, in particular, felt it undermined their traditional role. The 'base people' lost their privileges: no longer could they get by with the produce of their fruit trees and the vegetable plots beside their houses because now, like everything else, these were communally owned. Their carts and oxen were seized. So were private grain stocks, fish-nets, bicycles and anything else which might set the individual apart from the mass. In many villages, the larger houses – which also often belonged to 'base people' – were dismantled to provide wood for the new communal dining halls, and uniform, smaller huts, barely big enough to sleep in, built in their place.

Communal eating, while intended to be the most egalitarian of policies, in practice deepened the divide between the 'haves' and 'have-nots' of the new society. Pol might inveigh against 'authoritarianism, mandarinism, show-off-ism, high-rank-ism' and 'lording it over the people', but as the radicalisation drive accelerated, all these phenomena increased.

In the countryside, those with power – the *chhlorp*, the soldiers, commune and district officials – ate separately and well. Some had four meals a day and personal cooks to prepare their favourite dishes. Railway workers and certain other privileged groups were given special rations of meat and rice. At the Foreign Ministry, senior officials also benefited from a separate regime. Still more pampered were the 'elders', the regional leaders who came to B-1, accompanied by servants and bodyguards, before being sent abroad as Democratic Kampuchea's first ambassadors. Laurence Picq, with all the naïve innocence of her May 1968 Parisian radicalism, was scandalised by their behaviour:

> They all had quantities of suitcases, boxes and trunks . . . [in contrast to] the rest of us, who had had to give up everything we possessed . . . In the kitchen, despite the penury of supplies, the cooks prepared special dishes for them. [Sometimes] they deigned to put in an appearance. But in general . . . they preferred to eat among themselves. They had real feasts, with chicken, sucking pig, wine and sticky rice . . . and each morning, one of their bodyguards would go to collect freshly baked bread, that was made for the foreign diplomats, to bring for their breakfast . . . During the day, [the wives] went rummaging in abandoned houses and came back with fine clothes, silk underwear and bric-à-brac which they said were for the co-operatives. One day I overheard them discussing what they could get for some jewels they had found. It was a strange world . . . These people lived a life apart, in a style beyond anything one could imagine in a country so puritan and poor. Dinners, excursions, parties, liquor – and first choice in whatever plunder was going. Like the conquerors they were, they never went without.

At the highest level, everything was available. Thiounn Mumm recalled how at Vorn Vet's headquarters 'there was always a basket of fresh fruit on the table. I never ate better in my life.' When an aide's wife was pregnant, Son Sen's wife Yun Yat sent round a gift of pears. Sihanouk remembered the Central Committee commissariat providing 'Japanese biscuits, Australian butter, French-style baguettes, ducks' eggs . . . and succulent Khmer crabs', together with locally-grown tropical fruits, 'oranges from Pursat, durians from Kampot, rambutans and pineapples'. When Ieng Sary returned from a trip to the UN, he brought with him a hamper of foie gras and Swiss cheeses. All the leaders grew fat. Contemporary photographs show Pol and Nuon Chea looking bloated. Khieu Samphân put on weight and acquired an unhealthy, reddish complexion.

In the countryside, meanwhile, the ideological thumbscrews were being tightened still further.

Foraging, which had helped many villagers avoid starvation in the first year of Khmer Rouge rule, was now denounced as a manifestation of individualism and banned on the grounds that it would result in some having more than others. For the same reason, local officials refused to allow villagers to fish, or to kill the monkeys and wild boar that raided their plantations.

Picking a coconut without authorisation was an anti-revolutionary act. Ieng Sary had a Foreign Ministry official dismissed for doing so. Fruit that fell to the ground should be allowed to rot, rather than be gathered for individual use. 'That belongs to Angkar,' the soldiers would say as they forbade anyone to touch it.

From the summer of 1976 onward, children above the age of seven were separated from their parents to live communally with Khmer Rouge instructors who taught them revolutionary songs and assigned them light tasks in the fields – much as earlier generations of Cambodian children had gone to live as Buddhist novices at a *wat*. Parents were not allowed to discipline their children. That right, too, belonged to Angkar on behalf of the collectivity, not to the individual.

Yet among the revolutionary elite, 'familyism' and 'siblingism', as Pol called them, grew apace. Ieng Sary was one of the worst offenders, systematically placing his children and nephews in high posts for which they were unsuited. Son Sen, on the other hand, behaved with a rigour matching the severity of his image. As highly placed a man as Nuon Chea, the number two in the regime, authorised his mother, a devout old lady who lived near Battambang, to keep a Buddhist monk, almost certainly the only practising bonze in the country, to recite the sutras for her. Even more striking was an experience that befell Sihanouk one day when Khieu Samphân was accompanying him on a provincial tour.

> Suddenly our driver pulled over to the side of the road and stopped to let past another vehicle . . . We were in the company of the Khmer Rouge Head of State, which should have meant we had an absolute right of way. Who, then, was this other person, in a car flying not just a pennant but a large red flag of Democratic Kampuchea, to whom even a president had to give way? . . . To my astonishment, I saw a woman in her 60s, with greying hair, and a small boy, perhaps a grandchild, beside her . . .

The Prince never did work out the passenger's identity. She was Pol's (and Ieng Sary's) mother-in-law.

At less exalted levels, cadres' positions in the hierarchy were reflected in the quality of the *kramas* they wore, silk or checkered cotton; or the number of pens in their breast pocket. Commune secretaries had bicycles; district secretaries, motor-bikes; regional secretaries and above, cars.

Other human longings also tarnished the immaculate, selfless existence to which Khmer Rouge ideology aspired. At a time when husbands and wives were supposed to show no public sign of affection and even to stand several yards apart, local cadres seduced attractive young women and then executed them for moral turpitude. One girl turned the tables on her accuser, claiming that she had also had intercourse with two other village tyrants. She was killed, but so were they. Her fellow deportees regarded her as a heroine. As in China and North Korea, the revolutionary art troupes which put on propaganda performances were a source of nubile young women.

They enjoyed special rations, and in a country deprived of any other form of entertainment, were the equivalent of film stars. Tiv Ol, the handsome young Deputy Information Minister, fell from grace after his superior, Hu Nim, learnt that he had been 'caressing the breasts and vulvas' of the Ministry's performing artists. Nuon Chea, who was consulted, recommended taking no action. But Nim insisted, saying the incidents were too widely known simply to be brushed aside. Thiounn Thioeunn remembered a woman hospital director being executed for procuring nurses to work at a clandestine brothel for Khmer Rouge cadres.

Such abuses occur in all countries with dictatorial systems where privilege depends on power and no checks and balances exist to ensure a minimum of social justice. It is a characteristic not of communism but of tyranny, whatever its political colour.

But in Democratic Kampuchea the contrast was so flagrant that it became a caricature. Not only did a tiny, cosseted elite preside over the destinies of a nation of slaves. But the regime which that elite imposed made ideological purity, abstinence and renunciation, material detachment and the repression of the ego, the foundations of national policy, outweighing all other considerations.

The ban on foraging was not an oversimplification by uneducated local officials. It was approved by the national leadership in Phnom Penh. When the choice was between allowing starving people to feed themselves, and observing absolute egalitarianism (in the process letting food go to waste), the regime chose egalitarianism. It may be argued that this was an aberration, that the leadership never envisaged the ban being enforced in districts where there was hunger. And it is true that Pol spoke often of the need to raise living standards. In August 1976, he exhorted regional leaders to recruit good cooks, 'so that no one can criticise the notion of collectivism, saying that the food . . . made collectively tastes bad . . . If they make tasty food, people's stomachs will be full.' Revealingly, however, his concern was not that, if collectivism failed, people would be discontented, but that individualism would re-emerge. He certainly knew that, in some areas, there was acute privation – detailed reports from the Zone leaders arrived on his desk each week – but either he did not wish to think about it or he regarded it as unimportant.

This was not an exception: it was the rule. Whenever ideological principle and practical benefit came into conflict, principle won out, regardless of the material cost.

The emptying of the towns had resulted in the abandonment of a capital stock of housing, commercial buildings and factories that represented a substantial part of the national wealth of one of the world's poorest countries. Pol had initially given instructions that 'the beauty of the towns must not be spoiled', but by late 1976, any thought that they would ever be repopulated had been definitively abandoned. Visitors to a saltworks at Kampot found '5,000 young girls and women . . . living in makeshift barracks, [while] in the town only half a mile away hundreds of well-preserved houses stood empty'. The past had been repudiated and was never to rise again. The leadership spoke of rebuilding every rural village in the country within ten years, so that the peasants' individualistic, wooden homes, each slightly different from the other, would be replaced by a uniform, small, model, family dwelling, identical from one end of Cambodia to the other. Similarly the traditional rice-paddies, small plots which followed the topography of the terrain, were to be levelled and amalgamated into square one-hectare fields, grouped in units of a hundred, in perhaps unconscious imitation of the checkerboard pattern utilised at the time of the Angkorian kingdom, five hundred years before. Like many Khmer Rouge innovations, the giant fields had mixed results: they were easier to irrigate and plough, but harder to make level, which is essential for rice cultivation.

This 'irrational radicalism', as a Yugoslav visitor called it, permeated the entire economy. Cars, including Mercedes and other luxury vehicles, were cut in two by village blacksmiths: 'the metal . . . was melted down to make ploughshares; the motor was adapted to drive a water-pump; the wheels were attached to ox-carts'. Often there was no petrol for the pump and no oxen for the cart, but no matter. Pin Yathay, formerly Sihanouk's Director of Public Works, watched a convoy of wagons being pushed by teams of men, taking goods from the coast to the interior. As the radicalisation drive gathered speed, autarky was the watchword. Mechanisation was increasingly disdained. In Pol's mind, it was a sign of weakness, of lack of confidence in the peasants' strength.

Intellectual resources were squandered too. Doctors, schoolteachers, lawyers, mechanics, airline pilots, electricians, merchant seamen, even factory workers – all, with few exceptions, ended up working in the co-operatives as labourers, if they survived at all.

Two hospitals in Phnom Penh, headed by Thiounn Thioeunn and his long-time partner In Sokhan, treated senior leaders and foreign diplomats. Central Committee members often went for medical treatment to China. Khmer Rouge cadres in the provinces had access to Western medicines, as did some other privileged groups. The rest of the population relied on rural clinics, where untrained nurses administered intravenous drips of coconut juice, vitamin injections, and pills containing a herbal remedy against malaria. The school system was in a similar state. Ping Sây and two colleagues were put to writing revolutionary textbooks for the day when secondary education would begin. But that day never came. In the cooperatives, former students taught children the rudiments of literacy and arithmetic for a few hours a week, but even that depended on the attitude of the village chief.

Technicians from the 'old society' were not trusted and therefore not employed. Ieng Sary told the Chinese Ambassador, Sun Hao, in the spring of 1976: 'Our principle is to use qualified people to run the factories. But it is a very difficult problem, because, as well as being technically qualified, they must also have a revolutionary background. Our enemies know this, and try to infiltrate their agents.' Shortly afterwards the Standing Committee approved the sending of half a dozen intellectuals to work in industrial enterprises. More followed during the summer. But by September the leadership had had second thoughts and they were all withdrawn. A Central Committee directive warned:

> We must heighten our revolutionary vigilance [towards] . . . professors, doctors, engineers and other technical personnel. The policy of our Party is not to employ them . . . [Otherwise] they will infiltrate our ranks each year more deeply . . . For the workers of the old regime, we [also] do not employ them any longer [unless] we know their background quite well.

Pol's answer was to recruit and train young people, whose minds were judged to be ideologically pure. Children barely into their teens were brought in from the countryside to become factory workers, radio operators, photographers and seamen. It was not a complete answer. In practice, some of the old technicians had to be kept on because the factories would not run otherwise. But the regime's aim in the long term was to eliminate them altogether.

In the new Khmer Utopia, everything, material or spiritual, that was contaminated by the past, had to be jettisoned so that a new and more beautiful world could emerge. The key which would unlock this radiant future was not technology, but political consciousness:

> Is the possession of technical skills a result of education and culture, or does it come from the stance of socialist revolution? It comes from the socialist revolution.

> By cultivating good political consciousness, we can all learn swiftly . . . Formerly to be a pilot required a high school education . . . [Now it takes three months]. It's clear that political consciousness is the decisive factor . . . As for radar, we can learn to handle it after studying for a couple of months . . . We can also learn about navigating ships . . . We can learn anything at all, and we can learn it fast.

These were the beliefs Pol had developed in the 'liberated areas' ten years earlier. If people could only develop the right mentality, the rest would follow. Like all metaphysical theories, it was an article of faith. Ideology was primary. Everything else took second place.

In line with Pol's injunction to 'build and defend' the new Cambodia, the nation's efforts were now devoted entirely to two linked goals: strengthening its military capability, which was being achieved through massive aid from China (a singular exception to the rule of self-reliance, justified on the grounds of necessity); and the building of a vast network of irrigation channels to expand the area under rice cultivation. 'With water we have rice,' went a Khmer Rouge jingle, 'with rice we have everything!' (or, in a later, more ominous version, 'with rice we can make war!').

Irrigation had been the basis of the prosperity of Angkor, and both Sihanouk and Pol Pot wished to emulate that achievement. It is certain, moreover, that if Cambodia is ever to prosper, a nationwide irrigation system is indispensable. Sihanouk spoke endlessly about the need 'to master water resources', but most of his schemes remained on paper and those which were implemented often failed because of poor planning. The Khmers Rouges achieved more, at vastly higher human cost, but the absence of technical expertise meant that the results were uneven. A huge dam in the Eastern Zone, 800 yards long and 40 yards wide, on which 20,000 people had laboured for five months, was successful in preventing flooding during the exceptionally heavy rains of 1978. But later, after the regime fell, it collapsed, like many others, for lack of maintenance. 'Major dams were constructed on the same principles as small ones across streams,' one worker recalled. 'They were built without the use of theodolites or other instruments and by men with little or no technical training . . . Practical knowledge gained on the job, through trial and error, was prized above anything to be found in books.' Often a dam would be built, would then collapse, and finally, at a second or third attempt, would hold. A vast reservoir in the north-west, built by joining up three mountains, failed completely because each year the enormous volume of water coming down the hillsides swept away the retaining walls. The idea itself was sound: the mountain basin could have been the centre of an irrigation network covering hundreds of square miles. But the machinery and know-how for such an immense project were lacking.

There will probably never be a final verdict on the pharaonic labours the Khmers Rouges undertook. All that can be said for certain is that their irrigation system was an improvement on that which had existed in Sihanouk's day.

Why, then, at a time when the number of people working on the land was larger than ever before, was there so little rice that, in less than four years, a million Cambodians died of malnutrition or related diseases?

This is one of the central mysteries of the Khmer Rouge period. The generally accepted explanation – that famine ensued because huge quantities of rice were exported to China to pay for arms shipments – was concocted by Vietnamese propagandists for their own political purposes and replayed unthinkingly by Western academics. It is wrong. China – along with Vietnam itself, France, the United States and Thailand – shared the moral responsibility for the tragedy that enveloped Cambodia. But rice exports, whether to China or elsewhere, were not a material factor. Ieng Sary acknowledged at the time that, contrary to the regime's hopes, there was no exportable grain surplus in 1975 or 1976. The following year, some tens of thousands of tons of rice were sold to Madagascar, Senegal and Singapore, a fraction of the annual exports of 200 to 400,000 tons during the Sihanouk period. In 1978, Cambodia hoped to export between 100 and 150,000 tons of rice to China, but the contract was never fulfilled. Apart from rubber, wood and ingredients for traditional medicines, no other natural produce was exported either. Singapore offered to buy processed fish from the Tonle Sap, but the deal fell through after the Cambodians pleaded 'problems with logistics'.

The truth lay elsewhere.

The root of the problem was that the co-operatives produced less than the regime and most outside observers believed. This was, in part, because the younger and stronger men and women spent much of the year in mobile brigades building irrigation works rather than tending their fields – with the result that, even if the rural population as a whole had increased (by the addition of urban deportees), the effective manpower had diminished. China experienced a similar shortfall and an even more terrible famine in the late 1950s, when part of the rural population was diverted to running backyard iron furnaces. But more important was the lack of motivation. Even under intense pressure, slaves work less well than free men. Again the Chinese experience is salient. When, in 1980, Deng Xiaoping introduced what was termed the 'household responsibility system', allowing peasant smallholders the responsibilities and rewards of growing their own produce instead of working collectively, China's grain harvest shot up by 40 per cent. In Cambodia, the peasants endured a reverse transition from total free enterprise to a system without incentives of any kind. Overseers may have been able to enforce a daily quota for moving earth, but they could not control the quality of transplanting, the application of fertiliser, the depth of ploughing or any of the thousand-and-one other things that determine the final yield. During the Khmer Rouge years, probably between a third and a half of the population was sick, hungry or both, and in no state to work hard. The rest, while physically capable, had every reason to do only the minimum their guards would let them get away with.

How much the co-operatives really harvested in Democratic Kampuchea is uncertain. No reliable statistics were kept. Some specialists have guessed around 60 per cent of the pre-1970 crop, or 1.5 million tons of rice a year, others somewhat more, but they may all have been too optimistic. What is sure is that many rural cadres, fearing punishment if they admitted low yields, claimed to have fulfilled or over-fulfilled the three-tons-per-hectare target and, on that basis, the state assessed its levies to supply the army and administration, and to rebuild the strategic reserves which had been run down in 1975. The inevitable result was that rice poured out of the countryside into state granaries in the towns, leaving starvation rations for perhaps 40 per cent of the rural population.

To Pol, the rural penury was incomprehensible.

In all his public statements, he set out a Utopian vision of uninterrupted progress. In Democratic Kampuchea, everything was for the best in the best of all possible worlds. He spoke of 'outstanding successes' in eradicating illiteracy and malaria and 'solving the agricultural problem'; of an educational system where children, adults and old people 'study full-time day and night'; of rural clinics, staffed by devoted nurses, with twenty beds for every hundred families; a guaranteed food supply for every citizen of 312 kilograms of rice a year; and even, humourlessly, of the progress of 'a seething mass movement to collect and produce natural fertiliser'.

It was the ideal, not the reality. Yet Pol certainly believed that, under his leadership, Cambodia was heading towards those goals. How, then, was it possible that, as he acknowledged at a closed meeting of Party leaders at the end of 1976, serious food shortages existed in three-quarters of the country's communes? If 'political consciousness' was the key, if human will-power, rightly harnessed, could accomplish anything, such failures should not happen. 'This is our fault,' he told them. 'The problem stems from personal factors within the Party . . . [Our] revolutionary stance and consciousness are not yet strong . . . The line must seep in everywhere until it is effective.'

The notion that the line might be wrong, that Kampuchea's 'model for the world' might be fatally flawed, that ends and means, ideology and practice, were in such total opposition that the system would eventually implode, that radicalisation, far from being the answer, was making every problem worse, was not even considered. The solution, Pol determined, was to be still more thorough and intransigent. 'There are people in charge,' he declared, 'who question the stance of independence-mastery and self-reliance . . . This is a shortcoming . . . If we solve . . . this problem everywhere, we will be able to advance.'

The stage was being set for a witch-hunt. The next act of the Cambodian tragedy was about to commence.

11

Stalin's Microbes

ON SUNDAY, FEBRUARY 25 1976, a series of explosions ripped through the centre of Siem Reap, blowing up a munitions depot. Two days later, the Standing Committee announced that American aircraft had made two bombing runs over the town, five hours apart, killing fifteen people and destroying a number of buildings. Protest meetings were held in Phnom Penh and elsewhere. In March, the Swedish Ambassador, Kaj Bjork, was taken with other visiting envoys to inspect the damage. Mr Bjork prudently declared that he was not sufficiently versed in military matters to know whether what he was being shown was a recent bomb crater.

His caution proved justified. Years later, Ieng Sary acknowledged that there had been no bombing. 'There was an uprising,' he said. 'The bomb craters were old. They dated from the war.'

Ever since the Khmer Rouge victory the previous April, there had been isolated minor revolts. At Koh Kong, in the Western Zone, a dissident Khmer Rouge regional chief had gathered a force of three hundred men and was carrying out small-scale attacks from bases along the Thai border. Pol's one-time commander, Prince Chantarainsey, held out for a time in his old fiefdom in the mountains of Kompong Speu until he was killed in an ambush near Kirirom. More serious were a spate of village rebellions by Cham Muslims protesting against Khmer Rouge insistence that they abandon their religion and culture, notably in the district of Krauchhmar, on the Mekong in the Eastern Zone. But none of this went beyond the low-level insurgency that had plagued all Cambodian governments, including Sihanouk's, during their first years in power.

Siem Reap was different. Pol suspected that highly placed army officers might have been involved. Above all he was uneasy because it proved impossible to establish who was responsible. Two weeks later, the regional secretary, Soth, told the Standing Committee: 'We still cannot find the root of [this] event.'

Other untoward developments soon followed.

At the end of March, Hu Nim informed Pol of a scandal involving Koy Thuon, the former Northern Zone Secretary who was now Minister of

Commerce. Thuon, like his friend the disgraced Tiv Ol, liked women. In the early 1970s, he had established a revolutionary arts troupe to provide young female companions for the pleasures of his bed. After the Khmers Rouges took power, Thuon arranged for one of his ex-girlfriends to be married off to a cadre named Long. This was afterwards said to be a manoeuvre to detach Long from another girl, whom Thuon himself now fancied. The young man was furious and, in revenge, spread stories about the Minister's conduct. When Koy Thuon learnt of this, he had Long killed.

To Pol, this raised serious questions. Thuon's behaviour went against everything the revolution stood for.* Siem Reap was in the Zone he used to head and Soth was a long-time associate. Could Thuon have been implicated in the Siem Reap 'event'? On April 8, the Minister was placed under house arrest at K-1, the former Bank Buildings where Pol had made his headquarters. Another Northern Zone veteran, Doeun, the Director of the Central Committee's General Office, was appointed to act in his place. Soon evidence emerged that Doeun had been privy to Thuon's activities and might have covered up for him. In the hothouse world of Democratic Kampuchea, it began to look as if there were a Northern Zone conspiracy to overthrow the regime.

Six days before Koy Thuon's arrest, another puzzling event occurred.

At about 4 a.m. on April 2, a grenade exploded outside the Royal Palace. Because Sihanouk's bedroom had air-conditioning, he heard nothing. But the explosion woke the palace staff. Khieu Samphân told Long Nârin and the Prince's major-domo, Chhorn Hay, that it had been an assassination attempt. What he did not say was that, under torture, the soldier who allegedly threw the grenade claimed to have acted on the orders of two officers of the 170th division, which was garrisoned just north of the palace. They were arrested on April 12 and implicated, in turn, the former division commander – the flamboyant ex-monk Chan Chakrey – and another Eastern Zone leader, Chhouk, who headed Region 24 on Cambodia's southern border with Vietnam.

Pol had had doubts about Chakrey for some time. The previous autumn he had brought him to Phnom Penh to work in the General Staff Office

---

* Koy Thuon's removal from the position of Northern Zone Secretary in May 1975 and his appointment as Commerce Minister, a less powerful post, suggests that Pol already distrusted him. His philandering may have been one reason; he may also have been blamed for the débâcle in Kompong Thom in 1974, when 40,000 'base people' fled the 'liberated areas' to take refuge with Lon Nol's forces. In later years it became the rule that whenever a provincial official was suspected of disloyalty, Pol's first step was to detach him from his local power base and bring him to Phnom Penh to work in one of the ministries.

in order to deprive him of command responsibilities. After the grenade incident, he was sidelined completely.

In May 1976, Cambodian and Vietnamese negotiators held talks in Phnom Penh to try to reach agreement on delineating their common border. The meetings were intended to pave the way for a summit in Hanoi to sign a border treaty.

But the atmosphere had changed since the last summit between the two countries nine months earlier.

The Cambodian leaders were still determined to avoid provoking Vietnam. Nuon Chea told the Standing Committee that spring that the guiding principle remained 'to prevent the situation getting bigger'. In the North-East, the Zone Secretary, Ney Sarann, instructed local troop commanders 'to solve the problem politically, not by bloodshed'. But the Cambodians also made clear that there were limits beyond which they would not be pushed around. 'Kampuchea will never allow any imperialist, small or large, near or far, to invade its territory,' Khieu Samphân declared in a speech on the first anniversary of Cambodia's 'liberation'. When the text of his remarks was read out at a celebratory meeting in Paris a week later, the Vietnamese representative conspicuously refused to applaud. The reference to an imperialism that was 'small' and 'near' was too blatant to ignore. More ominous – though the Vietnamese would not learn of it for another year – was the Standing Committee's decision in March to declare that the CPK had been founded in 1960 and not, as Vietnam insisted, in 1951.

This was not the arcane matter it might seem. If the CPK dated its foundation to 1951, it acknowledged Vietnamese paternity: the PRPK, which Nguyen Thanh Son had midwived that year, was entirely a Vietnamese creation. If the founding Congress occurred in 1960, it was an authentic Cambodian Party, created by Khmers without Vietnamese participation. Pol was right, both historically and politically: 1960 *was* the Party's birth date. But for the Cambodians to repudiate in this way the Vietnamese father figure was a bone in Hanoi's throat.*

The border talks failed and the summit was postponed. In public, the Cambodians redoubled their protestations of friendship. In private, confidence nosedived. Even before the meetings, the Standing Committee had been worrying about the possibility of an assassination attempt if the

---

* The persistence of Vietnamese feeling over this issue was shown a few years later, when one of Hanoi's first moves, once it had installed a more accommodating Cambodian government, was to change the date of the Party's foundation back to 1951.

summit were to take place – a preposterous idea, but one which reflected the paranoia that had gripped the Cambodian leadership. Now they started asking themselves how much longer they should continue with what felt more and more like a strategy of appeasement.

Ostensibly the problem concerned the sea border. The Cambodians were willing to accord *de jure* recognition of Vietnam's ownership of the offshore islands, a concession which Sihanouk had always refused. But Vietnam also sought changes to the maritime border itself, giving it an additional 130 square miles of seabed off the coast of Kampot. It later emerged that they thought the area might contain oil. But there were no valid grounds for the claim, and when the Vietnamese negotiators persisted, the Cambodians concluded that Vietnam was behaving as the neighbourhood bully. 'What this is really about,' Ieng Sary declared, 'is our conception of honour. Do we want to be Vietnam's lackeys, or not?'

Outwardly relations remained cordial. Friendship delegations exchanged visits. In July 1976, when Vietnam was reunified, the Cambodian leaders sent effusive congratulations. Scheduled air services began between Phnom Penh and Hanoi. Pol himself described the two countries' friendship as 'a strategic question and a sacred feeling'. In the face of such warmth, whatever anxiety Hanoi may have felt about the border issue was laid to rest. Vietnam 'deemed it necessary to have patience' with Democratic Kampuchea, a Vietnamese minister explained. Le Duan himself declared that friendship with Cambodia and Laos was 'the primary and basic content of Vietnam's foreign policy'.

It was all a smokescreen. The ardour of Pol's professions of goodwill was matched by his misgivings about Vietnam's intentions.

In mid-April, China's Vice-Premier Zhang Chunqiao, one of the ultra-radical 'Gang of Four' headed by Mao's wife, Jiang Qing, had paid a secret visit to Phnom Penh. He came to see for himself the policies Pol was applying and to reassure Beijing's closest ally that the political turmoil in China, which had culminated the previous week in the sacking of Deng Xiaoping, would not affect relations. Their discussions were reflected in a speech Pol made at the beginning of June, subsequently publicised throughout the Party, where, for the first time, he addressed the issue of internal enemies. In it, he used a political vocabulary strikingly similar to that then being employed by the Chinese leftists against Deng:

> There is a continuous, non-stop struggle between revolution and counter-revolution. We must keep to the standpoint that there will be enemies 10 years, 20 years, 30 years into the future . . . Are [these enemies] strong or not? That does not depend on them. It depends on us. If we constantly take absolute measures, they will be scattered and smashed to bits.

At the present time, he declared, the internal enemies 'have no big forces'. So long as the Party remained strong, they could do nothing. But if Cambodia were to weaken, it would risk attack not only from within, but also from without. 'Outside enemies are just waiting to crush us,' he said. 'Enemies of all kinds want to have small countries as their servants.' The allusion to Vietnam was transparent.

On May 19, the day after the Vietnamese delegation returned home, Chan Chakrey, the Eastern Zone general who had fallen under suspicion, was detained, followed over the next two months by six others.

Unlike Koy Thuon, who was treated with kid gloves through most of his confinement, Chakrey and his companions were taken straight to S-21, the regime's new security prison, which had been set up that winter in a disused secondary school at Tuol Sleng in the southern part of Phnom Penh. S-21 was the responsibility of the Defence Minister, Son Sen, who in turn answered to Nuon Chea. It was initially headed by an army offi-cer, but early in 1976 François Bizot's former jailer, Deuch, took over. Deuch was still the same true believer he had been when Bizot knew him, five years earlier, and carried out his task with a mixture of fanatical devo-tion and schoolmasterly precision. Chakrey was his first high-level pris-oner. He was interrogated under torture for four months and, in nearly a thousand pages of confessions, described a fanciful plot to assassinate Sihanouk and the CPK leadership. He also confirmed the accusations against the Region 24 Secretary, Chhouk, who was arrested on August 28. The latter implicated the Eastern Zone Secretary, So Phim, and three other veteran leaders: Ney Sarann, Keo Meas and Non Suon.

Chhouk's confession marked a watershed. For the first time a serving Central Committee member had charged other members of the leadership with treason.

Like all such documents from S-21, it was of little intrinsic value in itself. Pol was not so foolish as to put faith in statements extracted under torture. So Phim, who over the next year or so would be accused more than a dozen times of seeking to overthrow the regime, was left at liberty. Pol's former cook, Moeun, now married to Pich Chheang, the Khmer Rouge Ambassador to China, was accused of betrayal eight times because she had once been part of Koy Thuon's network. Pol ruled that the charges should be ignored. 'If Moeun is a traitor,' he said, 'then everyone is.' In the Foreign Ministry, it became a rule of thumb that a cadre fell under suspicion only after being denounced three times. Later, as the purges accelerated and the number of denunciations rose exponentially, the figure was increased to five.

The purpose of S-21 and the confessions it generated was not so much to provide information as to furnish 'proof' of treason which would then justify purges that the leadership had already decided to carry out.

By the time Chhouk was arrested, an insidious linkage had begun forming in Pol's mind between opposition at home and enmity abroad. Vietnam, he concluded, was bent on undermining his regime 'the way that weevils bore into wood'. Some time that summer, probably in July, he had discussed his concerns with Nuon Chea and Son Sen, the other two members of the ultra-secret Security Committee responsible for the suppression of internal dissent. Shortly afterwards, Sen told divisional commanders to prepare 'to deal with enemies buried within the country as well as with those without'. Those 'living in the warmth of the Party', he warned, were the most dangerous of all. The same month, Pol began emphasising the need for military preparedness against Thailand and Vietnam. They were 'lying in wait, looking for opportunities to make trouble', he said. 'Every day they are making plans to destroy us.'

Security was tightened in Phnom Penh. Army units were ordered to route radio messages through the General Staff HQ instead of communicating with each other directly. Soldiers were forbidden to carry weapons 'or anything which might be mistaken for a weapon' at meetings attended by Party leaders. A purge of 'no-good elements' was launched within the military.

But unexplained incidents continued.

In September, shots were fired near the palace and tracts attacking the regime were found scattered in the streets. A mastermind was at work, Son Sen declared:

> These leaflets were made here in Phnom Penh. They were made in official workplaces like division and regimental offices and ministries . . . The conflicts are getting sharper . . . The actions [of our enemies] are becoming so provocative that [we must expect them] to attack us without delay . . . We must get rid of those we suspect!

On September 20, Ney Sarann was detained and taken to S-21. Keo Meas followed. They were accused of conspiring with Chhouk to create a new, Vietnamese-backed 'Kampuchean Workers' Party' whose goal was to bring down the regime and install a revisionist government allied to Hanoi. No such party had ever existed, as Pol very well knew. But from then on membership of the phantom 'Workers' Party', like membership of the CIA or the KGB, became a portmanteau crime to which real and imagined adversaries were forced to confess.

Over time, the supposed conspiracy ramified. It was claimed that soldiers had been sent to assassinate Pol and Nuon Chea at the National Day meeting in April 1976, but that the plot had failed because the would-be assassins did not recognise their intended victims (or, in an alternative version, because their weapons had been discovered when they tried to enter the meeting place). Pol's driver allegedly tried to poison him by putting DDT in his drinking water. A second poisoning attempt was foiled when a guard tasted Pol's food and died. In the end, the regime claimed to have 'documentary proof' – meaning confessions extracted under torture – of no fewer than six bungled attempts on Pol's life.

Many years later Ieng Sary admitted that none of it had been true. 'There were no coup attempts,' he said. 'It was all greatly exaggerated. In Pol's mind, there were serious incidents. But in fact they were a pretext – a pretext for a crack-down.'

The crack-down was necessary, Pol believed, because those Party leaders who 'think that the socialist revolution is too deep and too extensive [and] . . . that class struggle is unnecessary', were the same men who doubted the necessity of resisting Vietnam – in other words, who advocated compromise with Cambodia's external enemies. The two attitudes were 'yoked together', he declared.

In simple language, moderates were traitors.

The convulsions within the Party were kept a tightly guarded secret. When, for the first time, Son Sen mentioned the arrests of Ney Sarann and Keo Meas at a meeting with senior army officers in October, he warned them: 'This matter must not get out. Don't let it become known at the lower levels.' Pol spoke of an 'uncompromising, bitter, life-and-death struggle' against class enemies 'who furtively steal their way into and hide themselves in our revolutionary ranks', and warned ominously that it would continue 'long into the future'. But it was not until December, in an address to Central Committee members and senior provincial leaders, that he spelt out the extent of the problem and his plans to deal with it:

There is a sickness inside the Party, born in the years [of struggle] . . . Because the heat of the revolution [at that time] was insufficient . . . we searched for the microbes without success . . . [Now], as our socialist revolution advances . . . we can locate the ugly microbes . . . If we scratch the ground to bury them, they will rot us from within. They will rot society, rot the Party and rot the army . . .

The string of traitors that we smashed recently had been organized secretly during [the years of struggle] . . . In the socialist era, [such people] must be cast aside.

1976 was a year of furious, diligent class struggle . . . Many microbes emerged. Many networks came into view . . .

> Sometimes there is no active opposition. There is only silence . . . We
> should ask: are there still treacherous, secret elements, buried inside the
> Party, or are they gone? According to our observations over the last 10 years,
> it's clear they're not gone at all . . . They have been entering the Party con-
> tinuously . . . They remain.

The language was pure Stalinism. Pol was harking back to his reading as a
student in Paris. Stalin, too, had compared his opponents to 'an ulcer in a
healthy body', and had described the cure to be applied: 'to be victorious
we must, before all else, purge the Party and its leading headquarters'. The
first step, he added, was 'the meticulous verification of the life histories of
all Party members'. Pol also now decreed: 'Everyone must be verified
accordingly, and the Party will be stronger.'

On September 9 1976, Mao Zedong died. Cambodia declared official
mourning, and at a memorial meeting just over a week later, Pol Pot
revealed for the first time that Angkar was a Marxist-Leninist organisation.
It was intended as a first step towards the public announcement of the
CPK's existence, long urged by the Chinese, which was to take place on
the anniversary of the Party's foundation at the end of the month. This
year's anniversary would be celebrated not as the 25th but the 16th, in line
with the Standing Committee's secret decision the previous March to date
the Party's establishment from 1960. But the campaign against 'traitors'
made Pol think again. Publicising the Party's existence would entail dis-
closing its new birth date, which would not please Hanoi. With an anti-
Vietnamese purge under way, this was not the moment to be openly
provocative. Accordingly, urgent messages were despatched on the eve of
the planned celebrations, ordering that they be put on hold. Finally, on
October 11, nearly two weeks later than usual, a scaled-down anniversary
meeting took place. The Party marked its sixteenth birthday as planned.
But its existence, and its new history, remained secret.*

---

*One aspect of this Byzantine affair remains to be elucidated. In late September or early
October, the journal *Revolutionary Youths* published an article marking the anniversary which
– in violation of the Standing Committee decision in March – took 1951 as the year of the
Party's foundation. Shortly afterwards *Tung Padevat* appeared, containing a text of Pol's
speech at the October 11 meeting, in which he not only affirmed 1960 as the Party's birth
date, but explained: 'We must arrange the history of the Party into something clean and
perfect in accordance with our stance of independence-mastery.' The conventional explanation that the discrepancy reflected a power struggle between Pol and Keo Meas is plainly
wrong. As we now know, Pol had complete control over the content of both journals, and
neither Keo Meas (who had been under surveillance ever since his return from Hanoi, fifteen months earlier) nor anyone else could have used them to criticise his leadership.

Amid these events it was announced that, 'because of ill-health', Pol had resigned as Prime Minister and Nuon Chea had taken his place. The resignation was effective from September 20. Four weeks later, Ieng Sary also dropped from sight.

If this was a diversionary manoeuvre intended to confuse Hanoi, it succeeded brilliantly. A jubilant Le Duan informed the Soviet Ambassador that Pol and his brother-in-law had been removed from power. They were 'bad people', he said. 'Nuon Chea is our man indeed and my personal friend.' The Soviets evidently believed him, for in Moscow Leonid Brezhnev referred favourably for the first time to 'the path of independent development [of] Democratic Kampuchea'.

It just went to show how out of touch the Vietnamese had become. Several more months would pass before Hanoi realised that Pol was not only still in power but carrying out a merciless purge of every potential Vietnamese sympathiser he could find.

The day after the Party's delayed anniversary, October 12, Cambodia, like the rest of the world, began to receive reports of astounding developments in Beijing. A few days earlier, Mao's successor, Hua Guofeng, had secretly arrested Jiang Qing, Zhang Chunqiao and the other members of the so-called 'Gang of Four'. Ieng Sary heard the news in Belgrade on his way back from the United Nations. The Yugoslav diplomat who briefed him remembered that the colour drained from his face. 'It can't be true,' he muttered. 'They are good people.' Pol was outwardly less concerned. China, in his view, had a strategic interest in Cambodia which was independent of ideology. None the less, he preferred the Left. Two weeks earlier he had personally drafted a congratulatory message to Hua on China's National Day, which attacked by name the disgraced reformist Deng Xiaoping, as 'anti-socialist and counter-revolutionary'. Common to both Pol's and Ieng Sary's appreciation was the fear that political turmoil in China would weaken Cambodia's ties with its only powerful ally at the very moment when relations with Vietnam were poised to go sharply downhill. The Khmer Rouge Foreign Minister was sent post-haste to Beijing to seek assurances from the new leadership that relations would remain unchanged.

In November 1976, Pol himself followed. The visit, like most of his journeys to China, was secret. Hua was waiting at the state guesthouse to

---

With hindsight there seem two possibilities. Either it was a simple mistake: the staff of *Revolutionary Youths*, unaware of the change of date, prepared a routine article on the anniversary which Pol or Nuon Chea approved unread. Or it was a deliberate attempt to persuade the Vietnamese, who had access to *Revolutionary Youths* but not to the restricted 'Five Flags' edition of *Tung Padevat*, that it was business as usual in Phnom Penh.

greet him, and in an effusive speech of welcome, congratulated him on having stripped the enemy's defences from Phnom Penh in April 1975 'like peeling a banana'.

Their talks covered both military co-operation and political ties. Afterwards Pol's delegation, comprising Vorn Vet, Ieng Sary, the North-Western Zone Secretary, Ruos Nhim, and the head of the Central Committee General Office, Doeun, set out on a provincial tour which took them first to the Great Wall – where they shivered memorably in the cold of the North China winter – and then on a pilgrimage around the country's revolutionary sites. From Shanghai, where the Chinese Party had been founded, they went to Yan'an, the communist headquarters during the civil war, and to Mao's birthplace in Hunan. By the time the visit ended, Pol's confidence in his Chinese ally had been confirmed. Only then did Radio Phnom Penh inform the Cambodian people that Hua had been appointed Party Chairman and that the 'counter-revolutionary Gang of Four anti-Party clique' had been resoundingly smashed.

In December Pol summoned the Central Committee for its annual plenum, preceded by a study session. The relationship between Cambodia and Vietnam, he told the delegates, was 'a constant, antagonistic contradiction'. Full-scale military conflict was not yet imminent. But the time had come to begin 'long-term preparations both for a guerrilla war and for warfare using conventional forces'. Military bases should be readied in remote areas, and urban deportees moved out of border districts and replaced with 'base people' who were more reliable.

The Defence Minister, Son Sen, conveying the same message to the army, was blunter:

> Before Vietnam was our friend, but 'a friend with a conflict'. Now it has become our real enemy. Before we did not know their plans clearly – but now we know for sure that they have established traitorous parties to fight against us. In future, they will do something else. They won't stop . . . This is the conflict between correct and fake revolutions . . . between the standpoint of independence and that of being a lackey.

By this stage the purges were generating a self-perpetuating cycle of suspicion and fear in which each new victim who disappeared into the maw of Tuol Sleng produced new 'evidence' of Vietnamese perfidy which fuelled new purges and new victims.

The Hanoi leadership did not help its own cause. The Vietnamese Party's Fourth Congress that month approved a resolution calling yet again for 'the preservation and development of the special relationship [with] Laos and Kampuchea' so that, as it put it, the three Indochinese states 'will forever be associated with one another in the building and defence of their respective countries'. The overtones of limited sovereignty, whether intentional or not, could not have been better chosen to raise Cambodian hackles.

The meat-mincer ground on. In the first half of 1976, four hundred people entered S-21. In the second half, more than a thousand. By the spring of 1977, a thousand people a month were being 'smashed'. Stalinism has its own logic. In Democratic Kampuchea, it was given free rein.

Nothing illustrated better the ghastliness of Pol's regime than S-21 and its associated institutions in the provinces. Not because of what they were – all totalitarian regimes torture and kill their opponents – but because they represented in its purest form a doctrine of extermination.

The word recalls the practices of Nazi Germany, a parallel artfully underlined by the Vietnamese propagandists who, after the regime fell, turned Tuol Sleng into what is today the equivalent of a holocaust museum. But the analogy is false. The role of S-21 was not to kill but to extract confessions. Death was the finality, but it was almost incidental. The officials in charge, Son Sen, Deuch and the Head of the Interrogation Unit, Mam Nay, all former schoolmasters, brought neat, orderly minds to the organisation of their work. But for the barbed-wire netting, covering the façade to prevent suicide attempts, it might have been an office block staffed by bureaucrats processing industrial statistics.

In that sense, much about S-21 is depressingly familiar.

It was not just a totalitarian phenomenon. Democratic governments have also gone down that road. The French army in Algeria set up torture centres where conscripts martyrised suspected fedayeen and then killed them 'to maintain secrecy', exactly the same justification as was used in Democratic Kampuchea. Five thousand Algerian prisoners were killed in this way in one interrogation centre alone. In the country as a whole, the number of such deaths probably exceeded the 15–20,000 who died in S-21. The factors that led young, Roman Catholic Frenchmen to violate every principle of justice and humanity they had learnt since childhood were not essentially different from those that governed the conduct of S-21 guards. Both were told, in the Khmer phrase, to 'cut off your heart' – an injunction which, to a greater or lesser extent, applies to soldiers everywhere. Both were under pressure from peers. The French conscripts faced court-martial if they refused to carry out orders; the S-21 guards faced torture and death.

It may be argued that for Khmers it was easier: their religion cultivates indifference. However, S-21 had French carceral antecedents. The shackles used in its cells were inherited from French colonial times. The torture that the Khmers Rouges called 'stuffing prisoners with water' had been introduced to Indochina by the French army, which called it 'la baignoire' ('the bathtub') and used it on the Viet Minh in the early 1950s. If the French connection is easy to draw – Cambodia was, after all, a former French protectorate – other Western countries have little cause to crow. Experiments carried out in American universities suggest that a majority of human beings, American, British, German, or any other nationality, will agree, under suitable conditions, to inflict physical torture on others. At a conservative estimate, more than half of all UN member states have, or have had in the recent past, prisons resembling S-21. Democratic Kampuchea was not a fatal exception in an otherwise kindly world.

Yet S-21 was different in ways that set it apart from all other institutions of its kind.

In Stalinist Russia, in Nazi Germany, in countries like Argentina, Indonesia and Iraq, the death camps were monstrous aberrations, growing from the dark side of societies which in other respects appeared more or less normal and where those outside the concentration camp universe enjoyed certain basic freedoms.

Tuol Sleng was not an aberration.

Instead it was the pinnacle, the distillation, the reflection in concentrated form of the slave state which Pol had created. Thiounn Mumm's uncle, the ex-Issarak leader Bunchan Mol, had written years before the Khmers Rouges came to power:

> In a civilized society, people understand what justice is. In our Khmer society, we do not . . . We still like to follow the savage ways of ancient times. If a man is condemned, we kill all his relatives lest one day they take revenge . . . If we knock down an opponent, we beat him until he dies. Victory, to us, means that our adversary is dead. If he lives, it is not victory. That is our Khmer mentality.

S-21's role derived from this approach to political conflict. It stemmed from what a Cambodian historian has called a 'conquer-or-be-conquered' tradition in Khmer politics that can be traced back through the Sihanouk years all the way to Angkor, and which continues to the present day. 'In the ancient kingdom,' another former urban deportee wrote,

> people had been buried alive, their fingers, hands, noses chopped off. The dead were left in the street, or tossed into fields to be devoured by wild beasts. What had changed?

Confessions of treason were needed for men like Ieng Sary and Khieu Samphân to read out at closed Party meetings, proving that Angkar had 'as many eyes as a pineapple' and that nothing could escape its vigilance. The climate of fear this generated helped to unmask new 'traitors', who were then tortured to make them identify other members of their 'strings', the *k'sae* or patronage networks which were the basis of political activity in Cambodia.* If they were important leaders, their close relatives were located and killed. 'Had I been arrested,' Deuch said later, 'my father, my mother, my sisters, my brothers-in-law, my nephews, would have been arrested too. That's the way it was.'

In this looking-glass world, the smallest gesture became suspect. Laurence Picq, at B-1, remembered how on one occasion a high official named Roeun gave her a loaf of freshly baked bread:

> I got up without thanking her, because one wasn't supposed to thank people any more, and instead uttered the ritual formula: 'My greatest happiness is to serve Angkar wherever and whenever I am needed' . . . The bread smelt terribly good . . . But when I got back, I had doubts and I started to puzzle over Roeun's behaviour. What did she want? The whole thing stank. It was a trap . . . I put the bread in a cupboard and went on with my work, promising myself not to touch it until I knew more . . . The next day one of Roeun's servants brought me another loaf . . . I put it with the first . . . In the climate of pyschological warfare and the politics of hunger amid which we all lived, those loaves of bread carried the germs of a fantastic plot.

She never learnt exactly what had been behind it. But in January 1977, the former Northern Zone Secretary, Koy Thuon, after languishing under house arrest for nine months, was transferred to S-21. His old subordinates followed: Roeun's husband, Doeun – who, like Thuon, was a member of the Central Committee; Roeun herself; their long-time associate, Sreng, now Zone Deputy Secretary, and Soth, the Siem Reap leader. All confessed to being agents of the CIA.

---

* There is a crucial distinction between 'strings' and factions. Even in orthodox Marxist-Leninist parties, true factional activity is relatively rare. The 1957 'anti-Party Group' in the Soviet Union and the 'Gang of Four' in China are exceptions that prove the rule. From the 1930s, in Stalin's case, and the 1940s, in Mao's, no serious factional challenge was ever mounted to their power. To both men, 'factionalism' was a convenient label to damn those of their followers whose devotion appeared to be flagging. In Democratic Kampuchea, Pol never used even the label, and though sometimes he sought to portray purge victims as having engaged in factional activity, in reality Cambodian communist politics was played out on feudal lines. Individual leaders attracted retinues of followers and jockeyed for personal advantage, but they did not join together to form cliques. It was each man for himself, which made Pol's task far easier.

Meanwhile arrests of alleged pro-Vietnamese elements continued, among them Sien An, the former Cambodian Ambassador to Hanoi – who was accused of working for the French counter-espionage service, the SDECE – and Keo Moni, the former Issarak leader who in the 1950s had been Khmer Viet Minh Foreign Minister.

The day after Koy Thuon was brought in, the Minister of Public Works, Toch Phoeun, was detained. His arrest marked the start of a new sweep, this time against the so-called 'intellectuals', former members of the Phnom Penh underground and the left-wing student movement, including Doeun's deputy, Phouk Chhay, and the Information Minister, Hu Nim. They, too, were accused of working for the CIA. In fact, Pol had decided that they were too prone to compromise and therefore, at a time of tension with Vietnam, not reliable. Shortly afterwards a KGB 'string' was uncovered, allegedly led by Phouk Chhay's friend Hak Sieng Layni, who, like Keo Meas, was charged with having created a rival Khmer Communist Party, this time supposedly answering to Moscow.

These early purges set the tone for everything that followed.

All who were taken to S-21, whatever the reasons for their arrests, were forced into an identical mould. They had to confess to being either CIA, KGB, Vietnamese agents or 'other', a category which came to include French, East German and Thai intelligence, and Chiang Kai-shek's Guomindang in Taiwan. Foreigners were treated like everyone else. An unfortunate young British yachtsman named John Dewhirst, who had been arrested by the Khmer Rouge coast guard, confessed:

> My course at the CIA college in Loughborough, England . . . ran concurrently with my teacher training course . . . from Sept 1972 to June 1976. It was held on Wednesday afternoons, Saturday afternoons and Monday mornings . . . The principal was Peter Johnson, a retired CIA colonel. The college was housed in a building disguised as the Loughborough Town Council Highways Department Surveyor's Office . . . [It] was the smallest of the six CIA colleges in England . . . The others are at Aberdeen, Cardiff, Portsmouth, Bristol and Doncaster . . . Every Monday morning we would receive a lecture-seminar from Johnson on the role of the CIA as an anticommunist force . . . The lectures were really like indoctrination sessions . . . [We were] assigned spying jobs for the CIA and we had to report to CIA contacts . . .

Dewhirst's confession, like those of the dozen or so other Westerners – Americans, Australians and New Zealanders – who died at Tuol Sleng, is revealing for the light it sheds on the methods of the S-21 interrogators. Prisoners first told their life-stories factually. Afterwards they were made to embroider their initial accounts with supposed links with foreign intelligence agencies until their interrogators felt they had incriminated themselves sufficiently. Then they were killed.

Cambodian prisoners were subjected to the same pitiless routine, with equally far-fetched results. Koy Thuon and many others ended up claiming that they worked not only for the CIA but also for the KGB or the Vietnamese. Pol saw no contradiction in that. He regarded himself at the head of a regime surrounded by malign forces which, by their very nature, had to be working in concert. As Nuon Chea put it, there was 'joint action by the USA, the KGB and Vietnam . . . The Vietnamese . . . accept anybody who fights the CPK, even CIA agents.' It was a very Khmer way of looking at things: Sihanouk, when he was in power, made similar statements.

By April 1977, Pol felt able to proclaim that 'the enemy's leadership machine has been basically wiped out'. But the Standing Committee maintained its call 'to continue to purge and sweep away adversaries', and it was not until the autumn that Pol finally declared the purges at an end. By then, he said, five Central Committee members, four division commanders and countless lesser fry had been eliminated. This was 'a great victory' which had left the Party 'purified and strengthened'. He neglected to mention that no convincing evidence had been found that any of those purged had been traitors and that, in some cases, like that of Siet Chhê, who had accompanied him to meet Mao two years earlier, it would never be clear why they had been arrested at all. The macabre jingle, 'Angkar kills but does not explain', was as true at the summit of the Party as it was among the ordinary people.

The period from mid-1976 to the late autumn of 1977 saw Pol's experiment in utopian socialism reach its zenith, creating the conditions for its collapse.

All that year, the firestorm of terror with its epicentre at S-21 billowed out across the country, reducing to ashes thousands of Party cadres and hundreds of thousands of 'new' and 'old' peasants. In a broadcast on Radio Phnom Penh, Pol surmised that 'between 1 and 2 per cent of the population' was irredeemably hostile and 'must be dealt with as we would any enemy' – not a reassuring thought for people who had seen how the Khmers Rouges had treated their enemies two years earlier, at the end of the civil war. By August 1977, according to the CPK's own figures, four to five thousand Party members had been liquidated as 'bad elements' and 'enemy agents'.

The movement began in the Northern Zone and Siem Reap, where every 'string' reaching out from Koy Thuon and his associates was meticulously dismantled and replaced by forces loyal to Ke Pauk, who had Pol's confidence. When there were signs of resistance, Mok's troops were sent in from the South-West to help the new leadership establish itself. That set a pattern of intervention which would repeat itself whenever Pol sought to move against an incumbent Party network that he regarded as disloyal.

Soon afterwards Ieng Sary's wife, Thirith, the Minister of Social Affairs, led a delegation to the North-West. She came back shocked by what she had seen. Conditions in the area were indeed bad: with almost a million extra mouths to feed as a result of the influx of 'new people', they could hardly be otherwise. But Thirith's conclusion was calculated to stoke the regime's paranoia. 'Conditions there were very queer,' she said later. 'The people had no homes and they were all very ill.' The cadres pretended to follow Party policy, but in fact they undermined it by forcing people to work in appalling conditions. The only possible explanation was that 'agents had got into our ranks'. A report in such terms was – and was intended to be – music to Pol's ears. It confirmed his worst suspicions. 'Hidden enemies seek to deprive the people of food,' he told the Central Committee in December 1976. 'They [distort] our instructions and mistreat the people . . . forcing them to work whether they are sick or healthy.' For some months he took no action while Mok sent trusted village cadres and their families from the South-West to settle in the area, ostensibly as ordinary peasants but in reality to pave the way for a purge. Finally, in June troops from the Western Zone and the South-West followed. They began by systematically smashing the existing cadre networks at district and village level, executing the incumbents and replacing them with South-Western officials. Then, over the following six months, higher-level leaders were targeted. By the end of the year, the leaders of five of the Zone's seven regions, standing committee members from the other two and at least thirty more ranking officials were despatched to S-21 to make their confessions and be killed.

Other Zones were not spared either. During the summer, the Eastern Zone Party Congress asserted that, there too, 'lackeys of the Vietnamese' were 'trying to starve the people and make them suffer, so that they lose confidence in the Party'. In the first half of the year, it said smugly, 'hundreds of these traitors have been swept away'. In the Western Zone, where at that stage only minor purges had occurred, Nuon Chea told senior cadres that the first priority was 'revolutionary vigilance'; economic development came second.

Pol wanted to have his cake and eat it.

He wanted a clean, pure, absolute Party, from which all doubtful elements had been expunged, and, at the same time, to unite the whole population for the coming struggle with Vietnam. He wanted everyone to be well-fed, to work reasonable hours and to have three, four, or even five days off each month, so that they would be 'sharp and keen', yet at the same time he insisted that the three-tons-per-hectare target be met, no matter what the cost.

To the cadres who had to administer his policies, the choice was clear. Terrorised themselves, they responded by terrorising the population under their control. In a state which held that human will-power was capable of any feat, failure was equated with sabotage. If the choice were between improving the people's livelihood – as Pol urged – and, in consequence, failing to meet Party targets; or achieving those targets – as Pol also urged – at the expense of living standards, most officials preferred the latter. Since the introduction of communal eating and the ban on foraging, most people lived badly anyway. When there were so few carrots, all that was left was the stick.

From late 1976 onwards, and especially from mid-1977, Cambodia slipped back into the barbarism of its antique past.

Attempts to 're-educate' alleged offenders, never widespread under Khmer Rouge rule, were abandoned altogether, both at national level, in Phnom Penh, and in the countryside. The Standing Committee's decision a year earlier to vest the 'authority to smash' in the Zone leadership and above was quietly forgotten. In theory, district secretaries approved executions, but in practice death was meted out at commune or village level. The 'Forest in the West', as the execution ground was often called, became the punishment of first resort.

What happened at S-21, which was subject to central control, was abominable enough. When the senior interrogator, Pon, reproached his underlings for excessive violence, he had to explain that what he meant was 'beating prisoners to death, cutting open their arms, their backs and their penises.' Inmates were drained of their blood for use in the city's hospitals. 'They used a pump,' one guard remembered. 'They went on until there was no blood left in them and they could scarcely breathe. You could just hear this wheezing sound, and see the whites of their eyes rolling as if they'd had a fit. When they were through, the corpses were thrown into a pit.'

The medieval savagery of the jails in the countryside, where there were no constraints of any kind on the interrogators' actions, made even such horrors seem tame. Haing Ngor was taken to one such prison in the North-Western Zone after being caught foraging for food:

> We stopped at a collection of buildings I had never seen before, at a clearing back in the woods . . . Some wrinkled black objects hung from the eaves of the roof but I was too far away to see what they were . . . In the

afternoon, the guards brought [in] a new prisoner, a pregnant woman. As they walked past I heard her saying that her husband wasn't a [former Lon Nol] soldier . . . Later [an] interrogator walked down the row of trees, holding a sharp knife . . . He spoke to the pregnant woman and she answered. [Then] he cut the clothes off her body, slit her stomach and took the baby out. I turned away but there was no escaping the sound of her agony, the screams that slowly subsided into whimpers and after far too long lapsed into the merciful silence of death. The killer walked calmly past me holding the foetus by its neck . . . He tied a string around [it], and hung it from the eaves with the others, which were dried and black and shrunken.

Khmer Rouge peasant cadres, like the Issaraks before them, used *kun krak*, or 'smoke-children', as magic talismans. They extracted prisoners' gall-bladders for medicine. They ate the livers of those they killed. Denise Alfonso, a Franco-Vietnamese woman who lived in a co-operative near Battambang, saw a young man die in this way. In a housewifely touch, she noted that 'the human liver, cooking on the stove, made little jerks like frying pancakes'.

The leadership in Phnom Penh knew of such practices. They were mentioned in telegrams to Son Sen from officials in the provinces. There is no reason to think that Pol and other Standing Committee members approved. But nor did they do anything to stop them. The 'seething class hatred' of the peasants, however hideous the forms it might take, had to be assumed and embraced. It was the same attitude that had led Pol to glory in the bloodshed of the war – a perverted machismo which, behind his gentle smile, took pride in ruthlessness. S-21 was viewed in the same way. Neither Pol himself nor Nuon Chea ever went there. But to each it was an essential instrument of the revolutionary state. Pol himself decided on the most important arrests, sometimes in consultation with Khieu Samphân. Ieng Sary's Foreign Ministry served as an antechamber to the prison, where provincial cadres would be brought, ostensibly to be 'trained as ambassadors' before being taken off to their deaths.

The generalisation of violence, the intensification of ideological pressures and the development of a psychological climate in which virtually the entire population lived in constant fear, meant that, by 1977, the regime's natural supporters were growing disillusioned. Not only had the Khmers Rouges failed to win over the 'new people', they had lost the goodwill of the old. In many areas, even the poorest peasants, in whose name the revolution had been launched, felt they had been cheated. Instead of the three meals a day they had been promised, there was watery rice soup. Police reports quoted hostile slogans: 'Serve the socialist revolution and eat rice mixed with morning glory. Serve the communist regime and eat morning glory alone!' Despite the risks, the numbers attempting to flee to Thailand and Vietnam steadily increased.

By the spring of 1977, the Vietnamese leaders realised they had a problem on their hands.

The year had begun with renewed border clashes, the first for many months. In February, Hanoi sent a Vice-Foreign Minister, Hoang Van Loi, on a secret visit to Phnom Penh. He offered co-operation in repatriating Cambodian refugees fleeing the Khmer Rouge regime – a singularly cynical move when the Vietnamese were well aware that anyone sent back would immediately be killed – and invited the Cambodian leaders to attend an Indochinese summit with Vietnam and Laos. The proposal was immediately rejected. Pol concluded that his tough stance was paying off. The Standing Committee agreed that henceforward national defence rather than the economy should be the Party's first priority.

In March and April, clashes continued, provoking an angry exchange of diplomatic notes. By this time Hanoi had belatedly realised that the Cambodians were undertaking a sweeping anti-Vietnamese purge. Then, on April 30, the second anniversary of the liberation of Saigon, Cambodian units, backed by artillery, crossed into Vietnam in force, slaughtering hundreds of local inhabitants and razing their villages. In the words of the official Vietnamese record: 'Most barbarous crimes were committed. Women were raped, then disembowelled, [and] children cut in two. Pagodas and schools were burnt down.'

There is no reason to doubt the truth of this account. There had been similar atrocities earlier in the year on the frontier with Thailand, where sporadic fighting had resumed after a coup the previous October had brought a right-wing military government to power. If the Khmers Rouges butchered Cambodian women and children they would hardly treat their ancient enemies, the Vietnamese and the Thais, any better. But it was not quite the unprovoked carnage that Vietnamese propaganda reported. Internal CPK military telegrams, believable to the extent that they were never intended to be made public, listed fifteen clashes allegedly provoked by the Vietnamese from April 1 to 29 on the southern part of the border. That month, in a speech marking the anniversary of the fall of Phnom Penh, Pol denounced 'the land-swallowing Y[uon] and their running dogs', using the traditional pejorative epithet to describe the Vietnamese. Not long afterwards he told the Thai communist leader, Khamtan, that Vietnamese expansionism was 'totally different from that in Eastern Europe. There the Soviet Union dominates everyone. But at least the subject peoples still exist.'

Ill-founded or not, Cambodian fears were real. After two years in which both sides had tried to avoid a collision – the Cambodians because they wanted time to make their regime stronger, the Vietnamese because they expected to achieve their ends by political means – all their ancient hatreds abruptly reignited. For centuries, Cambodians had equated powerlessness with periods of Vietnamese control, and empowerment or 'independence-mastery', as the Khmer Rouge termed it, with times when Vietnamese were slaughtered. Now that once again conciliation had failed, the only choice, in Pol's view, was what one long-time American Vietnam-watcher aptly called 'the bristly dog gambit':

> Cambodia's hostile, if not aggressive, behaviour towards Vietnam and Thailand is not entirely irrational. Cambodia has tried various means [over the centuries] to fend off its enemies. Nothing has worked well. What is left is . . . seemingly irrational behaviour . . . The rule, as it is for a small dog surrounded by bigger, stronger dogs, is to bristle, assuming an aggressive posture and appearing so fearfully troublesome, so indifferent to consequences, as to convince others to leave well alone. [The gambit] may not work, but it holds as much promise to the Cambodians as any other.

Hanoi's response came in stages. First, the Vietnamese air force carried out bombing raids on Cambodian border positions. Then, on May 12, it proclaimed a 200-mile exclusive economic zone along the Vietnamese coast. Since the Cambodians had refused to make concessions over the sea border, the Vietnamese presented them with a fait accompli. Finally, four weeks later, the Vietnamese Party Central Committee wrote to its Cambodian counterpart, calling for high-level talks to end these 'bloody incidents'. The Cambodians proposed instead a cooling-off period and mutual troop withdrawals. There the political negotiations stalled. But cross-border shelling continued from both sides, and tens of thousands of civilians were evacuated from the frontier areas in anticipation of worse troubles to come.

At this point, other interests began to come into play.

Cambodia's situation was straightforward: it relied on China, which saw it as a barrier to the spread of Vietnamese power.

Vietnam's position was more complicated. Its economy was a shambles and it needed all the aid it could get. The Russians were already giving generously and were willing to give more, although the quality of what they offered was not always satisfactory. The possibility of American assistance – which Nixon had proposed after the 1973 peace accords – was blocked because Vietnam insisted that aid must come first, diplomatic relations second. That left China. Despite the fiasco of Le Duan's meeting with Mao in 1975, the Vietnamese had not entirely given up hope of further Chinese assistance. In the early summer, Vietnam's Premier Pham Van Dong travelled to Moscow, where extensive new military and economic aid was agreed, and then to Beijing. There he was received by Vice-Premier Li Xiannian, the economics specialist in the Chinese leadership. If he expected a softening of China's attitude, he was disappointed. Li's statement was a monologue for the prosecution. Vietnam, he said, had slandered China, hurt the friendship between the two countries, provoked armed clashes along their common border, sabotaged the rail link between them, created disputes over the ownership of islands in the South China Sea and the demarcation of the maritime border, and had compelled Overseas Chinese citizens to adopt Vietnamese nationality. He concluded, unsurprisingly: 'We are in no position to provide new aid to the Vietnamese comrades . . . so I am not dealing with this question.'

Pham Van Dong's visits to Moscow and Beijing in May and June 1977 fundamentally altered the international context in which the Cambodia–Vietnam conflict was played out. Over the next nine months, there would be moments of vacillation, as both sides tried to escape the consequences of the choices they had made. But the die had been cast. Vietnam had chosen the Soviet camp. China found itself with no alternative but to support its awkward Cambodian ally.

In July the Vietnamese sent their entire top leadership to the Laotian capital, Vientiane, to sign a Friendship Treaty formalising the 'special relationship' between the two countries. It pledged enhanced mutual assistance in national defence, confirmed Vietnam's right to station troops on Laotian territory and opposed 'all schemes and acts of sabotage . . . by foreign reactionary forces', the new epithet for the Chinese. To Beijing it was a warning to stay out of Vietnam's sphere of influence. To Pol, it was proof of what Vietnam was planning for Cambodia if the Khmers let down their guard.

The same week the CPK Eastern Zone Committee passed a resolution asserting that the conflict with Vietnam could 'never be resolved politically' and that preparations should be made to send troops deep into Vietnamese territory to 'annihilate them on their own ground'. After that, it declared, 'they will no longer dare invade our country.' Two new military commands were created in the areas bordering Vietnam: the Highway 1 Front, in the south, headed by Son Sen; and the Highway 7 Front, stretching from Kompong Cham to Ratanakiri, under So Phim, with Ke Pauk as his deputy. Cambodian commanders began telling their men that their ultimate goal was to recover 'Khmer Krom', the former Cochin-China, ancient Cambodian lands which they claimed Vietnam was occupying illegally. This was not official CPK policy, but it helped motivate the troops.

On the other side of the border, Vietnam's Defence Minister, Vo Nguyen Giap, ordered his forces to intensify their counter-attacks.

Of the three countries most directly involved, China appeared least happy at the turn events were taking. Foreign Minister Huang Hua told a closed Party conference in Beijing that the conflict between Hanoi and Phnom Penh was 'trouble for them and trouble for us . . . If our handling of it is not right, we will find ourselves in a dilemma.' Beijing informed all three Indochinese governments that it wished to see Cambodia and Vietnam stop fighting and return to the conference table. It promised not to take sides in the dispute and said it was ready to use its good offices if the parties so desired. However, it went on, it would oppose any attempt by 'revisionist social-imperialism' to infringe Cambodian sovereignty or invade its territory.

There matters remained until September 1977.

On the 24th of that month, a Saturday, when many of Vietnam's senior officers at the border had left to spend the weekend in Ho Chi Minh City, as Saigon was now called, elements of two Cambodian Eastern Zone divisions crossed into Tay Ninh province. They penetrated about four miles, leaving behind them the usual trail of horror. A journalist who visited the area three days later found 'in house after house, bloated, rotting bodies of men, women and children . . . Some were beheaded, some had their bellies ripped open, some were missing limbs, others eyes.' Altogether, according to Vietnamese officials, nearly a thousand people were killed or suffered serious injuries.

Three days later, on the 27th, Pol Pot addressed a rally at the Olympic Stadium in Phnom Penh, where he made the long-awaited announcement that Angkar was in fact the Communist Party of Kampuchea. The speech, which lasted five hours, was not broadcast until the 29th, by which time Pol was in Beijing at the start of his first, and last, official visit abroad.

The Vietnamese Politburo ordered a total blackout on the Cambodian attack and retaliation was put on hold. The VWP Central Committee congratulated the CPK on its public emergence, expressed 'deep gratitude . . . for [its] valuable support and assistance' to Vietnam and pledged to defend the 'special relationship' between the two parties and peoples. Then, on Friday the 30th, Le Duan chaired an emergency meeting of the Politburo in Ho Chi Minh City. It decided to take up the Chinese offer of good offices and to seek a meeting with the Cambodians while they were in Beijing. At the same time General Vo Nguyen Giap was instructed to make plans for a reprisal, should the mediation effort fail.

Pol had meanwhile been explaining to Chairman Hua his own idiosyncratic view of the conflict and how it might eventually be resolved:

> The nature of the Vietnamese army has changed. They're no longer willing to bear hardships and to suffer as they did before. Now they rely more on arms – artillery, tanks, aircraft. Their infantry isn't strong. Their soldiers and officers are degenerate, they don't want to fight any more. Most of those who've come from the North have found themselves a new wife in the South, sometimes two wives. Like that, how are they going to fight? . . . We are not afraid of doing battle with them. The problem is that they constitute a permanent threat. The Vietnamese have an expansionist policy towards South-East Asia. We tried to negotiate with them, but it was useless . . . From a strategic point of view, only the development of the revolutionary movement in South-East Asia will really solve this problem. Otherwise, the difficulties between Cambodia and Vietnam will go on for who knows how many centuries . . . We have united with the Burmese, Indonesian, Thai and Malaysian [communists] . . . and in the North we have China to support us . . . This is our strategic beacon.

Next day, when Hua replied, he tried to indicate tactfully how far-fetched China found this approach. Ignoring Pol's remarks about the South-East Asian communist parties – whose role the Chinese were beginning to play down – he proposed that Cambodia should instead strengthen relations with South-East Asian governments, which alone, he suggested, could offer real support against Vietnam. From China's standpoint, he went on, the best outcome would be a peaceful settlement:

> We do not wish the friction between Vietnam and Cambodia to grow. We want the two sides to find a solution through negotiations in a spirit of friendship and understanding, and by making mutual concessions. That said, we agree with Comrade Pol Pot that resolving the problem by negotiations will not be easy. With Vietnam, it is necessary to be very vigilant.

A few hours after this second round of talks, China received Vietnam's request to send an envoy to discuss the latest border tension. In the light of Hua's remarks, the Cambodians had little choice but to agree, and on October 3, Vice Foreign Minister Phan Hien had two lengthy meetings with Ieng Sary. They got nowhere. Hien accused the Cambodians of atrocities along the border. Sary retorted that Vietnam was trying to overthrow the Democratic Kampuchea leadership, and that it would have to stop its 'acts of aggression, subversion and sabotage' if it wished to reduce tension. As they were meeting, Pol told a news conference that an unnamed 'enemy' was 'trying to strike [Cambodia] from within and without'.

Next morning, he flew to Pyongyang where North Korea's President Kim Il Sung received him munificently and was outspoken in his support.

'Those people [the Vietnamese] are really wicked,' he declared. 'I am shocked that Vietnam wants to put its hands on the whole of South-East Asia.' This was easy for Kim to say. Unlike China, North Korea was far from Vietnam and risked nothing by taking such a stand. The Koreans appreciated Cambodia's plight. They, too, were surrounded by powerful neighbours. In public, Kim praised his visitors for 'thoroughly smashing . . . counter-revolutionary subversion and sabotage'. In private, he told Pol, 'we regard your victories as our own.'

The Vietnamese leaders were in a quandary. To launch a full-scale punitive expedition risked triggering a border war. To do nothing was impossible.

In the end, Le Duan decided to make one last attempt to obtain Chinese help. The day before Pol's departure for home on October 22, Deng Xiaoping – now back in power following the fall of the 'Gang of Four' – had told a Western reporter that China wanted Cambodia and Vietnam 'to carry out good negotiations. We ourselves do not judge what is just or erronous.' General Giap was authorised to launch limited raids into Cambodian territory – which he did in Svay Rieng in October and Prey Veng a month later – but not to initiate large-scale retaliation. On November 21, Duan arrived in Beijing to a welcome which, to outward appearances, was not noticeably different from that given Pol Pot eight weeks earlier. He, too, was met at the airport by Mao's successor Hua Guofeng, who accompanied him on the drive into Beijing, through streets lined by several hundred thousand people, waving Chinese and Vietnamese flags and chanting slogans of friendship. But the talks that afternoon were acrimonious, and in a vituperative speech at the welcoming banquet, Duan accused his hosts of abandoning communist principles.

The rift was now out in the open.

In mid-December, 50,000 Vietnamese troops, backed by armour and artillery, poured across the border along a front stretching more than a hundred miles, from the Parrot's Beak in Svay Rieng to Snuol in the north. In the first week, they met little resistance and penetrated about twelve miles into Cambodian territory. Khmer Rouge soldiers who fell into their hands were systematically killed. Reinforcements were then sent in from the South-West, and in some areas Giap's forces were forced on to the defensive.

At dawn on December 31, Radio Phnom Penh announced that Cambodia was breaking off diplomatic relations with Vietnam because of its 'ferocious and barbarous aggression'. The decision, which had been taken by the CPK Standing Committee a week earlier, was designed to cause maximum damage to Vietnam's image internationally by depicting it as an expansionist power, bent on subjugating its neighbours, while it was *in flagrante delicto* with tens of thousands of its troops physically on

Cambodian soil. Hanoi was taken totally by surprise. Until then, both sides had kept the conflict under wraps. Now not only was it public but the Cambodians had drawn the first blood. Giap had never intended more than a brief incursion, but under the glare of publicity his troops returned home more precipitately than might otherwise have been the case, the last men crossing the border on January 6. The Cambodians crowed victory. In fact neither side had much reason for satisfaction. Khmer Rouge casualties had outstripped Vietnamese by a margin of three to two. Yet far from forcing Pol to the negotiating table, Giap's campaign had left Phnom Penh more bellicose than ever.

The focus of the conflict now moved elsewhere.

In January 1978, the American Secretary of Defense, Harold Brown, flew to Beijing to begin putting in place a network of military contacts between the United States and China which by the end of the year would develop into a *de facto* alliance against the Soviet Union.

The same month, President Carter's National Security Adviser, Zbigniew Brzezinski, described the Cambodia–Vietnam conflict, inaccurately, as 'a proxy war' between the USSR and China.

None of those involved yet admitted, even to themselves, that two hostile coalitions were forming which were moving irreversibly towards a wider war: The Chinese, in particular, were reticent. But the battle lines set that winter – the Khmers Rouges, China and the US on one side; Vietnam and the USSR on the other – would remain immovable for the next decade and beyond.

In late January and the first half of February, the Vietnamese Politburo held a series of meetings in Ho Chi Minh City. Prodded by Le Duan and others in the pro-Soviet wing of the leadership, it drew two ominous conclusions. The first was that Vietnam could not continue to coexist with a hostile government in Phnom Penh. Steps would therefore have to be taken to overthrow Pol Pot's regime – either by fomenting an uprising or by creating an exile movement to act as a front for the Vietnamese army to launch a full-scale invasion – and this would have to be done quickly, before the Khmers Rouges grew stronger militarily and were able to broaden their international support. The second was that nothing good could be expected from Beijing. China, the Politburo decided, intended to use Cambodia to put pressure on Vietnam to return to the Chinese fold. In this Le Duan was wrong. Had he paid more attention to the visit then being made to Phnom Penh by Zhou Enlai's widow, Deng Yingchao, he would have realised that the Chinese were bending over backwards to avoid envenoming the dispute. Mme Deng's emphatic restatement of the need for a peaceful settlement so infuriated the Cambodian leaders that Radio Phnom Penh delivered a public rebuke. But just as the Khmers Rouges were now interpreting every Vietnamese action through a prism of ancestral hatred, so Le Duan's view of Beijing was distorted by atavistic memories of Chinese suzerainty and repression.

The result was to generate a series of self-fulfilling fears.

China's military aid programme to Cambodia, launched two years earlier, now appeared to Hanoi in a new and sinister light. Vietnamese military planners noted with alarm that the new military airport being built at Kompong Chhnang, with camouflaged hangars and munitions dumps burrowed into the hills, was less than thirty minutes' flying time from Ho Chi Minh City. Border clashes were becoming increasingly frequent, not just with Cambodia, but also on Vietnam's frontier with China. In March, a dispute broke out over the status of the million strong Overseas Chinese community in South Vietnam. Hanoi saw them as a potential fifth column and, to break their economic power, announced the nationalisation of all private business. China retaliated by suspending economic aid to Hanoi and pulling out Chinese technicians. By June, 130,000 refugees had fled across the Chinese border. The stage was set for one of the most egregious tragedies of the latter part of the twentieth century – the exodus of the 'boat people'. A quarter of a million emigrants, stripped of their possessions by the Vietnamese police, set out in floating coffins to seek a new life abroad. Tens of thousands drowned or were murdered by Thai and Malay pirates. The operation was approved by Le Duan himself. By the time it ended, the moral high ground that Vietnam had conquered in the long years of struggle against the United States was definitively lost.

By the early summer of 1978, the two principals in the drama that was beginning to unfold – Vietnam and China – had put their uncertainties aside and begun preparing in earnest for the inevitable dénouement.

The Vietnamese set up training camps for Khmer refugees at former US military bases in the south. Le Duan and Le Duc Tho had their first meetings with potential leaders of the future Khmer resistance. Son Ngoc Minh, who had headed the Cambodian Party in the early 1950s, had died after a stroke in 1972, but some of his colleagues had stayed on in North Vietnam and since been joined by Khmer Rouge cadres who had fled after 1975. All were relatively junior figures: Pen Sovann had worked for the FUNK radio station in the early 1970s before becoming a major in the Vietnamese army; Bou Thang was an Issarak veteran from the North-East; Hun Sen, a young Khmer Rouge military commander, had defected in the summer of 1977. But they were the only material available from which to create the nucleus of a future post-Khmer Rouge regime. An intensive programme of indoctrination was started, and in April, the first battalion of the future rebel army was commissioned.

Three months later in Beijing, the Chinese Politburo approved contingency plans to 'teach Vietnam a lesson' for its mistreatment of the Overseas Chinese. A discreet build-up of Chinese forces was ordered along Vietnam's northern border. Le Duan travelled to Moscow to strengthen ties with the Russians. As a token of its good faith, Vietnam joined the Soviet-bloc economic grouping, Comecon, a step it had until then avoided for fear of needlessly antagonising China and the United States. Soviet arms and military advisers began pouring into northern Vietnam to bolster Hanoi's defences against what were now described as Beijing's hegemonic designs. Chinese arms, including 130-mm artillery, anti-tank weapons, armoured cars and complete sets of infantry equipment for an additional 60,000 men, were shipped to the port of Kompong Som as Chinese engineers raced to complete the new, more secure railway line under construction from the coast to Phnom Penh. Belatedly endorsing long-standing Khmer Rouge claims, the Chinese accused the Vietnamese of seeking to extend their overlordship not only in Indochina but to all of South-East Asia. Brzezinski's 'proxy war' formulation had struck a chord in Beijing. Vietnam was 'the Cuba of the East', a stalking horse for Soviet ambitions, undertaking in Asia the same role that Castro's forces were playing in Africa and Latin America. Behind the Cambodia–Vietnam conflict lay a Kremlin plot to dominate the entire region. No longer was it merely a local dispute. The outcome would affect the global balance of power.

Much of this was as self-serving and false as Le Duan's judgement of Chinese intentions. But it, too, became an unchallengeable truth.

For the umpteenth time in Cambodia's tormented history, the paranoid miscalculations of its leaders meant that its fate would be decided not by its own people but by outside powers.

After General Giap's forces had withdrawn, Pol sought to redefine Khmer Rouge strategy. He proposed the re-establishment of a united front, so as to maximise support for the regime at home; stepped up diplomatic efforts to win public and political sympathy abroad, notably in the West; and approved an easing of domestic policy.

Pol had first raised these ideas almost a year before. 'We have to gather all the forces that can be gathered,' he had said. 'Even feudalists, rich peasants, capitalists or whatever, if they are with us, they are not with the enemy and this is to our profit.' At the time, that had remained a dead letter. But now, in 1978, it had become a necessity:

How do we gather forces? We do so in the same way as [during the civil war]. But now it is more meaningful, because we hold power throughout the country . . . We must win over the petty bourgeoisie, the small capitalists and the landowners . . . and pull them to our side [without] discriminating against them . . . Why do we need to do this? In order to isolate the enemy . . . At the present time, we must do whatever we can to minimise the forces of the enemy [and] expand our own forces [so that] the Party will be stronger, the people will be stronger, the armed forces will be stronger, and the economy will be stronger. We should not reject [any] force that will join with us . . . We must apply [this] line correctly.

As part of this process, Pol toyed with the idea of taking a higher personal profile. It was not something that particularly appealed to him, but the experience of both China and North Korea showed that a personality cult was a powerful tool to rally a nation behind its leader. In the winter of 1977, a group of artists was ordered to paint his official portrait and to sculpt busts of him in a variety of materials including silver. It seems none was ever displayed, and a revolutionary monument, 25 feet high, showing Pol in a heroic pose leading a group of peasants, which was to have been erected at Wat Phnom, also remained at the design stage.

The search for broader international support went in tandem with the united front at home. It had begun with Pol's visits to China and Korea. In November 1977, Burma's Ne Win had become the first foreign head of state to visit Phnom Penh. Others, including President Ceauşescu of Romania, followed. Initially, the Chinese played the main role in urging the Khmers Rouges to be more open in their dealings with the outside world. But by early 1978, Pol had become a convert. Democratic Kampuchea had 'great need of friendly countries', he declared. It would make every effort to 'unite with progressive and revolutionary forces the world over'. Khieu Samphân remembered the Standing Committee holding lengthy discussions on the subject. 'It was not a decision that we took lightly,' he said, 'but in the end everyone realised it was necessary.'

Measures were taken to improve relations with Thailand, where the extreme-right-wing military government had been replaced by a mixed administration led by General Kriangsak. A stream of Marxist-Leninist groups from Western Europe, Latin America, Australia and even the United States began pouring into Democratic Kampuchea on goodwill visits aboard the now weekly flight from Beijing. Friendship delegations came from Japan and Scandinavia. A handful of foreign journalists and academics travelled to Phnom Penh, first from Yugoslavia, then from the United States and Britain. Weekly tourist flights were started from Bangkok offering half-day visits to Angkor. The UN Secretary-General,

Kurt Waldheim, was invited to visit the following year, and Japan agreed that a Khmer Rouge Ambassador should present his credentials to Emperor Hirohito at the Imperial Palace in Tokyo, becoming prospectively the first major industrialised power to open relations with the Phnom Penh regime.

The conflict with Vietnam was not the only factor at work.

By 1978, Pol was forced to recognise that the Khmer Rouge system was functioning poorly. Officially the difficulties were blamed on 'wrecking' by internal enemies. But he himself acknowledged that 20 to 30 per cent of the population was still not properly fed and that, in some areas, people were starving. Over the next twelve months a series of measures were taken to make life more tolerable. Foraging and family cooking were permitted again. The regime took a hesitant, first step towards honouring its promises of a better diet by introducing a 'dessert day', three times a month, when rice soup sweetened with palm sugar was served. The ban on coloured clothes was lifted. The system of one day off in ten was reaffirmed and, in principle, made universal. Marriages were permitted for the first time between 'old' and 'new' people and, in the summer of 1978, the distinction between the two groups was abolished as the whole population was granted full political rights. As always, these changes were introduced unevenly, at the whim of local cadres. In many areas, conditions got worse rather than better in 1978. None the less, in the country as a whole, there was a trend towards greater tolerance, however imperfectly applied.

The same applied to matters of discipline. By 1977, execution had become the standard punishment, even for minor offences. Now Pol signed a Central Committee directive, laying down that only 'those who are absolutely hostile to the Party, the revolution and the people, [and] who refuse to repent' need be killed. All others, not 'absolutely hostile', including even those who had served the CIA, the KGB and the Vietnamese, were to be educated to 'mend their ways, achieve illumination and return to the bosom of the Party'. The new rules did not exclude further purges when the Centre so decided. But arbitrary killings decreased. The directive was to be discussed in every unit 'at least five or six times', the Central Committee decreed, 'so that everyone understands it completely'. An air-force officer, who returned that summer after two years' training in China, was told by friends: 'You're lucky. Things are much better now. Before, everyone was worried about being arrested. Now, if you do something wrong, even if you have an illicit love affair, you're demoted, but you survive.' The change of policy was also felt in the co-operatives, where the pressures on intellectuals – former students and professional people – noticeably eased. Local cadres were ordered to stop referring to themselves as Angkar: that term was for the organisation, not for individuals.

Attitudes towards intellectuals changed in other ways. The returned students who had been reforging themselves through manual labour in the countryside were brought back to Phnom Penh and told they would be found jobs in the ministries. A school was opened in B-1 to provide language and secretarial training for future Foreign Ministry cadres. Technical instruction, until then scorned as a mark of the bourgeoisie, made its appearance again in the factories. Thiounn Mumm was put in charge of a new National Technical College, with three hundred pupils, who were to be trained as agronomists, engineers and scientific workers.

Much of this had been prefigured in Pol's speeches and writings during the previous two years. But now it was being put into effect. It might be inspirational to claim that 'revolutionary consciousness' could accomplish anything, but not if, as a result, the country had to rely on Chinese experts. Even the decision to do without money, which the CPK leadership had vaunted as the regime's most original feature, was examined afresh. When Democratic Kampuchean delegations travelled abroad, they had to carry with them suitcases full of US dollars, the symbol of American imperialism. Was that independence? As relations with Vietnam deteriorated, and Cambodia developed trade ties with non-communist South-East Asia, Japan and Europe, the arguments in favour of a national currency became stronger. That spring, Pol told a group of Yugoslav journalists that 'we have ceased to use money up to now . . . [but] we do not take the present system as a permanent one'. Money and wages could be reintroduced if the practical situation required it. According to Khieu Samphân, Pol and Ieng Sary decided in the autumn that money should indeed be used again, but by then it was too late for the decision to be implemented.

The changes introduced from the spring of 1978 – more openness; greater tolerance; a bigger effort to win domestic support – were incremental and small-scale, but by comparison with a year earlier they were a sea change. However they were only one side of the coin. The same year Pol and Nuon Chea launched the biggest and most murderous purge since they had taken power. Tens of thousands of people were bludgeoned to death in prisons and on execution grounds, accused of having 'Vietnamese minds in Khmer bodies', the same charge that had been hurled at the Hanoi returnees five years earlier.

This dichotomy went to the heart of the system Pol had created. It could not exist without terror, even when its leaders were convinced that a more moderate approach was needed. The two were linked by a dialectic in which the massacre of suspected opponents and calls for fewer executions were seen not as diametrical opposites but as complementary halves of the same whole. In Pol's mind, the united front against Vietnam had to be offset by an all-round tightening of discipline within the regime itself – just as, in the early 1970s, the establishment of a united front under Sihanouk had been counterbalanced by stricter class criteria for the Party.

'Our slogans should be, "Purify the Party! Purify the army! Purify the cadres!"' he told a meeting of his colleagues in January. But now there was a crucial difference. In the early 1970s, the united front and the Party had been distinct. In 1978, the Party controlled everything. The front Pol wished to enlarge was composed of the same people that he wished to purge. The leadership had set itself on two divergent and incompatible courses.

Having approved the principle of the purge, the meeting went on to discuss the fate of the Eastern Zone, whose failure to resist Giap's forces had rendered it, in Pol's eyes, objectively treasonous. Both the East and the North-East, Pol declared, must be 'watched with great care'. Part of the population was unreliable because it was made up of 'opportunists' and 'people who follow the Vietnamese'. He did not explicitly criticise the Eastern Zone Secretary, So Phim, but instead pointed to weaknesses in Regions 21, 23, 24 and 25, adjoining the Vietnamese frontier, and to serious problems in the North-East, where he accused the Zone Secretary, Vy, of 'taking things too lightly'. The East was not the only area to be censured. Takeo province (Region 13) in Mok's South-Western Zone was reproached for 'mediocre organisation'. But it was the Eastern Zone troops who were the leadership's main concern. They showed a tendency to 'pacifism', Pol said, which 'prevents us from attacking the enemy effectively'. It would be necessary to send in Central cadres to 'keep a solid grip on power'.

That turned out to be the signal for village and district cadres from the South-West to move into the East, following the same procedures as in the North and North-West a year earlier. Local patronage 'strings', descending from the Eastern Zone and Regional leaderships, were systematically smashed and new 'strings', answering to Mok and his cohorts, installed in their place. At the same time 60,000 villagers were moved out of the border areas in the Parrot's Beak and the Fishhook – another tongue of land which juts into Vietnam further north, near the point where Kompong Cham and Kratie provinces meet – to create a heavily mined *cordon sanitaire* of scorched earth and deserted fields along the length of the Vietnamese frontier as far as Mondulkiri.

But the purge did not end there.

In March 1978, the Western Zone Secretary, Chou Chet, was arrested. He had been the last survivor of the old Pracheachon group. Then the remaining Hanoi returnees were killed, along with several dozen of their children, who had been held since 1975 at a special camp near Rovieng, in Preah Vihear.

From there, the wave of suspicion rolled over the North-West. In a carbon copy of what had happened a year earlier, local cadres were accused of starving the people in order to turn them against the regime. But this time the North-Westerners were ready. When Mok's South-Western cadres moved in, the old village leaders resisted. In many areas, the new-comers were unable to impose their authority. The former system, which had relied on a monopoly of terror, was compromised. Each commune, each district, was now divided against itself.

But the worst of the self-inflicted blows the regime suffered that spring occurred in the East, where Pol's attempts to galvanise So Phim's forces had failed to produce the results he had hoped for. By the end of March, he had reached the conclusion that the root of the problem was the Eastern Zone Secretary himself. Phim was in poor health, and spent April and the beginning of May in hospital in Phnom Penh. During his absence, the Central Zone military commander, Ke Pauk, who was his deputy in the Highway 7 Front Command, was ordered to undertake a sweeping purge of the Eastern Zone military and civil administration. By April 20, more than four hundred Eastern Zone cadres were being held in Tuol Sleng.

Pol and Nuon Chea then called Pauk to the capital where they showed him 'documents' purporting to prove Phim's treason. Among them were the confessions Chou Chet had made under torture, accusing him of con-spiring with Vietnam and plotting a *coup d'état*. On Pol's instructions, Pauk returned to the Highway 7 Front HQ in Kompong Cham and began summoning the commanders and political commissars of the Eastern Zone divisions and regional brigades to 'meetings', where they were dis-armed and detained. The more important among them were sent to Tuol Sleng, the others killed on the spot. Around the middle of May, when So Phim returned, Pauk summoned him to a 'meeting' also. Phim angrily refused. 'I am the President of the Highway 7 Front,' he replied. 'What right does the Deputy President have to call me to a meeting? It should be the reverse. What does this mean?' Instead, he sent a bodyguard to find out what was going on. The man did not return. Two other emissaries, including Phim's nephew Chhoeun, also disappeared without trace. Finally, on May 23, Phim despatched Pol's old protégé Sok Knaol, now Director of the Eastern Zone Office, to confront Pauk directly. He, too, failed to return.

At that point, Phim concluded that Pauk was out to destroy him.

But he still refused to believe that Pol was responsible. Even two days later, when Pauk's forces crossed the Mekong and began closing in on his headquarters, Phim thought that his deputy was plotting to usurp the authority of the Standing Committee.

On the 28th, he set out for Phnom Penh, accompanied only by his family and bodyguards, to seek a meeting with Pol to try to set matters straight. When they reached the east bank of the Mekong, opposite the capital, they were attacked by Son Sen's forces and So Phim was wounded in the stomach. He managed to escape, taking refuge in the forest of Srei Santhor, north of Phnom Penh. But six days later, his hideout was surrounded. That night Phim shot himself. His wife and children were captured as they were preparing his body for burial in accordance with the Buddhist rites. They, too, were killed.

For the next two months, surviving Eastern Zone units staged hit-and-run attacks against the combined forces of Pauk, Son Sen and Mok. So many thousands of Eastern Zone soldiers were sent to Tuol Sleng that it was unable to cope with the influx. The S-21 chief, Deuch, remembered Nuon Chea issuing instructions that 'there was no need to interrogate them, just smash them'. Deuch was displeased. 'No such order had ever been received before,' he noted. 'Nor were we used to working in that way.' But the killings at Tuol Sleng were as nothing compared to the massacres that took place among the civilian population. A short time before, Radio Phnom Penh had spoken of the need to 'purify . . . the masses of the people', a significant addition to Pol's original formula which had called merely for a purge of the Party and the army. If an Eastern Zone village was suspected of aiding the rebels, the inhabitants were slaughtered. For years afterwards, survivors returning to their former homes would find areas of jungle carpeted with bones.

Hundreds of thousands more were deported to the Central Zone, the North and the North-West, where many were also killed. The death-toll will never be known: certainly more than 100,000, perhaps as many as a quarter of a million. Whatever the figure, it was the bloodiest single episode under Pol Pot's rule.

The leading rebels – the Zone deputy chiefs of staff, Heng Samrin and Pol Saroeun, and half a dozen district secretaries – eventually made their way to Vietnam to join the nucleus of exiles being groomed for leadership by Le Duc Tho. By the autumn, in most parts of the Zone, a semblance of order had been restored. But the population remained profoundly hostile.

And still the killings continued.

A week after So Phim's suicide, the North-Western Zone Secretary, Ruos Nhim, was detained and sent to Tuol Sleng. He and Phim had been close. Their children had married each other. Chou Chet had claimed in his confession that they had been working together to overthrow the regime. At a time when the regime was bent on cleansing itself no matter what the cost, that was enough. Nhim, So Phim and Chou Chet were 'thatched houses', not 'brick houses', Issaraks not intellectuals. That made them potential traitors. That there were no serious grounds for believing that any of them had plotted against Pol's regime,* any more than had all the others who ended up in Tuol Sleng, was beside the point. In the Stalinist scheme of things, considerations of innocence are irrelevant.

In totalitarian despotisms, a purge can strengthen a regime or fatally weaken it. Pol Pot's purges in 1978 bled Cambodia white. By August, only Mok's forces in the South-West and Pauk's in the Central Zone were still considered reliable. The Standing Committee was told that month that the armed forces were spending 60 per cent of their energy defending the regime against internal enemies.

In public, the CPK leaders whipped up a frenzy of patriotic fervour. Pol himself declared, in a commentary written for Radio Phnom Penh:

> In terms of numbers, [each] one of us must kill 30 Vietnamese . . . That is to say, we lose one against 30. We will therefore need two million troops for 60 million Vietnamese. In fact, [that] will be more than enough . . . because Vietnam has only 50 million inhabitants . . . We need only two million troops to crush the 50 million Vietnamese and we will still have six million Cambodians left. We must formulate our combat line in this manner in order to win victory . . . We absolutely must implement the slogan of one against 30.

The regime was getting back to basics. It was the same type of crude appeal to anti-Vietnamese racism that Lon Nol had used. Such language resonated in the Khmer psyche. The *Black Paper*, an indictment of Vietnamese treachery written by Pol that autumn, had a similar effect. Its vituperations against Hanoi were, in the words of one Western historian, 'beyond falsehood'. Yet to Khmers, they touched a chord of national pride which was among the regime's few remaining assets.

---

*It has often been claimed, on the basis of statements by both Vietnamese and Khmer Rouge sources, that So Phim attempted to rebel against Pol Pot with Vietnam's support and that it was the failure of his efforts which finally persuaded Hanoi that only a full-scale Vietnamese invasion would bring down the regime. There is no evidence for this. Phim, like Ruos Nhim, may have had reservations about Pol's domestic policies. He may also have doubted the wisdom of an aggressive military posture against Vietnam. But he was no more pro-Vietnamese than Pol himself. Vietnam's lack of contact with Phim – and, at that time, with other Eastern Zone cadres – is amply demonstrated by the fact that, four months after his suicide, the Vietnamese leaders believed he was still alive.

If Pol used such emotional props to the hilt, it was because he had little else to fall back on.

In private, at a Standing Committee meeting in August, he was uncharacteristically gloomy. 'We can hold on for a certain time,' he warned, 'but if the present situation continues, it will become impossible. We can now afford to sustain only partial losses. If things go on as they are, we will face the risk of collapse.'

In these bleak circumstances, Pol did what Stalin had done when the Germans attacked Russia in 1941. He sought strength in the ancient, immutable values of his people's culture, the bedrock of their national identity, formed long before the advent of communism and destined to endure long after it had passed.

Stalin turned to the Russian Orthodox Church to instil in the Soviet people a sacred mission to defend their homeland. Pol turned to the monarchy. On September 28, Khieu Samphân gave a banquet for Prince Sihanouk, who had not been seen in public for more than two years. The photographs taken on that occasion, transmitted around the world, showed the Prince and his wife, in good health, accompanied by Penn Nouth and other former members of his suite, apparently on the best of terms with Pol Pot's government.

To reach that point had taken two and a half years. Having cut his ties with the regime in the spring of 1976, Sihanouk had sat on his dignity and sulked. For the next eighteen months, he had received occasional visits from Khieu Samphân, but little else. Change came with the conflict with Vietnam. In September 1977, on Pol's instructions, the Prince was presented with a basket of lychees. He responded with a series of letters, praising the CPK Secretary's 'wise leadership' and condemning Vietnam's aggression. In January, Zhou Enlai's widow, Deng Yingchao, was permitted to see him being driven past in a limousine but not allowed to meet him. At the end of the summer, he was moved from the palace to a new, more secure residence in the area where Penn Nouth lived, ostensibly as a precaution against a Vietnamese kidnap attempt. Pol was keeping him in reserve, to be produced like a rabbit from a hat at a moment of his own choosing.

By September 1978 he could wait no longer.

For months the Chinese had been urging him to speed up preparations to counter what they now saw as an inevitable Vietnamese invasion.

This was a major theme of Son Sen's visit to Beijing in July, and was brought up again when Nuon Chea went there in August. But the most important discussions took place in the last ten days of September, when

Pol himself flew secretly to China to meet Deng Xiaoping.* According to the Khmer Rouge Ambassador, Pich Chheang, who was present at some, though not all, of the talks, Deng pleased and surprised his guest by the ferocity with which he condemned Vietnam. Le Duan, he said, was an ingrate – a crocodile, in Cambodian terms – who had to be punished for his treachery. But he also suggested that, in China's view, the Khmers Rouges were partly responsible for bringing these troubles on themselves by their excessive radicalism; the lack of discipline and 'putschist, anarchic behaviour' of their troops on the Vietnamese border; and their failure to unite the country behind them. When Deng made these remarks, Pich Chheang recalled, Pol smiled and said nothing. They did agree, however, on the importance of Sihanouk's role, the need for united front tactics, and the necessity of preparing for a protracted guerrilla war when the Vietnamese attack finally came. Deng also made clear, as he had done earlier to Son Sen and Nuon Chea, that while China would give the Cambodians all the military help it could, the conduct of the war would ultimately be Cambodia's responsibility. Whether Pol realised that this meant China would not send troops, and that the Cambodians would have to fight on their own, is uncertain. It appears that he did not.

Sihanouk's re-emergence was the most visible consequence of Pol's visit to Beijing but not the only one. Since January 1978, Khmer Rouge frontier units had been under orders to adopt an aggressive, forward posture. 'We must attack first, because otherwise they will attack us,' Pol said. 'Every Vietnamese attack must be met by a counter-attack.' After his return from Beijing in October, the front-line commanders were told to switch to a defensive strategy, to use mines against Vietnamese armour and infantry formations and to avoid decisive confrontations which carried a risk of heavy losses. Pol explained the tactics they should use by means of traditional imagery which the peasant soldiers could easily grasp. He told them to fight like 'a lake of floating water-hyacinths', which meant entangling the enemy in a mesh of small guerrilla groups in the same way as aquatic plants entangle and pull down a swimmer; or as 'multiplying snails', whereby two- or three-man groups would creep up on an enemy section, each taking a single Vietnamese soldier as its target, and then melt back

---

*Pich Chheang and his wife, Moeun, were unable to remember when the visit took place and the Chinese archives on the subject are sealed. The evidence for a late September dating is that the anniversary of the founding of the CPK appears to have been celebrated ten days earlier than usual, on September 19, yet when Pol's speech was broadcast, more than a week later, Radio Phnom Penh claimed that he had spoken on September 27. According to Pich Chheang, Pol's visit lasted about a week and was spent mainly in talks with Deng, who by this time, in fact if not yet in name, had eclipsed Hua Guofeng as China's paramount leader.

into the jungle. 'If we carry out guerrilla warfare,' he maintained, 'we can never be defeated':

> We must use the tactics of mobility and rapid attack, firing one or two shots and then disappearing before the enemy can locate us . . . We should attack from the flanks, avoiding engagement when their forces are strong. Occupying terrain is of no importance. What matters is preserving our strength . . . so that we can hit them at their weak spots.

As if to offset the regime's new-found caution, its propaganda became increasingly shrill. 'The Vietnamese stink to high heaven,' *Tung Padevat* told its readers. 'They are so degraded that they are despised as nothing, for [they] think only of carrying around a begging bowl . . . beseeching charity from all and sundry.' It was a poor argument against an enemy which was even then methodically preparing the Khmers Rouges' downfall.

While Pol was talking to Deng Xiaoping in Beijing, Le Duc Tho was meeting Heng Samrin, Pen Sovann and the other Khmer exiles at Thu Duc, a former US police camp in the suburbs of Ho Chi Minh City. He told them that Vietnam planned a full-scale invasion of Cambodia at the beginning of the coming dry season and that the newly formed Khmer resistance would fight alongside their Vietnamese 'brothers-in-arms'. In the meantime the exiles were to set up an umbrella organisation, the Khmer National United Front for National Salvation (KNUFNS), capable of assuming power when the Pol Pot regime fell. History was repeating itself. For the third time in as many decades, the leaders in Hanoi were building a clandestine Cambodian resistance movement to further Vietnamese interests.

In that same month of September 1978, the Vietnamese Premier, Pham Van Dong, set out on a hastily arranged regional tour to try to build diplomatic cover for the coming attack on Cambodia. He proposed a Treaty of Friendship and Co-operation with the non-communist South-East Asian states and solemnly assured each of his interlocutors that Hanoi had no expansionist ambitions. In Kuala Lumpur, he even laid a wreath to Malay soldiers who had died fighting the communist insurgency. But the treaty proposal was politely rejected. It was too much, too suddenly, too late.

Vietnam's efforts to woo the United States fared no better. In October President Carter decided that the China relationship took priority and normalisation with Vietnam would be put on hold.

Three weeks later Le Duan, accompanied by Pham Van Dong and a phalanx of VWP Politburo members, flew to Moscow, where they were given an unusually cordial reception by the Soviet leadership. Duan and Leonid Brezhnev signed a Friendship Treaty which provided, among other things, for the two countries to take 'appropriate and effective steps to safeguard [their] security' if either were attacked. The immediate purpose was to deter China from escalating its conflict with Vietnam. The 'international reactionaries', gloated the Vietnamese Party journal, *Tap Chi Cong San*, would now face 'heavy retaliation' should they recklessly attack a Soviet ally.

Cambodia was hardly discussed. The Vietnamese leaders told their Soviet counterparts merely that they expected the Khmer resistance to 'use the forthcoming dry season to make powerful attacks on the Phnom Penh regime' and that they did not believe China would be in a position to send troops to its aid.

Two days after the treaty was signed in Moscow, Deng Xiaoping set out in Pham Van Dong's footsteps to visit Thailand, Malaysia and Singapore. He found his hosts already half-convinced that a Vietnam which was now part and parcel of the Soviet bloc was a potential danger to the whole region. The battle to contain Hanoi, Deng told them, would be fought out in Cambodia. 'There is a possibility that Phnom Penh will fall,' he added. 'That would not be the end of the war, but the beginning.' The Vietnamese would invade Cambodia in force, but they would be unable to consolidate their gains and a long resistance struggle would follow. When that happened, he went on, China 'will not stand idly by. We will take appropriate measures.'

To Lee Kwan Yew in Singapore and Malaysia's Prime Minister Mahathir, Deng's analysis was persuasive. The Thai Premier, General Kriangsak, was warier. Thailand would be in the front line if conflict broke out in Cambodia. It would be able to support the Khmers Rouges only if it were sure of having China's backing. Deng assured him that that was the case and, by way of encouragement, indicated that China would reduce its support for the Thai Communist Party and persuade the Khmers Rouges to do the same.

While Deng was in South-East Asia, another top Chinese leader, the regime's security chief, Wang Dongxing, flew to Phnom Penh. Apart from demonstrating Chinese support, his mission was to appraise Pol's plans for resistance and to give whatever advice seemed necessary.

It was not the easiest of tasks. Hu Yaobang, the future Chinese Party Chairman, who accompanied Wang's delegation, found the atmosphere unreal. Throughout the deserted city, beds were being taken from empty houses to equip extra hospital wards for the wounded. Factory workers were receiving military training. Officials were digging trenches. But neither Pol nor anyone else seemed to have any clear idea of what they would do when the Vietnamese came. In his speech at the welcoming banquet, the Cambodian leader had planned to say: 'The government of Democratic Kampuchea and the CPK know that they can count on the help of the fraternal Chinese army if the need arises.' But the Chinese objected and the offending paragraph was deleted. Instead, Wang warned sombrely that the Vietnamese aggressors 'may run wild for a time', meaning that the Cambodians would probably be unable to stem their advance. At that point there was a power cut in the hall and all the lights went out.

In private Wang urged the CPK leaders to begin readying the population psychologically for the coming struggle, to distribute arms to the peasants and to prepare arms caches and stocks of rice. None of his recommendations was implemented.

One reason for this was that a new round of purges had begun, targeting the very men who would normally have been responsible for planning the resistance to Vietnam.

On November 1 and 2 1978, the CPK had held its Fifth Congress. The meeting was unusually brief — normally CPK congresses, including the preliminary meetings, lasted several weeks — and its main, if not its only function seems to have been to elect a new leadership. Mok, who now headed both the North-Western and the South-Western Zones, became the third-ranking leader, behind Pol and Nuon Chea, with the rank of Second Deputy Secretary, responsible for Agriculture and Rural Affairs. He was also appointed Vice-Chairman of the Party's Military Commission. Ieng Sary ranked fourth, and Vorn Vet, who was in charge of military supplies to the Eastern Front, fifth. Son Sen, who now finally moved up from being a candidate to a full member of the Standing Committee, was in sixth place; and Kong Sophal, the new Chief of the Army Logistics Department, seventh.

Next morning troops burst into the room where Mok, Sophal and Vorn Vet were meeting. 'Mok was shitting in his pants,' Ieng Sary recounted gleefully. 'He thought it was all over.' In the event, Vorn Vet and Kong Sophal were arrested and taken to Tuol Sleng. The reasons remain a mystery. It requires a peculiarly devious mentality to promote a man to the summit of power one day in order to arrest him the next, above all at a moment when the country was about to embark on a life-and-death struggle for survival. Kong Sophal may have fallen under suspicion because of his association with Ruos Nhim when he was military commander in the North-West. Vorn Vet's arrest is inexplicable. Like Pâng and Siet Chhê, he had been one of Pol's favourites.

The 'sickness in the Party' of which Pol had spoken two years earlier had become a sickly suspiciousness, a paranoid mistrust, infecting leadership at every level. The more desperate Cambodia's plight, the more the poison spread.

The regime's days were numbered, not only because of the war with Vietnam, but because the body politic had rotted from within. The microbes, 'the ugly microbes', as Pol had called them, were not, as he believed, the result of some political gangrene, blighting a healthy organism. They were the very essence of the system he had built.

For the next few weeks, the regime existed in a state of limbo.

At the end of November, the Chinese Party Central Committee confirmed Deng's decision not to send troops to Cambodia, but decided instead to entrust the Chinese People's Liberation Army with a punitive operation across Vietnam's northern border. The Russians, Deng argued, would not risk a world war to defend their Vietnamese ally, regardless of the security clause in their new Friendship Treaty. But there was a possibility they might launch a tit-for-tat attack into Xinjiang. Three hundred thousand people were accordingly evacuated from Kashgar and other sensitive areas on the Soviet border with Chinese Central Asia.

On December 2, several hundred Khmer exiles gathered near Snuol, in a clearing in a rubber plantation about two miles inside the Cambodian border, to inaugurate the new Vietnamese-backed National Salvation Front, headed by Heng Samrin. Le Duc Tho was on hand for the occasion, as he had been in April 1950 when, in very similar circumstances, Vietnam had created the Khmer National Liberation Committee, led by Son Ngoc Minh.

A week later, two American journalists, Elizabeth Becker of the *Washington Post* and Richard Dudman of the *St Louis Post Despatch*, and a British academic, Malcolm Caldwell, who was sympathetic to the Khmer Rouge cause, became the first non-communist Westerners, other than diplomats, permitted to visit Democratic Kampuchea. Dudman reported that officials were speaking openly of the possibility of having to abandon Phnom Penh.

Yet as each side prepared for war, on the battlefields there was an eerie silence. Radio Phnom Penh continued to broadcast its usual reports on the improvement of life in the co-operatives. At the Foreign Ministry, Laurence Picq recalled, 'We weren't worried . . . We thought everything would work out painlessly; there'd be no gunfire, no fighting, no bloodshed.' Even in the army, only units directly involved in the fighting knew what was going on. The head of the air-force radar repair unit, Kân, on a visit to the border area in late November, was shocked to find defeated Cambodian troops in retreat. 'Soon afterwards I heard that the Vietnamese had broken through, that our defences weren't holding,' he said. 'But all that was unofficial. Officially we were told nothing.'

On December 22, Pol received Becker and Dudman and gave them his version of the confrontation that was now looming. Vietnam, the Soviet Union and the Warsaw Pact were on one side, he declared. On the other were 'NATO [and] . . . Kampuchea, South-East Asia and the world'. He also saw Caldwell for what must have been, in the circumstances, an altogether surreal discussion of Khmer Rouge economic policy.

That night, after they had packed their bags for the following morning's flight to Beijing, an event occurred which provided the perfect metaphor for the disintegration of the regime.

At around 1 a.m. Becker was awakened by what she thought was the noise of dustbins being knocked over, followed by a gunshot and the sound of moaning. When she opened her door, she found herself face to face with a young man wearing 'clothes [that] seemed different [and] . . . a hat like a baseball cap'. He was armed to the teeth. She fled. Dudman, who was also now awake, saw from his window 'several shadowy figures running back and forth . . . in the dim glow of the streetlights'. At least one was carrying a pistol. The man in the baseball cap then reappeared, fired at Dudman as he stood outside his room, but missed. Afterwards several more shots were heard. Nothing further happened until an hour and a half later, when Pol's former aide, Phi Phuon, now Head of Security at the Foreign Ministry, arrived with a group of guards and broke down the door. They found Becker and Dudwell unharmed. Caldwell was sprawled on the floor, dead, with bullet wounds in the chest and head. Beside him was the body of a young Khmer – possibly, but not certainly, the man in the baseball cap.

At 4 a.m., Ieng Sary was informed. He awoke Pol, who said little, as was his wont, other than to express regret and to give instructions that Thiounn Thioeunn conduct an autopsy and preserve the body to be flown to Beijing.

Later the most outlandish theories were concocted to try to explain what had happened. British intelligence believed that Pol had ordered Caldwell's death. An internal Khmer Rouge inquiry found that one of the guards had been having an unhappy love affair. It suggested he had gone on a shooting spree and then committed suicide. Another guard, under torture at Tuol Sleng, implicated the Defence Minister, Son Sen. Pol himself later told aides he believed that Dudman was the killer. The American was a CIA agent, he said, and had murdered Caldwell to discredit the regime. None of these 'explanations' made much sense. But Phi Phuon noticed one troubling detail. Although the dead Cambodian was found with a pistol by his hand, making it look as though he had shot himself in the head, the position of the body was not right. Phi Phuon thought that he had been murdered and someone had tried to mask his death as a suicide.

The likeliest explanation, which, perversely, the regime refused to credit because of its obsession with traitors, was that the attack was the work of a Vietnamese commando unit. No one else had a comparable interest in showing up Khmer Rouge incompetence and no one else was as well-placed to do so.

Yet the overriding lesson of Malcolm Caldwell's death, however it occurred, was that by December 1978 security in Phnom Penh had broken down. The troops which had formerly guarded the capital had all been sent to the East, to the Highway 1 and Highway 7 Fronts, where they were dug into defensive positions, in an extended arc stretching from the Parrot's Beak to the Fishhook, awaiting the Vietnamese attack. To defend the city after their departure, a former Special Zone officer named Ponlâk had been appointed military governor, with Pol's nephew, So Hong, as his deputy. But the only troops at his disposal to man checkpoints and carry out patrols were youths barely into their teens. 'They used to fall asleep on guard duty,' Long Nârin remembered. 'They'd put down their rifles and you could take them away – and then watch them panic when they woke up and found they weren't there.'

A creeping neurosis set in. Even inside the Foreign Ministry compound, one Khmer Rouge official was so frightened of a Vietnamese attack that when he left his office each evening to go home, he made his wife, who was expecting a child, walk in front of him. 'They won't attack a pregnant woman,' he told her.

On Christmas Day of 1978, the invasion began. Vietnamese advance columns set out from Ban Me Thuot, in the Central Highlands, and from southern Laos, making for Kratie and Stung Treng. It was a replay of the Viet Cong offensive after Lon Nol's coup in the spring of 1970, only this time it was a lot quicker. Kratie fell on December 30 and Stung Treng four days later, putting the whole of the North-East in Vietnamese hands. But that was just a feint. After an intensive air and artillery bombardment, the Vietnamese main force, consisting of more than 60,000 men, commanded by General Le Duc Anh, smashed through the Khmer Rouge defence lines on January 1, heading up Highway 1 and Highway 7 to Phnom Penh.

They did not have things entirely their own way. On Highway 7, in Kompong Cham, Son Sen's forces blocked the advance for forty-eight hours. Then his headquarters were overrun and Sen himself narrowly escaped capture, taking refuge in the jungle before making his way back to Phnom Penh. Mok's forces also put up stiff resistance at the ferry crossing of Neak Luong, and along Highway 3, from Kompong Som to Phnom Penh.

But the Cambodian strategy was fatally flawed. By putting half of Democratic Kampuchea's best troops, more than 30,000 men, into stationary, forward positions, instead of adopting mobile, guerrilla tactics – as the Chinese had recommended and Pol had originally planned – the Khmer

Rouge High Command had offered the Vietnamese a sitting target. In less than a week, Son Sen's defensive shield was in shreds.

As the country erupted in flames, Pol immersed himself in routine.

On December 29, with the Vietnamese already in control of the upper reaches of the Mekong, he spent the evening hosting a banquet for the chairman of the Canadian Marxist-Leninist Communist League, a tiny pro-Chinese splinter group that had rallied to the Khmer Rouge cause. Next day he took time off to meet an obscure left-wing Peruvian newspaper editor.

At that point, the fall of Kratie was announced. A bodyguard unit was despatched to prepare for an eventual withdrawal to Tasanh, in the Cardamom Mountains, south of Samlaut, where Son Sen had built a complex of underground bunkers as an emergency HQ if Phnom Penh were abandoned. They took with them the regime's war treasury, several hundred kilograms of gold and silver confiscated after the 1975 victory.

On the evening of January 1, when it became clear that Kompong Cham was also about to fall, Pol ordered the Foreign Ministry security chief, Phi Phuon, to escort Sihanouk, Penn Nouth and their families to Sisophon. They were to leave at once. At the least sign of danger, Pol said, Phi Phuon should take the Prince and his party across the border to safety in Thailand, whence they would make their way to Beijing. Sihanouk, Phi Phuon remembered, took the news calmly. Less than an hour later, the cavalcade of two Mercedes, one each for Sihanouk and Penn Nouth, a Lincoln Continental for the entourage and two escort jeeps, set out through the darkness along the potholed road to the North-West.

The last days sped past in a blur.

Twenty-four hours after Sihanouk's departure, the entire diplomatic corps followed. So Hong, Pol's nephew, looking flustered and sweating profusely, told the Chinese Ambassador: 'The front line is critical . . . We think the Vietnamese intend to push forward and bombard Phnom Penh.' They were then all driven to Siem Reap in a fleet of government cars.

On the 4th, the Vietnamese offensive paused. The diplomats returned to their embassies, and Sihanouk and Penn Nouth were brought back from the Thai border. Then the advance resumed. The following evening, Pol met Sihanouk at the former French Governor-General's Residence, now known as House No. 1, and asked him to go to the UN to plead Cambodia's cause before the Security Council. The meeting, which was followed by a banquet, lasted four hours. It was the first time the Prince had been exposed at length to Pol's magnetic personality and despite himself he was impressed. 'He was waiting for me, smiling, outside the massive door of the residence,' Sihanouk wrote later. 'He placed his hands

together and greeted me in the traditional manner, with a slight genuflex-
ion, just like in the old society . . . Then immaculately dressed servants
served us tea and petits fours with fresh orange juice.' Sihanouk noted that
the Khmer Rouge leader employed the special court vocabulary, speaking
'easily and with flair . . . He had a certain charisma . . . and an eloquence
that was "sweet and persuasive".' Pol assured him that the Vietnamese had
walked into a trap. The Khmer Rouge army, he said, was deliberately
luring them deep inside Cambodian territory. 'It's a stratagem to make
them think that militarily we are very weak,' he explained. 'Once they are
all within our borders, we will cut them up into little pieces . . . drowning
them in a flood of popular resistance until they are leached out like salt in
running water.' He had spoken in similar vein in a radio broadcast earlier
the same day, in which he accused the Vietnamese of 'trying to exterminate our Cambodian race', and predicted that they would perish 'in a vol-
cano of national indignation'.

Sihanouk took this as just another of the deceits which underlay so
many extraordinary Khmer Rouge statements. But it seems on this occasion he was wrong.

Pol was certainly aware that Cambodia's forward defences had failed. He
was making a virtue out of necessity: mobile warfare was the only option
left. But he evidently remained convinced that once Phnom Penh had been
abandoned and the Vietnamese army tried to occupy the hinterland, it
would bog down and become an easy target for Khmer Rouge guerrillas.
The Vietnamese offensive, he declared, 'will last for only a short period of
time'. Other leaders shared this view. Khieu Samphân thought 'we would
just be leaving Phnom Penh temporarily, and then we'd be back'. At the
Foreign Ministry, So Hong told colleagues that it would 'all be over in a
few weeks'. That may have been whistling in the dark. But it also reflected
a widespread belief that, as In Sopheap put it, 'the army had the situation
in hand'.

The Chinese knew differently. Their technicians at the rubber plantation in Chhup, in the Eastern Zone, had already reported by radio that
'there was basically no more army.' They headed for Kompong Som, where
a Chinese merchant ship was waiting to evacuate them.

None the less, on Saturday January 6, the Chinese Civil Air Administration maintained its scheduled weekly flight to Phnom Penh. It brought out
Sihanouk, his entourage and about a hundred Chinese experts and other
visitors, including a group of hapless Chinese acrobats who had been tour-
ing Cambodia when the invasion began. A plan to send two more planes
to fly out Chinese technicians from Battambang was abandoned when it
was realised that the runway there was too short.

Khieu Samphân and Son Sen were at the airport to bid the Prince farewell. So were the Chinese and Yugoslav ambassadors. Not long afterwards, they too would depart.

Son Sen left the city that evening, making his way through Vietnamese lines to Kompong Cham, where he tried to rally what remained of the Khmer Rouge divisions on the Eastern Front. Pol, Nuon Chea and Khieu Samphân, accompanied by several jeep-loads of bodyguards, set out at dawn the following morning – Sunday January 7 – for Pursat, near the Great Lake, midway between Phnom Penh and Battambang. Pol travelled in a Chevrolet, which was higher off the ground and rode the potholes better than the Mercedes of his companions. Ieng Sary made for Battambang aboard a special train carrying several hundred Foreign Ministry personnel together with the Ministry archives, which had been hastily packed the previous day.

Many of the other ministries, including one of the biggest, Social Affairs, which had 2,000 staff members and was headed by Sary's wife, Khieu Thirith, were never informed that an evacuation was under way. Later trains were supposed to take out medical personnel from the city's four main hospitals – but most of the patients, including large numbers of severely wounded soldiers, were left behind because there was no room in the wagons. 'It was indescribable,' one man wrote later, 'a picture of human misery . . . The platforms were clogged with convoys of soldiers, with the injured, and with people desperately trying to flee.' Soon after 7 a.m. the same morning, the forty or so diplomats in the city left by road for the second time, together with six hundred Chinese technicians and about fifty North Koreans who had been working on agricultural and hydroelectric projects. They were accompanied by the Chief of Protocol, Son Sen's younger brother, Nikân, and a handful of other officials. They, too, headed for the Thai border, which they reached without incident the following day. After that, the only senior Khmer Rouge figure remaining in Phom Penh was Mok, whom Pol had belatedly ordered to help Ponlâk, the military governor, assure the city's defence. Shortly after 8 a.m. Mok was seen near the Foreign Ministry driving a jeep. But a few hours later, he also decided that nothing could be achieved by staying and set out for his old base on Mount Aural.

Thus, by the middle of Sunday morning, the rulers of Democratic Kampuchea had stolen furtively away, abandoning the capital to its own devices. The population of 40,000 workers and soldiers, plus the military units based in the immediate vicinity, was left, leaderless, to fend for itself.

The chaos and disorganisation of the final days – the sheer incompetence of Pol's administration; the absence of any coherent plan for resistance; the refusal to confront the reality of Phnom Penh's imminent fall; the failure to evacuate the wounded – showed the bankruptcy of the regime. It was doomed, whatever the circumstances, because it did not know how to rule.

Khmer Rouge policy, right up to the last hours, remained wholly consistent with everything that had gone before. The priority accorded to getting Sihanouk to safety, to protecting Pol and the other leaders, was merely the practical application of the principle expounded by Nuon Chea months before: 'If we lose members but retain the leadership, we can continue to win.' The corollary – that ordinary people were expendable – had been Khmer Rouge practice ever since the evacuation of Phnom Penh in April 1975. The lack of concern over loss of life and over the squandering of material resources was exactly the same as three and a half years earlier.

Yet if there were one, overriding reason for the collapse of Democratic Kampuchea in January 1979, it lay in the leadership's mania for secrecy.

Pol simply could not bring himself to tell the Cambodian people what was going on, even if it meant the destruction of the regime. The radio broadcast he made early on the morning of Friday January 5 was as revealing for its omissions as for anything he said. Apart from two brief references to 'temporary difficulties', he gave no hint that large parts of Cambodia were already under Vietnamese occupation. On the contrary, he implied that the 'valiant and invincible Cambodian army' was successfully resisting the aggressors. Still less was there any practical advice to the population about how to respond to the Vietnamese advance. Instead he intoned ritualistic formulae about 'relying on the worker-peasant alliance', developing production and strengthening national unity. It was a textbook example of how not to rally a nation to resist, and it followed months of similar mistakes. Pol had known since September that it was only a matter of time before the Vietnamese invaded. Yet apart from establishing a fallback base for the leadership at Tasanh, he had made no contingency plans. In a regime where mistrust had been institutionalised, trusting the population, or even the military, was unthinkable. Outside the inner circle formed by Pol, Nuon Chea, Mok, Ieng Sary and Son Sen, no one was adequately informed. Mey Mak, then head of civil aviation at Pochentong, remembered:

> Did we have any advance warning that the Vietnamese were so close? Well, two or three days before, on January 3 or 4, [the air-force commander] Mang Met told us to be prepared to deal with 'disturbances' . . . But he didn't say anything about Vietnamese soldiers. We knew that something was wrong, because, two weeks earlier, some of the pilots had told us that Vietnamese troops were in Memot . . . And then, Sihanouk left on January 6. But I thought that was [like the trips he had made] in 1975 . . . I still didn't have

any idea that the Vietnamese were about to attack Phnom Penh. I knew they were in Kompong Cham. But if you listened to the radio, it spoke every day about the Vietnamese being beaten back – it never talked about our forces retreating or anything like that. So even though there were rumours – people said the Vietnamese had reached this far, or had overrun that place – we still didn't really believe it. They were simply rumours.

Apart from Mang Met and his two deputies, Lvey and Phal, no one at Pochentong knew that the Vietnamese were approaching. No attempt was made to rebase the air force at Battambang, to move out the fuel reserves or even to fly out any of the planes. When the Vietnamese arrived, every aircraft the Cambodians possessed was lined up on the tarmac, theirs for the taking. Hundreds of armoured vehicles, quantities of munitions and strategic grain reserves fell into Vietnamese hands because, 'to maintain secrecy', no one had been ordered to move them. Confidential Party documents, which should have been destroyed, were left behind. Even the most secret of all the Khmer Rouge institutions – the S-21 interrogation centre at Tuol Sleng – continued its evil work, oblivious of the danger, until it was almost too late. Prisoners were still being interrogated on January 5 when Deuch received an urgent order from Nuon Chea to kill the remaining inmates. He complied. But there was no time to destroy the prison archives and most were recovered intact by the occupation forces.

Ironically, had Pol been less secretive, the secrecy he sought would have been far better preserved.

As it was, no sooner did word spread that Democratic Kampuchea's top leaders had fled than most of the senior officers followed. At 8 a.m. on Sunday, Mang Met's 502nd Air-force Division was ordered to block the Vietnamese advance from the south. Mey Mak went with them. Three hours later, when he radioed Divisional HQ for orders, there was no one there to answer. On the other side of the city, another battalion commander received a wireless signal from his regiment at 10 a.m., telling him: 'From now on, you are on your own. Don't wait for further orders. There won't be any.' Phi Phuon, who had been ordered by Ponlâk to defend the Foreign Ministry, assembled eight hundred factory workers and Ministry employees and issued them with rifles. By midday, Ponlâk, too, had fled. Phi Phuon's men – none of whom had ever fired a shot in anger before – held out near the railway station until evening and then headed westwards. Twenty years later, he was still outraged by the way the leadership had behaved. 'It was a complete shambles. They organised no defence at all. Even Ponlâk, who was supposed to be the City Governor, wasn't told anything. They trusted no one at that moment . . . Mang Met was under orders to defend the city too. What did he do? He ran away.' With no guidance from above, individual company commanders began leading their men away from the city as well. Even then, one officer recalled, 'it was totally disorganised. No one followed orders. Some groups fell back, others went ahead, until by dawn they'd all scattered in different directions.'

Mey Mak was shocked by the attitude of the villagers in the areas through which they passed. 'They hated us,' he said. 'They just wanted us gone.' There were cases of individual soldiers who became separated from their comrades being disarmed and beaten to death, and of revenge killings of local Khmer Rouge officials. But they were relatively few. After so much horror, people were sick of blood. The little energy they had left they needed for their own survival.

Three years, eight months and twenty days after the Khmers Rouges won power, the slave state which Pol Pot had created had come to an ignominious end. Old Madame In – the mother of In Sopheap and In Sokhan – summed it up at the railway station that morning. 'Didn't they win a glorious victory?' she said to her companions. 'But they wouldn't treat people properly, so now they've lost everything. Band of cretins!'

12

Utopia Disbound

AFTER TWO DAYS in Pursat, Pol and Nuon Chea travelled on to Battambang. There they met Ieng Sary, whom they decided to send at once to Beijing to discuss a plan of resistance with the Chinese. The problem was how to get him there. Foreign diplomats and aid workers had been permitted to enter Thailand, but no Cambodian had yet been allowed across. If the Thai government sealed the border or, worse, reached an understanding with Vietnam to establish a condominium over Cambodia, as had happened during a similar crisis a century and a half before, the resistance would be stillborn. Nikân, who had negotiated the diplomats' passage, was instructed to seek authorisation for Ieng Sary and his party to transit through Bangkok.

To Pol's relief, the Thai Premier, General Kriangsak, decided that an arrangement with the Vietnamese would not be in his country's interests. On the afternoon of January 11 1979, a military helicopter landed near Poipet, a few yards inside Cambodian territory, to take out Sary, Son Sen's wife, Yun Yat, In Sopheap and a group of broadcasters from Radio Phnom Penh. They were to set up a radio station in China, the 'Voice of Democratic Kampuchea', which for the next few months would be the regime's sole channel of communication with the outside world.

The Thais supped with a long spoon. The Cambodian delegation was set down after nightfall in a deserted area of Bangkok's Don Muang Airport. No Thai official was present. They were driven across the tarmac and hustled on to a commercial airliner for Hong Kong after all the other passengers had embarked. None the less the die had been cast. The decisions of those first few hours determined the course of a war which would last two decades.

In Beijing next morning, Ieng Sary met Deng Xiaoping. The Chinese leader gave him a dressing-down for the excesses of Khmer Rouge rule and its 'deviations from Marxism-Leninism'. But most of the discussion then and at a further meeting the following day was taken up with the practicalities of resisting Vietnam. The Cambodians, Deng said, would need to prepare themselves for a long war. Instead of modern weapons they would use 'the methods of the past', fighting in small groups to wear the Vietnamese down. It was important to win Thailand's agreement to allow arms shipments to traverse its territory. And they must 'examine with the greatest attention the idea of a united front with Sihanouk'. After his arrival in Beijing, Deng said, the Prince had harshly criticised the Khmers Rouges, and, he noted pointedly, 'there were reasons for that'. On the other hand he had done everything Pol Pot asked, travelling to the UN to give a rousing speech in Cambodia's defence, after which the Security Council had voted by thirteen to two (the dissenters being the USSR and Czechoslovakia) to condemn Vietnam's aggression; and he had deftly deflected journalists' questions about Khmer Rouge atrocities. The CPK Central Committee, Deng went on, should seriously consider naming Sihanouk Head of State and bringing non-communists into the government to canvass support abroad.

It was a reprise of the united front which Sihanouk had headed after the 1970 coup. As though to underscore the parallel, Deng offered Sary five million dollars to defray immediate expenses, the same sum that Beijing had given the Khmers Rouges each year during the civil war. The only question was whether Sihanouk would agree to play the same role a second time. 'Say nothing to the Prince,' the Chinese leader told Sary, 'because it's not sure he will accept. If you agree with our idea, we will try to help [persuade him].'

They proved to be prescient words.

That same evening, as Sihanouk was returning with his Khmer Rouge minders to his hotel room in New York, he slipped a short note into the hand of the American policeman who had been assigned to guard him. It was a request for political asylum.

At 2 a.m., four burly secret servicemen escorted the Prince from his hotel to a waiting police car. For the next two weeks, he remained cloistered in a private suite at New York's Lenox Hill Hospital. The press was told that he was suffering from 'extreme stress and exhaustion'. The United States was as anxious as China to avoid doing anything which might weaken international opposition to Vietnam. American diplomats remained silent over the asylum request, and eventually, after France, too, proved unwilling to accept him as a political exile, Sihanouk agreed to return to Beijing. The deal was clinched when Deng Xiaoping, in the midst of a triumphal visit to America that month to celebrate the establishment of US–Chinese diplomatic relations, invited him to dinner at Blair House, the official residence for state guests in Washingon, and promised – untruthfully, as they both knew – that China would never again put pressure on him to co-operate with Pol Pot.

The main effect of Sihanouk's escapade was to persuade the Chinese to take a tougher line with the Khmers Rouges, whom they held responsible for the Prince's conduct. In Beijing, Chairman Hua summoned Ieng Sary and upbraided him in terms harsher than any Chinese leader had used before.*

> The problem was that when you achieved victory and Sihanouk returned, you weren't very clever in the way you treated him . . . He had joined you in the struggle against the Americans . . . and what did you do? You were unjust to him . . . He asked to see his daughter. You didn't let him. He wanted to see Penn Nouth. You didn't let him. He wasn't allowed to have newspapers or to see foreigners . . . Why did Sihanouk ask for asylum? Because for three years he suffered . . . There is a lesson to be drawn from this . . . In future, if Sihanouk says bad things about the Khmer Rouge leaders, you should [let it pass]. When the wolf is at your door, you don't worry about the fox.

Not only should Khmer Rouge policy change towards Sihanouk, Hua declared. Khmer Rouge policy towards the Cambodian people should change too:

> Will the war [in Cambodia] end in victory? That depends on whether the people's hearts are with you or not. For that reason, [you] must re-examine [your] previous experience to see what was done well and what was done badly. Only thus can one build a broad, unified national front against Vietnam and attract the majority [of the people] . . . The puppet [Vietnamese-installed] government has elaborated its programme on the basis of the errors in your policies. Of course they are doing so to deceive the people . . . But . . . you must make efforts to improve people's living standards in the liberated zones . . . to bring them democracy and happiness . . . This is a struggle for their hearts . . . You must also draw political lessons from your earlier campaigns against counter-revolutionaries. It is true that [such people existed] but they were very few. In [such matters], one must always be very cautious . . . In the present situation you must chart a new strategy and a new political direction . . . because, in guerrilla war, without the support of the people you can do nothing.

---

* Ieng Sary was more deeply implicated in the events in New York than the Chinese realised. Sihanouk wrote later that the final straw which made him defect was a message from Beijing, shortly after his speech to the Security Council, advising him that Sary would lead the Cambodian Delegation to the UN General Assembly and proposing that he stay on as his deputy. Sihanouk by this stage loathed Sary with a consuming, visceral hatred. That such an 'execrated, despised individual' should try to take precedence over him, Sihanouk wrote, was 'an offence which my dignity could not tolerate'. It was exactly the same kind of problem that had triggered Sihanouk's resignation as Khmer Rouge Head of State almost three years earlier. Then, too, Sary had been responsible.

While Deng concentrated on bringing Sihanouk back into the Khmer Rouge fold, the Secretary-General of the Chinese Party's Military Commission, Vice-Premier Geng Biao, flew to Thailand to see Prime Minister Kriangsak.

Geng found his host nervous. 'He kept stressing that everything must be kept secret,' he told Hua on his return to Beijing. 'He isn't at all confident. During our talks he kept asking again and again whether the Cambodians could really hold out. He seems to be full of worries.' At the Thais' insistence, they met not in Bangkok but at Utapao military airbase on the coast, 90 miles to the south. Kriangsak confirmed that Ieng Sary would be allowed to pass through in transit on his way back to Cambodia, but said he would not be allowed to stop over in Bangkok or to meet any Thai official. Messages between Cambodia and the Thai government would be routed via China and a single designated Thai official would liaise with the Chinese Embassy in Bangkok for that purpose. No other communications channel would be authorised.

However, Geng reported to Hua, on the issue that was of overriding importance – the shipment of Chinese aid to the Khmers Rouges – the Thai Premier was much more forthcoming:

> He proposed three routes. The first would be . . . for China to send merchant ships, flying a foreign flag, to Cambodian waters off the coast of Koh Kong, where the arms could be transshipped and brought ashore in small boats . . . I told him I thought that was possible . . . The second, he said, would be for . . . Chinese aircraft to parachute arms into northern Cambodia . . . But that would be difficult to keep secret. The third method would be for China to ship arms and other aid in small quantities through the commercial port of Bangkok . . . They would be packed to look like consumer goods . . . The Thai army would unload and store them in military warehouses, after which they would be transported by road to Ubon, west of Preah Vihear. From there Kriangsak would arrange for them to be taken into Cambodia.

The Thai government, Kriangsak indicated, would also allow the Khmers Rouges to buy arms and other supplies from Sino-Thai merchants in Bangkok.

The day that Geng Biao was in Thailand, January 15, the vanguard of the Vietnamese invasion force reached Sisophon. They had been held up not, as the Chinese believed, by Cambodian defences, but because they had advanced so much faster than expected that their armoured columns ran out of fuel. Except at Siem Reap, where they encountered significant guerrilla attacks, the Khmer Rouge army put up even less of a fight after the fall of Phnom Penh than it had in the East.

The progress of the invasion force was in a sense deceptive: Vietnam had seized only the urbanised skeleton of Cambodia – the main roads and the towns – but none of the countryside between. None the less, the appearance of the first Vietnamese infantrymen at the Thai border concentrated minds in Bangkok. On January 21, the Foreign Ministry announced that Thailand would continue to recognise 'Democratic Kampuchea', thus placing itself alongside China and the US squarely in the anti-Vietnamese camp. The other non-communist South-East Asian nations followed suit. By the time Ieng Sary arrived, a few days later, Kriangsak's injunction that he have no contact with Thai officials had been quietly forgotten.

To escape the Vietnamese advance, Pol, Nuon Chea and Khieu Samphân moved to Pailin on the Thai border and then, in late January, to Tasanh, further to the south, where Ieng Sary joined them.

There, on February 1, the Central Committee convened a two-day work conference, attended by divisional and regimental commanders, to discuss future strategy.

The discussion showed that Pol had learnt very little from the setbacks of the previous weeks. Sihanouk's name was not mentioned. In lip-service to the united front, there was praise for the role of 'Cambodian Buddhists', a term not heard since 1975. But the main thrust of Pol's remarks was that Vietnamese-installed district administrators should be 'wiped out' (Hua had urged that they be 'won over'); Vietnamese spies and agents should be killed; and the army should 'keep tight control' over the civilian population. All the old Khmer Rouge instincts had resurfaced. Hua's warning that a guerrilla war was unwinnable without mass support was ignored.

But whatever their shortcomings, the Khmers Rouges were the only Cambodian asset China had with a significant capacity to wage war against Vietnam, and Beijing was determined to make the most of them.

On the night of February 9, eight Chinese diplomats, led by Ambassador Sun Hao, each carrying a 40-pound rucksack, crossed into Cambodia near Poipet. They were greeted by Nikân and Pol's nephew, So Hong, who led them on foot through the jungle to Malay, a then almost uninhabited area twelve miles to the south. There the 'embassy' was received by Ieng Sary. A week later they moved again, this time by car, to another stretch of empty jungle near Pailin, where Pol briefed them on the military situation. Finally, on February 23, they donned black Khmer Rouge outfits and *kramas*, and set off in a convoy of jeeps for Tasanh. But, contrary to their own and Beijing's expectations, they were not based at Pol's headquarters. Instead yet another isolated jungle clearing was prepared for them, with four open-sided thatched huts as embassy residences.

Even in the middle of a war, the CPK kept its allies at arm's length. Pol's command centre was only two miles away, but Ieng Sary assured the Ambassador that the journey 'took three hours and was unbelievably difficult', so Khmer officials would come to them rather than the other way round. Over the next five weeks, Pol visited the 'embassy' twice and Ieng Sary once. The diplomats' only other contact was with a liaison officer, to whom they gave a daily briefing note for the Cambodian leaders on the basis of the coded telegrams they received each morning by radio from Beijing. The rest of the time they spent digging an air-raid shelter and clearing land for a vegetable garden.

Much of the cable traffic that month was devoted to the 'appropriate, limited lesson' which Deng Xiaoping had promised to administer to Vietnam.

It had started on February 17, with a sustained pre-dawn artillery barrage pouring 130-mm shells and rockets at a rate of one a second across the Chinese–Vietnamese border. This was followed by 85,000 Chinese troops, who headed for the five provincial capitals in the border region. Over the next two weeks they penetrated Vietnam to a depth of about fifteen miles. By the time the last Chinese soldier withdrew a month later, the Vietnamese had lost 10,000 dead, their military infrastructure along the border had been destroyed and their already weak economy crippled. Politically, the invasion had discredited the Soviet Union, which had conspicuously failed to come to the aid of its ally; it had cemented the growing Sino-American military entente; and it had given substance to Deng's bold assertion, made during his visit to the US, that 'we Chinese mean what we say.'*

But its immediate goal – to make Vietnam withdraw regular units from Cambodia to reinforce the border with China, reducing the pressure on the Khmers Rouges and allowing them to establish a 'liberated zone' where the new Chinese Embassy could be based, so confirming their claims to be regarded as the legitimate government – proved a failure. Not only did the Vietnamese expeditionary force remain in place but in mid-March it launched a new offensive against Pol's base at Tasanh. On March 27, the Chinese diplomats were asked to withdraw to a new site, a day's march away, higher up in the mountains. The following morning Ieng Sary arrived, gasping for breath, with the news that a

* More importantly in the long term, it strengthened Deng's hand in his struggle for power with Hua and other leaders who wanted to stick more closely to Mao's ideological legacy. The unsatisfactory performance of the Chinese army, which suffered 20,000 dead and wounded, enabled him to remove hundreds of leftist officers and to undertake the first fundamental reform of military policy since the 1940s.

Vietnamese special forces unit was nearby and they must set out at once towards the south. The same day Tasanh was overrun. Pol, Nuon Chea and Khieu Samphân had left a few hours earlier, abandoning part of the Central Committee archive, vehicles and weapons, reserves of rice and 3,000 tons of ammunition.

On April 8, after a gruelling twelve-day trek across the mountains, Ieng Sary and his Chinese charges reached the Thai border. There, to their astonishment, they stumbled upon a group of Khmer Rouge officials bathing in a river. Among them Sun Hao recognised Pol and Nuon Chea. The CPK leadership had established its new temporary headquarters just inside Cambodian territory. But the fate of the 'embassy' was already sealed. Beijing had decided the diplomats should be pulled out. Not only were the Khmers Rouges unable to guarantee their safety, but there was no longer a 'liberated zone' in which they could be based. Three days later, they bid Pol's 'government' farewell and crossed into Thailand, where they were detained by Thai border guards until urgent phone calls to Bangkok established their identity.

The Chinese diplomats were not alone in fleeing Cambodia that spring.

In the second half of March, Vietnamese units fanned out in an arc from Koh Kong to northern Battambang with orders to hem in the remnants of the Khmer Rouge army and the peasants they controlled – most of them 'old' people who had left their co-operatives more or less willingly to escape the Vietnamese advance – and to push them towards the border. The first groups crossed into Thailand in early April. Kriangsak's government was appalled but could do little to stop them. Bangkok had already chosen its side. After consultations with China and the United States, it was agreed that the refugees would be allowed to enter temporarily until the situation stabilised and they were able to return. Over the next few weeks, some 200,000 people, soldiers as well as civilians, flooded into the border areas. Some left almost at once, marching in disciplined columns along the frontier to re-enter Cambodia in areas free of Vietnamese control. The majority lived rough in primitive squatter camps, a couple of miles inside Thai territory.

In May, Pol, too, slipped across the border. He, Nuon Chea and Khieu Samphân were given the protection of the Thai army's 3rd Bureau, headed by the Military Intelligence Chief, General Chaovalit. Mok was still inside Cambodia, along with Son Sen, Ke Pauk and some 20–25,000 soldiers, most of them in the Eastern Zone, at Mount Aural, in Pursat, Koh Kong and parts of Battambang. But the majority were dispersed in small, isolated groups, hiding in the jungle, without contact among themselves and with no means of communicating with their leaders. The Khmer Rouge military command structure had been smashed in January. Now the movement's principal leaders, and the bulk of their followers, were in exile.

To the overwhelming majority of Cambodians in January 1979, the Vietnamese appeared as saviours. Hereditary enemies or not, Khmer Rouge rule had been so unspeakably awful that anything else had to be better. Vietnamese propagandists exploited this to the full. Vietnam's army, they claimed, had entered Cambodia not to occupy it but to deliver the population from enslavement by a fascist, tyrannical regime which enforced genocidal policies through massacres and starvation. That was of course untrue. The Vietnamese leaders had not been bothered in the least by Khmer Rouge atrocities until they decided that Pol's regime was a threat to their own national interests. But the notion of a 'humanitarian intervention' influenced opinion abroad and, for a time, coloured attitudes inside Cambodia as well.

Human gratitude, however, is fleeting. Within months the Vietnamese had outstayed their welcome.

In one sense, this was inevitable: foreign armies stationed in other people's countries are subject to the law of diminishing returns. In Cambodia, the alienness of the Vietnamese presence was all the more glaring because the Khmer figleaf, KNUFNS, was so small. A nominally Cambodian government had been established in January – headed by an ex-Khmer Rouge military commander, Heng Samrin, with a former Hanoi-based Issarak, Pen Sovann, Secretary-General of the revived People's Revolutionary Party of Kampuchea (PRPK), as his deputy – ruling a country which now called itself the People's Republic of Kampuchea (PRK). But policy was set by Vietnam, transmitted through a VWP Central Committee liaison group known as A-40, and implemented by Vietnamese 'advisers' who were in charge of every Ministry and provincial administration.

It was the same system that the Vietnamese had used in Laos since the early 1950s. The impression of a country under occupation was heightened by the way the army behaved. In the spring of 1979, Phnom Penh was systematically looted. Nayan Chanda, of the *Far Eastern Economic Review*, reported:

> Convoys of trucks carrying refrigerators, air conditioners, electrical gadgets, furniture, machinery and precious sculptures headed towards Ho Chi Minh City . . . The once busy Chinese business section of Phnom Penh looked like a scene after a cataclysmic storm. Every house and shop had been ransacked and remains of broken furniture and twisted pieces of household goods were strewn over the road. Damp nodules of cotton from ripped-open mattresses

and pillows covered the ground. Clearly marauders had gone through the households, searching for gold and jewellery.

Factories were dismantled and equipment sent back to Vietnam. As famine set in, rice from Khmer Rouge stockpiles left by the same route – or so, at least, many Khmers believed. When international organisations finally started sending food aid, part of that, too, was diverted to Vietnam.

Restrictions were placed on entry to the towns, which, with the exception of Phnom Penh, had been open during the initial months after the invasion. Former town-dwellers who had managed to return – often to discover that their old home had been requisitioned by a Vietnamese officer or a cadre in the new regime – were threatened with being packed off to the countryside to go back to working in the fields. Despite the government's promises that basic freedoms would be restored, there was no return to private farming.

Former civil servants and professional people who had survived the Khmer Rouge years and were now recruited to build the new administration found themselves under Vietnamese tutelage. At the obligatory indoctrination sessions it was made clear that their future depended on having a 'correct attitude' towards their Vietnamese comrades. Those who refused to co-operate, or were suspected of opposing the new regime, risked imprisonment in very harsh conditions.

As a result, in April and May 1979, tens of thousands of Cambodians, mostly 'new people' from the towns – former Sino-Khmer shopkeepers and their families and members of the pre-Khmer Rouge intellectual elite – voted with their feet. Thailand became the highway to a new life in the West. But if the Thais had turned a blind eye to the arrival of the Khmers Rouges and the peasant population they controlled – seeing them as a crucial defence against Vietnamese military pressure along the border – they took a very different view of a massive influx of civilian refugees who wished to leave Cambodia permanently and might end up spending years as uninvited guests before other countries agreed to take them. The lesson of the Vietnamese boat-people, washing up in their hundreds of thousands on South-East Asian beaches – to a great wringing of hands from the West but at that stage not much else – was already there as a warning. In June, most of the refugees were forcibly repatriated by the Thai army, often with great callousness. At Preah Vihear, in the north, 45,000 people were made to scramble down a precipitous mountainside into an uninhabited, heavily mined area of jungle. Several thousand died, either shot by Thai soldiers to prevent them trying to cross back or blown up in the minefields.

That finally got the attention of Western governments. But another four months passed before Thailand reached agreement with UNICEF and the International Red Cross on an orderly arrivals' programme – to be funded, Kriangsak's office emphasised, entirely by foreign aid – to deal with the refugee influx. For many, it was already too late. The famine which had spread through Cambodia that summer was as bad as, if not worse than, any in the Khmer Rouge period. To compound the misery, Vietnam initially refused to accept food aid from non-communist sources, fearing, correctly, that if it did so, relief would also be provided to the Khmers Rouges on the border. The upshot was that the number of refugees in Thailand jumped from 150,000 in October to well over half a million two months later.

Whatever else the Vietnamese were doing in Cambodia, they were not winning hearts and minds.

During the summer of 1979 the Khmers Rouges got their second wind. While the monsoon rains beat down, turning the roads into rivers of mud, and the Vietnamese remained in their barracks, the guerrillas and the population they controlled made their way stealthily back across the border. They had four months to reorganise before the next dry-season offensive began.

In July, Pol set up a new permanent headquarters, known as Office 131, on the western flank of Mount Thom, just inside Cambodian territory about twenty miles north-east of the Thai town of Trat in the coastal province of Chanthaburi. To mark the move, he changed his name to Phem.

Like the old HQ on the Chinit river, ten years earlier, Office 131 was a forbidden zone, protected by minefields and camouflaged pits filled with *punji* sticks. Access from Thailand was controlled by a Thai Special Forces group called Unit 838, formed by General Chaovalit to assure the Khmer Rouge leaders' protection. A network of well-camouflaged trails led across the mountains to Samlaut, which became a staging area both for Khmer Rouge units, making their way out of the jungle to try to reach the border, and for the messengers Pol despatched to re-establish contact with the scattered groups of soldiers still dispersed in the forests.

Many of those who emerged were walking skeletons, having survived on leaves and roots. Dysentery, malaria and oedema were rampant. The civilian population under Khmer Rouge control, especially 'new' people, accompanying them against their will, suffered even more. Mey Mak encountered cannibalism in the jungles of Pursat. In one case, which still made him shudder, a woman ate her own child. Tens of thousands starved. By October, in the words of the writer, William Shawcross, 'awful spindly creatures, with no flesh and with wide vacant eyes, stumbled out of the forests and the mountains into which the Khmer Rouge had coralled them . . . In many cases they were so badly starved that their bodies were consuming themselves . . . The lassitude of death had taken over.' Yet it was not just captive villagers who suffered. Men and women who had served the Khmer Rouge cause all their adult lives were in no better state.

Only the movement's leaders and their senior aides ate well.

In the makeshift camps on the border, Laurence Picq wrote in her diary, the rank and file subsisted on one daily bowl of watery soup made from the chopped-up stems of banana trees. But the top cadres were as 'fat and sleek as otters', dining on fish and fresh vegetables and rice. Photographs from the period show Pol and Ieng Sary looking stuffed.

Towards the end of the year, as relief supplies from the Red Cross and the UN began to reach the area, conditions improved. Peasants in ox-carts, loaded with sacks of rice, and long lines of porters made their way across the border passes. Chinese aid also started flowing in, not just arms and ammunition, but mosquito nets, water-bottles, uniforms, sugar and salt, packed biscuits, quinine and antibiotics.

Politically, two other events occurred to strengthen the Khmers Rouges' position. In November 1979 the UN General Assembly voted to seat the delegation of Democratic Kampuchea and exclude the Vietnamese-backed regime in Phnom Penh. The following month, Soviet troops invaded Afghanistan. To the West, this was the ultimate proof that the rulers in the Kremlin were committed to a policy of global expansionism. It redoubled non-communist South-East Asia's support for Thailand, which was seen as the next target in this new game of Russian roulette, and sealed a Faustian pact between the US, China and the Khmers Rouges to do whatever was necessary to make Vietnam's burden in Cambodia intolerable.

That winter's dry-season offensive failed to dislodge the Khmers Rouges from the border. New area commanders had been named – So Hong at Kla'ngop, Sok Pheap in Malay; Nikân in Sampou Loun; Phi Phuon in Kamrieng; and Y Chhean in Pailin. Thanks to China, their troops were now adequately armed, and each battalion had a signals unit. In the interior, as well, guerrilla activity was increasing and the military structure was being rebuilt. In January 1980, Son Sen transferred the Eastern Front HQ from the Chinit river, where he had spent the first year after the Vietnamese invasion, to Paet Um, an old Issarak base at the junction of the borders of Cambodia, Thailand and Laos. Ke Pauk headed a new Northern Front, with its HQ in Kompong Thom. Mok, at Mount Aural, retained command of the South-West. More significantly, young Khmer villagers began leaving their homes to join the maquis. By the middle of 1980, the Khmers Rouges claimed to have 40,000 troops in the field. Not all were well-trained. But neither were the Vietnamese.

Although their troop strength in Cambodia would soon reach 180,000, many were from regional units.

As the resistance expanded, so did Office 131. Wooden huts were erected to accommodate bureaux handling military planning, foreign policy, economics, health, information and social affairs, with a staff of more than a hundred and a large open assembly hall for seminars and meetings. A monitoring group provided Pol with daily summaries of broadcasts from foreign radio stations and translations from Thai and Western newspapers. He himself lived higher up the mountain, in an area that was off-limits to all except the *montagnard* bodyguards, protected by yet another minefield and a ditch full of sharpened bamboo stakes, patrolled day and night by a special security battalion.

Office 131 was the Khmer Rouge nerve centre. But it was not the seat of government of Democratic Kampuchea. That lay two hundred miles to the north-east, at a border camp called 808. Henry Kamm of the *New York Times* was taken there early in 1980. He found himself, he wrote, in a looking-glass world:

> [On] a table, decorated with flowers and greenery, placed under a handsome, thatched vaulted roof, hot coffee . . . was served with shy smiles by young Khmer Rouge soldiers . . . A courteous young man speaking flawless French collected our passports to issue us visas. Mine was returned bearing the only visa in longhand I have ever received. . .
>
> The Khmer Rouge guest-house was the very latest in jungle luxury. It was clearly modelled on the sumptuous hunting lodges to which French planters of the past invited guests for weekend shoots . . . [There were] four guest bungalows and paths linking them to the bath-houses, toilets, dining pavilion, meeting lodge and communications shack. Local materials had been tastefully used . . . Soldiers swept the entire camp daily to keep the falling leaves from cluttering. In front of each bungalow, our attentive hosts had placed trays of glasses, a thermos of hot water, a packet of Chinese tea and packs of American cigarettes . . . Vases of bamboo . . . were filled with fresh flowers . . . The plates of fruit brought from Bangkok were renewed each day . . . The best Thai beer, Johnnie Walker Black Label Scotch, American soft drinks and Thai bottled water were served.

At a time when many Cambodians were still close to starvation, Kamm found the display nauseating. That was not a thought that would have occurred to his hosts, Khieu Samphân and Ieng Sary. To them, 808 was the smiling, new public face of Democratic Kampuchea. Reporters were told it was the CPK Central Committee's headquarters. Pol himself went there to give interviews to favoured foreigners. The private face – Office 131 – was secret. In the first years not even Chinese journalists were told of its existence.

The Khmers Rouges purpose in arranging Kamm's visit, and many others like it at that time, was to persuade public opinion abroad that they had changed, to counter the atrocity stories filling Western newspapers and to make it easier for Western governments to continue upholding Democratic Kampuchea's right to be represented at the UN and in other international bodies. To that end, Pol and his colleagues were prepared to go a long way in publicly denying everything that their movement had once stood for. 'Our main duty is not to . . . build socialism,' Samphân declared, '[but] to drive all the Vietnamese forces out of Cambodia and to defend our nation, our people, our race.' Ieng Sary, a few months later, was even blunter, telling Kamm: 'We are abandoning the socialist revolution.' At the time most journalists covering the region, and most governments, assumed this was simply a ploy, just another of the endless tissue of lies and deceit which Pol and his colleagues had spun throughout their years in power.

They were wrong. Change was truly in the air. It was not what the regime pretended, nor could it have been. Sihanouk had told Deng Xiaoping, when the latter tried to persuade him that the Khmers Rouges now respected human rights: 'Vice-Premier, I am not able to believe you. Tigers don't change into kittens.' But the ultra-radical ideology that had underpinned the Khmer Rouge revolution, and which for years had seemed its *raison d'être*, was being quietly jettisoned, as though it had never been important, with hardly a backward glance.

The new-look Khmers Rouges shed their black peasant garb. The troops now wore jungle green, courtesy of their Chinese allies; the cadres, white shirts and dark trousers. Pol did the same until he discovered the attractions of safari suits, which were made to measure for him in Bangkok. He liked pastel colours, especially pale blue. Ministers affected business attire, rather than high-collared Mao jackets, when travelling abroad. Laurence Picq remembered putting on a short-sleeved pink blouse for the first time in July 1979. 'I felt indecent,' she wrote. 'It was like wearing a disguise. We weren't ourselves any more.' The young men and women recruited that winter to work at Office 131 were chosen, not on the basis of class, as would have been the case in the past, but ability. They had to have some secondary education and were made to take an exam in Khmer, French and English – skills which, one of them observed, 'would have got us killed before'. In October, Pol gave orders that there should be no more executions and, for the most part, these stopped. Ieng Sary told closed Party seminars that there had to be 'a new beginning'.

The refashioning of Khmer Rouge social behaviour was accompanied by a reorganisation of the movement's political institutions.

In September 1979 Khieu Samphân announced the creation of a new united front body, memorable mainly for the clumsiness of its name, the Patriotic Democratic Front of Grand National Union of Kampuchea (known by its French initials as FGUNDPK). More significantly, three months later, Samphân took over the Prime Ministership, ostensibly to allow Pol to concentrate on his role as Commander-in-Chief of the Armed Forces but in fact to try to give the Khmers Rouges a more acceptable public image. It was the opening gambit in a long-drawn-out political game.

That autumn, Pol had belatedly come round to accepting Deng Xiaoping's suggestion that Sihanouk should be made Head of State. But the Prince, infuriated by Chinese entreaties that he co-operate with 'those people who killed my children and grandchildren', was sulking in Pyongyang. For another year, neither side blinked. But in February 1981, after a further Vietnamese dry-season offensive had failed to crush Khmer Rouge resistance, Sihanouk took the bait.

By then his political options had narrowed. It had become clear that neither Vietnam nor the Phnom Penh authorities was willing to make a separate deal with him and his attempts to build a credible, non-communist third force had got nowhere. Unless he wished to retire from politics altogether, forfeiting any hope of ever seeing the Cambodian monarchy restored, he had no choice but to come to terms, for the second time in his life, with his hated communist opponents. Accordingly he proposed the creation of a tripartite coalition, composed of the Khmers Rouges; a non-communist resistance group headed by former Prime Minister Son Sann; and his own movement, the United National Front for an Independent, Neutral, Peaceful and Cooperative Cambodia, known by its French acronym, FUNCINPEC. The offer came with numerous face-saving conditions and, unsurprisingly, when Khieu Samphân met Sihanouk in North Korea in March, they failed to agree. But a dialogue had begun. All those involved understood that, after a suitable interval, it would lead to an accord.

In August 1981, Pol travelled to Beijing to meet Deng Xiaoping and Premier Zhao Ziyang. A specially chartered Chinese airliner was sent to Bangkok to collect him. Security was so strict that the half-dozen aides who went with him carried passports in false names.

'We think you should be flexible,' Zhao told him at their first meeting. 'You have to adapt your policy to the twists and turns of the road ahead.' According to Mey Mak, who was present, Pol bristled. 'We know we have suffered a defeat,' he replied. 'But we still adhere to the stance of independence-mastery. It will be up to our Central Committee to decide what policy we follow.' Later, at a meeting from which the rest of the delegation was excluded, Deng explained what Zhao had meant. In order to retain the support of non-communist South-East Asia, he said, the Khmers Rouges' differences with Sihanouk – in particular, their objections to giving a pledge to disarm after an eventual Vietnamese withdrawal – should be papered over. In return he promised that China would use its influence to ensure that, in the detailed negotiations that would follow, Khmer Rouge interests were protected.

Two weeks later, on September 4 1981, Sihanouk, Son Sann and Khieu Samphân met in Singapore and issued a joint statement announcing their intention to form a coalition government and wage a common struggle 'for the liberation of Cambodia from the Vietnamese aggressors'.

In December, the Communist Party of Kampuchea announced its self-dissolution. This was not, as was widely assumed, a public relations stunt. Had it been, the movement would have continued to operate in secret, as happened in other countries in similar circumstances. It did not. The CPK became the first and only Party in the history of international communism to terminate its own existence.

The decision, taken by Pol and Nuon Chea, with little discussion beyond the inner circle, caused consternation among the Party rank and file. 'People were very shocked and disoriented,' one of Son Sen's aides recalled. 'We tried to convince them that, even without a Party, it was still possible to organise. Son Sen told them the main problem was the survival of the Cambodian nation. 'Do you want to keep the Party and continue to struggle alone?' he asked them. 'Or is it better to unite with other national forces?'

One problem was that Party membership conveyed a certain status. To get round that, Pol proposed the creation of a 'Movement of Nationalists' to which former full-rights Party members would be given automatic entry. Even if the Party itself no longer existed, he said, there needed to be a mechanism to form 'progressive elements'. But the nationalist movement never caught on. 'It was too like a political game,' one man said. 'People just lost interest and it folded after a few months.' In fact, it seems Pol decided that any formal political structure would be counter-productive at that stage and quietly dropped the idea.

In many ways the dissolution of the Party was a very odd move. It removed part of the glue that held the Khmer Rouge movement together. Abroad, it brought no benefit because no outsider believed it had happened.

Yet at home it made sense. No Party meant no Angkar. The 'new' Khmer Rouges were now, in theory and to a large extent in practice, a purely military organisation dedicated to fighting the Vietnamese. The movement's ruling body, the CPK Standing Committee, was replaced by a Military Directorate comprising Pol, Nuon Chea, Mok, Son Sen and Ke Pauk. The new Khmer Rouge radio station was named the 'Voice of the National Army of Democratic Kampuchea'. Its broadcasts were a mix of traditional Khmer music and military communiqués. Political propaganda was out; what mattered was the progress of the war.

As loyal foot-soldiers, defending the Khmer nation, the 'new' Khmers Rouges wished to divest themselves of the nightmarish memories associated with communist rule. Pol had finally taken to heart Hua's warning that a guerrilla war was unwinnable without popular support. From 1981 onwards, his overriding goal was to win back the support of the countryside that he had squandered during his years in power. To achieve that, he explained, it was necessary to wage armed struggle but 'not to accumulate military successes. We [are] fighting . . . to build our forces politically and weaken those of the enemy.' The aim, a Khmer Rouge officer recalled, was 'to win the hearts and minds of the villagers in order to bring them to the side of Democratic Kampuchea'. In many areas the policy succeeded. A year later a Vietnamese officer complained: 'In certain places where we have no permanent military presence . . . the Khmer local authorities are two-faced. One face smiles at us, the other smiles at the Khmers Rouges.'

There was a second reason for the dissolution of the Party. The bulk of Democratic Kampuchea's diplomatic support at the United Nations and elsewhere came from capitalist countries – notably the United States and its allies – while the supply lines which kept the Khmers Rouges alive passed through pro-Western Thailand. Most of the communist world except China was hostile to the Khmer Rouge cause. And even China, in Pol's view, was already by 1981 well on the capitalist road. 'One day China will have a capitalist system,' he told In Sopheap. 'That's not a criticism. But we must take it into account. It's no good trying to comfort ourselves because their system still contains crumbs of socialism.' The point he wished to make, Sopheap concluded, was that 'we must adapt our policy in the light of the dominant trend in the world'. If Democratic Kampuchea retained a communist system, it would be out of step with its main allies. A few years later, Pol put it more succinctly: 'We chose communism because we wanted to restore our nation. We helped the Vietnamese, who were communist. But now the communists are fighting us. So we have to turn to the West and follow their way.'

At one level, the decision, and Pol's explanation for it, provided confirmation, were any needed, that the veneer of Marxism-Leninism which had cloaked Cambodian radicalism had only ever been skin-deep.

Disbanding the Party meant changing a label, little else.

It also reflected the perpetual Khmer tendency to take things to extremes. Almost three years earlier, Deng Xiaoping had recommended that in the interests of the united front, the Khmers Rouges should 'not put the Communist Party in the foreground' but emphasise patriotism, nationalism and democracy instead. Pol took that literally. If the Communist Party had become a hindrance, better to get rid of it altogether.

In documents destined for a wider audience and in his speeches at political seminars, he was less explicit. 'The method has changed, but the spirit remains the same,' he told one meeting. The movement's 'ideals' had not altered, merely 'to a certain extent, the form of the struggle'. The ambiguity inherent in such lapidary formulae was deliberate. Apart from Pol's natural preference for obliquity, he could not expect men who had spent all their adult lives fighting for socialism to change their ideas overnight. Instead, each person was left to work out for himself exactly what the movement's 'spirit' and 'ideals' now consisted of.

The changes were real. The goal of communism was abandoned. Offenders were re-educated rather than killed. The ban on individual possessions was lifted. Collective eating ended. Families lived together normally again. Young people chose their own marriage partners. Social restrictions were eased. In many ways even more striking – because it marked a break not only from previous Khmer Rouge practice but from the conduct of the military under Lon Nol, under Sihanouk and every other regime in Khmer history – captured Phnom Penh government soldiers were no longer executed. Instead they were invited to choose between joining the guerrillas or being freed and allowed to return home. 'Each person you kill has a family,' Pol explained. 'Each family will bear a grievance . . . That way you increase the number of our enemies, and we will have fewer friends.'

In most other respects, however, the Khmers Rouges remained as before.

Despite promises, soon after the Vietnamese invasion, to 'draw lessons from past mistakes', Pol never admitted responsibility for the 1.5 million deaths under his rule, nor did he repudiate the policies that had caused them. Once, in a moment of honesty, he admitted that the movement had been immature, 'drunk with victory and incompetent' and had shown itself not up to the task of running the whole country. But usually the most he would say was that 'the line was too far to the left' and that he had placed too much trust in those around him: 'They made a mess of everything . . . They were the real traitors.'

The basic strategy – to win power by forging an alliance of intellectuals and poor peasants – was unaltered. If he now eschewed political violence, it was not because he thought it morally wrong but because, at a time when the first priority was to build popular support, it was inopportune.

In the Khmer Rouge guerrilla camps, whether at the border or in the interior, the military hierarchy continued to impose a totalitarian regime of unparalleled severity. The same methods that had been used in the past to indoctrinate Party members – isolation from the outside world; rigid compartmentalisation between units; restrictions on movement; the use of hunger as a punishment and food as an incentive; the subordination of the individual to the collective; and the renunciation of personal advantage – were now applied to the training of an army imbued, as Khieu Samphân put it, with 'razor-sharp patriotism' and 'an absolute determination to make any sacrifice for the nation'.

Even in its new, more moderate guise, the movement remained the personal despotism of one man, whose views could not be challenged and whose hold over his followers was undiminished by defeat. It was less awful than before, but the change was relative: in place of terror, Pol ruled by fear.

The negotiations to form a coalition government dragged on for nine more months. Periodically, China knocked heads together, insisting that the new arrangements, whatever form they took, 'must not weaken the anti-Vietnamese forces who are fighting on the front line' (in other words, the Khmers Rouges), and threatening to block arms deliveries to the other two movements if they refused to compromise. Finally, in Kuala Lumpur on June 22 1982, the three parties announced the formation of the Coalition Government of Democratic Kampuchea with Sihanouk as Head of State, Son Sann, Prime Minister, and Khieu Samphân, Vice-Premier with responsibility for foreign affairs – which, in a government without domestic jurisdiction, was the only post that mattered.

The creation of the CGDK, as it was known, brought a number of changes.

Ieng Sary was sidelined, publicly at first but also gradually in the movement's private councils. His last major appearance had been at the UN General Assembly in the autumn of 1981. In December, he lost his post on the Standing Committee, which ceased to exist when the Party was dissolved. Thereafter, being neither a member of the Military Directorate nor of the new coalition government, he had no official role. He claimed later that he had been excluded because he advocated a political settlement to end the conflict rather than a purely military solution, but like many of his statements that appears to have been untrue. He was probably pushed aside because Sihanouk detested him, and because his name was too closely linked abroad with the horrors perpetrated during the Khmers Rouges' years in power. He continued to participate in leadership meetings, but his influence waned.

Base 808, the former Khmer Rouge seat of government, was closed, and over the next two years, most of the civilian ministers who had worked there, including Thiounn Mumm and his brother, Chum, went into exile in China or France. Sary himself moved to the Thai village of Tamoun, near Soy Dao, the 'Mountain of Stars', twenty miles north of Chanthaburi, where he was in charge of an ultra-secret base called D-25, which now replaced the old facilities at Kamrieng as a permanent transshipment point for all Chinese military aid sent through Thailand to the Khmers Rouges.

Sihanouk, meanwhile, after three years waiting in the wings, returned to centre stage in his new role as Head of State.

Thailand and the other non-communist South-East Asian states welcomed it as a first step towards a negotiated end to the conflict. China had mixed feelings. Sihanouk was not as easy to deal with as he had been in the early 1970s. Having allied himself once with the Khmers Rouges, only to be marginalised after their victory, he was not going to be burned a second time. His interests coincided with those of the Khmers Rouges to the extent that both wished to force Vietnam to withdraw its troops from Cambodia. But it was clear to Beijing that the moment a political settlement loomed, they would have very different agendas.

At this stage, moreover, China did not want peace. Nor did the United States.

The object was not to end the war against Vietnam, but to prolong it. Deng had told the Japanese Prime Minister, Masayoshi Ohira, early on in the conflict: 'It is wise for China to force the Vietnamese to stay in Cambodia because that way they will suffer more and more.' His Vice-Foreign Minister, Han Nianlong, urged that nothing be done 'to lighten [the Russians'] burden'. Only when that burden became intolerable and Moscow could no longer bear the cost of supporting Vietnam, he said, would a political solution become possible. Nor did the Chinese have any illusions about how long this would take. In the summer of 1983, they told Sihanouk that the guerrillas would need to go on fighting 'for another four or five years'. The implication – that peace talks might begin in 1987 or 1988 – would prove remarkably accurate.

The US administration was less frank, and less than truthful. Zbigniew Brzezinski, President Carter's National Security Adviser, acknowledged: 'I encouraged the Chinese to support Pol Pot . . . Pol Pot was an abomination. We could never support him, but China could.' It was not very brave.

At the UN General Assembly, the Secretary of State, Alexander Haig, and his aides ostentatiously walked out when the Khmer Rouge delegate stood up to speak. But while they held their noses in public, they worked overtime in private to canvass diplomatic support to enable the Khmers Rouges to keep their UN seat. China could never have persuaded right-wing African countries like Kenya and Malawi to vote for Pol Pot, still less to receive a Khmer Rouge Ambassador. The United States could and did. 'All you [Americans] had to do was to let Pol Pot die,' Prince Sihanouk said later. '[In 1979] Pol Pot was dying, but you brought him back to life . . . and sent him into battle to kill and kill and kill . . . But now you say the Khmers Rouges are unacceptable. What hypocrisy! What hypocrisy!' For America, as for China, the aim was to make Vietnam bleed and through Vietnam's pain to weaken its patron, Russia. The 'proxy war' Brzezinski had spoken of had finally become a reality, and it was partly of America's making.

There was a clear if unwritten division of labour. China provided a billion dollars' worth of military aid to the Khmers Rouges over the course of the decade. The US kept the coalition afloat politically, and along with Malaysia, Singapore and Thailand, gave more limited help, totalling about 215 million dollars in all, to the two non-communist military forces – the 5,000-strong Sihanoukist National Army and 9,000 men belonging to Son Sann's National Front for the Liberation of the Khmer People. Neither group was very effective, but they created the illusion that it was not just the Khmers Rouges doing the fighting.

In practice, even after the CGDK had been established, there was little military co-ordination on the ground. The Khmers Rouges stood by and did nothing when Son Sann's forces were attacked. The latter refused any contact with the Sihanoukists. But the overall strength of the resistance was growing. In 1983, guerrilla attacks increased and in many areas con trolled by the Heng Samrin government the security situation deteriorated.

That year Pol travelled to Bangkok for a medical check-up. He was found to have Hodgkin's disease, a cancerous condition which attacks the lymphatic system. The Thai army doctors who examined him warned that he would need prolonged treatment, and it was decided that he should go to China once the military situation permitted. That looked like being quite soon. The Khmers Rouges were continuing to make gains – in two spectacular incidents the following spring, a Vietnamese army fuel depot was destroyed near Battambang and the town of Siem Reap was attacked – and towards the middle of 1984, Pol felt confident enough to move Office 131 to a new base, higher up in the mountains, several miles inside Cambodian territory, near a stream known locally as O'Suosadey, the 'Good-day River'.

Nevertheless, the discovery that he had cancer gave him pause.

The six months he spent at O'Suosadey were a time of personal and political reflection. He would soon be sixty. He had no family. Khieu Ponnary was living with her mother, her sister, Thirith, and Ieng Sary at the transshipment base at Soy Dao. Her condition had worsened. Chinese specialists had examined her but had concluded that her schizophrenia was so advanced that nothing further could be done.

In the summer of 1984 Pol decided that he wanted to remarry and have children.

For a man who, throughout his political career, had preached the renunciation of family ties, and who, even now, urged his soldiers to delay marrying until victory had been achieved 'lest they think of their wives and families to the detriment of the struggle', it was an extraordinary departure. Whatever it said about social policy, or about the leadership's double standards, it confirmed that the ideological rigour of the past was rapidly disappearing.

No less striking was Pol's choice of a go-between: the Eastern Zone Commander, Son Sen. At the end of 1978, after the murder of Malcolm Caldwell, it had been rumoured that Sen's days were numbered. Now he was back in favour. He sent to O'Suosadey two young women from one of the all-female transport battalions which carried military supplies from the border to Khmer Rouge units in the interior. One of them, a tall, well-built peasant girl named Meas, Pol decided he liked. She was twenty-two years old. Soon afterwards she joined his household as a cook.

Then, in December 1984, the Vietnamese launched the biggest dry season offensive for six years. In a matter of weeks, every Khmer Rouge base was overrun and much of the infrastructure built by the forces fighting for Son Sann and Sihanouk was destroyed as well. O' Suosadey was abandoned and, for a second time, Pol was forced to flee into Thailand.

For the remainder of the decade, he did not set foot on Cambodian soil.

His new headquarters, K-18, was on a rubber plantation a few miles outside Trat. The land was paid for by the Cambodians, using money provided by China, but registered in the name of a Thai general. It was guarded by the same Thai Special Forces unit, 838, that had helped protect Office 131. The Thai army also arranged the purchase of two other properties, half an hour's drive to the north along the road from Trat to Chanthaburi: B-50, where Pol lived; and 'House 20', a larger complex, with two brick houses and a number of wooden bungalows for visitors, which served as residence and offices for Khieu Samphân. The geography held the clue. Pol was preparing his succession. One of Samphân's aides recalled:

Khieu Samphân looked after diplomatic work . . . . But at K-18, Son Sen was in charge . . . [There was an idea in the air] that Sen would become the top leader of Democratic Kampuchea, while Samphân would be responsible for government matters. It was just a feeling, but there were lots of little signs. For instance, when Nuon Chea needed money, he had to get it from Son Sen. On practical questions, even though Nuon was the Number Two in the leadership, it wasn't he who decided. The work system, all the mechanisms that Pol established at K-18 – they were all built around Son Sen. And Pol himself? He gave me the clear impression that he was withdrawing.

It was a very gradual withdrawal. Pol kept a house at K-18, where he stayed when he held political seminars with cadres from the interior. He still took all the major decisions. But he no longer micromanaged Khmer Rouge policy as he had in the past.

The new arrangements received their public consecration in September 1985, when it was announced that, 'having reached his 60th birthday, the mandatory age for retirement', Pol was stepping down as Commander-in-Chief in favour of Son Sen, but would continue to work in an advisory capacity. Khieu Samphân was confirmed as President of the Khmers Rouges' civilian wing, now rebaptised the 'Party of Democratic Kampuchea', a paper organisation which served as the vehicle for the movement's participation in the coalition government.

Like the dissolution of the Communist Party, the news of Pol's retirement was widely disbelieved. Sihanouk called it 'a farce'. And it was certainly true that, like Deng Xiaoping in China, Pol continued to be the movement's ultimate authority, even without any official position. Nevertheless the change was more than cosmetic. The nature of the struggle was evolving. For the last five years, it had been essentially military. During the months Pol spent at O'Suosadey, he became convinced that the emphasis would soon shift back to politics and that the time had come for new men to take the fore. His personal circumstances had also changed. During the summer, he and Meas married. They held no wedding ceremony. But at a reception at K-18, attended by Nuon Chea, Son Sen, Samphân and two or three others, where the couple toasted each other with orange juice, he gave a hint of his own new priorities. 'I want you to be a good mother,' he told her. The following spring, their daughter was born. Pol named her Sitha, after the heroine of the Khmer religious epic, the Reamker. Some time afterwards he left for China, where he remained for almost a year, undergoing cancer treatment at a military hospital in Beijing followed by a prolonged convalescence.

*　　*　　*

By the mid-1980s, the strategy of Beijing and Washington – to hurt Vietnam in order to hurt Moscow – was beginning to pay off. The cost of strategic rivalry with NATO, military tension with China and the never-ending war in Afghanistan was more than the flagging Soviet economy could stand. When, in March 1985, Mikhail Gorbachev came to power, one of his first priorities was to cut back on Moscow's overseas commitments. Vietnam was one of these. Hanoi might continue to claim that the situation in Cambodia was 'irreversible', but the boast sounded increasingly hollow. The question was not whether peace negotiations would begin, but when.

Gorbachev was not the only or even, for Cambodians, the most important new leader to emerge that winter. In Phnom Penh, the Vietnamese appointed Hun Sen, the former Khmer Rouge deputy regimental commander who had been serving as Heng Samrin's Foreign Minister, to take over as Prime Minister. Hun Sen was then thirty-four years old. He had a glass eye, the result of a wound sustained during the Khmer Rouge offensive against Phnom Penh in April 1975. He was ambitious, capable, devious and, as events would show, extremely ruthless. To Vietnam, he represented the middle ground in a regime which was split on factional lines between ex-Khmer Rouge leaders like Heng Samrin and ex-Issaraks, like Pen Sovann, neither of whom had performed entirely to Hanoi's satisfaction. In practice, most of Samrin's power now passed to his younger rival.

By the time Pol returned from China in the summer of 1988, Hun Sen and Sihanouk were already well engaged in a diplomatic minuet around the possibility of direct negotiations. Most of the parties to the dispute – the Sihanoukists, Son Sann's group, the Phnom Penh authorities and Vietnam – favoured formal peace talks, as did Thailand and the other South-East Asian states. China bowed to the inevitable. Agreement was finally reached on an informal meeting with Hun Sen, 'en famille', as Sihanouk put it, at a country hotel at Fère-en-Tardenois, on the edge of the champagne country an hour's drive east of Paris. The Prince was accompanied by his wife, Monique, and his son, Ranariddh; Hun Sen by two aides. The three days of discussions ended with a banquet, prepared by Sihanouk himself in the kitchens of the hotel's world-renowned restaurant.

Beyond agreeing on the need for a political solution, little of substance was achieved. But that was not the point. The ice had been broken. A further meeting followed in January 1988, opening the way for talks in Jakarta six months later which brought together for the first time the leaders of all four Cambodian factions: Sihanouk, Hun Sen, Khieu Samphân and Son

Sann. Nearly ten years after the Vietnamese invasion, serious negotiations on a political settlement had finally begun.

From the Khmers Rouges' standpoint, the process had started too soon.

Their efforts to win back support in the countryside, which had begun in 1981, had intensified over the previous three years. But Pol estimated that only about 1,000 out of Cambodia's 7,000 villages supported the Khmer Rouge cause, most of them in remote mountainous or jungle areas where the writ of the Phnom Penh authorities did not run. In reality even that figure may have been too high. His goal was to win over at least a third of the rural population by 1990. This did not mean creating 'liberated zones' as in the early 1970s. Now the movement's tactics were to suborn the village chief, and then to build core groups of supporters, first at the level of the family, later of several families and finally of the whole village. The network so formed operated in clandestinity and had no name. But it guaranteed Khmer Rouge control – which meant that, if a political settlement were followed by elections, such villages would vote for Khmer Rouge candidates. Pol explained the new strategy in a speech at a political seminar that winter:

> Suppose there are 100 seats in the Kampuchean National Assembly. It would not be bad if we have 20 [representatives], better than that if we have 30 and even better if we have 40 . . . At the least we will have 10 or 20 or 30 voices there belonging to us . . . [And if we have] representatives in parliament we will inevitably have some representatives in government [and] in the major ministries . . . [That] is the only way in which it will be possible to protect to an important extent the interests of the people.

Later he spoke of the Party of Democratic Kampuchea holding 'perhaps 15 per cent of ministerial posts'. The goal was to obtain a foothold in power – on the premise that the movement mirrored the interests of the peasantry, who made up 80 per cent of Cambodia's population, and that the demographic majority they formed would eventually translate into majority political support. 'The towns will follow the villages,' Pol declared. 'Whoever is able to gather the force [of the villages] will be the winner.'

Given time, this strategy had a chance of success. In much of rural Cambodia, a combination of war taxes, military conscription and forced labour was making the Phnom Penh authorities increasingly unpopular.

But time was precisely what the Khmers Rouges did not have.

Pol wanted a negotiated settlement 'only when the situation on the domestic battlefield is ripe'. If elections took place before the guerrillas had got control of a big enough part of the rural population, it would be a disaster, he said. 'This is a big worry. It's why we must speed up our activities and Khieu Samphân must try to slow down the progress of the negotiations until we have accomplished . . . our objectives.'

But over the next eighteen months, that option disappeared.

After making several token troop withdrawals from Cambodia in the early 1980s, Vietnam finally pulled out most, if not all, of its forces in September 1989. Two months later the Berlin Wall came down, the Soviet Empire proceeded to fall apart and relations between Russia and China were normalised. There were even the beginnings of a thaw between China and Vietnam.

In short, the Cold War ended, and with it the rationale for the United States and its allies to continue backing the Khmers Rouges.

For some time President Bush had been ill at ease with such unpleasing bedfellows. Now his Secretary of State, James Baker, announced that America would stop supporting the Coalition Government's claim to occupy Cambodia's seat at the UN and start giving humanitarian aid to the authorities in Phnom Penh. Between the lines, the message was clear: the Faustian pact was over. It was left to the French Foreign Minister, Roland Dumas, to spell out the implications. 'The international community,' he told Hun Sen and Khieu Samphân in December 1990, 'cannot indefinitely focus on the fate of Cambodia if the Cambodians themselves do not show the political will to reach a settlement.' In plain language, the window of opportunity for a peace settlement was about to close.

Pol now faced an impossible dilemma.

If the Khmers Rouges dragged their feet, the negotiations might break down or, worse, Sihanouk and Son Sann might do a deal with Hun Sen on their own. The new Thai Premier, Chatichai Choonhavan, was more interested in business ties with Vietnam than in supporting ousted revolutionaries and hinted that Thailand might halt arms shipments if the Khmers Rouges refused to co-operate. Even China could no longer completely be relied on.

On the other hand, the guerrillas were still far short of the support of the two to three thousand villages Pol had hoped for.

The Gulf War, in the spring of 1991, distracted the West's attention and provided a few months' respite. But the day of reckoning came in June, when the leaders of the four Cambodian factions met at the Thai resort of Pattaya to iron out the last remaining problems. For the first time since the peace process had begun, Pol left B-50 to stay near by. If the Khmers Rouges were going to dig in their heels, this was their last opportunity to do so. At each stage of the discussion, Khieu Samphân sought Pol's agreement. But by then the negotiation had developed a momentum of its own.

To pull back without good reason had become extremely difficult. On June 26, the meeting decided that the Supreme National Council (SNC) – the body in whose name Cambodia would be ruled until a new government was elected – should be established in Phnom Penh, and approved an indefinite ceasefire and an end to foreign military aid.

Pol accepted the deal on offer because, of the two alternatives – fighting on in isolation, without foreign support, probably against the combined forces of Sihanouk, Son Sann and Hun Sen; or trying to make the best of a peace settlement which offered at least the possibility of the Khmers Rouges having a role in mainstream political life – the latter was less bad. At the time he evidently did not realise the extent to which the settlement was flawed. On the crucial issue of how the elections should be conducted, Hun Sen, despite his youth, had outwitted Sihanouk, Son Sann and Khieu Samphân combined, men far older and more experienced than himself. The PRK – or 'State of Cambodia', as the Phnom Penh regime now called itself – would not be dissolved, as the resistance wanted, but would remain in place until a new government was formed. As a result, voting would be 'organised' by the UN and 'supervised' by the SNC, but in practice it would use 'the existing structures' of the Phnom Penh administration. Politics is a practical art and Hun Sen a practical person. The agreement gave his government a head start by allowing it to control the mechanics of getting in the vote.

On October 23 1991, the 'Agreement on a Comprehensive Political Settlement of the Cambodian Conflict' was signed in Paris, and the UN began gearing up for the biggest and most expensive peace-keeping operation in its history.

Three weeks later, Prince Sihanouk flew back in triumph to the capital he had fled during the Vietnamese invasion in 1979. He travelled from Beijing aboard a Chinese airliner, escorted by the same senior Chinese diplomat who had come to take him to safety all those years before. As he drove into Phnom Penh, along streets lined with cheering crowds, in a pink Chevrolet convertible – a relic of his former rule, refurbished for the occasion – children cried out excitedly, their eyes shining, 'The King! The King has returned!' And for most of the population, after twenty years of civil war, Khmer Rouge despotism and Vietnamese occupation, that was indeed how it seemed. The following morning, Sihanouk and his suite, wearing traditional court dress and reclining on rattan quilts, watched a display of classical Khmer dance in the palace gardens. Among them, seeming slightly ill at ease, was a man who looked exactly like Pol Pot. It was Loth Suong, his elder brother, with whom he had lived as a child. Suong's wife, Chea Samy, had helped revive the royal dance troupe after her brother-in-law's regime had been overthrown. For a fleeting moment, it seemed that the Cambodia of the 1960s was really back again.

After the Vietnamese withdrawal in 1989, the Khmers Rouges had occupied a strip of territory along the border stretching northward from Pailin, where Pol established his new headquarters.

A two-storey Thai-style village house, with a galvanised iron roof, was built for him, fifty yards from the stream that marked the frontier, in the forest ten miles west of the town. It was spacious but extremely simple – a large L-shaped sitting room, with a brick-tiled floor and perforated walls; two upstairs bedrooms and a study; a primitive kitchen with a wood stove and an outhouse. In the garden, he planted a jackfruit tree. An underground bunker, capable of resisting artillery fire and big enough to take half a dozen people, was dug nearby, reinforced with tree trunks and packed earth. The building itself was hidden from view by a thicket, beyond which lay two other houses for aides and secretarial staff and a row of small huts for the bodyguards.

From this vantage point Pol watched events unfold in Phnom Penh. He did not much like what he saw.

Immediately after returning, Sihanouk went on the warpath. He told a news conference that he regarded Hun Sen as a son; that 'without Vietnam we would all be dead'; and that the Khmer Rouge leaders should be put on trial. He then endorsed the claims of the State of Cambodia to be the country's *de facto* government and proposed an alliance between FUNCIN-PEC, led by his son Prince Ranariddh, and Hun Sen's PRPK, now renamed the Cambodian People's Party (CPP), which, like Pol's own movement, claimed to have become an avid convert to pluralism, liberal democracy and the free market. None of this augured well for the 'neutral political environment' envisaged by the Paris accords. Nor did the reception given to Khieu Samphân when he came to inaugurate the Khmer Rouge mission in Phnom Penh ten days later. A mob, organised by Hun Sen's security police, broke into the building, forcing him to hide inside a wardrobe. His life was never in danger: men with walkie-talkies discreetly controlled the proceedings. But he was beaten and humiliated. Television pictures showed him, with blood streaming down his face, 'protected' by government soldiers, crawling into the back of an armoured personnel carrier which had been sent to 'rescue' him.

The incident had long-term repercussions. The other member of Pol's new leadership team, Son Sen, who had arrived in the capital a week earlier, had apparently heard rumours of the impending demonstration. But no action had been taken. To Pol's suspicious mind that raised questions about Sen's loyalty. Soon afterwards, he reclaimed the authority he had devolved in the late 1980s and resumed direct control over Khmer Rouge decision-making.

It also offered a foretaste of Hun Sen's ruthlessness. As the months passed, Pol would discover that his youthful adversary was not only as hard-bitten and tough as himself, but hungrier for power.

At a meeting held in Pailin on December 13 to discuss these developments, Pol set out the movement's strategy. It would continue to observe the provisions of the Paris accords, but in its own fashion. The 70 per cent of Khmer Rouge troops who were to be demobilised, along with the same proportion of the other factions' forces, would remain on standby await-ing cantonment, but nearly 10,000 men would be passed off as civil police, entitled to keep their arms. Meanwhile the movement must redouble its efforts to 'liberate' the villages, replacing CPP headmen and local officials with pro-Khmer Rouge elements. As Pol well knew, this was a violation of what had been agreed. However, he could argue that Hun Sen's government had also refused to disarm its police. It, too, used violence and intimidation to repress opponents in the countryside. In reality, neither side intended to honour the Paris accords to the letter. But Hun Sen had a major advantage: the support of Sihanouk. The Prince had experienced Pol's rule once. He was determined to prevent him ever holding power again, even if it meant allying himself with a regime installed by the Vietnamese.

By February 1992, Pol had recognised the danger.

If the Khmers Rouges allowed themselves to become isolated, he warned his colleagues, the UN and the Western powers 'will drag the other forces into joining with Phnom Penh. It will become an alliance of the West, Vietnam, Hun Sen, FUNCINPEC and Son Sann – and the Chinese, the Thais and [the other] South-East Asian nations will [have to] accept it, whether they like it or not.' The answer, he decided, was to follow a two-pronged policy – a posture of cautious co-operation', as one observer described it – designed on the one hand to prove to the outside world and the two other former resistance factions that the Party of Democratic Kampuchea would play the democratic game so long as the Phnom Penh government did the same, and on the other to show what would happen if the movement were backed into a corner. Accordingly, the movement's troops committed innumerable ceasefire violations; it attempted forcibly to repatriate refugees from Thailand to territories under its control; and it was refractory in permitting access by UN military observers – while at the same time continuing to obey the rules just enough to make the UN believe that it wished to remain part of the peace process.

But then in June Khieu Samphân informed the Supreme National Council that Khmer Rouge troops would not disarm. The pretext was that Vietnamese forces had not completely withdrawn. The charge was untrue but impossible to disprove and politically rewarding. Over the past decade, with the Phnom Penh government's encouragement, an estimated 400,000 Vietnamese settlers had come to Cambodia. They now formed a highly visible minority whose presence lent vicarious credibility to the idea that Vietnamese troops had remained behind in disguise.

In fact, the allegations of a Vietnamese presence were a red herring.

The real problem for the Khmers Rouges was the UN's failure to control the Hun Sen administration. The head of the peace-keeping operation, Yasushi Akashi, acknowledged that the 'neutral political environment' required by the Paris agreement had not been achieved. This was partly due to the limitations imposed by the UN's charter, which requires its troops to serve as 'peace-keepers, not peace-enforcers', and its civil servants to find ways round problems, not meet them head on. The result was that bureaucratic sleight of hand substituted for political choice. By the summer, Pol had begun to doubt whether, in such circumstances, even a modest place in the next government – in his eyes the one merit of the parliamentary process that the Paris Accords laid down – was still a realistic goal.

The decision not to disarm marked a fundamental change in Khmer Rouge strategy. From then on, the movement adopted a much more con-frontational stance, putting pressure on the UN Transitional Authority to rein in the Phnom Penh government while at the same time, in total vio-lation of the Paris accords, aggressively expanding the territory under its control. Future Khmer Rouge military co-operation, Akashi was told, would depend on the UN creating the 'neutral political environment' all sides claimed to want. Over the next nine months, matters went from bad to worse. The Khmers Rouges organised sporadic massacres of Vietnamese settlers, causing tens of thousands to flee in terror across the border. Political violence by Hun Sen's CPP likewise continued. The peace-keepers were no better able to deal with the one than with the other.

In January 1993, Sihanouk retired in disgust to Beijing, declaring that he would have nothing further to do with the UN or the Phnom Penh authorities until the intimidation stopped. 'None of the conditions for the election has been met,' he said. 'None!' The UN's insistence on going ahead was 'a hideous comedy'.

The Khmers Rouges went through the motions of preparing to take part in the vote, announcing the formation of yet another new political body, the Cambodian National Union Party, to put up candidates. But their refusal to disarm made it seem increasingly unlikely that they would actually do so.

Pol confirmed his movement's decision to boycott the election towards the end of March. A few days later he moved his headquarters from Pailin to Phnom Chhat ('Umbrella Mountain'), a low hill on the Thai border, twenty miles north-east of Aranyaprathet, where Khieu Samphân soon joined him. In April, just as the election campaign was about to begin, the Khmer Rouge delegation withdrew melodramatically from Phnom Penh, claiming inadequate security. As the movement seemed poised for a return to illegality, the normally impassive Akashi warned angrily that it was taking 'a dangerous step towards outlaw status . . . There should be no more sanctuaries for that party and no more chances.'

The Khmers Rouges now controlled about a fifth of Cambodia's territory (but only 5 per cent of the population), in an easterly arc along the Thai border from the Cardamom Mountains to Preah Vihear. They had money: the cross-border trade in gems from Pailin and in tropical timber, cut by Thai companies – in disregard of a UN embargo – brought in tens of millions of dollars a year. China no longer supplied weaponry, but there were still large stocks in the warehouses, which had been moved from Soy Dao to the frontier area near Kamrieng, and whatever was lacking could be bought through the Thai army. Most important of all, the Thai government, which like everyone else now expected Hun Sen's party to win the election, bringing to power a pro-Vietnamese government in Phnom Penh, had decided its interests would best be served by having a Khmer Rouge buffer zone along the border. Son Sen established his headquarters at Oda, halfway between Pailin and Malay, while Nuon Chea took charge of the area around Samlaut. Together they controlled what was known as the Southern Front, while Pol and Mok were in command in the North.

In short, if the civil war were to resume, the Khmers Rouges had everything they needed in order to fight: arms, financial resources and the discreet support of a friendly foreign power.

When the election results were announced at the beginning of June 1993, however, these calculations were put in doubt. Contrary to expectations, Prince Ranariddh's FUNCINPEC emerged the winner, with 58 seats in the 120-seat assembly to 51 for Hun Sen's CPP. Hun Sen refused to recognise the results, prompting ten days of feverish manoeuvring until Sihanouk imposed a Cambodian-style solution: the country would have not one Prime Minister but two. Ranariddh and Hun Sen would jointly head a coalition government in which each ministry would have twin incumbents.

That was not what the people of Cambodia had voted for. But the UN, having invested 2.8 billion dollars and sent 20,000 soldiers and civilian administrators to oversee the peace process, had no intention of imperilling its success by standing on principle. Hun Sen learnt a lesson he would never forget: that whenever he played fast and loose with the rules of democracy, the international community would sit on its hands and look the other way. Sihanouk was rewarded by the restoration of the monarchy with himself as King, which through all the vicissitudes of the previous quarter-century, had been his one constant and overriding goal.

The Khmers Rouges' situation was almost equally bizarre.

Their representatives returned to Phnom Penh and talks were held on how they might re-enter the peace process. But at the same time, the new Cambodian National Army – now including former FUNCINPEC and Son Sann troops as well as Hun Sen's forces – launched a military offensive to try to reoccupy the territories which the Khmers Rouges had seized since the Paris accords. Initially, it was highly successful. In August Phnom Chhat was overrun – sending Pol and Khieu Samphân scurrying into Thailand – and then, six months later, Anlong Veng and Pailin. But the bicephalous royal government was unable to hold on to these gains, and one after another they passed back into Khmer Rouge hands. By May 1994, Son Sen's troops were in control of almost as much territory as before the offensive began. There was a stalemate. Neither side had the strength to do decisive damage to the other.

Having failed to solve the problem militarily, Hun Sen and Ranariddh tried political pressure. In June, the Khmers Rouges were ordered to close their mission in Phnom Penh. The following month, parliament unanimously passed legislation declaring them 'outside the law'. The wheel had gone full circle. The insurrectionary movement Pol had launched in the 1960s had returned to the maquis from which it came.

Peace had never been helpful to the Khmer Rouge cause.

The three years during which they held power, from 1975 to 1978, were so ghastly that most Cambodians wanted nothing to do with them ever again. The three years after the Paris agreement, from 1991 to 1994, rotted the movement from within.

After a quarter of a century of warfare, the rank and file had had enough. 'They wanted to be with their families, to raise their children and farm,' one regimental commander remembered. Markets reopened, private agriculture resumed, the more go-ahead villagers bought saws and ox-carts and started logging for the Thais. Radio broadcasts from Phnom Penh brought a seductive whiff of debauchery and corruption. The draconian internal controls which had always been the movement's strength began to crumble. The desertion rate, which had been running at about three hundred men a year in the 1980s, rose tenfold. Even the election boycott which Pol had decreed was honoured in the breach. In many areas, local Khmer Rouge commanders allowed villagers and even, in some cases, their own troops, to vote for FUNCINPEC. Pol's long-time aide, Phi Phuon, reflected with some bitterness:

> Most people at that time were against continuing to fight. The vast majority thought that the Paris accords were the last chance for Cambodia, and the decision not to take part in the elections shocked them. A lot of us had sent our families to our home villages, or had children studying in Thailand. Now we were told to bring them back, otherwise we would be considered traitors. How could Pol Pot make such a serious error of appreciation about the reality of the situation – about the way the people on our side really felt? . . . It was because anyone who disagreed with him was accused of being ideologically backward, or of falling under the influence of enemy propaganda. So everyone kept quiet.

That was not quite true. Pol was well aware of the popular mood. His own private secretary, Keo Yann, told him he felt that the struggle was over and he intended to stay and farm in Pailin. Pol allowed him to do so, a reaction that would have been unthinkable a few years before. But he did not change his mind about fighting. It was a decision that puzzled many of those around him. 'He ought to have known that resuming armed struggle wouldn't work,' Long Nârin said later. 'I don't know why he did it. But he did.'

The next problem was how to reimpose wartime discipline. Pol's answer was that everyone should once again take the poorest peasants as their model, as they had in the early 1970s. The old slogan of 'independence-mastery' was revived, and red flags, bearing a sickle but no hammer, were flown in Khmer Rouge villages. The aim of 'peasantisation', as it was called, was to bolster military morale. 'If the soldiers saw that the villagers in the rear areas were getting rich by selling logs to Thailand, while they were risking their lives,' a cadre explained, 'they would lose heart. The rear had to support the front. It couldn't be left loose.'

Tightening discipline in the rear, however, meant stopping cross-border trade. To that end, in the autumn of 1994, Pol issued a directive, signed with his personal code, '99', ordering the confiscation of privately owned means of transport. Initially, ox-carts and lorries were targeted, because they could be used to take logs across the border. But soon afterwards private cars and motor-bikes were seized, too, and stored in makeshift entrepôts. In some areas, the new rules were enforced more strictly, in others less. On the surface, they were accepted. 'What could people do?' a cadre asked. 'They didn't have guns.' But throughout the Khmer Rouge areas, there was deep-seated, sullen, peasant anger. The population had not wanted to resume fighting in the first place. Now, the first glimmer of prosperity after twenty years of privation had been brutally snuffed out. 'The ox-carts were the peasants' life,' Long Nârin remembered. 'And Pol Pot took them away.'

After the fall of Phnom Chhat, Pol moved to Anlong Veng. When that base, too, was overrun during the spring of 1994, he retreated to Kbal Ansoang, on the crest of the Dangrek Mountains, abutting the Thai border, eight miles further north.

It was an idyllic setting. Pol's house stood on the edge of a cliff, a thousand feet above a perfectly flat plain that stretched away to the horizon in the south. It was built of brick, with ceramic tiles and bathroom fittings from Thailand; there was a terrace, where he sat in the evenings, with an iron balustrade, shaded by creepers, and orchids growing in coconut shells, hanging from the trees; and below, blasted out of the rock, a basement sealed with iron doors, where documents and weapons were stored. The interior was furnished simply with heavy tropical wood armchairs, in the French colonial style, and a chaise-longue made from rattan and bamboo.

Nearby stood a traditional Khmer wooden house for Tep Khunnal, a young engineer with a doctorate from Toulouse who had taken Keo Yann's place as Pol's secretary. Slightly further away were other dwellings: for Khieu Samphân, for Thiounn Thioeunn, the apolitical aristocrat who, alone of the Thiounn brothers, had remained faithful to the Khmer Rouge cause, and for four intellectuals – Chan Yourann, In Sopheap, Kor Bunheng and Mak Ben – who had been among the leaders of the short-lived Cambodian National Union Party, formed for the elections. In July 1994 Pol had appointed them ministers in a fictive 'government' of the Khmer Rouge territories, which no one ever recognised and whose existence was quickly forgotten.

Just beyond the outer perimeter, protected by a minefield, stood an open-air meeting hall, with dormitories for visiting cadres. Pol conducted political seminars less often than in the past, but when he did so he was as convincing as ever. One participant remembered:

> Every time we returned from a seminar, we felt full of gratitude and loyalty towards Pol Pot . . . He made a tremendous impression, especially on those who came for the first time. They always wanted to come back and study more . . . As a teacher, he was brilliant. He has a sense of humour and he's warm-hearted towards you . . . He gives you confidence in yourself . . . He always left us feeling illuminated by his explanations and his vision . . . Even

the other leaders felt he was the heart and soul of the movement . . . [We] worried that one day he would die and there would be no one to replace him.

In 1994, Pol was nearing seventy. Until the previous year, while K-18 remained open, he had been able to get follow-up treatment for his cancer from Thai doctors in Trat. At Kbal Ansoang, that was not possible. He also developed heart trouble. Thiounn Thioeunn diagnosed aortic stenosis, a congestive condition in which the aortic valve no longer functions properly. In the West, such patients are usually given open-heart surgery. But in Pol's case, Thioeunn said, he had left it too long and it had become inoperable. Already at Trat he had sometimes required an oxygen cylinder in order to breathe. At Kbal Ansoang, he needed oxygen frequently and, the following year, suffered a minor stroke which impaired his vision and left him partly paralysed down his left side.

As his illness worsened, he spent more time with his family, especially with his daughter, Sitha, who was then eight years old. He taught her to read and write Khmer and cooked her dishes that she liked. Like old men everywhere, he started to reminisce. In Sopheap remembered days when he would call them to a meeting and spend the afternoon regaling them with stories about his youth in Phnom Penh. Later he got Tep Khunnal to read to him extracts in Khmer translation from his biography, *Brother Number One*, by the American historian David Chandler. Shortly afterwards he began dictating his own version of his life, but the notebooks later disappeared. He drank whisky or cognac, when the Thais brought him a bottle, and spent hours listening to traditional Khmer music, which he had loved since learning to play as a child. 'He appreciated the finer points,' an aide remembered. 'As he listened, he'd comment on the musicians' technique.' He also received newspapers and magazines sent in from Thailand, including, improbably, the French weekly *Paris-Match*. He told In Sopheap that it interested him because, when the political struggle resumed, the Khmers Rouges, too, would need to publish a glossy magazine promoting their cause. The real reasons are impossible to fathom. In Pol's youth, *Paris-Match* had been widely read in Cambodia for its caricatures of Sihanouk, depicted as Saint-Exupéry's character, the Little Prince. But one can only wonder what he made of the stories of philandering rock stars and film actresses, the intrigues of European royalty and the skulduggery of French politicians, that filled the magazine's pages in the 1990s, as he presided from his mountain lair over the dwindling fortunes of the most radical revolutionary movement of modern times. As Ieng Sary once observed, 'Pol Pot had a very complex character.'

Age had not mellowed him, however, nor given him a moral sense extending beyond his own and his movement's interests.

In September 1994, the gentle old man who doted on his small daughter ordered the execution of three young backpackers – a Briton, a Frenchman and an Australian – who had been captured by Khmer Rouge forces in an attack on a train during the summer. There was no particular reason to have them killed. However, negotiations with the Royal Government had failed to elicit any offer which made it worth keeping them alive. Pol might have abandoned communism as a goal, but the line of demarcation between friends and enemies, between those who should be preserved and those whose lives had no value, was as absolute as ever.

That winter, the fates began closing in. Their agent was Son Sen, the studious, bespectacled military commander who had spent the latter part of his career being alternately suspected by Pol of treason and groomed as his successor.

Son Sen was particularly zealous in applying the 'peasantisation' policy. In Samphou Loun, a few miles south of Malay, where he had transferred his headquarters after the battles of the previous spring, communal eating was reimposed and private trade banned. On Sen's instructions, Mam Nay, Deuch's former deputy at the Tuol Sleng interrogation centre, established a prison to which recalcitrant peasants were taken for 're-education', a term which soon acquired the same sinister connotation that it had had in the 1970s. Those who refused to mend their ways, about forty in all, were bludgeoned to death. So were a group of traders at Bavel, twenty miles south-west of Battambang, who ran an open-air market in the no-man's-land between government and Khmer Rouge territory. Son Sen ordered their arrests as spies. Fifty-two people, including women and small children, were executed.

Two of Son Sen's principal subordinates, Y Chhean at Pailin and Sok Pheap in Malay, disapproved of these methods. In their own areas, they implemented the confiscation policy half-heartedly, and when Sen called meetings of the front commanders, they stayed away. Over the next year, relations between the three men became increasingly strained.

Other factors exacerbated the tension. Pailin and Malay were the main centres for trade in gems and timber with Thailand. The local commanders were unwilling to give up their share of the proceeds. Then, in 1995, Hun Sen and Ranariddh set up a special military committee to make contact with potential Khmer Rouge turncoats. For a long time nothing happened. But in February 1996, a Khmer Rouge commander at Mount Aural defected with his men. Shortly afterwards Y Chhean and Sok Pheap travelled secretly to Chanthaburi for a meeting with the committee's vice-chairman, Nhek Bunchhay of FUNCINPEC, and two senior CPP generals. They were told that if they changed sides they and their troops would be granted an amnesty, and they would be allowed to retain command of their areas. This was the same procedure that Sihanouk had employed half a century earlier, when Issarak defectors like Dap Chhuon and Puth Chhay were given commissions in the Royal Army and allowed to keep control of the districts where they had been based. Agreement was reached in principle, but no time limit was set. In the summer Chhean and Pheap attended another secret meeting at Chanthaburi, this time with Ieng Sary. Since the Paris accords, Sary's eclipse had become total. He gave the plan his blessing.

Matters came to a head in July 1996. Son Sen reported to Pol that Y Chhean was refusing to obey orders. Mok was sent to investigate.

But Mok was not a conciliator. As one of Pol's aides put it: 'He went to put out the fire and he made it worse . . . Mok was good at messing things up. He just said what came into his head, cursing and blaming people. He was not a thoughtful man.' Son Sen then sent troops to put down what the Khmer Rouge radio described as a rebellion by traitors. But by this stage it was hard enough to get the soldiers to fight Hun Sen's forces; they had no interest in killing each other. The majority mutinied. On August 15 1996, it was announced that Ieng Sary, Y Chhean and Sok Pheap had severed their ties with the Khmers Rouges and formed a new political movement which would co-operate with the government. All the remaining bases along the southern part of the border, from Samlaut to Phnom Chhat, joined them. Sary received an amnesty from the King for 'a good deed worth the lives of thousands of people', and thereafter divided his time between Pailin, where he became unofficial satrap, and Phnom Penh. Some four thousand soldiers – nearly half the total Khmer Rouge troop strength – were integrated into the Royal Army.

Ieng Sary's defection was a body-blow from which the Khmers Rouges never recovered.

By the end of the year they had also lost almost all their bases in the interior, which left them hemmed in to a narrow band of territory spread over a few hundred square miles of jungle along the country's northern border. 'We are like a fish in a trap,' Pol told his aides. 'We cannot last like this for very long.'

The way forward, he concluded, was to make the transition from armed to parliamentary struggle that he had rejected three years earlier. But had he done so then, it would have been from a position of strength: in 1993, the movement was still intact, it had international support and Sihanouk and Hun Sen both paid lip-service to the idea that the Khmers Rouges should have a role in the nation's political life. Now it would be from a position of weakness: the movement was outlawed. Its numbers were fast declining and the Thais, sensing the end approaching, had cut back their support. By this time it must have been clear to Pol that his refusal to implement the Paris accords had been a capital error. But whatever thoughts he had on that subject he kept to himself.

Ieng Sary was denounced as a traitor and accused of having embezzled large amounts of Chinese aid. Nuon Chea and Son Sen were blamed for the loss of the southern bases, stripped of their responsibilities and assigned to what were known as the 'Middle Houses', an isolated cluster of dwellings half-way down the mountain, not under arrest but out of power. Mok retained his command. But he too was under a cloud. Having decided that the older generation had failed him, Pol now turned to more junior members of his dwindling entourage. At a mass meeting in February 1997, it was announced that two veteran division commanders, Saroeun and San, were to head a 'Peasant Party' which would operate in the rural areas, while Khieu Samphân and a group of younger intellectuals would form a 'National Solidarity Party' as the movement's parliamentary face.

It all smacked of desperation. Pol's health was rapidly deteriorating. He needed oxygen every day, and attended meetings with tubes fixed to his nose. In Sopheap remembered him telling them, 'We are at the crossing of a river. If I can get you to the other side, you can go on by yourselves.'

Succour came from an unexpected quarter.

The previous year, at about the time Y Chhean was preparing to talk to Nhek Bunchhay, FUNCINPEC had held a party congress at which Prince Ranariddh threatened to withdraw from the government unless his party was given a bigger share of power. Shortly afterwards, senior FUNCIN-PEC leaders met secretly in Kompong Som and decided to try to build a political alliance with three other small parties – one of which was led by Sam Sary's son, Rainsy – and, more importantly, a military alliance with the Khmers Rouges.

This was less far-fetched than it might sound. Ranariddh's forces and the Khmers Rouges had been allies against the Phnom Penh government in the 1980s. What had been done once could be done again. However, news of the Kompong Som meeting reached Hun Sen, who warned Ranariddh that splitting the coalition would carry a high political price. To show that he meant business, in March 1997 he sent a group of body-guards to break up an anti-government demonstration by members of Sam Rainsy's party. They used hand-grenades – a method that succes-sive Cambodian governments have favoured for dealing with political opponents since Ieu Koeuss's assassination in 1950. Four were thrown into the crowd, killing fifteen people and wounding scores of others. Meanwhile Ranariddh's efforts to put out feelers to the Khmers Rouges got off to a bad start when a helicopter carrying a FUNCINPEC negotiating team landed in the mountains above Anlong Veng, ostensibly for talks within the framework of the government campaign to promote defections, and the entire delegation was detained. It was later claimed that the Khmer Rouge commander who had authorised the landing had omitted to inform Pol Pot, who, suspecting betrayal, had sent in his own troops. The envoys were held in 'tiger cages', free-standing iron cells used as military prisons in the jungle. By the time they were freed five months later, only four of the fifteen were still alive.

The two incidents illustrated the climate of extreme tension that had developed. To Hun Sen, all means were good to prevent a FUNCINPEC–Khmer Rouge alliance and, in the process, to humble Ranariddh. Pol wanted a deal with FUNCINPEC but feared that by negotiating he would encourage other leaders to follow Ieng Sary's lead and seek a separate accommodation with Hun Sen. Only Ranariddh himself seemed oblivious to the dangers. His insouciance would cost him dear.

On May 16 1997, a FUNCINPEC emissary travelled from Bangkok to meet Pol's secretary, Tep Khunnal, at the border. Agreement was reached in principle for Khieu Samphân's National Solidarity Party to join FUNCINPEC in a united front. On June 1, Samphân and Ranariddh met over lunch at the house of a Thai general in Prasa, twenty miles north of the border in Surin province, and confirmed the accord. Samphân said later that after this meeting, 'I began to believe that what I had been waiting for was finally happening – the parliamentary road was becoming a reality'.

At this point the Prince made a serious misjudgement. Without consulting Samphân, FUNCINPEC announced that, as part of the agreement, Pol Pot, Mok and Son Sen would go into exile. The aim was to present the accord to Cambodians not as an electoral manoeuvre but as a statesmanlike effort to end the insurgency by bringing Khmer Rouge 'moderates' into the fold while banishing those viewed as hardliners. Indeed, Ranariddh was angling for something even better than banishment. With his blessing, Nhek Bunchhay had been negotiating with the US military attaché in Bangkok. As he explained,

> the plan was to seize Pol Pot and bring him to our base at Tatum, which is on the Thai-Cambodian border about twelve miles west of Anlong Veng. The US would send a helicopter from a naval ship in the Gulf of Thailand and fly him back to the ship. A unit of my troops actually set out from Tatum, but to reach the area where Pol Pot was, they had to travel through Thai territory –

and as soon as they crossed the border Thai units pushed them back. I had arranged things with the Thai military on the border and they were prepared to cooperate. But then a senior commander – one of Chaovalit's men – arrived from Bangkok by helicopter and vetoed the idea. So they wouldn't let our troops come across. But it was close: we nearly succeeded.

There is no reason to believe that Pol ever got wind of the plot. But the talk of enforced exile evidently troubled him. On June 7, the Khmer Rouge radio formally denied that any negotiations had ever taken place. Two days later, Sihanouk issued a statement, ruling out pardons for Pol Pot and Mok but not for Son Sen. The latter was still in disgrace for his part in the loss of Pailin and Malay. His position had not been helped by the defection of two of his brothers, Nikân and Son Chhum, the former Khmer Rouge Ambassador to North Korea. The combination of events reawakened in Pol's mind his old suspicions about Sen's loyalty. Sihanouk's remarks – making it appear that Sen was in a different category to the others – were the final straw.

At about midnight Pol summoned his division commander, Saroeun, informed him that Son Sen and his wife were traitors and pronounced the fateful words which over the years had signalled the liquidation of so many of his associates: 'I would like you to take care of it.' In the early hours of the morning, In Sopheap heard the sound of distant gunfire. Son Sen, Yun Yat, and thirteen other family members and aides, including a five-year-old grandchild, were shot to death in the 'Middle Houses' by Saroeun's troops. Pol later told an interviewer that he had given orders 'only for Son Sen and his wife to be killed', as though those killings were acceptable; the others, he said, were 'a mistake'.

It was a murder too far. Khieu Samphân dutifully endorsed it. Nuon Chea kept silent. But Mok felt that if Son Sen could be killed, no one was safe.

On June 11, he rallied his troops at the district centre of Anlong Veng, telling them that Pol Pot had betrayed their movement and that his tyranny must end. Twenty-four hours later, the vanguard of Mok's forces reached Kbal Ansoang. They met virtually no resistance. That afternoon Pol, his wife, eleven-year-old daughter and another child left on foot with twenty bodyguards along a dirt track leading eastward along the crest of the mountains towards the ancient temple complex of Preah Vihear. Pol was in no state to walk and the bodyguards had to carry him on their backs. In Sopheap remembered their flight as 'a total shambles. It wasn't organised – it was chaos.'

They were tracked by Thai air-force L-19 spotter planes. Two or three days later, probably on June 15, several of the bodyguards were detained by

Thai troops when they crossed the border to get water. They were found to be carrying rucksacks containing several hundred thousand dollars in cash. When Pol himself was eventually located, he was being carried in a hammock, slung from a bamboo pole. In Sopheap remembered that next morning he met Saroeun's deputy, San. 'Elder Brother,' San said to him, 'our movement is finished now, isn't it?' Sopheap could not bring himself to answer, but they both knew he was right.

In the event, the death throes of the Khmers Rouges dragged on for almost two more years. Pol was placed under house arrest in a small cottage near the 'Middle Houses' where Son Sen had died. Khieu Samphân, Nuon Chea and the 'ministers' in Pol's imaginary government rallied to Mok's support. The talks with Ranariddh continued and on July 3, Khunnal and Bunchhay initialled an agreement, which the Prince and Khieu Samphân were to sign three days later, formally integrating what was left of the movement into Ranariddh's new united front.

But it was not to be. On July 5 1997, Hun Sen staged a military coup, summarily executing dozens of FUNCINPEC officials, including two ministers, arresting hundreds of others and driving Ranariddh into exile. His action nullified the Paris peace accords and destroyed what remained of the UN's multi-billion-dollar effort to impose 'democracy' on Cambodia. The West looked away in embarrassment and accepted the fait accompli.

At the end of July Pol and the three Khmer Rouge commanders who had remained loyal to him, Saroeun, San and Khon, were brought before a mass meeting near the Thai border crossing at Sang'nam, half a mile from the 'Middle Houses', at which the movement's new leadership solemnly proclaimed its attachment to liberal democratic values and vilified Pol for all the horrors committed during his time in power. The American journalist Nate Thayer, who was invited to film the proceedings as proof of the Khmers Rouges' change of heart, found the atmosphere very odd:

> [He sat] in a simple wooden chair, grasping a long bamboo cane and a rattan fan . . . an anguished old man, frail eyes struggling to focus on no one, watching his life's vision crumble in utter, final defeat . . . Pol Pot seemed often close to tears, [while] the three [detained] commanders, in contrast . . . had menacing, almost arrogant expressions, staring coldly and directly in the eyes of. . . the speakers and members of the crowd. They showed no fear . . . The crowds, though robotic, appeared to be both entertained and awestruck by the event, [but many of] those who had overthrown Pol

Pot [were] deferential . . . [They] spoke in almost gentle, respectful terms about their deposed leader. . . [When he left], some people bowed . . . as if to royalty.

Pol was 'sentenced' to life imprisonment. The three commanders were executed.

Three months later, Mok arranged for Thayer to return to interview Pol. It was his first meeting with a foreign journalist for fourteen years.

Thayer found him slowly dying, but 'chillingly unrepentant'. He had nothing to apologise for, he said. 'My conscience is clear . . . I'm old and ill . . . My life is over politically and personally . . . The Khmers have a saying about old age, illness and death. Now only death remains, and I don't know the date. The following spring, Mok presented him to two other journalists, apparently to prove that he was still alive and available as a bargaining chip.

But there was no longer anyone to bargain with. Ranariddh was out of power and Hun Sen was too smart to waste time on a movement which was collapsing anyway. In March, one of Mok's divisional commanders seized the district centre of Anlong Veng and defected with about a thousand Khmer Rouge troops. Ke Pauk and the former Ambassador to China, Pich Chheang, joined them. Mok himself and the remnants still loyal to him retreated into the mountains. On April 15, as government forces came within artillery range of the 'Middle Houses', guards dyed Pol's hair brown in case they had to flee into Thailand. That night he died peacefully in his sleep. The cause was heart failure.

His body was preserved with ice and formaldehyde so that journalists could come to witness the funeral. Thai forensic specialists took finger-prints, dental photographs and hair samples. An American correspondent wanted to remove one of his teeth, supposedly for purposes of identifi-cation. Three days afterwards Pol's widow and his daughter carried out the Buddhist rites. Then his body was cremated on a pile of rubbish and car tyres. In Sopheap, and many others, found the spectacle 'sickening, simply disgusting'. Even those, like Ieng Sary, who had broken with Pol, were shocked by the squalor of his end. Yet it was a far, far gentler death than those which Pol had meted out to the million and a half Cambodians who perished under his rule. Mok was blunter. He told a Khmer reporter:

Pol Pot has died like a ripe papaya [falling from a tree]. No one killed him, no one poisoned him. Now he's Wnished. He has no power, he has no rights, he is no more than cow shit. Cow shit is more important than him. We can use it for fertiliser.

Thus the Khmer Rouge era ended. In May, the radio station fell silent and the staff fled to a Thai refugee camp. Thiounn Thioeunn and his family, In Sopheap, Chan Yourann and the other 'ministers' followed. In October, Tep Khunnal left with Pol's widow, Meas, for Malay, where they married and started a family. In December, Khieu Samphân and Nuon Chea were allowed to settle under Ieng Sary's protection in Pailin. Mok was captured in March 1999. He alone of the former leadership refused to surrender, and he alone was imprisoned to await an aleatory trial.

Afterword

Almost a century ago, a French doctor, struck, like many of his compatriots, by the torpor of the Cambodian population, wondered to himself whether a nation capable of creating the wonders of Angkor 'might not, after all, one day rediscover the spark that will rekindle the brilliance of its former genius'. Angkor and the grandeur it represents have been both an inspiration and an encumbrance to successive Cambodian governments. The temple complex, the largest and one of the most sumptuous religious edifices in the world, shows what Cambodians were capable of and cruelly underlines their subsequent decline.

National humiliation and the frustration it engenders among an educated elite are an almost infallible recipe for violent revolution. The Chinese, the Koreans, the Russians, the Germans under Hitler, all went down that road. In Cambodia, it produced the Khmers Rouges.

The countries concerned have judged these regimes in very different ways. The Germans repudiated Nazism, holding it to be an aberration, a monstrous perversion of their culture. The Chinese and the Russians have not repudiated Mao or Stalin, any more than they have disowned the First Emperor of Qin or Ivan the Terrible, arguing that, although tyrants, they represented, in times of trial and national renewal, the aspirations of their peoples. Pol Pot, like Hitler, led his country into darkness, Yet he was also, for a time, an authentic spokesman for the yearning felt by many Khmers for the return of their former greatness. The French missionary François Ponchaud called the revolution which Pol launched, 'an explosion of Khmer identity'. A Yugoslav journalist, visiting Democratic Kampuchea in 1978, struggled to express a similar idea when he compared the Cambodian communists' behaviour to that of 'a quiet, introverted person, whose opinions were never listened to before, but who now speaks out unexpectedly and passionately'.

The Khmers Rouges leapt the gulf from diffidence to mass murder.

The violent ideology in whose name they acted was bequeathed to them by the French Revolution, by Stalin and by Lenin. But the peculiarly abominable form it took came from pre-existing Khmer cultural models.

Every atrocity the Khmers Rouges ever committed, and many they did not, can be found depicted on the stone friezes of Angkor, in paintings of the Buddhist hells or, in more recent times, in the conduct of the Issaraks – just as Mao drew on Chinese antecedents. Yos Hut Khemcaro, the head of the Khmer Buddhist Foundation, asserts: 'The Khmer Rouge was born out of Cambodian society, it is the child of Cambodia.'

The harshness of Pol Pot's regime can be ascribed in part to the sheer weight of Cambodian history. Even now, when the Khmer Rouge whirlwind and the wars that preceded and followed it are past, rural life in much of Cambodia is not essentially different from what it was five centuries ago. In the 1970s, the strait-jacket of feudal tradition was stronger. Sihanouk had been unable to smash the invisible shackles of patronage and corruption that prevented Cambodia from becoming a prosperous, modern state. To Pol and his colleagues it must have seemed that, without extreme methods, change was impossible. The perception that Cambodia's survival was at stake stiffened their resolve still more. Like a cornered animal, which turns instinctively to confront pursuing predators, Pol viewed policy in terms of a fight to the death. The alternative was to be devoured.

A multitude of other factors was also at work. In Cambodia, institutional restraints against wrongdoing are weak. Law was, and remains, whatever the power holders say it is. The impersonal fatalism of Theravada Buddhism erects fewer barriers against evil than the anthropomorphic God of Christianity or Islam who sits in judgement and threatens sinners with hell-fire. The attraction of power played its part too. Pol was seduced by the prospect of remaking Cambodia and reforging the minds of its people in accordance with a vision all his own. Khmer society has always been based on the principle of unquestioning obedience – of woman to man, of subject to ruler. Under the Khmers Rouges, orders were carried out unhesitatingly, regardless of whether they made sense. From the Head of State, Khieu Samphân, down to the humblest soldier in the ranks, people were not expected to ask themselves questions and in general they did not do so.

All that is true, but it is also a little too pat.

It is too simple, too comforting, to blame Khmer Rouge atrocities on the peculiar feudal culture of an exotic tropical land, just as it is to attribute them to the individual perversity of a handful of warped leaders. State-sponsored evil flourishes wherever democratic checks and balances are absent. Pol Pot's Cambodia, Hitler's Germany, Mao's China and Stalin's Russia all illustrate the point.

But while democracy offers protection against moral collapse, it is not foolproof. France was a democracy when its troops carried out mass murder in Algeria. So was the United States when it condoned slavery. American slave-owners may have treated their chattels less cruelly than Pol Pot treated his, but the principle was the same.

Sadly – and inconveniently – evil is not a discrete condition that can be isolated and set apart. It is part of a sliding scale of values, the negative counterpart of good, with a vast grey area between.

That is one reason why the United States and other Western countries have sought to use the charge of genocide to label the Pol Pot regime a special case requiring a special kind of justice. That Nuon Chea, Ieng Sary, Khieu Samphân and other Khmer Rouge leaders committed crimes is beyond dispute. But if they are to be put on trial it should be for crimes against humanity, of which they are guilty and for which they may legitimately be convicted, not for genocide, of which they are innocent. The Khmers Rouges did not set out to exterminate a 'national, ethnic, racial or religious group', whether their own, the Vietnamese, the Chams or any other. They conspired to enslave a people. That they did so believing that their ends were noble is irrelevant. Such an undertaking, carried out on so grand a scale and with such unrelenting savagery, is by definition, if words have any meaning, a 'crime against humanity'.

That term, however, is exceedingly broad. The West has skeletons in its cupboard too. The US Army's conduct in Iraq (as earlier in Vietnam) merely lengthens the catalogue of inhumanities perpetrated in the service of democratic ideals. The United States, whose allergy to supranational justice is so highly developed that it rejects it out of hand for American citizens, is not alone in believing that the jurisdiction of international tribunals should be limited to exceptional crimes such as genocide and not allowed to spill over into areas where the actions of 'normal' governments might come under scrutiny.

If the term 'genocide' has been widely accepted in Cambodia's case, it is because the enormity of what was done in this small Asian country seems beyond the power of ordinary words to convey. Yet from the very start there has been a political subtext. The term was first used by the Vietnamese in the spring of 1979, when they were turning the Tuol Sleng interrogation centre into a museum cleverly designed to recall images of Belsen. It touched a chord of guilt and horror in the Western subconscious that was politically extremely rewarding. The US, too, found 'genocide' to its advantage. The equation, 'No Vietnam war, no Khmers Rouges', is simplistic, but it reflects an undeniable truth. America's role in Indochina in the 1960s and '70s was instrumental in bringing Pol Pot to power and its support for the anti-Vietnamese resistance in the 1980s helped him to endure. For fifty years, ever since John Foster Dulles started taking an interest in Cambodian affairs, America's relationship with Cambodia has been an unhappy story. To officials like Madeleine Albright, President Clinton's Secretary of State, who launched the American effort to bring the surviving Khmer Rouge leaders to trial, their condemnation for genocide, the most heinous of crimes, would allow the US to turn the page with honour and regain the moral high ground.

That should not be seen as mere posturing. There has always been a strong moral component in US foreign policy. America sees itself as 'the shining city on the hill', the upholder of universal truths, bringing light to less fortunate peoples, just as Britain did, when it was the sole superpower, a century earlier.

But the end result has been to make genocide a political commodity, to be exploited by each outside institution, each outside power, in whichever way best fits its own interests.

For Cambodians, this is nothing new.

For centuries their country's fate has been determined by the whims of foreign powers. The one ruler who rejected that logic, Pol Pot, brought even worse disaster. That the international community should look to its own needs, rather than those of Cambodia, in its efforts to make the crime fit the punishment, is merely what they have learnt to expect. Nor is there any sign that this will change. When Hun Sen's coup in 1997 sounded the death knell for parliamentary democracy in Cambodia, the outside world acquiesced because, as Singapore's Prime Minister, Lee Kwan Yew, remarked drily, 'No country wanted to spend US$2 billion for another UN operation.' Since then, Western embassies in Phnom Penh have been under instructions not to make waves. That the present system is utterly corrupt, that what is left of the country's natural wealth is being plundered by those in power, that hundreds of millions of dollars creamed from foreign contracts end up in their private bank accounts, that there is a culture of impunity – applying not merely to ministers' wives who disfigure their husbands' mistresses by pouring acid over their bodies, but at every level of society – is seen as regrettable, but unavoidable. Impunity may start at home, but foreign governments do nothing to discourage it. Every year that aid donors gather and pledge another five or six hundred million dollars for Cambodia's development is another year that Hun Sen need not worry about cleaning up his act.

In such circumstances, trying the surviving Khmer Rouge leaders for past crimes offers an alibi for doing nothing about present ones.

There are multiple reasons for this stance. Maintaining the status quo is always the easiest option. The international community's attention is limited. Cambodia has already had more than its fair share. At least some foreign help gets past the grasping hands of Cambodian politicians and trickles down into projects which might actually benefit the people. And there is the claim, so often used to justify propping up rotten governments, that if we do not do so, others will.

For there should be no illusion: the present Cambodian government is rotten.

The two most powerful men in the country, Hun Sen and Chea Sim, the President of the Senate, are both former Khmers Rouges. Lee Kwan Yew, not the most sentimental of men, has described them as 'utterly merciless and ruthless, without humane feelings'. Neither has repudiated his Khmer Rouge past. Prince Ranariddh has been pardoned and serves as window-dressing. Sihanouk has become an impotent symbol. In any case, the King's own democratic convictions have been less than constant and are of recent date. Hun Sen has been described as his 'best pupil' for the way that he has used intimidation and murder to manipulate elections, techniques which to many older Cambodians recall Sihanouk's own cavalier treatment of the parliamentary process. Hun Sen's rule is certainly preferable to the horror that enveloped Cambodia in Pol Pot's time. But the authoritarian mind-set remains essentially the same.

If foreign powers have their part of responsibility for the Cambodian nightmare, the principal roles were taken by local actors.

Pol Pot was the supreme architect of his country's desolation. But he and his colleagues did not act alone. In the words of the Buddhist leader Yos Hut Khemcaro, 'Millions of Cambodians, including Buddhist clergy, worked with [them]'. Most of the best and brightest of the country's intellectual elite bought into the vision that Pol held out. Sihanouk shares the blame for having closed off the possibility of legal political opposition during his years in power. Later, fired by the desire for revenge and the restoration of the monarchy, he allied himself with Pol Pot twice: in 1970, when Khmer Rouge goals were still concealed, and again ten years later, when their crimes were known to all.

That, too, is a Cambodian tradition. All through history, Khmer monarchs have allied themselves with their enemies, usually Thais or Vietnamese, disregarding atrocities committed against their own people, in order to topple domestic rivals.

The Cambodian sociologist Ros Chantrabot has written that 'since the fall of Angkor, the Khmers have been caught in an ineluctable spiral of self-destruction, of self-suicide . . . We know the vectors of this process, the struggles of princes . . . who appeal to neighbouring [powers] for help . . . We are still at this stage today. But what is worse is that the process of self-destruction is now so much a part of Khmer being that it sucks us in, it dictates to us the most aberrant forms of behaviour . . . The Khmers are like a man about to drown, whose struggles merely hasten his drowning.'

That judgement is too bleak. Over the last few decades, Cambodians have shown a resilience equal to their suffering, a will to survive equal to the threats against them. But like a porcelain vase, shattered into a thousand fragments and then restored, the country is fragile. It is too weak to make more trouble.

The fire next time will be somewhere else.

Dramatis Personae

Saloth Sâr (1925–98), alias Pol Pot, Pol, Pouk, Hay, Grand-Uncle, First Brother, '87', Phem and '99':

1st marriage = Khieu Ponnary (b. 1920; m. 1956; d. 2003)
2nd marriage = Meas (b. 1962; m. 1985)
          ch. Sitha (b. 1986)

Deuch (b. 1942), real name, Kaing Khek Iev: Schoolteacher. Imprisoned for two years by Sihanouk. Entered the maquis in 1970. From 1975 to 1979, director of S-21, the Khmer Rouge torture centre at Tuol Sleng. After the Vietnamese invasion, worked for Radio China International in Beijing. Converted to Christianity in the 1990s. In detention awaiting trial since 1999.

Haing Ngor (1940–96): Cambodian medical doctor who won an Oscar for his role as a Khmer journalist in the film *The Killing Fields*. Having survived the Khmer Rouge regime, he was murdered at his home in Los Angeles while resisting a robbery by three drug addicts.

Heng Samrin (b. 1934): Joined the communists as a messenger in 1959, rising to become a Khmer Rouge divisional commander in the Eastern Zone. Fled to Vietnam in 1978. Head of State of the Vietnamese-installed People's Republic of Kampuchea, 1979–91. After the mid-1980s lost power to Hun Sen.

Hou Yuon (1930–76): Member of the Cercle Marxiste in Paris, where he obtained a PhD in economics. Member of parliament and junior minister under Sihanouk after 1958. Fled to the maquis with Khieu Samphân in 1967. Subsequently Minister of the Interior of the GRUNC. An outspoken critic of the excessive radicalism of the policies of Pol Pot, to whom he was none the less personally loyal. Under house arrest after 1975. Died in unexplained circumstances.

Hu Nim (1932–77), alias Phoas: Director of Customs under Sihanouk. Elected to parliament in 1958, afterwards a junior minister. Fled to the maquis in 1967, shortly after Khieu Samphân and Hou Yuon. Minister of Information of the GRUNC and Democratic Kampuchea. Purged and killed at Tuol Sleng.

Hun Sen (b. 1952): Deputy Khmer Rouge regimental commander. Fled to Vietnam in 1977. Foreign Minister of the Vietnamese-installed Cambodian government 1979–86; Prime Minister 1985–93. Co-Prime Minister (with Prince Ranariddh) 1993–97; thereafter Prime Minister of the Royal Government.

Ieng Sary (b. 1924), real name, Kim Trang, alias Van, Thang and Nenn: Co-founder and head of the Cercle Marxiste, member of the French Communist Party. Married Khieu Ponnary's sister, Thirith, in 1953. Alternate member of the CPK Standing Committee in 1960; full member in 1963. Khmer Rouge Vice-Premier for Foreign Affairs 1975–79. Marginalised after 1981. Defected to Hun Sen in 1996. Now lives as a private citizen in Phnom Penh.

In Sopheap (b. 1943): Scion of an aristocratic family, most of whose members supported the Khmers Rouges. His elder brother, **In Sokhan**, was a close friend of Ieng Sary. Worked at the Khmer Rouge Information and Foreign Ministries before becoming Ambassador to Egypt in the 1980s. Now lives as a private citizen in Pailin.

Ke Pauk (1933–2002), real name, Ke Vin: Ex-Issarak. Re-joined the communist movement in 1957, rising to become military chief and eventually CPK Secretary of the Northern Zone. Member of the CPK CC from 1976 and of its Standing Committee from November 1978. With Mok, one of Pol Pot's two principal military supporters. Defected to Hun Sen in 1998, becoming a general in the Royal Army. Died of a liver ailment.

Keng Vannsak (b. 1926): Pol Pot's mentor in Paris and the moving spirit behind the informal study circle which developed into the Cercle Marxiste. Led the Democratic Party campaign for the 1955 elections. A dyed-in-the-wool republican who became one of Sihanouk's *bêtes noires*. Served as Lon Nol's Ambassador to France in the early 1970s. Now lives in the Paris suburb of Montmorency.

Keo Meas (1926–76): Ex-Issarak. Head of the clandestine Phnom Penh Committee of the communist movement in 1954, afterwards leader of the

Pracheachon group. Member of the CPK CC in 1960, dropped at the Second Congress in 1963. From 1969 onwards, Khmer Rouge representative in Hanoi. Purged as pro-Vietnamese and killed at Tuol Sleng in 1976.

Khieu Ponnary (1920–2003), alias Yim: Daughter of a judge. In the early 1950s, Democratic Party activist and liaison agent with the Khmers Viet Minh. Married Pol Pot, five years her junior, on July 14 1956, and followed him into the maquis in 1965. President of the Democratic Kampuchea Women's Association. Alternate member of the CPK CC from 1971. Incapacitated by chronic schizophrenia.

Khieu Samphân (b. 1931), alias Hem, Nân: Head of the Cercle Marxiste in Paris after Ieng Sary's departure. PhD in economics. Member of parliament and minister under Sihanouk from 1962. Fled to the maquis with Hou Yuon in 1967. Alternate member of the CPK CC from 1971; full member from 1976, the year in which he became Khmer Rouge Head of State. Pol Pot's most faithful lieutenant. Defected to Hun Sen in December 1998. Now lives as a private citizen in Pailin.

Khieu Thirith (b. 1930), alias Phea: Younger sister of Khieu Ponnary. Married Ieng Sary in Paris in 1953. Followed him to the maquis in 1965. Khmer Rouge Minister of Social Affairs. Now lives as a private citizen in Phnom Penh.

Kong Sophal (1927–78), alias Keu, Chheang: Schoolteacher. Joined the communist movement in Phnom Penh in 1958. Head of the Democratic Kampuchea Youth League before fleeing to the maquis in the North-West Zone where he became deputy to Ruos Nhim. Played a key role in fomenting the Samlaut uprising in 1967. CPK CC member from 1971, promoted to the Standing Committee in November 1978. Arrested immediately afterwards and killed at Tuol Sleng.

Koy Thuon (1933–77), alias Khuon, Thuch: Schoolteacher, childhood friend of Hu Nim. Joined the communist movement in the summer of 1960. CPK CC member from 1971. Secretary of the Northern Zone from 1965 until 1975, when he was replaced by his deputy, Ke Pauk. Arrested in 1976 and killed at Tuol Sleng.

Le Duan (1907–86), alias Anh Ba: Railway worker. Helped found the ICP in 1930. Imprisoned by the French. Headed the communist movement in southern Vietnam. Took refuge in Phnom Penh for several months in

1957. Appointed Secretary-General of the Vietnamese Workers' Party in 1960. Succeeded Ho Chi Minh in 1969 and ruled Vietnam with an iron hand for the next seventeen years.

Le Duc Tho (1911–90): Founder member of the ICP who became Le Duan's closest collaborator in southern Vietnam. VWP Politburo member responsible for relations with the Cambodian communists. Negotiated the Paris peace accords with Henry Kissinger in 1973, for which he was awarded, but refused to accept, the Nobel Peace Prize.

Lon Nol (1913–85): Defence Minister and Chief of the General Staff under Sihanouk, whom he overthrew in a *coup d'état* in March 1970. Six months later turned Cambodia into a republic, of which he became President. Suffered a debilitating stroke in 1971, but clung to power with US support. Flown to exile in Hawaii in April 1975, sixteen days before the Khmer Rouge victory.

Long Visalo (b. 1947): PhD in cartography from Budapest. Returned to Cambodia after the Khmer Rouge victory. Interned until 1979. After the Vietnamese invasion joined the PRK administration, becoming Ambassador to Cuba and Vice-Minister of Foreign Affairs.

Mey Mak (b. 1947), real name Nuon Chanthân, alias Nuon Bunno: Joined the Khmers Rouges after Lon Nol's coup in 1970, rising through the ranks to become a company commander. Based at Pochentong Airport 1975–79. One of Pol Pot's secretaries at Office 131 in the 1980s. Deputy Khmer Rouge Military Representative to the Supreme National Council 1991–94. Defected to Hun Sen in 1996.

Mey Mann (1921–2001): Member of the Cercle Marxiste in Paris. Followed Pol Pot into the maquis to join the Khmers Viet Minh, returning with him to Phnom Penh in August 1954. Expelled with the rest of the population of Phnom Penh in 1975, but remained a Khmer Rouge sympathiser until his death.

Mok (b. 1925), real name Chhit Chhoeun, alias Nguon Kang, Ta 15: Ex-Issarak. Member of the CPK CC from 1963, Secretary of the South-Western Zone from 1968, CPK Second Deputy Secretary, ranking just behind Pol and Nuon Chea, from 1978. With Ke Pauk, he was one of Pol Pot's two principal military supporters. Rebelled against Pol's leadership in 1997. In detention awaiting trial since 1999.

Ney Sarann (1925–77), alias Achar Sieng, Men San, Ya: Ex-Issarak. Worked as a teacher in Phnom Penh in the 1950s. Joined Office 100 in 1964. Member of the CPK CC and Secretary of the North-Eastern Zone from 1971. Accompanied Pol Pot to meet Mao in 1975. Purged as a pro-Vietnamese element and killed at Tuol Sleng.

Nikân (b. 1940), real name Son Nhan: Youngest brother of Son Sen. Schoolteacher and communist activist in Siem Reap. Entered the maquis in 1967 and worked at Pol's headquarters in Ratanakiri. In 1978 he became Chief of Protocol at the Khmer Rouge Foreign Ministry. After the Vietnamese invasion, commander of Khmer Rouge forces at Samphou Loun, on the Thai border. Defected to Hun Sen in 1996.

Non Suon (c.1927–77), alias Sen, Chey Suon: Ex-Issarak. Chairman of the South-Western Zone in 1952. Spokesman for the Pracheachon group. Probably elected to the CPK CC in 1960, but dropped three years later. Imprisoned in 1962. Amnestied after Lon Nol's coup in 1970 and became a CPK Regional Secretary. Khmer Rouge Minister of Agriculture. Purged as a pro-Vietnamese element and killed at Tuol Sleng.

Norodom Ranariddh (b. 1944): Son of King Sihanouk. Spent the Khmer Rouge period as a research fellow at the University of Aix-en-Provence. Leader of FUNCINPEC and First Prime Minister from 1993, but ousted four years later by the Second Prime Minister, Hun Sen, in a *coup d'état*. Since 1998, President of the National Assembly.

Norodom Sihanouk (b. 1922): King of Cambodia 1941–55, when he abdicated in favour of his father, Suramarit. Head of State 1960–70. After being overthrown in a coup in March 1970, allied himself with his former Khmer Rouge opponents against the US-backed government of Lon Nol, which was defeated in April 1975. Returned to Phnom Penh as Head of State in October, but resigned the following spring. Held incommunicado by Pol Pot's government until January 1979. Under pressure from China, renewed his alliance with the Khmers Rouges in 1982, opening the way to the Paris peace agreement of 1991. Became King of Cambodia for the second time in 1993.

Nuon Chea (b. c.1923), real name Long Bunruot, alias Long Rith, Nuon, Second Brother, Grand-Uncle: Studied law at Thammasat University in Bangkok. Member of the Thai Communist Party. Joined the Khmers Viet Minh in 1949. Worked undercover in Phnom Penh from the 1950s.

Appointed CPK Deputy Secretary in 1960. Responsible for Party and state security. President of the Standing Committee of the National Assembly of Democratic Kampuchea 1976–79. Defected to Hun Sen in 1998. Now lives as a private citizen in Pailin.

Pâng (1944–78), real name Chhim Sam Aok: Recruited into the communist movement by Son Sen while a seventeen-year-old schoolboy in Phnom Penh. Worked at Office 100 at Ta Not and in Ratanakiri. After 1970, Pol's chief assistant for administrative matters, a post which he continued to hold after the Khmer Rouge victory. Purged and killed at Tuol Sleng.

Penn Nouth (1906–85): Veteran Cambodian statesman. Democratic Party stalwart before rallying to Sihanouk's Sangkum. Prime Minister of the GRUNC 1970–76. Spent the entire Khmer Rouge period in Phnom Penh, officially as an adviser to the Democratic Kampuchea government. Died in exile in France.

Pham Van Dong (1906–2000): The son of the private secretary to Vietnam's Emperor Duy Tan. Imprisoned by the French as a communist agitator. Joined Ho Chi Minh in China in 1942. Headed the Vietnamese delegation at the Geneva talks in 1954. Vietnamese Prime Minister 1955–87.

Phi Phuon (b. 1947), real name Rochoem Ton, alias Cheam: Of Jarai nationality. Joined the revolutionary movement in Ratanakiri while a teenager. In 1968 served as a bodyguard to Pol Pot and later his aide-de-camp, a post which he conserved until the Khmer Rouge victory. Chief of Security under Ieng Sary at the Foreign Ministry 1975–79. Defected to Hun Sen in 1996. Currently deputy governor of Malay.

Pich Chheang (b. c. 1945), alias Tho: A protégé of the Northern Zone Secretary, Koy Thuon. Founded a guerrilla force in 1969, rising to the post of Zone Chief of Staff. In 1975 succeeded Non Suon as director of the National Bank. Subsequently Ambassador to China. Survived the purge of Northern Zone officials thanks to his marriage to Pol's former cook, **Moeun**. Defected to Hun Sen in 1998. Now lives in Anlong Veng.

Ping Sây (b. 1926), alias Sang, Chheang: Member of the Cercle Marxiste and the French Communist Party. In the 1950s, editor-in-chief of the Democratic Party newspaper, *Ekhepheap*. Twice imprisoned by Sihanouk.

Attended the CPK's founding congress in 1960. Subsequently a member of the communist underground in Phnom Penh. Entered the maquis in 1973 but fell into disfavour. Now lives as a private citizen in Phnom Penh.

Rath Samoeun (1930–*c*.1972): Co-founder of the Cercle Marxiste and member of the French Communist Party. Returned to Cambodia to join the Khmers Viet Minh. After the Geneva accords in 1954, lived in Vietnam. Died, probably of illness, in the 'liberated zone'.

Ruos Nhim (1922–78), real name, Moul Oun, alias Moul Sambath: Ex-Issarak. Aide to Sieu Heng in 1948. Member of the CPK CC from 1963 and Secretary of the North-Western Zone. With Kong Sophal, instigated the Samlaut uprising in 1967. CPK Standing Committee member from 1975. Purged and killed at Tuol Sleng.

Siet Chhê (1932–77), alias Tum: Buddhist monk, worked as a school-teacher in Phnom Penh 1954–64. Joined Office 100 at Ta Not. Subsequently an Eastern Zone regional secretary. Accompanied Pol to meet Mao in 1975. The same year appointed Logistics Chief at General Staff HQ. Purged and killed at Tuol Sleng.

Sieu Heng (*c*.1920–75): Ex-Issarak. Cousin of Nuon Chea. Founding member of the PRPK in 1950. After the 1954 Geneva accords, appointed by the Vietnamese to head the provisional Cambodian communist leadership with responsibility for the rural areas. Defected to Sihanouk's government in 1959. Killed after the Khmer Rouge victory in 1975.

Sirik Matak (1914–75): Cousin of King Sihanouk. Minister of Defence and of Foreign Affairs in the 1950s. Subsequently Cambodian Ambassador to China. Principal architect of Lon Nol's coup against Sihanouk in March 1970. Killed immediately after the Khmer Rouge victory.

So Phim (*c*.1925–78): Ex-Issarak, military leader of the Eastern Zone. Founder member of the PRPK in 1951. Alternate member of the CPK Standing Committee, ranking fifth in the hierarchy, from 1960; full member three years later. CPK Secretary of the Eastern Zone from 1960 onwards. Committed suicide to avoid arrest after Pol Pot ordered a massive purge of the Zone hierarchy.

Son Ngoc Minh (*c*.1910–72), real name allegedly Pham Van Hua, alias Achar Mean, Kim Bien: Born in South Vietnam of mixed Khmer-Vietnamese parentage, became the first authentic Cambodian communist. Inducted into the ICP in 1949. Leader of the PRPK from its formation in 1951. After the Geneva accords, withdrew to Vietnam. Elected in absentia to the CPK CC in 1960. Died in Beijing after a stroke.

Son Ngoc Thanh (1908–77): Early Cambodian nationalist. Co-founder of the first Khmer-language newspaper, *Nagaravatta,* in 1936. Prime Minister in August 1945. Arrested and exiled by the colonial authorities. Returned in triumph to Phnom Penh in 1951. Led a right-wing rebel group, the Khmer Serei, initially against the French, then against Sihanouk. Afterwards based in Thailand and South Vietnam. Prime Minister under Lon Nol 1972–73. Died under house arrest in Vietnam.

Son Sen (1927–97), alias Khieu, Khamm, Aum: Schoolteacher. Member of the Cercle Marxiste in Paris. CPK CC member from 1963. With Pol Pot at Office 100 in Ta Not and Ratanakiri. CPK North-Eastern Zone Secretary 1970–71, then Chief of the General Staff of the Khmer Rouge army. Minister of Defence from August 1975. Alternate Standing Committee member, responsible for the Tuol Sleng interrogation centre. Chosen by Pol Pot as his successor in the 1980s but then fell from favour. Killed as a traitor on Pol's orders near Kbal Ansoang.

Suong Sikoeun (b. 1937): Member of the Cercle Marxiste in Paris in the 1960s. Joined Sihanouk in Beijing after the 1970 coup. Inducted into the CPK by Ieng Sary, with whom he was associated throughout his career. After 1975, head of the press section of the Democratic Kampuchea Foreign Ministry. Defected to Hun Sen in 1996. Now lives as a private citizen in Malay.

Thiounn Mumm (b. 1925): The second of four brothers from one of Cambodia's wealthiest aristocratic families, all of whom espoused the Khmer Rouge cause. The eldest, **Thiounn Thioeunn**, became Minister of Health. **Thiounn Chum** was notional Finance Minister 1979–81. **Thiounn Prasith** was Ambassador to the UN. In Paris, Mumm was co-founder of the Cercle Marxiste and its head throughout the 1960s. Joined Sihanouk in Beijing following the 1970 coup and returned with him to Phnom Penh after the Khmer Rouge victory. Notional Minister of Science 1979–81. He and Chum then returned to France. Mumm now holds French citizenship and lives near Rouen; Chum lives just outside Paris; Prasith lives in New York State; Thioeunn, who defected to Hun Sen in 1998, lives in Phnom Penh.

Tiv Ol (1933–77), alias Penh: Student activist, then secondary school teacher, in the 1950s and '60s. Joined Pol Pot in Ratanakiri in 1968. From 1970, Deputy Minister of Information in the GRUNC. Purged and killed at Tuol Sleng.

Tou Samouth (c.1915–62): Former Buddhist preacher. Ex-Issarak. Founder member of the PRPK in 1951. Head of the Urban Committee of the communist movement from 1954. Elected CPK Secretary at the founding congress in 1960. Detained and killed on the orders of Lon Nol.

Vorn Vet (c.1934–78), real name Pen Thuok, alias Sok, Mean, Te, Kuon, Veth and Vorn: Joined the Khmers Viet Minh in 1954 after dropping out of secondary school. CPK CC member and head of the Phnom Penh CPK Committee from 1963. CPK Secretary of the Special Zone from 1971. Member of the Standing Committee. After 1976, Vice-Premier for the Economy. Purged and killed at Tuol Sleng.

Yun Yat (c.1937–97), alias Ath: Schoolteacher. Married to Son Sen. From the early 1970s, responsible for the Party journal, *Tung Padevat*. In 1976, Minister of Culture, Education and Propaganda. Spent the 1980s in Beijing as director of the Khmer Rouge radio station. Killed as a traitor with her husband on Pol Pot's orders near Kbal Ansoang.

Notes and Sources

This book is based in large part on primary sources, notably several hundred hours of interviews with former members of the Khmer Rouge movement—anging from Khieu Samphân, the Head of State of Democratic Kampuchea, and Ieng Sary, the Foreign Minister, to bodyguards and cooks—s well as original documents in Chinese, Khmer, French, Russian and Vietnamese, held in state and Party archives in Aix-en-Provence, Beijing, Hanoi, Moscow, Paris and Phnom Penh. The aim has been to tell the story of the Cambodian nightmare, to the extent that that is feasible, from the vantage point of those who created it, rather than solely from that of the victims. Such an endeavour would have been impossible without the substantial body of scholarship on the Khmers Rouges and their antecedents produced over the past quarter-century by historians like David Chandler, Stephen Heder, Ben Kiernan, Serge Thion and Michael Vickery. Many others have also put their shoulders to the wheel. The bibliography that follows is far from comprehensive. It is intended essentially as a *vade mecum* for the notes, detailing those works which are referred to so frequently as to make the use of a short title desirable. Other titles, to which reference is made more rarely, are cited as they occur. Most have been quoted for the primary source material they contain. With few exceptions, works of analysis based on secondary sources are not listed, even though in some cases they may offer illuminating insights.

The notes which follow provide sources for citations and give an overview of the reference materials and arguments which underpin the narrative. Complete archival and source notes may be obtained on request by e-mail from anatomy-ofanightmare@wanadoo.fr .

Ablin, David A., and Hood, Marlowe (eds.), *The Cambodian Agony*, M. E. Sharpe, Armonk, NY, 1987 (*Agony*)

Allman, T. D., 'Anatomy of a Coup', in Grant et al., *Widening War* (*Anatomy*)

Ang Chouléan, *Les êtres surnaturels dans la religion populaire khmère*, Cedoreck, Paris, 1986 (*Etres surnaturels*)

Annotated Summary of Party History, issued by the Eastern Zone Military-Political Service, n.d. but 1973, translated in Jackson, *Rendezvous*, Appendix A.

Ayres, David, 'The Khmer Rouge and education: beyond the discourse of destruction', *History of Education*, vol. 28, no. 2, 1999 (*Education*)

Becker, Elizabeth, *When the War Was Over: Cambodia and the Khmer Rouge Revolution*, Simon & Schuster, New York, 1986 (***When the War***)

Bektimirova, N. N., Dementiev, Yu. P., and Kobelev, E. V., *Noveishaya Istoriya Kampuchii*, Nauka, Moscow, 1989 (***Istoriya***)

Bilan de Norodom Sihanouk pendant le Mandat Royal de 1952 à 1955, n.d., n.p. but Phnom Penh, 1955 (***Bilan***)

Bizot, François, *Le Portail*, La Table Ronde, Paris, 2000

Black Paper: Facts and Evidences of the Acts of Aggression and Annexation of Vietnam against Kampuchea, Ministry of Foreign Affairs of Democratic Kampuchea, Sept. 1978 (reprinted by the Group of Kampuchean Residents in America, New York)

Brown, David E., 'Exporting Insurgency: The Communists in Cambodia', in Zasloff and Goodman, *Conflict* (***Exporting Insurgency***)

Brown, MacAlister, and Zasloff, Joseph J., *Cambodia Confounds the Peacemakers, 1979–1998*, Cornell University Press, Ithaca, NY, 1998 (***Cambodia Confounds***)

Bunchan Mol, *Kuk Niyobay*, Phnom Penh, 1971

—*Charek Khmer*, Editions Apsara, Paris, n.d.

Burchett, Wilfred, *Mekong Upstream*, Red River Publishing, Hanoi, 1957

—*The China Cambodia Vietnam Triangle*, Zed Books, London, 1981 (***Triangle***)

Caldwell, Malcolm, and Lek Tan, *Cambodia in the Southeast Asian War*, Monthly Review Press, New York, 1973

Carney, Timothy M., *Communist Party Power in Kampuchea (Cambodia): Documents and Discussion*, Cornell University, Ithaca, NY, Jan. 1977 (***Communist Party Power***)

Chanda, Nayan, *Brother Enemy: the War after the War*, Macmillan, New York, 1986

Chandler, David P., *The Tragedy of Cambodian History: Politics, War, and Revolution since 1945*, Yale University Press, New Haven, CT, 1991 (***Tragedy***)

—*A History of Cambodia*, 2nd edn., Silkworm Books, Bangkok, 1993 (***History***)

—*Facing the Cambodian Past: Selected Essays, 1971–1994*, Silkworm Books, Chiangmai, 1996 (***Facing***)

—*Brother Number One*, Westview Press, Boulder, CO, 1999 (***Brother***)

—*Voices from S-21: Terror and History in Pol Pot's Secret Prison*, Silkworm Books, Bangkok, 2000 (***Voices***)

Chandler, David P., and Kiernan, Ben (eds.), *Revolution and its Aftermath in Kampuchea: Eight Essays*, Yale University South-East Asia Studies, no. 25, New Haven, CT, 1983 (***Aftermath***)

Chandler, David P., Kiernan, Ben, and Boua, Chanthou (eds.), *Pol Pot Plans the Future*, Yale University Southeast Asia Studies, Monograph no. 33, New Haven, CT, 1988 (***Pol Pot Plans***)

Chandler, David P., Kiernan, Ben, and Muy Hong Lim, *The Early Phases of Liberation in Northwestern Cambodia: Conversations with Peang Sophi*, Monash Working Paper no. 10, Clayton, Victoria, 1976 (***Peang Sophi***)

Chhang Song, *Buddhism under Pol Pot*, 1996, unpublished ms (***Buddhism***)

CWIHP, *77 Conversations between Chinese and Foreign Leaders on the Wars in*

Indochina, 1964–1977, ed. Odd Arne Westad, Chen Jian, Stein Tonnesson, Nguyen Vu Tung and James G. Hershberg, Woodrow Wilson Center Working Paper no. 22, Washington, DC, May 1998 (**77 Conversations**)

Corfield, Justin, *Khmers Stand Up! A History of the Cambodian Government, 1970–1975*, Monash University, Clayton, Victoria, 1994 (**Stand Up!**)

Criddle, Joan D., and Teeda Butt Mam, *To Destroy You Is No Loss*, Atlantic Monthly Press, New York, 1987 (**Destroy**)

Deac, Wilfred P., *Road to the Killing Fields: The Cambodian War of 1970–1975*, Texas A & M University Press, College Station, TX, 1997 (**Road**)

Debré, François, *Cambodge: La Révolution de la Forêt*, Flammarion, Paris, 1976 (**Revolution**)

Delvert, Jean, *Le Paysan Cambodgien*, Mouton, Paris, 1961 (**Paysan**)

De Nike, Howard J., Quigley, John, and Robinson, Kenneth J. (eds.), *Genocide in Cambodia*, University of Pennsylvania Press, Philadelphia, 2000

Ebihara, May M., *Svay: A Khmer Village in Cambodia*, Columbia University PhD dissertation, 1968 (**Svay**)

—'Revolution and Reformulation in Kampuchean Village Culture', in Ablin and Hood, *Agony* (**Revolution and Reformulation**)

—'A Cambodian Village under the Khmer Rouge', in Kiernan, *Genocide and Democracy* (**Village**)

Ebihara, May M., Mortland, Carol A., and Ledgerwood, Judy (eds.), *Cambodian Culture since 1975: Homeland and Exile*, Cornell University Press, Ithaca, NY, 1994 (**Cambodian Culture**)

Edwards, Penny, 'Ethnic Chinese in Cambodia', in *Interdisciplinary Research on Ethnic Groups in Cambodia*, Preah Sihanouk Raj Academy, Phnom Penh, 1996 (**Ethnic Chinese**)

Elliott, David W. P., Kiernan, Ben, Hy Van Luong, and Mahoney, Therese M. (eds.), *Indochina: Social and Cultural Change*, Keck Center for International and Strategic Studies, Claremont, CA, 1994 (**Indochina**)

Elliott, David W. P. (ed.), *The Third Indochina Conflict*, Westview Press, Boulder, CO, 1981

Engelbert, Thomas, and Goscha, Christopher E., *Falling out of Touch: A Study on Vietnamese Communist Policy Towards an Emerging Cambodian Communist Movement, 1930—1975*, Monash University, Clayton, Victoria, 1995 (**Falling**)

Evans, Grant, and Rowley, Kelvin, *Red Brotherhood at War: Indochina Since the Fall of Saigon*, Verso, London, 1984 (**Brotherhood**)

Fiche d'étudiant, Echols Collection, Cornell University Library

Forest, Alain, *Le Cambodge et la colonisation française: histoire d'une colonisation sans heurts (1897–1920)*, L'Harmattan, Paris, 1980 (**Colonisation sans heurts**)

Furuta, Motoo, 'The Indochina Communist Party's division into Three Parties: Vietnamese Communist Policy towards Cambodia and Laos, 1948–51', in Furuta, Motoo and Shiraishi, Takashi, *Indochina in the 1940s and 1950s*, Cornell University South East Asia Programme, Ithaca, NY, 1979 (**Division**)

Gettleman and Kaplan, *Conflict in Indo-China: a reader on the widening war in Laos and Cambodia*, Random House, New York, 1970 (**Conflict**)

Ghosh, Amitav, *Dancing in Cambodia: At Large in Burma*, Ravi Dayal, New Delhi, 1998

Goscha, Christopher E., *Le Contexte Asiatique de la Guerre Franco-Vietnamienne: Réseaux, Relations et Economie (d'Août 1945 à Mai 1954)*, PhD thesis, Paris, 2000 (**thesis**)

Grant, Jonathan S., Moss, Laurence A. G., and Unger, Jonathan (eds.), *Cambodia: The Widening War in Indochina*, Washington Square Press, New York, 1971 (**Widening War**)

Haing Ngor, *A Cambodian Odyssey*, Macmillan, New York, 1987 (**Odyssey**)

Heckman, Charles W., *The Phnom Penh Airlift: Confessions of a Pig Pilot in the early 1970s*, McFarland, Jefferson, NC, 1990 (**Pig Pilot**)

Heder, Stephen, *Kampuchean Occupation and Resistance*, Chulalongkorn University Institute of Asian Studies, Bangkok, 1980 (**Occupation**)

—'The Kampuchean-Vietnamese Conflict', in Elliott, *Third Indochina Conflict* (**Conflict**)

—'Kampuchea: From Pol Pot to Pen Sovann to the Villages', in Khien Theeravit and Brown, *Indochina* (**Pol Pot to Pen Sovann**)

—*Pol Pot and Khieu Samphân*, Centre of South-East Asian Studies, Monash University, Clayton, Victoria, 1991

Hinton, Alexander Laban, 'Why Did You Kill? The Cambodian Genocide and the Dark Side of Face and Honor', *Journal of Asian Studies*, vol. 57, no. 1, Feb. 1998 (**Why?**)

Ieng Sary, *Imprimé de la collection des documents sur le Cambodge*, Bibliothèque Militaire, Hanoi, 1979, Doc. 32(N442)/T724, 'Sur l'Histoire de la Lutte de notre peuple Cambodgien', talk between Ieng Sary and Jacquet, General Secretary of the French Communist Party (Marxist-Leninist), Phnom Penh, Sept. 9 and 15 1978, VA (**Talk with Jacquet**)

—'Interview with Adrian Maben', Pailin, Aug. 1999 (**Maben interview**)

In Sopheap, *Khieu Samphân: aggrandi et réel*, unpublished typescript

Institut Bouddhique, *La Vie du Paysan Khmer*, Phnom Penh, 1969 (**Paysan Khmer**)

Ith Sarin, 'Life in the Bureaux of the Khmer Rouge', in Carney, *Communist Party Power* (**Bureaux**)

—'Nine months with the Maquis', in Carney, *Communist Party Power* (**Nine Months**)

Jackson, Karl D., 'Cambodia 1978: War, Pillage and Purge in Democratic Kampuchea', *Asian Survey*, 1979 (**Cambodia 1978**)

Jackson, Karl D. (ed.), *Cambodia, 1975–1978: Rendezvous with Death*, Princeton University Press, NJ, 1989 (**Rendezvous**)

Jennar, Raoul, *Les Clés du Cambodge*, Maisonneuve and Larose, Paris, 1995 (**Clés**)

Kampuchea Dossier, vols. 1–3, Vietnam Courier, Hanoi, 1978–9

Ke Pauk, 'Autobiography of a Mass Murderer', *Phnom Penh Post*, Mar. 1–14 2002 (**Autobiography**)

Khien Theeravit and Brown, MacAlister (eds.), *Indochina and Problems of Security and Stability in South-East Asia*, Chulalongkorn University Press, Bangkok, 1983 (*Indochina*)

Khieu Samphân, *Cambodia's Economy and Industrial Development*, trans. Laura Summers, Cornell University, Ithaca, NY, Data Paper 111, Mar. 1979 (*thesis*)

Khin Sok, *Le Cambodge entre le Siam et le Vietnam*, Ecole Française d'Extrême-Orient, Paris, 1991 (*Cambodge*)

Khing Hocdy, *Ecrivains et Expressions Littéraires du Cambodge au 20ème Siècle*, L'Harmattan, Paris, 1993 (*Ecrivains*)

Khmer Armed Resistance, Khmer Peace Committee, n.p. but Beijing, Oct. 1952

Kiernan, Ben, *The Samlaut Rébellion and its Aftermath, 1967–70: The Origins of Cambodia's Liberation Movement*, University of New South Wales, 1975 (*Samlaut*)

—'Origins of Khmer Communism', *South-East Asian Affairs*, 1981 (*Origins*)

—*Cambodia: the Eastern Zone Massacres*, Center for the Study of Human Rights, Columbia University, NYC, n.d. (*Eastern Zone Massacres*)

—'Pol Pot and the Kampuchean Communist Movement', in Kiernan and Boua, *Peasants and Politics* (*Communist Movement*)

—'Wild Chickens, Farm Chickens and Cormorants: Kampuchea's Eastern Zone under Pol Pot', in Chandler and Kiernan, *Aftermath* (*Chickens*)

—*How Pol Pot Came to Power*, Verso, London, 1985 (*How Pol Pot*)

—'Kampuchea's Ethnic Chinese Under Pol Pot: A Case of Systematic Social Discrimination', *JCA*, vol. 16, 1986 (*Chinese*)

—'Rural Reorganization in Democratic Kampuchea: The North-West Zone, 1975–1977', in Elliott et al., *Indochina* (*Rural Reorganization*)

—*The Pol Pot Regime: Race, Power and Genocide in Cambodia under the Khmer Rouge, 1975–79*, Yale University Press, New Haven, CT, 1996 (*Regime*)

Kiernan, Ben (ed.), *Genocide and Democracy in Cambodia*, Yale University Press, New Haven, CT, 1993 (*Genocide and Democracy*)

Kiernan, Ben and Chanthou Boua (eds.), *Peasants and Politics in Kampuchea, 1942–1981*, Zed Press, London, 1982 (*Peasants and Politics*)

Kirk, Donald, 'Revolution and Political Violence in Cambodia, 1970–1974', in Zasloff, Joseph J., and Brown, MacAlister, *Communism in Indochina: New Perspectives*, Lexington Books, Lexington, MA, 1975 (*Revolution*)

Kropotkin, Pëtr Alekséevitch, *La Grande Révolution, 1789–1793*, Stock, Paris, 1909

Lancaster, Donald, 'The Decline of Prince Sihanouk's Regime', in Zasloff and Goodman, *Conflict* (*Decline*)

Laurent, Maurice, *L'Armée au Cambodge et dans les pays en voie de développement du sud-est asiatique*, Presses Universitaires de France, Paris, 1968 (*Armée*)

Lee Kwan Yew, *From Third World to First: The Singapore Story, 1965–2000*, HarperCollins, New York, 2000 (*Third World to First*)

Locard, Henri, *Le Petit Livre Rouge des Khmers Rouges*, L'Harmattan, Paris, 1996 (*Petit Livre Rouge*)

Mabbett, Ian, and Chandler, David P., *The Khmers*, Blackwell, Oxford, 1995

Mamm, Kalyanee E., *An Oral History of Family Life under the Khmer Rouge*, Working Paper GS 10, Yale University, 1999 (***Family Life***)

Mao Zedong, 'On New Democracy', in *Selected Works*, vol. 2, Foreign Languages Press, Beijing, 1967

—'Some Questions concerning Methods of Leadership', in *Selected Works*, vol. 3, Foreign Languages Press, Beijing, 1967 (***Some Questions***)

Martin, Marie Alexandrine, 'L'Industrie dans le Kampuchéa Démocratique (1975–1978)', *Etudes Rurales*, Paris, nos. 89–91, Jan.–Sept. 1983 (***Industrie***)

—'La riziculture et la maîtrise de l'eau dans le Kampuchéa Démocratique', *Etudes Rurales*, no. 83, July–Sept. 1981 (***Riziculture***)

—'Le Gouvernement de Coalition du Kampuchéa Démocratique: Historique, Bilan et Perspectives', *Bulletin de l'ASEMI*, vol. 13, nos. 1–4, 1982 (***Gouvernement***)

—'La Politique Alimentaire des Khmers Rouges', *Etudes Rurales*, nos. 99–100, July–Dec. 1985 (***Alimentaire***)

—*Cambodia: A Shattered Society*, University of California Press, Berkeley, CA, 1994 (***Shattered***)

—*Les Khmers Daeum: 'Khmers de l'Origine'*, Presses de l'Ecole Française d'Extrème-Orient, Paris, 1997 (***Khmers Daeum***)

Meyer, Charles, *Derrière le Sourire Khmer*, Plon, Paris, 1971 (***Sourire***)

Migot, André, *Les Khmers*, Livre Contemporain, Paris, 1960

Mok, interview with Nate Thayer, Anlong Veng, 1997 (***Thayer interview***)

Morris, Stephen J., *Why Vietnam Invaded Cambodia*, Stanford University Press, CA, 1999 (***Why Vietnam***)

Mosyakov, Dmitri, *The Khmer Rouge and the Vietnamese Communists: A history of their relations as told in the Soviet archives*, Yale University, New Haven, CT, 2000 (***Khmer Rouge***)

Nuon Chea, 'Statement of the Communist Party of Kampuchea to the Communist Workers Party of Denmark', July 30–31 1978, in *Journal of Communist Studies*, vol. 3, 1987 (***Statement***)

Ong Thong Hoeung, *Récit d'une Illusion*, unpublished typescript (***Récit***). A revised version was published in 2003 (*J'ai cru au khmers rouges: Retour sur une Illusion*, Buchet-Chastel, Paris)

Osborne, Milton, *Sihanouk: Prince of Light, Prince of Darkness*, University of Hawaii Press, Honolulu, 1994 (***Prince of Light***)

—*Politics and Power in Cambodia: The Sihanouk Years*, Longman, Sydney, 1973 (***Politics and Power***)

—*Before Kampuchea: Preludes to Tragedy*, Allen & Unwin, London, 1979 (***Before Kampuchea***)

Pannetier, Adrien, *Notes Cambodgiennes: Au Coeur du Pays Khmer*, Payot, Paris, 1921

Peschoux, Christophe, *Les 'Nouveaux' Khmers Rouges: Enquête, 1979–1990*, L'Harmattan, Paris, 1992

Phillips, Herbert P., 'Social Contact versus Social Promise in a Siamese Village', in Potter, Jack M., Diaz, May N., and Foster, George M., *Peasant Society*, Little

Brown, Boston, 1967, pp. 348–9 (*Social Contact*)

Picq, Laurence, *Beyond the Horizon: Five Years with the Khmer Rouge*, St Martin's Press, New York, 1989 (*Horizon*)

—Original uncorrected typescript from which the published French and English versions, *Au delà du Ciel* and *Horizon*, were taken (*typescript*)

Pin Yathay, *Stay Alive, My Son*, Macmillan, New York, 1987 (*Stay Alive*)

Pol Pot, 'Interview with Tran Thanh Xuan, Vice-Director of the Vietnam News Agency', July 20 1976, *JCA*, vol. 7, 1977, pp. 418–22 (*Tran Thanh Xuan interview*)

—'The Party's Four-Year Plan to Build Socialism in All Fields, 1977–1980', July Aug. 1976, in Chandler et al., *Pol Pot Plans* (*Four-Year Plan*)

—'Preliminary Explanation Before Reading the Plan, by the Party Secretary', Aug. 21 1976, in Chandler et al., *Pol Pot Plans* (*Preliminary Explanation*)

—'Summary of the Results of the 1976 Study Session' (undated but autumn 1976) in Chandler et al., *Pol Pot Plans* (*Study Session*)

—'Report of Activities of the Party Center According to the General Political Tasks of 1976', Dec. 20 1976, in Chandler et al., *Pol Pot Plans* (*Report*)

—'Abbreviated Lesson on the History of the Kampuchean Revolutionary Movement Led by the Communist party of Kampuchea' (undated but early 1977) in Chandler et al., *Pol Pot Plans* (*Abbreviated Lesson*)

—'Pol Pot présente les expériences du Cambodge à Khamtan, Secrétaire-général du PC Thailandais', Aug. 1977, Doc. 32(N442)/TVN 7808, VA (*Talk with Khamtan*)

—'Statement by the CPK Secretary at 27th September [1977] mass meeting in Phnom Penh marking the CPK's 17th anniversary', BBC SWB FE/5629/C2/1-9, 5631/C2/1-6 and 5632/C/1-7 (*September 27 speech*)

—'Interview with Yugoslav Journalists', Radio Phnom Penh, Mar. 20 1978, in *JCA*, vol. 8, 1978, pp. 413–21 (*Yugoslav interview*)

—'Interview with Cai Ximei', May 1984 (*Cai Ximei interview*)

—'Interview with Nate Thayer', Anlong Veng, 1997 (*Thayer interview*)

Ponchaud, François, 'Cambodge Libéré', *Echange France-Asie*, no. 13, Jan. 1976 (*EFA 13*)

—'Le Kampuchéa Démocratique: Une Révolution Radicale', *Exchange France-Asie*, no. 17, May 1976 (*EFA 17*)

—*Cambodia:Year Zero*, Holt, Rinehart & Winston, New York, 1978 (*Year Zero*)

—'Vietnam-Cambodge: Une Solidarité Militante Fragile', in *Temps Modernes*, vol. 35, Jan.–Mar. 1980 (*Vietnam-Cambodge*)

—*La Cathédrale de la Rizière*, Fayard, Paris, 1990 (*Cathédrale*)

Porter, Gareth, 'Vietnamese Communist Policy towards Kampuchea, 1930–70', in Chandler and Kiernan, *Aftermath* (*Vietnamese Policy*)

—'Vietnamese Policy and the Indochina Crisis', in Elliott, *Third Indochina Conflict* (*Crisis*)

Prasso, Sherry, *Violence, Ethnicity and Ethnic Cleansing*, Department of Social Anthropology, Cambridge University, May 1995

Puangthong Rungswasdisab, *Thailand's Response to the Cambodian Genocide*, Yale

Center for International and Area Studies, Working Paper GS12, New Haven, CT, 1999

Qiang Zhai, *China and the Vietnam Wars: 1950–1975*, University of North Carolina Press, Chapel Hill, NC, 2000 (***Vietnam Wars***)

Quinn, Kenneth M., 'The Khmer Krahom Program to Create a Communist Society in Southern Cambodia', Airgram A-008, American Consulate, Can Tho, to US Department of State, Feb. 20 1974 (***Khmer Krahom Program***)

—'Political Change in Wartime: the Khmer Krahom Revolution in Southern Cambodia', in *Naval War College Review*, Spring 1976, pp. 3–31 (***Political Change***)

Reddi, V. M., *A History of the Cambodian Independence Movement, 1863–1955*, Sri Venkateswara University Press, Tirupati, 1970

Robequain, Charles, *The Economic Development of French Indo-China*, OUP, Oxford, 1944

Ros Chantrabot, *La République Khmère (1970–1975)*, L'Harmattan, Paris, 1993

Ross, Robert S., *Indochina Tangle*, Columbia University Press, New York, 1988 (***Tangle***)

Schanberg, Sydney H., *The Death and Life of Dith Pran*, Elizabeth Sifton Books, New York, 1985 (***Death and Life***)

Schier, Peter, and Oum-Schier, Manola, *Prince Sihanouk on Cambodia*, 2nd edn., Mitteilungen des Instituts für Asienkunde, Hamburg, 1985 (***Sihanouk***)

Shawcross, William, *Sideshow: Nixon, Kissinger and the Destruction of Cambodia*, Hogarth Press, London, 1991 (***Sideshow***)

—*The Quality of Mercy*, Simon & Schuster, New York, 1984 (***Quality***)

Sher, Sacha, *Le Parcours Politique des Khmers Rouges: Projet et Pratiques, 1945–1978*, PhD thesis, University of Paris X, Nanterre [draft dated 2001] (thesis). A later version, with different pagination, is dated Sept. 2002. The first part has since been published as *Le Kampuchéa des Khmers Rouges: Essai de comprehension d'une tentative de révolution*, L'Harmattan, Paris, 2004

Short, Philip, *The Dragon and the Bear*, Hodder & Stoughton, London, 1982 (***Dragon***)

—*Mao: A Life*, Henry Holt, New York, 2000 (***Mao***)

Sihanouk, Prince Norodom, *Paroles de Samdech Preah Norodom Sihanouk*, Ministère de l'Information, Phnom Penh, 1964–1967 (***Paroles***)

—*L'Indochine Vue de Pékin: Entretiens avec Jean Lacouture*, Le Seuil, Paris, 1972 (***Indochine***)

—*My War with the CIA: Cambodia's Fight for Survival* (as related to Wilfred Burchett), Penguin, Harmondsworth, 1973 (***My War***)

—*Le Calice jusqu'à la Lie* (English version), typescript, 1980 (***Calice***)

—*War and Hope: The Case for Cambodia*, Random House, New York, 1980 (***War and Hope***)

—*Souvenirs Doux et Amers*, Hachette, Paris, 1981 (***Souvenirs***)

—*Prisonnier des Khmers Rouges*, Hachette, Paris, 1986 (***Prisonnier***)

—*Sihanouk Reminisces: World Leaders I Have Known*, Duong Kamol Publishing, Bangkok, 1990 (***World Leaders***)

Smith, Frank D., *Interpretive Accounts of the Khmer Rouge Years*, Center for Southeast Asian Studies, Madison, WI, 1989 (**Interpretive Accounts**)

Snepp, Frank, *Decent Interval*, Random House, New York, 1977

Somboon Suksamran, 'Buddhism, Political Authority and Legitimacy in Thailand and Cambodia', in Ling, Trevor (ed.), *Buddhist Trends in South-East Asia*, Institute of South-East Asian Studies, Singapore, 1993 (**Buddhism**)

Someth May, *Cambodian Witness*, Faber and Faber, London, 1986

Stalin, Josef V., *Histoire du Parti Communiste (Bolchévik) de l'URSS: Précis Redigé par une Commission du CC du PC (b) de l'URSS, approuvé par le CC du PC (b) de l'URSS*, 1938, Moscow, Editions de Langues Etrangères, 1949 (**Histoire**)

Stanic, Slavko, 'Kampuchea: Socialism without a Model', *Socialist Thought and Practice*, Belgrade, vol. 18, no. 10, 1984 (**Without a Model**)

Stuart-Fox, Martin, and Ung, Bunheang, *The Murderous Revolution*, Alternative Publishing Cooperative, Chippendale, NSW, 1986

Swain, Jon, *River of Time*, Heinemann, London, 1995 (**River**)

Szymusiak, Molyda, *The Stones Cry Out: A Cambodian Childhood, 1975–1980*, Hill & Wang, New York (**Stones**)

Thierry, Jean-Pierre, *Vergès et Vergès*, JC Lattès, Paris, 2000

Thierry, Solange, *Le Cambodge des Contes*, L'Harmattan, Paris, 1985

Thion, Serge, 'The Pattern of Cambodian Politics', in Kiernan, *Genocide and Democracy* (**Pattern**)

Thompson, Ashley, *The Calling of the Souls: A Study of the Khmer Ritual Hau Bralin*, Monash University, Clayton, Victoria, 1996 (**Calling**)

Truong Nhu Tang, *A Viet Cong Memoir*, Vintage Books, New York, 1985 (**Memoir**)

Vandy Kaonn, *Cambodge: 1940–1991*, L'Harmattan, Paris, 1993 (**Cambodge**)

—*Cambodge: La Nuit Sera Longue*, Editions Apsara, Paris, 1996 (**La Nuit**)

Vann Nath, *A Cambodian Prison Portrait: One Year in the Khmer Rouge's S-21*, White Lotus Press, Bangkok, 1998 (**Portrait**)

Vergès, Jacques, *Le Salaud Lumineux*, Michel Lafon, Paris, 1994 (**Salaud**)

Vickery, Michael, 'Looking Back at Cambodia [1945–1974]', in Kiernan and Boua, *Peasants and Politics* (**Looking Back**)

—'Democratic Kampuchea: Themes and Variations', in Chandler and Kiernan, *Aftermath* (**Themes**)

—*Kampuchea: Politics, Economics and Society*, Frances Pinter, London, 1986 (**Kampuchea**)

—*Cambodia, 1975–1982*, Silkworm Books, Chiangmai, 1999 (**Cambodia**)

Y Phandara, *Retour à Phnom Penh*, Métailié, Paris, 1982

Yi Tan Kim Pho, *Le Cambodge des Khmers Rouges: chronique de la vie quotidienne* (avec Ida Simon-Barouh), L'Harmattan, Paris, 1990 (**Cambodge**)

Yun Shui, 'An Account of Chinese Diplomats Accompanying the Government of Democratic Kampuchea's Move to the Cardamom Mountains', in *Critical Asian Studies*, vol. 34, no. 4, 2002, pp. 497–519 (**Diplomats**)

Zasloff, Joseph J., and Goodman, Allan E., *Indochina in Conflict: A Political Assessment*, Lexington Books, Lexington, MA, 1972 (**Conflict**)

Confessions, unless otherwise indicated, are from the Tuol Sleng Archives, Phnom Penh. Other abbreviations are employed as follows:

CPK	Communist Party of Kampuchea
FUNK	National United Front of Kampuchea
GRUNC	Royal Government of National Unity of Cambodia
ICP	Indochinese Communist Party
PRPK	People's Revolutionary Party of Khmerland (subsequently Kam puchea)
VWP	Vietnamese Workers' Party
AOM	Archives d'Outremer, Aix-en-Provence
ASEMI	Asie du Sud-est et le Monde Insulindien
BBC SWB	British Broadcasting Corporation Summary of World Broadcasts
BCAS	*Bulletin of Concerned Asian Scholars*
CWIHP	Cold War International History Project
DC–Cam	Documentation Center of Cambodia, Phnom Penh
EMIFT	Etat-Major Interarmes des Forces Terrestres en Indochine
JCA	*Journal of Contemporary Asia*
MAE	Ministère des Affaires Etrangères
QD	Archives du Quai d'Orsay, Paris
RC	*Réalités Cambodgiennes*
SDECE	Service de Documentation Extérieur et de Contre-Espionnage
SHAT	Service Historique de l'Armée de Terre, Vincennes
VA	Vietnamese Archives, Hanoi

PROLOGUE

Page

3 *The news reached . . . surrendered:* This account is drawn from interviews with Ieng Sary in Phnom Penh on Nov. 30 2000, Mar. 9 and Nov. 12 2001.

5 *If you preserve:* Interview with Mey Mak, Pailin, June 25, Sept. 20 and 21 2000; Mar. 13, 14, 15, 16 and 17 2001. *'Patriotic intellectuals':* See Caldwell and Lek Tan, pp. 418–33, where the text of the declaration and the list of signatories are reproduced.

6 *Disaffected schoolmaster: RC*, Mar. 1 1968. *Cropped up again:* The list was issued on Mar. 23 1972 (see Serge Thion, 'Chronology', in Chandler and Kiernan, *Aftermath*, p. 300). *During Sihanouk's visit: China Pictorial*, June 1973. *'The enemy is searching':* Sien An, confession, Feb. 25 1977. *'Knew who I was':* Pol Pot, *Yugoslav interview.* **On April 17:** The following account is drawn from interviews with Khieu Samphân (Pailin, Mar. 28 and 29, Apr. 2, 3 and 20 2001) and Phi Phuon (Malay, May 4 and 6, Nov. 14 and 15 2001); and from conversations with villagers during a visit to Sdok Toel on Dec. 16 2001.

7 *It would build . . . gone before: Der Spiegel*, May 2 1977.

8 *There the assembled . . . Buddha:* Phi Phuon, Khieu Samphân, interviews. *Fateful decision:* Phi Phuon, interview.

10 **What I saw**: Ong Thong Hoeung, *Récit*, p. 8.

One and a half million: Estimates of the number of deaths under Khmer Rouge rule from April 1975 to January 1979 range from 250,000 to 3 million. The 'unbearable uncertainty of the number', as one demographer has put it, stems from two main causes.

Estimates based on sampling—in other words, interviews with individual survivors about the numbers of their family members who died—may be inflated by double-counting and, more importantly, fail to take into account the enormous disparities which existed not just between zones and regions, but from one district to another and even, within districts, from one co-operative or village to another. Moreover, a disproportionate number of refugees interviewed were former city-dwellers, who accounted for only 800,000 out of a total population of about 7 million in 1975 and who suffered a far higher mortality rate than any other group in Democratic Kampuchea. (It must be noted that of the estimated 3 million people living in Cambodia's towns in April 1975, the vast majority were peasants who had taken refuge there to escape the fighting and who returned to their home villages as soon as the war ended.)

Estimates based on demographic trends are bedevilled by uncertainties over the exact population in 1970; over the death toll from the war and the natural rate of population increase from 1970–5; over levels of emigration and over the numbers of famine victims after the Vietnamese invasion in 1979.

I have taken the figure of 1.5 million deaths as representing a reasonable midpoint. I suspect, but cannot prove, that the true death toll may have been lower. If the entire population of former city-dwellers had died (which it did not), there would have been 800,000 deaths; and if 10 percent of the remaining 6.2 million peasants died (again almost certainly an overestimate), the total woudl be 1.42 million. It is certainly possible therefore, that the actual death toll was of the order of one million.

That is surely horrific enough. Whether the true figure is 3 million, 1.5 million or 'only' 750,000 in no way alters the barbarism of a regime which brought about the demise of between 10 and 40 per cent of its own people.

CHAPTER ONE: SÂR

15 **Prek Sbauv . . . civil war**: This account relies mainly on my own visits to Prek Sbauv and on interviews with Saloth Nhep on Nov. 29 and Dec. 27 2001. Regarding Sâr's change of birth date, Ieng Sary and Suong Sikoeun, among others, made themselves younger for the same reason (Ieng Sary, Suong Sikoeun, interviews). **March 1925**: Pol Pot gave this date when he recounted his life-story to the Chinese journalist Cai Ximei, in May 1984. In 1997 he told Nate Thayer: 'They wrote it on the wall in my home. The month *bos*, the year, *chluv* [ox]. January'. According to Thayer, he repeated the word in French: 'janvier'. The problem is that January 1925 fell in the Year of the Rat; the new lunar year of the Ox began in the month *cet*, in the last days of March 1925. The only way the different accounts can be reconciled is if Pol Pot meant the first month, not of the lunar year, but of the cyclical year, which would indeed correspond to March/April 1925 (see Institut Bouddhique, *Cérémonies des Douze Mois*, Phnom Penh, n.d., p. 15 and calendar).

16 **French missionary**: Khin Sok, pp. 239–40.

18 **Keng Vannsak endured . . . fainted**: Keng Vannsak, interview.

19 **Sâr's earliest memories . . . powers of protection:** In Sopheap, interview. See also Ang Chouléan, *Etres surnaturels.*

21 **Each year . . . religious obligation:** This account draws on an interview with the Abbot of Wat Botum Vaddei, Nhun Nghet, on Sept. 27 2001; on visits to the monastery that year; and on Chhang Song's reminiscences of his childhood in a *wat* in Takeo in the late 1940s (interview, Phnom Penh, Oct. 25 2001).

21–2 **In those days . . . beaten:** Nhun Nghet, interview.

22 **Never turn your back:** Saveros Pou, *Une Guirlande de Cpap*, Cedoreck, Paris, 1988, pp. 411–51.

23 **Your eyes:** Khing Hocdy and Jacqueline Khing, *Les Recommandations de Kram Ngoy*, Cedoreck, Paris, 1981; see also Khing Hocdy, *Ecrivains*, pp. 14–15. **They taught us:** Nhun Nghet, interview. See also Migot, *supra.* **Catechism:** 'Bref aperçu sur l'Ecole Miche, 1934–42' by Fr. Yves Guellec, unpublished ms held at the Archives Lasalliennes, Lyons; interviews with Ping Sây in Phnom Penh, Nov. 25, Dec. 1 and 4 2000; Mar. 6, Apr. 25 and Oct. 30 2001. Sây, who spent several months at the Ecole Miche during the winter of 1944–5, remembered the catechism but not the prayers.

24 **The street traffic:** H. W. Ponder, *Cambodian Glory*, Butterworth, London, 1936, pp. 155–6.

25 **Didn't surprise us:** Saloth Nhep, interview. See also Kiernan, *How Pol Pot*, p. 25.

26 **Royal audiences:** Meyer, *Sourire*, pp. 112–13.

27 **Nostalgia:** In Sopheap, interview. **Joke:** *Searching for the Truth*, no. 4, p. 8.

28 **Politeness:** Saloth Nhep, interview. See also Meyer, *Sourire*, pp. 32–3. **'Nice to be with':** Ping Sây, for example, remembered: 'He was a very, very nice person [in those days] . . . It was always really pleasant to be with him' (interview). See also interviews with Nghet Chhopininto, Paris, Feb. 17 and 22 2001; Mey Mann; and Khieu Samphân. Saloth Nhep said Sâr and Chhay were both 'good fun'. **'Adorable child':** Interview with Saloth Suong (Loth Suong), Phnom Penh, Nov. 1991; Chandler, *Brother*, pp. 9 and 204 n.5; and Kiernan, *How Pol Pot*, p. 27.

31 **At the college Preah Sihanouk . . . theatrical troupe:** The following account is taken from Khieu Samphân, Ping Sây and Nghet Chhopininto (interviews).

32–3 **School was closed . . . breath away:** Khieu Samphân, interview.

33 **'I can still remember':** Khieu Samphân, interview. **Found a job:** In Sopheap, interview.

34 **Riensouth:** Pierre Lamant, interview, Paris, Mar. 25 2002; and David Chandler, personal communication. Other Frenchmen who taught in Cambodia in the late 1990s and early 2000s, such as Henri Locard and Claude Rabear, experienced similar frustrations in dealing with the current generation of Cambodian students. Keng Vannsak, in the late 1950s, noted the same lack of initiative among the staff of the Phnom Penh Teacher Training College.

36 **Ieng Sary . . . Sisowath:** Ping Sây, Thiounn Mumm and Ieng Sary, interviews.

38 **Communist Manifesto:** Keng Vannsak and Ieng Sary, interviews. **Conflict of a different kind:** The following section is drawn mainly from Christopher E. Goscha's illuminating thesis on the First Indochina War, *Le Contexte Asiatique de la Guerre Franco-Vietnamienne: Réseaux, Relations et Economie (d'Août 1945 à Mai 1954).*

42 **In the summer:** Ping Sây, interview. See also Mey Mann and Ieng Sary, interviews. **'Most students':** Khieu Samphân, interview.

43 **On the eve:** The following account is from the recollections of Mey Mann (interview).

44 **'Indefinable half-smile'**: Meyer, *Sourire*, p. 33.

45 **The morning after:** The following account is taken from Mey Mann and Nghet Chhopininto, interviews.

CHAPTER TWO: CITY OF LIGHT

48 **'Policemen who gesticulate'**: *Khemara Nisut*, no. 8, Dec. 1949, pp. 19–20.

49 **Sâr was lucky:** Mey Mann remembered: 'He had a friend, or a cousin, I'm not sure what exactly . . . who took him off to stay with him . . . somewhere not in the Latin Quarter' (interview). Nghet Chhopininto thought Sâr spent the first year staying with the sons of the governor of Kratie (Em Samnang and Em Samrech) in an apartment near the Jardin des Plantes (which is close to the Ecole de Radio-Electricité in the rue Amyot), in the 5th arrondissement of Paris (interview). Vannsak (interview) thought it was 'probable' that he had spent the first year with Somonopong. In fact, it seems certain that he stayed at 17 rue Lacepède, where Samnang and Samrech were both still living in 1955, together with two of Somonopong's relatives, Prince Sisowath Monichivan and Prince Sisowath Vongvichan (côte 19800042, art 21, dossier 1912, AS de l'Association Khmer, 13 avril 1955, Centre des Archives Contemporaines, Fontainebleau). **Bon vivant:** Mey Mann and Ping Sây, interviews. See also Ieng Sary, interview. **Girlfriend:** The account of Sâr's relationship with Son Maly is taken from Keng Vannsak, interview.

50 **'Quite good marks'**: Pol Pot, *Cai Ximei interview* and *Thayer interview*.

51 **Camping holiday:** Pol Pot, *Thayer interview*. **'Progressive students'**: Pol Pot, *Cai Ximei interview*. **One of these . . . had left:** Ieng Sary, *Fiche d'étudiant* and interview with Henri Locard, Pailin, 1998; Keng Vannsak, interview. **Pay his respects . . . daily injections:** Keng Vannsak, interview.

52 **'Patriotic and against'**: Pol Pot, *Cai Ximei interview*.

55 **Statutes:** 'Statuts du Parti Révolutionnaire du Peuple du Cambodge' and 'La ligne politique du Parti', translated in 'le Parti Ouvrier Vietnamien', SDECE, c. 10H620, SHAT.

57 **'Lack qualities'**: 'Rapport du Général Viet Minh Nguyen Binh sur le Front Cambodgien'. Aug. 11 1951, c. 10H636, SHAT. **'Truly paradoxical'**: Commandement des Forces Terrestres du Cambodge, EM/3B, No. 2371/3, 'Synthèse d'exploitation', undated, c. 10H5585, SHAT.

59 **'Gathering of friends'**: Keng Vannsak, interview

60 **They screwed me:** Keng Vannsak, interview. **Young working men and women:** 'Festival Mondial de la Jeunesse', Berlin, 5 au 19 août, in c. BA2275, Archives de la Préfecture de Police, Paris.

61 **Armed struggle:** Vandy Kaonn, *La Nuit*, p. 182. **'[They] came back convinced'**: Keng Vannsak, interview.

62 **Thiounn Mumm had invited:** Nghet Chhopininto, interview. Mumm (interview) confirmed making a report after his return from Berlin but did not specify the circumstances.

63 **'The main question'**: Mey Mann, interview. **Selected participants:** Nghet Chhopininto, interview. **Too doctrinaire:** Keng Vannsak, interview. **Rue Lacepède:** Sâr himself claimed that 'I and some of the other students organised a small group called the Cambodian Marxist [Circle]', and dated its foundation to July–August 1951 (*Cai Ximei interview*). Ieng Sary (interview) said: 'Initially, Saloth Sâr did [not

take part] . . . Only later did his views start to change'; and (*Maben interview*): 'We tried to bring him into our group . . . but he did not want to come. Finally he joined us before he left France.' The truth no doubt lies somewhere between—Sâr trying to pretend falsely that he was a founder member, Sary exaggerating his reluctance to join because of his links with Vannsak and Son Ngoc Thanh. For the location of Sâr's cell, see Sher, *thesis*, p. 120; and Ieng Sary (interview with *Phnom Penh Post*, July 3–16 1998), who stated: 'Chandler made quite a few mistakes. He did not have knowledge of Pol Pot's role in rue Lacepède.'

64 **Masturbate:** Sher, *thesis*, p. 134. **Out of wedlock:** Thiounn Mumm, interview.

65 **'I did not wish':** Pol Pot, *Thayer interview*: 'That is my nature . . . I never talked much. [Someone] wrote that he knew me [in Paris] to be a polite, discreet, smiling young man. So, I did not want to show myself as a leader.' **'Out of his depth':** Keng Vannsak, interview. **That summer failed:** Pol Pot, *Cai Ximei* interview; Saloth Sâr, *Fiche d'étudiant*. **'Middle school certificate':** Pol Pot, *Thayer interview*.

66 **'Big, thick works':** Pol Pot, *Cai Ximei interview*. **Sâr joined:** Sâr himself told a Chinese interviewer in 1984 that he had joined the PCF in Paris (Pol Pot, *Cai Ximei interview*), and this is confirmed—though apparently on the basis of hearsay—by both Mey Mann and Keng Vannsak (interviews). Pham Van Ba, who in the early 1950s headed an Indochinese Communist Party cell in eastern Cambodia, also stated that Sâr had a PCF membership card (Chanda, *Brother Enemy*, p. 58). Thiounn Mumm, who insists that, contrary to widespread belief, he himself was never a PCF member, has questioned Sâr's claim, and some Western specialists, including Christopher Goscha, have likewise expressed doubts. To muddy the waters further, Ieng Sary, whose PCF membership is not in question, has also denied ever having held a Party card (*Maben interview*). Until the PCF follows the example of the Soviet, Chinese and Vietnamese parties and permits broader access to its archives, questions will remain. However, given the state of Sino—Soviet relations in the early 1980s, it is hard to see why, if it were untrue, Sâr should have invented PCF membership in an interview destined to be read by the Chinese leadership. Until proof to the contrary emerges, therefore, it should be assumed that his version is correct. For an overview, see Mey Mann, interview; and Pol Pot, *Talk with Khamtan*. **Easier to understand:** Pol Pot, *Cai Ximei interview*.

67 **Six basic lessons:** Stalin, *Histoire*, pp. 391–402. The six points are enumerated in the book's conclusion as guidelines that all militants should learn. All are depicted as essential, but 'revolutionary vigilance' and the need for a flexible approach to Marxism-Leninism are given pride of place.

68 **He confided:** Debré, *Révolution*, p. 86. See also Sher, *thesis*, pp. 133–4, quoting an unnamed former comrade of Sary. David Chandler, following Debré (whose source was Keng Vannsak), attributes these remarks to Saloth Sâr, and accordingly speculates that Sâr's ambition to become the pre-eminent Cambodian communist leader dated back to the 1950s. I find the evidence unpersuasive. Vannsak himself says he was referring to Sary (interview). **He gave talks:** Pol Pot, *Cai Ximei interview*. **He helped . . . Sisowath:** Ieng Sary, interview. For the parallel with Lenin's *Iskra*, see Thiounn Mumm, interview. **L'Humanité:** Pol Pot, *Thayer interview*. Referring to *l'Humanité*, he said simply, 'It frightened me'—which I have taken to be a reference to the newspaper's hectoring tone. Whatever Saloth Sâr's faults, stridency was not one of them. Ieng Sary, by contrast, named *l'Humanité* as one of his favourite news-

papers (*Maben interview*) and it was at his initiative that it was made compulsory reading in the Cercle.

70 **Seminal influence**: Pol Pot told Cai Ximei (*interview*):'When I read Chairman Mao's books, I felt they were easy to understand. I understood Stalin's books more easily too.' According to Ping Sây (interview), *On New Democracy* was the first of Mao's works that members of the Cercle studied. **'Democratic Cambodia'**: See the document issued by the 'Comité représentatif du Sud-Est Cambodge démocratique' on Sept. 24 1948, Haut Commissaire, Indochine, c. 77, AOM.

72 **Only book . . . understand all of it**: Pol Pot, *Thayer interview*. **Opening paragraph**: Kropotkin, pp. 1–2. The phrase I have translated as 'peasants and labourers' is, in the original, 'des paysans et des proletaires dans les villes'. However, in the eighteenth century the industrial proletariat did not yet exist and Kropotkin made clear (p. 283) that he was referring to 'les artisans et toute la population laborieuse des cités.' In this context, to use the literal translation, 'proletarians', would be misleading. The eighteenth-century French proletariat was the equivalent of the *cyclo-pousses* and coolies of 1950s Phnom Penh, not of any proletarian workforce that Marx ever dreamed of.

73 **Surrealistic encounter**: *Le Monde*, Dec. 31 1998. **Robespierre's personality**: Suong Sikoeun, interview. See also *Phnom Penh Post*, Nov. 15 1996; and Sher, *thesis*, p. 62.

74 **To the Russian . . . centre ground**: Kropotkin, pp. 312, 406, 433 and 707–9. **Ambivalence**: This is a constant theme throughout Kropotkin's book. 'The bourgeoisie and the educated classes would have done nothing . . . if the mass of the peasants had not risen up and . . . given the discontented elements among the middle classes the possibility to fight the King and the Court' (p. 5); 'the bourgeoisie constantly distrusted its ally of a day, the people' (p. 76); 'so began, on the part of the bourgeois leaders, the systematic treason that we shall see occurring throughout the Revolution' (p. 100); 'in short, the bourgeoisie and the intellectuals, the defenders of property rights, worked so hard to break the élan of the people that they halted the Revolution altogether' (p. 288). See also, *inter alia*, pp. 107–8, 178, 206 *et seq.*, 255, 279–81, 285, 405, 431–3, 615–16, 658. **'Never stop half way'**: Ibid., pp. 646 and 738–9.

76 **On June 4**: The official French-language version of the speech, which Sihanouk delivered in Khmer, is reproduced in *Bilan*, pp. 125–36. Nhiek Tioulong gives unrevised excerpts in 'Chroniques Khmères', *supra*, p. 11.

78 **Special issue**: 'Lettre de l'Association des Etudiants Khmers en France à Sa Majesté Norodom Syhanouk [*sic*], Roi du Cambodge', July 6 1952, in *Khemara Nisut*, no. 14. Unlike earlier editions, which were cyclostyled or printed in French, this issue, dated Aug. 1952, was handwritten on wax stencils in Khmer. The text quoted is from a contemporaneous French version of the letter, kindly supplied by Ben Kiernan, and from a later ms translation made by Mey Mann.

79 **Old Khmer**: The usual, and literal, translation of this term—which is used to describe the autochthonous peoples inhabiting the Cardamoms and other remote parts of the country—is 'Original Khmer'. But it would be wrong to attach too much significance to that: it does *not* indicate an atavistic yearning for a primitive, golden age. According to Keng Vannsak (interview), 'It was a term that was in common use. It simply meant "Old Khmer", or "Ancestor", and it conveyed the image of a Brahman. It had no revolutionary significance . . . The idea was rather that of a sage.' Other students, writing in the same issue, used the pseudonyms *Khmer Neak*

Ngear (Khmer hereditary slave)—an allusion to the plight of the population under the monarchy—and *Khmer Serei* (Free Khmer). **'Monarchy or Democracy?':** *Khemara Nisut*, no. 14, Aug. 1952 (d. D00084, DC-Cam).

82 **'Reconnaissance':** Pol Pot, *Cai Ximei interview.* **Second task:** Ping Sây, interview.

CHAPTER THREE: INITIATION TO THE MAQUIS

85 **Regimental despatch:** 'Compte-rendu de Combat du 22 Décembre 1952', A.R.K., 4ème Bataillon, 2ème Compagnie, No. 1025/C3, pp. 1–3, in 'Opérations de Pacification au Cambodge, Décembre 1952–Janvier 1953', Etat-Major, 3ème Bureau, No. 146/3, c. 10H285, SHAT. **Before I went away:** Pol Pot, *Thaver interview;* See also In Sopheap, *Khieu Samphân.* **To Sâr:** See *Sammaki*, Nov. 24 1954 (in c. HCC 27 [Surveillance de la presse Cambodgienne, 1951–1955], AOM), cited in Sher, *thesis,* pp. 610–11, where the 'essential task' of internal policy is described as 'achieving national independence and internal sovereignty'.

88 **Colonial troops:** Bunchan Mol, *Charek Khmer,* pp. 44–67; 'Proclamation Royale', June 21 1952, in *Bilan,* p. 149. For Viet Minh accounts of French atrocities, see SDECE, Bulletins de Renseignements Nos. 17574/1 of Oct. 2 1949 and 18431/1 of Oct. 24 1949, in c. 10H4120, SHAT. On Nov. 18 1951, the French commander, General Dio, felt it necessary to issue orders—'to be read, understood and *explained* regularly to the cadres'—for the maintenance of 'strict discipline. Plunder, robbery, pillage, rape, abuse of power and taking food without payment are absolutely to be avoided.'

90 **Saloth Chhay:** Pol Pot, *Cai Ximei interview.* In Sept. 1951 French intelligence located Keo Moni's SE Zone HQ as being 'at Krâbao, 50 kms ENE of PreyVeng town' (Note de Renseignement No. 1919/2, Sept. 5 1951, c. 10H4122, SHAT). In the summer of 1954, when Mey Mann went there, it was still in that area (interview). **While Sâr .. . into reality:** De Langlade to Salan, 156/CAB, Mar. 24 1953, c. 10H285, SHAT.

92–4 **On June 6 . . . Laos and Vietnam:** Unless otherwise indicated, the following account is based on 'Politique Intérieure, Mois de Juin 1953', c. 10H613, SHAT. The document is unsigned, but Chandler (*Tragedy,* p. 328 n.53) attributes it to De Langlade on the basis of a copy sent to Washington by the US Embassy in Saigon.

92 **Secret memorandum:** 'Note Personnelle redigée par Norodom Sihanouk de Cambodge à l'intention des Etats-Unis d'Amérique et de la Grande Bretagne', c. 10H613, SHAT.

94 **On July 3:** De Langlade, 'Politique Intérieure', *supra.*

96 **Bona fides:** 'Rapport [oral] du camarade Khieu Minh, fonctionnaire-cadre de l'Ambassade Vietnamien à Phnom Penh, fait au sujet de Pol Pot et son Parti à la délégation des cadres du Comité de Recherche sur l'idéologie du CC', Phnom Penh, May 10 1980, Doc. 32(N442)/T8243, VA. **Sâr remembered:** Pol Pot, *Cai Ximei interview.* His story of having worked as a cook is confirmed by aVietnamese source ('Biographie de Pol Pot', Doc. 32(N442)/ T8313, VA). **Yun Soeun:** He added: 'Because I was a student from France, I was not a trustworthy cadre as far as those in the resistance group were concerned . . . So, I was not assigned any work to do.' (Yun Soeun, confession).

97 **'Six Rules':** 'Les Six Règles de Vie du Membre du Parti Communiste', Comité Exécutif Central du Parti Lao Dong, 1951, c. BA 2346, Archives de la Préfecture de Police, Paris.

98 **'Real difficulty'**: 'Recherche sur le Parti Cambodgien', Doc. 3KN/T8572,VA. *Sâr himself*: Pol Pot, *Cai Ximei interview.*

99 **Ba remembered**: Quoted in Kiernan, *How Pol Pot*, p. 123 (translation amended). *Visit nearby villages*: Pol Pot, *Cai Ximei interview*. *He made friends*: Ibid.; Mey Mann, interview; 'Implantation Rebelle au 15 mai 1952', EMIFT map, c. 10H4122, SHAT.

100 **After a fashion**: Pol Pot, *Cai Ximei interview*. *Unruffled manner*: Both In Sopheap and Suong Sikoeun (interviews) stressed Pol Pot's serene, monk-like demeanour as one of the sources of his charisma and hence of his power. *Principal aide*: Mey Mann, interview.

102 **The engine ... 30 monks**: Haut Commissariat Royal du Cambodge, No. 054A, Apr. 21 1954, c. A-O-I 166, QD.

104–5 **Sâr, Mey Mann ... set out last**: The following account relies on Mey Mann (interview). Pham Van Ba, in his interview with Kiernan (*How Pol Pot*, p. 155), appears to inflate his own role.

105 **Three young Khmers**: Mey Mann, interview.

CHAPTER FOUR: CAMBODIAN REALITIES

106 **Already ... end of Cambodia**: 'De Langlade à Monsieur ... le Commandant en Chef des Forces Terrestres ... en Indochine', Nov. 11 1953, c. 10H285, SHAT.

107 **Sâr was chosen ... coming elections**: In his confession (Oct. 7 1976), Keo Meas indicates that the assignment of tasks in the winter of 1954 was undertaken 'on instructions from the brothers higher up ... which were conveyed at first through the Vietnamese, and later on through Comrade [Saloth Sâr]'. Of the 'brothers higher-up', Son Ngoc Minh was in North Vietnam, and Sieu Heng in southern Vietnam (until 1956). That leaves only Tou Samouth—whom Meas noted soon afterwards took charge of the Phnom Penh Committee—as the source of these directives. Sâr's role in liaising with the Democrats is confirmed by Keng Vannsak and Thiounn Mumm (interviews).

108 **Sâr had gone ... united force**: Keng Vannsak, interview. *'Important role'*: Ping Sây, interview. *'Manipulating Vannsak'*: Thiounn Mumm, interview.

109 **Abdication**: *La Grande Figure, supra*, pp. 385–8.

111 **Evil genius**: Keng Vannsak, interview.

112 **'Slaves for centuries'**: Keng Vannsak, interview. *Sâr recalled*: Pol Pot, *Cai Ximei interview*.

113 **'Taking part in elections'**: Pol Pot, *Cai Ximei interview*. *New instructions*: 'Recherche sur le Parti Cambodgien', Doc. 3KN.T8572,VA.

115 **'Rouges'**: In 1956, Sihanouk used the term 'pro-Easterners' to designate the Pracheachon ('La Subversion au Cambodge', Nov. 7 1956, c. CLV 20, QD). The terms 'rouge' and 'rose' occur several times in the series of articles Sihanouk published in *RC* on Mar. 1, 15 and 22 1958. The first printed use of the term 'Khmer Rouge' appears to have been in *Neak Cheatniyum* of July 30 1960 (see Gorce to MAE, No. 380 AS/CLV. Aug. 3 1960, c. CLV 20; and *Les Echos de Phnom Penh*, Aug. 4 and 11 1960, quoting Sihanouk's speech of Aug. 2 at Thnal Rokar, Kompong Speu). *Initially the group ... serving foreign masters*: Gorce to MAE, No. 130/CX, Mar. 28 1956, c. CLV 7; No. 248/R, June 14 1956, c. CLV 112; No. 618/CX, Sept. 21 1956, c. CLV 8; Direction Générale des Affaires Politiques, 'Situation Politique au Cam-

bodge', Feb. 16 1957, c. CLV 112, QD; and Chandler, *Tragedy*, pp. 85—7. In May 1956,
the Pracheachon also set up a 'Support Committee for Cambodian Neutrality',
whose members included Hou Yuon — who had returned from France that spring
—and Sâr's brother Chhay. It proposed a government of national union, including
the Sangkum, the Pracheachon and the Democratic Party ('La Subversion au Cambodge', Nov. 7 1956, c. CLV 20, QD).

116 *After his return . . . from Paris*: Ping Sây, Thiounn Mumm and Mey Mann, inter-
views. For another description of the swamp areas of Phnom Penh in the 1950s, see
Chhang Song, interview, Phnom Penh, Oct. 25 2001. *Even Non Suon*: Keo Meas
(Oct. 7 1976), Non Suon (Nov. 7 1976) and Ney Sarann (Oct. 1 1976), confessions.
Black Citroën: Keng Vannsak, interview. Ping Sây was less impressed, describing the
car as 'a heap of old iron' (interview).

116–17 *It enabled him . . . to marry*: Keng Vannsak, interview.

117 *'Dances very well'*: Suong Sikoeun, interview. *She dumped him . . . equal to his
own*: Keng Vannsak, interview. *Sâr and Khieu Ponnary . . . married*: This account
relies on Ping Sây (interview), especially concerning Ponnary's role as an intermediary with the maquis; see also Keng Vannsak and Ieng Sary, interviews.

117–18 *'Made in heaven'*: 'Rapport [oral] du camarade Khieu Minh . . . le 10 Mai 1980',
Doc. 32(N442)/T8243, VA.

118 *Very odd union . . . scars*: Chandler (*Brother*, p. 50); Keng Vannsak (interview) says she
was nicknamed in French 'la vieille fille'. *Yet marry . . . Ponnary's family*: Mey
Mann, Ping Sây, interviews. *As the high point . . . No one could understand*: Ieng
Sary, interview. *One of her students*: Long Nârin, interview at Malay, June 18 2000
and May 4 and 5, 2001. *'They lived . . . appreciate that'*: Ieng Sary, interview.

119 *More outgoing . . . on her behalf*: Lim Keuky, quoted in Chandler, *Brother*, p. 50.
Cancer: Thiounn Thoeunn, interview; Moeun, interview at Anlong Veng, Dec. 12
2001.

120 *I still remember*: Quoted in Chandler, *Brother*, p. 52 (translation modified). *'Lifelong
friend'*: You Sambo, quoted in ibid., p. 51.

121 *'It gave us the chance'*: Pol Pot, *Cai Ximei interview*. Judging by the situation in
neighbouring Laos, where the Vietnamese had remained in force in the Pathet Lao
zone, this assessment was correct. A French intelligence report, quoting a senior
Pathet Lao defector in 1955, gives a vivid picture of the extent to which the Vietnamese dominated the Laotian revolution: 'All important posts, both civil and military, are held secretly by Viet Minh [although] they are kept out of sight as much as
possible . . . The Viet Minh advisers are all-powerful . . . The Pathet Lao [leaders] can
decide nothing without their approval . . . Radio reports from Pathet Lao battalion
commanders are sent . . . to Hanoi, which sends back orders by the same channel.
Souphanouvong and his ministers are frequently kept in ignorance of these
exchanges.' (Guibaut to Etassociés, No. 1618/CAB, Vientiane, Oct. 20 1955, c. A-O-I
166, QD). *Ieng Sary claimed*: Ieng Sary interview. I am grateful to Chris Goscha for
helping to make the connection between Hay So and Nguyen Van Linh. The *Black
Paper* (pp. 7, 20–21 and 70) states merely that in 1970 Hay So was one of the seven
members of the COSVN and that by 1978 he had become a member of the
VWPCC. The same source identifies Linh's deputy in Phnom Penh, Teur Kam (or
Tu Kun), as Nguyen Da Giang. *Angker*: Ping Sây, interview.

122 *We used to meet*: Suong Sikoeun, interview. *He organised . . . political stance*: You
Sambo, quoted in Chandler, *Brother*, p. 51; Ping Sây, interview.

124 *'Sulfurous'*: Quoted in Chandler, *Tragedy*, p. 99. **This time he beat . . . immediate recall**: Ibid., p. 100; *Daily Mirror*, London, June 7 and 17, *Sunday Pictorial*, June 15 1958 and Keng Vannsak, interview. Vannsak identified her as Soeung Son Maly and said her role in the scandal was well known in Cambodia. British newspapers, however, gave her name as lv Eng Seng and said she was 22 years old, considerably younger than Maly at that time.

126 **Six months later . . . South Vietnam**: Mathivet de la Ville de Mirmont to MAE, Telegram Nos. 696—7, Sept. 1, and *idem*, No. 420/AS, Sept. 7 1959, c. CLV 12, QD. See also Chandler (*Tragedy*, pp. 106—7), who states incorrectly that the parcel was addressed to Sihanouk; and Tran Tim Kuyen's recollection in Cao De Thuong, *Lam te . . . ton*, Saigon, 1970, p. 313.

127 **Most serious of all . . . it was lifted**: The best overview is again that of David Chandler, who has combed the US archives and, as a US diplomat, based in Phnom Penh in the early 1960s, was able to watch from the inside the two countries' slow divorce (*Tragedy*, pp. 93, 98—9 and 101—7). See also Jennar, *Clés*, pp. 58—63. On the blockade, see Gorce to MAE, 'Rapport sur l'évolution de la situation politique au Cambodge du 13 janvier au 20 mai 1956', A/S No. 248/R, June 14 1956, pp. 21—2, c. CLV 112, QD. Sihanouk himself wrote at length about the incoherence of US policy in *RC* on Mar. 29 1958, well before Washington's decision to resort to extra-legal means to try to bring him down.

128 *'Bleus'*: Sihanouk used the term 'bleu' in *RC* of Mar. 15 and 22 1958, but it may well have had currency earlier.

131 **Celebrated incident**: See Gorce to MAE, Nos. 75 AS/CLV, Feb. 22; 90 AS/CLV, Feb. 26; and 566 AS/CLV, Dec. 12 1960, c. CLV 13, QD. Sihanouk himself unwittingly cast light on what had really happened, when he explained that the young man, Reath Vath, had been found carrying a pistol and a hand-grenade at a rally where he was to speak at the end of 1959 (Sihanouk, *My War*, p. 113). He turned up at the US Embassy in Feb. 1960.

132 **Chinese empress**: Zhou Enlai and Pham Van Dong, Beijing, Apr. 10 1967, CWIHP archives, Washington, DC. **He was always punctual**: Someth May, *Cambodian Witness*, p. 88. **His younger brother**: Quoted in Laura Summers's introduction to Khieu Samphân, *thesis*, p. 12.

133 **French girl**: The portrait relies on my own meetings with Khieu Samphân in Pailin, on the recollections of Suong Sikoeun (interview) and of other former Khmers Rouges who prefer to remain anonymous. For the French girlfriend, recollection of Nghet Chhopininto's first wife, Nicole Bizeray, quoted in Sher, *thesis*, p. 143.

134 *'Thirsty for power'*: Gorce to MAE, No. 41 AS/CLV, Jan. 29 1960, c. CLV 13, QD.

135 **Charcoal burners**: Keng Vannsak, interview.

136 **The issue . . . proletariat**: Engelbert and Goscha, *Falling*, esp. pp. 129—30 and 136—8. Asked why the Party focused its efforts on the peasantry, Ping Sây gave the obvious response: 'Because [in 1960] there were very few workers. There was no industry and there were no factories' (interview).

137 **Two weeks . . . smell**: Ieng Sary, Ping Sây, Nghet Chhopininto, interviews; *Tung Padevat*, Sept.—Oct. 1976, pp. 1—32. **The 'feudal ruling class' . . . suppress [us]**: Engelbert and Goscha, *Falling*, pp. 125—42.

139 *'Excluded themselves'*: Ping Sây, interview. **Reapply**: Ping Sây, interview; 'Recherche sur le Parti Cambodgien', Doc. 3KN.T8572,VA.

141 **Who betrayed**: In July 1977, Ros Mao alias Say, who had been one of Samouth's

bodyguards in the early 1960s, confessed under torture at Tuol Sleng that he and five others—including Sieu Heng—had kidnapped the Party leader and taken him to Lon Nol's house (confession, undated but July 1977). Another of the five, Som Chea alias Sdoeung, gave an almost identical description of the circumstances in a confession dated May 4 1978. However, both men remained loyal Party members for the next fifteen years and it is hard to see why either should have obeyed a traitor (Sieu Heng) to act against a Party leader who, by all accounts, was well-liked and respected. Interrogators at Tuol Sleng sometimes showed prisoners previous confessions in order to pressure them to admit their own guilt; if Sdoeung was shown Say's confession, it would explain why the two coincide so exactly (too exactly, in fact, for unconnected recollections of events sixteen years earlier). Nuon Chea later described Samouth's death in terms consistent with, if not drawn from, the Tuol Sleng confessions (Mey Mann, interview), as did Pol Pot in his interview with Nate Thayer. Sieu Heng himself, questioned about Tou Samouth's death by an American diplomat in 1972, replied, 'Lon Nol knows what happened' (US Embassy, Phnom Penh, airgram A-2, Feb. 17 1972, quoted in Chandler, *Tragedy*, p. 338 n.98)—which, if it confirms Lon Nol's involvement, does nothing to clarify Heng's own role. In Sopheap says that Pol Pot and Nuon Chea told him in the 1990s that Tou Samouth's courage in keeping silent during his interrogation had saved the urban movement from destruction (interview), and Khieu Samphân (interview) makes a similar claim. The only conclusion that can be drawn is that allegations of Sieu Heng's involvement began to circulate within the Party between 1973 and 1978—precisely the time when the Party's history was being rewritten to make it appear that the Pol Pot leadership had been its driving force ever since its foundation. In 1979, shortly after the overthrow of the Democratic Kampuchea regime, Vietnamese officials suggested that Saloth Sâr himself had been responsible for Samouth's death (Kiernan, *How Pol Pot*, pp. 198 and 141 n.135). The claim does not withstand close scrutiny. **Sâr argued:** Pol Pot, *Cai Ximei interview*.

141–2 **The meeting . . . full members:** Ieng Sary, *interview*. According to Ruos Nhim (confession, undated), Koy Thuon—who had not attended the 1960 Congress—was among those present in 1963.

142 **Four new:** Mok said he, Ruos Nhim and Vorn Vet joined (*Thayer interview*). Kiernan (*How Pol Pot*, p. 201) quotes Nguyen Xuan Hoang as saying that Son Sen and Phuong, an Eastern Zone leader, also entered the CC at this Congress: that appears to be correct in the case of Son Sen, but not of Phuong, who entered the committee in 1971. **Workers' Party:** Ieng Sary, interview. This second change of name, like the earlier use of 'Labour Party', was kept secret from the Party at large and from the Vietnamese.

143 **Thirty-four named leftists . . . surveillance:** Keng Vannsak (interview) and Siet Chhê (confession, July 18 1977) both said police guards were posted at their homes. They were respectively among the best- and least-known figures named. It is hard to believe that they were singled out for such treatment, so I have assumed that the measure applied to all thirty-four.

143–4 **Ieng Sary . . . a day later:** Ieng Sary, interview. See also In Sopheap, *Khieu Samphân*, p. 60, where Sary is quoted as saying that he argued that the Party should have its own rural bases and a solid network in the cities before the leadership moved to the countryside.

144 **Oracle:** Massenet to MAE, June 26; and De Beausse to MAE, No. 1527 AS/CLV,

Sept. 24 1962, c. CLV 15, QD. The latter contains the text of a Cambodian government memorandum, detailing a prediction by an oracle at Kratie that 'bloody battles will break out' on Cambodia's border with Thailand in April 1963, but that the country would emerge from the trial strengthened. A minute in Sihanouk's hand ordered that the prediction be made known to the cabinet, the General Staff of the Armed Forces and members of parliament. **Royal oxen:** On May 19 1957, by Circular No. 35/PCM/2B/C, Sihanouk informed his cabinet and all the provincial governors: 'The choice of nourishment by the *asopareach* [royal] oxen after the ploughing of the sacred furrow authorises the prediction that the coming rains will be unfavourable for the harvest ...According to the official astrologers the rains will end early ... and the harvest will only be one sixth of that obtained last year ... I feel I must therefore draw the attention of the competent ministries and services (Agriculture, Public Works, Veterinary Services etc.) to the imperious necessity of drawing up, with immediate effect, practical measures to enable us to ward off the hideous spectre of famine ... All those who succeed in giving our people and our peasantry a real chance of avoiding famine and misery will be rewarded with official honours' (annexed to Gorce to MAE, No. 710/CX, May 24 1957, c. CLV 9, QD). See also Meyer, *Sourire*, pp. 86–96.

CHAPTER FIVE: GERMINAL

145 **Message:** Ieng Sary, interview. **Spartan:** Truong Nhu Tang (*Memoir*, p. 128) described in these terms his first impressions of the COSVN (Central Office for South Vietnam) HQ on the Cambodia-Vietnam border at Memot in 1968. The camp where the Khmers lived was probably less elaborate.

146 **Sâr persuaded:** Sdoeung, confession, May 4 1978. Ieng Sary (interview) said that in negotiating with the Vietnamese, 'Pol Pot was very good at that. He could manoeuvre; he was very subtle—very clever at tactics.'

147 **Copies ... police:** The following account of the operations of the 'printing office' is taken from Nikân (interview). He worked there from late 1967 to mid-1968 after it had been transferred to Ratanakiri. See also Ieng Sary, interview; Pâng, confession, May 28 1978; Sdoeung and Siet Chhê, confessions. *'After 1963'*: Pol Pot, *Cai Ximei interview. **In Paris ... the problems:** Pol Pot, *Thayer interview. **'We applied ourselves'*: Pol Pot, *Talk with Khamtan. **'Mixture [of influences]'*: Pol Pot, *Thayer interview.

148 *'Resides within'*: Pol Pot, *Talk with Khamtan*. Mao spoke of the experience of the Chinese people 'enriching and developing' Marxism-Leninism, but he never claimed, as Pol Pot did, that the masses could 'create' it on their own.

149 **Systematically refused:** Pol Pot, *Talk with Khamtan*. **No choice:** Khieu Samphân, interview. **Viññān:** Thompson, *Calling*, p. 2.

150 **Intensely introspective:** Robert S. Newman, *Brahmin and Mandarin: A Comparison of the Cambodian and Vietnamese Revolutions*, La Trobe University, Melbourne, 1978, pp. 7–8; Migot, pp. 351–2. *'Worker-farmers'*: *Revolutionary Youths*, Aug. 1973, pp. 9–20, quoted in Carney, *Communist Party Power*, pp. 30–3, refers repeatedly to the 'worker-farmer class'. The same term is used in the Sept. 1973 issue. **Proletarianised ... position:** Khieu Samphân, interview.

151 *'Black time'*: Pol Pot, *Talk with Khamtan*. *'Enemy furiously'*: Pol Pot, *Cai Ximei interview*. **Operating secretly:** Nuon Chea, *Statement*, pp. 28–30.

152 **'Several hundred'**: Meyer, *Sourire*, pp. 191–5. No accurate figures exist for the number of members of the CPK's urban underground killed by the regime in the 1960s, but scattered references in interviews with former Khmers Rouges and confessions from Tuol Sleng suggest that it was probably in the order of several dozen. Sihanouk himself acknowledged that his 'Buddhist neutralism, tinted with Hinduism, could not work without a few drops of violence' (Sihanouk, *Indochine*, p. 73), and at the beginning of 1964 warned bluntly that 'Khmers Rouges and left-wing intellectuals, accused of communism and sabotage' would be summarily shot (De Beausse to MAE, No. 243/AS, Feb. 4 1964, c. CLV 113, QD). **2,000**: Pol Pot, *Cai Ximei interview*. He told Le Duan in 1965 that the Party had 3,000 members, a figure which was almost certainly inflated ('Recherche sur le Parti Cambodgien', Doc. 3KN.T8572, VA).

153 **Public ridicule . . . scandalous**: De Beausse to MAE, No. 2019/AS CLV, Dec. 19 1962, QD.

153–4 **The most committed . . . existing government**: Phal, interview.

156 **Delegation to Hanoi**: Sâr said he had been 'delegated by the Cambodian communists to have a meeting with them [the Vietnamese]' (Pol Pot, *Cai Ximei interview*). Ieng Sary (interview) confirmed this. **Up till then**: 'Les Perspectives, les Lignes et la Politique Etrangère du Parti Communiste Cambodgien', Doc. TLM/165, VA. **Sâr set out . . . two and a half months**: Vorn Vet, confession, Nov. 24 1978; Pâng, confession (quoted in Chandler, *Brother*, p. 69); Pol Pot, *Cai Ximei interview*.

157 **On arrival . . . dozen times**: Pol Pot, *Talk with Khamtan* and *Cai Ximei interview*. **Le Duan tried**: See the text of Le Duan's talk with Saloth Sâr on July 29 1965, in Engelbert and Goscha, *Falling*, pp. 143–55. **Hobby-horses**: The same phrases are to be found in 'Instructions Viet Minh pour la Campagne au Laos et au Cambodge', a document obtained by the French SDECE in 1953 (No. 3749/234, June 22 1953, c. A-O-I 165, QD).

157–8 **The Cambodian Party's stress . . . solidarity**: Engelbert and Goscha, *Falling*, pp. 143–55.

158 **To bolster . . . reach a common view**: Pol Pot, *Cai Ximei interview*.

159 **He stayed**: I am grateful to Youqin Wang of the University of Chicago for this information. **Official host . . . Zhou Enlai**: Pol Pot, *Cai Ximei interview*; Ieng Sary, interview. Sâr himself said in 1984 he had seen 'other Politburo members', but without mentioning names (*Cai Ximei interview*); they may have included the Foreign Minister, Chen Yi, and Kang Sheng, the Head of the CPC International Liaison Department and concurrently Mao's security chief. According to Sary, Sâr had extended conversations with Kang Sheng only during his subsequent visit in 1970. An internal Chinese Party document, which notes his meetings in 1965 with Chen Boda and Zhang Chunqiao (neither of whom were then Politburo members), makes no reference to his seeing Kang either in 1965 or 1970. **Seminal article**: *Peking Review*, Sept. 3 1965, pp. 9–30. Although the article was published under Lin Biao's name, he played no part in the writing of it, which was carried out by a propaganda group under the leadership of Luo Ruiqing.

160 **Principal contradictions**: *Peking Review*, *supra*, p. 10. Le Duan had made clear when he met Sâr in July that, on this point, Vietnam disagreed with the Chinese (and by implication Cambodian) stance (Engelbert and Goscha, *Falling*, p. 145). Subsequently, Vietnamese historians condemned the January 1965 Cambodian Party CC resolution for 'putting in first place the contradiction between imperialism and the

oppressed peoples; emphasising the contradiction between the peasants and the feudal landowners; and putting the contradiction between imperialism and socialism last' ('Recherche sur le Parti Cambodgien', Doc. 3KN.T8572, VA). *Two younger men... dictatorship:* Unpublished internal Chinese Party document. *Material support:* Doc.TLM/165, *supra*, apparently quoting from a transcript of Sâr's discussions in Beijing which he gave the Vietnamese on his way back through Hanoi.

161 *He told Keo Meas:* Keo Meas, confession, Sept. 30 1976. *'Reassured':* Pol Pot, *Talk with Khamtan. At Loc Ninh ... his back:* 'Rapport [oral] du camarade Khieu Minh ... le 10 Mai 1980', Doc. 32(N442)/T8243,VA.

163 *'Malaise':* Malo to Manac'h, Paris, June 11 1966, c. A-O 1965-78 438, QD.

164 *A week after ... armed struggle:* 'Recherche sur le Parti Cambodgien', Doc. 3KN.T8572, VA; Chheang [Kong Sophal] (confession) confirms the decision in October 1966 to 'seize authority in the villages and communes'. *'Live together':* Pol Pot, *Abbreviated Lesson*, pp. 218–19. For a contemporary expression of the same idea, see the communist pamphlet quoted in *Le Sangkum* (July 1966), which stated: 'Don't have too much confidence in Sihanouk! That should be the motto of every Party member.'

165 *Impossible:* The North Vietnamese Premier, Pham Van Dong, told Zhou Enlai on Apr. 10 1967: 'We still do not know fully to what extent the struggle is organised and to what extent it has been provoked by the enemy' (CWIHP Archives). *'Pushing the peasants':* Chheang [Kong Sophal], confession. Ben Kiernan quotes an official Party history, circulated in the South-Western Zone in early 1972, as saying: 'From 1967, the Party resumed the armed struggle ...The events at Samlaut were prepared in advance' (*Communist Movement*, p. 256).

166 *At that point ... was over:* Kong Sophal and Say, confessions, *supra*. According to Say, senior monks fom Wat Thvak and Wat Treng took part in the negotiations. Kiernan (*Samlaut*, Part 1, p. 30) said the abbot of a monastery in Battambang, Iv Tuot, was also involved. In a speech at Siem Reap on June 20, Sihanouk paid tribute to 'the efforts made by the clergy of Battambang' to bring the unrest to an end (Argod to MAE, No. 1377/AS-CLV, July 4 1967, c. A-O 1965–78 439, QD). According to the North Vietnamese Premier, Pham Van Dong, the COSVN also sent emissaries to the CPK in April (or possibly earlier) to try to persuade the Cambodian leadership to call off the struggle (talks with Zhou Enlai, Apr. 11 1967, CWIHP Archives).

167 *By May:* Kong Sophal (confession, Nov. 12 1978) quoted the leadership as saying: 'If Battambang just does this alone, the enemy will be able to destroy all the revolutionary forces.' *'The pacification ... headquarters':* Lancaster, *Decline*, p. 52. *'Ghoulish details':* Osborne, *Before Kampuchea*, p. 43.

168 *He told guests:* The Reuters' correspondent Bernard Hamel was present at the dinner; I am grateful to Sacha Sher for this anecdote. See also Hamel's despatch for Reuters, 'Mystery about Cambodian communist leader Khieu Samphân', Phnom Penh, Apr. 24 1974. Milton Osborne (*Before Kampuchea*, p. 80; *Prince of Light*, p. 194) quotes Khim Tit, a former Defence Minister with close links to the Prince, as telling a similar story. *That evening ... peasant life:* Khieu Samphân, interview. A slightly different account appears in In Sopheap, *Khieu Samphân*, pp. 86–7.

170 *We have reached ... victories:* 'Lettre du Comité Permanent du CC du CPK au Bureau politique du CC du CPC', Oct. 6 1967, Doc. TLM/175, VA.

172 *Sâr himself ... available:* Phi Phuon and Ieng Sary, interviews. Pâng (confession, May 28 1978) said: 'In late 1966 (around July or August 1966) [*sic*], Office 100 was ..

. dissolved . . . The group travelling to the north-east was led by Brother Van [Ieng Sary]'—but this is evidently an error for 1967. Ieng Sary (interview) said the move to Ratanakiri took place in 1967. Engelbert and Goscha refer to Sâr receiving treatment in Vietnam in 1968 at 'the Central Committee's Southern Bureau Hospital', which was presumably the same place as 'Hospital No 5' (*Falling*, p. 83). *Malaria was . . . attack*: Khieu Samphân, interview; In Sopheap, *Khieu Samphân*, p. 90. *Relapses*: Phi Phuon, interview; Pâng, confession, May 28 1978; Mey Mann, interview.

172–3 *In the North-East . . . hunting*: Moeun, Phi Phuon, interviews.

173 *Unusual excitement*: Khieu Samphân, interview. Isolated incidents had occurred, both in Battambang and in the South-Western Zone, even before the 'official' outbreak of the rébellion (see the account of Sihanouk's visit to Kompong Tralach district, near Oudong, on January 9, in *RC*, Jan. 13 1968).

175–6 *Sihanouk himself . . . Khmer-language press*: Speech at Andaung Pich, Bokeo, on Feb. 1 1968 (*Paroles*, Jan.–Mar. 1968, p. 72); Argod to MAE, Telegram Nos. 350–7, Mar. 7, and Nos. 669–75, May 24, and Dauge to MAE, No. 157/AI, July 2 1968, c. A-O 1965-78 439, QD; Kiernan, *How Pol Pot*, pp. 274 and 293 n. 164; *Le Monde*, Nov. 20 1969.

176 *An Eastern Zone . . . palm tree*: Kiernan, *How Pol Pot*, pp. 265 and 276. Ten years later, the Khmers Rouges were alleged to be executing suspected spies using the same method. The stories may be apocryphal, but in both cases they were widely believed. *At K-5 . . . fetch him*: Phi Phuon, interview; Pâng, confession, May 28 1978.

176–7 *Rarely moved . . . she visited*: 'Alone Amongst Brothers: The Story of Khieu Ponnary, Revolutionary and First Wife of Pol Pot', *Cambodia Daily*, Oct. 20, 2001.

177 *Sâr took over*: Phi Phuon, interview. The 'Biography of Pol Pot', broadcast by Radio Pyongyang on Oct. 3 1977, said he was North-Eastern Zone Secretary 'from 1968 to March 1970' (BBC SWB FE/5634/B/4). *'Problem of unity'*: 'Recherche sur le Parti Cambodgien', Doc. 3KN.T8572, VA. At a meeting with Thai communists in August 1977, Sâr also spoke of the disunity caused by the CPK's dual origin (Pol Pot, *Talk with Khamtan*). *'Separatist tendencies'*: Pol Pot, *Talk with Khamtan*.

178–9 *I had been told . . . body*: In Sopheap, *Khieu Samphân*, pp. 89—90. Ill-health was a constant problem. Toch Phoeun remembered arriving at Phnom Pis in the South-West Zone in 1970 to find 'most of our comrades were sick, lying in their hammocks' (confession, Mar. 14 1977).

181 *America says*: *RC*, Nov. 11 1967.

182 *Exceed 20 million*: Conversation between Mao Zedong and Pham Van Dong, Beijing, Nov. 17 1968, CWIHP Archives. The North Vietnamese Premier said the money was paid 'to Sihanouk' which raises the question of whether the Prince himself benefited from these transactions. Until the minutes of this meeting became available, it had been assumed that Sihanouk himself was honest but lacked the will (or the inclination) to discipline those around him. It is of course possible that Pham Van Dong used the Prince's name merely as a synonym for the Cambodian administration. There is no way to be sure.

183 *Lon Nol, now back . . . to escape*: Except where specified elsewhere, this account of the raids, which took place between Aug. 11 and Sept. 6 1968, is drawn from *RC*, Aug. 30, Sept. 13 and 20 1968). *Forty suspects . . . subsequently executed*: Vorn Vet (confession, Nov. 24 1978) said 'more than twenty people' were arrested. Six of those

he identified—Dam Pheng, Leang Kim Huot, Pa Sieng Hay, Kum Saroeun, Chhoeun and Kac Sim—were also named by *RC*. The two sources together cited a further sixteen names. Vorn Vet's account stated that all except one woman, Kac Sim's wife, were 'killed by the enemy', which would normally mean that they were condemned by the Military Tribunal and shot. The Bokor story is told by, among others, Milton Osborne, in *Prince of Light*, p. 197; Kiernan, *How Pol Pot*, p. 276; and Meyer, *Sourire*, p. 193.

185 *'Not [too] optimistic'*: 'Zhou Enlai, Kang Sheng and Pham Van Dong, Hoang Van Thai, Pham Hung and others in the COSVN delegation', Beijing, 20 and 21 Apr. 1969, CWIHP Archives.

188 *'Very tense'*: *Black Paper*, p. 32. **Likewise deflected**: Ibid., pp. 32–4; Pol Pot, *Talk with Khamtan*. During his visit to Hanoi in the winter of 1965, Sâr had asked to meet the Soviet Ambassador. A meeting was arranged but, to his annoyance, only with a Third Secretary (Mosyakov, *Khmer Rouge*, p. 12).

CHAPTER SIX: THE SUDDEN DEATH OF REASON

190 **Pouk:** Phi Phuon, Suong Sikoeun, interviews.

191 *'You're asking me . . . principle'*: Phi Phuon, interview.

192 **So was the system . . . uniquely Khmer:** Engelbert and Goscha, *Falling*, pp. 123–4. In another, revealing Confucian allusion, the Vietnamese Party in the 1960s referred to Sâr as *Hai Thien*, '[First] Brother with a Like Mind'. The Confucian doctrine of the 'rectification of names' holds that if the name of a person or thing is changed, their behaviour will change accordingly: by referring to Sâr as 'like-minded', the Vietnamese leaders were expressing the hope that he would be so. This was not the only such case of a soubriquet conveying wishful thinking: the Vietnamese called Ieng Sary, the most devious of the CPK leaders, the 'Brother of Straight-forwardness'. For the Vietnamese use of *Anh Hai* in 1965, see 'Texte du Camarade Nguyen Huu Tai, spécialiste de B68 à Phnom Penh', Doc. 32(N442)/T7917, VA. Keo Meas, who represented the CPK in Hanoi after 1969, referred to Sâr as 'Comrade Hay' in his confession (Sept. 30 1976).

193 **Translate Marxist:** Sâr's explanation, some years later, was that Marxism-Leninism sprang from 'revolutionary practice', which implies that any revolution, regardless of its goals, is by definition Marxist (Pol Pot, *Talk with Khamtan*). See also Nuon Chea *Statement*, p. 26.

198 *'I am going to return'*: In *My War* (p. 29), Sihanouk says he told Zhou on March 19: 'I am going to fight and fight till the end'. Chinese documents confirm that he did speak in those terms, but do not make clear when ('Zhou Enlai and Prince Sihanouk', Beijing, Mar. 22 1970, CWIHP Archives). *Zhou Enlai nianpu* (vol. 3, p. 356) quotes the Prince as saying on Mar. 19 that he 'wished to return immediately to his country' and adds that Zhou advised him not to. **'Long, hard'**: Sihanouk, *Indochine*, p. 109. *'I think Sihanouk . . . reaction'*: François Ponchaud, interview, Phnom Penh, Dec. 2 2001. In a press statement on Mar. 20, Sihanouk was already complaining of the new regime's 'monstrous calumnies concerning . . . my private life' (*Peking Review*, Mar. 30 1970). **On March 21 . . . us to do:** 'Zhou Enlai and Pham Van Dong', Beijing, Mar. 21 1970, CWIHP Archives.

199 **Monarchical-communist:** Interview with *RC*, quoted in Gorce to MAE, No. 37/CX, Jan. 26 1960, c. CLV 11, QD. **Also met Sâr:** *Black Paper*, p. 38. **The problem**

was: Sâr wrote later that the Prince was 'on the defensive' during his first two days in China (*Black Paper*, p. 35). *We should . . . Kompong Som:* 'Zhou Enlai and Pham Van Dong', Mar. 21 1970, *supra*. The CIA reported the same day that Lon Nol had instructed his forces 'to avoid friction with [Viet Cong/North Vietnamese] forces . . . . as talks are continuing with [their] representatives in Phnom Penh' (quoted in Shawcross, *Sideshow*, pp. 124–5). The Chinese Ambassador in Phnom Penh, Kang Maozhao, told Lon Nol in April that China would recognise his government if he maintained the communist sanctuaries, allowed weapons' transit and aided the Viet Cong in their propaganda; not surprisingly, Lon Nol refused (Qiang Zhai, *Vietnam Wars*, pp. 189–90). *'On oath':* Etienne Manac'h, Pékin, to MAE, Telegram Nos. 1194–9, Apr. 1, and Nos. 1264–72, Apr. 6 1970, c. A-O-1965-78 442, QD.

199–200 *Two days later . . . near and far:* Sihanouk, 'Message to Compatriots', in Grant et al., *Widening War*, pp. 105–9.

200 *As the language:* The reference to 'the pure working people' bears the hallmark of Sâr's style. 'Pure' was one of his favourite adjectives; it was not a word Sihanouk used, nor was it Chinese communist jargon. See also the commentary in *RC*, May 28 1971. *References to socialism:* Sâr claimed in the *Black Paper* (pp. 35 and 38) that he 'examined and modified' the text (which he called the FUNK 'political pro-gramme' because it contained what the Khmer Rouge described as a 'five-point programme' of action), and that this was why 'there was no question of socialism or communism in that document'. The claim is credible. The Khmers Rouges went to great lengths throughout the civil war to hide their communist goals. See also Sihanouk, *Calice*, Ch. 6, p. 45. *During the meeting . . . no persuading:* Zhonghua ren-min gongheguo waijiaoshi, p. 74. This source says that Sâr met 'many members of the CPC Centre'. Sâr himself speaks only of meeting Zhou Enlai (*Black Paper*, pp. 35 and 38). While in China in 1970, he also had frequent contact with Kang Sheng (Ieng Sary, interview), but this took place before the coup. *Never told:* Sihanouk, *Calice*, Ch. 6, p. 44.

200–2 *Political matters . . . to the interior:* This account relies essentially on the recollec-tions of Thiounn Mumm (*supra*). For details of the Indochina Summit, see Xinhua News Agency, Apr. 25 and 26, and *Renmin ribao*, Apr. 26 1970; for the GRUNC cab-inet, see *Peking Review*, May 18 1970, and Jennar, *Clés*, p. 70.

204 *'They told us . . . have nothing':* 'Rapport [oral] du camarade Khieu Minh', *supra*. This was confirmed by Kuong Lomphon, who spent nine months with Ith Sarin in the Special Zone in 1972 and early 1973. Arguing that the Khmers Rouges did not want a quick victory, he wrote: 'They realise that the people do not yet know them . . . Thus they are preparing for a long drawn-out struggle. If they won quickly it would be meaningless' (quoted in Kiernan, *How Pol Pot*, p. 399 n.133).

205 *Some Vietnamese . . . supervision:* Former Khmer Rouge commune chief who wished to remain anonymous (hereafter 'Mekhum'), interview, Phum Chinik, Prek Kabas district, Takeo, Mar. 10 2001. *Sâr complained:* Black Paper, pp. 54–7. *No choice:* Siet Chhê, then CPK Secretary of Region 22 in the Eastern Zone, recalled that after the coup, 'The Vietnamese came in all over the place, everywhere in the Zone . . . with working groups for this and that. They had letters of authorisation from the Zone [Secretary, So Phim] . . . They organised some village authorities, but I did not recognise them . . .' (confession, May 11 1977). Sdoeung, in Region 25, remembered: 'In April 1970, the Vietnamese organised the village and commune authorities . . . The district chief of Koh Thom was a Yuon [Vietnamese] . . . and he

assigned me to be a member of the commune committee' (confession, May 4 1978). According to the *Black Paper* (p. 56), Vietnamese-installed local administrations were widespread in the Eastern Zone and existed to a lesser extent in the South-West. See also Mey Mak, interview. ***COSVN urged***: 'The Vietcong March–April 1970 Plans for Expanding Control in Cambodia', US Mission, Saigon, Vietnam Documents and Research Notes, No. 88, Jan. 1971, quoted in Kiernan and Boua, *Peasants and Politics*, pp. 257–61. The documents betray the same patronising tone toward Khmers as in the 1950s. Then the Viet Minh spoke of the 'insufficiency of their intellectual level' (see Ch. 2). Now Viet Cong cadres were told: 'because [the Khmers'] capacity for learning is slow, we must use explanations that suit their level of understanding.' Although the texts quoted by Kiernan and Boua were from lower-level units, they reflected COSVN guidelines.

207 ***When cannon fodder . . . were raped***: Robert Sam Anson, *War News: A Young Reporter in Indochina*, Simon & Schuster, New York, 1989, pp. 116–28 and 135–42; AP, Neak Luong, Apr. 15, quoted in Sihanouk, *My War*, p. 72; and UPI, Phnom Penh, Apr. 10 1970, quoted in Sihanouk, *Calice*, pp. 60–1; Ponchaud, *Cathédrale*, pp. 136–7. See also Dauge to MAE, Telegram Nos. 801–4, Apr. 14 1970, where the Ambassador, whose reporting was generally sympathetic to the new regime, warned of the risk of 'a real genocide'. The following day, he speculated that the killings were becoming 'more selective' because two priests, crossing the Mekong at Neak Luong, had counted 139 male bodies in the water, considerably fewer than on previous days (Telegram Nos. 846–8 Apr. 15). The Judicial Affairs Division of the French Foreign Ministry advised that 'the acts currently being perpetrated in Cambodia could come within the scope of the UN Convention against Genocide' (Direction des Affaires Juridiques, Note 420, Apr. 21 1970), all in c. A-O-1965-78 442, QD. ***It looked and smelt . . . not the outside***: *Observer*, Apr. 19 1970.

208 ***Only possible way out***: Phillips, *Social Contact*, pp. 351–5. ***Groslier***: Quoted in Shawcross, *Sideshow*, p. 127. ***Terrible explosions***: Sihanouk, *Indochine*, pp. 90–1; see also Sihanouk, *Prisonnier*, pp. 379–82. ***Radio broadcast***: Lon Nol, 'Message to Buddhist Believers', May 11 1970, in Grant et al., *Widening War*, pp. 109–12. The original broadcast was in Khmer. A French translation was issued by AKP on May 12 (c. A-O-1965-78 442, QD).

209 ***There was a price . . . resistance army***: Kiernan, *How Pol Pot*, pp. 306–10; and *Communist Movement*, pp. 262–3; Shawcross, *Sideshow*, pp. 174–5; Sheldon Simon, *War and Politics in Cambodia: A Communications Analysis*, Duke University Press, Durham, NC, 1974, pp. 40–1. Sosthène Fernandez was quoted as saying at the end of 1970: 'South Vietnamese troops rape, they destroy houses, they steal, they loot pagodas and they beat the Buddhist monks' (Bernard K. Gordon, 'Cambodia's Foreign Relations: Sihanouk and After', in Zasloff and Goodman, *Conflict*, p. 163).

210 ***Sâr bade farewell***: *Black Paper*, p. 55; Pâng, confession, May 28 1978. ***So anti-Vietnamese***: Interview with Chen Xiaoning, Beijing, July 9 2000. ***Stretcher***: Pâng, *supra*. ***Schizophrenia***: Thiounn Thioeunn, interview.

210–11 ***Sâr's cook . . . atrocities***: Moeun, interview; and 'Alone among Brothers', *Cambodia Daily*, Oct. 20 2001.

211 ***Friends remembered***: Moeun, interview. ***Trigger***: Ibid. ***During the talks***: *Black Paper*, p. 34. ***1,500 exiles***: Kit Mân, interview; Yun Soeun, confession, May 26 1977.

212 ***Before leaving . . . pocket lights***: Kit Mân, interview. ***Sâr himself***: Phi Phuon, interview; Tiv Ol, confession, June 14 1977 et seq. ***On the eve . . . Khieu ('Blue')***: This

account of the taking of new revolutionary names is drawn from Phi Phuon, interview. Khmers will also change their names if they are frequently ill, or narrowly escape death, 'in order to deceive the evil spirits' that threaten them (Ponchaud, *Cathédrale*, p. 213). **Pol:** David Chandler (*Tragedy*, p. 370 n.64; and *Brother Number One*, p. 209 n.25) quotes Keng Vannsak as saying that Sâr was known as Pol (or Paul) in Paris and speculates that this might have been the name by which he was known at the Ecole Miche. Vannsak's memory was at fault in this case: Sâr never used the name Pol in Paris. According to a missionary who taught at the Ecole Miche, it was not the school's practice to give Christian names to Cambodian children who studied there ('Bref aperçu sur l'Ecole Miche, 1934–42' by Fr. Yves Guellec, unpublished ms held at the Archives Lasalliennes, Lyons).

213 *The resolution . . . to be used:* Extracts from the text are given in 'Recherche sur le Parti Cambodgien' (*supra*) and, more fully, in Doc. TLM/165, 'Les Perspectives, les Lignes et la Politique Etrangère du Parti Communiste Cambodgien', VA.

214 *Fifteenth salvo:* Dauge to MAE, Telegram Nos. 2720–5, Oct. 9 1970, c. A-O-65-78 443, QD.

CHAPTER SEVEN: FIRES OF PURGATION

215–16 *Nothing the guerrillas:* Truong Nhu Tang, *Memoir*, pp. 167–70 and 177.

218–19 *The French . . . attackers to flight:* Bizot, *Portail*, pp. 46–51.

219 *Um Savuth:* Shawcross, *Sideshow*, p. 202; see also Donald Kirk, *Tell it to the Dead*, Nelson-Hall, Chicago, 1975, pp. 137–8.

218–20 *His first attempt . . . slaughtered:* See the eyewitness description in Chantrabot, pp. 86–7.

220 *I remember:* 'Mekhum', interview. *Wearing black:* Mey Sror, interview.

221 *But for those . . . oppressing classes:* Mey Mak and Mey Sror, interviews. Both men remembered Khmer-speaking Vietnamese instructors addressing political education meetings in Mok's South-Western Zone.

222 *Surrealistic years:* Deac, *Road*, p. 89; Shawcross, *Sideshow*, p. 186.

223 *Week-long meeting:* Black Paper, pp. 58–9. Pol's claims in this work, which he dictated to a group of Foreign Ministry officials (Suong Sikoeun, interview), must be treated with the greatest caution: some are pure invention—like his claim that, at this meeting, the Vietnamese tried to have him poisoned; others contain interesting nuggets of truth. *Caveat lector.*

Three decisions . . . all-Khmer units: This interpretation runs counter to the *Black Paper*'s claim (p. 58) that the Vietnamese military training programme was carried out 'secretly' and closed down as soon as the CPK discovered its existence. The fact that Vietnamese instructors were operating freely in Mok's South-West Zone until the summer of 1971, and that mixed units continued to exist both in the South-West and the East until at least 1972 — if not, in some cases, 1973 — indicates CPK acceptance of those policies at the highest level. Mok met Pol in January 1971. Had the guideline then been to prevent such co-operation, Mok would certainly have stopped it, as he did when CPK policy towards the Vietnamese tightened a year later. The fact that he did not suggests that the November 1970 meeting endorsed the training programme. Moreover, any other decision would have been against the CPK's own interests and would not have been understood by the Party rank and file, most of whom at that time regarded the Vietnamese as loyal allies.

The decision to phase out the mixed units, which had been created during the Vietnamese advance in April–May 1970, and to replace Vietnamese administrative cadres with Khmers, were both, in contrast, commonsense measures which would have been difficult for the COSVN to refuse. Indirect confirmation of this view comes from a US State Department source, who reported that 'late in 1970, Vietnamese advisers to FUNK [administration] committees were instructed to assume a lower profile' (Kiernan, *How Pol Pot*, p. 313; Brown, *Exporting Insurgency*, p. 129); and from General Tran Van Tra's subsequent claim that the VWP CC 'wanted to reconcile differences with [our CPK] friends' (quoted in Engelbert and Goscha, *Falling*, p. 100). Shortly after Pol's meeting with Nguyen Van Linh, a senior Vietnamese official, Hoang Anh, spoke in similar terms at the December 1970 VWP CC plenum in Hanoi: 'The matter of Cambodia is very important. For its successful resolution we must enhance our military efforts there and materially aid the local patriotic forces' (Morris, *Why Vietnam*, pp. 48 and 255 n.3, quoting a Russian translation of Hoang's report held in the Centre for the Preservation of Contemporary Documents, Moscow).

A later, hostile, Vietnamese account of Pol's meeting with Nguyen Van Linh stated: 'In essence, he said he did not agree with the way the General Staff had organised things to help the Cambodian revolution develop strongly after Lon Nol overthrew Sihanouk. After the meeting, [they] dissolved the forces and units that we had spent a long time helping to build for them, and they asked us to transfer to them completely all [Khmer] units which were being led by [Vietnamese] cadres' (Le Quang Ba, 'Un sommaire de la situation Cambodgienne', Doc. 32(N442)/T8807, VA).

224–5 *Ping Sây worked . . . own headquarters*: Ping Sây, interview. Most of the account that follows is drawn from Ping Sây's recollections, except the detail about the Zone secretaries' bodyguards, which comes from Phi Phuon, interview.

224 *Gastric . . . to take it*: Moeun, interview; and 'Alone among Brothers', *Cambodia Daily*, Oct. 20 2001.

225 *'Khmers cannot'*: Khieu Samphân, interview.

225–6 *In mid-January . . . inner councils*: Ibid. and Phi Phuon, interview.

226–7 *Pol's message . . . eventually went home*: Except where otherwise indicated, this account is taken from Phi Phuon, interview.

226 *Party line . . . struggle*: Quoted in Engelbert and Goscha, *Falling*, pp. 96–7.

227–8 *Apart from . . . Dângkda*: Unless otherwise indicated, the following account is drawn from Phi Phuon, interview.

228 *His message*: See also the CPK directive quoted in Kiernan, *How Pol Pot*, p. 323. Kiernan's claim that the Congress approved policies of 'war communism', however, is mistaken. Had such a decision been taken in August, it would have become apparent before the end of 1971; it did not. *The burden . . . new regime*: *Tung Padevat*, Dec. 1975/Jan. 1976, *supra*. This account is extrapolated from the meagre information available; however, it would hardly have been necessary for the CC to issue an 'emergency directive' unless Pol had discovered weaknesses which he believed required urgent correction. Kiernan (*How Pol Pot*, pp. 328–9) details some of the May 1972 decisions, but attributes them to the Third Congress in 1971. (See also *Tung Padevat*, Sept.–Oct. 1976, pp. 1–33, quoting Pol's speech on the Party's 16th anniversary, and Sreng, confession, Mar. 13 1977.)

229 *For the first two . . . support the resistance*: Except where otherwise indicated, the following account is drawn from Quinn, *Khmer Krahom Program*, pp. 11–17, and

Kate G. Frieson, 'Revolution and Rural Response in Cambodia: 1970–1975', in Kiernan, *Genocide and Democracy*, pp. 33–47, esp. p. 43 *et seq*. See also Brown, *Exporting Insurgency*, p. 128; and Quinn, *Political Change*, p. 19. On credit co-operatives, see Khieu Samphân, interview: on harvest-time mutual aid, Nghet Chhopininto, interview; Kiernan, *How Pol Pot*, p. 321; and Ebihara, *Revolution and Reformulation*, pp. 18 and 23. **Pick fruit:** Former Lon Nol district chief Chhing Nam Yeang, quoted by Kiernan in *How Pol Pot*, p. 319. **If a peasant . . . friendliness:** Ith Sarin, *Bureaux*, p. 46.

230 **Opposing . . . beaten to death:** Bizot, *Portail*, pp. 73–6 and 87–9; Quinn, *Khmer Krahom Program*, p. 19. **Mass graves:** According to the French chargé d'affaires, Gérard Serre, the graves may have contained altogether as many as 500 bodies (Serre to MAE, No. 20/DA.AI, Sept. 17 1971, in c. A-O-1965-78, vol. 134 ns, QD). **Exceptions:** Kenneth Quinn, on the basis of refugee interviews, concluded: 'The brutality of Khmer Rouge cadres . . . [was] quite limited in the early phases of FUNK control [in] 1970–71 and even 1971–72' (*Political Change*, p. 22). The former government district chief Chhing Nam Yeang, quoted by Kiernan, said that 'in 1970–71, the [Khmers Rouges] did not kill people' (*How Pol Pot*, p. 319).

232 **'Wild-looking boys' . . . 1962:** Vickery, *Cambodia*, pp. 1–2. **Forty years later . . . hated it:** Private communication from Bill Herod, whose companion, Bopha, lived at the village as a child from 1975–9. **'National failing':** *RC*, Mar. 29 1958. He had used the same phrase two years earlier in a speech to the Third Sangkum Congress (Agence Khmère de Presse, Apr. 21 1956, in c. CLV7, QD). **'Fundament':** Ith Sarin, *Nine months*, pp. 40–1.

232–3 **Years later . . . jealousy:** Ly Hay, interview, Paris–Phnom Penh, Sept. 18 2000. See also Ponchaud, *Year Zero*, p. 141.

233 **Organisation of life:** The lack of 'communal spirit' was already a problem noted by the Viet Minh in 1951, who wrote that 'Cambodians . . . don't like living collectively and don't regard desertion [from their units] as a matter of any great importance' (Comité des Cadres de l'Est au Comité des Cadres du Cambodge, Telegram No. 4/E, June 5 1951, c. 10H4122, SHAT). See also Ebihara, *Svay*, p. 92. Thai peasants show similar behaviour: see Herbert P. Phillips, *Thai Peasant Personality: The Patterning of Interpersonal Behaviour in the Village of Bang Chan*, University of California Press, Berkeley, 1965, p. 17, and *Social Contact*, pp. 348–9. **Co-operative tradition:** 'A striking feature of Khmer village life is the lack of indigenous, traditional, organised associations, clubs, factions or other groups that are formed on non-kin principles . . .' (Ebihara, *Svay*, p. 181).

234 **Comrades . . . into tears:** Bizot, *Portail*, pp. 84–6. **'Party theoreticians':** Ibid., p. 162. **In place of . . . the people:** Ith Sarin, *Bureaux*, pp. 50–1; Chandler, *Tragedy*, pp. 209 and 357 n.51; Haing Ngor, *Odyssey*, pp. 112–13; and Radio Phnom Penh, Jan. 31 1976, quoted in Ponchaud, *Year Zero*, pp. 117–18. Ponchaud uses the term *viney* rather than *sila* ('Social Change in the Vortex of Revolution', in Jackson, *Rendezvous*, p. 173). The Chinese 'Three Rules and Eight Points' may be found in Mao's *Selected Works*, vol. 4, Foreign Languages Press, Beijing, 1969, pp. 155–6.

234–5 **Angkar . . . the spirit:** Bizot, *Portail*, p. 163.

236 **Disbandment:** Mey Mak (interview) recalled that in the South-West, orders for the disbandment of mixed units were issued by Mok in 1972: 'They just gave us the order to do that . . . [They] said we had enough people ourselves to fight, we had the support of the people and we had the liberated areas . . . We didn't need the Vietnamese so much.' In Non Suon's area, Region 25, in the Special Zone, there was also

pressure from below. Mey Sror (interview) remembered: 'It wasn't that we had orders from above. It was just that we soldiers had come to hate the Vietnamese . . . We saw [them] taking Cambodian goods to Vietnam, and that made us angry with them. When I walked through the villages in Region 25, I heard the people complaining that the Vietnamese wanted to control everything.'

237 **By the beginning . . . highest level:** Ben Kiernan has written that the Third Congress approved a decision to 'expel the Vietnamese' and treat them as the CPK's long-term 'acute enemy' (*How Pol Pot*, pp. 328–30); see also Heder, *Pol Pot to Pen Sovann*, p. 19; and Morris, *Why Vietnam*, pp. 56 and 59–60. This is contradicted by Non Suon's confession, by CPK internal documents from 1972 onwards and by the subsequent development of CPK–VWP relations — all of which indicate clearly that, while there was mistrust of Vietnamese intentions, the CPK sought to avoid an open split until at least 1976. In this context, it is noteworthy that a hostile Vietnamese account quotes Ieng Sary as reassuring the Vietnamese leaders in 1971 and again in 1974 that Vietnamese–Cambodian solidarity was 'vital' for the revolution (Le Quang Ba, 'Un sommaire de la situation Cambodgienne', Doc. 32(N442)/ T8807,VA).

238 **Reasserting sovereignty:** Already in late 1971, the Secretary of one Eastern Zone region wrote to 'Ba Hai' [Pham Van Ba], the head of the Vietnamese Liaison Committee: 'I do not think it is right for your men to use military force against our men [to resolve disputes] and *thereby impair our sovereignty*' [emphasis supplied] (Morris, *Why Vietnam*, p. 57, quoting a document in the Indochina Archive, University of California, Berkeley).

240 **He said privately . . . they have won:** *Tribune de Genève*, Dec. 10 1971; *Far Eastern Economic Review*, Aug. 5 1972; 'Interview with Oriana Fallaci', *New York Times*, Aug. 12 1973.

241 **April 1971:** Ieng Sary said he arrived in Beijing in April 1971, and spent three months there in secret before his arrival was announced officially (interview). Thiounn Mumm (interview) and Van Piny (confession, Feb. 16 1978) both dated his arrival to July 1971. Sihanouk knew of his return in the first half of July (*Indochine*, p. 93). **Sary was . . . he loathed:** Ponchaud, interview; Shawcross, *Sideshow*, p. 255–6.

242 **'Absolutely no negotiation':** Ruos Nhim, confession, June 14 1978. **Acrimonious:** *Black Paper*, pp. 72–4. **Pol's view . . . 'liberated zones':** 'Directive de 870', Feb. 2 1973, in Doc. 32(N442)/T8053,VA. Sihanouk himself has given a very different account of the Khmers Rouges' decision to let him return to Cambodia (*War and Hope*, pp. 123–5; see also Chanda, *Brother Enemy*, p. 70). **'Bare-arsed':** Ith Sarin, *Sronoh Pralung Khmer*, pp. 5–6.

244 **Ill-health:** 'Excerpts from the minutes of the meeting between Comrade Le Duan and Ieng Sary', Apr. 8 1973, in Doc. TLM/165, 'Les Perspectives, les Lignes et la Politique Etrangère du Parti Communiste Cambodgien', VA. **From China . . . to the region:** A Vietnamese text quoted Zhou Enlai as telling Ieng Sary in the summer of 1973: 'Experience has shown that sitting down to negotiate does not mean compromising; because we have more advantages, in negotiation they must accept our requirements; thus we would negotiate in a more advantageous position, it does not mean compromising' ('Excerpts . . . from a series of meetings between Ieng Sary and Brother Le Duc Tho in July and August 1973', Doc. TLM/165, *supra*). A few months later, according to another Vietnamese transcript, Zhou said, 'US imperialism is tending to shrink; the Soviet Union is tending to expand' — causing the Vietnamese editor to comment: 'In truth . . . China wants Cambodia to yield to the United

States in order to resist the so-called "Soviet expansionism in South East Asia" '('Excerpts from the meeting between Ieng Sary and Brother Le Duc Tho in November 1973', Doc. TLM/165, *supra*). In Sopheap also thought part of the Chinese message to the Cambodians at that time was, 'When you chase away the wolf, don't forget the tiger' in the shape of the USSR (interview).

246 *Even in the Eastern . . . land of their own*: Quinn, *Khmer Krahom Program*, pp. 32–3.

247 *Twist the figures*: Pol Pot, *September 27 speech*. See also Carney, 'The Organization of Power', in Jackson, *Rendezvous*, pp. 99–100.

248 *I met . . . wasn't tough enough*: Ping Sây, interview.

249 *Until late 1972*: See, for example, the photographs published in *Le Nouvel Observateur*, Jan. 11 1971.   *They, too, killed*: Someth May recalled meeting a Khmer Rouge in the North-West who eventerated a monkey to show him 'the way I used to kill the Lon Nol soldiers when we caught them and the way to get the liver out' (*Cambodian Witness*, pp. 160–1).

250–1 *At the same time . . . Cambodia was lost*: The following is drawn mainly from Deac, *Road*, Ch. 8. See also Pol's account, in a speech in June 1976, in Chandler et al., *Pol Pot Plans*, pp. 31–2.

251 *'Friend with a conflict'*: Siet Chhê, confession, May 11 1977; Tiv Ol was quoted as saying that year that Vietnam was a friend, but 'not very loyal' (Kiernan, *How Pol Pot*, p. 388). For the date of the plenum, see Non Suon, confession, Jan. 14 1977.

251–2 *Chrok Sdêch . . . surrounding plain*: This account draws on visits to Chrok Sdêch, Boeng Var and Ra Smach in December 2001 and on conversations with local villagers. See also Thiounn Thioeunn and Thiounn Maly, interviews.

252 *We built . . . camouflage*: Nikân, interview.

253–4 *I had a guide . . . on the poor*: Kong Duong, interview.

254 *Exemplary severity*: Comité Permanent de la Zone Est, 'Directives Complémentaires: Pour faire face au mouvement Khmer Islam (d'origine Cham). . . en supplément du directive No. 20 du 25 novembre 1973', Dec. 6 1973, in Doc. 32(N442)/T8053, VA. Given the propensity of all Cambodian leaders, including Sihanouk, Pol and Hun Sen, to micromanage policy, it is inconceivable that such a directive would have been circulated without a text having first been issued in the name of the Standing Committee. Pâng said there was widespread discontent in the Northern Zone in late 1973/early 1974, 'especially along the Mekong', and 'at one time the Cham almost rose up against the revolution' (confession, May 28 1978).

255–6 *At the end of March . . . tightening*: This account relies on Phi Phuon, who accompanied Pol to Kep (interview). In 1978, when a Yugoslav journalists' delegation visiting Democratic Kampuchea was taken to the beach at Kep for a swim, their Khmer Rouge bodyguards waded fully-dressed into the sea after them carrying their weapons (conversations in Beijing in the summer of 1978 with Drago Rancic of *Politika*, who was a member of the group).

256 *The town market . . . robbery*: Yun Soeun, confession, May 26 1977. *Two years . . . in the fields*: *Tung Padevat*, Aug. 1975, pp. 1–23.

257 *It worked well*: Phi Phuon, interview. *All through history . . . similar views*: For an excellent discussion of this topic as it relates to the Cambodian revolution, see Vickery, *Cambodia*, pp. 299–309, and Ghita Ionescu and Ernest Gellner, *Populism: Its Meaning and National Characteristics*, Weidenfeld & Nicolson, 1969, pp. 106–9.

258 *New currency*: Phi Phuon, interview.

259 *Penance*: Phi Phuon, Ping Sây, interviews. *Matters came . . . Thai border*: See Vorn

Vet, confession, Nov. 24 1978; Phouk Chhay, Mar. 20 and 24 1977; May Sakhan, confession, Oct. 9 1976; Toch Phoeun, confession, Mar. 14 1977; Non Suon, confession, Nov. 19 1976; Phi Phuon, interview; Tan Hao, cited in Kiernan and Boua, *Peasants and Politics*, pp. 274–6. **Early in 1974 . . . CIA:** Phi Phuon, interview.

259–60 **Mok, in particular . . . killed him:** Ibid.; Bizot, *Portail*, pp. 383–5.

260 **Prasith . . . like us:** Phi Phuon, interview.

264 **By early April . . . incandescent revolution:** Except where otherwise indicated, the following account is drawn from Deac, *Road*, Ch.10; Chandler, *Tragedy*, pp. 233–5; Swain, *River*, esp. pp. 122–32. **While rice . . . wines:** *Baltimore Sun*, Apr. 17 1975; Haing Ngor, *Odyssey*, p. 73. See also George Hildebrand and Gareth Porter, *Cambodia: Starvation and Revolution*, Monthly Review Press, New York, 1976, pp. 7 and 19–38. **Some 800 . . . went with them:** Corfield, *Stand Up!*, pp. 218–23.

265 **Over lunch . . . the other two:** Phi Phuon, interview. **On Monday . . . failed to appear:** Swain, *River*, pp. 126–8; Nikân, interview; Corfield, *Stand Up!*, pp. 224–5; Deac, *Road*, pp. 222–3. **Eerie calm:** Criddle and Butt Mam, *Destroy*, p. 3; Yasuko Naito, in De Nike et al., p. 96; Ponchaud, *Year Zero*, p. 3. **Continuing bombardment:** Schanberg, *Death and Life*, p. 16; Swain, *River*, p. 131. **By dawn:** Kân, interview.

CHAPTER EIGHT: MEN IN BLACK

266 **The young men . . . St Laurent:** Composite accounts of the events of the morning of Apr. 17 are given by Justin Corfield in *Stand Up!*, pp. 225–31, and Kiernan in *Regime*, pp. 34–40. See also Ponchaud, *Year Zero*, pp. 4–5; Swain, *River*, pp. 136–7; Bernard Hamel, *De Sang et de Larmes*, Albin Michel, Paris, 1977, pp. 58–9; Ros Chantrabot, pp. 124–7.

267 **Harsher voice:** Radio Phnom Penh, Apr. 17 1975 in BBC SWB FE4881/A3/1–3.

268 **Soundlessly:** Ponchaud, *Year Zero*, p. 6. **We moved in:** Nikân, interview. **'Slab of lead':** Ponchaud, *Year Zero*, p. 6. **Newcomers . . . forest:** Criddle and Butt Mam, *Destroy*, p. 11; Fenella Greenfield and Nicolas Locke (eds.), *The Killing Fields: The Facts behind the Film*, Weidenfeld & Nicolson, London, 1984, p. 86; Ponchaud, *Year Zero*, p. 9.

269 **'Never seen money':** Quoted in Kiernan, *Rural Reorganization*, p. 45. **Toilet bowls:** Mey Mak, interview; Haing Ngor, *Odyssey*, p. 122. **They were scared . . . toothpaste:** Chandler et al., *Peang Sophi*, p. 3; Szymusiak, *Stones*, p. 50. **Excrement:** Bizot, *Portail*, p. 263. **Shook his head:** Thiounn Mumm, interview.

270 **It was not money . . . thrown aside:** Pin Yathay, *Stay Alive*, p. 52; Ponchaud, *Year Zero*, pp. 8–10 and 32; Criddle and Butt Mam, *Destroy*, pp. 11–12 and 15–18; and Szymusiak, *Stones*, p. 50. **'The city is bad':** Ponchaud, *Year Zero*, p. 21. Such views are common to all cultures. Julio Caro Barojo notes that the writers of classical antiquity held: 'In the city are found vice, corruption and artifice; in the country the ancient virtues . . . ' ('The City and the Country: Reflections on Some Ancient Commonplaces', in Julian Pitt-Rivers (ed.), *Mediterranean Countrymen*, Mouton, Paris, 1963, p. 28). **American bombing:** Kiernan and Boua, *Peasants and Politics*, p. 340. David Chandler goes a step further — in my view, a step too far — by arguing that 'the bombing . . . provided the CPK with the psychological ingredients of a violent, vengeful and unrelenting revolution' (*Facing*, p. 225). **In Battambang . . . stop them:** Chandler et al., *Peang Sophi*, p. 3; Mey Mak, interview. **'Something excessive':** Haing Ngor, *Odyssey*, pp. 79–80.

272 **It was a stupefying . . . the previous day:** Ponchaud, *Cathédrale*, pp. 160–1. Shane and Chou Meng Tarr, a New Zealand-Cambodian couple who were vocal supporters of the Khmers Rouges, took three days to cover the eight miles (*News from Kampuchea*, vol. 1, no. 1, Apr. 1977).

273 **'Hallucinatory':** Ponchaud, *Year Zero*, pp. 6–7.

Hospitals: The evidence is contradictory. Most reports of sick and wounded patients being turned on to the streets came from the area under Northern Zone control. Pin Yathay, who travelled south, reported seeing two patients on hospital beds being wheeled along by relatives in the middle of the city. Marie Alexandrine Martin quotes medical staff as saying the Khmero-Soviet hospital was evacuated on Apr. 17, but that l'Hôpital Calmette, in the north, continued functioning until May 6 (*Shattered*, pp. 171–2; see also Someth May, *Cambodian Witness*, p. 107).

Prosecution documents from the Vietnamese-orchestrated 1979 'trial' of Pol Pot and Ieng Sary, a hostile source if ever there was one, say only that 'some hospitals' were evacuated, implying that others were not (De Nike et al., p. 325).

A medical student, working at the Lon Nol government's temporary medical facility at the Olympic Stadium, which was taken over on Apr. 17 by South-Western Zone forces, has described how he and other staff there spent the next two months working under communist direction at different clinics and hospitals in Phnom Penh (*Bangkok Post*, Feb. 22 1976).

Haing Ngor has given a graphic account of young Khmer Rouge soldiers bursting into an operating theatre and demanding 'the doctor', but his assumption that they wanted to kill him may have been wrong; it is equally possible they had been ordered to round up any doctors they could find to treat Khmer Rouge wounded (*Odyssey*, pp. 78–9). Apart from Someth May (p. 111), who saw a doctor being taken away and later found his dead body, there appear to be few credible reports of doctors being singled out for execution or maltreatment because of their profession in the early stages of the new regime.

274 **Chakrey told him:** Mey Mann, interview.

276 **'Fearful explosion':** Bizot, *Portail*, p. 278. If what he heard was indeed the bank being blown up, which seems almost certain since no other major explosion was reported during this period, it must have occurred on the afternoon of April 19 or 20 (see also Stanic, *Without a Model*, p. 77, and Drago Rancic, writing in *Politika*, Belgrade, excerpted in *Seven Days*, May 19 1978). Official claims that the blasts were the work of saboteurs are cited in Robert Brown and David Kline, *The New Face of Kampuchea*, Liberator Press, Chicago, 1979, p. 34. For the charge that the CIA was responsible, see In Sopheap, *Khieu Samphân*, p. 101.

276n **One certainty:** Non Suon, the first Khmer Rouge National Bank Chairman, began work in the damaged building on May 12 1975 (confession, Jan. 16 1977).

278 **Angkar needs . . . rode off:** Pin Yathay, *Stay Alive*, p. 34.

278–9 **'Shiny new Peugeot' . . . suicide:** Haing Ngor, *Odyssey*, p. 96. Butt Mam also witnessed the family's suicide (*Destroy*, p. 41).

280 **Technicians and skilled workers:** Ponchaud, *Year Zero*, p. 28; Pin Yathay, *Stay Alive*, p. 38; Hu Nim, confession, May 28 1977, in Chandler et al., *Pol Pot Plans*, p. 277; Martin, *Industrie*, pp. 88–90. Technicians were also recalled to Kompong Som (Ung Pech's testimony in De Nike et al., p. 75).

281 **Sugary words:** Szymusiak, *Stones*, p. 182.

281–2 **Yet there were . . . unfailing courtesy:** Pin Yathay, *Stay Alive*, pp. 47 and 102.

282 **Humane gesture**: Criddle and Butt Mam, *Destroy*, p. 32. **A soldier helping**: Szymusiak, *Stones*, pp. 16–17; another incident involving 'good' Khmers Rouges is related on pp. 8–11.

284 **'If we worry'**: Mey Mak, interview. **'Cut off their hearts'**: Hinton, *Why?*, pp. 95 and 113. See also the statements of S-21 prison guards in Righy Pann's film, *S.21: La Machine de Mort Khmère Rouge*, transmitted by ARTE on June 2 2003.

285 **Kum**: Haing Ngor, *Odyssey*, p. 9. **Puth Tumniay**: Smith, *Interpretive Accounts*, pp. 18–23; Pin Yathay, *Stay Alive*, pp. 105–6. **'500 Thieves'**: Mamm, *Family Life*, p. 1. **Black crows . . . brief duration**: Pin Yathay, *Stay Alive*, p. 106; Carol A. Mortland, 'Khmer Buddhists in the United States: Ultimate Questions', in Ebihara et al., *Cambodian Culture*, pp. 81–3.

CHAPTER NINE: FUTURE PERFECT

286 **Three days . . . honour guard**: Phi Phuon, Nikân, Khieu Samphân, interviews. **Open work area**: Khieu Samphân, interview.

287 **CIA officials**: Heckman, *Pig Pilot*, pp. 339–40. See also Snepp, *Decent Interval*, pp. 339–40. Spy mania was part of the rationale for the expulsion of the 1,000 or so foreigners – mainly aid workers, businessmen, diplomats, journalists and planters — who found themselves in Phnom Penh at the moment of the communist victory ('Options fondamentales dans la discussion avec les représentants du Parti Communiste Chinois', in Doc. 32(N442)/T8300,VA). Eyewitness accounts of the foreigners' expulsion, and the events leading up to it, may be found in Bizot, *Portail*, pp. 225–371; Ponchaud, *Year Zero*, pp. 11–17 and 34–9; Schanberg, *Death and Life*, pp. 27–33; and Swain, *River*, pp. 145–70. **Paris Commune**: Ieng Sary, interview.

287–8 **Most . . . three years**: Cited by Long Visalo, interview in Phnom Penh, Nov. 26 and Dec. 8 2001.

288 **'Extraordinary measure'**: Doc. 2.5.01 in De Nike et al., p. 379. **'Agriculture is the key'**: In Sopheap, *Khieu Samphân*, p. 110, quoting a speech by Pol to the 'Party Centre' in September 1975. It may be objected that this was four months after the meetings in May, but there is no doubt that he already held these views at that time. In the following account, I have cited extracts from speeches Pol made over the next fifteen months where I am convinced that they are a restatement of positions originally adopted in May.

289 **Beg for help**: Pol Pot, *Four-Year Plan*, p. 47. **'Imported iron'**: Pol Pot, *Preliminary Explanation*, p. 152. His remark is worth comparing with Khieu Samphân's 1959 statement: 'While it is true that it is more advantageous for a backward country to import industrial goods rather than to produce them at any given point in time, it is equally true that in the long run such a country can never really improve its industrial overhead' (*thesis*, pp. 78–9). **Preserve our independence**: Ieng Sary, interview with James Pringle, *Bulletin du GRUNC*, Beijing, Sept. 4 1975, pp. 12–13.

289–90 **Individuals are grouped . . . in production**: Khieu Samphân, *thesis*, pp. 30, 53 (trans. amended) and 75–6.

290 **'Blueprint'**: *Bangkok Post*, Feb. 15, 17, 19, 21, 23 and 25 1976. **'Makes sense'**: Chandler, *Facing*, p. 213. **'Were they found'**: Joel R. Charny, 'Appropriate Development Aid for Kampuchea', in Ablin and Hood, *Agony*, p. 250. **Object lesson**: Meyer, *Sourire*, pp. 211–17, and 283–4.

291 **'Not irrational'**: Pierre Brocheux, in Camille Scalabrino et al., *Cambodge, Histoire et*

Enjeux: 1945–1985, L'Harmattan, Paris, 1985, pp. 230–1. **'Boldly to encourage . . . machines'**: Pol Pot, *Report*, pp. 206–7; see also Standing Committee meeting of Mar. 30 1976, in Chandler et al., *Pol Pot Plans*, p. 3.

292 **'Last . . . political rights'**: Heder, *Occupation*, p. 6; Ebihara, *Revolution and Reformulation*, p. 25.

293 **'If our people'**: Pol Pot, *September 27 speech*. **Convinced him**: In Sopheap, *Khieu Samphân*, pp. 99–100. **'Run really fast'**: Minutes of Standing Committee meeting, Feb. 4 1976, in Doc. 32(N442)/T8355,VA. **'No let-up'**: In Sopheap, interview. He gives a slightly different version in *Khieu Samphân*, p. 103.

294 **How must we organise**: Pol Pot's report to the Western Zone Party Conference, *Tung Padevat*, June 1976. A translation is given in Chandler et al., *Pol Pot Plans*, pp. 13–35; for the quoted section, see pp. 20 and 26. **Cutting-edge**: CPK CC Resolution, June 1976, Doc. 32(N442)/T8310,VA. **'Simplistic'**: Ieng Sary, interview.

295 **Six months**: Khieu Samphân, *thesis*, p. 79; Smith, *Interpretive Accounts*, p. 5. **Theravada Buddhism**: Jerrold Schecter, *The New Face of Buddhism*, Coward-McCann, New York, 1967, p. 17. **Recounted the experience**: Sihanouk, *My War*, pp. 123–4. **Palm sugar**: Ly Hay, interview. **He explained . . . following orders**: Pol Pot, *Talk with Khamtan*. **'Inert'**: Kirk, *Revolution*, p. 222.

296 **Immense apparatus**: Quoted in Burchett, *Triangle*, p. 95. **Closer and closer**: Pol Pot, *Report*, p. 207. **Necessity for Work**: Ieng Sary, *Der Spiegel*, May 2 1977.

296–7 **Two days later . . . behind them**: Unless otherwise specified, this account of the *Mayaguez* affair is drawn from Robert Rowan's book, *The Four Days of Mayaguez*, Norton, New York, 1975.

297 **Malaria**: Pâng, confession, May 28 1978. **To the Silver Pagoda**: Phi Phuon, interview. **Reassure Vietnam**: Pol Pot, *Talk with Khamtan*. **June 2 . . . geography**: *Kampuchea Dossier*, vol. 1, p. 67.

298 **Pol offered . . . victories to come**: Mosyakov, *Khmer Rouge*, p. 26. **'Cordial'**: *Nhan Dan*, Hanoi, Aug. 2 1975. **Repatriation . . . other way**: It is worth stressing that the repatriations did not begin in April 1975; they had been under way since August 1973. For the figure of 150,000, see Chanda, *Brother Enemy*, p. 16. Most sources agree that the departure of Vietnamese continued until late 1975 or early 1976 (*Black Paper*, p. 73; Serge Thion, 'Chronology', in Chandler and Kiernan, *Aftermath*, p. 304; Ponchaud, *EFA 13*, p. 17, and *Vietnam-Cambodge*, pp. 1237–8). **Playing for time**: Khieu Samphân, interview.

298–9 **Pol flew . . . not clear**: These details were furnished by a Chinese historian who wishes to remain anonymous; see also Pâng, confession, May 28 1978. Siet Chhê was known to the Chinese as Du Mu, from his revolutionary alias, Tum; and Ney Sarann as Ming Shan, from his alias, Men San. Pâng was also present. Citations are taken from the transcript of the meeting held in the Chinese Central Archives. Extracts are cited in CWIHP, *77 Conversations*, p. 194.

299 **'Better to kill'**: For a description of Chinese communist extremism in the late 1920s and early 1930s, see Short, *Mao*, pp. 223–4, 268–75, 277–81, 306, 308–9 and 314. The slogan about killing the innocent resurfaced in Vietnam in the early 1950s, but in attenuated form: 'Better to kill ten innocent people than let a guilty person escape'. Under the Khmers Rouges, the wording was identical to that in Jiangxi. It is unlikely that the Jiangxi slogan was known to the Vietnamese, and still less to the Khmers. One must conclude that peasant-dominated revolutions lead, in their early stages, to similar types of excesses.

300 **Entranced**: See the transcript in the Chinese Central Archives of Mao's meeting with Sihanouk, Penn Nouth, Khieu Samphân and Khieu Thirith on Aug. 27 1975, at which he explicitly endorsed the policy of evacuating the cities. **'No. We couldn't'**: Transcript of Mao's meeting with Le Duan, Beijing, Sept. 24 1975, held in the Chinese Central Archives.

301 **Non-committal smile**: Transcript of Zhou Enlai's meeting with Sihanouk and Khieu Samphân, Beijing, Aug. 26 1975, held in the Chinese Central Archives. See also Sihanouk, *World Leaders*, pp. 99–100. **Failed to agree**: See the transcripts of Pol's meetings with Hua Guofeng in Beijing on Sept. 29 and 30 1977 for an example of one such disagreement over the role of non-ruling communist parties in South-East Asia (Doc. 32(N442)/T8300, VA). **Four days later . . . greet them**: Ieng Sary and Mey Mak, interviews.

301–2 **Deng told him . . . discontinued**: According to the Vietnamese-language text (Doc. 32(N442)/T8300, *supra*), the military agreement was signed in Beijing on Feb. 6 1976 by Son Sen and Wang Hongwen, then ranked third in the Chinese leadership and Vice-Chairman of the CPC CC Military Commission. Given the content and importance of the agreement, a leader at Wang's level would have been expected to participate (Deng Xiaoping could not sign because by then he was under house arrest). De Nike et al. (p. 381) mistakenly identify the Chinese signatory as Wang Shangrong, a Deputy Chief of the Chinese General Staff who led the negotiating team which drew up the accord.

302 **More than three hundred . . . to China**: Ibid. Chinese technicians were normally rotated through Cambodia for stays of three to six months (Quan Yuhui, interview). According to Tuon, a Jarai cadre who handled liaison between '870' (the CPK CC General Office) and the Chinese and North Korean aid missions, there were never more than a thousand Chinese in Cambodia at any one time (interview, Pailin, Nov. 20 2001). In 1976, Cambodia sent 471 air-force trainees and 157 naval trainees to China. According to Kân (interview), they remained there for up to two years. **300 million**: Fang Weizhong (ed.), *Zhonghua renmin gongheguo jingi dashiji*, Social Science Press, Beijing, 1984, p. 552, quoted in Ross, *Tangle*, p. 75.

303 **'Greatly eased'**: Chandler et al., *Pol Pot Plans*, p. 15 (where this phrase is translated as 'maximally softened'). **Medical check-up**: Pâng, confession, May 28 1978.

304 **Hou Yuon . . . house arrest**: Ping Sây and Suong Sikoeun, interviews.

305–6 **We must fix . . . masses**: Cited in In Sopheap, *Khieu Samphân*, pp. 108–10.

306 **Three tons**: Ibid. For the reference to paddy, and not milled rice, see Pol Pot, *Report*, p. 187, and *Abbreviated Lesson*, p. 220. **Two tons**: Sihanouk, speech to parliament, quoted in Massenet to MAE, No. 1295/AS, July 23 1963, in c. CLV 16, QD. **In May . . . state power**: Pol, quoted in In Sopheap, *Khieu Samphân*, p. 106. **Non Suon**: Non Suon, confession, Jan. 16 1977. **That summer**: Criddle and Butt Mam, *Destroy*, p. 50. Denise Alfonso also remembered being shown specimens of the new currency at a village thirty miles south of Phnom Penh, apparently in July 1975 (De Nike et al., p. 443). See also Pich Chheang, interview, Anlong Veng, Dec. 10–11 2001; and Doc. No. 3, Sept. 19 1975, quoted in Kiernan, *Regime*, p. 94.

307 **Mok favoured . . . views**: Phi Phuon, interview. **The State . . . this matter**: In Sopheap, *Khieu Samphân*.

308 **September 19**: Doc. no. 3, Sept. 19 1975, quoted in Kiernan, *Regime*, p. 99. Laurence Picq was told when she arrived in Phnom Penh in October 1975 that 'money had been abolished' (*Horizon*, p. 11). **I found myself . . . kept**: Thiounn Mumm, inter-

view. *He once told*: Pol Pot, *Preliminary Explanation*, p. 129. *'Shortages of food . . . different regions'*: Quoted in In Sopheap, *Khieu Samphân*, p. 109. At the CPK Standing Committee meeting in Kompong Som he also noted the plight of the urban deportees (Dossier L01022, Aug. 20–4 1975, DC-Cam).

309 *Ox*: Pin Yathay, *Stay Alive*, p. 170. See also Stuart-Fox, *Murderous Revolution*, p. 53, where the animal is described as a buffalo. *'Slaves we are'*: Yi Tan Kim Pho, *Cambodge*, p. 113.

310 *Along the roadside*: Picq, *typescript*, pp. 9–11. *Convoys*: Ponchaud, *Year Zero*, pp. 31–2; Haing Ngor, *Odyssey*, p. 100. Both describe goods being sent to the Eastern Zone (which they assumed, wrongly, meant they were taken to Vietnam). That plunder was also sent to other Zones is clear from the discussions between Zone leaders on how the 'booty' should be shared out.

311 *Foreign Ministry . . . work for diplomats*: This account of B-1 is drawn largely from Picq, *typescript*.

312 *Bank Buildings . . . increasingly close*: Ieng Sary and Phi Phuon (interviews); Pâng, confession, May 28 1978. *Lived apart . . . chores*: Ieng Sary, interview.

313 *Cathedral*: Father Ponchaud remembered having been told by an elderly colleague when he had arrived in Cambodia in 1965 that, to Khmers, the Phnom was a site of mystical power, 'the religious and spiritual nexus, assuring the community of Heaven and Earth'. 'If ever this country gets a nationalist government,' the old priest had added, 'the Cathedral will be the first thing to go' (interview). But it was solidly built and took many months to demolish (In Sopheap, interview; Ong Thong Hoeung, *Récit*, p. 31). *Rest of . . . coconut palms*: Szymusiak, *Stones*, p. 50; Yi Tan Kim Pho, *Cambodge*, p. 227; Pin Yathay, *Stay Alive*, p. 76; Martin, *Alimentaire*, p. 358; Y Phandara, *Retour*, p. 67.

314–15 *Boot camp . . . hungry all the time*: Long Nârin, interview. According to Laurence Picq, two students were allowed to return in December 1972 and fifteen more a month later. A third group returned in December 1973. Suong Sikoeun left Beijing in May 1974 (interview).

315 *'There will always . . . kill them'*: Long Visalo, interview.

316 *'Thin as nails'*: Ong Thong Hoeung, *Récit*, p. 10. *They told us . . . mentality*: Long Visalo, interview.

316–17 *How do we . . . reasonable*: Ibid.

317–18 *Ultimate aim . . . evil*: Picq, *typescript*, pp. 241; Ong Thong Hoeung, *Récit*, pp. 20–1.

319 *That first year*: Martin, *Alimentaire*, p. 349. See also Yi Tan Kim Pho, *Cambodge*, pp. 74–5; Pin Yathay, *Stay Alive*, pp. 100 and 130. There was also severe hunger in Siem Reap (Schanberg, *Death and Life*, p. 45), Preah Vihear (De Nike et al., p.95) and no doubt other areas. Laurence Picq at B-1 heard reports of starvation for the first time in the spring of 1976 (*Horizon*, p. 67), Sihanouk a few months earlier (*Prisonnier*, pp. 46–7).

320 *'Too much'*: Chandler et al., *Peang Sophi*, p. 7; see also Kiernan, *Rural Reorganisation*, p. 52. *Pursat . . . year was out*: Szymusiak, *Stones*, p. 95; Kiernan and Boua, *Peasants and Politics*, p. 354; Pin Yathay, *Stay Alive*, pp. 102, 131–2 and 140; Schanberg, *Death and Life*, p. 45. *'Narrow path'*: Pol Pot, *Report*, p. 188.

321 *Leadership recognised . . . per day*: 'The rice ration should be two milk cans per person per day . . . If there is a shortage it will affect people's health, and then the workforce will be reduced' (minutes of the CPK Standing Committee meeting, Feb. 28

1976, DC-Cam). See also Pol Pot, *Four-Year Plan* (pp. 111–12), which sets the ration at between 1.5 and 3 milk cans per person. Given that these documents, especially Standing Committee minutes, which were circulated to fewer than ten people, were highly restricted and never intended to go further, one may assume that the views Pol expressed were those he genuinely held. **'Most important medicine . . . among us':** *Tung Padevat,* June 1976; Pol Pot, *Preliminary Explanation,* p. 127. **One free day . . . and up to fifteen:** Pol Pot, *Four-Year Plan,* p. 112. See also Criddle and Butt Mam, *Destroy,* p. 158; Pin Yathay, *Stay Alive,* p. 89; Stuart-Fox, *Murderous Revolution,* p. 45; Haing Ngor, *Odyssey,* p. 274; and Kiernan, *Rural Reorganisation,* p. 65. **'There's not enough':** Pol Pot, *Preliminary Explanation,* p. 158.

322   **Those we surprised:** Quoted in Martin, *Shattered,* pp. 167–8.   **Couplet:** Locard, *Petit Livre Rouge,* p. 175. Keng Vannsak argued that the phrase was intended to be taken literally—'man was reduced to an object of profit and loss' (quoted in Burchett, *Triangle,* p. 94).

323   **In Samphân's words:** Quoted by Long Visalo, interview.   **Incantation:** Forest, *Colonialisation sans heurts,* p. 493.

324   **Like the monks:** Minutes of CPK Standing Committee meeting, June 1 1976, DC-Cam. **Called for 'renunciation':** Ponchaud, *EFA 17,* pp. 4–5. **'Renunciation of feelings':** This citation is from Pin Yathay but I have misplaced the reference to the text in which it occurs.

325   **The whole aim:** George Orwell, *1984,* Penguin Books, Harmondsworth, 1970, pp. 45–6. **'Entangled':** Pol Pot, *Preliminary Explanation,* p. 158.

326   **150,000:** Dossier L01045, Nov. 30 1975, in which an Eastern Zone official complained to Pol that the 'dispersal strategy' was being obstructed by Northern and North-Western Zone leaders who were 'refusing to accept Islamic villagers' (DC-Cam). See also Stuart-Fox, *Murderous Revolution,* p. 87, and Kiernan, *Eastern Zone Massacres,* pp. 39–41. It may be argued, of course, that 'dispersal' was itself a form of racism; but in that case the same label must be accepted for such measures as school bussing in the United States to achieve desegregation. That, too, involved the dispersal of pupils of one race among those of another. **Not racism:** Serge Thion makes this point well in his essay, 'Genocide as a Political Commodity', in Kiernan, *Genocide and Democracy,* pp. 171–2.

327   **Glasses:** I owe this detail to Michael Vickery. **Not America:** Prasso, p. 4. In the same spirit, when Samphân was teaching in the 1960s, he was puzzled that one of his students, an Indian girl from Pondicherry, stayed in Cambodia rather than 'going home to India' (I owe this anecdote to Henri Locard). **'Not hard':** Vann Nath, *Portrait,* p. 24. See also Smith, *Interpretive Accounts,* p. 5; Ben Kiernan, 'Letter to the Editor of *The Times*', Aug. 11 1977, in *JCA,* vol. 7, 1977, p. 547, quoting Peang Sophi as saying that working conditions in Cambodia in 1975–6 were less arduous than in his Melbourne factory.

327–8   **Even usually critical . . . spend money:** Pin Yathay, *Stay Alive,* p. 47; Stuart-Fox, *Murderous Revolution,* p. 46; Haing Ngor, *Odyssey,* p. 269; Ponchaud, *Year Zero,* p. 183, and *Cathédrale,* pp. 236–7; Edwards, *Ethnic Chinese,* p. 145.

CHAPTER TEN: MODEL FOR THE WORLD

329   **'Do you intend':** Transcript of Mao's meeting with Khieu Samphân, Ieng Sary, Sihanouk and Penn Nouth, Apr. 2 1974, Chinese Central Archives, Beijing. **'Don't**

be frightened . . . disagreement': Transcript of Mao's meeting with Sihanouk, Penn Nouth, Khieu Samphân and Khieu Thirith, Aug. 27 1975, Chinese Central Archives, Beijing. According to Sihanouk (*Calice*, Part 2, Ch. 1, p. 3), Kim Il Sung also raised with the Cambodians the issue of his return.

331 *To say nothing*: Ong Thong Hoeung, *Récit*, p. 9. *More truthful . . . abroad*: Osborne, *Prince of Light*, p. 230. See also Sihanouk, *Prisonnier*, pp. 17–18, for his account of similar discussions with his family in Europe in December. *December 31 . . . ridiculous*: Sihanouk, ibid, pp. 18–19.

333 *Diplomatic missions*: 'Speech by the Party Secretary to the Council of Ministers', Apr. 22 1976, in Dossier D695, DC-Cam. *'Bowled me over' . . . Jurgens*: Sihanouk, *Prisonnier*, pp. 41, 66 and 70; see also pp. 32–3.

334 *Memoirs*: Sihanouk, *Prisonnier*, pp. 82 and 85.

334–5 *But then . . . react negatively*: Ibid., pp. 88–9; Minutes of CPK Standing Committee meeting, Mar. 11 1976, Dossier D7562, DC-Cam. Sihanouk referred in particular to the accreditation of Meak Touch, the new DK Ambassador to Vientiane, whose arrival to take up his post was reported by Radio Phnom Penh on Mar. 6. The timing, while not conclusive, supports the view that the credentials issue was an important factor.

334 *Untrustworthy*: These comments were made at a Standing Committee meeting on Mar. 30 1976 (Doc. 32(N442)/T8322, VA: this version gives details not contained in the Khmer-language text, Dossier D693, at DC-Cam).

336 *To Pol . . . except us*: Minutes of the CPK Standing Committee meetings of Mar. 11 and 13 1976 (Dossier D7562); 'Speech by the Party Secretary to the Council of Ministers', Apr. 22 1976 (Dossier D695), DC-Cam.

337 *Fictitious*: *Far Eastern Economic Review*, June 25 1976. This was not, as has sometimes been suggested, a journalist's error. Cambodia continued to deny that Pol Pot was Saloth Sâr until the regime fell. Y Phandara was told by the Ambassador to China, Pich Chheang, in the spring of 1978 that Saloth Sâr 'had died during the war'; Chinese officials at that time repeated the same thing.

337–8 *If we lose . . . struggle*: Nuon Chea, *Statement*, p. 31.

338 *Always smooth*: Ieng Sary, interview. *'Seduced you'*: Sihanouk, *Prisonnier*, p. 320. *Very likeable*: Kong Duong, interview. *Parable*: Mey Mak, interview.

339 *Complicated*: Ieng Sary, interview. *[Pol] demanded . . . disgrace*: Vandy Kaonn, *Cambodge*, p. 137; Chou Chet, confession, May 20 1978.

340 *He would listen*: In Sopheap, *Khieu Samphân*, pp. 95–6; I have condensed the citation, but without changing the sense. Sopheap, who gave a similar account from his own experience of attending meetings with Pol, said there was little real exchange of views after 1975 (interview). *Pol Pot liked*: In Sopheap, interview.

341 *'Not what I expected' . . . monkhood*: Becker, *When the War*, pp. 424–5; In Sopheap, interview. See Martin Stuart-Fox, *Buddhist Kingdom, Marxist State*, White Lotus, Bangkok, 1996, p. 80, for the importance of the monks' ceremonial fans in neighbouring Laos. *'In the entire world'*: 'Long Live the Marvellous Revolutionary Armed Forces of the Communist Party of Kampuchea', *Tung Padevat*, Aug. 1975.

341–2 *Island of purity . . . learns from us*: Pol Pot, *Report*, p. 188; 'Extraits de quelques textes du Bureau 870', Doc. 32(N422)/T8318, VA. Although Pol himself never publicly criticised China in these terms, in a speech to a closed Party meeting in August 1976 he paraphrased Mao's remark to him the previous summer—that China was 'a capitalist country with no capitalists'—asserting that China and North Korea 'have socialism as a base, but they [are] not clear of the capitalist framework' (*Four-Year Plan*, p. 107). Such views explain why Pol's tribute to Mao during his visit to China in September 1977 was not re-broadcast by Radio Phnom Penh (Chandler, *Seeing Red*, p. 45).

342 **Not using money . . . victory:** 'Extraits de quelques textes du Bureau 870', *supra;* Henri Locard, untitled typescript, p. 11; Chandler, *Facing*, p. 231. **'Growing capability':** David Morell and Chai-anan Samudavanija, 'Thailand's Revolutionary Insurgency: Changes in Leadership Potential', *Asian Survey*, vol. 19, no. 4, Apr. 1979, p. 332.

343 **'Without precedent':** Ieng Sary, *Der Spiegel* interview, May 2 1977. **We do not have . . . any book:** Pol Pot, *Yugoslav interview; Four-Year Plan*, pp. 46 and 49. **'We want to . . . practical way':** Ieng Sary, *Der Spiegel* interview, *supra; News from Kampuchea*, vol. 1, no. 4, Oct. 1977, p. 35. **'Certain [foreign] comrades':** Pol Pot, *Talk with Khamtan*. He may well have been thinking of members of Khamtan's own party. David Chandler quotes Thai Communists as saying of the Khmers Rouges: 'Their understanding of Marxism, of socialism and class analysis was terrible'; '[Theirs] was the revolution of the downtrodden, pure and simple' (*Tragedy*, p. 280).

345 **Inveigh against:** *Revolutionary Youths*, July 1976, pp. 17–31 and Nov. 1976, pp. 1–15.

347 **Ieng Sary . . . sutras for her:** Thion, *Pattern*, pp. 158–9; Becker, *When the War*, p. 171; Nikân, interview. Thiounn Thioeunn (interview) gave a scathing assessment of the medical qualifications of Sary's daughters. **Suddenly our driver:** Sihanouk, *Prisonnier*, p. 263. **Mother-in-law:** This is guesswork, but Madame Khieu fits Sihanouk's description (see Ong Thong Hoeung, *Récit*, p. 3), the one difference being that she was then in her late seventies, rather than her sixties, as the Prince thought. Sihanouk insisted that the mysterious passenger was not Khieu Ponnary, whom he knew by sight, and it is difficult to think of anyone else who would have warranted such exceptional treatment.

348 **Detailed reports:** 'Report of the Eastern Zone Congress, July 17 1977', Doc. 32(N442)/T8294, VA, which speaks of the dangers of 'people starving and suffering, and losing confidence in the Party'. See also the regular telegrams on the economic situation in the regions in the 'Khmer Rouge Communications File', DC-Cam. By mid-1976, food supplies were deteriorating even in the Foreign Ministry in Phnom Penh. At the end of the year Laurence Picq and other Ministry workers were suffering from oedema caused by malnutrition (Picq, *Horizon*, pp. 67–8, 78 and 84).

350 **'Our principle . . . agents':** 'Minutes of meeting between Ieng Sary and Chinese Ambassador', undated but apparently early 1976, Doc. 32(N422).T8188, VA. **We must heighten:** 'Directive No. 32 of the Party Standing Committee of the Eastern Zone', Sept. 5 1976, Doc. 2.5.06 in De Nike et al., pp. 385–6. The timing is important. Pol had said in late July: 'We don't use old workers, because if we [did] there would be many complications politically' (*Four-Year Plan*, p. 47). But that had been the position since late 1975. The Central Committee directive on which the Eastern Zone document was based—extending the prohibition to intellectuals—was presumably issued in the last days of August or the very beginning of September. Ong Thong Hoeung and at least thirty colleagues were sent to the factories at precisely that moment and withdrawn a month later. **Is the possession . . . learn it fast:** *Tung Padevat*, Sept.–Oct. 1976, pp. 1–32; Pol Pot, *Talk with* Khamtan; *Preliminary Explanation*, p. 160.

352 **Between a third and a half:** Although there is no way of proving it, I tend to agree with Michael Vickery that between a half and two-thirds of the population were, at least in relative terms, reasonably fed until 1978 (*Themes*, p. 131).

CHAPTER ELEVEN: STALIN'S MICROBES

354 **Soth:** Minutes of the CPK Standing Committee meeting, Mar. 8 1976, Dossier D684, DC-Cam.

354–5 **At the end . . . Long killed:** Hu Nim, confession, May 28 1977, in Chandler et al., *Pol Pot Plans*, pp. 289 and 293–6.

355 **Evidence emerged:** Hu Nim, confession, May 28 1977, in Chandler et al., *Pol Pot Plans*, p. 295. Doeun, in his confession, insisted that he did pass on the information to Pol Pot, but without making clear how quickly he did so. **At about 4 a.m. . . . Vietnam:** This account is based on Long Nârin, interview, and Kiernan, *Regime*, pp. 321–3. While I do not agree with Kiernan's interpretation, he provides a useful summary of the known facts.

356 **In public:** See Nuon Chea, letter to Pham Hung, May 23 1976, quoted in *Kampuchea Dossier*, vol. 1, pp. 130–1.

357 **But there were . . . lackeys or not:** 'Talk between Ieng Sary and Sunao Sonoda, Foreign Minister of Japan, in Tokyo, June 12 1978', Doc. 32(N442)/T8297, VA. Kiernan gives an account of the negotiations which is much more sympathetic to Vietnam (*Regime*, pp. 115–20), based on his interpretation of the minutes of the CPK Standing Committee, May 14 1976. **'Sacred feeling':** Pol Pot, *Tran Thanh Xuan interview*. **Zhang Chunqiao:** These details were furnished by a Chinese historian who wishes to remain anonymous.

357–8 **In it, he used . . . servants:** Pol Pot, 'Keynote opinions of the Comrade delegate of the Party Organisation at the [Western] Zone Assembly', *Tung Padevat*, June 1976, pp. 14–65.

358 **S-21:** The following account draws on Chandler, *Voices*, and on Deuch, interview with Nate Thayer, Battambang, April 1999. **First time:** According to Ney Sarann (confession, Sept. 30 1976), Chhouk joined the CC at the CPK's Fourth Congress in January 1976. **Pol's former cook:** Moeun, interview. **Rule of thumb:** Suong Sikoeun, interview; Picq, *typescript*, p. 222.

359 **Shortly afterwards . . . destroy us:** Dossiers L01373, Aug. 2, L01374, Aug. 3 and L01442, Sept. 2 1976, DC-Cam; and Pol Pot, *Preliminary Explanation* (Aug. 23 1976), p. 161. **Tracts . . . those we suspect:** Dossier L01445, Sept. 9 1976. According to Son Sen, seditious pamphlets were discovered on at least five occasions that year, in April, June, July and August/September.

360–1 **There is a sickness:** Pol Pot, *Report*, pp. 183–5.

362 **Resignation:** BBC SWB FE5323/B/1. Pol's resignation, announced by Radio Phnom Penh on Sept. 27, was backdated to the 20th, the day of Ney Sarann's arrest. It was allegedly approved by a cabinet meeting that day, but whether in fact such a meeting ever took place is unclear. Twenty years later, neither Nuon Chea nor Mok had any recollection of these events (interviews with Nate Thayer). Ieng Sary, however, did remember, which, as David Chandler has noted, tends to confirm that it was linked to a foreign policy issue (*Brother*, p. 180 n.44). Had Pol really been ill—or had it been an internal manoeuvre to turn the tables on political opponents—the last thing he would have done would be to have the news broadcast by Radio Phnom Penh. **November 1976:** The following account is drawn from Phi Phuon (interview), who named the members of Pol's delegation and his interlocutors identically in separate conversations, several months apart. Pich Chheang confirmed that the visit took place, but was unable to remember the details (interview). The delega-

tion stayed at Diaoyutai, a well-guarded walled estate, west of the Forbidden City, containing villas for high-level visitors.

363 **Relationship . . . reliable:** Pol Pot, *Study Session*, p. 172, and *Report*, p. 191. **Before . . . lackey:** Dossier L01500, Oct. 9 1976, DC-Cam.

364 **Algeria:** The existence of such centres, long a taboo subject in France, was discussed in a series of articles in *Le Monde* in 2001, and in television documentaries broadcast by Antenne 2 and the Franco-German channel ARTE. **Both were told . . . torture and death:** See Hinton, *Why?*, pp. 95 and 113–15; and Rithy Pann's film, *S-21: La Machine de Mort Khmère Rouge*, transmitted by ARTE on June 2 2003.

365 **Baignoire:** Peter Scholl-Latour, *Death in the Ricefields*, St Martin's Press, New York, 1981, p. 32. **In a civilized:** Bunchan Mol, *Charek Khmer*, pp. 177–82. **'Conquer-or-be-conquered':** Thun Saray, quoted in Prasso, p. 20. See also Mabbett and Chandler, *Khmers*, pp. 160–1.

366 **'In the ancient kingdom':** Criddle and Butt Mam, *Destroy*, p. 213. **'Had I been arrested':** Deuch, interview. **Bread:** Picq, *typescript*, pp. 188–90.

367 **John Dewhirst:** 'Details of my course at the Annexe CIA college in Loughborough, England', Dossier D1444, Sept. 5 1978, DC-Cam.

369 **Soon afterwards . . . into our ranks:** Becker, *When the War*, p. 236; Vickery, *Themes*, p. 117. Khieu Thirith remembered the visit as being in mid-1976. I suspect it was later —probably in November or early December. Pol alluded to her findings so clearly in his speech of Dec. 20 that one may reasonably deduce he had only recently been made aware of them. **'Hidden enemies':** Pol Pot, *Report*, p. 207. **'Lackeys . . . swept away':** 'Resolution of the Eastern Zone Congress, July 17 1977', Doc. 32(N442)/T8294, VA. See also Kiernan, *Eastern Zone Massacres*, pp. 16, 27, 37, 48, 51 and 88; and Kiernan, *Chickens*, pp. 185 *et seq.*

370 **'Authority to smash':** Minutes of the CPK Standing Committee, Mar. 30 1976, Dossier D693, DC-Cam. **Pon:** Untitled 1978 notebook with entries by Pon and Tuy, DC-Cam. **Inmates . . . into a pit:** Interview with an S-21 guard in Rithy Pann's film, *S21: La Machine de Mort Khmère Rouge, supra.*

370–1 **We stopped . . . black and shrunken:** Haing Ngor, *Odyssey*, pp. 217–18 and 222–3.

371 **Antechamber:** Picq, *typescript*, pp. 217, 230 and 238.

373 **'Bristly dog gambit':** Douglas Pike, testimony before the US Congress House Committee on International Relations, Oct. 4 1978, cited in Ablin and Hood, *Agony*, p. xl.

375 **On the 24th . . . serious injuries:** MTI correspondent Gyori Sandor, quoted in Chanda, *Brother Enemy*, p. 194; Pham Van Dong, 'Interview by Vietnam News Agency', undated but January 1978, *JCA*, vol. 8, p. 263. **'Deep gratitude':** Pham Van Dong, ibid, p. 268.

376 **The nature . . . vigilant:** This account of the talks between Pol and Hua is taken from Doc. 32(N442)/T8300, VA.

377 **Kim Il Sung . . . victories as our own:** 'Talks with Pol Pot, Ieng Sary and Vorn Vet, Pyongyang, Oct. 5 and 6 1977'. Doc. 32(N442)/T8307, VA; BBC SWB FE5633/A3/2.

378 **Crowed victory:** See Pol Pot's speech of Jan. 17 (SWB FE5717/A3/2), where he speaks of 'a monumental victory . . . [which] may be compared to the great victory of April 17 1975'.

380 **'We have to gather':** Pol Pot, *Abbreviated Lesson*, p. 224.

381 **How do we gather:** 'Pay attention to pushing ahead with the work of building the

forces of the Party and the collectivity and make them strong and stronger', in *Tung Padevat*, Mar. 1978, pp. 37–53. **Personality cult:** Vann Nath, *Portrait*, pp. 42–82 and 86; Testimony of Ung Pech, in De Nike et al., p. 81. **Marxist-Leninist groups:** Details of these and similar visits are recorded in BBC SWB FE, *passim*.

383 **'We have ceased':** Pol Pot, *Yugoslav interview*.

384 **'Our slogans ... grip on power':** 'Réunion particulière du Comité Central du Parti du 22 Janvier 1978', Doc. 32(N442)/T8302, VA.

385–6 **But the worst ... profoundly hostile:** By far the best account of So Phim's fate, and the terrors wrought afterwards on the population in the East, is given in Kiernan, *Regime*, pp. 392–416, from which the following is largely drawn. The only point on which I take issue with him is the claim that, in the final days, Phim wished to seek help from the Vietnamese. This rests mainly on a 1992 statement by Heng Samrin, who by then had long since thrown in his lot with Hanoi and therefore had his own interests to defend. Samrin's claim is all the harder to swallow because, until the late summer of 1978, he was himself on record as holding strong anti-Vietnamese views (see Heder, *Pol Pot to Pen Sovann*, p. 25).

386 **So many thousands ... in that way:** Deuch, interview with Nate Thayer; see also Vann Nath, *Portrait*, pp. 79–81.

387 **60 per cent:** 'Excerpts from the Meeting of 870, August 5 1978', in De Nike et al., p. 412. **Khmer psyche:** In Sopheap commented: 'To Europeans, his arguments may sound far-fetched, but for Khmers they made sense ... In emotional terms, Pol Pot knew exactly how to speak in order to touch Khmer hearts' (interview).

388 **On September 28 ... own choosing:** This account of Sihanouk's reappearance and the events leading up to it is taken mainly from *Prisonnier*, pp. 209, 212–17 and 259–93. On his isolation from April 1976 to September 1977, see pp. 125–45, 168 and 174–5; and Schier, *Sihanouk*, pp. 21–2. **Deng Yingchao:** Norodom Sihanouk's unpublished 'Memoirs' quoted by Julio A. Jeldres in 'China's Growing Influence in Cambodia', *Africana: rivisti de studi extraeuropei*, no. 8, Pisa, 2002, p. 8.

388–9 **Last ten days ... he did not:** Pich Chheang and Moeun, interviews. The date of Pol's speech marking the CPK's 18th anniversary is given as Sept. 19 in Doc. 32(N422)/T8318, VA. For the broadcast version, see SWB FE/5930/C/1–6 and FE/5931/C/1–13. On Sept. 29, Pol received the Chinese Ambassador, Sun Hao, in Phnom Penh (SWB FE/5933/A3/12), and on Oct. 2 he attended a Standing Committee meeting (Doc. 32(N422)/T8318, *supra*). Puzzlingly, neither he nor Nuon Chea was present at the Sept. 30 National Day reception at the Chinese Embassy, but this may have been for other, unconnected reasons. If the Sept. 19 date is correct, it suggests that he was in Beijing from the 20th or 21st until about the 28th. However, it is also possible that the visit took place in early October.

389–90 **Pol explained . . . into the jungle:** '870 to 12', Jan. 20 1979, Doc. 32(N442)/T7293, VA.

390 **'If we carry out ... weak spots':** 'Réunion particulière du Comité Central du Parti du 22 Janvier 1978', *supra*. I have cited these excerpts here since in practice they were not implemented earlier. **'Vietnamese stink':** 'The National Duties of All of Us', *Tung Padevat*, July 1978, pp. 1–3.

391 **In his speech ... deleted:** Picq, *typescript*, pp. 340–1.

392 **'May run wild':** BBC SWB FE5962/A3/2–5. **On November ... seventh:** The only known details of the Fifth Congress are contained in a cadre's notebook, of which a partial translation exists in the VA (Doc. 32(N442)/T8389). A note by the Vietnamese

editor, presumably based on an untranslated section, suggests that the notebook may have belonged to Ieng Sary.

394 ***That night . . . man in the baseball cap:*** This account is taken from Becker, *When the War*, pp. 427–9; Dudman, *St Louis Post Despatch*, Jan. 15 1979; and Phi Phuon, interview. Significantly, Phi Phuon's account was consistent with those of Becker and Dudman on all important details. ***At 4 a.m. . . . Beijing:*** Phi Phuon, interview. ***Pol had ordered:*** This was the version given to me by British diplomats in Beijing in February 1979.

395–6 ***On Christmas Day . . . in shreds:*** Unless otherwise specified, this account of the invasion relies on Chanda, *Brother Enemy*, pp. 341–3.

396–7 ***Pol met Sihanouk . . . running water:*** Sihanouk, *Prisonnier*, pp. 316–20.

397 ***He had spoken . . . short period of time:*** Pol Pot, recorded appeal to the Cambodian people, broadcast at dawn on Jan. 5, local time, BBC SWB FE6009/A3/1-3. ***Chinese knew differently:*** Yun Shui, *Diplomats*, pp. 499–501.

398 ***Son Sen left the city:*** Phi Phuon, interview. ***Set out at dawn:*** Ibid., Khieu Samphân, interview. David Chandler, relying on Y Phandara's memoir, describes two helicopters passing over Phnom Penh that morning, 'carrying Pol Pot and his close associates to exile in Thailand'. Sadly—the image is so evocative one wishes it were true —reality was more prosaic. According to Mey Mak (interview), who headed the civilian sector at Pochentong Airport, one helicopter left the military sector of the airport on the evening of Jan. 6, but it was never established who was in it. Two of the remaining helicopters were apparently flown out by their pilots on their own initiative the following morning (ibid.; and Ong Thong Hoeung, *Récit*, p. 164), but most remained on the ground and were captured by the Vietnamese, along with the rest of the Democratic Kampuchean air force. ***Special train:*** Long Visalo, interview, and Y Phandara (*Retour*, pp. 179–89) both say they saw Ieng Sary aboard the train. He himself claims to have travelled to Battambang by road with Khieu Samphân (*Maben interview*), but Samphân has denied this (interview).

399–400 ***Did we have . . . simply rumours:*** Mey Mak, interview.

400 ***Prisoners . . . occupation forces:*** An American, Michael Deeds, was among the last to be interrogated at Tuol Sleng. His final confession was dated Jan. 5 1979 (*Cambodia Daily*, Apr. 15–16 2000). See also Deuch, interview with Nate Thayer. ***'On your own':*** Kân, interview.

401 ***'Band of cretins':*** Ong Thong Hoeung, *Récit*, p. 163.

CHAPTER TWELVE: UTOPIA DISBOUND

402 ***To Pol's relief . . . had embarked:*** Nikân, interview; In Sopheap, interview; Henry Kamm, *Cambodia: Report from a Stricken Land*, Arcade, New York, 1998, pp. 153–6. ***Dressing-down:*** In Sopheap, ibid.

402–3 ***But most of the discussion . . . help persuade him:*** The following account is drawn mainly from the summary of Ieng Sary's meeting with Deng and Geng Biao on Jan. 13 in Doc. 32(N422)/T10.622, *supra*.

403 ***That same evening . . . Pol Pot:*** Sihanouk, *Prisonnier*, pp. 342–5 and 365–71. See also Chanda, *Brother Enemy*, pp. 363–9; and the summary of Chinese Foreign Minister Huang Hua's meeting with Ieng Sary on Jan. 15 in Doc. 32(N422)/T10.622, *supra*.

404 ***The problem . . . do nothing:*** Doc. 32(N422)/T10.622, *supra*.

405 ***Geng found . . . authorised:*** Ibid. Lee Kwan Yew also noted that Kriangsak was 'prone to worrying, especially over the fall-out from Cambodia' (*Third World to First*, p. 297). ***He proposed . . . merchants in Bangkok:*** This account combines Geng's

report of Kriangsak's remarks with additional details of their talks provided by Han Nianlong to Ieng Sary at their meeting on Jan. 18.

406 **On February 1 ... was ignored**: 'Report of the Conference on Feb. 1 and 2, 1979' in Doc. 32(N442)/T724,VA.

406-8 **Eight Chinese diplomats ... established their identity**: This account is drawn from Yun Shui, *Diplomats*, pp. 504–19.

409 **Convoys of trucks**: Chanda, *Brother Enemy*, pp. 370–1.

410 **Factories**: Stuart-Fox, *Murderous Revolution*, pp. 173–4. **Rice**: Heder, *Occupation*, p. 31; Someth May, *Cambodian Witness*, p. 266. Michael Vickery disputes Heder's account of the looting of Cambodian rice stocks (*Cambodia*, p. 235), but he agrees that this was what most Khmers believed and politically that is what counted.

410-11 **Finally got the attention ... two months later**: By far the best account of the famine and the refugee exodus is Shawcross's meticulously researched *Quality*, Chs. 5–10. His judgement that the extent of the famine was exaggerated in the West (where alarmist headlines spoke of 'two million dead by Christmas') does not invalidate the conclusion that it was worse than in the 1975–8 period. The death toll in the Khmer Rouge years was due primarily to a combination of overwork, lack of food and lack of medical treatment. In 1979, the main cause of death was hunger.

411 **New permanent headquarters**: Phi Phuon visited Office 131 for the first time for a meeting with Pol in July (interview). The area was also known as Châ-2 and 505. The description that follows is taken from interviews with Kong Duong, Kân, Mey Mak and Suong Sikoeun—all of whom worked there—and from an interview with Phann, who was with one of the groups hiding in the forest in the Eastern Zone. **Walking skeletons**: Kong Duong, Chor Sokhan, interviews. **Cannibalism**: Mey Mak, interview.

411-12 **'Awful, spindly'**: Shawcross, *Quality*, p. 170. Stephen Heder (*Occupation*, pp. 70 and 115) and Serge Thion and Ben Kiernan (*Khmers Rouges! Matériaux pour l'Histoire du Communisme au Cambodge*, Albin Michel, Paris, 1982, p. 299), relying on refugee interviews in Thailand, put the civilian population under Khmer Rouge control at 500–800,000, and suggest that as many as half may have died. On the basis of interviews with surviving Khmer Rouge officials, it seems more likely that the civilian population was of the order of 200,000, of whom perhaps a quarter died.

412 **'Fat and sleek'**: Picq, *typescript*, pp. 441, 445 and 453–4. See also her description of the 'chubby faces' of Ieng Sary and other leaders in July 1979 (ibid., pp. 466–9), and photographs taken of Sary at the meeting of the non-aligned movement in Colombo the same month. The earliest photographs of Pol, taken by Chinese journalists, date from December 1979. They, too, show him looking plump and overweight.

413 **Looking-glass world ... nauseating**: Kamm, *Stricken Land*, pp. 178–81.

414 **'Our main duty ... socialist revolution'**: Ibid., pp. 181–2. I have taken the liberty of changing Kamm's rendering, 'we abandon,' to 'we are abandoning', since Sary does not speak English and the phrase must therefore have been translated from French or Khmer. **No more executions**: Mey Mak said categorically that 'after 1980 there was no more killing' (interview). Deuch, who dated the change to October 1979, said they stopped for a time but then resumed (interview with Nate Thayer). See also Peschoux, *'Nouveaux' Khmers Rouges*, pp. 25–6 and 168–71.

415 **'New beginning'**: Picq, *typescript*, pp. 478–9.

415-16 **August 1981 ... interests were protected**: This account is from Mey Mak, interview. Ieng Sary accompanied them to Bangkok, but neither he nor any other senior CPK leader went with Pol to Beijing.

417 *'In certain places'*: Martin, *Gouvernement*, p. 470. *'We chose communism'*: Kân, interview.

418 *Offenders were re-educated . . . fewer friends*: Peschoux, *'Nouveaux' Khmers Rouges*, pp. 141 and 180–5. *'Draw lessons'*: Kân, Mey Mak, interviews. *'Drunk with victory'*: From a document circulated in March 1993, quoted by Nate Thayer in 'Whither the Khmer Rouge?', *Phnom Penh Post*, June 6–12 1993. *But usually . . . real traitors*: Chandler, *Brother*, p. 163.

420 *D-25*: Kong Duong, Mey Mak and Suong Sikoeun, interviews.

421 *'What hypocrisy'*: *Vanity Fair*, Apr. 1990. *Make Vietnam bleed*: A Khmer Rouge diplomat explained to Henry Kamm why the sharpened bamboo stakes the guerrillas placed in man-traps did not have poisoned tips. 'That would kill them,' the diplomat said. 'A wounded man takes four others to carry him and then he cries and cries and cries. It makes the others begin to think.' 'So much,' Kamm commented, 'for the finesse of Khmer Rouge diplomacy' (*Stricken Land*, p. 179). Yet that was the US strategy in Cambodia. By wounding the Vietnamese, America hoped to make the Russians think. *That year . . . situation permitted*: Interview with Saut, a Jarai medical assistant who treated Pol, at Pailin, 21 Nov. 2001; Thiounn Thioeunn, interview.

422 *No less striking . . . cook*: Ieng Sary, Mey Mak, Kong Duong, interviews. *His new headquarters . . . Samphân*: Kân, Kong Duong, Moeun, Mey Mak and Phann, interviews. All five worked at K-18 or House 20, or visited the area, between 1985 and 1990.

422–3 *One of Samphân's aides . . . major decisions*: Phann, interview.

423 *He and Meas . . . good mother*: Moeun, interview. She was among those present at K-18 that day.

425 *Their efforts to win . . . Khmer Rouge candidates*: The Khmer Rouge strategy for the reconquest of the villages in the second half of the 1980s is discussed at length by Christophe Peschoux in *'Nouveaux' Khmers Rouges*, Ch. 5. *Suppose there are*: From a speech to the Democratic Kampuchea Women's Association in December 1988, cited in Heder, 'Were the KR Serious about the elections?', *Phnom Penh Post*, Mar. 24–Apr. 6.

427–8 *Three weeks later . . . really back again*: This is drawn from my own recollections of Sihanouk's return, which I covered as the BBC's Far East correspondent.

428 *Incident . . . Sen's loyalty*: Phann, who was an aide to Son Sen at the time, believed he had failed to take the reports seriously (interview). Stephen Heder's understanding is that Son Sen did report the rumours of trouble, but Pol Pot said no action should be taken (private communication). Either way, Sen was blamed for what happened. Phi Phuon recalled Pol speaking at a seminar at Phnom Chhat in July 1993 about 'an internal problem in the movement' that came to the surface when Samphân was attacked. He said this was taken at the time as being a reference to Son Sen (interview).

430 *Not disarm*: Brown and Zasloff, *Cambodia Confounds*, pp. 137–8.

431 *Decision to boycott*: Mey Mak, interview. According to In Sopheap (interview), Pol hoped 'right up to the last minute that the Paris accords would be applied correctly —correctly, that is, from the Khmer Rouge point of view'.

433 *Most people . . . kept quiet*: Phi Phuon, interview.

434 **Kbal Ansoang:** The following sketch of Kbal Ansoang draws on my own visit in November 2001 and on In Sopheap's recollections of life there (interview). Both Sopheap and Kor Bunheng used the word 'idyllic' to describe the area.

434–5 **Every time . . . replace him:** Peschoux, 'Nouveaux' Khmers Rouges, p. 140. Although the speaker, a former Khmer Rouge cadre, was describing Pol's seminars in the 1980s, those who attended seminars at Kbal Ansoang, including In Sopheap, said his gifts of oratory were undiminished.

435 **He also developed . . . left side:** Thiounn Thioeunn, interview. See also Pol Pot, *Thayer interview.* **He spent more time . . . youth in Phnom Penh:** Kong Duong and In Sopheap, interviews. Kân also remembered Pol telling stories of his childhood (interview). **Later he got . . . disappeared:** Tep Khunnal, interview. Khunnal said he filled nine notebooks with Pol's reminiscences, but they were lost, along with other papers, when Mok overturned Pol's leadership in June 1997. Some were subsequently recovered and are now in posession of Stephen Heder (private communication). **Whisky:** In Sopheap, interview. Khieu Samphân also remembered Pol drinking whisky when they were in the maquis (interview). **He appreciated . . . technique:** Kong Duong, interview; interview with Meas Somneang, Pailin, Mar. 27 2001. At Office 131, in the early 1980s, a traditional orchestra was assembled to play for the Khmer Rouge radio station, and Pol would invite them to play for him. One of the group, a man then in his early eighties, was living at a *wat* in Pailin in 2001. **Paris-Match:** In Sopheap, interview.

436–7 **Their agent was . . . never recovered:** Except where specified elsewhere, this account relies on Kong Duong, Mey Mak, Phi Phuon, and Phann interviews.

437 **'Like a fish':** Kân, interview.

438 **Nuon Chea and Son Sen . . . cloud:** Interview with Mok's driver, Chhun, Anlong Veng, Dec. 12 2001; In Sopheap, interview. **Rapidly deteriorating:** Kân, Moeun, interviews. **'Crossing of a river':** In Sopheap, interview.

439 **May 16 1997:** Letter from Long Sarin to Prince Ranariddh, May 18 1997 (Nhek Bunchhay personal archive, Phnom Penh).

440 **The plan was to seize:** Nhek Bunchhay, interview.

440–1 **At about midnight . . . was right:** Unless otherwise stated, the following account is taken from interviews with Seng (Pailin, Mar. 14 2001), In Sopheap, Kân, Keo Yann, Meas Somneang and Phann, all of whom were at Kbal Ansoang on the day Mok's forces attacked. The chronology is confused. Pol's order for the killing of Son Sen shortly after midnight on the night of June 9 is confirmed by Tem's statement on June 24 1997 ('Anlong Veng Papers', *supra;* see also *Phnom Penh Post*, Aug. 15–28 1997). Mok said he started organising his forces at the Anlong Veng district centre on the morning of June 10 ('Anlong Veng Papers', meeting of Sept. 9 1997) and continued on the 11th. The Khmer Rouge radio at Kbal Ansoang broadcast for the last time on the morning of June 12. Pol must therefore have fled that afternoon. In Sopheap remembered spending 'three or four nights' on the run—i.e. until June 15 or 16—by which time it appeared to him that Pol had already been captured. Mok said the crisis had been resolved on June 14 (*Phnom Penh Post*, June 27–July 10 1997), implying that Pol had been caught that day. Meas Somneang's account also suggests that Pol must have been captured on June 14 or 15 (interview).

440 **Pol later told:** Pol Pot, *Thayer interview.*

442 **Pol Pot has died:** Chandler, *Brother*, p. 186. I have taken the liberty of changing the translation, 'cow shit', into 'cowpat'.

AFTERWORD

444 *'Explosion'*: Ponchaud, interview. He used the French term *sursaut*. *'Quiet, intro-verted'*: Drago Rancic, writing in *Politika*, Belgrade, excerpted in *Seven Days*, May 19 1978.

445 *Yos Hut Khemcaro*: *Phnom Penh Post*, Mar. 21–Apr. 3 1997.

446 *Actions of 'normal' governments*: For example, in 1945 the US Army granted an amnesty, in exchange for their research results, to Japanese germ warfare specialists who had carried out thousands of experiments on prisoners of war as horrific as any of the atrocities of Josef Mengele in Auschwitz (see Sheldon H. Harris, *Factories of Death: Japanese Biological Warfare, 1932–45, and the American Cover-up*, Routledge, London, 1994). Granting an amnesty in those circumstances was certainly a 'crime against humanity' and would be prosecuted as such under an international system of justice worthy of the name.

447 *Culture of impunity*: On July 6 1999, a film actress named Piseth Pelika was shot in Phnom Penh and later died of her injuries. It transpired that she had been the mistress of Hun Sen. The French weekly *l'Express*, accused the Prime Minister's wife, Bun Rany, of ordering her execution. She threatened to sue *l'Express* but did not do so. No police investigation of Pelika's murder was ever undertaken (*Phnom Penh Post*, July 23–Aug. 5, Oct. 15–28 and Oct. 29–Nov. 11, 1999, and July 7–20 2000).

448 *'Utterly merciless'*: Lee Kwan Yew, *Third World to First*, p. 328. *'Millions of Cambodians'*: *Phnom Penh Post*, Mar. 21–Apr. 3 1997. *'Since the fall of Angkor'*: Ros Chantrabot, p. 149.

449 *Like a porcelain vase*: The simile is Lee Kwan Yew's (*Third World to First*, p. 327).

Index

Page numbers in **bold** refer to the dramatis personae section, pages 450–8.

About the Author

PHILIP SHORT has been a foreign correspondent for the London *Times*, *The Economist*, and BBC in Uganda, Moscow, China, and Washington. He is the author of the definitive biography of Mao Zedong, and lived in China and Cambodia in the 1970s and early 1980s, where he has returned regularly ever since. He now lives in southern France with his wife.